The Unit Leader and Individually Guided Education

Juanita S. Sorenson
Max Poole
Lloyd H. Joyal
University of Wisconsin—Eau Claire

Addison-Wesley Publishing Company
Reading, Massachusetts • Menlo Park, California
London • Amsterdam • Don Mills, Ontario • Sydney

This book and the correlated films and filmstrips are in the Leadership Series in Individually Guided Education, Herbert J. Klausmeier, Editor.

Development of this series was funded by The Sears-Roebuck Foundation.

 Printed in the United States of America. Published simultaneously in Canada. Library of Congress Catalog Card No. 75-12102.

ISBN 0-201-19711-1
ABCDEFGHIJ-HA-79876

The authors dedicate this book
to
Herbert J. Klausmeier
who so willingly gave of
his time, effort, and talent
to make the
Leadership Series
in Individually Guided Education
a reality.

Editor's Foreword

These are exciting and challenging times in American education. Personnel in local school districts, intermediate education agencies, state education agencies, and teacher education institutions are cooperating as never before to improve the quality of education for children, high school youth, and college students. Bringing Individually Guided Education, a new approach to education, to an ever-increasing number of students provides the focus for many of these cooperative efforts. This Leadership Series in Individually Guided Education is designed to help teacher educators and other educational leaders in their improvement efforts. It comprises ten sets of printed materials and correlated films and filmstrips. The materials have been developed for use both in credit courses conducted on college campuses and local schools and in noncredit staff development programs carried out in the local schools.

The set of materials for *The Unit Leader and Individually Guided Education* consists of this textbook; two sound/color films, *The Unit Leader in Individually Guided Education* (17 min) and *Making Unit Meetings Effective* (23 min); and three sound/color filmstrips (12-15 min each): *The Unit Leader's Role in Planning Instruction, The Unit Leader's Role in Implementing Instruction,* and *The Unit Leader's Role in Evaluating Instruction.* Other audiovisuals that can be used effectively with this set of materials include two filmstrips: *The Multiunit School Organization* and *Instructional Programming for the Individual Student.* An accompanying instructor's guide provides aids to instructors for meeting the needs of their students in their particular situations.

The authors of this book, Juanita S. Sorenson, Max Poole, and Lloyd H. Joyal, have been involved in preparing unit leaders and IGE teachers for many years. They have been leaders in developing performance-based graduate courses for IGE and a master's degree with an IGE emphasis. In addition, they have helped conceptualize aspects of IGE related to the unit leader role and instructional programming. The authors have secured able contributing authors, each of whom has expertise in a particular area related to unit leader responsibilities, to assist in writing this book.

I have enjoyed the cooperative and productive working relationships with these scholars, the film producers, the publisher, and others in developing this comprehensive set of multimedia materials. To ensure that the users of this and other sets of materials in the Leadership Series get attractive, high quality, usable materials and also are not presented with conflicting interpretations of IGE in either the books or the visuals, I personally reviewed each book from its first chapter outline, through its several field-tested drafts, and the final manuscript. I did the same for each visual from the initial content outline, through the several drafts of the script, rough cuts, and fine cuts. Many other persons also participated in the production, review, and quality control process.

In this regard I am pleased to recognize the many school personnel, state education agency personnel, professors, and students who participated in field tests and review sessions; the consultants with expertise in the various subject matter fields or in the filmic quality and instructional effectiveness of the visuals; Anthony E. Conte, James M. Lipham, Wesley C. Meierhenry, and William Wiersma for serving on the Project Publications Board; Judith Amacker, William R. Bush, James R. Dumpson, Martin W. Essex, Nancy Evers, Lovelia P. Flournoy, John R. Palmer, Edward C. Pomeroy, Richard A. Rossmiller, B. Othanel Smith, Lorraine Sullivan, and James Swinney for serving on the Project Advisory Committee; Leslie C. Bernal, G. R. Bowers, Eleanor Buehrig, Xavier Del Buono, Lee M. Ellwood, G. W. Ford, Marvin J. Fruth, George Glasrud, James Hixson, Ronald Horn, Terry Jackson, L. Wayne Krula, Max Poole, Kenneth B. Smith, James Stoltenberg, Michael F. Tobin, Philip Vik, James E. Walter, S. Edward Weinswig, and William Wiersma for serving on the Project Steering Committee; and the staff of the IGE Teacher Education Project. Particular recognition is given to the members of minority groups who reviewed the visuals so as to avoid having any racism or sexism appear in them.

The development of these materials became possible through a grant made by The Sears-Roebuck Foundation in 1973 to the IGE Teacher Education Project at the University of Wisconsin—Madison. The authors, editor, and others associated with the Project receive no royalties from the sale of these materials. However, the royalties that accrue will be returned to the University of Wisconsin—Madison to support continuing research, development, and implementation activities related to Individually Guided Education.

Herbert J. Klausmeier
Series Editor and Director, IGE Teacher Education Project
The University of Wisconsin—Madison

Preface

This book has been written for existing and prospective unit leaders. It is also valuable for teachers, principals, superintendents, curriculum coordinators, board members, and anyone else interested in understanding the role and responsibilities of the unit leader in an Individually Guided Education (IGE) school.

The role of the unit leader is unique to the IGE concept. Until this time, information about the role of the unit leader could be found only in articles, pamphlets, filmstrips, and other miscellaneous sources. This book brings all this information together into an organized format and combines it with other pertinent educational information which is of interest to a unit leader. Two films and three filmstrips have been correlated with this book to provide the reader with "live" examples of the unit leader role in IGE.

The background information and experiences utilized in writing this book came from the existing IGE literature; interviews and interactions with experienced unit leaders; supervision of preservice teachers in smoothly functioning IGE schools; development and subsequent teaching of IGE courses at the University of Wisconsin—Eau Claire, the University of Toledo (Ohio) and Southwest State College (Marshall, Minnesota); participation in and coordination of inservice sessions, workshops, and institutes in a variety of settings throughout the United States; and experience in research and development of IGE procedures and products.

If a person is not familiar with the IGE concept, it will be helpful to study Part I of this book carefully. The first chapter gives background information concerning the development of the IGE concept, its definition, and the description of its seven components. Chapter 2 explains four basic change theories and how they may be utilized in effecting an educational change. Viewing the film, *The Unit Leader in Individually Guided Education,* will give the reader an overview of the various aspects of the unit leader role in an IGE school.

The chapters in Part II of the book explain the various roles and responsibilities of the unit leader. These include the unit leader as an instructional leader of a teaching team, a communicator between the teachers and the administrators, and a coordinator of teaching resources and materials. Viewing the film, *Making Unit Meetings Effective,* demonstrates the unit leader's role in helping adults develop skills so they work together more effectively. The last chapter in this section tells how a teacher can prepare to become a unit leader and keep abreast of educational changes.

In Part III, the role of the unit leader and the instructional program are brought together. Each chapter in this section is a step in the sequence of establishing and maintaining an excellent instructional program according to the IGE system. The emphasis is on meeting the educational needs of the individual student. The concluding chapter in Part III deals with a detailed case study of how one school implemented instructional programming in mathematics along with one motivational procedure. Correlated to the instructional sequence are three audio filmstrips entitled *The Unit Leader's Role in Planning Instruction, The Unit Leader's Role in Implementing Instruction,* and *The Unit Leader's Role in Evaluating Instruction.*

To aid the reader in studying the material covered in this book, the objectives which the reader should master are stated at the beginning of each chapter. After completing a chapter, the reader should review the stated objectives to check on comprehension and ability to apply the material presented in the chapter. References are listed at the end of each chapter. If the reader wishes to study a topic in depth, these listings form a good reference point. Further detailed information, too lengthy to be included in the text of the book, is placed in Appendix A. Appendix B is entitled *Form for Determining Preferences for School Library/Media Center Services.*

The book concludes with a *Glossary* of terms relevant to the study of Individually Guided Education.

University of Wisconsin—Eau Claire J.S.
January 1976 M.P.
L.J.

To the Reader

It is valuable for you as a reader to give some thought to the purpose and structure of this book before beginning to read it for the information it contains.

The unit leader is a new role in education and is unique to Individually Guided Education (IGE). Until now, information about this role has been available only from scattered sources: films, workshops, booklets, printed handouts, and practicing unit leaders. In this book we have undertaken to collect all the best information available from these sources and organize it into a single reference.

This is a handbook. As such, it provides guidance for the position of unit leader. Readers should recognize that the book is not exhaustive. Neither is it a directive explaining each step a unit leader should take. Rather, it is intended to provide a comprehensive picture of the unit leader role and can be used as a source of information which can be applied or adapted to all IGE schools.

The book is directed to several audiences. Some readers may be full-time college students or practicing teachers who are using the book as a text for a course. Others may be practicing teachers who are increasing their knowledge of IGE through workshops or institutes. The book may also be used by those who need a reference to which they can turn for answers to questions or for ideas about specific school situations. Although the unit leader is the focal person of the book, others who are involved in IGE (staff teachers, principals, curriculum coordinators, etc.) are also encouraged to use the information contained herein.

The book is organized into three parts. Part I (Chapters 1 and 2) summarizes the background information necessary for unit leaders and others involved in changing to IGE. Chapter 1 ends with an overview of the book and can be used as an organizer for the rest of the book. Chapter 2 deals with the process of change which is so vital to success in IGE. Part II (Chapters 3—9) discusses the personal qualities and knowledge which unit leaders need. Greater detail about how to prepare for the role is given in Chapter 9. Part III (Chapters 10—17) deals with the instructional aspects of the unit leader's role. It begins with a chapter on planning strategy. The next six chapters are devoted to Steps 1 through 7 of the Instructional Programming Model (IPM) and Chapter 17 is a case study in which a unit leader explains how one unit planned and carried out their mathematics program over a period of two years using instructional programming for the individual student.

As a reader, you may find it helpful to look through the Contents and note the chapter titles in each part. This will help you recognize the overall organization of the book.

It should be pointed out that many different authors have contributed chapters to this book. At times, this may seem to be a handicap as the style of writing changes somewhat from writer to writer. However, we hope that the collaborative effort of many authors who have shared their expertise contributes a diversity and strength of information which exceeds that which would be possible by a single author.

Each chapter begins with a list of objectives. These are included to help you know the intent of the chapter before you read it. The objectives can be used as a self-evaluation upon the completion of each chapter. You might create questions from each objective by asking, "Am I able to . . . ?", completing the questions by filling in an objective. When you feel uncertain about your response to an objective you might (1) bring up the topic in your next class session, (2) ask your IGE colleagues for help or clarification, or (3) pursue one of the references listed at the end of the chapter.

A summary is given at the end of each chapter. Many people find it helpful to read the summary before reading the rest of the chapter. Used in this way, the summary becomes an advance organizer for the chapter.

Chapter headings can also be useful for organizing information. If outlining serves as a useful learning tool for you, the headings and subheads can be used as a skeleton outline. You can then fill in relevant information under each topic to create an outline for your own use.

Most chapters include some figures. Basically, these are of two types: (1) examples of materials being discussed and (2) diagrams and models. Figures are used because they can present certain kinds of information in less space and can be more easily comprehended than many sentences of text discussion.

Example figures give you the exact form or outline the author is discussing. As you study examples and the accompanying text, you may realize that they would be appropriate for use in your own situation. You are encouraged to adapt and use examples to suit your needs.

Diagram and model figures are included when they can help present an idea in a clear and concise manner. They are explained and discussed in the body of the text. You are encouraged to study the diagram or model while reading the explanatory narrative to acquire a complete understanding of the concept.

A reference list follows each chapter. These lists include only the sources referred to in the chapter. The references can be used for further information on specific topics. They can also serve to guide you to other sources of information on topics of special interest or need.

We hope you enjoy your journey through this book and that you find the information helpful in your work in an IGE school.

University of Wisconsin—Eau Claire J.S.
January 1976 M.P.
L.J.

Acknowledgments

The authors wish to acknowledge the contributions of the following persons: Mary Melvin and Kathleen Nolan for their "practical" classroom examples and the long hours they willingly spent in editing and rewriting the manuscript; the 19 teachers, unit leaders, and principals in the class that reviewed the initial version of the text and whose valuable suggestions formed the basis for revision; Esther Henton who reacted to one school's implementation of IGE; Nancy Sandburg and Clifford Wing in New Hampshire and Richard Lappert and Edward Weinswig in Connecticut who tried out the revised version of the text, and whose subsequent suggestions contributed to the final version of the book and the instructor's guide; Ruth Bullis, Virginia Reece, and Dolores Martinek who typed and formatted the many versions of the manuscript; Douglas Sorenson who read and edited many chapters. In addition, we appreciate the suggestions of numerous students and colleagues who read the manuscript, and the administration of the University of Wisconsin—Eau Claire who supported our efforts in the undertaking.

Contents

Part I

IGE as an Alternative Form of Education

Through the consolidated contributions of teams of researchers, developers, evaluators, and school personnel, an educational concept has been created that combines principles and practices dealing with learning theories, student abilities, teacher abilities, and instructional methods. This concept is Individually Guided Education (IGE). It focuses on individual differences among students in terms of achievement, rate of learning, learning styles, motivational levels, and other personal characteristics.

Educational research contributed to the rationale for many of the basic concepts in the Individually Guided Education system. These included individualized instruction, team teaching, differentiated staffing, multiage grouping, nongrading, varied instructional grouping patterns, efficient use of multimedia materials, criterion reference evaluation, shared decision making, individual student motivation, better home-school-community relations, and supportive facilitative environments. In IGE, these elements are synthesized into seven basic components:

- Multiunit school instructional-administrative arrangements
- Instructional programming for the individual student
- Evaluation for educational decision making
- Curricular materials compatible with individualized instruction
- Program of home-school-community relations
- Facilitative intraorganizational and extraorganizational environments
- Continuing research and development

The change from the traditional approach to education to the IGE alternative will require many modifications in present schools. Elements from four basic change theories can be utilized to assist in this transition. Such a dramatic change from one teacher and 25 to 30 students to the more complex IGE system with so many components functioning simultaneously must be undertaken gradually. In order to make the change effectively, those involved in the change—students, teachers, administrators, parents, and the community—must understand the advantages and responsibilities involved. These individuals should be able to participate in the decision-making process on how and when IGE will be implemented, how the change will affect them, and how it will better meet the needs of the students and the values of the community. The change to IGE can be greatly enhanced by total commitment and cooperation by all persons involved in the change process.

1

Definition, Development, and Description of IGE: An Overview

Juanita S. Sorenson
Herbert J. Klausmeier
James M. Lipham

Objectives

After reading this chapter, the reader will be able:

- To define IGE and briefly describe its development since 1966.
- To identify the seven components of IGE and briefly describe the function of each.
- To describe the hierarchical multiunit organizational arrangement component (MUS) indicating the three organizational levels along with their personnel composition and primary responsibilities.
- To describe the seven sequential steps of the instructional programming model (IPM) component indicating which group of persons within the multiunit organization is primarily responsible for carrying out each step.
- To identify four sets of curriculum materials developed for IGE at the Wisconsin Research and Development Center and briefly describe the scope and content of each.

IGE has created a new role for the elementary teacher—that of unit leader. The unit leader is a teacher and an instructional leader who heads a team of three to five certified teachers, paraprofessionals, and student teachers or interns. Some 75-150 students with a 3-4 year age span are also under the instructional leadership of the unit leader.

The unit leader is a key person both in initiating the change to IGE and in further refining the educational program once it is underway. The role is a challenging one that offers new and rewarding opportunities for the teacher. IGE provides an environment in which the unit leader and teachers have opportunity to share professional ideas and problems not only within their building but with other professionals in the system, region, state, and nation. Teachers who assume the unit leader role need to fully understand the meaning of the IGE concept in order to develop skills and attitudes necessary to perform effectively and efficiently.

The purpose of this chapter is to acquaint prospective and practicing unit leaders with the definition, development, and description of IGE as an educational system. IGE is conceptualized as a comprehensive alternative system of schooling designed to produce higher educational achievements through providing well for differences among students in rate of learning, learning style, and other characteristics.*

The topics of this chapter expand the definition of IGE presented above and are discussed in the following sequence: (1) the history of IGE; (2) the seven components of IGE; and (3) an overview of the understanding, skills, and attitudes required for effective performance of the unit leader in the IGE school.

HISTORY OF IGE

To understand the development of IGE, consideration must be given to certain conditions prevailing in American schools which suggest an urgent need for a viable alternative form of education. Description of these conditions is followed in this section by a discussion of desirable conditions for teaching and learning. Then, the origin and historical development of IGE are traced.

Prevailing Conditions in American Education

By any criterion, the American educational system is remarkable. The progress made in education is evidenced by many statistics. For example,

---

* H. J. Klausmeier 1975. IGE: an alternative form of schooling. In H. Talmage (ed.), *Systems of individualized education.* The National Society for the Study of Education series on contemporary educational issues. Berkeley, Calif.: McCutchan, Chapter 3.

75 percent of the pupils entering the fifth grade in the fall of 1964 graduated from high school in 1972 and about 23 percent of them are expected to graduate from college with a bachelor's degree. Data in a report from the United States Department of Health, Education, and Welfare (1973) indicates the percentages for students graduating from high school ten years earlier, in 1962, were about 67 and 17 percent, respectively.

The quality of the product of American schools also compares favorably with that of other nations. For example, recent findings of the International Association for the Evaluation of Educational Achievement indicate that in reading comprehension the top 10 percent of American high school seniors performed better than similar groups in 15 other nations, including Australia, England, France, West Germany, Sweden, and Japan (Thorndike 1973). Further, many children of low socioeconomic status in the United States get more schooling than do their counterparts in 19 other nations. In reporting these findings, it was stated (Hechinger 1973, p. 12):

> The increasingly vocal critics of our schools, in keeping with the current mood of American self-criticism, have assumed an isolationist or at least a provincial tone. It is, of course, true that American schools have discriminated against the poor and against minority groups. American educational policy has not always made the climb up the ladder of success as easy or as equal as envisioned by the American dream. But a look at the schools of Germany, England, and France, where stratification is still far more rigid, puts the American achievement in a much brighter light, clearly at the head of the international parade.

The achievements of the schools, however, cannot allay concerns about inadequacies in American education. The critics of education can point to statistics which indicate education in the United States has not been a successful experience for some young people (United States Department of Health, Education, and Welfare, Office of Education 1969). These include:

- 25 percent of the students in our nation have a significant reading deficiency.
- 50 percent of our unemployed youth are functionally illiterate.
- About 2.5 percent of our youth drop out of school by the eighth grade.
- Over 1.5 percent of the people (3 million) in the United States are illiterate.

These disturbing findings appear to be related to practices and conditions which are typical in too many schools such as:

- Students are required to adjust to uniform educational programs and provisions for differences in rate of learning, style of learning, and other characteristics are inadequate.
- Students are placed in age-graded classes and are expected to attain the same instructional objectives by studying the same graded basic textbooks and supplementary materials.
- Students are frequently evaluated using norm-referenced tests of intellectual ability and educational achievement, and such tests are often used for categorizing and grading students, and not for improving their instruction.
- Teachers are treated as if they are equally competent in all subject fields and in all media and methods of instruction; and appropriate provisions are seldom made for differences among teachers in interests, knowledge, experience, and expertise; there is no differentiated staffing or a true career opportunity for dedicated elementary school teachers.
- Teachers spend nearly all their time throughout the school day with children, leaving little time for planning and evaluating instructional activities.
- The principal tends to be a building manager rather than an educational leader; the teacher is an independent ruler of a classroom rather than a cooperative team member; and administrative arrangements discourage cooperative planning and decision making.
- The staff spends most of its energy in keeping school going, and little effort is devoted to research and development activities that are essential to continuous improvement of educational practice.
- The staff of each school functions in relative isolation from other schools while communication networks for sharing creative ideas, materials, and instructional approaches function only sporadically, causing many "to reinvent the wheel."
- The typical school building is not well adapted to effective instruction. Access to library, audiovisual, and other instructional materials and aids is circumscribed. Such space configurations impede varied types of grouping and learning activities.
- Parent contact with the schools tends to be largely negative, being concerned primarily with problems of school finance or student discipline; and the primary means for communication between the school and the home is by report cards or parent-teacher conferences, supplemented occasionally by a school newsletter.

It was recognized early that the preceding obsolete conditions should be remedied without destroying public education or eliminating any effective practices. One solution was seen as being a new form of tax-supported education within local school districts to serve as an alternative to the self-contained, age-graded system of elementary education which has not changed much since 1850. The development of a suitable, carefully designed, and tested alternative to the traditional school would facilitate the adoption of practices conducive to more effective teaching and learning in the schools. IGE was conceived and developed as a response to the need for such an alternative.

Desirable Conditions for Teaching and Learning

First and foremost, the educational process should focus attention on the individual learner as a person with unique characteristics, capabilities, concerns, need-dispositions, and motivations. Focusing attention on the individual learner can be accomplished by the following four operations:

1. Assessing the level of achievement, learning style, and motivation of each student by the use of criterion-referenced tests, observation schedules, and work samples prior to beginning instruction.
2. Setting specific instructional objectives for each student to attain over a short period of time.
3. Planning and conducting instructional activities suitable for each student through varying the amount of guidance by the teacher, the amount of time spent in interaction among students, the use of resources, materials, equipment, and direct experience, and the amount of time spent by each student in different types and sizes of learning groups.
4. Assessing each student for attainment of initial objectives in order to set the next instructional objectives to be attained.

Teachers and principals will immediately recognize that such a system of individualized instruction eliminates heavy dependence on standardized texts and tests for structuring the form and content of instruction. Instead, a wide variety of quality curricular materials, audiovisual equipment, and assessment devices is required; sizes of groups, use of time, and teacher and student activities are varied to meet the needs of individual students. For example, some concepts may be introduced to a large group through a sound motion picture, extended in a smaller group through slide films and discussion, and developed independently through use of printed or audiovisual sets of curricular materials or programmed instructional packages. Although a wealth of materials may be available, in many instances it will be necessary for the principal and unit leaders, working as a leadership team, to provide teachers the time and encouragement to develop and refine curricular materials and assessment instruments and procedures.

To implement a system of IGE, the principal and unit leaders must demonstrate one of the essential qualities of leadership—that of initiating change in the organizational structure of the school. While the principal is responsible for initiating change at the building level, the unit leaders act as agents of change for the teams they lead.

The organizational design of the school should foster open communication, systematic planning, cooperative decision making, intergroup coordination, and instructional accountability at all levels. Moreover, the administrative and instructional divisions should be small enough to allow each person to be known and treated as an individual, yet large enough to permit role differentiation and complementary contributions. The organizational structure must designate role responsibilities and clarify working relationships among administrators, unit leaders, teachers, specialists, aides, student teachers/interns and other participants in the educational process. In addition, the organizational structure of the school should provide for adequate and appropriate involvement of each participant in the decision-making process.

To identify and satisfy the educational needs of individuals, the principal, unit leaders, and staff teachers must employ systematic problem-solving processes. Each step in planning, developing, conducting, and evaluating instruction should be treated as a problem to be solved. The inputs, processes, and outcomes of each division within the school must be coordinated with those of (1) other divisions within the building; (2) other schools in a district; and (3) other agencies, such as state education departments, teacher education institutions, and research and development centers which foster and sustain educational change. Continuous research and development utilizing problem-solving processes are vital to the success of IGE in a school.

The activities of the unit leaders, staff teachers, and principal in planning instructional activities, developing curricular materials and assessment procedures, and conducting research and development activities obviously provide the core of a continuous program of staff development. The principal and unit leaders must assume the primary leadership responsibility not only for staff development, but also for staff identification, selection, orientation, assignment, and evaluation. These activities are of critical significance since communication, interaction, and interdependence are increased in schools that individualize instruction.

To provide a desirable environment for learning, the principal plays a key role in obtaining the necessary financial and physical resources. Buildings must be planned, or in many instances remodeled, to permit maximum flexibility and an environment conducive to the many types of learning activities. Large instructional spaces which permit varied types of instructional groupings are required, as is a central Instructional Materials Center which includes library and audiovisual materials and equipment readily accessible to staff and students. Even in older buildings, inexpensive alterations, imaginative use of corridors, and ingenious adaptation of space to educational needs may improve the total climate for learning.

Increasingly, parents and citizens want ensurance that the schools are productive, that children are achieving well in the 3Rs and other curricular areas, and that they are developing culturally, socially, and emotionally as responsible individuals and productive citizens. Major attention must be given to increased involvement of parents and citizens in planning educational programs, providing educational activities, and evaluating educational outcomes. Parents should be able to convey information, values, and attitudes; teacher, parent, and student should be involved in reporting practices; and a systematic program of teacher-home and home-school relations should be developed.

Origin and Development of IGE

The system known as IGE was started by personnel of the Wisconsin Research and Development Center for Cognitive Learning and cooperating school systems as an efficient alternative to age-graded, self-contained schooling at both elementary and middle school levels. Every element and phase in the development, refinement, and implementation of the system is designed to create the conditions and stimulate the activities essential to effective educational planning, teaching, and learning.

IGE started in embryonic form when a project called Maximizing Opportunities for Development and Experimentation in Learning in the Schools was begun at the Wisconsin Research and Development Center, under the direction of Herbert J. Klausmeier as principal investigator (Klausmeier, Goodwin, Prasch, and Goodson 1966). As a first practical result of this project, four school districts, with the assistance of R & D personnel, started the first 13 nongraded, Instruction and Research (I & R) units as replacements for age-graded classes in schools of Madison, Janesville, Milwaukee, and Racine, Wisconsin in the second semester of the 1965-66 school year (Klausmeier, Cook, Goodwin, Tagatz, and Pingel 1967). In 1966-67, the number of functioning I & R Units was increased to 19.

In 1967-68, for the first time, seven elementary schools were completely organized into I & R Units, and the term "multiunit" elementary school (MUS–E) was coined to designate these schools (Klausmeier,

Morrow, and Walter 1968). Also, the other two elements of the organizational-administrative arrangements, the Instructional Improvement Committee (IIC) in each school building and the Systemwide Program (policy) Committee (SPC) in each school district, were formed.

The Wisconsin Department of Public Instruction selected the MUS-E for statewide demonstration and implementation during the 1968-69 school year. Thereafter, as implementers were educated regarding IGE and as materials and programs were developed to help local schools change to IGE, many agencies became involved and the number of IGE/MUS-Es increased rapidly: 50 in 1969-70; 500 in 1971-72; and over 1700 in 1973-74. Projections for the future indicate that accelerated expansion will continue throughout the 1970s. Some events associated with this rapid and continuous growth merit attention.

In 1968, the staff of the Wisconsin Research and Development Center, with assistance of personnel of the Wisconsin Department of Public Instruction and the local schools, developed a book and 15 videotapes for use in implementing IGE by state education departments, teacher education institutions, and other interested educational agencies. These materials were used until 1971. In 1969, the Wisconsin Research and Development Center and the Institute for Development of Educational Activities (/I/D/E/A/) signed an agreement whereby /I/D/E/A/ was authorized to use the preceding materials in producing a more sophisticated set of inservice materials. /I/D/E/A/ incorporated into the new materials insights from their own study of educational change. In 1970-71 and thereafter, /I/D/E/A/ used these IGE "Change Program" materials to prepare "facilitators" to establish multiunit schools (National School Public Relations Association 1972).

The Wisconsin Research and Development Center also used the same materials until 1972 when the requirements of /I/D/E/A/ for using the "Change Program" materials were found to be incompatible with the federally funded implementation activities of the Wisconsin Center. The Wisconsin Research and Development Center then had to develop new inservice materials in order to continue its implementation of IGE as provided for in an agreement with the Office of Education.

Early in 1971, the MUS–E was selected by the United States Office of Education for nationwide implementation. This brought the Research and Development Center into its first wide-scale implementation effort. The Research and Development Center was funded by three federal agencies to carry out certain parts of a comprehensive implementation strategy during 1971-72 and 1972-73. The National Institute of Education funded a small effort during 1973-74. In preparation for the national effort, a four-phase implementation strategy was formulated consisting of the following stages: (1) awareness; (2) first-year changeover; (3) maintenance and refinement; and (4) institutionalization.

The awareness phase was carried out by the Research and Development Center only in 1971. First-year changeover was carried out primarily by IGE coordinators of nine state education agencies—Colorado, Connecticut, Illinois, Indiana, Minnesota, New Jersey, Ohio, South Carolina, and Wisconsin—and of other agencies in California, Nebraska, New York, and Virginia. Sufficient funding was not available to respond to the interest in the other states. Approximately 275 IGE schools were started each year in these states. Maintenance and refinement activities, in the form of one-week institutes for experienced IGE personnel, were conducted by seven teacher education institutions in Connecticut, Ohio, and Wisconsin. Approximately 700 unit leaders, 300 building principals, and 100 reading staff teachers of functioning IGE schools attended these institutes (Sipes 1972). Institutionalization (defined as teacher education institutions developing on-campus programs and preparing building principals and unit leaders for their IGE roles) was started in 1971-72 with federal funding. The support was provided, however, only for that year.

In 1972, The Sears-Roebuck Foundation invited a proposal that led to funding of the project of which this book is a part—the University of Wisconsin/Sears-Roebuck Foundation IGE Teacher Education Project (Klausmeier 1972). The major activity of this project is to develop printed and audiovisual instructional materials for use in undergraduate programs to prepare teachers for IGE schools and in graduate programs to prepare staff teachers, unit leaders, and building principals and other administrators for IGE service. The second activity of the project is to assist personnel in various states to form state IGE networks which are coordinated by the state education agency. The mutual expectations are that the educational agencies and teacher education institutions of each state will have the capability to start and maintain IGE schools, to prepare prospective IGE teachers through on-campus programs, and to prepare unit leaders and building principals for service in IGE schools through on-campus graduate programs and continuing inservice programs.

Another significant event was the establishment, by the IGE coordinators of 12 states, of a national IGE organization. In November 1973, the Association for Individually Guided Education was organized and held its first annual meeting which was attended by over 400 persons representing state education departments, teacher education institutions, and public and private schools in 30 states. New theoretical conceptualizations, reports of research, and practical ideas for the refinement of IGE were shared and exchanged.

As the chronicle of preceding developments indicates, continuing cooperative efforts by many persons and agencies have been required to develop the various components of IGE, start the early IGE schools, and carry out the implementation process in numerous school districts in many states. Unlike a curriculum package that can be distributed commercially and then used by teachers without inservice education, IGE requires many changes within schools that are possible only if there is early inservice education, followed by continuing staff development within each IGE school. Each of the major components of IGE has far-reaching implications for school board members, superintendents, principals, unit leaders, teachers, specialists, students, parents, and others vitally concerned with improving the educational process.

COMPONENTS OF IGE

The system of IGE includes seven basic components, each of which is relatively complex. This section provides the reader with an introduction to each component which will be treated more fully in the remainder of this book. The components are:

1. **the multiunit school organization—administrative arrangements**
2. **instructional programming for the individual student**
3. **evaluation for educational decision making**
4. **selected curricular materials compatible with IGE**
5. **a program of home-school-community relations**
6. **a system of facilitative environments for IGE**
7. **a program of continuing research and development to improve IGE**

The components are shown in Figure 1.1.

The Multiunit Organization (MUS)

The multiunit organization was designed to produce an environment in a school building that would facilitate instructional programming for the individual student, as well as introduction and utilization of the other components of IGE (Klausmeier, *et al.* 1968). A prototypic multiunit organization is shown in Figure 1.2.

The multiunit school is a new organizational structure that has emerged from a synthesis of organizational theory and practice in education. The multiunit structure is designed to articulate vertical and horizontal relationships, affix organizational roles and responsibilities, fa-

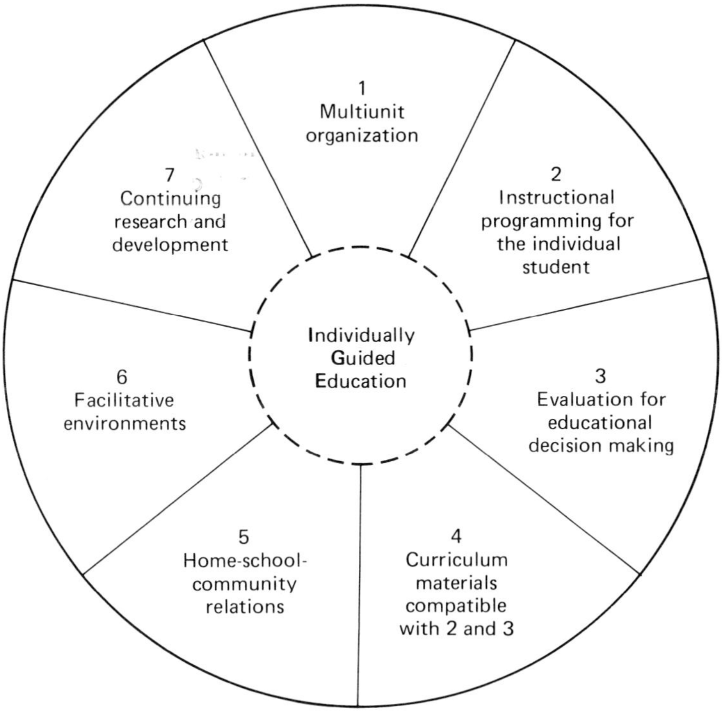

Fig. 1.1 Major components of individually guided education. (Adapted from H. J. Klausmeier, M. R. Quilling, J. S. Sorenson, R. S. Way, and G. R. Glasrud, 1971, *Individually guided education and the multiunit elementary school: guidelines for implementation.* Madison, Wisc.: Wisconsin Research and Development Center for Cognitive Learning, Chapter 2.)

cilitate immediate and long-range planning, increase involvement in educational decision making, and improve communication among school personnel. The anticipated results are fuller commitments to shared goals, higher educational achievement, and increased satisfaction for each person involved in the educational process. Admittedly, organizational change alone cannot meet simultaneously such ambitious theoretical and practical goals. Significant changes of the kinds described are possible, however, if other essential supportive components are combined with substantial restructuring to create an environment which motivates and reinforces contributions to learning. A description of the three levels of the multiunit organization follows.

The Instruction and Research (I & R) Unit. At the classroom level in the multiunit organization is the I & R Unit. This nongraded I & R

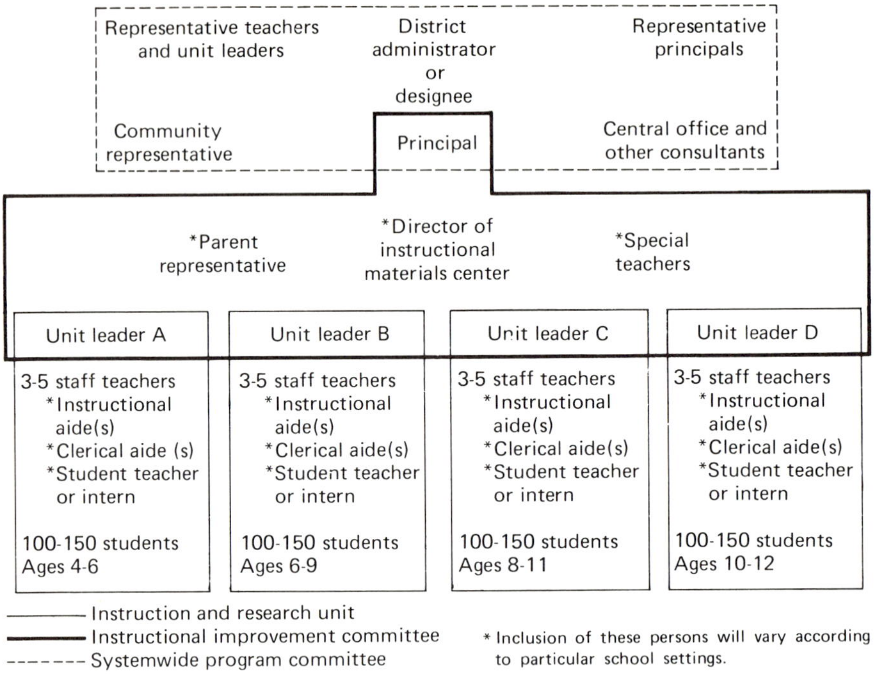

Fig. 1.2 Organization chart of a multiunit school. (Adapted from H. J. Klausmeier, R. G. Morrow, and J. E. Walter 1968, *Individually guided education in the multiunit elementary school.* Madison, Wisc.: Wisconsin Research and Development Center for Cognitive Learning.)

Unit replaces both the age-graded, self-contained classroom and departmentalized forms of organization for instruction. A typical I & R Unit includes the following personnel: a unit leader, three to five staff teachers, an instructional and/or clerical aide, student teachers or interns, and 100-150 students.

The main functions of the I & R Unit are to (1) plan, carry out, and evaluate instructional programs for each student in the unit; (2) engage in continuous inservice staff development activities; (3) provide preservice teacher education activities; and (4) plan and conduct cooperatively, perhaps with other agencies, a systematic program of research and development. Since all units must continuously conduct practical research to devise and evaluate an instructional program appropriate for each student, research is included in the title to reflect this emphasis.

The Instructional Improvement Committee (IIC). At the second level of organization, the school building level, is the IIC. The IIC is comprised of the principal and the unit leaders, and in some schools, a parent representative, the IMC director, and/or special teachers. It is organized and chaired by the principal. Other personnel are involved in meetings by invitation.

The four main functions for which the IIC takes primary initiative are (1) stating the general educational objectives and outlining the educational program for the entire school building; (2) interpreting and implementing systemwide and statewide policies that affect the educational program of the building; (3) coordinating the activities of the I & R Units to achieve continuity in all curricular areas; and (4) arranging for the use of the time, facilities, and resources that are not managed independently by the units. The IIC thus deals primarily with the planning, decision making, and coordinating functions that are related to instruction.

The Systemwide Program Committee (SPC). The SPC is at the third or district level of the organization. In earlier IGE literature this structure was called the systemwide policy committee since policy changes are often necessary to move from a self-contained classroom form or organization to that of the I & R Unit and the IIC required in IGE. Since the board of education is the policymaking body, the name, systemwide *program* committee, is more appropriate. The SPC is chaired by the district administrator or his or her designee and includes representative central office and other consultants, principals, unit leaders, teachers, and community representatives.

The four decision-making and facilitative responsibilities for which the SPC takes primary initiative are (1) identifying the functions to be performed in each IGE school of the district, (2) recruiting personnel for each IGE school and providing for their inservice education, (3) providing the essential physical resources and instructional materials, and (4) planning an effective program of home-school-community relations. A central office structure other than the SPC may be responsible for these functions; considerable flexibility is required since local school districts differ greatly in size and other characteristics.

Differentiated roles. Unlike some differentiated staffing programs that create a complex hierarchy and call for a proliferation of new roles and titles for personnel, the multiunit organizational pattern establishes only one new position, that of unit leader or lead teacher. However, basic changes are made in the roles of the principal and teacher and in other roles that are integrated into the unit such as the teacher aide, the instructional secretary, and the student teacher or intern. The multiunit structure does not preclude the identification and establishment of other specialized roles, such as those concerned with instructional media, pupil personnel services, or home-school-community relations. It does assume, however, that the unit leader and the staff teachers who work directly with the students and their parents are the key individuals in the instructional process. The multiunit pattern also calls for a direct concentration of the personnel and financial resources of the school district in the daily program of instruction. In the discussion that follows, the key roles of unit leader, staff teacher, and principal are described briefly.

The *unit leader* is a member of the IIC, the leader of a unit, and a teacher in the unit. As a member of the IIC, the unit leader contributes to planning the entire program of the school, primarily by defining the program for the unit in relation to that of other units. The leader of the unit has the following responsibilities: (1) planning and coordinating the instructional activities in the unit, (2) allocating and managing materials and resources, (3) fostering and maintaining effective working relationships within the unit and between the unit staff and others, and (4) instructing unit members, including beginning teachers, instructional aides, and student teachers/interns. The unit leader teaches from 60 to 80 percent of the time, the proportion depending upon the size of the unit and the amount of research and development and teacher education conducted in the unit. In addition, the unit leader is a career teacher who takes the initiative in developing and trying out new materials and instructional procedures.

The role of *staff teacher* is changed considerably in the multiunit organization. The staff teacher participates in unit planning sessions, is involved with a large number of children in the unit, and performs more professional and less routine work. The collaborative planning, instruction, and evaluation called for in IGE demand specialization of tasks according to the capabilities and interests of each staff member. For example, the teacher who is strong in a curricular area takes greater initiative in planning the unit activities in that area, in teaching other staff members, and in the actual teaching of children. Teachers may also be stronger or weaker in certain instructional groupings. One may be excellent in tutorial activities, another in small group activities, and still another in large group activities. The tasks of identifying instructional materials, developing assessment tools and procedures, planning home-school-community activities, or conducting other specialized functions are assigned according to each teacher's characteristics. Although teachers take initiative in areas of their strengths and interests, they do not become completely specialized. Most teachers teach in all curricular areas.

The role of the *principal* is also changed in the multiunit organization in that it includes greater and more direct leadership responsibility for the improvement of instruction. The principal organizes, structures, and chairs the IIC which serves as the vehicle for open communication and systematic planning, and assists the IIC in making decisions which can be implemented effectively. The principal selects, assigns, and orients the various staff members to their differentiated roles and encourages each staff member to participate in a meaningful program of professional growth and development. As the administrator of the school, the principal is responsible for obtaining and managing the financial and physical resources required for the program. In addition, the principal initiates extraorganizational relationships and utilizes these resources to provide effective programs of home-school-community relations, preservice and inservice training, and continuing research and development to improve instructional programming for the individual student.

Instructional Programming for the Individual Student

At the heart of IGE is instructional programming for the individual student. The model for this process was originally described by Klausmeier, *et al.* (1971) and is presented in revised form in Figure 1.3. It specifically takes into account each pupil's beginning level of performance, rate of progress, style of learning, motivational level, and other characteristics in the context of the educational program of the school. Instructional programming for the individual student must be appropriately planned and implemented in the cognitive, affective, and psychomotor domains. It can be used either with explicitly stated instructional objectives that specify mastery, or with expressive or more general instructional objectives that imply either activities to be carried out or progress to be made, rather than a prescribed level of mastery. Thus, the IPM is a model which suggests how objective-based instruction may proceed in various curricular areas, rather than prescribing that objective-based instruction should proceed in an identical manner in all curricular areas. Regardless of the specificity of the objectives and whether or not the same level of mastery is desired of every student, seven sequential steps are followed in implementing the model as outlined in Figure 1.3.

Step 1 involves setting general educational objectives to be attained by the student population of a school within a period of a year or longer. Objectives deal with level of achievement or other performance related to each curricular area and in accordance with acceptable value orientations and desirable action patterns. The initiative for setting schoolwide objectives is taken by the IIC with appropriate input from unit staff members, central office personnel, parents, and others concerned with the educational priorities of the school. In formulating the general objectives, attention is given not only to priorities but also to the programs to be utilized and the criteria to be accepted as evidence that the objectives have been attained.

Step 2 concerns identification of the range of instructional objectives

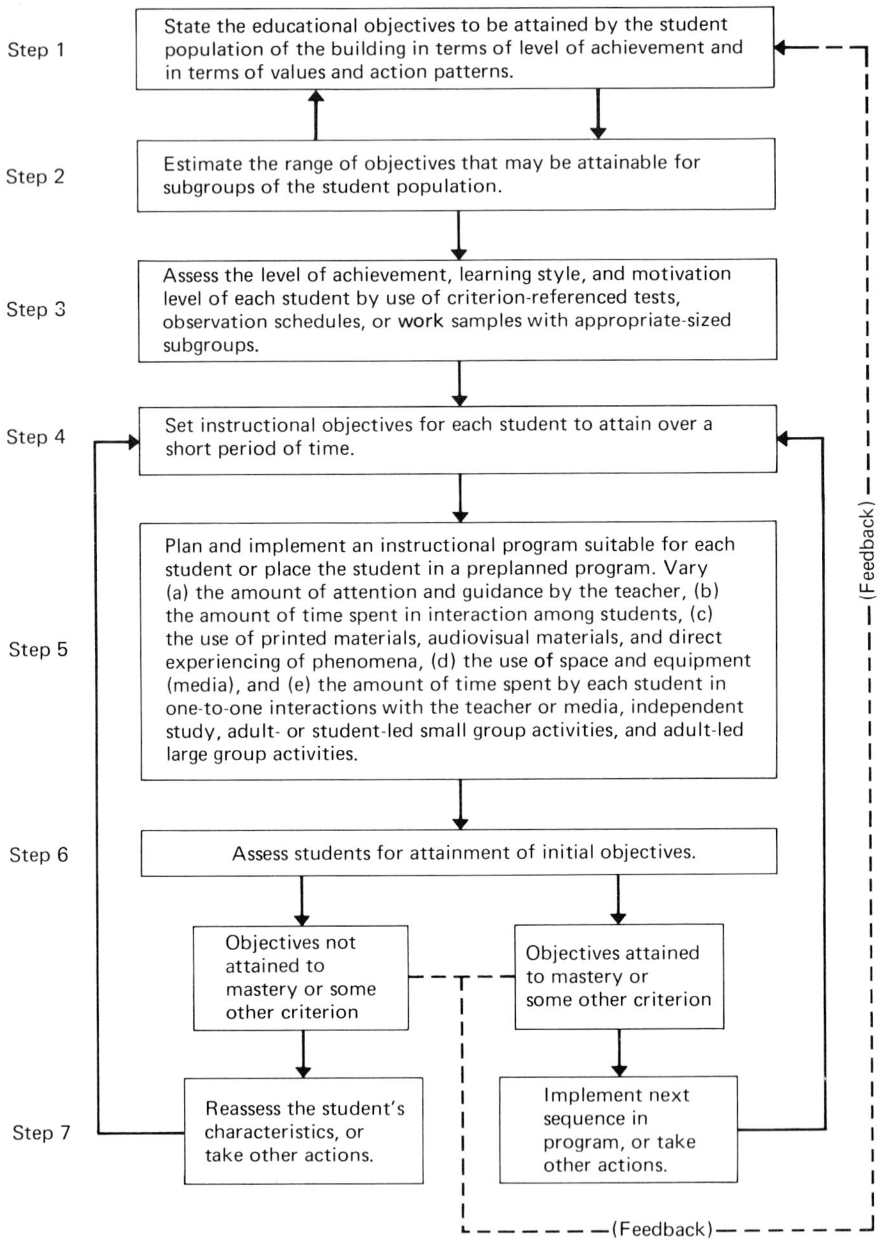

Fig. 1.3 Instructional programming model in IGE. (Adapted from H. J. Klausmeier, M. R. Quilling, J. S. Sorenson, R. S. Way, and G. R. Glasrud 1971, *Individually guided education and the multiunit elementary school: guidelines for implementation.* Madison, Wisc.: Wisconsin Research and Development Center for Cognitive Learning, p. 19.)

that may be attainable for subgroups of the student population. The initiative for this step is taken by the unit leader and staff teachers of each I & R Unit. For example, the unit staff must decide which of the mathematics objectives dealing with computation are appropriate for the 8- to 11-year-olds in their unit.

Step 3 involves actual assessment of each student's level of understanding, skill, or attitudinal development, either by observing performance or by administering tests and other measures. Criterion-referenced tests are particularly useful for assessing mastery of instructional objectives related to clearly delineated skills, such as reading, spelling, and arithmetic computation. When the appropriate subset of objective-related tests is administered, the needs of each student can be pinpointed, and the instructional objectives for the individual student can be identified.

Step 4 deals with setting instructional objectives for each student in the unit to attain over a short period of time. Particular objectives which the student has not yet attained become that student's instructional objectives.

Step 5 involves planning and implementing an instructional program in which the student attains objectives. The plan is implemented by varying (a) the amount of attention and guidance by the teacher; (b) the amount of time spent in interaction among students; (c) the use of printed materials, audiovisual materials, and direct experience; (d) the use of space and equipment; and (e) the amount of time spent by each student in one-to-one interactions with the teacher or media, in independent study, in adult- or student-led small-group activities, and in adult-led large-group activities.

Generally, each teacher instructs one or more groups of students who are working toward mastering the same objective or set of objectives. In each small group, materials, methods, and use of time are matched to individual pupils with consideration given to their present level of skill development, rate of learning, preferred learning style, and other characteristics. Personal characteristics, such as sociability, motivation, and emotional maturity, are also considered. To the extent that staff is available, individual tutoring and goal-setting conferences are provided for each student.

Step 6 involves assessment of students following their participation in the instructional program to determine their attainment of objectives.

Step 7 deals with decision making for both groups of students—those who attained their objectives and those who failed to attain their objectives. If a student failed to attain an objective, the appropriateness of the objective for the student along with his or her readiness to attain it must be evaluated. Other parts of the instructional programming sequence should also be reviewed for clues to student nonattainment of the objective. If the student has attained the instructional objective, he or she moves ahead in sequence to the next objective or to objectives in another related area. In a mastery-based, sequenced curricular area, the desired level of mastery and the successive objectives in the sequence are predetermined and are the same for all students. Other curricular areas may not have a fixed sequence for attaining objectives nor require all students to attain full mastery of objectives.

Implementation of the seven steps of the IPM requires a schoolwide effort. In the IGE school, instructional programming is carried out by the unit leaders and staff teachers with assistance from the staffs of other I & R Units and the central office. However, specialized assistance should also be provided in developing suitable instructional materials in the various curricular areas, preparing criterion-referenced tests and other measurement techniques, and in obtaining and summarizing the evaluative information needed for decision making.

Evaluation for Educational Decision Making

The third major component of IGE is a model of evaluation for decision making at all levels of the organization. Evaluation processes pervade the IGE school, relating to such essential functions as staff personnel, curriculum development, resource management, and home-school-community relations, but they converge critically on the individual student in the IPM.

A general model for analyzing decision making as a rational process includes the following six stages (Lipham 1974):

1. Identify the problem: define and set priorities for the decision to be made.
2. Set the decision criteria: determine what information and values are relevant to the decision.
3. Obtain information: utilize appropriate mechanisms to collect, summarize, and deliver the required data at the appropriate time.
4. Formulate alternatives: relate the data to the decision criteria.
5. Make the decision: choose one alternative.
6. Implement the decision: assess progress and outcomes.

A model for evaluating student learning and acting on the evaluated information has five phases as follows (Klausmeier and Goodwin 1975):

1. Formulate instructional objectives and set related criteria for attainment.

2. Measure.
3. Relate measurement to criteria.
4. Judge.
5. Act on judgment.

This sequence may be applied to both cognitive and affective learning. It also applies either to short parallel instructional sequences or to completely sequenced programs extending through an entire level of schooling. In IGE, the evaluation of the student's learning characteristics and performance is aimed at providing information at three stages: (1) at the beginning of a unit of instruction, (2) at key stages in the instructional sequence, and (3) at the end of a unit of instruction.

In the IPM, *initial evaluation* of each individual student is carried out before instruction starts. The evaluative information is used in setting objectives for the student and in planning an appropriate instructional program or in placing the student in a preplanned program. When a preplanned instructional program is used, as is often the case, each student is assessed on a number of specific instructional objectives directly related to that program. The placement test, or battery of tests and observations, usually consists of a number of items keyed directly to the objectives of the program. In this connection, short achievement tests are given early in the year, or when children transfer into the unit, to place students properly in the sequenced instruction. Other information from accumulated observations may also be used in placing students and in planning programs for them.

Formative evaluation which can be carried out during an instructional sequence involves assessing what the student is learning. This information is useful in identifying any problems that may need to be overcome by the student, the teacher, or both, so that the student may continue to make progress. Although students may provide some information, the skillful teacher is quick to recognize and overcome unforeseen problems.

Continuous systematic assessment of the student's progress is required in order to arrange appropriate instruction. For example, if an error in early placement has been made, it should be detected and corrected immediately. Or a student may be correctly placed but after initial success may experience difficulty with the pace of the instruction. The proper pacing of instruction requires continuous progress assessment, not only concerning the acquisition of the content of skills, but also regarding the student's level of motivation. Student progress is assessed mainly through the use of work samples and the daily observation of learning activities. Evaluation so integrated within the instructional program provides corrective feedback.

The final stage in the evaluation process, *summative* or *outcome evaluation,* involves determining the effectiveness of the instructional program. Such judgments are based on student outcomes.

To summarize, in instruction based on the IPM, criteria are set for determining attainment of the objectives, student achievement is measured, and the student's achievements are compared with the criteria. Decisions and actions follow. It is important, of course, that various alternatives have been planned in advance since outcome evaluation affects subsequent curricular and other decisions. Different options must be provided since all students cannot be expected to attain mastery of an objective at the same time or through the same program.

Curricular Materials Compatible with IGE

The success of IGE depends heavily on the availability of curricular materials compatible with the IPM and the model of evaluation for educational decision making. Curricular materials, whether developed for IGE or any other instructional system, should incorporate four main attributes (Klausmeier 1975).

First, the content incorporated in the material should be accurate and reliable. For example, scholars in the particular discipline should agree that the content is free of cultural bias, factual errors, and possible misinterpretations of the information.

Second, the content should be learnable by the particular students for whom it is prepared. Here, the concerns are that the content items—facts, concepts, and skills—are properly paced sequentially and that the steps in the sequence are not so large or abrupt that the student cannot accomplish them, or so small and repetitive that student curiosity and creativity give way to disinterest and distaste.

Third, materials and related activities should be teachable. To be compatible with the IPM and the evaluation needed, each set of materials in any curricular area should include (1) clearly stated objectives, either behavioral or expressive; (2) assessment tools and procedures directly related to each objective that will aid teachers in the initial, formative, and summative evaluation of student learning; (3) print and nonprint instructional materials that will enable students to attain each objective; and (4) suggestions to teachers concerning possible instructional activities that effectively combine the use of the materials with student and teacher activities. This last attribute of curricular materials assumes that each teacher, in order to attain any particular objective that may be common for students, must be able to vary the instructional activities for particular students in order to provide for individual differences.

Fourth, the materials should be suitable in terms of cost, attractiveness, and the amount of inservice teacher education required. Neither IGE nor any other form of schooling will improve education when the materials of instruction are either unattractive to children and teachers, or so costly that school districts cannot afford them. Similarly, while it is expected that new materials will require some inservice training, it is futile to incorporate new content and methodology which will require massive inservice education before it can be handled by teachers.

Many professors, scientists, and other personnel at the Wisconsin Research and Development Center have developed curricular materials that meet these criteria and are particularly suitable for use in IGE schools. Presently, programs are available in reading, prereading, mathematics, and student motivation and each program is described briefly below. These, as other programs, require careful evaluation prior to adoption for use in any particular school or school district.

The *Wisconsin Design for Reading Skill Development* (WDRSD) identifies essential reading skills and related instructional objectives and provides machine-scorable, criterion-referenced tests for assessing student mastery of the objectives (Otto and Askov 1973). The program is organized into six areas: Word Attack, Study Skills, Comprehension, Self-directed Reading, Interpretive Reading, and Creative Reading. The first three areas include explicitly stated objectives and mastery learning. The last three areas incorporate expressive objectives and participation in suggested activities rather than mastery of skills or content. Except for the tests, the WDRSD materials are intended for use by teachers, not by children. WDRSD is available to schools commercially from the National Computer Systems Company, Minneapolis, Minnesota.

The *Prereading Skills Program* (PRS) is chiefly designed to prevent reading failures by identifying and overcoming deficits in prereading skills at the preschool and kindergarten levels (Venezky *et al.* 1974). Diagnostic tests have been developed for three visual skills (letter order, letter orientation, and word detail) and two auditory skills (sound matching and sound blending). Instructional packages to help children learn these skills include games, songs, and other activities. Informal assessment procedures and a handbook for teachers are also included. PRS is available commercially from the Chicago Encyclopaedia Britannica Educational Corporation.

The *Developing Mathematical Processes* (DMP) program is a comprehensive instructional and management program that integrates arithmetic, geometry, and probability and statistics (Romberg and Montgomery 1974). Based on sound learning theory and empirical analyses of how children learn mathematics, DMP incorporates an activity approach which utilizes the manipulation of objects and symbols in a carefully sequenced program of mathematics instruction for grades K–6. Geometry is integrated with the study of arithmetic by taking a measurement approach where the students generate the numbers with which they work. Because students are constantly generating numerical data they also learn elementary probability and statistics as they organize and analyze data. DMP is available commercially from the Rand McNally Corporation.

The *Individually Guided Motivation* (IGM) program is designed to increase children's interest in learning related to any curricular area and also to enhance their self-direction (Klausmeier, Jeter, Quilling, Frayer, and P. Allen 1975). The IGM system includes four motivational-instructional procedures to assist teachers in raising the motivational level of their students: encouraging children to read independently, goal-setting conferences in content areas, encouraging self-directed behaviors, and older children tutoring younger children. All of these procedures utilize the motivational principles of goal setting, modeling, feedback, reinforcement, and reasoning. These principles and their incorporation into motivational-instructional procedures are explained and illustrated in the inservice materials, which include five 16 mm films, a text, a book to teach children to become tutors, and a manual for instructional aides.

Since the IGM procedures are designed for use with children low in motivation, a school may use a particular procedure with only a few children or with many children. IGM procedures can be used effectively with WDRSD, DMP, and other instructional programs. IGM inservice materials are available from the CCL Copy Shop, 1025 West Johnson Street, Madison, Wisconsin 53706.

In addition to the materials described here, many publishers are distributing high-quality instructional materials compatible with instructional programming for the individual student. The complete sets of materials usually include statements of objectives, assessment tasks and procedures, materials for students and guides for teachers.

Home-School-Community Relations

Since no system of public education is any better than the public's understanding of the school program, the successful implementation of IGE depends in large measure upon an active program of home-school-community relations. (Fruth, Bowles, and Moser in press.) Three general aims of a home-school-community relations program have been identified:

1. To make the staff more aware of available resources and more responsive to the educational expectations of the community, parents, and children.

2. To make the community, parents, and children more aware of and responsive to the requisites of the instructional program implemented through IGE.
3. To identify and utilize ways and means of actively involving both staff and community in the awareness, commitment, changeover, refinement, and renewal (institutionalization) of IGE.

The program of home-school-community relations operates at three interdependent levels: the school district level, the local school level, and the I & R Unit level. The first level is the larger community of the school district. At this general level the community controls the schools through its willingness to expend its power and resources on programs which mirror its values and interests. If the values held in the broader community are communicated and if the school is responsive to these educational expectations, then the community will use its power and resources to support the instructional program. If the school does not meet the expectations of the community—whether because of dissimilarities in values, lack of expertise, or faulty communication—the community will likely withdraw its support and will use its power to reallocate resources or to replace the staff with personnel who will accomplish the expected tasks in a manner acceptable to the community. The staff, on the other hand, has power in its expertise. The staff expects that the community will furnish the resources to implement the instructional program. Although the staff has power to withdraw services if it does not receive adequate resources, staff members are, in the final analysis, agents of the community and ultimately must either accommodate its demands or set about to change them. Open and clear channels of communication must be initiated and maintained in order to maximize the success of the instructional program.

The second level focuses on the local school community. At this level, particular attention is accorded parents. It is the parents who hold expectations for the school which are often more specific and less objective than those of the wider community. Parents also have a greater and more direct effect upon the input of each child into the instructional program. Taken collectively, and because of their intense interest in the school's means and projected ends, the parents generally constitute the most influential school-related group; they have the greatest impact upon community awareness and potential political actions within the larger community.

At the third level, the focus is directly on instruction. Because task and expertise are systematically allocated in IGE, parents must have a clear understanding of the school's aims regarding the cognitive, affective, and psychomotor development of their children. They also must understand the organization, program, and procedures used. To provide such understanding, the unit staff must devise an effective program of home-school-community relations. From the standpoint of the I & R Unit, the family directly affects the individual child's abilities, skills, and attitudes, thus the teachers must appreciate and understand these influences. Not only must the unit teachers understand the home to understand the child, they are also dependent on parents to accept and commit themselves to an individualized instructional program.

Facilitative Environments

It was recognized early that a system of supportive and facilitative environments is required to maintain and strengthen each IGE school so that, in fact, each school becomes increasingly self-renewing. The system of facilitative environments is conceptualized as consisting of the requisite inputs, personnel, material, and resources, in two categories: intraorganizational system variables and extraorganizational system variables.

At the intraorganizational level, the multiunit organization structure was conceptualized to produce the facilitative environment at the building and school district levels. Intraorganizational facilitative environments focus particular attention on obtaining, providing, and managing the physical and material resources which constitute the learning environment. The change to an IGE school often requires that existing school facilities be remodeled or that projected facilities be planned to provide maximum flexibility in learning spaces. Moreover, to maximize the instructional accountability inherent in the system of IGE, attention must be given to systematic planning, programming, budgeting, and evaluation of the equipment and materials that facilitate the teaching-learning process.

The system of extraorganizational facilitative environments includes the linkages and relationships which must be established and sustained between the school district and the larger environment including other school districts, the state education agency, teacher education institutions, and other groups, such as teacher associations and parent organizations, which share in policy development and program implementation processes. As in the multiunit organizational structure, a trilevel hierarchical arrangement is utilized to structure extraorganizational relationships. This network arrangement is shown in Figure 1.4.

At the lowest level in this structure are the SPCs of school districts which, it will be remembered, include the administrative officer of the school district or his or her designee, other members of the central office staff, representative building principals, teachers, and unit leaders of the IGE schools of the district.

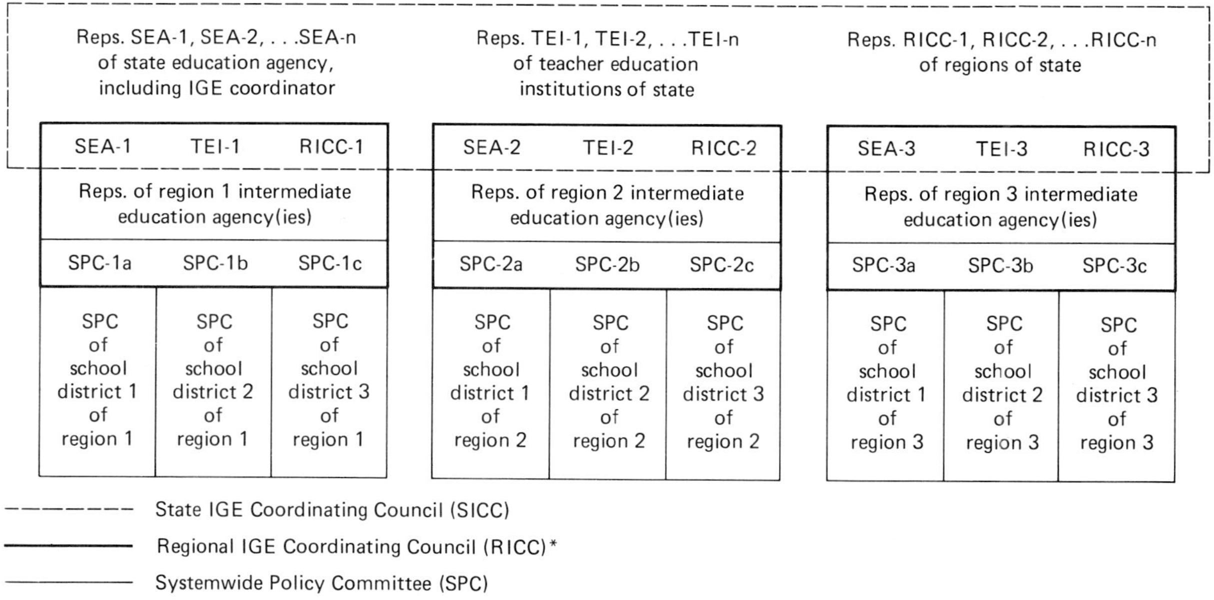

*These are often formed from existing leagues of IGE schools by including teacher educators and school district personnel.

Fig. 1.4 Prototypic organizational arrangements of a state-regional-local IGE network. (Klausmeier, Walter, and Lins 1974, p. 22.)

At the second level of organization is the Regional IGE Coordinating Council (RICC) comprising representatives of SPCs of a region, and a representative of a teacher-education institution of the region, one or more representatives of the regional educational agency (REA), and a representative of the state education agency (SEA). The RICC has responsibility for starting and maintaining IGE schools in a particular region of a state. The SPC representatives provide the linkage between the RICC and the individual IGE schools of each district. In many instances already existing leagues of schools will become the RICC. The SEA representative on the RICC provides the linkage with the state education agency.

At the third organizational level is the State IGE Coordinating Council (SICC). Chaired by the chief state school officer or his or her designee, the SICC includes at least one state IGE coordinator and key personnel of the state agency, representatives of teacher education institutions from the various regions of the state, and representatives of each RICC. Two important criteria for membership are: (1) having the specialized knowledge to contribute to the success of IGE, and (2) having the authority to represent the particular agency. For example, when providing a preservice IGE teacher education program the persons responsible for teacher certification, the teacher education program in a college, and the placement of student teachers in local IGE schools are essential participants in the program.

This pattern of facilitative environments was used as the frame of reference by personnel in 23 states where IGE state networks were formed in 1974. A recent comparative study of the facilitative environments in three states (Connecticut, Ohio, and Wisconsin) revealed that the greater the dynamic linkages, the clearer the coordinating structures, and the greater the resource capabilities between and among agencies, then the more complete the diffusion and integration of IGE into the target user system, the public schools (Paul 1974). Also, variations in the structure of the SICC were found to be necessary among the states because of differences among them in kinds of governmental units, constitutional and legislative provisions regarding education, area, population, and other characteristics.

Continuing Research and Development

The seventh and final component of IGE is that of a program of continuing research and development to produce validated instructional materials and procedures. Research to generate knowledge and theory dealing with the various components of IGE is essential since it is a dynamic system that must change and continuously improve. Various kinds of research and development related to IGE must be conducted by many individuals and agencies.

Local schools continuously conduct evaluative research when implementing the IPM and evaluating its effectiveness. Larger school districts and state education agencies also evaluate their IGE programs. Development and development-based research are conducted by the Wisconsin Research and Development Center to develop each component of IGE, including curricular materials and measurement tools. The development and refinement of the specific components of IGE and of other comprehensive educational systems and products require the specialized capabilities found in colleges and universities, research and development centers, regional educational laboratories, state education agencies, and other profit and nonprofit organizations.

Knowledge-generating research has many variants, including short-term horizontal descriptive research and controlled experimentation. Usually this type of research is not directly related to the instructional program of the school, although it could be, and the results sometimes have neither immediate nor long-term implications for improving IGE or any other form of schooling. Despite this, such research may be of great significance in extending knowledge about a component of the instructional system and in refining administrative and instructional theory and practice in education.

OVERVIEW OF THE UNIT LEADER'S ROLE

In this chapter, the unit leader's role has been discussed in the context of the total IGE concept. In subsequent chapters, the emphasis will be on skills and knowledge the unit leader and staff teachers, as prospective unit leaders, will need to assume the role.

Chapter 2 focuses on strategies for bringing about change—in this case from a traditional, self-contained classroom pattern of organization and instruction to the more complex IGE program with many components functioning simultaneously.

Chapters 3, 4, and 5 deal with personal aspects of the unit leader's role and responsibility. These include the desired characteristics for and responsibilities of the unit leader role in Chapter 3, as leader of other teachers in coordinating the unit in Chapter 4, and as representative of the unit to the IIC and SPC to communicate and make decisions in Chapter 5. Other chapters related to the role emphasize the unit leader's involvement in staff development, both inservice and preservice, in Chapter 6, research and development in Chapter 7, and home-school-community relations in Chapter 8. Information and vehicles to help unit leaders prepare for the role and keep up to date once they assume it are presented in Chapter 9.

Chapters 10 through 16 deal with the unit leader and staff teacher roles in planning, managing, and evaluating instruction according to the IPM. Chapter 10 deals with a general planning strategy for the unit and is followed by information and procedures for setting general educational objectives in Chapter 11 and specific instructional objectives in Chapter 12. Chapter 13 focuses on procedures for assessing student learning and Chapter 14 suggests strategies for grouping children according to assessment and other kinds of data. Practical activities and ideas for carrying out instruction are given in Chapter 15. Chapter 16 focuses on evaluating the total IGE program in a building.

How one I & R Unit implemented the IGE program over a period of several years as told by a unit leader is the subject of the concluding chapter.

Two instructional films, three filmstrips/cassettes, and an instructor's guide have been developed to accompany this textbook. Titles and a brief description of each are presented below:

The Unit Leader in Individually Guided Education is a 16 mm film which provides an overview of the new role of unit leader. It is designed for use with graduate students in elementary education classes and for teachers, principals and others who want to know more about the role in the inservice or workshop setting. The film focuses on the unit leader as a teacher of children and adults, as a coordinator of home-school relations, and as an instructional leader as chairperson of the I & R Unit and member of the Instructional Improvement Committee.

Making Unit Meetings Effective is a 16 mm film that deals with skills the adult members of the I & R Unit need to function smoothly and effectively as a team. These team-building skills include getting acquainted, developing trust, clarifying values, identifying strengths, listening to and helping each other, and reaching agreement on decisions. The film focuses on a team of adults carrying out activities to develop these skills and subsequent application of the skills to an instructional problem at an I & R Unit meeting. This film is designed to be used both in graduate classes in elementary education and in the inservice setting.

The Unit Leader's Role in Planning Instruction is a filmstrip/cassette which shows one I & R Unit staff in the process of planning a social studies unit of instruction on Latin America. It includes discussion of: (1) how general objectives were identified for the school; (2) how instructional objectives were developed for this unit of instruction; and (3) how the unit staff arrived at consensus on objectives, instructional activities and materials, and evaluation procedures. The major portion of the filmstrip is devoted to scenes of actual unit meetings in which plans are discussed and developed.

The Unit Leader's Role in Implementing Instruction portrays the role of the unit leader during the implementation of a unit of instruction on Latin America. The unit leader is shown as a resource person to the unit staff as she (1) discusses possible solutions for an instructional problem posed by one of the teachers; (2) demonstrates techniques for teaching a lesson on longitude and latitude; and (3) provides leadership in identifying alternative actions when an unexpected problem situation arises.

The unit leader role of coordinating space, materials, and equipment is illustrated in a unit meeting. Coordinating available human resources is shown as the unit leader discusses plans with the IMC director, the physical education teacher, and the music teacher. As a liaison with school and community personnel, the unit leader is shown in planning sessions with the principal and with parent volunteers.

Throughout the filmstrip, children are shown as they are involved in the instructional activities which have been planned by the I & R Unit under the leadership of the unit leader.

The Unit Leader's Role in Evaluating Instruction demonstrates how the unit leader works with the unit staff in evaluating a unit of instruction about Latin America. Evaluation activities include a discussion with the IMC director, discussion and demonstration of methods of evaluation for unit staff, identification of assessment instruments, and a final staff evaluation of the unit of instruction. The unit leader is also shown discussing conference procedures with parents.

An instructor's guide has also been prepared to help professors in colleges and universities prepare a syllabus and class exercises for using the book and correlated audiovisual materials in their graduate courses and for inservice sessions with staff in elementary schools. The *Instructor's Guide to the Unit Leader and Individually Guided Education* enumerates objectives, suggested activities to meet objectives, and ways to illustrate mastery of the objectives for each chapter of the book. It also indicates optional activities, other books, and audiovisual materials that might be useful in teaching a course or developing inservice activities about the unit leader role.

SUMMARY

This chapter has attempted to introduce present and prospective unit leaders to IGE. The following topics have been discussed.

- definition and description of IGE
- the history of IGE from 1966 to 1974
- the seven components of IGE and a brief description of the function of each
- a description of the multiunit school (MUS) component indicating the three organization levels and responsibilities of personnel within the organization
- a description of the seven steps of the Instructional Programming Model and personnel responsible for carrying them out
- curriculum products developed for IGE at the Wisconsin Research and Development Center that are compatible with IGE

REFERENCES

Fruth, M. J., D. Bowles, and R. H. Moser in press. *Individually guided education: concepts and principles,* H. J. Klausmeier, R. Rossmiller, and M. Saily (eds.).

Hechinger, G. 1973. U.S. schools *are* number one. *NEA Reporter* **2:** 12 (October).

Klausmeier, H. J., J. T. Jeter, M. R. Quilling, D. A. Frayer, and P. Allen 1975. *Individually guided motivation.* Madison, Wisc.: Wisconsin Research and Development Center for Cognitive Learning.

——— 1975. IGE: An alternative form of schooling. In H. Talmage (ed.), *Systems of individualized education.* National Society for the Study of Education series on contemporary educational issues. Berkeley, Calif.: McCutchan.

———, and W. Goodwin 1975. *Learning and human abilities; educational psychology.* (4th ed.) New York: Harper & Row.

———, J. E. Walter, and L. J. Lins 1974. *Manual for starting and maintaining state IGE networks.* Madison, Wisc.: University of Wisconsin/Sears-Roebuck Foundation IGE Teacher Education Project.

———, 1972. An invitation to the Sears-Roebuck Foundation to improve elementary schooling through implementation, refinement, and institutionalization of IGE/MUS–E. Madison, Wisc.: School of Education, University of Wisconsin.

———, M. R. Quilling, J. S. Sorenson, R. S. Way, and G. R. Glasrud 1971. *Individually guided education and the multiunit elementary school: guidelines for implementation.* Madison, Wisc.: Wisconsin Research and Development Center for Cognitive Learning.

———, R. G. Morrow, and J. E. Walter 1968. *Individually guided education in the multiunit elementary school: guidelines for implementation.* Madison, Wisc.: Wisconsin Research and Development Center for Cognitive Learning.

———, D. M. Cook, W. L. Goodwin, G. E. Tagatz, and L. Pingel 1967. *Individualizing instruction in language arts through development and research in R & I units of local schools, 1965-66.* Technical Report No. 19, Madison, Wisc.: Wisconsin Research and Development Center for Cognitive Learning.

———, W. L. Goodwin, J. Prasch, and M. R. Goodson with an introduction by W. G. Findle, 1966. *Project MODELS: maximizing opportunities for development and experimentation in learning in the schools.* Occasional Paper No. 3. Madison, Wisc.: Wisconsin Research and Development Center for Cognitive Learning.

Lipham, J. M. 1974. Making effective decisions. In A. Culbertson, C. Henson, and R. Morrison (eds.), *Performance objectives for school principals.* Berkeley, Calif.: McCutchan.

National School Public Relations Association 1972. *Individually guided education and the multiunit school: an education USA special report.* Arlington, Va.

Otto, W., and E. N. Askov 1973. *Wisconsin design for reading skill development: rationale and guidelines.* Minneapolis: National Computer Systems.

Paul, D. A. 1974. *The diffusion of an innovation through interorganization linkages.* Technical Report No. 308. Madison, Wisc.: Wisconsin Research and Development Center for Cognitive Learning.

Romberg, T. A., and M. Montgomery 1974. *Developing mathematical processes: resource manual.* Chicago: Rand McNally.

Sipes, W. H. 1972. *Preliminary report on results of one-week institutes for experienced multiunit personnel.* Madison, Wisc.: Wisconsin Research and Development Center for Cognitive Learning.

Thorndike, R. L. 1973. *International studies in evaluation III: reading comprehension education in fifteen countries.* Stockholm: Almqvist and Wiksells.

United States Department of Health, Education, and Welfare, Office of Education 1969. *Digest of educational statistics.* Washington, D.C.

United States Department of Health, Education, and Welfare 1973. *American education.* Washington, D.C.

Venezky, R. L. *et al.* 1974. *PRS (The prereading skills program): teachers' guide folder #10 history of PRS.* Chicago: Encyclopaedia Britannica Educational Corporation.

2

Bringing About Change

Douglas A. Paul
Juanita S. Sorenson

Objectives

After reading this chapter, the reader will be able:

- To describe how the concept of change is involved with the unit leader role.
- To indicate how IGE has attempted to alleviate the research-practice gap in education and the unit leader's part in closing this gap.
- To indicate the overarching ideas and relationships to IGE of the four major strategies for planned change: (a) social interaction; (b) problem solver; (c) research (research, development, and diffusion: RD&D); and (d) linkage.
- To indicate how the unit leader role is involved with each of the four strategies listed in the preceding objective.

The unit leader holds a key position in bringing about the change to IGE. As indicated in Chapter 1, the unit leader has the only role responsibility actively involved at all three levels—the I & R Unit, the Instructional Improvement Committee (IIC), and the Systemwide Program Committee (SPC)—of the multiunit organizational component. The teacher who assumes the unit leader role must be prepared to change as an individual and to provide leadership for change cooperatively with other staff members.

The teacher who assumes the unit leader role must be prepared to change as an individual and to provide leadership for change cooperatively with other staff members.

The unit leader's responsibilities can be classified into two subroles: (1) teacher and (2) instructional leader. The first subrole includes the unit leader as a teacher of children and as a teacher of adults in the inservice setting and during unit meetings. Training for certification as a teacher and experience in the field prepared the unit leader for teaching children; they did not, however, prepare the unit leader for teaching other adults.

The unit leader assumes an instructional leadership role with adults in the I & R Unit, the IIC, and the SPC. As leader of the unit staff, the unit leader acts as a coordinator. This includes duties as chairperson for unit meetings and ongoing coordinator of personnel, time, space, equipment, and materials. Again, teacher training did not prepare the unit leader for these responsibilities.

As a member of the IIC and when elected to the SPC, the unit leader acts as a two-way communicator between the unit and the IIC and between the IIC and the SPC. As with the coordinating role, preparation for teaching did not contribute to the unit leader's understanding of these responsibilities.

Continual involvement in planned educational change requires the unit leader to have a thorough understanding of the concepts of change, the facilitative environments for change, and the role of the unit leader as an agent of change. This chapter focuses on these topics in relation to the unit leader role. It should be noted that the process of planned change in adopting IGE is continuous. It begins with the awareness, commitment, and changeover phases and continues throughout refinement and renewal of IGE. In fact, if the unit leader and IGE staff hold a naive or short-sighted view of the process of planned change, they may unintentionally thwart the change to IGE.

Change is discussed in this chapter under the following topics: (1) the need for planned change, (2) strategies of planned change, and (3) outcomes of planned change.

THE NEED FOR PLANNED CHANGE

Translation and institutionalization of research into viable and beneficial education programs is a major concern of educational practitioners and researchers. The lag between the creation and development of new educational programs and their implementation in schools has been estimated to be half a century (Mort 1964, p. 318). The promise of timely and efficient diffusion of research findings from their source to their users introduces the need for planned change. Local schools may not be aware of the need for change and may not know how to manage change, which is the reason to include the "facilitative environment" as a component of IGE.

Change should be instituted so that (1) the integrity of the change is protected, (2) the change is suited to the conditions in the school, (3) the conflict over the change is resolved, (4) the change results in improved performance, and (5) the consideration of future change is increased (Maguire 1970, p. 3). The need for planned change arises from the limited capabilities of local schools to become aware of and to manage planned change. It also rises from the broader need for translating new theory, knowledge, and techniques into improved role competence. There is a close relationship between the utilization of educational research developments, on the one hand, and improved educational practice, on the other. This section deals with planned change in terms of (1) the research-practice relationship and (2) IGE: a product of research and development.

The Research-practice Relationship

The question of the relevance and application of educational research has been voiced by many sectors of the educational community. There is a need for developing research products into relevant educational programs, and there is a need for moving these programs into the nation's schools. Relevant programs and proven mechanisms for installing the developments of research are two critical needs facing education today. The documentation of these needs has been mostly descriptive. Many people assume that once a new educational idea has been refined, there is a fairly straightforward process of developing it into an educational program and implementing it in the schools. However, this is not the case. Evidence shows this sequence is seldom followed in actual practice and that special efforts must be made to ensure that the results of research are applied (Carter 1966).

The link between inventor and user is probably one of the weakest interfaces in our contemporary educational system (Rogers and Svenning 1969, p. 5). Underlying the concern for linking inventors of educational techniques and programs with the school staff is the belief that education can be and will be improved. One means for improving education is the establishment of mechanisms for translating research into developments and in turn translating the developments into practice. The need for telling educational practitioners about the products of research is overriding, and it served as the basis for the implementation strategy of IGE. This need must also be considered in the refinement and renewal phases of IGE.

IGE: A Product of Research and Development

The instructional and supporting organizational arrangements of IGE may be viewed as a development or product of administrative and instructional theory and research. Learning and administrative theories provided the framework for the Wisconsin Research and Development Center's research. This research focused on many of the problems facing the elementary schools today which were cited in Chapter 1. A new alternative system of schooling, IGE, was developed to help solve these problems. Translating the theoretically based and research-derived development of IGE into practice in the nation's schools became a significant IGE component—extraorganizational facilitative environments.

Obviously, there is no single approach to planned change. Rather, several perspectives, each emphasizing particular aspects of the change process, may be used. By understanding the major strategies of planned change from which the Wisconsin Research and Development Center's strategy comes, the unit leader will have a conceptual basis to help narrow the research-practice gap.

The Wisconsin Research and Development Center has taken an eclectic approach to the diffusion of IGE from the research and development stages to practice in the schools. It has utilized selected concepts and relationships from four strategies of planned change—social interaction, problem solver, research (research, development, and diffusion: RD&D), and linkage—in this process.

For example, the importance of interpersonal relationships and peer group support identified in the social interaction strategy is one basis for the creation of the interlocking network structure in the facilitative environments component. The problem-solver strategy relates to IGE in terms of recognition of the problems associated with age-graded instruction, self-contained classrooms, homogeneous teaching roles, and minimal interlocking of staff effort which is treated, in part, during the awareness stage of implementation. Staff training for the new roles and behaviors needed to solve the problems is also a critical ingredient of the IGE implementation effort. These two needs, problem clarification and staff capability, are major ingredients of the problem-solver strategy.

The interorganizational relationships among the Wisconsin Research and Development Center, state education agencies, teacher education institutions, and local educational agencies are characteristic of the research strategy which emphasizes the orderly translation of research and development into practice. These are considered in the network plan presented in Figure 1.4.

The overall emphasis of the Research and Development Center's implementation strategy for IGE is to create and maintain productive relationships between sources of assistance and the users of IGE. The Research and Development Center, the teacher education institution, and the state education agency represent external sources of help. Central office personnel and the community also represent sources of help and support for the school staff undertaking the implementation of IGE. This emphasis on interlocking organizational and group relationships to facilitate implementation is emphasized in the linkage strategy. By creating a proper mix of face-to-face contact, training, and consulting activities at a mutually agreeable frequency, external agencies and school-related groups are able to provide facilitative environments for the implementation of IGE.

Because unit leaders have a critical part to play in the process of changing to IGE, they need to be knowledgeable about widely practiced strategies of planned change, appropriate uses of each strategy, strengths and weakness of the strategies, and alternative ways in which the change process can be carried out. Therefore, the next section deals with four widely practiced strategies with particular attention to how the unit leader might utilize each strategy.

STRATEGIES FOR PLANNED CHANGE

Difficulties associated with implementing, maintaining, and refining a complex instructional and organizational concept like IGE may be made more manageable and understandable by examining the four strategies of planned change and identifying the role of the unit leader in relation to each strategy.

Social Interaction Strategy

The social interaction strategy emphasizes the effects of influence patterns and communication. The unit leader should be aware of the sources and patterns of influence which will affect the decision to implement IGE and the initial phases of implementation. Opinion leaders such as the unit leader within the school district or networks, may influence the early awareness of IGE, the decision to accept or reject it, and the speed and extent of its implementation. Knowledge of the major opinion sources will provide a base from which the unit leader may predict and in turn manage the consequences of opinion leadership.

Five major phases toward adoption of an idea are described in the social interaction strategy (Rogers 1962, p. 81). These are (1) awareness of an innovation which may create a "need" for it, (2) interest in the innovation which results in actively seeking information concerning its viability and usefulness, (3) evaluation of the innovation by judging it in relation to present practice, (4) trial of the innovation which involves implementation on a small scale, and (5) adoption of the innovation which results in its continued use. Within this view, the social interaction between the potential adopters and their peer groups is the major source of communication about the innovation.

The essential feature of the social interaction approach is being aware of the sources of information about an innovation. Personal versus impersonal sources of information and influence are key distinctions in the social interaction process. For example, impersonal sources of information may be effective at the awareness and information-seeking stage of the social interaction strategy, while personal sources may be more effective at the later stages of evaluation, trial, and adoption. For example, a teacher may read an article about IGE and then discuss the idea with other teachers or the principal. If interest is generated within the group, they gather more information about the concept from printed sources and perhaps from official disseminators. If a trial is agreed upon, they seek personal sources such as unit leaders or teachers who are presently teaching in an IGE school. The individual who first learns about IGE and passes the information along to other members is considered an opinion leader. Within the social network of the school, opinion leaders play key roles in influencing others and contributing to the diffusion of innovations.

However, it should be noted that the new idea or innovation does not necessarily originate from a previously recognized need or search for solutions to specific school problems. The social interaction strategy implies that initial awareness of new ideas such as IGE originate from opinion leaders with outside sources of information. This view, therefore, focuses minimal attention on individuals who initiate searches for new ideas.

Problem-solver Strategy

This strategy focuses on the difference between that which exists and that which is desired. It views the user of an innovation as a client to be helped in a collaborative setting. It emphasizes the design of solutions to solve unique problems and the training of local staff to solve future problems. The need for clarifying the problems which are related to IGE and the importance of tangibly illustrating how an IGE staff solves these problems is a critical role of the unit leader and the principal. While working with the internal and external school groups, the unit leader should facilitate personal understanding of and identification with the problems related to IGE. Progress in moving through the implementation phases will be facilitated by acknowledgment of a felt need on one hand, and by the understanding of how IGE will reduce the need on the other. The unit leader is in a pivotal position between the unit teachers and the principal to help acknowledge needs, to understand how to reduce the needs, and to ensure that the design stays in line with the problems it was created to solve.

A seven-stage model of change which focuses on the deliberate search for solutions to identified school problems has been developed (Lippitt, Watson, and Westley 1958). These seven stages are presented in Figure 2.1. Stage 1 in the model is called developing a need for change. It includes problem awareness, desire for change, and desire for external help. Establishing relationships with outside sources is Stage 2 of the model. This stage is considered crucial since a collaborative relationship

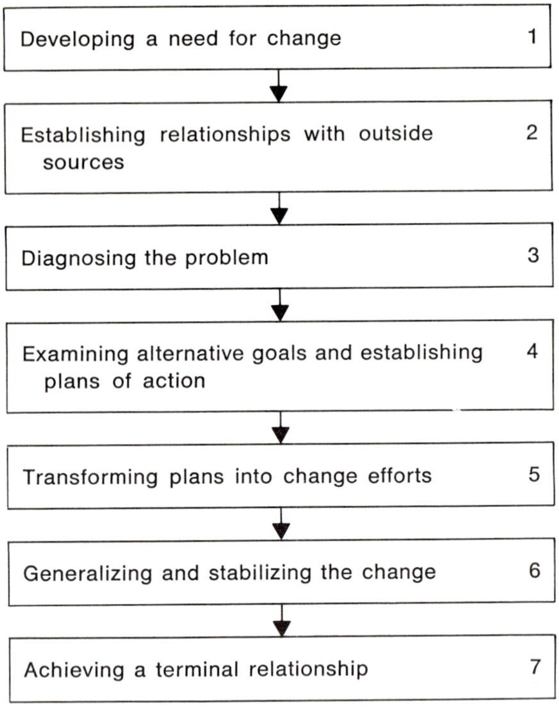

Fig. 2.1 Seven-stage model of change. Based on Lippitt, Watson, and Westley (1958).

between an outside change agent and the personnel of the school is the basis for the problem-solver strategy. In IGE, the outside source might be personnel in a regional or state education agency or a teacher education institution. "The success or failure of almost any change project depends heavily upon the quality and the workability of the relationship between the change agent and the client [school] system." (Lippitt, Watson, and Westley 1958, pp. 135-136)

In the first two stages, the problem-solver strategy distinguishes itself from the social interaction strategy. In the problem-solver strategy, the motivation for change comes from identification of a problem and a subsequent desire for external help to solve the problem. In the social interaction strategy, a preexisting innovation is transmitted through information channels regardless of the documented needs of the school.

Stages 3, 4, and 5 of the model deal with diagnosing the problem, examining alternative goals, establishing plans of action, and transforming plans into change efforts. The diagnostic stage provides a basis to suggest alternative solutions to the problem. At Stage 4, the client or school may wish to pilot test the alternative solution in order to minimize future failure and evaluate the effectiveness of the solution. At Stage 5 the best solution is transformed into action or implementation. This is the critical point in the change strategy. Continuous monitoring of the change is suggested in order to minimize premature discontinuance and in order to adjust the plan to unforeseen conditions. Input for these stages might come from a variety of education agencies, the central office of the school system, or teacher education institutions.

Stages 6 and 7 of the problem-solver strategy include generalizing and stabilizing the change and achieving a terminal relationship. In order to stabilize the change it is necessary to provide structural support and rewards for the client (school) system. Structural support includes a new or revised organizational configuration consistent with the change, and rewards include tangible benefits going to the staff. The multiunit organization within the building and system and the state network linking the local system to a variety of support agencies in the state help provide this stability.

The last stage, achieving a terminal relationship with the external change agent relationship, is needed because of the tendency for a school to feel dependent on the outside resource. New skills and role competencies needed to maintain and refine the change must be developed within the client system. When the school system is capable and confident of making the change, the outside change agent may diminish or terminate the relationship. However, since IGE is a dynamic concept, the relationships with other schools and agencies should not be terminated, but the demand for input from network agencies will diminish as the change stabilizes in a school. The state network and the national AIGE organization are designed to bring this stage about.

The seven problem-solving stages furnish a conceptual scheme for perceiving, analyzing, and planning the change process. There are also a number of important distinctions implied by this problem-solver strategy. Initially, the school must be self-motivated in order to facilitate the mutual relationship with the change agent. Without self-motivation the school cannot successfully progress through the logically interrelated stages of the problem-solver strategy. However, the source of the motivation also may come from the change agent. This means that a school's change to IGE might be initiated by school personnel or outside sources such as the state or regional education agency or teacher education institution. The school must be able to distinguish between self-motivation and external stimulus.

There is also a need to make a distinction between premature adoption of solutions which may not correspond to the problem and the tendency to establish committees which may never act on the problem. This need is somewhat related to the issue of school capability. Much time and energy must be devoted to training the school staff in the use of the planned change. Learning the new roles and techniques associated with the change is a critical issue. If ignored, it will eventually lead to the failure and discontinuance of the change. In IGE, a strong, in-depth inservice program is necessary to train unit leaders, teachers, and principals for the changed and/or new roles they will assume. This topic is explored in depth in Chapter 6.

The lack of problem identification and the failure to establish mechanisms for monitoring and refining an instructional innovation are two causes for the unsuccessful implementation of change (Gross, Giaquinta, and Bernstein 1971). It should be stressed that a short-range view of change will inevitably lead to innovation failure. This is particularly important with respect to IGE which is a long-term, comprehensive, and complex innovation. It is necessary, therefore, for the unit leader and the principal to understand the need for continuous feedback concerning the effectiveness of the change. By not taking a long-range view of the change process, the unit leader, the principal, and the IGE staff may unknowingly upset the implementation of IGE.

Although the seven-stage model discussed here has received considerable attention and has many proponents in the field of education, there are a number of difficulties in the approach of which the unit leader, principal, and other members of the IGE staff should be aware. For example, awareness of a problem, desire to solve the problem, and a search for external help depend upon the individual's ability to identify problems, the attitude that the problem can be solved, and the decision that outside change agents can help solve the problem. Many schools may have neither the capability to identify complex educational problems nor the determination to solve such problems. Moreover, outside change agents, as personnel from regional or state education agencies or teacher education institutions are frequently viewed by practitioners as impractical and theoretical. Conversely, educational agencies or institutions may not reward their personnel who participate in such action programs in terms of salaries and/or promotions within the agency.

Research (Research, Development and Diffusion: RD&D) Strategy

The research strategy is based on an interorganizational view of change. Here, the unit of analysis is the organization, as opposed to the individual in the two previous strategies. The major implication of this strategy for the role of the unit leader revolves around the basic need for closing the gap between research and practice on the one hand, and the need for understanding the interorganizational relationship involved on the other hand. Awareness of the broad role and national concerns of the Wisconsin Research and Development Center will enable the unit leader to place his or her role in perspective and to understand the pivotal position he or she holds between external sources of knowledge and the implementation of that knowledge.

This strategy of change is first discussed in terms of its four main stages—research, development, diffusion, and adoption. Then, some assumptions and critical components are reviewed. The research strategy considers the receiver of new ideas and practices initially as passive. It differs from the social interaction perspective in that the change process is viewed from an earlier point in time, i.e., at the research stage. It also differs from the problem-solver strategy. Instead of focusing upon school needs, it emphasizes the predetermined solution to problems, and centers upon closing the gap between research and practice.

The research stage includes depicting, relating, conceptualizing, and testing without concern for practical application. It has been asserted that the researcher "needs to be free from pressures for immediate payoff" (Guba 1967b, p. 8).

The development stage where problems are identified and solutions are invented, packaged, and field tested logically follows the research stage. The importance of maintaining a distinction between research, the discovery of new ideas, and development, the solution to problems, should be stressed. "It is this activity [the developmental stage] and not research, which is at the heart of change; for while research may make change possible, it is development that actually produces an innovation that may be adopted." (Guba 1966, p. 12) In IGE, the unit leader may be involved with some research in coordination with an outside agency, but will most likely be concerned primarily with development of materials and procedures for IGE in the I & R Unit.

The first two stages—research and development—assume that there are a variety of problems common to most schools and that solutions to these problems can be prepackaged for delivery. However, it should be noted that when developers become aware of the needs and problems of local schools they are then able to design relevant innovations. The balance between prepackaged solutions to general problems on the one hand, and solutions to unique individual school problems (problem-solver approach) on the other hand is a critical issue in the research perspective.

The diffusion stage includes telling, showing, helping, involving, training, and intervening. It is directed toward "building awareness and understanding of an innovation and causing practitioners to consider its features with a view to possible application" (Guba 1967a, p. 42). There are three critical issues: (1) the identification of problems the innovation is designed to solve; (2) the creation of demonstration centers in order to increase credibility and provide the practitioner an opportunity to determine whether the solution fits the problem; and (3) the training of staffs to train other teachers. All of these issues relate to IGE.

Making clear the problems that the innovation is designed to solve minimizes false expectations and helps to solve specific problems. The importance of problem identification at the diffusion stage is also related to the need for balance between prepackaged and unique solutions at the development stage. Credibility may be favorably influenced by demonstration centers—in the case of IGE, smoothly functioning IGE schools—but it is also related to the relevancy of the innovation with respect to the problems recognized by the potential adopting system and the system's perception of the researcher.

Adoption, the fourth stage, includes trial, installation, and institutionalization. The trial component of the adoption stage is based on the need for determining whether or not the innovation performs as claimed. The installation component assumes that modifying, training, equipping, and organizing are necessary prerequisites of institutionalization. The institutionalization component assumes that assimilation and acceptance will follow over time. The adoption stage of the research approach places the initiative on extraorganizational systems which are responsible for encouraging and supporting the target system throughout the adoption stage. The basic premise here is that the more help given to teachers in carrying out the innovation, the more successful it will be (Brickell 1964, p. 505). The degree of external intervention, involvement, and support is the primary focus and critical issue in the research perspective. The adopting system, as it progresses toward the implementation, refinement, and institutionalization of an innovation, must be supported by an outside enabling agency, and elaborate help must be given to teachers (Brickell 1966, p. 99). In IGE, the outside agency might be the local league, the regional or state agency, or a combination of the three acting as a network.

Linkage Strategy

The linkage strategy to planned change emphasizes the need for structured interaction between sources and users of knowledge. Linkage agents function to facilitate interorganizational cooperation and communication. The unit leader is in a position to encourage or discourage interorganizational interaction through the IIC and unit meetings. By understanding the role of linkage agents, the need for regular training and consulting on a face-to-face basis and the short-term inconveniences and the long-term benefits, the unit leader will be able to facilitate the changeover to IGE and help the principal work with internal and external groups.

Seven stages of the linkage approach are described as follows (Havelock 1971, pp. 21-29):

1. linkage, which signifies the degree of interpersonal connection and mutual communicative relations among two or more parties
2. structure, which signifies the systematic organization and coordination of elements within the research-utilization continuum
3. openness, which signifies readiness to give and to receive new information
4. capacity, which includes factors related to a broad range of human, fiscal, and political resources
5. reward, which represents positive reinforcement going to members of the systems involved in the research-utilization continuum
6. proximity, which signifies physical accessibility
7. synergy, which is a combined action of forces organized toward adoption of an innovation.

The significance of the linkage strategy is, in part, centered upon the introduction of organizational concepts within the seven stages. However, in order to understand the eclectic nature of the linkage strategy, references will be made to the social interaction, problem-solver, and research strategies.

The social interaction strategy, which emphasized the importance of the social relations network, the potential adopter within the network, the strengths of informal personal contact and the effect of group norms, has been integrated into the linkage concept. The factors of linkage, reward, proximity, and synergy are related in that (1) linkage corresponds to interconnections within the social relations network, (2) reward corresponds to the reinforcing effect of meeting group norms, (3) proximity corresponds to informal contact, and (4) synergy is related to the overall repetition of social contact within the social system network.

The problem-solver strategy is also related to factors within the linkage strategy. The problem-solver approach emphasized the mutual collaboration between change agents and practitioners, the awareness of the problem to be solved by the practitioner, and the capability of the practitioner to solve recurring problems. These three factors correspond to the linkage factors of openness (willingness to enter into collaborative relationships with external agents), reward (sense of accomplishment resulting from solving a problem), and capacity (the resources within and the capability of the user system).

The research strategy, which in part stressed the need for an orderly transition from research to use, is also related to two factors within the linkage strategy. The factor of linkage is concerned with the need for connecting the producers of new knowledge with systems that need and can use the knowledge. The factor of structure stresses the need for a coordinated and systematic approach to the process of knowledge utilization.

The linkage strategy, although receiving minimal empirical or descriptive verification, has focused attention on the major factor of linkage. The need for linking sources and users of knowledge can be described as follows (Chase 1970, p. 320):

> The building of organizational links to facilitate the flow of knowledge into educational practice is going forward slowly but persistently. Education not only suffers from inadequate knowledge-producing resources but also from the lack of closely linked agencies for moving knowledge through essential processes and phases to widespread and effective use.

The relationships among linkage, structure, and capability on the diffusion of IGE in three states have been explored (Paul 1974). Interviews conducted with personnel from the Wisconsin Research and Development Center, state education agencies, teacher education institutions, and IGE schools revealed that linkage between organizations possessing knowledge of IGE and capability to assist local school personnel in the changeover was an effective means for diffusing IGE. Frequent face-to-face contact and frequent training activities were found to be conducive to complete implementation of IGE. Teacher education institution (TEI) personnel played a major role in the linkage effort by visiting schools, and providing inservice and preservice training. In addition, student teachers or interns assigned to IGE schools helped get the TEI staff involved.

However, problems occurred with the linkage strategy. A number of the IGE school staff noted that university affiliated personnel were often too theoretical or that they disrupted the I & R Units' daily routine. Regardless of whether the TEI, State Education Agency (SEA), or Research and Development Center personnel visit and help the IGE staff, it should be mutually understood what the responsibilities and concerns are for both parties. Figure 2.2 illustrates the interorganizational nature of the Wisconsin Research and Development Center's change strategy which was studied by Paul. The direction of the arrows refers to one-way action and two-way interaction, while the density of the arrows refers to the frequency of action or interaction.

The greatest value of the linkage approach is its recognition of organizational variables as predictors of innovation adoption. The interorganizational theme of the linkage strategy provides a basis for the eclectic

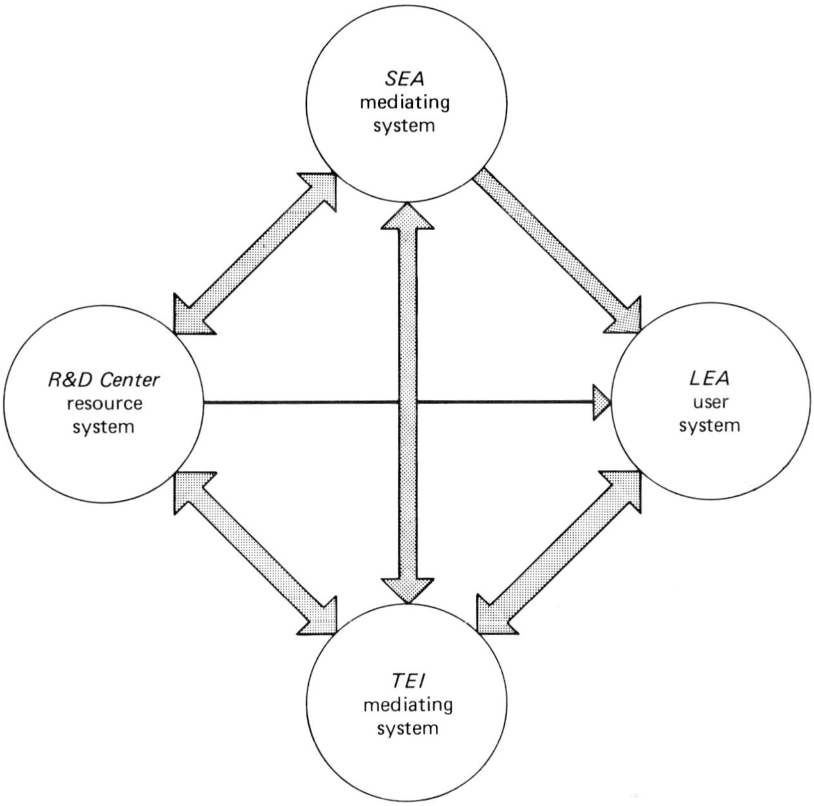

Fig. 2.2 Linkage relationships among resource, mediating, and user systems.

approach to innovation diffusion used by the Wisconsin Research and Development Center. The regional and state networks for IGE diffusion are interorganizational alliances and the phases of IGE implementation correspond not only to the social interaction approach but also to the broad concept of linkage between the sources of expert knowledge and the users of the knowledge.

OUTCOMES OF PLANNED CHANGE

The major outcome of planned educational change is the establishment of new practices which will bring about an improved state of affairs compared with previous practices. The strategies of planned change and the role of the unit leader in implementing IGE are directed, conceptually and behaviorally, toward the goal of institutionalization of new structures, interaction patterns, and role expectations. The role of the unit leader and the goal of improved educational opportunities as related to the research-practice gap and change strategies supporting IGE are discussed in this section.

Much rhetoric has been directed toward the slow, chaotic, and disappointing movement of educational developments, such as the creation of a new role, into practice. However, along with the minimal research done on the problem, there have been few practical programs for systematically and purposefully bridging the research-practice gap. The eclectic planned change strategy of the Wisconsin Research and Development Center represents one successful and realistic approach toward translating and installing the developments of research into viable and beneficial educational programs.

As mentioned in the beginning of this chapter, the unit leader's role in this effort includes teaching children, training the unit staff, coordinating unit activities, and communicating problems and concerns of the unit to and from the IIC, SPC, and on occasion other agencies in the state network.

A number of illustrations of the significance of the unit leader's role and the strategies of planned change may help reinforce the need for understanding these strategies. Although the linkage strategy calls for collaborative relationships between outside sources of help and the school staff, in some instances the principal or the IIC is not supportive of on-site visits by outsiders. One way the unit leader can help bring about planned change is by understanding the importance of external assistance. He or she may influence the principal and the staff to accept and support outside help. In such instances the unit leader must work hard to avoid disruptions which could result in some staff members complaining to the principal. Then, too, the unit leader must work closely with the principal in order to convince him or her not only of the need for additional help but also of the need for easy access to the school and staff by the external resource personnel.

Second, just as the unit leader must work closely with the principal in helping implement IGE, the unit leader must also work closely with the unit teachers. For example, the need for identifying educational problems, stressed in the problem-solver strategy, is important in the IGE implementation process. The problems characteristic of many elementary schools, and from which IGE emerged as an alternative solution, must not only be understood by the unit leader but also be communicated to the unit teachers. If the unit staff does not agree that the problems concerning IGE exist or are serious, then a fundamental basis for implementing IGE will be missing. The unit leader has a responsibility to help illustrate the problems which IGE is designed to solve.

A third illustration of the unit leader's role in planned change revolves around the interlocking membership structure of the IIC and SPC, and the Regional IGE Coordinating Council (RICC). The unit leader is not only a member of the IIC, but the position is also represented on the SPC and RICC. Consequently, the role of communicator between the unit and the IIC, SPC, and RICC is a critical responsibility. By identifying problems and concerns within the I & R Unit, the unit leader is able to communicate these concerns to planning, policy-, and decision-making bodies. Consequently, the unit leader acts as a linkage agent between the I & R Unit and the school (IIC), the school and the district (SPC), and the district and the region (RICC).

A fourth illustration of the unit leader's diverse role and the strategies of planned change centers upon the need for coordination. The various responsibilities and activities of the unit not only require coordination within the unit but also within the school. The linkage strategy of change includes the factor of structure which involves systematic coordination. The unit leader must systematically coordinate the various unit activities in order to ensure that the change is being effectively implemented. The assignment and movement of groups of students is a complex and difficult task which the unit leader must face in a systematic and fairly structured manner. If the coordination function is ignored, the process of implementing change will inevitably be hindered.

The unit leader and principal play central roles in implementing IGE. The principal may act as a gatekeeper between the networks, the central office, and the community on one hand and the unit leaders and unit teachers on the other hand. The unit leader may, in turn, act as a gatekeeper between the principal and outside resources, and the unit teachers. The degree to which the developed research product of IGE enters and is established within the school, the degree to which outside enabling groups enter into a collaborative relationship with the staff of the school, and the degree to which the community is involved with and committed to IGE are mainly the responsibility of the principal and the unit leaders. Consequently, the unit leader may directly and actively contribute to the need for planned change and for the removing of the research-practice gap in education—both important outcomes of planned change. The unit leader must understand the strategies of planned change, the need for extensive training to implement the change, and the advantages of working closely with the principal and the unit teachers.

SUMMARY

The need for planned change has been discussed with attention being directed toward the gap between the developments of research and their use in schools and toward IGE as a product of research which has been shown to be a significant educational program.

Four strategies of planned change were discussed and compared. Each approach emphasized a different place along the continuum from research to practice. The social interaction strategy emphasized communication channels and the stages of change from knowledge of the innovation to peer confirmation of the decision to accept or reject the innovation. The problem-solver strategy focused on the creation of solutions for individual schools which explicitly addressed well-documented local problems. The research strategy stressed a general view of change beginning at the research stage. The linkage strategy discussed the interorganizational dynamics associated with disseminating and using knowledge. Linkage agents were identified as a means for translating research developments into practice and for assisting users of the developments.

The major outcome of planned change was shown to be the narrowing of the gap between research developments and practice by successful implementation of a new program, IGE. The strategies of planned change were related to the role of the unit leader as teacher, coordinator, and communicator. Finally, the role of the unit leader was depicted as one of pivotal importance in the necessity for linking research products with practice.

REFERENCES

Brickell, H. M. 1964. State organizations for educational change. In M. B. Miles (ed.), *Innovations in education.* New York: Columbia University.

——— 1966. The local school system and change. In R. I. Miller (ed.), *Perspectives on educational change.* New York: Appleton-Century-Crofts.

Carter, L. F. 1966. From research to development to use. Santa Monica, California: Systems Development Corporation (ED 026741).

Chase, F. S. 1970. R and D in the remodeling of education. *Phi Delta Kappan* **51** (February).

Gross, N. D., J. B. Giaquinta, and M. Bernstein 1971. *Implementing organizational innovations: a sociological analysis of planned educational change.* New York: Basic Books.

Guba, E. G. 1967a. Development, diffusion and evaluation. In T. Eidell and J. Kitchel (eds.), *Knowledge production and utilization in educational administration.* Eugene, Ore.: Center for the Advanced Study of Educational Administration.

——— 1967b. *Development, diffusion, and evaluation.* Bloomington, Ind.: National Institute for the Study of Educational Change.

——— 1966. The change continuum and its relation to the Illinois Plan for Program Development for Gifted Children. Paper delivered to a conference on educational change, Urbana, Illinois (March).

Havelock, R. G. 1971. *Planning for innovation through dissemination and utilization of knowledge.* Ann Arbor, Michigan: Center for Research on Utilization of Scientific Knowledge.

Lippitt, R., J. Watson, and B. Westley 1958. *The dynamics of planned change.* New York: Harcourt.

Maguire, L. M. 1970. *Observations and analyses of the literature on change.* Philadelphia: Research for Better Schools.

Mort, P. R. 1964. Studies in education innovation from the Institute of Administrative Research. In M. B. Miles (ed.), *Innovations in education.* New York: Columbia University.

Paul, D. A. 1974. The diffusion of an innovation through interorganizational linkages: a comparative case study. Madison, Wisc.: University of Wisconsin Doctoral Dissertation.

Rogers, E. M. 1962. *Diffusion of innovation.* New York: Free Press.

———, and L. Svenning 1969. *Change in small schools.* University Park, N.M.: ERIC Clearinghouse on Rural Education and Small Schools.

Part II

Description of the Unit Leader Role

The one role unique to IGE is that of the unit leader. The unit leader has three main areas of responsibility—teaching children and adults, providing instruction leadership for the I & R Unit, and serving as a member of the IIC.

To be successful in this role, a person should be a master teacher who has demonstrated superior instructional and leadership expertise. This position requires a person that has a positive attitude toward curriculum improvement, research and development, and teacher education. A potential unit leader must demonstrate the ability to be flexible and inventive in adapting methods, materials, and procedures to fit the instructional situation. And a unit leader needs to relate well to other staff members, administrators, parents, and be respected in the community.

Leading the I & R Unit demands precise planning and coordinating. The unit leader, along with other unit teachers, plans the instructional program for 100-150 children in the unit. The unit leader role has the added responsibility to ensure that the plans are carried out smoothly and accurately and that they meet the needs of each individual child.

The unit leader assumes responsibility for leading the unit staff in developing and implementing a program of good home-school-community relations. Also, the unit leader should be aware of innovations in educational materials and methods and share this information with other staff members. In some situations, the unit leader coordinates practical research activities within the I & R Unit.

As a member of the IIC, the unit leader helps to plan and develop the instructional program of the building. Here, the unit leader provides two-way communication between the unit staff and the IIC, the principal, consultants, and the Systemwide Program Committee (SPC). The unit leaders and principal also have responsibility to develop and implement inservice and preservice programs for the building staff.

The most important responsibility of the unit leader, teaching children, should never be entirely removed from the instructional setting. Sixty to eighty percent of a unit leader's day should be spent in direct contact with the children of the unit.

3

Expectations of the Unit Leader Role

Max Poole
Kathleen L. Nolan

Objectives

After reading this chapter, the reader will be able:

- To describe opportunities the unit leader role offers for the elementary teacher.
- To describe the responsibilities of the unit leader in (a) instruction; (b) staff development; (c) research, development, innovation, and diffusion.
- To indicate personal qualities which a unit leader should possess and briefly explain the importance of each quality to effective teaching.
- To comprehend the difference between IGE and "typical" practices in the total educational program.
- To describe the general cognitive background and specific knowledge needed by the unit leader.

"I really have mixed emotions about accepting the principal's request that I become the primary unit leader. Naturally, I am flattered to be offered such a responsible position, but I'm not sure I want to do anything but work with children. Besides, I'm not sure I am qualified to be a unit leader."

These concerns of a prospective unit leader are understandable. How much contact will there be with children? Why *was* this person selected? Is he or she indeed qualified to be unit leader? These and similar questions have been asked frequently during the past several years. IGE has offered many new opportunities for career teachers. One of these is the position of unit leader.

It has been emphasized in the previous chapters that the unit leader is a new and changed role for the teacher which is unique to IGE. It is a role which includes teaching children and providing leadership for adults. This particular combination makes it possible for master teachers to continue to work with children and, at the same time, to share their expertise with other teachers and to provide leadership for effecting needed changes in the schools.

The unit leader is first of all a master teacher, but many other responsibilities are part of this role. They include guiding the I & R Unit in planning for and carrying out instructional programs for the students. Responsibilities such as representing the unit, keeping abreast of new curriculum developments, providing leadership for new plans for home-school-community relations, and guiding research and development activities are also part of this role.

Teachers who are, or may become, unit leaders should give serious consideration to the expectations of this position. Educators who have the responsibility of selecting unit leaders may find it helpful to have guidelines to aid them in choosing the most qualified person for each unit leader position. In the first section of this chapter, the unit leader position will be discussed as an emerging career opportunity. The remainder of the chapter will focus on the responsibilities of the unit leader, the desirable characteristics of a unit leader, and the guidelines for selecting unit leaders.

AN EMERGING CAREER OPPORTUNITY

It is self-evident that the emphasis on the teaching role of the unit leader calls for a master teacher—a career teacher whom staff members can look to as a resourceful and highly competent teacher of children. There are many such teachers in the elementary classrooms today. There have always been those persons whose performance has suggested that they are clearly outstanding among their peers. These teachers usually received little recognition or reward in the past. The only route to greater compensation in terms of salary, power, and prestige was to leave the classroom. It is likely that such positions as assistant principal, supervisor, or curriculum consultant have been filled by persons from that select group in our public schools.

The relationship between lack of status and lack of opportunity toward upward mobility causing teachers to leave the classroom has been studied (Bush 1971 and Geer 1966). Recommendations for alleviating some of these problems include the suggestion that schools move toward a differentiated staffing pattern in which a competent person could aspire toward a high level of position and still remain a teacher of children.

Another reason teachers leave the profession is the incompatibility between the assigned role and their particular qualifications and abilities. Schools are urged to provide more opportunities and conditions in which greater use could be made of individual teacher expertise. Many graduates of four-year teacher education programs have left teaching positions because of lack of adequate intellectual stimulation, insufficient support for carrying out innovative ideas, and improper expectations for the use of their individual skills, aptitudes, and abilities (Bush 1971).

There is a linkage between the historical conception of school and the increasingly diverse orientation of schooling in the United States today. The power of tradition is dwindling in the multiplication of alternative ways to operate schools. "Today curriculum consists of different approaches to teach a given subject or grade; the range of options extends to all aspects of schooling, from building design to staffing patterns, from grouping students to new instructional technologies." (Lorti 1973, p. 476) This movement is a change in status of the career teacher and suggests implications for new career teaching specialization. In addition, persons were drawn into education in the 1960s because of research and development attitudes which led to changes in traditional practices.

It is quite probable that IGE has attracted and will continue to attract outstanding teachers to work with children. Consequently, many of our best teachers will aspire to the challenging and rewarding position of unit leader. During the relatively short time that IGE has been in existence, this has occurred again and again. Whether recommended or elected by peers, appointed by administrators, or a combination of the two, their selection has demonstrated the vital relationship between the outstanding teacher and the responsibility of the unit leader.

IGE has indeed opened a new horizon for a very select group who aspire to leadership in their art—a group which can lead the way as dedicated professionals. "The professional teacher uses all he or she is

capable of learning to build bridges between theory and practice—between curriculum on paper and curriculum in fact—between the research of professional psychologists, sociologists, and philosophers and school practices that reflect these and the persistent factors and problems that characterize our times." (Wright, *et al.* 1971, p. v). In addition, the professional teacher does a better job of teaching by knowing and using sound practices in the process of designing a curriculum that is scientific in nature rather than one that is static and stereotyped (Wright, *et al.* 1971, p. vi). The role of unit leader teacher is well suited to carrying out such a proposition.

Although IGE is relatively new to the educational scene, it is increasingly apparent that the unit leader is vital to the successful implementation and subsequent effectiveness of the concept. The assignment of teachers to this role should never be taken lightly. It should be understood that the unit leader position is not being prescribed as "the unreachable goal." Rather, it is being suggested that the role is of such importance that it should be assumed by only the best teachers in our elementary schools.

RESPONSIBILITIES OF THE UNIT LEADER

In order to place the emerging career position of unit leader in its proper context, it is helpful to see how the role was envisioned in IGE (Klausmeier, *et al.* 1971, pp. 38-41). Excerpts from the description of the unit leader role are reproduced below:

> The unit leader has responsibilities as a member of the IIC, as a leader of a unit, and as a teacher. The responsibility of the unit leader is instructional, not administrative or supervisory. His leadership role is in planning and coordinating. As a member of the IIC, he helps to plan and develop the instructional program of the building. He serves as a liaison between the unit staff and the principal and consultants and he coordinates the efficient utilization of the unit staff members, materials, and resources.
>
> *Unit Leader Responsibilities*
>
> A. Instruction
>
> 1. Assumes leadership in developing, carrying out and evaluating a program of IGE in the unit, including objectives, materials,

---

IGE has indeed opened a new horizon for a very select group which aspires in its art—a group which provides dedicated and professional leadership.

equipment, and activities. The unit leader works closely with the unit staff, the building principal, subject-matter specialists, and others.

2. Coordinates the assessment of children's characteristics and progress in the unit and the placement of children in appropriate activities.

   The unit staff, building principal, and central office personnel are also involved, including research director, school psychologist, and subject specialists.

3. Assumes leadership in initiating, establishing, and maintaining good home-school relations. The unit staff, building principal, social workers, and other specialists contribute effectively to this area of concern.
4. Teaches about half or three-fourths time or in other ways is directly involved with the children.
5. Utilizes portions of the remaining time to (a) act as liaison between the principal and unit staff, (b) meet with unit staff members to plan instruction and to enhance the understanding and direction of IGE, and (c) meet with the IIC.
6. Keeps abreast of advances in subject knowledge, instructional materials, and other components of a system of individually guided education.

B. Staff Development

1. Inservice
   a. Develops, cooperatively with the IIC, the principal, and relevant central staff, a building program of on-the-job education for the certified personnel of the unit, including first-year teachers; carries out the relevant elements of the building program in the unit.
   b. Develops and carries out a similar program for instructional secretaries and aides.
   c. Coordinates the inservice training activities of the certified and noncertified personnel in the unit whereby capabilities of the aides are identified and improved and the certified teachers learn to work effectively with aides.
2. Preservice Education
   a. Develops, with the IIC, principal, relevant central staff, and representatives of teacher-education institutions, the building

program for interns; carries out the relevant elements in the unit.

b. Coordinates the placement of the intern in the unit and the instructional activities of the intern with the certified and noncertified personnel.

C. Research, Development, Innovation, Diffusion

1. Development

a. Plans the development activities of the unit with appropriate personnel of the unit, building, central office, and other agencies.

b. Coordinates the development of a system of individually guided education within the unit, including a statement of objectives, the assessment of the capabilities of students, the instructional program, and evaluation procedures.

2. Innovation

a. Coordinates the introduction of novel instructional materials, measurement and evaluation tools and procedures, instructional methods, etc.

b. Stimulates the invention of new instructional methods within the unit.

c. Keeps abreast of innovations throughout the school system, the state, and nation through visits, conferences, and reading.

3. Diffusion

a. Provides for the proper briefing of observers of the I & R Unit.

b. Participates in the planning and actual diffusion of promising practices within the building and system as appropriate.

4. Research

a. Plans research activities of the unit with appropriate personnel of the unit, the building, the central office, and other agencies.

b. Coordinates research activities within the I & R Unit.

c. Guides the administration of experimental treatments—instructional methods, materials, media—by subexperimenters (teachers or others) to ensure continuous adherence to the specified experimental design and to a schedule for collecting information.

d. Guides the collection and, as time permits, the analysis of information collected.

e. Keeps abreast of relevant research results and methods.

The responsibilities of the unit leader are many and varied. The position calls for a person who has strengths in diverse areas and has the ability to use these strengths in the IGE setting. The next section of this chapter will focus on characteristics which are found in people who have the ability to carry out the responsibilities of the unit leader.

DESIRABLE CHARACTERISTICS OF THE UNIT LEADER

What kind of a person should be considered for the role of unit leader? What are the characteristics of a person who exhibits excellence in teaching children, creates innovative teaching materials, knows current educational literature, carries out research activities, and is able to provide effective leadership for other adults who are working toward similar goals?

Research into the behavior of effective teachers has indicated they are able to (Hamachek 1969, p. 342):

1. be flexible, to be direct or indirect as the situation demanded.
2. perceive the world from the student's point of view.
3. "personalize" their teaching.
4. experiment and try out new ideas.
5. ask questions skillfully.
6. exhibit adequate knowledge of subject matter.
7. provide well-established examination procedures.
8. reflect an appreciative attitude (evidenced by nods, comments, smiles, etc.).
9. use conversational manner in teaching—informal, easy style.

The remainder of this section will further delineate the characteristics expected of the unit leader, using characteristics of successful unit leaders, principals, and others who have worked in IGE schools, and the literature as a base. The discussion will relate to (1) personal qualities and (2) knowledge requirements.

Personal Qualities

The importance of positive personal qualities for the unit leader cannot be stressed too heavily. These qualities include:

1. commitment
2. positive perception of self
3. positive perception of others
4. openness
5. facilitator of change
6. self-renewal
7. charisma
8. flexibility

Each of these qualities as it pertains to the unit leader role is discussed in detail below.

Commitment. The importance of a commitment to a career in teaching has already been stressed. In addition, there should be a commitment to IGE. This means that the unit leader thoroughly understands the concept, that the unit leader is in philosophic agreement with IGE as an alternative to the traditional approach, and that the unit leader is dedicated to carrying out the concept of IGE. Throughout the history of education, many new ideas and practices have been advanced. Although some enjoyed wide acceptance and success, others which appeared to be equally promising never reached fruition. Obviously, a number of reasons can be cited for their failures.

It is likely, however, that too many educators who sincerely believed that such changes would result in better learning lacked sufficient personal commitment to give sustained support to testing the ideas in the schools. New ideas should at least receive a fair opportunity in the educational forum. The unit leader should be dedicated to such a position in IGE. In Figure 3.1, the differences between IGE and typical practices in an elementary school are specified, and a prospective unit leader must know these distinctions. The reader should review these practices in order to assess his or her total commitment to IGE practices.

Positive perception of self. Another quality to look for is the candidate's perception of self. Psychologists have made many studies about the characteristics of persons who possess the so-called adequate self. Various terms have been used to describe such persons. They are often referred to as "self-accepting," "self-actualizing," "self-realizing," "fully functioning," "adequate personalities," and so on. It is especially appropriate to expand upon the latter two qualities. "Fully-functioning" is used to denote persons who feel that "they are enough." Such persons are referred to as being in a state of "movement" or "becoming" (Kelly 1962). This is most desirable for teachers involved in the IGE program.

Practice	IGE	Typical
Objectives	Educational objectives form basis of program	Often there is no statement of educational objectives
	Staff selects/adapts/develops objectives	Sometimes overall statements developed by outsiders are accepted as the school's objectives
	Individual student objectives	No individual student objectives
Physical facility	Instructional pods	Self-contained classrooms
	Instructional Materials Center	Library
	Space used flexibly	Space used inflexibly
Instructional staff	Differentiated staff	All teachers perform same tasks
	Principal is instructional leader	No instructional leader
	Staff complemented by student teachers, instructional aides, secretaries	Occasional aide, secretary, or student teacher
	Special teachers are part of units	Special teachers work independently
Other education personnel	Central staff personnel are involved in context of building planning	Central staff work independently
	Resource persons work directly with staff during school day	Resource personnel are used outside school hours
Teacher activities	Responsibilities differentiated among staff for instruction	Teacher responsible for total instruction of about 30 children except for special areas
	Unit planning	Individual teacher planning
Use of time and resources	Each child's program is determined by instructional objectives	All children in a room have the same learning experiences
	Time allocations set by unit staff	Time allocation set by central staff
Assessment and evaluation used	Child's readiness assessed	Little use of preassessment
	Child's progress compared to a mastery level	Child's progress compared to others
	Provided feedback to child	Assigned grades
	Comparisons made to improve the instructional system	Comparisons made among schools

Practice	IGE	Typical
Terminal behavior	Final student performances are stated in instructional objectives	No terminal performances predetermined
	Postassessment made before moving to next unit of instruction	Students move en masse to next unit of instruction regardless of previous achievement
Home-school communication	Reporting involves teacher, parent, child	Report cards sent home
	Systematic parent-school, teacher-home conferences and visits	Few parent-teacher conferences and visits
	Parents invited to unit and committee meetings to communicate their ideas	PTA deals with peripheral problems
Materials, media, supplies	Materials and media selected for individual and group needs	Textbooks adopted systemwide
	Large variety of AV materials	Limited amount of AV materials
	Teachers encouraged to develop additional materials	Few teacher-developed materials
Curriculum content and sequence	Staff selects content and plans sequence	Textbooks and systemwide curriculum guides determine sequence
Organization for instruction	I & R Units	Self-contained classrooms
	Students in a unit vary 3-4 years in age	Students assigned to grades by ages
	Unit meetings held during school day	No teacher planning time
	IIC	Ad hoc system committees
Student activities	Student readiness assessed	Student readiness not seriously considered
	Individual differences met daily	Little attention to individual differences
	Learning styles taken into account	Little emphasis on learning styles

Fig. 3.1 Relating IGE and typical practices. Condensed from Klausmeier and Ripple 1971, New York: Harper & Row, pp. 229-236.

They should continually move toward higher levels of function and purpose. Adequate personalities appear to be characterized as follows (Combs 1962, p. 70):

1. They tend to see themselves as generally liked, wanted, successful, able persons of dignity, worth, and integrity.
2. They perceive themselves and their world accurately and realistically. These people do not kid themselves. They are able to confront the world with openness and acceptance, seeing both themselves and external events with a minimum of distortion or defensiveness.
3. They have deep feelings of identification with other people. They feel "at one with" large numbers of persons of all kinds and varieties. This is not simply a surface manifestation of "liking people" or being a "hail-fellow-well-met" type of person. Identification is not a matter of polished social graces, but a feeling of oneness in the human condition.
4. They are well informed. Adequate people have perceptual fields which are rich, varied, and available for use when needed.

Reports on a study comparing good and poor teachers conclude (Combs 1969, p. 71):

1. Good teachers feel identified with, rather than apart from, others. They identify with people rather than being withdrawn or alienated from others.
2. Good teachers feel basically adequate rather than inadequate. They see themselves as having what is needed to deal with their problems.
3. Good teachers feel trustworthy rather than untrustworthy. They see themselves as essentially dependable, reliable, and having the potentiality for coping with events.
4. Good teachers see themselves as wanted rather than unwanted. They see themselves as essentially likeable, reasonable, personally attractive, wanted, and in general, capable of bringing forth a warm response from those people important to them.
5. Good teachers see themselves as worthy rather than unworthy. They see themselves as persons of consequence, dignity, integrity, and worthy of respect.

We can expect such teachers to understand themselves and to accept themselves—their limitations as well as their abilities. In short, their life experiences have caused them to feel that they are indeed persons of worth and dignity.

Positive perception of others. While previous conclusions dealt with self-perception of effective teachers, an extensive research review to determine how effective teachers viewed others was conducted (Hamachek 1969, p. 343). It was found that good teachers differed from poor teachers by viewing others in the following ways:

1. They generally have more positive views of others.
2. They do not seem to be as prone to view others as critical, attacking people with ulterior motives; rather, they see others as potentially friendly and worthy in their own right.
3. They have a more favorable view of democratic classroom procedures.
4. They seem to have the ability and capacity to see things from the other person's point of view.
5. They do not seem to see students as persons "you do things to" but rather as individuals capable of doing for themselves once they feel trusted, respected, and valued.

Inasmuch as a great deal of teaming and group decision making takes place in IGE, the unit leader must demonstrate the capacity to identify with the rest of the staff. Adequate persons can work harmoniously with others in either a leader or follower role (Combs 1962, p. 55). Since they feel adequate, they do not *have* to lead in order to prove their strength and power. Leadership for them is not a way of proving superiority, but a way of organizing to accomplish desirable ends. The feeling of identification produces trust in others so that adequate persons can lead or not as the situation demands. They are satisfied in either role.

Openness. Openness is an important human quality for those involved in successful educational innovation. Historically, innovations in education are subject to a considerable amount of resistance by teachers. The "tradition syndrome" has long been a benchmark of the teaching profession. Someone once said, "People are usually down on the things they are not up on!" This has been true of the IGE development. Openness to new ideas is consistent with the behavior of the adequate person. He or she does not feel threatened by change. Innovations such as IGE can be viewed objectively and realistically. Such persons can then turn their attention to their mission as teachers—to change the behavior of children in the most effective way. The difficulty of change can be expressed as follows (Wright, *et al.* 1971, p. 15):

> It is going to take courage to buck the tides that block individualization of instruction in the majority of the nation's schools, perpetuate antiquated

grading and marking systems; institutionalize level concepts of teaching and learning, and equate actual learning with the amount of time spent sitting in the classrooms.

Unit leaders who are open individuals will be alert to new knowledge, new methodologies, new technologies. They will assume leadership in recommending and implementing change in curriculum or instructional strategies which may lead to better learning opportunities for the children in their school. Openness implies that the unit leaders must at times take risks as they lead the staff from the familiar to the unfamiliar. At times they will likely experience failures.

Openness is the ability to listen to and consider others' ideas, to consider and accept differences of opinion, and to encourage the free generation of new ideas from the staff and students.

Facilitator of change. A facilitator of change is a person who practices and encourages new ideas and procedures when they are relevant to the ongoing situation. This quality is important for the unit leader as an agent of change. It has been observed that the initial enthusiasm with which schools implement IGE sometimes wanes as teachers labor to refine the concept. There are few knowledgeable educators who can, in all candor, dispute the fact that IGE is one of the most idealistic, comprehensive, and promising of innovations in the elementary school today. Realization of the purpose and goals of IGE is dependent upon the effectiveness in which the schools bridge the gap between theory and practice. The unit leader must continually attend to the task of interpreting, communicating, facilitating, and assessing IGE in accordance with the original definition, purpose, goals, and procedures.

Involvement in research may assist teachers to see how the "helping relationship" is related to student growth and learning (Combs 1962, p. 72):

> If teachers, administrators, counselors and other school personnel accept the premise that, to change behavior, perceptions must be changed, then education becomes more individual and more personal. The atmosphere within the school becomes more friendly; relationships change from authority figure-subordinate relationships to a person-to-person relationship. The classroom environment becomes less threatening and more facilitating and supporting, less content centered and more meaning centered. Such acceptance implies that classrooms become laboratories where facts, information, and the perceptual world of students are brought together in the presence of a catalyst (the teacher).

Self-renewal. A self-renewing person is a lifelong learner, motivated to reeducate himself or herself throughout a career, lest he or she become obsolete or pedestrian. Too often teachers think of a bachelor's degree as terminal insofar as their own learning is concerned. The motivation for further education is often monetary reward or advancement.

Perhaps teacher education needs to assume some responsibility for this attitude. Teacher education institutions need to reexamine their own programs to determine whether they are training "finished" teachers or whether they believe that "the good teacher is not a finished product but a human process" (Combs 1962, p. 116).

Earlier in this chapter is mentioned the desirability of teachers being "fully functioning" persons. It is absolutely necessary that unit leaders have the thirst for continuous learning. Continued research and development associated with IGE is rapidly adding to the stockpile of knowledge about the concept. The Research and Development Center at the University of Wisconsin—Madison spent years developing, testing,

A self-renewing person is a lifelong learner, motivated to reeducate himself or herself throughout a career. (Courtesy the Media Development Center, UW—EC.)

and refining IGE. In the ensuing years, continuing research and development have added to the original model, not only by the Research and Development Center, but by countless IGE schools throughout the United States. A number of universities and state departments have also added to the IGE base. Unit leaders must be aware of such changes, because, "Positive attitudes toward personal, continued learning make the difference between a professional career teacher and one who is just 'marking time'—lacking stimulation, ambitions, sensitivity, and motivation." (Wright, *et al.* 1971, p. 5)

One unit leader's view of self-renewal is presented below (Rossman 1975):

> I found that the dictionary defines *renewal* as "revival; to regain strength and vigor." I cannot hope to remain a vigorous and energetic leader of a team when I am drained of body and mind with little desire to do nothing more than maintain a satisfactorily functioning status-quo team. With those thoughts in mind, I agreed to renew my contract to be a unit leader only with the assurance that I would receive a second semester leave of absence. These periodic role changes have been invaluable to my professional and personal growth. Unless I can step back and explore and evaluate identity, role and goal, the upward momentum and challenge for tomorrow become lost in the dizzying 'busyness' of today.
>
> There are also other, more tangible needs more easily met during the semester or year long break from the unit leader role. I have the advantage of taking valuable university courses that need time and energies. I can visit schools and rap with professionals about goals, problems and new ideas. I can visit with consultants, review texts and read and write those articles which were merely 'more work' after an already too long day. A leave, a renewal, is also a goal in itself. It is something to look forward to and to use as a crutch on those insufferable days when I'd like to hang it all up forever. This renewal or leave has become an integral part of my professional life. I will return to my classroom a better and more enthusiastic teacher and a refreshed unit leader for my team with new ideas to help us grow together. I will have a better understanding of individual needs. And above all, I'll be a person I and others can live with for another four or five years.

Charisma. Charisma is a word that has only recently been associated with the teaching profession. Researchers have most often noted that effective teachers reflect warmth, enthusiasm, humor, sensitivity, and compassion. An extensive study reported in this context concluded that effective teachers are understanding, attractive, stimulating, kindly, alert, original, confident, fair, poised, responsible, steady, and democratic (Ryans 1960).

Use of charisma is especially appropriate in the context of the classification scheme presented in Figure 3.2 (Spady 1973, p. 5). Charisma

				Expertise dimension			
				Subject matter expertise			
				(low)		(high)	
				Pedagogical expertise		Pedagogical expertise	
				(low)	(high)	(low)	(high)
Charismatic dimension	(high)	Empathy concern	(high)	4	3	2	1
			(low)	8	7	(6)	5
Stimulation= excitement	(low)	Empathy concern	(high)	12	11	10	9
			(low)	16	15	14	13

Fig. 3.2 A classification scheme for attributes to maximize teacher legitimacy and effectiveness. (Reproduced from Spady 1973, p. 5.)

is combined as one of the conditions for determining teacher-effectiveness and teacher-expertise dimension. Effective teachers must (1) have something of substance and interest to say, and (2) be capable of saying it clearly and accurately. A good teacher must be capable of (1) communicating higher ideas in a stimulating and exciting manner, and (2) communicating on a highly personal teacher-student relationship.

To develop an understanding of the chart, look at the meaning of "number 6." Reading vertically, number 6 is to the right of center and would indicate high subject matter expertise. However, number 6 is not to the far right of the center and so indicates a low pedagogical expertise. This means that a teacher who is a "number 6" knows quite a bit about a particular subject, but does not present it in the best fashion. Reading horizontally, number 6 is above the center, and therefore indicates a high degree of stimulation excitement. However, number 6 is not far above the center and therefore fits into the low empathy concern cell. This means that, though this teacher provides an exciting atmosphere to the class, he or she does not empathize with the students' points of view. Readers can rate themselves simply by following these four steps:

1. *Start at the top of the chart.* Under the words, "Subject matter expertise" circle the eight cells to the right of center for "high" or the eight cells to the left of center for "low," depending on your personal feeling.

2. *Identify an area of four cells within the eight cells identified in Step 1 above* as follows. Consider how you present subject matter to your classes, then under "pedagogical expertise" circle the four cells in the "low" *column* or the four cells in the "high" *column.*
3. *Identify an area of two cells within the four cells identified in Step 2 above* by examining your "stimulation-excitement" quality on the horizontal grid. If you have exciting classes, circle the two cells above the horizontal line for "high" or, if you have a low key method of teaching, circle the two cells below the horizontal line for "low."
4. *Select one of the two cells identified in Step 3 above.* Across from "empathy-concern," circle the "low" or "high" cell, depending on the amount of empathy-concern you feel for your students.

By lining up your four "lows" and "highs" (and there is only one box which will accommodate all four), you will find the number which classifies your attributes for teacher legitimacy and effectiveness.

The most effective teacher would appear as "number 1." This indicates that knowledge mastery and expertise in methodology are combined with empathy for the personal needs of children and an exciting and stimulating manner of communicating. Unit leaders might well consider the implications of this design inasmuch as motivation is such an important element in IGE.

Flexibility. Flexibility is basic to innovation and team teaching and is a keystone to success in IGE (Hamachek 1969, pp. 341-343):

> By far the single most repeated adjective used to describe good teachers is 'flexible.' Either implicitly or explicitly (most often the latter), this characteristic emerges time and again over all others when good teaching is discussed in the research. In other words, the good teacher does not seem to be overwhelmed by a single point of view or approach to the point of intellectual myopia. A good teacher knows that he cannot be just one sort of person and use just one kind of approach if he intends to meet the multiple needs of his students. Good teachers are, in a sense, 'total' teachers. That is, they seem able to be what they have to be to meet the demands of the moment. They seem able to move with the shifting tides of their own needs, the student's, and do what has to be done to handle the situation. A total teacher can be firm when necessary (say 'no' and mean it) or permissive (say 'why not try it your way?' and mean that, too) when appropriate. It depends on many things, and good teachers seem to know the difference.

IGE demands teachers who are flexible. Differentiated staffing, nongradedness, space utilization, accommodation to each student's characteristics and needs, assessment and reassessment, shared decision making, and appropriate instructional materials immediately convey the extraordinary need for flexibility.

Commitment to IGE is obviously a necessary prerequisite for a successful unit leader. In addition, the unit leader must have those qualities which make it possible for him or her to work successfully with people —adults as well as children. Unit leaders who possess and demonstrate the personal characteristics discussed in the preceding section are those who are likely to be most effective in their roles.

Knowledge of the Field of Education

In addition to having desirable personal characteristics, good teachers must also be well informed. This is all the more true of the unit leader, who needs a liberal amount of study in general and professional education. In-depth studies in psychology, curriculum design, philosophy, history of education, and sociology are also recommended. The unit leader regularly draws upon his or her conceptualization in those foundations in order to translate theory into sound and workable practices. One of the most flagrant omissions on the part of the teaching profession in the past has been the inability or unwillingness of educators to draw upon the mass of theory which has been generated in these fields and to help teachers relate it to the school situation. The discussion here has been categorized into two parts: (1) general educational knowledge and (2) knowledge of IGE.

General educational knowledge. This category includes traditional areas of the educational curriculum such as psychology, curriculum design, philosophy, history of education, and sociology.

Psychology provides a substantive base which is fundamental to IGE. Knowledge of human growth and development, theories of learning and instruction, measurement and evaluation are important. Psychology can help the teacher develop skills to draw upon that body of knowledge in appropriate ways which will result in better learning opportunities for each child.

A basic knowledge of *curriculum design* is essential for the unit leader. One of the important changes which occurs with the implementation of IGE is that the development of curriculum for a particular school becomes the responsibility of the staff of that school. Objectives are identified for the specific school population. Using the Instructional Programming Model (IPM), the staff develops the plans necessary to implement the instructional program. To provide the leadership needed for this process, the unit leader must have a thorough knowledge of curriculum design.

Philosophy is a field which strongly influences curriculum design and is inexorably tied to IGE. The unit leader needs a broad philosophic background upon which to build an educational philosophy. This is, of course, tempered and altered by experiences. Some of the practices which are important to IGE may be opposite to philosophies of traditional classroom teachers. The study of philosophy helps one to strengthen or reject personal attitudes and beliefs.

The *history of education* relates philosophy to the trends and practices which have occurred in education and to the people who have influenced educational movements. The IGE concept becomes more meaningful when one knows the history of ideas and innovations which preceded it.

The study of *sociology* is of significant importance to IGE because of the home-school-community dimension. Emphasis on the community setting is a natural extension of the highly personal attention to needs of individual students. A great deal of effort goes into the assessment of each child's program in the context of his or her unique characteristics, concerns, and motivations. This implies that the unit leader must be aware of societal values, structure, changes, and function.

Knowledge of IGE. Specific knowledge and skills which unit leaders should possess can be generated from an analysis of the seven components of IGE. Each component, along with knowledge and skills relevant to it, is presented below.

The *multiunit organization* requires a comprehensive understanding of the rationale for unit organization, space utilization, and shared decision making. In turn, technical, procedural, and interpersonal skills are necessary to carry out the IGE program most effectively.

Instructional programming for the individual student integrates knowledge from human growth and learning, principles of learning, and use of educational objectives to design curriculum for each child. This is the most important task the unit leader carries out.

A thorough understanding of *evaluation* in terms of preassessment, the monitoring of progress, and postassessment to determine achievement according to criterion-referenced tests is essential for the unit leader. Knowing how to develop and use tests appropriate for a specific school population is a skill unit leaders must have. They must also be knowledgeable about evaluation processes related to staff personnel, curriculum development, resource management, and home-school-community relations.

Selection or development of *curriculum materials* compatible with IGE are part of the unit leader's duties. The unit leader should be a specialist in at least one curriculum area. The interdependent relationship of the teacher's conceptualization of the content area and its adaptation to the Instructional Programming Model is important in planning the instructional program. The effective unit leader will find knowledge of curriculum materials essential to orchestrate a program which is consistent with IGE.

The expectation of *home-school-community relations* in IGE is more extensive than most teachers have known in the past. The unit leader must be aware of the populations involved in home-school-community relations, as well as the means for communicating most effectively with them.

Facilitative environments are essential for unit leaders and others to acquire the help and support needed for carrying out IGE. Unit leaders need to know the supporting services which are available within and beyond the school district. These include the IGE league as well as regional, state, and national organizations.

The unit leader should have basic knowledge of the *research and development* which supports IGE. He or she should also have at least a minimal understanding of research and development techniques which can be used in ongoing research in the school.

Self-evaluation

The checklist presented in the following pages will help teachers evaluate themselves on the characteristics described as desirable for unit leaders in the previous parts of this section. It should be noted that responses to Part 1 should be "yes" and "no" only. Responses to Parts 2 through 4 are scaled on a five-space continuum. A check in box 1 indicates a high degree of a particular quality; a check in box 5 indicates a serious lack of that quality. A majority of the check marks in Yes boxes and in boxes 1 and 2 over the entire checklist indicates the profile of a teacher

Unit Leader Self-evaluation Checklist

Directions:

Part 1, Professional background: Respond either "yes" or "no" to each item.

Part 2, Personal qualities: A check in box 1 indicates possession of a high degree of each quality and a check in box 5 indicates a lack of that quality. Evaluate yourself on the five-space continuum for each item.

Part 3, Knowledge of education: A check in box 1 indicates that you rate yourself very high on the item and a check in box 5 indicates a very low self-rating. Evaluate your knowledge of each item on the five-space continuum.

Part 4, Knowledge of IGE: Mark the same as in *Part 3.*

Part 1. Professional background (Check either "yes" or "no")	Yes	No
a. Teacher certification		
b. Master's degree		
c. Three or more years successful teaching experience		

Unit Leader Self-evaluation Checklist—cont.

Part 2. Personal qualities (Check only one space for each item)

	1	2	3	4	5
a. Commitment					
(1) commitment to teaching					
(2) commitment to IGE					
b. Perception of self					
(1) see self in positive way					
(2) perceive self and world realistically					
(3) identify with other people					
(4) keep well informed about everyday events					
c. Perception of others					
(1) use democratic procedures in teaching					
(2) see things from another staff member's point of view					
(3) see things from the child's point of view					
(4) see things from the parent's point of view					
(5) see things from the administration's point of view					
(6) trust students					
(7) accept suggestions from others					
(8) recognize capabilities of staff					
(9) interact effectively with other staff					
d. Openness					
(1) assume leadership in implementing change					
(2) willing to risk failure					
(3) encourage free expression of other's ideas					
(4) willing to listen to others					
e. Facilitator of change					
(1) aware of recent educational research					
(2) encourage new, creative ideas					
(3) practice new instructional methods					
(4) use a variety of materials/media					
f. Self-renewal					
(1) have positive attitude toward continued learning					
(2) read current educational literature					
(3) attend conferences, workshops, inservice					
(4) take graduate courses					
g. Charisma					
(1) communicate in exciting and stimulating manner					
(2) communicate on a highly personal teacher-student basis					
(3) have sense of humor					

Unit Leader Self-evaluation Checklist—cont.

	1	2	3	4	5
h. Flexibility					
(1) use many teaching approaches					
(2) meet the demands of the moment					
(3) can be either firm or permissive at appropriate times					
i. Leadership					
(1) participate in curriculum development					
(2) work with administrator cooperatively					
(3) show leadership among staff					
(4) participate in inservice development					
(5) supervise university students competently					

Part 3. Knowledge of the field (Check only one space for each item)

a. Psychology					
(1) human growth and development					
(2) theories of learning and instruction					
(3) evaluation of pupil growth					
(4) group behavior					
b. Curriculum design					
(1) traditional elementary school curriculum					
(2) curriculum development within schools					
(3) subject matter sequences					
(4) planning sequence					
c. Philosophy					
(1) educational philosophy					
(2) philosophy of individual differences					
(3) team teaching philosophy					
(4) nongrading philosophy					
(5) IGE					
d. History of education					
(1) public education in the U.S.					
(2) developments which led to the self-contained classroom					
(3) movements away from the self-contained classroom					
e. Sociology					
(1) home-school communication techniques					
(2) community setting as a learning environment					
(3) community social values					

Part 4. Knowledge of IGE

a. Multiunit organization					
(1) unit organizational structure					

Unit Leader Self-evaluation Checklist—cont.

	1	2	3	4	5
(2) space utilization in schools					
(3) differentiated staffing					
b. Instructional programming					
(1) general educational objectives					
(2) instructional objectives					
(3) preassessment					
(4) postassessment					
(5) monitoring processes					
(6) purposes of criterion-referenced tests					
(7) alternatives to meet pupil needs					
c. Evaluation					
(1) problem identification					
(2) relevancy in problem solving					
(3) sources of accurate information					
(4) viable alternatives					
(5) objective means for choosing alternatives					
(6) implementation of decisions					
d. Curriculum materials					
(1) specialization in one curricular area					
(2) conceptualizing skills					
(3) conceptualizing objectives					
(4) available materials					
(5) *Wisconsin Design for Reading Skill Development* or *Developing Mathematical Processes*					
(6) motivational techniques					
e. Home-school-community relations					
(1) available resources in community					
(2) parental expectations					
(3) community involvement					
f. Facilitative environments					
(1) Systemwide Program Committee (SPC) responsibilities					
(2) IGE League or Regional IGE Coordinating Council (RICC)					
(3) State IGE Coordinating Council (SICC)					
g. Research and development					
(1) conducting research					
(2) development of instructional materials					

who has the qualities to become a successful unit leader. The same profile should exist for practicing unit leaders. The checklist is also useful for the prospective or practicing unit leader to evaluate weaknesses and to work to improve those weaknesses.

GUIDELINES FOR SELECTION OF UNIT LEADERS

The previous sections have looked at the unit leader both as a role and as a person. The next consideration must be matching the most qualified person available with a specific unit leader position. This section will be concerned with this task in relation to professional qualifications, role description, and "who selects the unit leader."

Professional Qualifications

Unit leaders should be those educators who are committed to IGE, are master teachers, have leadership skills, and are willing to spend increased time and energy on professional activities.

Delineating the qualities which combine to make a master teacher is a task which has often been undertaken, but has not been achieved with any degree of finality. As early as 1853, Horace Mann recognized the difficulty of describing characteristics of effective teachers when he wrote in his *First Annual Report*: "Teaching is the most difficult of all arts and the profoundest of all sciences. In its absolute perfection, it would involve a complete knowledge of the whole being to be taught, and of the precise manner in which every possible application would affect it."

Following an analysis of the research on teaching effectiveness, Klausmeier and Ripple reacted to the inconclusive findings on teacher effectiveness in this way: ". . . good teaching is so subjective, so intangible, so bound up with the nature of teachers as people that it will never be possible to reduce its components into factors that readily lend themselves to statistical analysis and conclusions" (Klausmeier and Ripple 1971, p. 252). Although it is difficult to explain why an excellent teacher is superior to other teachers, it is possible to recognize that he or she *is* superior.

The teacher has been defined as: " . . . a person engaged in interactive behavior with one or more students for the purpose of effecting change in the students. The change, whether it is to be attitudinal, cognitive, or motor, is intentional on the part of the teacher." Decisions about instructional *goals* may be made by legislators, school board members, or teachers. The teacher's responsibility extends beyond goal setting to determining the means for accomplishing desired ends. (McNeil and Popham 1973, p. 219) This statement focuses on one of the fundamental differences in the behavior of IGE teachers and typical elementary classroom teachers in their approaches to the act of teaching. IGE teachers, especially unit leaders, must be concerned not only that goals are identified, but also that appropriate means are developed for achieving those goals.

The role of the unit leader can be filled only by highly qualified teachers. The role is so specialized that possible certification of unit leaders could well be considered by state departments of education. Nine characteristics which should be taken into account in considering the unit leader role are (Klausmeier, *et al.* 1971, p. 41):

1. Certification as a teacher.
2. Three or more years of successful teaching experience.
3. Master's degree, or progress toward one.
4. Graduate education in human learning and development, curriculum and instruction, and research and development. A flexible program is recommended: the equivalent of 6-15 hours in curriculum instruction and learning; 3-9 hours in group dynamics and leadership; 3-9 hours in staff development and 6-12 hours in broad areas including measurement and evaluation and research and development. Some practicum work in unit operations is essential.
5. Commitment to a career in teaching.
6. Positive attitudes toward curriculum improvement, research and development, and teacher education.
7. Flexibility and inventiveness in the adaptation of methods, materials, and procedures.
8. Ability to recognize and utilize the capabilities of the unit personnel.
9. Ability to maintain effective interaction with all personnel of the unit, children and parents, the building principal, central office personnel, and other consultants in research and teacher education.

Increased expectations and rewards differentiate the unit leader from other positions in the school (Klausmeier, *et al.* 1971, p. 40):

> Certain rewards follow the responsibilities enumerated; also certain characteristics are desired of unit leaders. Unit leaders as a group should receive higher salaries than staff teachers because they meet expanded professional responsibilities of the type previously outlined. The unit leader knows more than the regular teacher about instruction, research and development, and teacher education. He works more hours per week and more weeks per year. It should also be apparent that the unit leader must continually improve his professional capabilities by pursuing further education and gaining relevant experience during the school year and summer. Many

teachers who are committed to a career of teaching (this is only a small percentage of the national total) could qualify as unit leaders if they wanted to assume the additional responsibilities, if they were willing to work eleven months each year, and if they continuously and systematically extended their knowledge and capabilities. It is critical to recognize that the unit leader is an instructional leader, not a supervisor or administrator.

Role Description

Administrators and staff members need to develop guidelines for selecting unit leaders appropriate for their particular building. These guidelines should clearly define the role qualifications necessary for the position and provide a means of assessing the teaching behavior of an applicant. A job description for selecting unit leaders should include (Bolton 1973, p. 6):

1. *the general nature of the position,* including the broad goals of the system, the organizational structure of the system, and general expectations of the teacher in and out of the classroom,
2. *the static and dynamic features of the position,* including what is important at the beginning, what is likely to change, what will affect these changes, the nature of the students, and how the position will be affected by other people,
3. *the teacher behaviors required and desired,* in the classroom and out of the classroom, and
4. *the teacher characteristics sought,* including aptitudes, skills, social requirements, interests, and physical requirements.

The following major situational factors which affect teacher performance should also be considered (Bolton 1973, p. 5):

1. pupil characteristics, including measures such as attitude, interests, abilities, motivation, morale, and prior learning;
2. principal characteristics, including orientation to change, ability and interest in helping teachers, human relations and organizational skills, and decision-making style; and
3. colleague characteristics, including general esprit, attitude toward newcomers and change, willingness to help new teachers, and willingness to plan programs cooperatively.

These guidelines must be considered in the context of the individual schools where the qualifications must be more carefully described according to the particular needs and circumstances.

Who Selects the Unit Leader?

In the past, new teachers have generally been interviewed and selected by central office personnel and the building principal. Because the unit leader will have much contact and interaction with the principal, staff teachers, and other unit leaders, it is important that all of these people be represented in the interviewing and selection of new unit leaders. Procedures for the selection of unit leaders differ, depending on the stage of IGE in the building under consideration and on the personnel practices of the school system.

When a school makes the initial decision to adopt IGE, one of the first steps which must be taken is to form unit teams. This is usually accomplished through cooperative decision making by the principal and building staff. After the teams have been identified, unit leaders are chosen. In some schools, the principal makes the choice and invites certain teachers to become unit leaders. In other schools, the team, with or without the help of the principal, selects one of its members as unit leader. This may be done through discussion, acceptance of a volunteer, achieving consensus, voting, or some combination of these procedures. Central office personnel may be involved in either of these methods.

After the original implementation of IGE, the approach for selecting unit leaders is somewhat different. Selecting several of the best prospects from the available applications may be handled by central office personnel. Following that, the principal should arrange for the unit staff and some (or all) of the IIC members to participate in interviews with the qualified applicants. Because the team and the IIC will be working closely with the new unit leader, it is imperative that they be involved in making the final selection.

SUMMARY

The comprehensiveness and complexity of IGE portends that far more skills and much more knowledge than appear in this chapter must be developed and applied by teachers who aspire to be unit leaders. Problem solving, interpersonal relationships, taxonomies, instructional objectives are illustrative of the ideas which are parts of the IGE philosophy. The blueprint for the unit leader role has barely been explored in this chapter. Unit leaders the authors envision will rigorously pursue the remainder of this text, read other IGE publications, visit IGE schools, and strengthen their perceptions and skills.

REFERENCES

Bolton, D. L. 1973. *Selection and evaluation of teachers.* Berkeley: McCutchan.

Bush, R. N. 1971. The status of the career teacher: its effect upon the teacher dropout problem. In R. J. Havighurst, B. L. Neugarten, and J. M. Folk (eds.), *Society and education: a book of readings.* Boston: Allyn and Bacon.

Combs, A. W. 1969. *The professional education of teachers.* (7th print.) Boston: Allyn and Bacon.

——— 1962. A perceptual approach to the truly adequate personality. In A. W. Combs (ed.), *Perceiving, behaving, becoming: a new focus for education.* (ASCD Yearbook) Washington, D.C.: Association for Supervision and Curriculum Development.

Geer, B. 1966. Occupational commitment and the teaching profession. *School Review* **74:** 31-47.

Hamachek, D. E. 1969. Characteristics of good teachers and implications for teacher education. *Phi Delta Kappan* **50:** 341-345.

Kelly, E. C. 1962. The fully functioning self. In A. W. Combs (ed.), *Perceiving, behaving, becoming: a new focus for education.* (ASCD Yearbook) Washington, D.C.: Association for Supervision and Curriculum Development.

Klausmeier, H. J., and R. E. Ripple 1971. *Learning and human abilities.* New York: Harper & Row.

———, M. R. Quilling, J. S. Sorenson, R. S. Way, and G. R. Glasrud 1971. *Individually guided education and the multiunit elementary school: guidelines for implementation.* Madison, Wisc: Wisconsin Research and Development Center for Cognitive Learning.

Lorti, D. C. 1973. Observations on teaching as work. In R. M. W. Travers (ed.), *Second handbook of research on teaching.* Chicago: Rand, McNally.

McNeil, J. D., and W. J. Popham 1973. The assessment of teacher competence. In R. M. W. Travers (ed.), *Second handbook of research on teaching.* Chicago: Rand McNally.

Rossman, Patricia 1975. Informal note. McFarland, Wisconsin (February).

Ryans, D. R. 1960. *Characteristics of teachers: their description, comparison, and appraisal.* Washington, D.C., American Council on Education.

Spady, W. G. 1973. Authority, conflict and teacher effectiveness. *The Educational Researcher* **1:** 4-10.

Wright, B. A., L. T. Camp, W. K. Stosberg, and B. L. Fleming 1971. *Elementary school curriculum: better teaching now.* New York: Macmillan.

4

Guiding the I & R Unit

William M. Bechtol

Objectives

After reading this chapter, the reader will be able:

- To describe the place of nongrading, multiage grouping, and team teaching in an IGE school.
- To describe briefly the general guidelines and factors to consider in assigning students and teachers to units.
- To list in sequence and describe briefly the activities used to build an effective team.
- To indicate the unit leader strategies for (a) managing the I & R Unit, (b) forming a family circle, (c) chairing the unit meeting, and (d) improving teaching in the I & R Unit.
- To lead a small group (3-6 people) in a simulated unit meeting situation (a) in two or more of the team-building activities, and (b) illustrating at least five positive strategies for conducting an effective meeting.

This chapter focuses on the instructional leadership aspect of the unit leader role. Here, the unit leader coordinates the activities of the certified teachers, aides, and student teachers or interns to provide an effective instructional program for the 75-150 students assigned to the I & R Unit. The unit leader's role within the I & R Unit is facilitated by the multiunit organization component of IGE.

The I & R Unit in the multiunit organization is distinctly different from the self-contained graded classrooms in a traditional elementary school. In the latter, the child was too often adjusted to curriculum instead of the curriculum to the child. In IGE, the I & R Unit structure has been designed so that a team of three to six professional teachers provides for the individual differences of each student. The unit leader is the key person on the unit team.

The idea of the I & R Unit is new to most students, parents, and community members. The I & R Unit has the following characteristics:

1. It is a new organizational structure; it replaces the graded or the self-contained classroom.
2. It occupies a specific geographic space within the school; this space is used in new ways.
3. The students in a unit are multiaged.
4. The students are taught by a team of 3-6 professional teachers who are charged with the total educational experience of the students assigned to the unit.

One of the leadership responsibilities of the unit leader is to help unit teachers, aides, students, parents, and the community to conceptualize the difference between the I & R Unit and the self-contained, graded classroom. Every student should understand and be able to explain to family and friends what the I & R Unit is, what it stands for, and what it does. Parents and community leaders should have a similar understanding of the I & R Unit.

In this chapter, the instructional leadership role of the unit leader is explored under the following topics:

- considering general educational concepts in IGE
- starting and maintaining the I & R Unit
- providing leadership for a positive environment
- chairing the unit meeting
- improving teaching within the I & R Unit

CONSIDERING GENERAL EDUCATIONAL CONCEPTS IN IGE

This section reviews briefly the concepts of nongrading, multiage grouping, and team teaching and suggests their implications for IGE.

Nongrading

In the traditional graded school, students of the same age move together at a regular pace from kindergarten through grade 12, one grade a year. In a nongraded organization, students progress at their own individual rates according to their achievements.

In the graded school, every child has been expected to learn fractions and study the United States in fifth grade. It is as if the school handed the fifth grade teacher thirty sets of size 10 clothes. In the graded school we say, "Wear the clothes. It's OK if they sag or if the shoes are tight. A little discomfort is good for children." Just the opposite happens in the nongraded school. The teacher is asked to measure the group and to find out what size of clothes they need.

Nongrading can be described as the vertical movement of students (NEA Research Memo 1965). Each student is allowed to progress at his or her own rate. Each student masters as much of an appropriate curriculum as possible during the year. At the beginning of the next year, the students start where they left off and again work at their own speed. No grade label is attached to work at any time. There are no promotions or retentions. Slow-learning students may take longer to master work, but are not "held back a year" or "pushed to keep up with the class." The academically talented students may master curriculum faster than they would in a graded school, but not skip material or mark time waiting for less able students to catch up with them.

Permitting students to progress through the curriculum at their own rates soon increases the achievement spread of students in an I & R Unit. After two years of IGE instructional programming in mathematics, more than one fourth of the students in the primary unit (ages 5-8), in Garfield Elementary School, Alexandria, Minnesota, were using the intermediate math packages. This meant that these students were at least one year ahead of the graded norm. The same spreading occurred in the schools in Tipp City, Ohio. Students entering high school ranged in mathematics knowledge from decimal fractions to algebra II, depending on each student's individual learning rate.

During the changeover to IGE, the unit leader should monitor unit instructional activities to make certain that graded concepts are not controlling decisions about instruction.

Multiage Grouping

Multiage grouping places children of several ages together in the same learning environment. Some of the characteristics of multiage grouping are (1) teachers become more aware of the needs of individual students and less dependent on meeting the standards of graded textbooks, (2) instructional programs are planned which allow children to learn at their own rates and in the ways which are most effective for them, (3) expectations that each child should learn the material designated for his or her grade level are decreased, (4) younger children benefit from the models provided by the older children, (5) older children can acquire an increased sense of responsibility by working with younger students, and (6) the age range is similar to that of peer associations outside the school situation.

Multiage grouping is not new to American education. The school band is a good example. What are the criteria for being in the school band? Are all 16-year-olds automatically in the band? No. To be in the band a student must be able to read music, play an instrument, march, etc. Maybe criteria similar to those for school band are appropriate for most learning activities. Multiage grouping really says that age is not the most important characteristic of students in school.

During the first years of IGE, the unit leader must monitor student grouping patterns closely. Student grouping should be based on data concerning appropriate instructional objectives. It is easy for the unit staff to fall back and use age or grade level grouping. Teaching the unit team members that age or grades should not be the controlling forces takes patience, consistence, and firm leadership by the unit leader.

Team Teaching

Team teaching or cooperative teaching is a logical plan for carrying out instruction. Team teaching is "a formal type of cooperative staff organization in which a group of teachers accepts the responsibility for planning, carrying out, and evaluating an educational program, or some major portion of a program, for an aggregate of pupils" (Anderson 1966, p. 83).

Somehow successful teaming occurs when "my" students become "our" students. One team member explained, "I used to teach 'Ms. Miller's students' social studies while she taught 'my' students language arts. That's not teaming; it's trading. Ms. Miller didn't really care what I taught. I never bothered to check what she taught. The students never became 'our' students."

There are many advantages to team teaching. It provides opportunities for (1) increased individualization of instruction; (2) better preparation and better instruction; (3) greater flexibility in grouping, scheduling, and use of space; (4) better utilization of the staff; and (5) increased inservice growth of the staff through interaction with team members.

If there are all these advantages to team teaching, why are schools primarily organized into self-contained classrooms? Teaming isn't easy; it is difficult to establish effective teaching teams. Team teaching has been compared to a marriage where someone else selects the partners.

One principal of a team-teaching school reports that he thought that each team would break up in October (Bechtol 1973). Teachers would come into his office and share "I can't work with John," or "I don't want to go to a team meeting tonight. Evelyn will make all of the decisions anyway," or "Jerry is constantly clearing his throat; I just can't stand to meet with him." Such matters as personal habits, sex, politics, religion, or decision-making procedures threatened to break up teams.

Since teaming by the adult members of an I & R Unit is an important function in the IGE school, it is essential that team members learn to work effectively together. A strategy for building effective teaching teams has been developed and is described in the next section of this chapter.

STARTING AND MAINTAINING THE I & R UNIT

In the previous section, the unit leader's role in handling general education concepts in IGE has been explored. This section deals with (1) how the unit leader provides leadership in the building as well as within the I & R Unit during the initial stages of forming units, and (2) continued leadership as the school and units function over a period of years. Specific topics discussed are assigning students and teachers to units and strategies for building a team of professionals who work effectively together.

Assigning Students to Units

Plans for assigning students to I & R Units vary in each IGE school. Some school staffs simply combine grades into a primary unit (grades 1 and 2), a middle unit (grades 3 and 4), and an upper unit (grades 5 and 6). Other school staffs use a very sophisticated plan that considers the needs of the students and the skills of the teachers. Some general guidelines that all schools should consider when assigning students to I & R Units, and that unit leaders must be alert to are (Bechtol 1973):

Size. How many students can a unit staff "know" so that an individual instructional program based on diagnosed needs and learning styles can be developed for each pupil? Size of the unit is important. IGE school staffs have found that the teaching team can efficiently manage an individualized program for 75 to 150 pupils. When a unit becomes larger than 150, management becomes more difficult.

Age levels. How many age levels should be included in a unit? Multiage grouping is an important element in IGE. Pupils of at least two age levels should be placed in a unit. A three-year age span seems ideal because it replicates a student peer group. Children play with other children who are their age or are one or two years younger or older than they. It is much more desirable to take 75 nine-year-olds, 75 ten-year-olds, and 75 eleven-year-olds and form two multiage I & R Units than to put all the pupils of one age together.

Achievement range. What range of achievement should be included in each unit? Each I & R Unit should have a wide range. There is no advantage and there are many disadvantages in developing a "smart" unit and a "dumb" unit. Many school staffs examine the achievement range of a particular age group within the unit. Then, pupils at similar achievement levels are divided between two or more units. For instance, a school which has 280 students in the 8- to 10-year-old age range, may choose to create two middle level I & R Units. Each of these units should include both high achievers and low achievers. It is unwise to consider placing the less able 9-year-olds in a unit with all 8-year-olds. This can lead to problem situations in that many of the 8-year-olds will perform at a higher level of achievement than the 9-year-olds; such a situation permits little opportunity to provide the support and encouragement needed by these 9-year-olds. It is much better to include children from all three age groups in each unit and assure that each unit has a range of achievement which represents the range of this total group of 8- to 10-year-olds. This wider range can provide a more supportive, helping environment for all children.

Special students. Are gifted or special education pupils placed in the units? Yes. Staffs of many IGE schools in Wisconsin and Minnesota have found that a single I & R Unit can accommodate pupils who perform at the extreme ends of the achievement range. It's surprising, but in contrast to self-contained classroom teachers, unit teams seem to be more able and willing to accept and teach special students. Some schools have found it efficient to put all pupils who qualify for special education in the same unit. In this way, the special education teacher can become a member of the I & R Unit team. Special education pupils can become functioning pupils in the unit and can also be given special attention. In one school when this arrangement was first used, a pupil who had previously been in a self-contained, special education classroom told the principal, "I don't think they (the unit team and other pupils) know that anything is wrong with me."

Balance. How do you achieve balance in the units? When assigning pupils to units, the staff must consider the personal characteristics of the pupils. Each unit should have some *sparklers* (pupils who have a positive attitude toward learning and who serve as leaders or models for other pupils). The staff should identify the sparklers and see that each unit has a share of them. Each unit should have some *problem pupils* (hard to teach). These are pupils who have some learning disability (emotional, physical, or intellectual) requiring excessive one-to-one teacher time. If all these pupils are put in the same unit, it becomes a difficult situation. There should also be approximately equal numbers of boys and girls in each unit.

Peer relationships. Peer relationships should be considered in placing pupils in a unit. Pupils who work well together can be kept together. Pupils who do not work well together or who are too dependent on each other can be separated.

Student-teacher relationships. Teachers' teaching styles must be considered. Pupils who need a special type of teacher can be placed in a unit with that kind of teacher. Whether a pupil works well or does not work well with a particular teacher should be considered during placement.

Age. The student's age must be considered. The unit is a family. Is it better that the child be the youngest in the "family," the middle child, or the oldest?

The delightful thing about the IGE school is that pupils and parents can have a voice in the assignment process. In the traditional elementary school, parents try to get their child into Ms. X's class or to avoid Ms. Y's class. Now the pupil's or parents' wishes can be considered. Is it better that Joey be the youngest pupil in the unit, since he is the oldest in the family? Will Judy and Pam learn better together or should they be separated? If, at a year-end parent conference, the parents or teachers believe that Albert will perform better with a male teacher, plans can be made to place him with a male teacher for many activities. The multiunit organization in the IGE school provides the opportunity to consider the many needs of the individual students.

Assigning Teachers to Units

IGE schools assign teachers to I & R Units in many ways. Ideally, instructional units should be formed by looking first at the learners and then assigning the teachers to the units to meet the learners' needs.

The goal of unit staff selection is to build an instructional team that has the greatest potential for planning and implementing IGE. This team is charged with the total educational experience and instructional process of the students assigned to the unit. The unit leader must lead this small problem-solving, decision-making society.

The first decision to make when a school adopts IGE is who on the staff will stay and who will leave. It is best if a school can adopt IGE with total staff consensus. But teachers who are unwilling to participate in a unit should be allowed to transfer to another school (Institute for the Development of Educational Activities 1971).

The second decision is the selection of the unit leaders, which is the responsibility of the principal. There are many guidelines for selecting unit leaders as described in Chapter 3. Briefly, the unit leader should (1) be properly certified and a career teacher; (2) have leadership capabilities and be willing to accept extra responsibilities; (3) command the respect of pupils, parents, and other staff members; (4) believe in IGE; and (5) want the job. It is suggested that the principal develop a job description for unit leaders and that formal applications be requested. Even though a teacher fits the formal criteria for the job, the principal should consider informal criteria. Is the teacher acceptable to the staff, skilled enough in group dynamics to keep the unit on target, able to follow through on tasks?

Two guidelines for the process of assigning teachers to units are: (1) once unit leaders are selected, an Instructional Improvement Committee (IIC) meeting should be held to make preliminary assignments of teachers to units, and (2) each teacher should be consulted to see if the assignment is suitable (Klausmeier, *et al.* 1971). If not, some shifting may be necessary.

Since the students in each unit range in age and represent a wide range of achievement and styles of learning, teachers assigned to the I & R Unit should have diverse talents, interests, and skills.

Unit teams should be deliberately organized to provide learning alternatives for students. One possibility is to ensure that each team has teachers who have the qualities necessary to (1) provide a very structured learning environment to serve those children who function best in directed activities, (2) provide a flexible environment in which children can make many choices, and (3) provide a warm, supportive environment in which each child feels needed and appreciated. Under the leadership of an effective unit leader, an I & R Unit which includes teachers who have these strengths can provide many learning options for children.

Three methods are suggested for assigning teachers to units: (1) by subject area strengths, (2) by skills in individualizing the instructional program, and (3) by teaching styles. Obviously, the needs of students must be considered when assigning teachers to units. Perhaps the least desirable way to organize units is to put two grades together and select the teachers of those grades to become the unit staff.

Some IGE schools use the teacher's student age preferences and subject area strengths to organize unit teams. Even though most teachers in the I & R Unit teach most subjects, the idea of having unit teachers serve as resource teachers in language arts, mathematics, science, and social studies has proven successful.

One interesting way to organize a unit team is to select members who have different specific skills in methods of individualizing the instructional program. The unit leader should have exceptional leadership and management skills. One unit member should be a diagnostician, with specific skills in assessment and prescriptive teaching. Another member should be a multimedia curriculum specialist who has the skills to develop instructional programs. A fourth team member should be a learning-process specialist who has skills in human relations, in small-group learning modes, and in educational climate development.

A more sophisticated plan for organizing a unit is to develop a team that has different teaching styles. The Wilson School staff in Janesville, Wisconsin (1973) has identified seven teaching styles as follows:

Task-oriented. The task-oriented teacher is teacher-centered and works to get the task done.

Child-centered. With this teaching style, teaching activities emerge from the interests of the students.

Cooperatively planned. This teacher respects children and integrates learner interest with teacher objectives.

Subject-centered. This teacher is interested in teaching a specific subject such as mathematics, science, or history.

Learner-centered. This teacher is process-oriented. His or her teaching focuses on how the student learns.

Emotional Involvement. An interpersonal relationship develops between this teacher and the students.

Dispassionate. This teacher is emotionally neutral.

Remember that one teaching style is not better than another. Students learn from and like all kinds of teachers. For example, one teacher in an I & R Unit yelled so much that the students gave her a descriptive nickname. The name sounded negative, but it actually wasn't. On the year-end student evaluation many students identified this person as the teacher who was "best" for them.

Each IIC will have to decide which teacher qualities are of most importance in assigning teachers to units. The above suggestions, combined with the needs of students, provide some ideas for possible approaches to this important and difficult step in organizing for IGE.

Building the Unit Team—"Making Unit Meetings Effective"

Changing from a group of three, four, or five self-contained classroom teachers into an effective unit team isn't easy. This section presents a sequence of team-building activities which have helped a great number of unit teams to begin and maintain effective IGE programs.

What makes an effective unit team? How does the effective team function? The effective team has open communication, a living philosophy of education, and a helping relationship. In a truly helping relationship, team members build more trust, and the more trust they build, the more they share and develop their potential. Trust is the key word in achieving a helping relationship and developing the effective unit team.

The Johari Window, which is presented in Figure 4.1 illustrates, in a simple way, what should be accomplished in the team-building sequence (Luft 1963).

The top, left box is called the "common knowledge box." This knowledge includes things that both you and I know about me: I am five feet eight, have blue eyes, etc. In the bottom, left box are the things I know about myself, but you don't know. Some of these things are my secrets, things I'm not going to let you know; some are things I haven't had time to tell you (give me time and I will). One caution: team building is not open, free-wheeling sensitivity training; team members cannot handle intimate personal details and work together daily.

Things about myself the other person —	Things about myself that I — know	don't know
knows	common knowledge	*my blind spots* such as bad breath, that my best friends haven't told me about yet
does not know	my secrets and things I haven't had a chance to tell yet	my hidden potential of things I never dreamed I could do or be

Fig. 4.1 The "Johari Window." (Adapted from *Group processes: an introduction to group dynamics* by J. Luft by permission of Mayfield Publishing Company, formerly National Press Books, 1963, pp. 10-15.)

The top, right box is the "blind spot box." These are the things you can see or have discovered about me, but of which I am unaware. The lower, right box is the "hidden potential box." These are the things I don't know about myself and you don't know about me either.

In a good team, the "common knowledge box" grows larger and larger. As it expands, it dips into the "hidden potential box," and gradually each team member becomes more effective. To speed up this process, a series of team building activities have been developed which include (Bechtol 1973):

1. getting acquainted (warm-up activities)
2. listening
3. developing trust
4. clarifying values
5. helping each other
6. identifying strengths
7. arriving at agreement ("We Agree")

These team-building activities can be accomplished in a number of ways. One way is for the principal to lead the IIC through the activities and then each unit leader leads his or her unit staff through the activities. Another way is to have the principal or a consultant lead all the I & R Unit teams through the activities in a workshop. A third alternative is for a unit leader to use the printed information presented here and in the correlated film, *Making Unit Meetings Effective,* to direct the activities with unit members. No matter which plan is selected, the sequence indicated below should be followed. Helping team members develop skills to function effectively as a team is a leadership responsibility of the unit leader.

Teams must be organized prior to the team-building skills sessions. All activities are designed to be completed within the unit team, and adequate time (6-10 hours) must be set aside to complete the activities.

Getting acquainted (warm-up activities). Three types of "whips" are described here. Whips are quick verbal exercises that help team members get to know each other.

1. *Proud Whip.* Each team member shares with the team something he or she owns, has done, or is particularly proud of and tells why he or she is proud of it.
2. *What My Name Means to Me.* Each team member states his or her name to the team and tells what it means to him or her.

3. *Hero Whip.* Each team member answers the question, "If you could be someone else in history, movies, novels, etc., who would you be, and why?"

Another kind of warm-up activity is unfoldment. Two types of unfoldment exercises are described below (Pestrue 1968). The team-building skills leader first models a personal unfoldment for the entire group. He or she will then direct each team member to do a personal unfoldment or a paired interview. These are equivalent activities; the leader will select the one that is better for the unit team(s) being trained.

1. *Personal Unfoldment.* The following narrative is used to introduce this exercise: "We are now going to do depth unfoldment. I will model the unfoldment process for you. I will have six minutes, as will each person here, in which to unfold myself in a personal way so that you will all become better acquainted with who I am as a professional leader and who I am as a person. During the unfoldment, each of us should share those experiences from early in life to the present moment that we feel have contributed to our being the persons we are now. These need not necessarily or even primarily be traumatic experiences, but you may include them. Sometime during the unfoldment, perhaps during the last minute, share the peak experience in your life."

   Each team should appoint a timer. If a person is unable to use the full six minutes, the team should use the remaining time to ask questions. The leader should enforce the time limit in order to accomplish the goals of the session and in order to protect a participant from taking an undue share of time, thus creating group hostility or personal anxiety. Because a positive feeling usually exists following the unfoldment, a break is not recommended unless the group is very tired.
2. *Paired Interviews.* This activity is done as follows: Choose a member of your team whom you do not know well. It is your task to find out in an interview as much about your partner as possible. Take notes, and ask any questions you wish. The person being interviewed has the right to refuse to answer any questions. After an eight- to ten-minute interview, return to the group and tell about the person you interviewed. Stand behind the person as you tell about him or her, place your hand on his or her shoulder, and report in the first person. Then change roles and repeat the procedure.

Listening. One of the skills effective teams must have is the ability to listen to each other. In this exercise, all team members should feed back to the first person who shared in an unfoldment or an interview report just how much they remember. The feedback should continue around the group in the order that they shared.

This exercise focuses on both listening skills and empathy. Group members may discover how well they listened or should listen. In addition, the persons who are being talked about will discover that the group already knows a lot about them.

Developing trust (nonverbal trust walk: blind). The leader directs the group to pair off in twos and asks one member of each pair to close his or her eyes and allow himself or herself to be led by the partner. The pair may go out of the room and even out of the building, but they should return to the room in five to ten minutes. When they return, the partners switch roles and repeat the exercise. Throughout the exercise, the partners should not talk, but rely on nonverbal communication to accomplish the guidance. A feeling of cooperation and trust is the desired outcome of this exercise.

Clarifying values. By completing the form on "Preferred Qualities of Children" in Figure 4.2, team members become aware of their different values (Hurley and Randolph 1971, pp. 1-10). Considering these qualities helps unit members to look at discipline.

When each member of the team has completed the form, team members should compare their answers freely. When all teams have compared their answers, the leader should instruct each participant to

Instructions: After reading completely through the qualities or characteristics of children, as listed below, assign number "1" to the quality which you believe would be the most desirable quality in this list for a ______-year-old child. Then assign "2" to the attribute which you regard as second most important, "3" to the third most important, and so on until you have assigned a number to all ten of those listed qualities. You may, of course, change your mind or correct any assigned numbers as you go along. Please assign a number to each of these ten attributes, even if you find it quite difficult to make some choices. No tie scores, please.

Characteristic	*Rank*	
responsible and trustworthy	______	A
neat and clean	______	B
curious	______	C
interacts well with others	______	D
considerate and cooperative	______	E
assertive and self-reliant	______	F
able to make friends	______	G
respectful toward adults	______	H
fun-loving and carefree	______	I
imaginative and creative	______	J

Fig. 4.2 Preferred qualities of children. (Adapted from Hurley and Randolph 1971.)

add his or her scores for B, E, and H (structured) and compare the total with the total for C, F, and J (unstructured). There are no right answers, but different values of team members may become apparent.

Helping each other (helper-helpee). This exercise demonstrates how an effective team functions. Each team member takes a turn at being the helpee, while the other team members serve as helpers. The helpee shares a real problem with the team, such as "I have trouble teaching vowels in phonics," or "I'm not successful teaching boys like Billy," or "I can't manage learning stations." Then the helpers try to help him or her solve the problem. The following process is used (1) clarification—the helpers ask the helpee questions to clarify the problem, (2) alternatives—the helpers present alternative solutions to the problem while the helpee listens quietly, and (3) application—the helpee selects the best of the alternative solutions and describes how he or she may use this plan. Adequate time must be provided for the completion of this activity.

Identifying strengths (strength bombardment). By this time in the sequence of team-building activities, the unit members should be getting to know a lot about each other. It is now appropriate to ask them to identify the personal strengths of the other team members (McHolland and Pestrue 1968).

For this exercise, each team member will need a sheet of newsprint. The sheets are taped to the wall, and each one is divided into two columns (the column on the right should be only four to six inches wide). At the top of the larger left column is written *Strengths Others See in Me* and at the top of the right column, *Strengths I See in Myself.* The name of the person whose strengths are to be identified is written at the top of the newsprint.

Next, the chairs should be arranged so that each person can easily walk up to the newsprint and write. The first segment of the exercise is nonverbal; no talking is allowed. The team members take turns writing the strengths of the team member on the newsprint with a felt pen. When the newsprint is filled or no one else wants to record a strength, the verbal phase begins. Each person who listed a strength will look at the person and explain why he or she wrote the strength or will clarify what the strength means. Finally, the person whose strengths have been listed stands and validates (or negates) the strengths by checking them in the column titled *Strengths I See in Myself.* He or she also verbalizes why these are seen as strengths. When he or she finishes, one of the team members should remove the newsprint from the wall and present it to him or her. The process continues until every member of the unit team has a record of his or her personal strengths.

Arriving at agreement ("We Agree"). This is the most important of the team-building skills. In this situation, each I & R Unit team must be given adequate time to complete this activity fully. The purpose of the "We agree . . ." activity is to build a living team philosophy. The words "We agree" should be written on a chalkboard or on newsprint. Then the team should generate as many statements as possible that all can agree on, such as "Children learn . . . ," "The role of the teacher is . . . ," "The school should . . . ," "The team will . . . ," "The student outcomes for our unit this year are . . ." The "We agree" activity helps each team member build and internalize the team philosophy.

It cannot be overemphasized how crucial this activity is. Every statement suggested for the "We agree" philosophy must become a state-

The purpose of the "We agree. . . ." activity is to build a living team philosophy.

ment that is acceptable to each member of the unit team. Much discussion within an open atmosphere is necessary to allow team members to explain their feelings toward a statement. Also, each teacher should thoroughly understand the meaning of the statement before agreeing to it. Many changes and compromises may have to be made before a statement becomes acceptable to all the members of the I & R Unit. If a teacher does not agree to the philosophy expressed in a statement, this statement is not acceptable. The statements which are agreed upon are combined to form the unit team's philosophy. This philosophy should later be made public to the other I & R Units, the students, and to the parents.

If all of the I & R Units in the school are participating in the team-building sequence, a building philosophy can be developed from the "We agree . . . ." statements. Each unit's statements should be edited and reproduced on a transparency. Special teachers who are not attached to a unit should develop "I agree" statements which should be shared and discussed at an IIC meeting. A committee including the principal can combine these statements to form a philosophy of education for the building.

The completion of the "We Agree" step completes the team-building skills sequence. The student outcomes identified by the unit team during the activities should be translated into objectives. This process directly relates the team-building sequence to the Instructional Programming Model.

PROVIDING LEADERSHIP FOR MANAGEMENT AND COMMUNICATIONS

How do we get started in instructional programming for the individual student in IGE? A unit staff is encouraged to implement instructional programming in only one or two subjects during the first year of implementation. For example, a school might select mathematics skills for the first semester and, if instructional programming was functioning effectively, add social studies during the second semester. The two subjects differ considerably since many objectives in mathematics are sequential, while only a few are sequential in social studies.

While implementing instructional programming and focusing on the individual child in one subject area, the team should also discuss and share their teaching activities in other areas. This provides the opportunity for them to develop skills and insights which will be valuable as they begin to plan together for instructional programming in other subject matter areas in the future. Trying to operate under two different organizational systems (self-contained classroom and the multiunit organization) can cause much confusion and many hard feelings.

The unit staff, under the leadership of the unit leader, should study student needs to determine which subjects should be implemented during the first and subsequent years. A three- to five-year plan for implementing institutional programming in subject areas should be developed. In order to plan and implement instructional programming in one or more curriculum areas and develop long-range plans for implementing it in other areas, a system of management of instruction as well as personnel, space, and materials must be developed. In addition, communication channels must be kept open among unit members, among the entire school faculty, and with the parents and community. These concerns are the focus of this section.

Managing the I & R Unit

Changing a school from graded, self-contained classrooms into individualized, nongraded, multiaged, team-taught I & R Units is a major change for teachers and students. The managing of such a program is an example of the unit team's philosophy of education and goals ("We Agree") put into practice.

In the effective I & R Unit, management is based on trust. It is based on the principle that both students and teachers are trustworthy. *Unit teachers trust students.* They believe students want to learn and will learn if given an opportunity. *Unit teachers trust each other.* They believe that each unit teacher will do a fair share to make the IGE instructional program effective. They trust the unit leader to fulfill his or her role. The unit leader trusts, respects, helps, and supports fellow unit members. *Unit teachers trust the other teachers in the school.* Through the IIC all teachers share the responsibility for the education of the students in the school. The concept of management based on trust is the self-fulfilling prophecy in action. How can a person become trustworthy unless someone trusts him or her? The unit leader must model this concept. The unit leader must trust others and be trustworthy.

In a traditional school, students gained identity by being able to say, "I'm in grade five," or "I'm in Ms. Butler's room." In managing an I & R Unit, the unit leader should strive to build a unit with identity for both staff and students. The unit staff should utilize the following management strategies in this process:

1. *Emphasize the goals of the unit.* A student should know what the unit stands for. The unit staff should emphasize and explain the unit's goals, the desired student outcomes, and the philosophy of the unit

team. When students understand these goals and are focused to achieve them, an *esprit de corps* or sense of pride begins to develop.

2. *Place the emphasis on learning not teaching.* Focus unit meetings and instructional activities on what the learner will do, not what the teacher will do. Help students to understand the objectives that they are working on and why. Give students feedback about how they're doing. Take time to give students recognition for achievements. Share with them when the work is more challenging or when they have been given increased responsibility. Emphasize growth and development of students, not teaching.
3. *Keep the schedule simple and flexible.* The schedule should not be so complex that the unit team spends the majority of its meeting time scheduling. A simple schedule with large, interchangeable blocks of time is the easiest plan for a unit staff to manage.

    Dividing the school day into three or four large blocks of time has proven to be manageable and is necessary for carrying out instructional programming. The block schedule provides flexibility for the unit staff and permits more efficient use of instructional aides and specialists. The daily schedule shown below is an example of how large blocks of time can be scheduled.

Time	*Block*	*Contents*
8:30- 8:50		Advisory group
8:50-10:10	Block A	Reading—language arts
10:10-11:30	Block B	Mathematics
11:30-12:15		Lunch
12:15- 1:35	Block C	Special subjects
1:35- 2:55	Block D	Science, social studies, health
2:55- 3:15		Advisory group

One unit team used the block schedule in the following way. Block A was used for skill-development groups in reading and for language arts activities. Block B was used for skill-development groups in mathematics. During Blocks A and B, instructional aides and special education teachers were scheduled into the unit to provide more instructional options. Block C was used for special subjects, such as physical education, art, and music; specialists in these areas were scheduled into the unit during this time. (In schools where such specialists are not available, unit teachers, with parent volunteers and older students, can teach the special subjects.) Block D was used for science, social studies, health, or an interdisciplinary combination of these subjects.

A flexible schedule such as this enables the IIC to schedule special teachers and instructional aides efficiently. It also enables the unit team to change what occurs in each block readily, so that scheduling does not demand a high percentage of the unit staff's planning time.

4. *Don't try to have each student at a different place.* If students have common instructional needs, put them together in a small group. Build skill groups that use most unit team members, resource teachers, and instructional aides to provide students with options. For example, during the language arts block, four unit teachers can aid the reading resource teacher and an instructional aide so that the 110 students can be grouped into six small groups. For example, Mr. A has 22 students in a "possessives" group. Ms. B with the instructional aide has two skill groups, 18 in Base Words and 14 in Plurals. Ms. C has 25 students in Consonant Blends. The reading resource teacher has 15 students in Sight Vocabulary. The unit leader has 16 students in Independent Activities. These students will work at learning stations, in tutoring roles, or in independent study. As students complete the objectives of their skill group, they will join the Independent Activities group. At a time agreed upon by the unit team (two or three weeks) all students will be regrouped.
5. *Train students to work efficiently in an individualized program.* Teach students the component parts of the IGE instructional program. Students should be able to explain the Instructional Programming Model (objectives, preassessment, diversified learning activities, postassessment). They should be able to state the objectives that they are currently working to achieve. They should be able to use learning stations and interest centers efficiently. Time should be provided in each subject to teach students what they need to learn, what they may choose to learn, the alternatives for learning, and how responsible students use these alternatives. Students should be given feedback and encouraged to discuss their progress in the individualized program.
6. *Train older students to help younger students.* The helping relationship should be emphasized. Instead of being resentful of younger students, older students should be taught to assume roles as tutors and models. They can assume some of the responsibility for helping younger students learn and adjust. Tutoring makes the tutee feel special. It bolsters the self-confidence of the tutor. Tutoring improves learning for both the tutor and the tutee.
7. *Build a special identity for the unit.* Use large group meetings to emphasize unit goals, for morning exercises, to preview the day's

activities, or to introduce units of instruction or learning stations. I & R Unit names or mascots—such as the Beavers, the Big Dipper Unit, the Zoo Unit, and the Kopy Kats—have been used to give the unit identity. Some units have selected songs to open the school day, or chosen unit colors, or ordered unit sweat shirts. Other units have elected students to represent the unit at building student council meetings. All efforts made to give the unit identity should help the student achieve the goals of the unit and enhance each student's self-concept.

8. *Build family circles to personalize the unit program.* Each unit member should serve as a teacher-advisor for a "family" of 20 to 25 students. Use the family group for human development activities, for program planning and contracting, and for reporting to students and parents.

9. *Don't keep problems to yourself.* If the unit staff thinks that a student is too noisy or not doing appropriate work, the teacher-advisor should share the problem with the student or his or her parents. If students are using a learning station or another area in the unit improperly, teach them to use it correctly. The I & R Unit staff should discuss problems as they arise and make plans to solve them. Many teams have used *Individually Guided Motivation* materials to plan for and carry out activities to help students become more self-directive (Klausmeier, *et al.* 1975).

Forming a Family Circle

A student may get lost among the 75-150 students in an I & R Unit. It is the responsibility of the unit leader to help unit staff members build a monitoring system so the team can account for each student. One way to handle this is to establish a "family circle" in which each unit staff member serves as a teacher-advisor to 20 to 25.

Good teachers have always counseled students. Students come to teachers they know and trust. The family circle, which includes one-to-one conferences, provides structure to help students solve instructional or personal problems or conflicts. Students need a home base, an adult friend, and a model.

The unit leader and staff can use the following steps to start family circles within the I & R Unit:

1. Assign students to advisors. This can be done by a random method for a trial period, by matching students' learning styles with a unit teacher's teaching styles, or by permitting students to select their own teacher-advisors. Whichever method is used, assignment should

never be regarded as permanent, and changes should be made when necessary.

2. Schedule a place and a daily time(s) for family circles to meet. The beginning and the end of the school day seem to be the best times for elementary students. A place where students can be seated in a circle makes discussion most effective.
3. Conduct a sequence of human development activities so that students get acquainted and begin to develop trust.
4. Begin recording insights. For program planning, teacher-advisors need expanded cumulative records. Begin anecdotal records for only a few students first. Record learning styles, personality traits, strong points, weak points, peer group, etc. Don't try to collect too much data at first.

The family circle is a way that the unit staff can (1) develop conducive learning environments, (2) analyze student needs, (3) determine student's learning styles, (4) provide motivation, (5) design instructional programs to meet a variety of needs, and (6) develop student responsibility and accountability within the total setting.

Possibly the key concept that the teacher should recognize in the family circle is that the teacher is a model. The teacher should deliberately model the behaviors wanted from students.

Three activities that occur within the family circle are human-development activities, program planning and assessment, and parent-student-advisor conferences (Huber, *et al.* 1974). Each is described in detail below.

Human-development activities. An I & R Unit staff makes the basic assumption that all students can succeed. This staff assumes that every student has inherent strengths and potential. The teacher-advisor transmits a sense of confidence to each advisee in the family group through regular human-development activities. These activities help each student focus first on self and then on others.

In many ways, the human-development activities are similar to the team-building activities. Students must get acquainted, clarify values, identify strengths and achievements, and set goals as the family group becomes a problem-solving, peer-support group. The unit leader should arrange for inservice training so that the unit staff has appropriate skills to direct initial human development activities.

Program planning and assessment. The teacher-advisor is responsible for ensuring that each student learns how to learn. Once students develop these basic learning skills, individualized and personalized instruction begins. More than any other member of the I & R Unit staff, the teacher-advisor is responsible for coordinating and monitoring the instructional program for each student in a manner which best accommodates that student's needs, interests, and abilities.

To personalize the instructional program, the teacher-advisor needs assessment data. Setting realistic expectations for students and getting students to set their own realistic expectations are important functions of the teacher-advisor.

So that students and the teacher-advisor can cooperatively plan instructional programs, the unit leader should ensure that some advisory group meetings are spent discussing how achievement is measured and evaluated within the I & R Unit, what measurement criteria are used, how standards differ from student to student, and why the standards differ. In one-to-one conferences the teacher-advisor should check to see if each student recognizes how his or her instructional program differs from others in the advisory group and why it differs. The teacher-advisor should check to see if and how students evaluate their own progress and how they feel about progress or lack of it.

Planning IGE instructional programs for 20 to 25 student advisees seems to be a tremendous responsibility. Fortunately, the teacher-advisor will have help and advice from the other team members, the principal, students, and parents. Together, this group can help the teacher-advisor and the student plan meaningful and appropriate programs.

Parent-student-advisor conferences. Conferences or written progress reports bring most parents as close as they will ever be to the school. Reporting is important. It is a vital function of the teacher-advisor who is the logical person to maintain the home-school liaison.

It has been suggested that parents have every right to know what their child is doing, what he or she is capable and incapable of doing. The student has a right to know these things, also. The student should know first. This is why many I & R Unit staffs have chosen to replace report cards and parent conferences with the parent-student-advisor conference.

One of the goals most frequently accepted by I & R Unit staffs is that students should become more independent, self-directed learners. Even kindergarten-age students should be able to develop a sense of responsibility for their own actions. The unit leader should encourage even the smallest children in the unit to participate in the reporting process. As the students mature they should take an ever-increasing responsibility in the reporting process.

It is the teacher-advisor's responsibility to arrange the most useful conference for the student and parent. Three or four parent-student-advisor conferences should be scheduled each year. Prior to a conference, the teacher-advisor should review the student's progress with the student. Then at the parent-student-advisor conference the student is able to report progress to the parent. The student conducts the conference. The teacher-advisor's role is one of assisting the student to prepare for the conference and supporting the student while the student reports. The parents can make suggestions and ask questions about the student's learning program and progress. All three parties should use the conference to talk about matters of mutual concern and to decide on plans for the next several months.

The teacher-advisor should use the conference and other contacts with parents as a means to collect additional data about advisees. Parents are important resources. They can identify their child's needs, interests, reasoning patterns, motivation, etc. In IGE, the teacher-advisor needs these data.

CHAIRING THE UNIT MEETING

The I & R Unit is a structure in which the cooperative strengths of the unit team members are blended into a program for meeting the individual needs of the students. Within this structure, unit members plan and evaluate the strategies and techniques necessary to make learning meaningful for each student. *The heartbeat of any I & R Unit begins in the unit meeting.* It is here that the instructional program is designed and redesigned. It is here that IGE moves from theory into practice.

Chairing the unit meeting is the responsibility of the unit leader. This includes ensuring that unit meetings are effectively planned, conducted, and evaluated. It also includes coordinating the strengths of each unit member to see that the unit functions effectively.

Each unit member must assume an active role in the unit meeting. Planning the instructional program for 75 to 150 students requires the cooperation and active contribution of all unit members. *Sharing responsibilities is important.* Units do not function well when the unit leader assumes all the responsibility. Meetings during which the unit members sit passively as the unit leader tells each staff member what to do are not effective. One of the difficult tasks for the unit leader to learn is the delegation of responsibility. The unit leader does not have to perform each task, but has the responsibility to see that activities are completed. Further descriptions of the unit leader's role in unit meetings are presented below.

Planning for the Unit Meeting

There is a limited amount of time for the unit team to conduct meetings. For efficient use of time, an agenda should be prepared and distributed to each member at least one day prior to the meeting.

An agenda such as the sample presented in Figure 4.3 permits the unit leader to organize the unit meeting and to communicate to the unit members, the principal, and other resource personnel.

Building an agenda is an easy way for the unit leader to share the responsibilities for planning and developing successful unit meetings. By using this sharing process the unit leader is not required to plan all of the meetings alone. Instead, sharing responsibility provides a structure to coordinate the strengths of the unit staff to see that tasks are completed. Agendas for a series of unit meetings are presented in Chapter 10 and in Appendix A.

Conducting the Unit Meeting

"Plan your work and work your plan." After the agenda for the unit meeting has been set, it is the responsibility of the unit leader to see that identified tasks are completed. Good premeeting planning is not enough if these plans are not realized during the unit meeting. Conducting the unit meetings can be a most satisfying or a most frustrating experience for the unit leader.

"Our unit meetings are great," explained one teacher. "We're so close and open that we can focus on the kids' needs all the time."

"I don't know how I ever taught before team teaching," stated a unit leader. "Together we can teach so much more effectively than any one of us could individually."

Apollo Unit Meeting

________ Date　　　________ Time

Task	Responsibility of	Resources needed	Objective	Time
1. Assign students to skill groups	Entire team	Keysort cards, pupil folders, other assessment data	To place every student, in an appropriate skill group	40 minutes
2. Brainstorm ideas for science unit	Ms. White	None	To get ideas for topics to use in teaching science processes	20 minutes

Fig. 4.3 Sample unit meeting agenda.

"They (team members) just sit there waiting for me to tell them what to do," complained the unit leader.

"What's the use of having a unit meeting if Helen's got all the answers anyway?" asked the teacher. "If she's going to ignore our comments, she could just give us an outline of what we're to do."

These comments indicate that teaming can be effective or it can be frustrating.

Establishing unit meeting procedures. A set of "team ground rules" must be developed to make a good unit meeting. The "We Agree" session is an ideal time to do this. If procedures have not been established, time must be spent at the first unit meeting to develop these ground rules. Unit teams must agree on meeting times and a decision-making model.

The I & R Unit should meet at least three hours each week. Here are some alternate meeting strategies. Some units use a sequence of four short meetings and one long meeting each week. The short meetings (15-30 minutes) are used to complete certain housekeeping (ongoing or situational) functions. The longer meeting (40-80 minutes) is used to deal primarily with various aspects of instructional programming. Other units use three shorter meetings and two longer meetings. One effective unit uses three shorter meetings and one long after school or evening meeting that ends with the team having dinner together.

The I & R Unit is a small decision-making society. Decisions must be made daily. A decision-making model that is efficient and that permits active participation by all unit members must be adopted and used. Since unit teams are usually small enough to permit much group interaction, the consensus decision-making model is often adopted. In this model, problems are presented to the group and all are involved in discussing, clarifying, and deciding. The rationale for this model is that consensus decisions provide more alternatives, develop greater individual commitment to the decision, improve interpersonal relationships and communication, encourage cooperation rather than competition, and facilitate the delegation of responsibilities.

How does the unit leader use this model? In an informal way, the unit leader can encourage discussion and clarification of the problem, seek alternative solutions, and poll each member for his or her position. A more formal way to involve unit members in the consensus decision-making model is through hand signaling as follows:

1. Five fingers—total agreement with the decision.
2. Four fingers—you have some reservations about the decision but will support it.

3. Three fingers—you have no strong feeling either way and will support the decision.
4. Two fingers—you still have some questions concerning the decision and you will need more information before you can support the decision.
5. One finger—you have serious questions concerning the decision and you will not support the decision at this time.
6. Closed fist—you are totally opposed to the decision and will not support it.

If any member of the group indicates a signal of two, one, or a closed fist, the decision-making process must stop. A decision cannot be made until all members of the unit team indicate a signal of three, four, or five.

The dynamics of teaming is based on the concept that "more heads are better than one." Group decisions tend to be considerably more accurate than individual decisions (Hall and O'Leary 1971).

It should be interjected here, however, that no system or model can ensure success unless the discussion of the team members brings out important problems, and issues are clarified. It is the unit leader's responsibility to keep the discussion oriented toward these ends.

Teams should avoid the decision-making techniques of minority control and majority vote. In minority control a single team member or small minority is less able to make as good a decision as a majority of the unit team. Majority vote, when used regularly, may split the unit team into two factions.

The consensus technique, although time consuming, results in decisions of superior quality when compared with the other two. Also each staff member has made a commitment to an item and has a stake in its implementation.

After adopting a decision-making model, the team should also agree about the types of decisions the team will make. When does an individual teacher make the decision? Which items require team action?

Involving all unit members. The unit leader is responsible for seeing that each unit member takes an active part in the unit meeting. It was described above how each member can be actively involved in decision making. Another way to encourage active participation is through role responsibilities. Composition of the unit will facilitate this. Units with a mathematics resource teacher have distinctly defined a role responsibility. Unit meeting tasks relating to mathematics become this teacher's responsibility. Other role responsibilities can be assigned. A unit member can perform the *on-task role.* The member has the responsibility to see that unit members stay on task and inform the unit when the discussion is not on the topic. Another role is the *timekeeper.* Before each unit meeting, approximate time limits are established for agenda items. It is the responsibility of the timekeeper to inform the unit team when they have exhausted the allotted time. These roles keep members actively involved and also help unit meetings to be effective and efficient.

It is crucial that the unit leader listen closely to team members and that their needs are not disregarded for the "good" of the unit. Occasional sessions should occur which are for the purpose of encouraging team members to share their needs and concerns. The unit leader who wishes to ensure relevant involvement should make certain that each team member has opportunities for expressing personal concerns.

Evaluation of the Unit Meeting

Evaluating the unit meeting is an ongoing task of the unit team. The I & R Unit's effectiveness is based on how well it carries out and completes its tasks. The unit leader must establish a process to analyze and critique the effectiveness and efficiency of the unit meeting. Time must be set aside for the unit team to analyze its own behavior.

One way to achieve this is to schedule a unit meeting about every three months for the purpose of analyzing its function and evaluating past meetings. Questions that can be used to evaluate the unit meeting's operation are as follows: (1) Are we practicing our philosophy? (2) Are we focusing on meeting unit goals and objectives? (3) Are we using our time efficiently? (4) Are we fulfilling our roles as unit members? (5) Are our programs meeting the needs of the students? (6) How am I doing as unit leader?

The unit leader must make certain that the unit staff critiques its operation. Evaluation continually refocuses the I & R Unit on its goals and objectives.

IMPROVING TEACHING WITHIN THE I & R UNIT

How can the I & R Unit study, critique, and improve its overall team operation? How can it survive and prevail in a society where knowledge is increasing and rapidly changing, where new movements are creating new problems or are emphasizing old ones, where team members are bombarded with new curriculum materials and techniques, and where demands are being made on the teachers or the unit to do more—better and faster? Obviously, the I & R Unit must have a system of continuous improvement.

Every unit needs a self-renewal system if it expects to keep abreast of a changing world and to have a positive impact on the children assigned to the unit. The unit leader is responsible for seeing that the unit adopts and uses a program of continuous improvement.

The self-renewing I & R Unit and its team members have the following characteristics (Rankin 1967): (1) clarity of and commitment to one's goals, (2) awareness of the consequences of one's actions, (3) openness in accepting what others think about one's action, (4) honest appraisal of one's feelings about such feedback, (5) constant search for better ways to accomplish one's goals, and (6) the ability to change one's behavior when such change seems in order.

The unit must devote part of its time to analyzing its own day-to-day performance. It is not the unit leader's responsibility to evaluate the other team members' performances. The unit leader is not a supervisor. It is his or her responsibility to see that the unit members adopt or develop a system of peer supervision. The unit must schedule time so that, on a regular basis, the performance of each member can be observed and critiqued.

Early observations should be used to collect data to determine (1) each teacher's predominant teaching styles, (2) each teacher's effectiveness with various learning modes, (3) each teacher's effectiveness in utilizing different teaching strategies, techniques, and media, and (4) each teacher's effectiveness in working with different students. Later observations will be used to help each unit teacher improve teaching performance.

The climate within the I & R Unit team should be one that encourages continuous improvement. Only the individual teacher can make changes in his or her teaching performance (Amidon and Flanders 1967). By studying his or her own behavior in some systematic, objective manner, the unit teacher can gain insight to understand and improve teaching behavior. Others may help the individual in the process of change, but they cannot do so unless the teacher desires to change. The unit leader can help the unit develop a positive climate by modeling appropriate behaviors in the continuous improvement process. The unit leader should be first to volunteer to have his or her teaching studied and critiqued.

A good system for analyzing and improving the unit team's ongoing operation is the observation cycle (Goldhammer 1969). It is based on the following key concepts: (1) the provision of feedback is useful to the unit team, to the individual teacher, and to the individual teacher in a group role, to improve teaching performance; (2) peer supervision is a powerful and effective stimulant for ongoing professional growth; (3) in-depth study of teaching performance provides team members needed experience in the often neglected functions of planning and evaluation;

(4) by observing and analyzing a team member's teaching, an individual teacher gains in understanding his or her own teachng competency and how it may be modified.

The observation cycle can be used by two teachers at a time or by the entire I & R Unit team. Each of the five steps in the cycle is described below.

Preobservation Conference

The purposes of the preobservation conference are (1) to identify the teacher's intentions (objectives of the lesson, plans, criteria for evaluation, etc.); (2) to develop a contract between the observer(s) and the teacher (items or problems on which the teacher wants feedback); and (3) to agree on any ground rules that might be needed (use of video- or audiotape, time limits, etc.). This meeting usually lasts 10 to 15 minutes. It gives the unit teacher who will be observed a chance to identify what will be observed and how.

Observation

The first rule in observation is for observers to write down what they see, not how they feel about what is going on. Prior to the observation the observer(s) should have agreed where and how to locate themselves and how to record. Use of audiotape or videotape is helpful. Written notes describing the dialog verbatim are very helpful. Remember the purpose of observation is to collect objective data. The actual observation period should be limited to a maximum of 15 minutes.

Data Organization and Analysis

The purposes of this session are to (1) reconstruct the observed events (essentially as an historian, attempting to agree on what actually happened); (2) assess the observed lesson in terms of the teacher's own intention, pedagogical criteria that have been generated in the unit's "We Agree," and the teacher's own teaching style and history; and (3) develop a plan for helping the teacher improve. The observer(s) should identify the points, questions, ideas, and problems to be raised during the conference and the roles to be played (by the unit leader, observer, etc.) during the conference. The observed teacher should also record as accurately as possible his or her recollections of the lesson and reactions to it.

The analysis must include determination of priorities. What will be emphasized? What will be ignored? It is not good practice to bombard the observed teacher with all the possible criticisms and suggestions that could be presented at the postobservation conference.

Postobservation Conference

This session must be open-ended. It should last as long as necessary. The central purposes of the conference are to provide feedback and to provide a basis for the improvement of future teaching. First, the observer's notes or the audio- or videotapes should be reviewed. Next, the teacher's notes and reactions should be studied. Then the observer's working notes of analysis and strategy should be used.

Remember, the observed teacher may be threatened by this conference. The observer or the unit team must aim to establish a climate within which a helping relationship can take place. The teacher must be ready to hear what the observer has to say. To eliminate perceived threats to the teacher and negative self-perception, the observer must create an atmosphere of credibility and trust. The observer can be credible if the analysis is supported by concrete evidence. The observer can be trusted if the focus is on behavior, not the teacher's competence.

The climate for continuous improvement or self-renewal can be enhanced by (1) using inquiry teaching—examining ideas without the intent of hurting people and being open, objective, and flexible; (2) assigning priority to those items of teaching behavior that are amenable to change in the time and under the conditions available; (3) dealing with behavior, not the person—without psychological analyzing or moralizing; (4) selecting only a few behaviors on which to work—choosing those tasks which are manageable and can be achieved; and (5) working with strengths rather than weaknesses.

The postobservation conference provides feedback and a sense of direction for improving future teaching. Other purposes are to provide the teacher with rewards and satisfaction, to identify issues in teaching, to offer didactic help, to train the teacher in techniques for self-improvement, and to develop incentives for professional self-analysis.

The burden for ensuring that goals are reached for maintaining the pace of the conference, for coping with problems that arise, and for departing from strategies or terminating rests with the observer(s).

Critique

This is usually a private session and its purpose is in effect self-criticism or group criticism. The observer and the teacher may be involved; or the entire unit team may be present. The postobservation conference should be analyzed. The observer should try (1) to reconstruct the postobservation conference; (2) to assess the conference to see if the observer(s) achieved his or her intentions and to see if the teacher was helped; (3) to consider if the observation cycle developed greater professional skills within the unit team; and (4) to evaluate the observer(s) skill in handling the several phases of the cycle. Several key questions should be answered. How was the observed teacher helped? How was the observer(s) helped? How should more help be provided in the future?

"We don't have time to critique our unit's performance," explained the unit leader. "How can we free someone to observe? What will the children do while the observer is gone?"

Let's look at the observation cycle. Note that the observation period (only 15 minutes) is carried out during the actual student day. Here's the time involved in each step of the cycle:

(1) Preobservation conference—10-15 minutes
(2) Observation period—10-15 minutes
(3) Data organization and analysis—30-45 minutes
(4) Postobservation conference—20-45 minutes
(5) Critique—10-20 minutes

The continuous improvement model is described above for two unit teachers. Whenever the entire unit team is involved in the observation cycle, one member should assume the role of observer. This person can then observe one or more of the unit team members. This role should rotate so that all members have the opportunity to conduct the postobservation conference.

To find adequate time for the observation process, the unit team may arrange for one observation in each three- or four-month period. In this way, each member of the team will be evaluated every two years.

There are other systems that can be used to provide teachers with objective feedback and analysis about their teaching performance. Two of these are interaction analysis (Amidon and Flanders 1967) and teacher self-appraisal (Robertson 1967). Both systems are effective, but they require more intensive training of the observer than the one described above. None of the systems is effective unless it is used on a regular basis. It is the responsibility of the unit team to adopt a system for continuous improvement and to build time in the unit schedule so that it can be used.

SUMMARY

In this chapter the role of the unit leader in starting the I & R Unit and keeping it functioning effectively has been described.

The I & R Unit was presented as a new organizational structure that replaces the grade or the self-contained classroom. Nongrading, multiage grouping, and team teaching are organizational practices that are used within the I & R Unit.

Assigning individual students to the appropriate I & R Unit is one of the key tasks in a new IGE school. This task should consider size of units, student age levels, achievement range, special students, balance, peer relationships, student-teacher relationships, and student age in relation to the total unit.

Several plans for assigning teachers to I & R Units are described. Factors to consider here are subject area strengths, skills in individualized instruction, and teaching styles.

A sequence of activities to build an effective, problem-solving unit team is described in detail.

Management based on trust is the most effective way to develop an efficient I & R Unit. Nine steps that the unit can utilize are presented.

A plan that the unit leader can follow to form family circles is suggested. Each unit member serves as advisor for 25 to 30 students.

Procedures that the unit leader should follow while chairing the unit meeting are described. These include a sample agenda, a consensus decision-making model, a meeting schedule, a process that encourages active participation, and an evaluation plan.

Once the I & R Unit has begun, a system for continuous improvement of teaching must be adopted. A five-step observation cycle which can be used by two unit members or the entire team is described.

REFERENCES

Amidon, E. J., and N. A. Flanders 1967. *The role of the teacher in the classroom.* Minneapolis: Association for Productive Teaching.

Anderson, R. H. 1966. *Teaching in a world of change.* New York: Harcourt.

Bechtol, W. M. 1973. *Individualizing instruction and keeping your sanity.* Chicago: Follett.

Goldhammer, R. 1969. *Clinical supervision: special methods for the supervision of teachers.* New York: Holt.

Hall, J., and V. O'Leary 1971. Excerpts from the utilization of group resources in decision-making. *PETCI Skill Training.* Portland: Northwest Regional Educational Laboratory, pp. 314-317.

Hubel, K., P. Tillquist, R. Riedel, and C. Myrbach 1974. The teacher-advisor system. Dubuque: Kendall/Hall.

Hurley, J. R., and C. C. Randolph 1971. Behavioral attributes preferred in eight-years-olds. *JSAS Catalog of Selected Documents in Psychology,* fall.

Institute for the Development of Educational Activities 1971. *The principal's handbook.* Dayton, Ohio.

Klausmeier, H. J., J. T. Jeter, M. R. Quilling, D. A. Frayer, and P. Allen 1975. *Individually guided motivation.* Madison, Wisc.: Wisconsin Research and Development Center for Cognitive Learning.

———, M. R. Quilling, J. S. Sorenson, R. S. Way, and G. R. Glasrud 1971. *Individually guided education and the multiunit elementary school: guidelines for implementation.* Madison, Wisc: Wisconsin Research and Development Center for Cognitive Learning.

Luft, J. 1963. The Johari window. In *Group processes: an introduction to group dynamics.* Palo Alto, Calif.: National Press.

McHolland, J., and J. Pestrue 1968. Human potential seminars. Mimeographed, Evanston, Ill.: Kendall College.

National Education Association 1965. *Nongraded schools: NEA research memo.* Washington, D.C.: NEA Research Division.

Rankin, S. C. 1967. MOREL annual report, Vol. 4, MOREL position on self-renewal. Mimeographed, Detroit: Ohio Regional Educational Laboratory.

Robertson, E. W. 1967. *Teacher verbal and nonverbal classroom behavior.* Tucson: The University of Arizona.

Wilson School, Jamesville, 1973. *Individually guided education in a multiunit organization.* Unpublished brochure, Janesville, Wisc.

5

Representing the I & R Unit

Joan D. Inglis

Objectives

After reading this chapter, the reader will be able:

- To describe how the interrelated structure of the multiunit organization (MUS) contributes to effective communication, coordination, and decision making.
- To describe the unit leader's responsibilities in communication and coordination as a member of the IIC.
- To describe the unit leader's responsibilities as a member of the SPC and other organizations in the facilitative environments component of IGE.

The leadership role of the unit leader within the I & R Unit has been described in Chapter 4. However, the unit leader's role does not end in internal leadership. Rather, the unit leader assumes external responsibilities by representing the I & R Unit staff in other policymaking and coordinating groups where decisions affecting the I & R Unit are made. The comprehensive structure of the multiunit organization (MUS) provides an arrangement of interrelated groups at three levels of operation: (1) the I & R Unit at the instructional level, (2) the IIC at the building level, and (3) the SPC at the system level. The composition and function of these groups were described in Chapter 1. The interrelationship of these groups provides the vehicle to improve communication among school personnel, to coordinate educational efforts and organizational relationships and to provide increased involvement in decision making.

The I & R Unit, the IIC, and the SPC, as the decision-making bodies in IGE, cannot function independently of each other. A link must exist between each of the groups so that all involved personnel are working for a common purpose rather than at cross purposes. That connecting link exists primarily in the person of the unit leader, who functions as the official representative of the unit staff to the other policymaking committees. These connections are illustrated in Figure 5.1.

The overlapping membership in the multiunit organizational structure is a complex system designed to bring about shared decision making at each level. As the official representative for the unit staff, the unit leader accepts responsibility for three functions: communication, coordination, and decision making at the school level as well as at the system level, if chosen to do so. It must be remembered that the unit leader

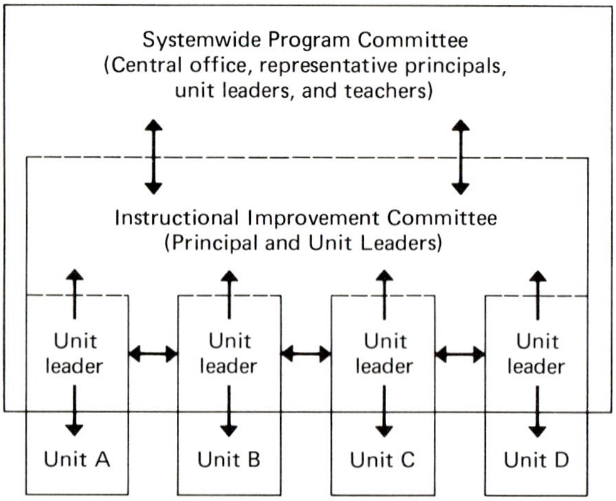

Fig. 5.1 The unit leader: the connecting link.

As the official representative of the unit staff, the unit leader accepts responsibility for three functions: communication, coordination, and decision making at the school (IIC) level.

performs these functions for the unit members and that he or she speaks, not as an individual, but as the designated representative for the I & R Unit. This chapter will focus on the unit leader's responsibilities in communication, coordination, and decision making in the IIC and SPC.

COMMUNICATING: A TWO-WAY PROCESS

The unit leader's role in educational improvement is the central theme of this text. In this role the unit leader is continually involved in change and innovation. Although educational change is not accomplished easily, there are practices which facilitate the process.

In three phases of change—(1) the initial planning for change, (2) the designing of procedures to be used in implementation, and (3) the implementation itself—the real measure of success is determined by the degree of input given by the staff to be affected in the change (Reichart

1969, p. 125). In order to obtain active staff participation in each of these phases, an open system of communication must be established. This requires identification of channels or persons in key positions through which information and suggestions may flow and the development of processes for clarification of purposes and coordination of individual and group efforts. Successful implementation occurs only through interaction of the persons involved in development, evaluation, adoption, use, and continuing improvement of innovations. Effective communication is essential to fruitful interaction.

Several school conditions which encourage communication and therefore change, are (Lippitt 1967, p. 319):

1. school arrangements which provide a reasonable amount of time for teachers to spend with each other.
2. structural arrangements which provide the opportunity for teachers to be physically close together.
3. an environment in which a notable degree of influence is exercised by the teachers.
4. arrangements which define a line of open communication among support systems.
5. arrangements which provide face to face communication in small groups.

Innovation relates to two patterns of communication—hierarchical and diffused (Lippitt 1967, p. 319). The hierarchical or vertical communication pattern is one in which professional ideas may travel quickly from designated leaders to the followers, yet little innovation takes place. Traditionally organized schools have had this "top-down" type of communication system. Decisions made by central office personnel are given to teachers through their principals at monthly faculty meetings. The part relegated to the teacher is limited to implementation. This practice is highly unlikely to produce teacher involvement or innovative behavior.

Conversely, in those schools where the communication structure is diffused or lateral, and where almost everyone is linked to someone, teachers innovate and share more than in schools with a nondiffused structure (Lippitt 1967).

However, in a diffused structure "messages" do not travel quickly down the ranks. Rather, the process is relatively slow as personnel at all levels in the hierarchy become involved in face-to-face conversation in both the sharing and decision-making processes.

Face-to-face communication is the most effective way to communicate one's ideas, feelings, and attitudes. It is not always the most efficient in terms of time. However, if the "manager" is concerned about organizational effectiveness, as opposed to efficiency, "eyeball-to-eyeball" communication is desirable whenever possible (Bellon 1971, p. 102). Because there is some personal risk involved in innovation and change, the need for supportive communication and involvement is obvious.

The multiunit organization component of IGE utilizes facets of both the hierarchical and diffused patterns into a communication linkage in the following ways:

1. The unit meetings offer a biweekly formal communication format in which teachers share and plan for the instructional program in a face-to-face relationship.
2. The I & R Unit structure provides a physical arrangement compatible with open communications. Many IGE teachers operate in instructional pods or areas, others in extended classrooms in which traditional walls have been removed, while others remain in clustered yet traditional classrooms.
3. Unit teachers share jointly in decision making for the unit and for the school through their unit leaders.
4. There is a formal structure of communications at I & R Unit, building (IIC) and system (SPC) levels.
5. Face-to-face communication exists in both the formal and informal arrangements.

In an IGE school, many decisions affecting teachers and children in the I & R Units are made in the IIC. In order for the school to function effectively the lines of communication must be structured, dependable, and provide for leadership. Communication must take place within the unit, between the principal and the units, and between the units. In Figure 5.1 the two-pronged arrows indicate that communication in this model is considered as a two-way process—(1) that of carrying input from the unit and (2) that of providing feedback to the unit.

Communicating from the I & R Unit to the IIC

The unit leader, as a communication agent, represents the I & R Unit and participates in the decision-making process according to the wishes of the unit members as expressed in the unit meetings. The unit leader reports the unit needs, ideas, and problems that may affect the total building program. Topics to be considered by members of the IIC are often generated in the unit. In the following example, "Science Curriculum—Articulation among Units" a problem was identified by an intermediate unit (Unit C) and given priority on the IIC agenda for the regular weekly meeting.

The problem had its roots in Unit C. Here, many of the nine- and ten-year-olds had completed the two-year cycle of science concepts originally selected for this segment of the school population. Two of the four teachers in Unit C felt the children should be able to go on with the science curriculum selected for the upper intermediate unit (Unit D). Another teacher felt this was infringing on the next year's work and was therefore unfair to the Unit D staff. This teacher called attention to the science guide which mentioned something about horizontal development as well as vertical planning. Lacking specific science expertise, the unit staff was unsure of how to proceed. They were also concerned about the opinion of other teachers in the building. Consequently, they asked the unit leader to take the problem to the IIC.

The IIC was not expected to make a decision at this first meeting. Rather each unit leader, after thorough discussion to clarify the issue, was asked to place the problem on the agenda of their next I & R Unit meeting. The opinions and suggestions of the teachers in all units were to be reported back to the IIC by the respective unit leaders.

In the succeeding IIC meeting, each unit leader reported that the teachers wanted to retain the originally planned scope and sequence of the science curriculum. They felt it best to develop plans for horizontal or enrichment curriculum and in-depth study in science rather than vertical development. One unit leader reported that a member of her unit had volunteered to help Unit C design such science activities. Another indicated that the unit staff he represented wanted more inservice education in science. The decisions were made quickly. In order to expedite the decisions, the Unit C leader agreed to obtain a list of science needs from the Unit C staff and the principal was directed to investigate inservice possibilities.

In this illustration, a specific problem from one I & R Unit was brought to the IIC by the unit leader for solution. The problem was a total school problem and could not be solved in the unit where it had occurred. It should be noted that while the problem was solved in this school by providing for horizontal enrichment, this is only one alternative. A school that was implementing instructional programming in science might have selected instead vertical development utilizing high school and college tutors and community resource persons. However, not all matters considered in the IIC must come initially from the unit staff as the next example will demonstrate.

Communicating from the IIC to the I & R Unit Staff

Some items on the IIC agenda may be generated by the principal as chairperson of the IIC and be placed before the members of the IIC. In other words, the items for consideration may come from the "top—down" as well as from the "bottom—up." An item on the "Metric System" appeared on the March IIC agenda in a particular building. The principal announced that he had received a communication from the central office stating that the Board of Education had issued a policy statement at its last meeting that the metric system would be taught to all elementary students, beginning September of the next school year. A metric system brochure, as well as a scope and sequence chart assigning specific content to pupil levels in the school, and necessary materials would arrive in the schools in about two weeks. Each school was asked to "tool up" for metric for fall.

The principal gave copies of the memorandum to each unit leader to distribute to the respective unit staffs. The meeting was open to discussion which largely focused on clarifying the administrative directive. This situation is quite different than the one presented in the previous example. The message came from central office as a statement of fact. Neither the teachers nor principal were in a decision-making situation. Materials, as well as the scope and sequence, were being sent. The unit leaders were expected to interpret the policy statement to the unit staff and to commence planning procedures for fall implementation.

The unit leader is responsible for communicating the decisions of the IIC to the unit staff and students, consultants, parents, and others affected by the decision. It is crucial that everyone affected by the decision is aware of what is happening so that any future action that needs to be taken will be fully supported. Not all matters placed on the agenda by the principal are limited to teacher decision making regarding implementation procedures. This is illustrated in the following example where a more involved *two-way* communication problem is undertaken.

Two-way Communication: A Case Study

The principal of a school had placed only one item—the school budget—on the weekly IIC agenda. The principal explained that central administration was considering decentralization of a portion of the system's operating funds. Under the proposed arrangement, each school would have control over its own budget, excluding salaries. The principal in each school was to discuss the proposal with the teachers in his or her building and report opinions at the next principals' meeting. The communication pattern was as follows: (1) the "message" was given to the principal; (2) the principal discussed the advantages and disadvantages with the unit leaders at the IIC; (3) the "message" was then carried by each unit leader to the unit meeting for discussion and decision: (4) the result was fed back again by the unit leader, to the IIC; and (5) the principal reported the IIC decision, as a school consensus of opinion, to the general meeting of principals chaired by the superintendent. The final decision was not to be made at this meeting of the principals but at the central office. The principal then reported the central office decision to the unit leaders in the IIC, who in turn reported the shared decision back to the unit. This process is depicted in Figure 5.2. In this instance, it was decided that individual schools would control their own budgets, the amount to be allocated at the central office. Further decisions would now be the responsibility of the individual schools.

Following the decision, the IIC in this case devoted several meetings to budgetary matters. Under the guidance of the principal, the unit leaders studied the total picture of the school operations including material inventories and costs, replacement costs, etc. The unit teachers were asked to delay discussion about the budget in the unit meetings until the unit leaders had the opportunity to become knowledgeable about these unfamiliar matters.

Within a week, the unit leaders presented the total situation to the the staff teachers and sought answers to the following questions they had prepared in the IIC:

Should the total allocation be divided evenly among the units?
Should the number of children in each unit be the criterion (cost per child)?
How should the money be spent? All at once or dispersed over the year?

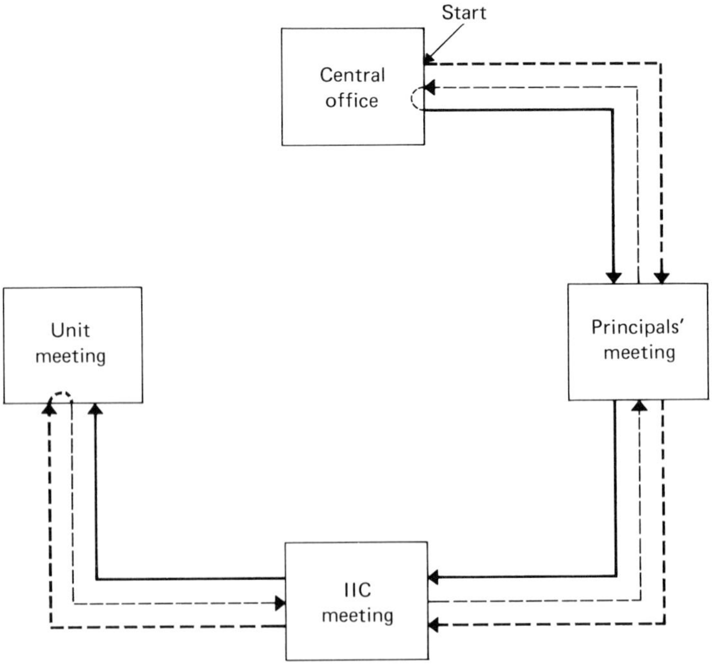

Fig. 5.2 Pattern of communication within a system.

How should units determine what is critical?
Should units set priorities?
Must all units adopt the same textbook series in each subject area?

Each unit staff attended to the serious business of compiling a list of recommendations which was then reported to the IIC. With this input and the help of the principal, whose experience in budgeting was valuable in this matter, the following decisions were made:

All units would conduct an inventory of supplies on hand, and based on past records from the principal's office, estimate needs for the coming year.

All units would compile a reasonable list of desired purchases and rank them as to priority.

All units would reserve a reasonable sum for instructional needs during the year and inservice consultants if desired and indicated.

Allocation need not be divided equally if the total building program could be best served by unequal distribution.

These decisions were then acted upon in each unit meeting and the needed information carried back again to the IIC for final decision.

At this point, it is appropriate to pause in the case study to consider the unit leader's position. The unit leader must represent the unit and in this case try to secure the materials desired by the staff. At the same time, the unit leader must also be willing to compromise and still maintain the cooperation of the unit members. This situation demands wide open communication so that residual hard feelings can be avoided. The IIC cannot become a battleground in which each unit leader attempts to "get the most." The unit leader, as the liaison between both groups, must possess several basic skills in communication. The unit leader will need to:

- be pleasant, approachable, and sensitive to the feelings of others,
- express himself or herself in such a way that members can understand what is being said,
- be accurate in communicating ideas,
- listen attentively to team members and unit leaders,
- clarify statements for all when necessary,
- encourage others to speak and contribute,
- recognize and praise good contributions,
- exhibit tact and maintain poise,
- offer alternatives in order to gain compromise when needed,
- explain his or her actions to ensure openness and avoid suspicion of secrecy, and
- keep the group on task while problem solving.

Return now to the case study. It was decided in the IIC that the total school program should be considered above that of individual units. Therefore funds would not be divided evenly. As reading was the first curriculum area to receive attention the preceding year, the primary units had received many new diagnostic tools and instructional materials. In September of next year, the school would concentrate on science. The intermediate units had few up-to-date materials and no multimedia or discovery kits. Therefore, it was decided that a larger allocation should be given to them. Furthermore, the inventories revealed that a large surplus of art supplies existed in the building and by sharing across units very little paint, glue, etc. needed to be purchased. The primary units were thus able to cross out a high priority budget item. The IIC continued to work out the distribution of funds to the satisfaction of all concerned, with the total school program having top priority.

Effective joint decision making, as described in the preceding case study, depends to a large extent on the unit leader's ability to perform as a communications expert within the school community. However, the communication role also extends beyond the school to include the parents and the general community.

Communicating between the I & R Unit and Parents and Community

The unit leader functions as a liaison to parents and community. Parent and community attitudes vary regarding innovation and experimentation. Change is viewed as a negative condition by some, while others react positively. However, providing avenues of communication with parents cannot help but strengthen the positive support, neutralize negative feelings and ward off possible antagonism. Not only is this a wise plan but it is also an obligation of the school.

Again, the unit leader assumes responsibility for several functions. These include analyzing, informing, and involving the parents and community. These will be described in detail in Chapter 8.

As has been stated many times before in this text, the unit leader does not operate alone. This would not only be impossible but it would also be contrary to the team approach in IGE. However, the unit leader must direct attention to the process of involving the parents and community. The unit leader guides the unit as it makes plans to improve communication links with the larger population involved in schooling. The unit leader contributes his or her talents and encourages staff members to offer theirs. It is important that the unit leader create a generally positive attitude toward involving parents and community and toward helping them to understand the operations of an IGE school.

Unit leaders, as well as the staff teachers and principal, are responsible for improving home-school-community relations. We are primarily concerned here with the role of the unit leader as a communication agent between the parents and the I & R Unit to which their children are assigned. The unit leader responsibility in this regard is to report unit activities to the parents and to encourage active parent involvement in the unit. One way of doing this is through a newsletter such as the one presented in Figure 5.3 or in a letter like the one in Figure 5.4.

Disney World's Happenings

NEWSLETTER #1

Disney World Unit

Our unit has undergone a name change this fall. We are no longer Unit III but rather the Disney World Unit.

Our unit consists of 4 rooms and each has been decorated in Disney fashion. We have Marine Land, Tomorrow Land, Frontier Land and, of course, Fantasy Land.

Parent-Teacher Conferences

Preparations are being made for parent-teacher conferences which will be held November 11th and 12th.

This is a time which provides an opportunity for parents and teachers to become better acquainted as well as to discuss your child's progress in the Disney World Unit.

We surely hope that you will plan to attend your child's conference and we are looking forward to seeing each of you.

Open House

The Disney World teachers wish to thank all parents for their great response to the Open House. We hope it has answered a few questions about the Individually Guided Education system we operate under.

Any questions or suggestions you would like to make would be welcome. If you would like another Open House sometime in the future please feel free to let us know.

Asia

The next area of study in social studies we will be discussing will be Asia. Six topics that possibly will be involved in this unit are:

1) Life-style
2) Geography
3) Problems of Asia
4) Economy
5) Contrast of people
6) Government

If you have any pictures, items, or other information that we could use, we would be very pleased to have you come and share them with us.

Through this unit and the other continents we will be discussing throughout the year we hope to broaden the child's scope of the world, and the general life-style of other people.

Mold Unit

For the past few weeks the children of Disney World have been learning about molds, mushrooms, and other nongreen plants. Each child has been able to grow his or her own mold garden and we have had some amazing results.

Fig. 5.3 Sample I & R Unit newsletter from the Thorp Elementary School, Thorp, Wisc.

Toledo, Ohio
September 30, 1975

Dear Parents,

The upper intermediate program is, for the most part, based on individualization. We feel this is best for the children because they work at a level which is not frustrating to them and they progress at their own rate.

The students in room 101-102 are considered one whole class and the teachers and student teacher are all available to help the children at all times. We also have our aide and an intern who are invaluable to our program and work with the children in some areas.

We have a vast amount of reading material. The material is of varying levels and each child has been tested to determine at which level he or she will function most efficiently and with as little frustration as possible.

In language arts an assignment sheet is handed out each Monday and the students are expected to complete these assignments by Friday. Every week the assignment sheet included reading for conferences, vocabulary words, and spelling exercises. Other assignments vary from week to week. Quest activities are also included for those who complete the required assignments.

A spelling pretest is given to all students on Monday. If a child gets 100 he or she takes another pretest on the next unit on Tuesday. If the child should get another 100 he or she is finished with the spelling work for the week. If, however, the child misses words either Monday or Tuesday, then there is a spelling exercise for the child to do for the week and a final test to take on Friday on the words missed on the pretest. As you can see, we have students in many different units each week. When all units in the spelling book are completed, we have extension spelling words we give the children weekly. We also have task groups periodically for all students having difficulty in any one area and who need more help.

In mathematics, which is also individualized, the students are pretested in an area, such as addition, subtraction, multiplication, etc. Depending on how well they do on the pretest they either pass out of that area and go on to the next or are given assignments to do with teacher instruction and assistance. Those who have assignments will then be given a posttest when the assignments are completed. If they do well on this posttest, they take the next pretest. If, however, the student does not do as well as expected, indicating lack of understanding of a particular concept, the student is then given more instruction, followed by another posttest.

We also have large group mathematics which consists of activities that need more structured guidance and reinforcement or fun activities involving mathematics concepts not necessarily included in the weekly work.

Our science and social studies are not as yet completely individualized. We do have lectures, discussions, projects, activities, and small group work so the students have a nice variety in these subjects. Many of the projects, activities, or small group activities are on a more individual basis and often student-selected.

Our long-range goal is to have each child learn and progress as much as possible this year. We are grateful to have the number of adults available to help the children and also feel lucky to have cooperative parents.

We would be happy to answer any questions you have during the school year.

Sincerely,

Fig. 5.4 Sample parent information letter.

Parents are better able to support their children and consequently the unit if, in simple words, "they know what's going on." They should know how, when, and why children are being tested. They should know why their children are asking for old candles or clothespins, or why it's important to talk to the mailman, or to dig a hole in the yard. They should know why their youngsters are not always working with the same groups of children. It would be well to talk to parents about:

- the goals and focus of an IGE program.
- the research data on individual differences.
- the importance of instructional objectives.
- the various diagnostic procedures used in the unit.
- the importance of varied grouping configurations.
- the learning activities designed to accommodate varied learning modes and learning styles.
- the evaluation and reporting techniques used in the unit.
- the advantages and difficulties of team teaching.
- the differentiated staffing employed in the unit.
- the methods used in developing curriculum.
- the use of the Instructional Programming Model (IPM).

The unit leaders and staff teachers must help the parents to see how their children, in terms of academic achievement, social development, personality, and self-concept relate to the principles and practices which exist in the unit.

The unit staff should be continually aware of opportunities to involve parents in unit activities, to define the principles of IGE, and to demonstrate the practices used in the unit. Parent conferences and other reporting devices, although inherent procedures in schooling, are only the bare minimum for establishing open communications with parents. The unit leader in one school listed the topic of improving parent communication on the unit meeting agenda and suggested that it be dealt with in a brainstorming session. The following list of ideas was generated:

- morning coffee to explain the IGE program—release the unit leader or a teacher.
- afterschool get-together.
- mothers organize "coffees" in homes—release unit leader or teacher to attend.
- invite small groups to watch "a unit morning"—prepare list of "what to look for"—grouping configurations, varied learning activities, independent learning, peer learning, teacher-pupil conferences, etc.

- invite small groups to observe at unit meeting and IIC.
- inservice morning for parents. Children remain home while teachers go through "IGE day."
- seek parent volunteers.
- open-door policy at all times.
- unit newspaper or newsletter.
- invitation to parents for plays, reports, experiments, etc.
- class logs sent home.
- a monthly letter or phone call to each parent.
- ask several parents to be "an advisory committee" for the unit.

Goodwill, understanding, and support from parents are most valuable elements in a successful unit. The unit leader must make every effort to build and maintain positive parental attitudes for the good of the children and the staff. It becomes a matter of creating communication opportunities for the parties involved.

Effective communication among unit leaders, teachers, principal, and parents results in improved cooperation on school policies and activities. Although it is difficult to separate coordination from communication, for they appear generally to be interlocking conditions, the role of the unit leader as a coordinating agent will be considered briefly in the following section.

COORDINATING: IIC AND SPC

The unit leader, as a member of the IIC and the SPC, shares the responsibility for coordinating the building program and systemwide activities respectively. The vital leadership aspect of this position is especially apparent in this function. It is also true that many teachers new to IGE are inexperienced in this role. Therefore, it is likely that unit leaders will desire additional training in such areas as elementary curriculum planning, instructional programming in the subject areas, group dynamics, and teaching and learning strategies. Such training can be arranged through inservice programs or college courses. However, released time from teaching responsibilities is needed if unit leaders are to take part in "on the job" study. It is one thing to be able to engage in the processes of communication, coordination, and decision making, but without the basic information and knowledge of curriculum, instruction, and organization, decisions are of little value. The unit leader's coordination responsibilities are described below.

Coordinating at the IIC

Coordination at the building level, which takes place in the IIC, involves four main functions. "(1) stating the educational objectives for the entire school building, (2) interpreting and implementing systemwide programs, (3) coordinating I & R Units to achieve continuity in all curriculum areas, and (4) arranging for the use of time, facilities and resources that are not managed independently by the units." (Klausmeier, *et al.* 1971) The unit leader as a member of the IIC has coordinating responsibilities in each of these functions. The following vignettes illustrate ways in which unit leaders can be involved.

Stating the educational objectives for the school. As a result of financial cutbacks a small, suburban K–4 school in northeast Ohio found itself without a full-time physical education teacher, as did the other four schools in the system. The regular staff in each school was required to assume instruction in the psychomotor segment of the curriculum. The schools had had a full-time physical education specialist in each building for a number of years. Many teachers had never taught physical education, and the long-tenured teachers had taught a social-games type of program. The schools were also in the first year of IGE implementation. The principal put the topic "What about the physical education program?" on the agenda for the newly formed five-member IIC and the meeting proceeded somewhat as follows:

Unit Leader 1: Our unit would like some additional large balls for Dodge Ball and Keep Away. We're thinking in terms of games.

Unit Leader 2: The primary teachers would like the 10 o'clock time in the gym as a break for the children in the morning.

Unit Leader 3: Did anyone find the old physical education guides? We could surely use them.

Unit Leader 4: Wait a minute. I think this conversation is going the wrong way. Shouldn't we take the physical fitness route by really attempting to improve psychomotor skills. Our unit started to observe the children doing skipping and hopping exercises last week to see which children in the unit do or do not have these gross motor skills. But we really don't know where to go from this point. And anyway, shouldn't whatever we do be coordinated among units?

Unit Leader 2: Not a bad idea! Working on skills, that is.

Unit Leader 3: Organizing is the answer. But how?

Principal: What would you think about making this our first area for instructional programming for individual students in

IGE? I know that most schools start with reading or math, but we have a real need here.

Unit Leader 4: I'll wager the other schools would be thrilled if we come up with something. Why don't we all go back and talk to the teachers? Let's look over the material we received during the workshop this summer so we all know how to begin.

Unit Leader 1: OK with me, but will we have time for games? I'm sure that's what our unit will want.

At the meeting of the IIC the following week it was reported that the unit staffs had supported the proposal and that a physical education program for the building would be designed according to the IPM and the IGE model. The staff teachers were willing to work on the project, especially in terms of critiquing, using, and revising, but agreed that the IIC should initiate and coordinate the design. The unit leaders and principal recognized that the first task to be performed by their committee was to prepare the educational objectives for the building. This was discussed at the following meeting somewhat as follows:

Unit Leader 2: We have agreed that physical education is the curriculum area in which we will use the IPM. We have also accepted the job of setting the broad objectives. Now what?

Unit Leader 4: Well, first we have to consider the characteristics of the children and then we have to take a look at the particular phase of physical education that we judge to be appropriate for them.

Unit Leader 3: The children aren't too hard to work with. They're approximately five through nine years old and from middle-class families. Most parents are interested in the school and in the progress of their children. Some of the children are overprotected, I think. But many, not all of course, have had lots of physical experiences, like swimming and ice skating.

Unit Leader 1: What we really don't know much about is physical education. Although I do think gross motor skills are right as target areas for our young children.

Unit Leader 4: According to what I've read, it's appropriate to include resource persons in the IIC, especially in matters of this kind. I suggest that we invite the physical education specialist from the system to help us on this. I'd be willing to search for objectives from other systems and to review them and report back to you.

Principal: I like what we are doing here. If it is agreeable with you, I'd like to ask a couple of parents, too. They can help us with background information on the children, especially their out-of-school activities. How about a month from today as a deadline for having a tentative set of objectives that we can give the staff to review?

As suggested, the IIC expanded its membership temporarily in order to get the assistance and support it needed. The following statement of general educational objectives was prepared and accepted:

As a result of the physical education program, the pupils (K–4) should develop:

1. organic fitness by means of activities which are selected to increase strength, vigor, and vitality.
2. neuromuscular skills and abilities through developmental activities which progress from the use of large muscles to the use of small muscles.
3. desirable recreational attitudes and interests which will be of value in current and future recreational pursuits.
4. desirable and lasting physical health habits.
5. the skill of accurately following directions and instructions.
6. emotional control and an initial sense of personal values toward physical exercise.
7. an understanding of the activities which will enable them to achieve and maintain physical fitness.

From these objectives each I & R Unit staff and the IIC generated instructional objectives in walking, running, skipping, jumping, and ball handling. For example, 20 instructional objectives in ball bouncing were established: the first being, "Bounce an 8-inch rubber ball with two hands continuously five times in succession without stopping," and the last being, "Dribble an 8-inch ball down to a line 25 feet away, using the dominant hand going down and the other hand coming back." Teachers, parents, aides, the physical education specialist, and the principal joined in the preassessment of performance for each child. The children were to be grouped according to identified need regardless of age.

Interpreting and implementing systemwide policies. The administration of a small suburban system which had only two high schools was considering a program in which high school students acted as aides. The purpose was two-fold: (1) to help several IGE elementary schools to carry out more effective instructional programming by providing aides, and (2) to increase senior offerings, especially for those students who had completed many of their high school requirements early and had few courses left to study as seniors. Moreover, these administrators had contacted the university in the area to suggest that these seniors enroll in a freshman course, "Career Decisions" offered by the College of Education. Before making final decisions certain questions had to be answered. Would the elementary I & R Units want high school aides? If such a policy were adopted, would the units agree to supervise and keep records of the performance of the aides as directed by the college training course and the high school requirements? Would the unit staff assist, critique, and evaluate? Would the unit staff plan for the effective use of these aides?

The administrators approached the elementary principals who took the proposal to the IICs. The unit leaders viewed the idea enthusiastically and interpreted the proposed policy to the unit teachers. The teachers reacted positively and accepted the terms. Eighty seniors signed up for the system's *High School Aide Program* and 40 of those who signed up enrolled for college credit. Both groups were trained by the cooperating university. The topic of the *High School Aide Program* appears on the IIC's agenda twice a month in each of the elementary schools using these aides. In this way the unit leaders coordinate the implementation of the aide program and oversee its effectiveness, in terms of servicing the units and meeting the supervisory functions required in the aide course at the college level.

Coordinating the I & R Unit to achieve continuity in all curriculum areas. A functioning IGE school had undergone some major personnel changes after its second year of implementation. The principal of the school had been moved to another building for the purpose of implementing IGE in a new setting. One of the excellent unit leaders moved to the same building. In addition, because of decreased enrollments, reassignment within the building had changed the composition of another well-functioning I & R Unit.

The new principal and unit leader were assigned to the experienced IGE school under the transfer policy within the system. Although both were successful professionals, neither had experience in IGE and neither person was given inservice education in IGE prior to transfer. The first three months of the new school year gave rise to deterioration in the total IGE program, especially in reading. The school had previously adopted an objective-based reading and language arts program for the teaching of skills, along with an independent, self-selected period using children's literature. The children had not been grouped by ability for two years, nor had they used the basal reader. However, in the three months of the new year there was general laxity about pre- and post-testing, grouping according to assessment results, and record keeping. The reading program was not being coordinated. Students and parents began to report unfavorable comments about the failure of all teachers to use the checksheets used previously in parent conferences. They also objected to ability grouping in basal readers begun in one unit and limited pupil access to the library.

Although the IIC had continued to meet weekly, the composition had changed, and informed leadership was absent. The emphasis on the meeting had switched from curriculum to general building materials. The parents had brought the problems to the principal and at the succeeding IIC the principal forced an open discussion of the situation. As a result both he and the new unit leader sought additional training in IGE. They, with the cooperation of the other members, began the process of reviewing and coordinating the reading program to resemble the one with which the parents and students had found satisfaction.

Arranging for the use of facilities, time, materials, and resources that are not managed independently by the units. A particular school had procured funds, through the central office and parents, to develop an instructional media center in the building. Central Office had committed funds for removing a wall, for carpeting and for electrical work as well as for a part-time director. The Parent Teacher Association had organized a fund-raising drive to collect money for initial supplies. Planning the physical area, such as electrical outlets for carrels, determining the kinds of equipment and materials to be included, outlining the procedures for student use, and organizing the volunteers to man the center were clearly matters for the unit leaders, as members of the IIC. All considerations were discussed with each unit staff until all opinions were known. The unit leaders and the principal worked with the system's plant and facilities personnel and electricians. Second, they prepared three lists of materials and equipment: (1) necessary materials, (2) desired materials, and (3) materials desired in the future. Third, they established a job description for the personnel who would maintain the center. Last, they established school-policy statements for the use of the center.

Coordinating at the SPC

All unit leaders participate in coordinating functions in the building's IIC. Some unit leaders represent the IIC at the SPC level of coordination which will be described below.

Coordination at the SPC (or alternate systemwide committee) level focuses on program matters which are likely to be constant for all schools and units. The responsibilities to be assumed by this committee are: (1)

identifying the functions to be performed in all IGE schools in a district, (2) recruiting personnel for IGE schools and arranging for inservice, (3) providing instructional materials, and (4) disseminating relevant information within the district and community (Klausmeier, *et al.* 1971).

Consider the first responsibility in the following illustration of program evaluation as it originated in an urban school system. Pressure from the parents of children in the IGE schools in the district forced the administration to consider a systemwide evaluation of the program. The purpose of the evaluation program was to evaluate the progress of each IGE school in the system as well as the total IGE effort in the district. The evaluation considered pupil achievement and attitude, teacher and parent attitudes, and the effectiveness of the unit meetings and the IIC. Such an evaluation could not take place unless all personnel were involved. Obviously, the coordination of such an effort was vital to its suc-

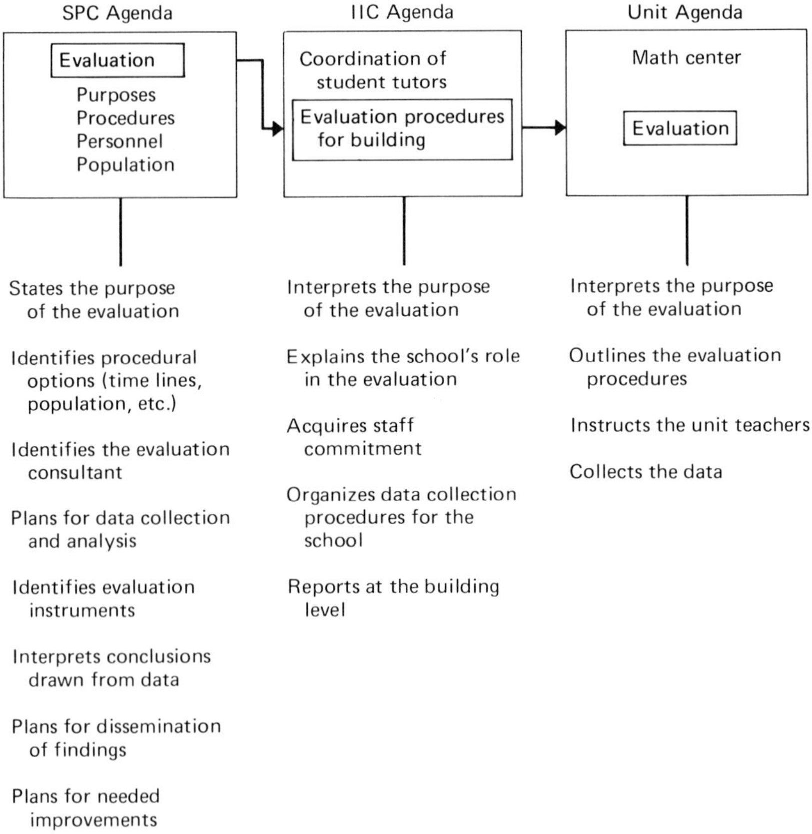

Fig. 5.5 Trilevel coordinating functions of the unit leader.

cess. The unit leaders, with memberships in each group, provided the coordination linkage. The trilevel coordinating functions of the unit leader are represented in Figure 5.5.

Here the unit leader, as a member of the SPC, is involved in preparing a statement of purpose, designating time lines and school populations, selecting outside evaluation personnel, and planning for data dissemination and curriculum improvement based on the data. Moreover, the unit leader also assists the evaluation consultant in planning for data collection and analysis, and interpretation of conclusions.

Within the building, the unit leader, as an IIC member and leader of the I & R Unit must keep the evaluation procedures operating in a consistent manner. That is, the unit leader must be faithful to the design and report unit findings as requested and in the agreed upon format. The coordination responsibilities at this point call for keeping everyone on task and operating in like manner. Following the data collection, the unit leader may be involved in organizing and comparing the data and will surely have reporting and interpreting responsibilities. Finally, the unit leader will be concerned with making and implementing decisions based on evaluation. It is highly unlikely that coordination will take place across schools or within schools without open communication and shared decision making.

Before terminating this chapter on the unit leader's role as the official representative of the unit, attention should be given specifically to the process of effective decision making which is, after all, the primary ongoing function in all groups in which the unit leader holds membership.

DECISION MAKING: A PRIMARY FUNCTION

The importance of a two-way system of communication and overlapping group membership is ultimately realized in the manner in which decisions are reached in the policymaking groups, the IIC and SPC. This is equally true of unit operations, of course, but that is not the focus of this chapter.

In the final analysis, a group decision results only when all members of the group feel that sharing has taken place and that they are willing to make a commitment to act on the decision. Five ways in which decisions are made and the consequences of these actions are (Chin and Hadley 1971, pp. 92-93):

1. *Lack of response.* Members make suggestions without discussion and several "clutch" at a suggestion which passes as a group's decision. This may result in feeling of group desperation or feelings of individual inadequacy by members whose ideas were not considered.

2. *Authority rule.* One person makes the decision after hearing what is considered sufficient discussion. This action produces low involvement and a negative effect on implementation.
3. *Minority rule.* A minority which has agreed upon their objectives manipulates the group by the very fact of their agreement. This often results in lack of response by others, feelings of desperation and low involvement or antagonism.
4. *Voting or polling* (majority rule). This method is highly conventional and although it may appear rational, its disadvantages include resentment and frustration on part of those whose "ideas were not understood." The win–lose conflict is apparent and those who have lost often battle to win the next issue.
5. *Consensus.* Although time consuming, this is considered to be the most effective decision-making procedure. In a consensus situation, it is possible for all persons to feel that they understand the situation, have had sufficient influence, are able to compromise without losing face, and are willing to implement the decision.

Therefore, it would appear that each unit leader, as a representative of the unit staff, must speak for the unit, but must still be free to compromise in order that "group decisions" can be made in the IIC and SPC. In addition, once a decision is made, the unit leader must be able to translate the details of the process in such a way that the unit staff will also feel committed and cooperatively implement the decision. It follows that consensus must be the watchword in both the IIC and SPC lest the unit leader become resentful or frustrated in the process and communicate this attitude to the staff.

Inherent in the decision-making process is the need to compromise and to collaborate. But so it is also inevitable that conflict situations will arise. Not always is conflict completely damaging to group processes. Conflict, as disagreement, may lead to the creation of new ideas but only if the lines of communication are open. The unit leader, as a representative decision maker, would be wise to encourage that adequate attention be given to each step in the problem-solving process. These steps are identification of the problem, thorough analysis of the problem (including the use of professional literature, research, and experience to contribute to better understanding), presentation of alternative solutions to the problems, testing alternatives when possible, and adopting a final solution.

When conflict or disagreement does arise, it is imperative that action be delayed until the issue is discussed, analyzed, and resolved. The IIC and SPC, as well as the unit staff, must be concerned with the task at hand and the maintenance and stability of the group. The goals are consensus and commitment. Therefore, at any point of disagreement in the decision-making process, these groups would be well advised to surface the conflict and open it to thorough discussion. In this regard, the unit leader has the responsibility to:

1. present the opinions of the unit and school that he or she represents. Inability or unwillingness to place these opinions before the respective group would be a serious omission and could only lead to eventual discord in the unit, IIC, or SPC.
2. encourage open discussion on the part of all participating members. The unit leader must avoid the tendency to dominate the group.
3. listen to and consider the opinions of other group members in the desire to reach a satisfying solution. The unit leader must view the situation with some objectivity.
4. negotiate and reach a decision by informal consensus whenever possible. Causing cleavages, taking sides, and forcing a voting "show down" is damaging to the decision-making process.
5. come to the meeting well prepared. The unit leader cannot represent the unit, or the IIC, unless the "homework" has been done in these groups prior to attendance at the larger group.
6. be willing to postpone a decision over more than one meeting when consensus appears impossible in terms of time constraints.

The unit leader also has some rightful expectations in the role of unit, IIC, or SPC representative in decision making. These include:

- an agenda that will be available several days prior to the meeting.
- regular scheduling of both the SPC and IIC meetings including hour and place.
- a reasonable allocation of time that does not pressure decision making on an item.
- cooperation and preparation of all members to contribute to the decisions in terms of prior consideration of agenda items and a cooperative attitude.

Decision making is not a quick or momentary action since the decisions made in the interlocking system of the IGE multiunit organization presuppose implementation by many persons in the system. Unit leaders should keep this consequence clearly in mind as they participate in decision making. A favorable working situation, a representative system of communication and positive attitudes toward consensus will facilitate the leader's role in the decision-making process. An example of cooperative decision making that illustrates this situation is presented below.

Cooperative Decision Making: An Illustration

During the first year of IGE implementation it became apparent to the teachers in an urban elementary school that the previously used methods of reporting to parents were not satisfactory. Assessment of student progress had changed from a norm-referenced approach to a criterion-referenced approach, with emphasis on individual student progress. Many teachers in the building were questioning the use of letter grades as specified in the "old" report cards. Several units had begun to develop, in an ad hoc fashion, what they considered to be a better way to report to parents. One unit leader asked that the topic of reporting to parents be put on the IIC agenda for discussion. The principal and a unit leader, who represented the school, checked at the SPC whether an earlier decision that permitted the several IGE schools in the district to develop individual reporting procedures still held. It did.

When the four unit leaders came to the IIC meeting in which a common reporting system was on the agenda, there was no agreement among them and the ideas they brought from their units. Teachers in the primary unit (5- and 6-year-olds) wanted only parent conferences and had designed a short checklist of general topics for discussion. Teachers in the lower intermediate unit (7- and 8-year-olds) had decided on growth reports in the basic subjects with growth being reported in terms of Satisfactory (S), Unsatisfactory (U), and Needs Improvement (NI). Teachers in the intermediate unit (9- and 10-year-olds) wanted evaluation and reporting based on specific objectives in all content areas. They did not want to report a reading level nor use the S, U, and NI. Teachers in the upper intermediate unit (11- and 12-year-olds) felt obligated to equate all work to A, B, or C grades in order to prepare the pupils for the graded junior high school.

During the IIC meeting, each unit leader spoke for the teachers in his or her I & R Unit. The principal, acting as chairperson, encouraged each member to discuss all suggestions with candor. Although the principal was anxious to adopt a common school reporting system, she avoided any tendency in the meeting that might move the group to a vote. The units were so far apart that it would be impossible to serve more than a single unit in this way.

Although convinced of the worth of their own ideas, the unit leaders agreed to postpone a decision until a more thorough investigation of reporting systems used in other IGE schools could be made. They volunteered their unit members to do this job, and in addition agreed to review pertinent literature. The topic was to be placed on the agenda of the IIC to be held three weeks later.

At this later meeting, the unit leaders brought some examples of reporting forms which the unit members had selected as possible alternatives. Members of the several units had discussed the suggestions of the other units and were better able to consider the opinions of the others. Moreover, they had studied the problem of reporting to parents through reading and discussion. The atmosphere was one of enthusiasm to share all the information they had collected as well as of conviction that they could come to agreement on a procedure.

With very little discussion, they now agreed that the goals of the primary age children were probably better served by parent conferences only and that delaying the entire "report card" idea would be wise in serving the young child. The unit leaders did suggest that the discussion checklist used for the conference be organized by objectives and include the specific skills judged as desirable in language, reading, and mathematics. The primary unit had read a great deal on evaluation, and the unit leader was quick to support this idea. In addition the primary unit leader asked that other members of the units critique the checklist when completed.

The three remaining unit leaders all agreed that they wished a printed report for parents as well as a parent conference.

The upper intermediate unit, as reported by the unit leader, agreed that evaluation of pupil progress should be reported in terms of demonstrated mastery of cognitive and affective objectives, based on specified criteria. However, they were still concerned about possible methods to use to equate progress to letter grades. Prior to the IIC meeting the unit had invited parents to join in a discussion of the problem. Although most of the parents understood the situation and supported the elimination of letter grades, a few were still concerned about transition problems.

The discussion at the IIC meeting was lively. The inconsistency of normed letter grades with individual pupil progress was again reviewed. The pressure of future schooling practices on the elementary program received a great deal of attention. One of the unit leaders brought up the fact that the school received very few complaints from the junior high about the preparation of the children coming from this elementary school. The unit leader from the upper unit proposed that the elimination of letter grades for the older children be tried for a period of one year. The members of the IIC were quick to accept this proposal.

The unit leader representing the intermediate teachers expressed the opinion that their original idea of a growth report was not unlike that being proposed and that the teachers would be willing to work on such a report form. However, they would insist on a grade equivalent in reading to be included on the form. The other unit leaders compromised this point. They then decided that each unit would keep a record of suggestions for improving the reporting system when it was reevaluated at the close of the school year.

The IIC in this illustration resolved their earlier disagreements. With consensus reached in this meeting, the unit leaders could use all the information collected and actually begin the design of the physical format of the reporting form to be used along with the parent conference.

This narrative illustrates cooperative, informed decision-making efforts, open communication, and positive attitudes toward compromise and acceptance.

SUMMARY

The interrelated group structure in the multiunit organization is designed to encourage shared decision making within the school building and system. However, the three groups—the I & R Unit, IIC, and SPC—must be linked together for the system to operate for a common purpose. This linkage exists primarily in the person of the unit leader who represents the unit in the IIC and SPC and who also provides feedback from these groups to the unit. The unit leader's ability to establish a strong liaison among the decision-making bodies depends on the effectiveness of the communication process, the combined efforts toward coordination, and the quality of the decision making itself.

REFERENCES

Bellon, J. 1971. Team leaders and professional management. In *Perspectives on the role of the teacher corps team leader.* Project Report. Toledo: The University of Toledo.

Chin, R. and H. Hadley 1971. Group process in task teams. In *Perspectives on the role of the teacher corps team leader.* Project Report. Toledo: The University of Toledo.

Klausmeier, H. T., M. R. Quilling, J. S. Sorenson, R. S. Way, and G. R. Glasrud 1971. *Individually guided education and the multiunit elementary school: guidelines for implementation.* Madison, Wisc.: Wisconsin Research and Development Center for Cognitive Learning.

Lippitt, R. 1967. The teacher as innovator, seeker, and sharer of new practices. In R. Miller (ed.), *Perspectives on educational change.* New York: Appleton-Century-Crofts.

Reichart, S. 1969. *Change and the teacher.* New York: Crowell.

6

Strengthening Staff Development

Joan D. Inglis

Objectives

After reading this chapter, the reader will be able:

- To discuss verbally or in writing, the role of the unit leader in the process of change.
- To present a plan for assessing, formally and informally, the strengths and weaknesses, needs and interests of a teaching staff.
- To prepare an outline for training auxiliary personnel including responsibilities and possible functions of paraprofessionals.
- To outline the major components and concerns of an inservice program for IGE staff and contrast this outline with more traditional inservice programs.
- To discuss, verbally or in writing, the broad role of the unit leader in the preservice program.

The complexity of the unit leader's responsibilities becomes obvious as the roles and functions of this new teaching position are identified and discussed. The unit leader has been described as a self-renewing, master teacher who is innovative, flexible, knowledgeable, and open. The unit leader functions as a coordinator, communicator, and facilitator of the shared functions of diagnosis, problem solving, decision making, and evaluation.

The successful implementation and refinement of IGE in a school depends to a considerable degree on the capabilities of the unit leader as an educational leader possessing indepth skills necessary to bring about instructional change. The unit leader assumes leadership for the continuing professional development of the staff, and in addition, serves as the external representative of the teachers to the IIC and the SPC. This requires knowledge of individualization techniques, curriculum development procedures, and skills in interpersonal relationships and decision making. The unit leader, as an agent of change, is a teacher educator in both inservice and preservice education.

This is not to say that the unit leader operates unilaterally or makes decisions about professional development alone. Such behavior would be discrepant with the basic philosophy of shared decision making which is intrinsic to the multiunit organization. Members share the planning, organizing, and evaluating of all staff activities in which the unit engages. However, the unit leader accepts the responsibility to ensure that this is taking place and serves as a catalyst to mobilize and maximize the talents, abilities and personalities of the teaching unit.

Therefore, the unit leader actually becomes an agent of change and as such becomes deeply involved in the process of educational reform and renewal. Since change is difficult and sometimes painful, it is important that the person who assumes this role (1) believe in the program to be implemented, (2) have a commitment to the program, (3) be capable and trained in the necessary procedures, and (4) have the personality and qualities necessary to lead in this change effort.

CHANGE PRINCIPLES REVIEWED

Although the topic of change theory was discussed earlier in Chapter 2, it is appropriate to review several aspects of change as it relates to staff-development activities at both the inservice and preservice levels.

Educational change does not take place quickly nor easily. It certainly does not evolve without a certain amount of human disturbance, for all the forces which contribute to stability in personality and social systems, such as security, habit, comfort, and personal interests can be seen as resisting change (Watson 1969, p. 488).

It is also basic to the evolution of change that each person to be affected by the change be involved in the process. In order to change curriculum in the schools all teachers must perceive themselves as important persons in the curriculum-planning process. "The real measure of success will eventually be determined by the degree of input by the staff most affected by the change strategies." (Reichart 1969, p. 125)

Several principles for groups involved in change and the reeducative process have been cited (Chin 1969, p. 44-45):

1. Persons affected by change must be involved in working out programs of change and improvement.
2. Changing is not considered a technical problem alone, but one which may also involve attitudes and values.
3. Those involved must work together to identify needs and problems and their solutions.
4. Elements which impede change must be brought out and dealt with openly.

The following steps for change provide a base for the unit leader to consider role responsibilities and procedures in staff development (Alexander 1967, p. 346):

1. Identify needs, strengths, and weaknesses of staff and pupils as:
   a. staff strengths and weaknesses in planning and presentation.
   b. staff identified needs.
   c. pupil needs in terms of pupil outcomes and attitudes.
2. Determine curriculum priorities.
3. Select innovative practices.
4. Experiment with and evaluate these practices.
5. Formulate plans for diffusion.

The basic question for all unit members should be: What learning opportunity can we as teachers provide which will help the children in our unit to become able and eager learners?

Changes in philosophy, organization, and methodology in teaching do take place when IGE is implemented. Good traditional classroom teachers are expected to change their orientation and styles to enjoy contributing as members of a team. Teachers are expected not only to recognize the concept of individual differences, but to replace the age-graded, normed organization and materials with learning materials appropriate for instructional programming for individual students. The unit leader must encourage deviation from the comfort of the status quo and encourage alternative patterns of learning and problem solving.

Several other changes will obviously take place in IGE schools. The potential of technology is being applied to instruction. Technology can be used to improve learning in some areas and to free educators for individual teaching. Unit leaders will be assuming an important role in training for increased use of technology.

Teachers should expect to receive assistance as they change from a textbook course of study to instructional programming for individual students in IGE. They will need help in establishing educational objectives and finding appropriate materials for teaching these objectives. They will need assistance to employ strategies for grouping which result from the use of the IPM. Teachers will need help in curriculum planning and unit of instruction design, in evaluation techniques and record keeping and in designing optional instructional programs for children.

Will the real teacher please stand up? In some classrooms today one would be hard pressed to find the teacher in that position. Real teachers in IGE schools are exhibiting behaviors unlike those in a traditional setting. The stand-up teacher who lectures in front of the class is hard to find. Thirty children, boxed in neat rows with their textbooks opened to the same page, facing a teacher standing in front of the room, are not part of the physical image of an IGE school. The traditional scene of recitation, teacher questions followed by student answers, identical assignments for all, which were all devices for teacher control, are replaced by a more open classroom atmosphere.

Some change simply occurs as a matter of chance, or nature. But there are also rational ways to bring about change. It is important that changes take place in an organized fashion—that the talents and abilities of all teachers are used and that needs for continuing staff development are met.

LEADERSHIP FOR CHANGE

In order for any number of people to function as a group, someone has to take charge and a kind of formal or informal leadership evolves. It is as simple as that.

The End of the School Year picnic needs an organizer—someone to plan the right amount and variety of food, adequate physical facilities, and group activities. Without someone to coordinate these activities, the operation will probably be a flop and the likelihood of a repeat performance the next year is questionable.

Moreover, a group will probably malfunction without a clear purpose for its existence, whether that purpose is simplistic, (e.g., to have a good time at the picnic) or complex, (e.g., to modernize a city). Appointed or emerging leaders must examine the capabilities and interests of all who participate in the group and, while keeping the purposes clearly in mind, maximize and facilitate the contributions of each participant.

Thus the unit leader must develop a plan and then accept responsibility for organizing the members of the I & R Unit to see that there is direction to their activities. The unit leader must also be able to delegate responsibility.

Change is a disconcerting phenomenon, for when persons change their behaviors they are actually negating a previously held belief or practice. In order to facilitate desired change in education, the unit leader should possess certain leadership qualities to bring about goal achievement and group satisfaction. The leader is involved in two strategies (1) initiating structure, and (2) group maintenance through consideration (Fiedler 1967). The unit leader attempts to establish well-defined patterns of organization, channels of communications, and methods of procedure. Furthermore, the unit leader is very much concerned with staff morale.

Therefore, the unit leader must observe, listen, reinforce, and exhibit competencies to assist in the following group functions:

- identifying unit goals.
- identifying a degree of progress toward these goals.
- refining the quality of interaction and sharing within the group.
- creating group identity and cohesiveness, and
- collecting and making resources available to the teachers.

The unit leader attempts to clarify and resolve personal issues by reducing tension and encouraging sharing and willingness of team members to express themselves. The unit leader (1) demonstrates warm respect to members of the team, (2) encourages analysis and evaluates procedures and compromising behaviors, (3) attempts to develop sensitivity and skill in performing necessary functions and techniques of problem solving, and (4) tries to develop a positive group climate of trust in which team members feel free to experiment, disagree, and state honest opinions.

The vehicles available to the unit leader as an agent of change and as an instructional leader exist within the role in inservice and preservice staff development in the I & R Unit and school.

THE UNIT LEADER'S ROLE IN INSERVICE EDUCATION

In the inservice area, a unit leader in an IGE school must be willing to (1) assess the strengths and interests of members of the teaching unit, (2) develop and plan for staff growth in all areas of curriculum development, (3) design and participate in preservice as well as inservice programs, (4) orient and provide training for beginning teachers, teachers new to the unit, and auxiliary personnel, and (5) provide liaison functions with outside agencies and personnel.

Assessing the Strengths and Interests of I & R Unit Members

An important benefit to both the children and teachers on a team is the maximum use of the diverse abilities and talents of the teachers. In an IGE school, children have an opportunity to associate with several teachers, each with unique personalities, interests, and talents. It is unreasonable to expect an elementary teacher to be equally versed and personally interested in all areas of the curriculum. In teaming, there is a greater possibility that all content subjects will be presented with enthusiasm and expertise.

The task of the unit leader is to identify the diverse abilities of the teachers on the team. Some teams may have the good fortune to be composed of teachers who have known each other for some time, both in and out of school. However, the fact that teachers are social and personal friends may not ensure that the team will be compatible professionally.

Identification of teacher strengths and needs is too important to be left to chance. It is vital to the unit operation. The unit leader will need a plan to collect data during the initial stage of team operations. As the leader of the group, the unit leader should capitalize on both formal and informal assessment measures to ensure maximum use of each member's potential contribution to the team functions.

Formal Assessment. Prior to the initial planning by a newly formed team, the unit leader should design a form, or use a form previously compiled, to collect data about the members of the unit. Each team member should take the time and interest to complete the form with care, keeping in mind that the information is important to the functioning of the team. The form should include items pertaining to academic training, subject matter interest, previous teaching experience, special talents and hobbies, teaching style, life experiences, and self-assessment. Teachers are also persons; they are no more alike than the children they teach. Their special talents and experiences are valuable to the motivation, education, and sheer delight of children. One teacher may be a member of the Audubon Society and be the nature buff in the community. Another may be an amateur artist who has studied in varied media, and yet another teacher may spark a social studies unit because of special knowledge of music and composers. The uniqueness of the teacher as a person can make the team a special one. A form that a unit leader could use for collecting data about teachers on the team is presented in Figure 6.1.

Informal assessment. The unit leader has the opportunity to assess the strengths and weaknesses of the unit staff in informal ways too. These occur during the unit meeting, during periods of observation, and during staff self-evaluation. Action which takes place during the unit planning presents the unit leader with an excellent opportunity to assess the strengths and needs of the members of the teaching unit. In the case study of a unit meeting which follows, certain staff needs can be identified by the unit leader.

In August, prior to the opening of school, the four teachers in Unit C met in the unit leader's home to plan and outline major goals and topics for the coming fall. These teachers had never worked together. Each had a self-contained classroom in the previous academic year. In the spring of the previous year, a team of college professors conducted a workshop in initial organization for IGE. Following the workshop, the entire school staff was excited about the opportunity to improve instruction for their pupils and made a commitment to implement the program. Decisions for teaming assignments were made at the close of the school year. The central office agreed to take down several walls, and the principal and unit leaders attended institutes during the summer.

The teachers decided to initiate instructional programming for individual students in reading and language arts. As a result of the meeting (detailed below) they identified the following units of study as appropriate for the first semester:

Poetry—approximately 4 weeks
Figurative language—approximately 2 weeks
Critical reading (Fact versus Fiction)—2 weeks
Reading study skills in the content areas—3 weeks
Undecided—2 weeks

Thelma: Poetry seems so important for children, but I can never get them interested in reading anything other than what I assign. And then when I have them write some poems, they moan and groan and just put something on paper. There are never more than a handful who seem to get much out of it—except that they are exposed—I suppose that's something. I guess part of the problem is that I don't know much about poetry. I couldn't have cared less when I was in school. But I do think it's a shame that kids don't like it—it's a real art form.

Name ____________________ Degree __________

Area of Specialization ____________________

Certification(s) ____________________

1. *Academic training:*

A. *Curriculum:*

General ☐ Curriculum Development ☐

Concentration:

Soc. Sci. ☐ Math ☐ Reading and Lang. Arts ☐

Science ☐ Art ☐ Music ☐ Phys. Ed. ☐ Other ☐

Children's Literature ☐

Specific course in:

Individualization ☐ Interaction Analysis ☐ Ed. Media ☐

Testing & Evaluation ☐ Inquiry ☐ Competency-Based Education ☐

Others: ____________________

Comments: ____________________

B. *Foundations:*

General ☐

Concentration:

Ed. Psych. ☐ Social Foundations ☐ Philosophical Foundations ☐

Research and Testing ☐

Specific courses in:

Behavior Management ☐ Learning Theory ☐

Child Growth and Development ☐ Group Processes ☐

Problem Solving and Creativity ☐ Personality ☐

Assessment ☐ Instructional Systems ☐

Others: ____________________

Comments: ____________________

C. *Administration and Supervision:*

Public School Supervision ☐ Educational Leadership ☐

Community Analysis ☐ Public Relations ☐

Others: ____________________

Comments: ____________________

Fig. 6.1 Teacher strengths assessment form.

____

____

2. *Previous experience:*
   Grade levels (ages) taught: ____________
   Administrative assignments: ____________
   Special areas taught: ____________
   Other than teaching experience: ____________

3. *Teaching self-assessment:*
   My best teaching area is ____________.
   My second best teaching area is ____________.
   I work best with bright children ☐ average children ☐ slower children ☐
   I work best with large groups of children ☐ small groups of children ☐ one-to-one ☐
   I am a good initiator ☐ diagnostician ☐ stimulator ☐ record keeper ☐ skill teacher ☐ advisor ☐ evaluator ☐
   The team could use my special skill of ____________.

4. *Personal resources:*
   Hobbies: ____________
   Collections: ____________
   What I read during my spare time: ____________
   What sports do I know about? ____________
   Have I ever designed a publication ☐ a newspaper ☐ written a song ☐ directed a musical ☐ led a choir ☐ played an instrument ☐
   Other experiences: ____________
   Travels: ____________
   Talents: ____________

5. *Personal self-assessment:*
   I would like to share ______ with the children in the unit.
   I would like to share ______ with the teachers in the unit.
   I'm really good at ____________.

Fig. 6.1 Teacher strengths assessment form (*Cont.*).

Jane: What you're saying, Thelma, is that we should try to get them interested before we do anything else and I agree!

Ethel: At a conference last spring, I heard someone talk about rock music and poetry—but I can't remember who it was.

Jane: That's an idea! How about lyrics and songs. I don't know much about poetry either, except what's in the text, but I've got my guitar and lots of ballads and stuff.

Ethel: Why don't we work on the *Melody of Language in Poetry* and use some of Bill Martin's material. Al Caiola plays the guitar while Bill Martin recites.

Unit Leader: Well, not many of us think we know too much about poetry. But when we pull it all together, it isn't too bad. As I see it, the emphasis will be on motivation—creating an interest in poetry through a study of the *Melody of Language*. Right?

Thelma: Sounds good!

Unit Leader: Jane, your talent with the guitar and songs will be exciting and, Ethel, you've listened to Bill Martin. Why don't you collect some of these materials. We've got the *Sounds Of* series in the library. Ethel, I think the person you referred to was Nancy Larrick, and I may have her book in the office. Thelma, you really started something. We'll all lend a hand on this one. Let's gather material this next week and think about other goals, in addition to motivation, that we want to achieve. Who wants to do the initial planning?

Jane: Why don't I get something down on paper for the next meeting. Remember I'm only starting it—I couldn't do it alone.

Thelma: Agreed—I know I couldn't do it at all.

Unit Leader: Let's think about figurative language. In what context will we handle that?

Ethel: I think we should work on language development and help the children develop colorful and powerful language—but somehow, it can't just be isolated lessons. If they don't use language development, what good is it simply to be able to identify similes and metaphors.

Jane: You're right. I'll bet there'll be some good examples of language development in the poetry unit we're going to do. How about oral language.

Thelma: Wait. I've got it. I took a great class in oral communication and we studied persuasive speech. I've got a good unit I prepared. I think parts of it would work out well.

Ethel: Those topics would lead right into critical reading and thinking. Let's do it by studying the difference between news reporting and editorializing. Then, I'd really like to get the kids to produce a neat newspaper. All those summers I worked on the *Gazette* and the year as editor of the *Collegian* would seem worthwhile if I could help these children really put something together. I'll start working on it.

Jane: My neighbor is Tom Gray. Maybe he'd let us come down to the news office one day.

Unit Leader: We've really talked about a lot of things. Let's see if I can put it together. We should have a wonderful semester if we can transfer all this enthusiasm to the children. We're really going to have to help each other though. Will each of you give some thought to the areas you mentioned? Next week, we'll talk more and begin to develop the materials together. We'll have to identify objectives and ways to assess the achievement and interests of the children. Then we need to plan learning options and evaluation strategies.

What did the unit leader find out regarding the strengths and weaknesses of the team during this informal unit meeting?

1. Ethel had had experience organizing a newspaper and really wants to try it with children.
2. Jane has musical talent, plays the guitar, likes to sing, and she didn't put the singing on her personal data sheet.
3. Thelma has had more work in speech than the others and thinks speech is worthwhile for elementary children.
4. Thelma feels really weak in poetry, maybe in many things.
5. Jane is a very practical person—this practicality will help us keep things going.
6. The unit staff might benefit from a refresher course in children's literature with an emphasis on poetry.

As teachers began to work together, their interests and abilities, as well as their professional needs, became better known to the unit leader as indicated in this case study. As written plans for the instructional designs were submitted to the unit staff for critiquing and further refinement, the unit leader continued to assess the strengths and weaknesses of the members of Unit C. These included:

1. Ethel has terrific organizational skills. She may be able to teach these skills to the whole staff.
2. Thelma needs help in attending to details, tends to overgeneralize—will be unable to give firm directions.
3. Jane really knows how to find excellent media and likes to search them out. I wonder if she would accept the media specialist function in the unit and give us some direction.
4. No one is good at writing worthwhile evaluation strategies for observing performance of students. We need some outside help here.

Observation is also a technique for noting the strengths and weaknesses of unit teachers. The unit leader is continually observing teammates and being observed by them. However, the unit leader must go one step beyond general observing and observe for the purpose of planning staff development. The unit leader in this case study observed the following characteristics of the staff.

1. Jane talks too much in small group instruction—(maybe she should do a large group presentation)—I'll ask her to observe the inquiry lesson that Ethel is doing tomorrow—perhaps we could all use a Flanders assessment.
2. Thelma is a great listener and wonderful with individual children—they like to be with her and she has such an easy, warm way of helping them to understand themselves.
3. Jane is an expert in math. I've known that. She's a sheer genius at seeing what it is that a child doesn't understand in a mathematical process and so quickly, too. She can get them off that stumbling block so fast, it's like magic.
4. No one is really doing very well with social studies. Everything is chaotic—the learning centers aren't really much. I need to put that on the agenda for this week's meeting. And I shouldn't forget some way to get help in evaluation strategies.

Staff self-evaluation at the end of the week provides still another informal tool to identify the strengths and weaknesses of the unit staff. The unit team can stop at the end of the week and ask themselves, "How'd we do?" Some focusing questions are:

1. How did we do as a team—did we plan and teach well together?
2. Did we remember to compliment each other when one of us did something pretty special?
3. Are we really providing instructional programming for individual students? What could we do better next week? Are we ready to try something new?
4. How did we do as individuals?
   What did I do well this week?
   What did I do poorly this week?
   Where do I need help?
   Who can give me the help I need?

Answers to these questions may aid the unit leader in identifying individual staff needs and also group needs. The effectiveness of a teaching unit is also measured by pupil outcomes in terms of attitudes, enthusiasm, and achievement. Based on these data, a unit can also have a "How'd we do with the children?" end-of-the-week evaluation. Some guidelines include:

- Did the children enjoy the week?
- How well did each child achieve the objectives for the week in each subject area where instructional programming is carried out?
- Why did they do well (poorly) this week?
- Did the children *ask us* questions?
- Did they have the opportunity to work in small groups and independently?

In the above case study, the unit leader employed three strategies—the unit-planning session, observation, and self-evaluation to identify the following staff needs:

- children's literature review (poetry in particular).
- writing evaluation strategies.
- learning centers in social studies.
- organizational skills.
- interaction analysis skills.

In addition, several individual strengths, which may be used to instruct others, were identified. These were:

- organizational skills.
- media familiarity.
- math skills.
- musical talent.

It is the unit leader's responsibility to help unit teachers to recognize their strengths and weaknesses. However, assessing the strengths and weaknesses of teachers is useless unless the information gathered is used as a basis for planned inservice activities.

Planning for Inservice Activities

As noted earlier in the chapter, change is unlikely to take place unless the teachers are involved in the change process themselves. It was also stated that the unit leader does not plan or make decisions unilaterally. This is also true in planning an inservice program for staff development. But the responsibility for organizing, determining staff needs, for helping the team to agree and set priorities, and for identifying the manner in which these processes are to be accomplished belongs to the unit leader.

Teacher education is no longer limited to a four-year campus program and summer graduate study. Rather, teacher education for change is continuous and ongoing in terms of inservice activities for teachers on the job. Inservice activities are designed to help teachers solve on-the-job problems and acquire skills essential to the roles they assume in the classroom. This is especially true in the implementation of new programs such as IGE. "Inservice of the future will be seen as aiding, supporting, and encouraging each teacher's development of teaching capabilities that he (she) values and seeks to enhance." (Tyler 1971, p. 16)

Inservice education can take many forms such as:

- systemwide sessions on new curriculum adoptions.
- school-building sessions focusing on the specific needs of a school staff.
- on-campus graduate programs.
- professional growth courses offered by a school system.
- summer or preschool teacher institutes.
- informal workshops offered by college personnel assigned to buildings to supervise undergraduate students.
- visitations and professional leave days.
- demonstration teaching.
- rap sessions with other teams within the building or from other schools.

Inservice activities can be conducted before school, after school, or in released time periods during the school day. Participants can be rewarded in terms of money, professional growth credits, graduate credit, or by no extrinsic reward at all. Inservice sessions can be directed by college personnel, school supervisors and administrators, teachers, unit leaders, specialists, or outside consultants. Inservice activities can be general or specific, on college campuses or in schools. They can be required or voluntary.

But in an IGE setting, where decision making at the I & R Unit and IIC level is encouraged, teachers should have the opportunity to define their own inservice needs. Teachers involved in innovation should be the persons most able to identify their needs and have some control over their own professional activities. It has been said that it is very difficult to teach and think about teaching at the same time. But teachers can identify what it is they would like to think about. Inservice sessions should supply the thinking time.

Too often teachers have complained about required meetings that are of no value to them either because the topic was irrelevant to their job or the "presenter" was inadequate. Inservice activities, in the form of command performances which have no meaning for those attending, should cease to exist. It is within the realm of the unit, under the leadership of the unit leader, to identify the kinds of problems encountered in the classroom in order to promote inservice activities which are relevant. There is psychological validity in this approach as well. When an individual or group of individuals identify their own purposes for learning, it is likely that more learning will take place.

Granted that this is so, then the unit leader, as the professional leader of the unit, should help teachers come to closure on identifying inservice needs. These needs can be generated from a number of situations such as unit meetings, committee members suggesting ideas, tabulation of common problems, or recognition of an everyday problem.

The unit meeting. Of course, this is a most viable mechanism. The "How'd We Do?" staff self-evaluation described previously offers the unit leader the opportunity to note unit weaknesses and to discuss methods of correction with the staff. Thc emphasis for successful team analysis must be "openness."

Coupled with an open attitude the unit could use any one of several interaction analysis techniques (Flanders Interaction Analysis, Whithall's Social Emotional Climate Index) to evaluate their verbal teaching patterns. Unit members can also tape their lessons, analyze the recordings individually or submit them to group critique.

As unit teachers identify their own needs for professional development one basic principle is established—*that inservice education should be directed to the actual problems encountered by teachers on the job.*

Committee action. The unit leaders in a school were appointed by the principal to develop a list of topics for the two hours of building inservice each week. One hour was released time, and teachers would contribute one hour of their own. Unit leaders got ideas from their unit members. The four unit leaders in the building compiled the following inservice topics:

- diagnosis.
- grouping procedures.
- measuring student outcome (achievement, attitudes, social values).
- curriculum design in content areas.
- curriculum materials and resources.
- use of paraprofessionals.
- student teachers and interns.
- communication problems.
- teaming skills.
- use and flexibility of teacher time.

A second principle is served—*that identification of inservice programs is best when done by the group involved.* The unit leader reports unit preferences and any pertinent discussion about inservice to the members of the IIC. The IIC in turn reviews the judgments made by each unit and identifies the topic most highly ranked across the units. The initial plans for a long-range program including coordination, sequencing, and evaluating activities are begun. At each point the unit leader is the communication agent from the IIC to the unit and from the unit to the IIC.

Common problems. Inservice activities can be arranged from unit discussions and assessment, as discussed previously, when there are no formal plans for professional growth programs. Once a need has been identified among the teachers in the unit, the unit leader presents the problem to the IIC. The primary purpose here is to see if others in the school have similar needs and, if so, whether time can be arranged compatibly and a reward system established.

For example, Unit D asked for help in developing evaluation techniques. The unit leader asked the principal to enter the topic on the IIC agenda for distribution prior to the weekly meetings. At the IIC, it was established that many teachers in the other units would appreciate similar help. Sixteen teachers indicated that they would be willing to attend a series of afterschool meetings if (1) the meetings could be held in their building, (2) the principal would keep the heat going, (3) they could earn two professional growth credits, and (4) a favorite instructor from the college would teach the series. These conditions were then established in the units. The unit leaders acted as reporters to the IIC and at this point the principal took over. This inservice need was then reported to central administration with the suggestion that the course be advertised and open to other schools so that the 25 teachers required to offer the course could be recruited. The central office administrators decided to support the proposal and agreed to (1) contact the professor so that a contract could be negotiated, (2) recruit the additional nine persons needed, (3) keep the heat on, and (4) give two professional growth credits. The teachers were enthusiastic and asked that the professor meet with the teachers before organizing the sessions. The third principle is acted upon—*that teachers establish, when involved, the time, place, and reward involved in inservice activities.*

Recognition of an obvious problem. A unit staff in a first year IGE school knew that they were not using paraprofessionals well. They wanted time to think about it and especially to talk with the teachers in a sixth year IGE school. They asked for a day off to visit the established I & R Unit. The unit leader carried this communication to the principal in the IIC. The principal agreed to teach the children, with several volunteer aides and a student teacher, for the day and arranged for the visitation activity. In this case, the inservice activity took the form of a visitation and release time for the activity was provided by the principal and paraprofessionals taking over instruction for a day.

Presenters of inservice programs. Inservice instruction can be carried out by a variety of persons, including experienced unit leaders, teachers, administrators, college faculty, and state department personnel. In fact, throughout the IGE schools, unit leaders often are hired by central offices to conduct inservice instruction. Moreover, unit leaders and teachers can provide many inservice sessions in their own buildings. For instance, a unit leader might attend a systemwide workshop on the teacher-advisor concept in IGE, and in turn give inservice to the school faculty and assist with implementation in the building. Two unit leaders might attend the National Association for Individually Guided Education (AIGE) Conference and return with a sufficient number of new ideas to hold an afternoon workshop for building teachers. As another illustration, the principal might attend a Leadership Institute conducted by the State Department of Education and subsequently hold inservice sessions for the unit leaders in the building.

One highly successful technique for inservice is the use of an instructional team consisting of a college instructor and a unit leader. The college instructor has a broad conceptual and practical base from which to draw and the unit leader has the immediate results of field experimentation. The unit leader offers credibility to the instruction and the daily experience of solving problems in the classroom.

In summary, the identification and development of inservice programs for IGE should be organized with the teams under the direction of the unit leader and building principal. All activities should be based on cooperative assessment and collaborative planning.

Training Paraprofessionals and Teachers New to the Unit

Paraprofessionals. The differentiated staffing in an IGE school may include, in addition to the unit leader and staff teachers, a number of paraprofessional personnel—paid and volunteer instructional and clerical aides, high school aides, undergraduate students from colleges and universities.

The noncertified instructional aide can be one of many types and can serve the team in a variety of ways. A retired biologist or historian may serve as an aide in the elementary school. A mother whose children are now in school may have been a nutritionist or a student in linguistic science. Instructional aides need not have degrees—some may have little

The unit leader's responsibility extends to the training of the paraprofessionals and to guiding the team in appropriate utilization of these assistants.

training beyond high school while others may have three years of college training. The naturalist, who is an expert by personal experience rather than formal training, is valuable as an instructional aide. (Highly trained professionals in fields other than education are often used as resource persons rather than aides.)

Clerical aides vary in much the same way—a former secretary, filing clerk, or a willing person with few clerical skills. Consider the high school aide who is a science or mathematics major. Although his or her regular duties may be mainly clerical, he or she could be an excellent tutor for children working in mathematics or science.

In order for the team to make the most efficient use of all available personnel, it is critical that all members understand their professional roles and that they can identify the differentiated tasks performed by professional and paraprofessional members of the team. In too many instances, auxiliary personnel have simply been added to a school staff without the necessary training and planning. Additional hands are welcomed in an elementary school, but without planning, it is doubtful that maximum use of the extra human resources will be achieved. The unit leader's responsibility extends to the training of the paraprofessionals and to guiding the team in appropriate use of these assistants. The unit leader, therefore, has to consider (1) aiding the unit and/or the IIC to develop criteria for the selection and assignment of aides or paraprofessionals, (2) training the aides, (3) establishing a set of general guidelines for the aides, and (4) assisting the aides in self-evaluation.

Selection and assignment of paraprofessionals, based on developed criteria, is an appropriate task for the IIC. However, it must also be recognized that larger school systems may have a school aide program in which central administration screens, hires, trains, and assigns aides to the schools with little individual school input. However, it would also seem appropriate for the school to have the privilege of accepting or rejecting those persons appearing for job interviews based on the wishes of the team. The relationship between a unit staff and their aide must be a positive and pleasant one. The purpose for hiring additional personnel is to help the teachers carry out more effective instruction. Friction between the teachers and aides places an additional burden upon the teachers. With this in mind, it is apparent that each teacher must also have something to say about the assignment of paraprofessionals to the unit.

In some ways, the role of aide in an I & R Unit may be a difficult one at times. The aide, especially if highly qualified, must take a rather subservient position during times of disagreement. At no time can an aide take sides when the members of the team find themselves deadlocked in opposing views. The aide does not have a vote. Nor can the aide criticize or gossip to members of the unit about a teacher in the unit. Maintaining neutrality and professional distance when appropriate is not always easy. Nor can the aide take the privileged information about children or teachers out to the neighborhood or community. The aide is bound by the same ethical code that binds the teacher.

If it is possible for the building to set its criteria for selection, the IIC should determine the kind of persons needed—in terms of skills as well as personal qualities. Since the primary role of the teacher aide is to be a friendly adult who respects and accepts each child, who is anxious to assist the teacher in a warm and quiet way, who elicits respect from children and teachers, it might be well to establish a list of personal qualities to look for, such as personableness, intelligence, enthusiasm, willingness, child-centeredness, reliability, etc. Although judging these qualities is a difficult task during interview sessions, some joint determinations can be made by the unit leaders, principals, and teachers.

The instructional and clerical skills desired in the unit will depend on the tasks which the teachers want the aides to perform. These tasks should be identified and listed by the team, under the direction of the unit leader, and used as additional criteria in choosing an aide for the unit. The suitability of the aide should be judged in relation to the potential to do the job needed. A listing of appropriate tasks for an aide is given below. This list is not exhaustive nor is it applicable to all aides. The tasks performed will be those selected by the unit, and those for which the aide has adequate skills.

Tasks for Aides (Paraprofessionals)

With Children	*Supportive Services*
Help children in personal duties	Clerical work
Supervise lunchroom and playground activities	Dittoes
Take attendance and lunchroom count	Record keeping
Work one to one with a child (listening, tutoring, taking dictation)	Filing
Teach games and play games with children	Prepare materials
Work with small skill or task groups	Typing
Present a slide presentation of an event or experience	Distribution and repair of audiovisual equipment
Give students special attention when needed	Repair games and independent activity materials
	Prepare work on chalkboard
	Locate materials
	Set up audiovisual materials
	Collect and record money intake
	Plan and assist on field trips

It is unfair to both paraprofessionals and teachers to expect them to function without adequate training. The degree of training will depend on the entry skills of the paraprofessionals and the tasks they will perform. In addition, the provision or lack of provision for formal training programs prior to coming to the classroom will affect the on-the-job training given by the unit leader.

Topics for formal or informal inservice for paraprofessionals are presented below. They include orientation to the unit, organization, the children in the unit, instructional procedures, building facilities and policies, and unit and building resources.

Topics for Aide Inservice Programs

The structure of the public school and its many personnel—from the local board, superintendent, curriculum directors to the custodian
The role descriptions and responsibilities of all personnel in differentiated staffing patterns
Professional ethics and public relations
Parents and the school
The teaching-learning process
- Intelligence
- Motivation
- Experiential background
- Reinforcement—reward and punishment
- Testing

Appropriate playground activities (accidents)
Individual differences
Manuscript or cursive writing
Child development
Visual aids
Preparation of materials
Use and repair of audiovisual equipment (projectors, recorders)
Classroom management
Purposes of teacher aides
Clerical tasks
Supervision of children
Record keeping
Drill and practice
Grading papers
Language arts, math, science, and social studies methodology
Games

It would also be wise for the unit teachers and/or the unit leader to develop a set of guidelines to help the aide in the performance of classroom duties. A suggestive guide from the Fremont, California, Title I Project is given below (National School Public Relations Association, 1972).

Guidelines for Aides

1. Learn the names of pupils immediately.
2. Learn as much as you can about each pupil as quickly as possible.
3. Lend personal assistance to pupils wherever possible.
4. Consult often with the teacher as to how you can help.
5. Give encouragement to pupils wherever and whenever you can.
6. Praise pupils' efforts and successes.
7. Be patient in dealing with pupils.
8. Become familiar with the school building, grounds, personnel.
9. Learn the routine of the school day.
10. Get acquainted immediately with emergency procedures.
11. Learn the location, use, and operation of equipment.
12. Get acquainted with school policy as it applies to you and your work.
13. Learn the routines of lighting, ventilation, and custodial service.
14. Assume responsibility with teachers' permission for calendars, books, etc.
15. Practice observing in a meaningful way every chance you get.
16. Inform the teachers with whom you work of any special talents or interests and of special experiences you have had.
17. Watch carefully how the teacher deals with and directs pupils.
18. Exchange telephone numbers with your teacher.
19. Get acquainted with other staff members.
20. Be mature in your conduct and demonstrate that you are a responsible person.
21. Ask for clarification when you do not understand an assignment or suggestion.
22. Be on time and leave at an appropriate time.

Finally, it is the unit leader's duty to help paraprofessionals evaluate their performance in the instructional setting. A self-evaluation checklist may serve as a tool for the evaluation conference to be held periodically. Some guiding questions include:

	Always	Usually	Seldom
1. Do I get along with teachers in the unit?			
2. Do I really free them to give attention to instruction?			
3. Do I enjoy being in the classroom?			
4. Are the children happy when they are with me?			
5. Am I better as a tutor than as a small group instructor (vice versa)? Why?			
6. Do I fulfill my duties on time?			
7. Am I able to find appropriate material?			
8. Can I use the assessment and record-keeping techniques adequately?			

Planning for selection, training, and evaluation will ensure more efficient use of paraprofessionals. In addition, the unit leader has development responsibilities to beginning teachers or transfer teachers newly assigned to the unit.

First-year teachers in the unit. The unit leader's responsibility to a first-year teacher in the unit is to assume leadership to provide maximum opportunity for professional growth and decision making as well as maximum use of talents and expertise. However, the unit leader has the opportunity to lessen the shock that occurs between the role of the beginning teacher and the role of the experienced teacher. For the most part, there is no bridge between the security of being a student and the unprotected role of being a first-year teacher. Too often the beginning teacher is expected to possess all the competencies necessary for teaching on the first day of permanent employment.

It is possible for a unit leader in a team structure to individualize a first-year teacher's entry into the profession based on observed entry behavior and identified needs as stated by the beginning teacher. The resourceful unit leader can usually provide most of the following "assisting and supporting" experiences within the unit such as:

- Constructive criticism of planning for instruction by all members of the team relative to the experience and needs of the children in the unit.
- Continual inservice growth in knowledge of subject matter, growth and development of children, instructional strategies, and materials and resources within the context of the unit meeting.

- Critical analysis of implementation of planned lessons by the unit leader and/or several members of the team.
- Opportunity to communicate with other professionals about student performance as well as teaching strategies.
- Automatic orientation to the many duties expected of teachers.
- Opportunity to observe several teaching styles and to model behavior of the master teacher (unit leader) when appropriate.
- Opportunity to be released from teaching duties during a portion of the day when judged to be an effective method for assisting the beginner. The new teacher may stop and assess his or her teaching, observe others, redesign, teach, and reassess under the direction of the unit leader and the team.

Experienced teachers new to the unit. It is the responsibility of the unit leader to assist such teachers in becoming familiar with unit procedures and with IGE principles and practices if they are not already familiar with them. The unit leader can ask other members of the unit to help in these matters. Experiences that were listed for first-year teachers can be adapted to help experienced teachers new to the unit and/or IGE feel "at home" in the I & R Unit or school.

THE UNIT LEADER'S ROLE IN PRESERVICE EDUCATION

Programs for preservice education differ among the teacher education institutions. No attempt will be made here to outline the many programs designed at various institutions. The concern of this section is the unit leader's role in preservice teacher education. Therefore, the focus is on the field component of teacher training. Even here there is a wide variance in the amount of time education students spend in elementary schools as well as the kind of experience, the manner in which these experiences are organized, and the degree to which these experiences are jointly planned by the educators in the schools and those in the colleges.

> After a half century of teacher training it has become profoundly clear that teachers learn to teach not in the training institution but in the schools where they serve. What goes on in the training institution may provide a preface to the real world of the classroom but it does not produce an able practitioner . . . the teacher in training must spend more time with children and less time with the abstractions of the lecture hall. A larger percentage of the training must be given by master teachers, rich in successful experience. (Rubin 1971, p. 192)

Preservice education for IGE schools should be field based. Limited experiences should be provided in the early college years and continue to increase through the student teaching experience.

Field activities in the instructional setting may vary from programs which have only student teaching and intern programs, to those which have laboratory experiences at the freshman, sophomore, and junior levels as well. In addition, there may be differences in the numbers of preservice students assigned to the I & R Unit or teaching team. A unit may have a single student teacher, a student teacher and several other undergraduates, or no student teacher and as many as six to ten other undergraduates. Or, a unit may have an intern who serves half-time in the school for the entire year or full-time for a semester and is paid one-half a regular teacher's beginning salary and is supervised by the school and college or university.

Differentiated staffing within an I & R Unit is a basic component of the IGE school. Students from teacher education institutions function within the differentiated staffing framework in the I & R Units. The wishes of the members of the unit and the needs of the cooperating college are to be considered in making decisions about the organization of preservice experiences in the schools. These decisions are to be made jointly by all personnel involved.

In any case, the unit leader does not function alone in (1) identifying or designing the activities in which preservice students will engage, (2) providing the field experiences the students are assigned, or (3) evaluating the progress of the students. In each case, the unit leader functions again as a coordinator, representing the needs and desires of the members of the unit, as the field components of the college program are designed and implemented.

Unit leaders in schools which serve as laboratories, or teacher centers, for teacher education institutions expand their roles to include that of classroom teacher educators. A teacher educator is defined as one who is engaged in the preparation of teachers. Probably the most influential teacher of teacher education students is the educator in the classroom. Although research indicates that this is true, especially in the relationship between student teachers and cooperating teachers, little has been done to recognize the classroom teacher as a teacher educator, or to aid in the professional development of this role. The unit leader, as a recognized teacher educator, assumes prime responsibility for the guidance and coordination of the preservice teachers assigned to the I & R Unit.

The Unit Leader and the Lower Division Student

An early field experience may be provided for lower division (freshman, sophomore) students. The student, at this initial stage, is usually enrolled in a college class having two component parts: (1) an on-campus seminar in which the teaching profession, its characteristics and its problems, and the curriculum, instruction, and social milieu of the school is examined and (2) an off-campus field experience during which the student can get involved in the "real" world of the classroom—with the children, teachers, and administrators in the school.

The purpose of such a program is to aid the student in making three decisions: (1) whether or not to become a teacher; (2) at what age level to teach; and (3) in what subject area(s) to specialize.

The lower division student in the public school classroom generally serves as a teacher aide, often in noninstructional duties although occasionally in tutoring and in small group situations depending on each student's qualifications.

The unit leader's role in this field experience is one of coordination and communication with the teaching members of the team, with course instructors from the college, and with the beginning student.

The organization of this experience should be jointly planned by the elementary school and college. This can be accomplished in one of several ways:

- The IIC (unit leaders representing the teachers in the units) can meet with the college instructors to plan the field experience for the school.
- Each unit as a whole can meet with college personnel to plan for the unit.
- The unit leader, as representative for the unit can meet with college instructors to plan the field experience.

In any case, the unit leader's responsibility is to place on the meeting agenda the topic of how best to use these students.

It is important that teachers recognize that college students are beginners with no prior commitment to teaching, that they are not paid, trained aides. The unit leader as a teacher educator, encourages teachers to provide a variety of experiences—clerical, such as operating video equipment and keeping records, and also experiences with children such as tutoring, or assisting a teacher in instruction. A tentative list of possible activities for lower division aides should be prepared at the unit meeting to be used when the IIC, the unit staff or the unit leader meet with college personnel. A typical list for first and second quarter/semester experiences follows:

Responsibilities and Experiences
for Lower Division Students*

First Quarter/Semester

1. Prepare paint, paste; easel, playdough, and clay.
2. Help children with outer clothing.
3. Greet children upon arrival.

---

* This list taken in part from Career Decisions Programs, CBTE, The University of Toledo, College of Education.

4. Check attendance.
5. Be able to name the pupils and be able to classify the basic socioeconomic characteristics of classroom, school, community.
6. Help in lavatory procedures.
7. Examine instructional materials.
8. Describe fire-drill and tornado-alert procedures.
9. Investigate school policies concerning dress, arrival times, etc.
10. Demonstrate printing techniques at the primary level, if appropriate.
11. Score objective-type tests and assist in record-keeping procedures.
12. Assist in grouping and regrouping children for instruction.
13. Operate standard classroom equipment. Listen to working vocabulary of children. Talk with individual children.
14. Make a bulletin board, if possible, with children.
15. Write a story dictated by a child.
16. Write an experience chart dictated by a child.
17. Read a story to a group of children.
18. Listen to a child read.
19. Tutor a child in any needed area.
20. Share a hobby or talent with children; if appropriate.
21. Assist teacher in project work.

Second Quarter/Semester

(In addition to First Quarter/Semester Prerequisites above)

1. Develop an art project with one child.
2. Do an experiment in science with one child or a small group.
3. Do a taping session with one child or a small group.
4. Help a child complete a research project.
5. Write a skit with a group of children.
6. Help produce a puppet show or practice a play with a group.
7. Teach a song, game, or folk dance to a group of children.
8. Conduct a spelling test.
9. Listen to a child's individual report.
10. Teach a child a physical skill, e.g., skating, swimming, skipping, jumping rope, etc.

In addition to taking part in instructional activities, it would be well for lower division students to do the following.

- observe and attend a unit meeting.
- observe an IIC (Instructional Improvement Committee) meeting.
- observe a local league meeting.
- observe a teacher center meeting.
- attend a Board of Education meeting.
- attend a PTA meeting.
- attend a professional education meeting (education association or federation meeting, a curriculum workshop or conference).

Name of student: ______________________________

Name of participating teacher: ______________________________

Field school placement: ______________________________

Each student is expected to develop a written contract with his/her participating teacher each quarter. The contract will include the specific classroom and school responsibilities which he/she agrees to fulfill during the field assignment that quarter. Lists of suggested tasks and responsibilities will be supplied by the unit leader and/or be found in the field handbook. The unit leader and the student will discuss various possibilities and note mutually agreed upon experiences for the quarter.

Three copies should be prepared by the student. One copy of the completed and signed student field contract is to be returned to the university seminar instructor. The others will be retained by the participating teacher and the student. The contrast will be used by the teacher to aid in the student's final evaluation.

List below the specific responsibilities and tasks of the contract.

Signed (Student) ______________________________ Date ____________

Signed (Teacher) ______________________________ Date ____________

Fig. 6.2 Student field contract.

Preplanning by the unit leader and college instructor is vital to the efficient maintenance of the program. Several forms and procedures are helpful in preplanning techniques. The *student field contract* which is shown in Figure 6.2 provides a structuring device for an initial conference between the unit leader and the lower division student during which time, goals, abilities, needs and interests can be discussed by both parties. Furthermore, it provides direction for both students and teachers for the entire field experience. Data gathered at this conference can also assist the unit leader when assigning the students to various unit members throughout the quarter/semester and for evaluation. Changes can be made in the contract by mutual agreement.

Name ____________________ Course and section ____________

Quarter/semester and year ____________________

Unit leader ____________________

	Date	House (From ______ to ______)	Total
1.			
2.			
3.			
4.			
5.			
6.			
7.			
8.			
9.			
10.			
			______ Total

Student ____________________ Date ____________

Teacher ____________________ Date ____________

Fig. 6.3 Lower division field experience calendar.

		Always	Usually	Seldom
1.	Was the student's attendance satisfactory?	☐	☐	☐
2.	Were the contract tasks fulfilled?	☐	☐	☐
3.	Did the student show flexibility and adaptability to school routine?	☐	☐	☐
4.	Did the student interact well with others?	☐	☐	☐
5.	Did the student show responsibility?	☐	☐	☐
6.	Did the student exhibit positive attitudes?	☐	☐	☐
7.	Would you like this student in your classroom again?	☐	☐	☐

Student's name ______________________________

Teacher's signature ______________________________

School ______________ Semester/quarter ______, 19 ______ Course ______________

Fig. 6.4 Lower division student evaluation form.

The *student field calendar* which is presented in Figure 6.3 serves the unit teachers, the university course instructor and the student. It provides documentation that the student attended on the dates required and performed the service indicated. A *daily log,* to be kept by the student, is also a useful tool for managing the field component. A log can include an account of the student's observations and impressions. The student should report description as well as interpretation. The log can be used as a reference point in seminar classes and in the conference discussions between the unit leader and student.

Finally, it is important that the unit leader again cooperate with the college in formulating and maintaining a system of evaluation. The unit leader is responsible for assessing the performance of the student in the field in terms of attendance, rapport with children and adults, and completion of assigned tasks. An *evaluation form* that is concise, simple, and takes very little teacher time is given in Figure 6.4.

The unit leader assumes responsibility for assigning and monitoring the lower division student's field experience in partnership with appropriate personnel from the college. This works smoothly in an IGE school since problems can be handled at the IIC level.

The Unit Leader and the Upper Division Student

The experiences of the upper division student include (1) the prestudent teaching experience and (2) the student teaching/intern experience.

Prestudent teaching experience. As the college student moves into upper division status, his or her role changes, and so does that of the classroom teacher educator. Although the unit leader continues to function as coordinator, supervisor, and evaluator, there is a change in focus.

The upper division student does not serve as an aide to the unit as in earlier experiences. The unit staff, especially the unit leader, aids the student to plan, teach, and evaluate a successful learning encounter with children. It is at this point that the college instructor and classroom teacher educator work most closely. The college students are learning how to design objectives, plan learning programs, select methodology, and plan for assessment and teaching strategies using varied instructional media. They must now test their understanding of the teaching-learning process by implementing planned strategies and activities and evaluating pupil outcomes as a result of teaching. Unlike the earlier experiences, the upper division student's planned teaching encounter must be cordinated with the ongoing teaching activities in the I & R Unit. This task is not always a simple one. During the upper division field component there are basic planning questions which neither the unit leader nor college professor could answer alone. These are:

1. For what purpose is the student participating in the classroom?
2. What kind of an experience is most appropriate to provide the opportunity to fulfill this experience?
3. In what subject area will the student work?
4. When and how often will the student be in the classroom?
5. In what instructional grouping pattern should the student work?
6. How will the student's field experience be absorbed into the unit's teaching plans?

The unit leader has an educational responsibility for this experience in terms of the college student and also in terms of the pupils in the unit. The unit leader must preplan with both the college instructor and the college student so that the student's experience will be worthwhile and have every chance to be successful. But the unit leader is first a teacher of children and as such must ensure that the contact with the college student is meaningful and rewarding to the children.

The unit leader, as the instructional leader of the unit, works with the teachers, college instructor, and college student in a variety of ways which are discussed below.

Identifying an appropriate topic within a subject area is, of necessity, carried out so it does not upset the long- or short-range plans of the team. Adjustments in these plans must be made willingly by the teachers involved. Moreover, for the sake of both the children and college students, the lesson should not be a complete repetition of what has been done at a previous time. "Appropriateness" must therefore include a consideration of the topic, the age of the children, their previous experience, and the likelihood of interest in the topic. For example, the preservice student is studying reading and language arts and teaching a lesson as required in the language arts module. In the preplanning conference with the instructor and the student, the student suggests vocabulary development as a possible topic. The unit leader agrees that indeed the children could benefit from additional work in this area. The student offers several suggestions for activities learned on campus—sentence extension, diamonte, haiku, Mary O'Neill's *Hailstones and Halibut Bones* or *Words, Words, Words*. The unit leader, as team representative, reports the previous experiences of the children—they have written cinquain and used Mary O'Neill's books; they tried haiku but were discouraged by the tight syllabic control. However, they have never experimented with *diamonte*. This would be something entirely new and might be fun if presented in an interesting way. The student agrees—the appropriate topic is therefore selected. Had this preplanning not taken place, the children might have been subjected to repeated initial instruction, and the college student might have had considerable difficulty generating interest and participation in that children would be going through a repeated lesson as if it were initial instruction. The preplanning session protects both the children and the student and permits the unit leader to function as a teacher educator and team representative.

A group of students is identified for the student to work with. The unit leader will need to decide the number of students and which particular students should be involved and the most effective time schedule based on several factors: (1) the number of college students assigned to the I & R Unit, (2) the educational and personal needs of the children, and (3) the "teaching" experience of the college student. The student who selects vocabulary development is one of a four-member student team assigned to a unit composed of fifty-two students, two staff teachers and the unit leader. Each student member has agreed to plan for this activity. Based on knowledge of the children in the unit, the unit leader has identified 14 children who are not yet ready for a written activity such as diamonte. These 14 children will be assigned to one regular staff teacher and an instructional aide for small group instruction. Under the direction of another staff teacher, each of the members of the student teams will teach diamonte to 12 children. This will permit the students to (1) function as a team in planning the lesson and (2) have teaching experience in the small group pattern. The unit leader will be free of teaching responsibility in order to critique the students' teaching.

The lesson taught needs to be critiqued carefully. This responsibility is also shared jointly by the college instructor and unit leader. However, it is more likely that the unit leader will assume a great deal of the supervisory duty so that all prestudent teachers have the implementation phase of their experience evaluated. The team teachers, unit leader, and university instructor, under leadership of the unit leader, will need to organize the teaching day to free a member or members of the unit to critique the students.

It is important that the unit leader and teachers help the student analyze the lesson in terms of the behaviors of the children receiving instruction:

Were the children interested and involved?
Did they understand what was expected of them?
What did they learn?
Did they learn what I expected them to learn?
Will they continue to pursue on their own what was taught?
Which children will need additional help (after examining the product)?
What might have been done to improve the learning encounter?
How will the format be changed for children who need further instruction?
What provision has been made for students to pursue this activity independently?

There is little doubt that the unit leader is functioning as a teacher educator in the guidance of the prestudent teaching experience of the upper division student.

The student teacher/intern experience. The student teaching phase of preservice teacher education is the final experience before entry into the profession as a full-time teacher. The unit leader's role as a teacher educator during this phase is crucial if the student teacher is going to have the opportunity to practice the behaviors needed as a first year teacher (MacDonald 1971, p. 53).

> There exists a disparity in student teaching in that first-year teacher behavior suggests the continuing orientation of the student teacher as student rather than as teacher with an abrupt change in identification occurring some time during the first year of teaching.

In IGE schools where a partnership exists with teacher education institutions, the student teachers (this term will represent student teacher or intern) have probably had classroom experience throughout their previous training. They have acted as aides, observed, and participated as well as taught lessons and studied the teaching-learning act. They bring considerable experience to the student teacher phase. It is the unit leader's responsibility to see that the student is able to bridge the gap between theory and practice, thus becoming a producer of ideas as well as a consumer. The student should also be encouraged to offer criticism as well as to accept it, and to make decisions, act on them, and be responsible and answerable for them. Ultimately, the unit leader helps the student teacher to experience the satisfying feeling of being a fully functioning teacher.

The unit leader accepts the student teacher as a *new member* of the teaching unit. And as a new member, the student teacher is encouraged to plan, implement, and evaluate instructional procedures for children in an IGE setting. However, in an IGE school, these procedures are shared by a team of teachers and in this way student teachers are supported and helped to make sound decisions. The unit leader is responsible for (1) absorbing the student teacher into the functions of the unit (both in the unit planning and teaching) and (2) for supervising the teaching performance of the student teacher.

Three important factors that must be taken into consideration are (1) supervision is defined as helping and assisting the student to be successful, (2) the student is recognized as an individual, and (3) the unit leader is conscientious in the evaluation process.

Typical "cooperating teacher" type questions arise immediately. When should the student start actual teaching? With what subject should the student begin? Should the student start with large or small groups first—with bright or slow children first? When should the student teacher be left alone in the classroom? Should the student be involved in grading and parent conferences? Should the supervising teacher take notes when observing? Should the student be under the direction of the college or the school? Does the student teacher need to do detailed lesson plans? Does every plan need checking before teaching? How are grades determined?

The very structure of team planning and teaching in an IGE school provides the answers to some of these questions. In fact, the teaming structure, differentiated staffing, and instructional programming for individual students in IGE schools probably negate the questions themselves.

The student teacher begins actual teaching of children based primarily on previous experience. The student teacher who has had field experience in an IGE setting prior to student teaching will not benefit from prolonged observation and participation experiences once associated with student teaching programs. On the other hand, if the prestudent teaching courses have not included an emphasis on early laboratory experiences, the student will probably assume teaching duties more slowly. Student teachers assigned to an I & R Unit in which they have participated

It is the unit leader's responsibility to see that the student teacher is able to bridge the gap between theory and practice.

in a prestudent teaching experience should be able to function rather quickly as the other teachers, children, and classroom environment are familiar. These decisions belong to the student teacher/intern and the unit leader. However, from the first day the student should be assisting the team in actual teaching in small groups or one-to-one instruction. This includes becoming a member of the planning team with immediate access to the teachers and their long- and short-range plans as well as their discussions of the children's needs and progress. At the first unit meeting, students should identify the subject area and grouping pattern area in which they feel ready to participate. As children are not grouped according to generalized ability, the questions of teaching bright or slow children first is largely academic. The important concern is that the student teacher identifies a particular skill or activity to teach—one in which there is a reasonable opportunity for success.

The question of lesson plans is also academic. Members of the team assume responsibility for initial planning of curriculum areas identified by the team members, which they themselves critique and revise. As a recognized member of the team, the student teacher functions in the same way, and from the very beginning assumes the duty of initial planning. The unit leader responds critically as do all unit members in order that the final product is appropriate to the needs of the children in the unit.

Whether or not the student teacher is left alone in the classroom depends largely on the physical structure of the school. In large teaming areas or pods, no teacher is really alone as small groups of children and their teachers function in various sections simultaneously. In IGE schools that operate in rooms with walls, the student teacher may in fact be alone while teaching a specific lesson. However, in no case should a student teacher be isolated with a group of children for entire days without the critiquing expertise of the unit leader or staff teachers. The matter of supervision of the student teacher belongs on the agenda of the unit planning sessions. Teachers and student teachers agree together how to regroup children often in order to provide periods free of instruction, during which time the unit leader and teachers can evaluate the student's implementation of planned teaching strategies and teaching behaviors. The unit leader must see that planned observation time is accounted for in unit activities.

The procedures for observing and evaluating the student teachers are too important to be left to chance. In addition to providing the time for direct observation, a planned supervisory procedure increases both the efficiency and potential effectiveness of the observation. The unit leader might consider the supervisory act as a five-step process, referred to in Chapter 4 of this text under peer observation (Goldhammer 1969). It will be recalled that these steps include a preobservation conference, in which the student teacher identifies the pupil and teacher behavior to be observed, such as questioning strategies and reinforcement techniques. In this way objectives for the observation are established. The conference is followed by the observation itself, during which the unit leader collects data to be analyzed in light of the objectives. The unit leader then plans for the conference by noting which of the student teacher's behaviors are to be reinforced and which are to be modified. During the conference itself, the student teacher also analyzes the data and together with the unit leader identifies needed changes in instructional strategies and teaching acts. Finally, they evaluate the effectiveness of the supervisory procedure.

Supervision by objectives is effective when the student teacher identifies the objectives, focuses on a few rather than global abilities, emphasizes self-improvement, and understands the relationship between pupil outcomes and teacher behavior. It is the unit leader's responsibility to guide or assign other experienced teachers to guide the student teacher to this level of self-awareness. This process is vital to the success of preservice teachers.

SUMMARY

It has been said in this text that the unit leader is primarily a teacher and an instructional leader among teachers. The leadership role is especially evident in the area of staff development. The unit leader's responsibilities as a leader and an agent of change for promoting staff development have been described in this chapter.

It is important to both the children and the unit teachers that the maximum use be made of the diverse abilities and talents of each team member. The unit leader needs to identify the strengths and weaknesses of each team member. The unit teacher should be allowed to lead other team members in areas of their strengths and be provided assistance in areas where he or she is weak. The unit leader should use both formal and informal assessment measures to discover each team member's potential contribution to team functions.

The unit leader shares in the responsibility for organizing, determining staff needs, and for helping the team agree and set priorities in inservice activities.

It is the responsibility of the unit leader to assist aides, paraprofessionals, and teachers new to the unit in becoming familiar with unit procedures and with IGE principles and practices. Along with this responsibility the unit leader, as a recognized teacher educator, assumes major responsibility for the guidance and coordination of the preservice teachers assigned to the I & R Unit. In this capacity the unit leader provides liaison functions with colleges in the training of future teachers.

REFERENCES

Alexander, W. M. 1967. The acceleration of curriculum change. In R. I. Miller (ed.) *Perspectives on educational change.* New York: Appleton-Century-Crofts.

Career Decisions Program 1972. CBTE, The University of Toledo, College of Education.

Chin, R. 1969. Parts of planned change. In W. Bennis, K. Benne, and R. Chin (eds.) *Planning for change.* New York: Holt.

———, and K. Benne 1969. General strategies for effecting changes in human systems. In W. Bennis, K. Benne, and R. Chin (eds.), *Planning for change.* New York: Holt.

Fiedler, R. E. 1967. *A theory of leadership effectiveness.* New York: McGraw-Hill.

Goldhammer, R. 1969. *Clinical supervision: special methods for the supervision of teachers.* New York: Holt.

MacDonald, J. 1971. Student teaching: benefit or burden. *Journal of Teacher Education,* Spring.

National School Public Relations Association 1972. Professionals in the schools. Arlington, W. Va.

Reichart, S. 1969. *Change and the teacher.* New York: Crowell.

Rubin, L. (ed.) 1971. Teacher training and educational reform. *Improving inservice education: proposals and procedures for change.* Boston: Allyn and Bacon.

Tyler, R. W. 1971. Inservice education for teachers. In L. J. Rubin (ed.), *Improving inservice education.* Boston: Allyn and Bacon.

Watson, J. 1969. Resistance to change. In W. Bennis, K. Benne, and R. Chin (eds.), *Planning for change.* New York: Holt.

7

Becoming Involved in Research and Development

Mary R. Quilling
Joan D. Inglis

Objectives

After reading this chapter, the reader will be able:

- To explain why IGE is called a research-based system of education and give several examples to support the explanation.
- To state reasons for utilization of research findings and for I & R Unit participation in research and development activities.
- To identify at least three roles the unit leader assumes in research and development activities.
- To describe at least two useful strategies for carrying out research comparing two or more instructional procedures or programs in the I & R Unit.
- To indicate at least two situations which are appropriate for an I & R Unit to carry out development activities.

This chapter is concerned with the role of the unit leader in research and development. These responsibilities have been described as follows (Klausmeier, *et al.* 1971, pp. 39-40):

For research:

1. Plans research activities of the unit with appropriate personnel of the unit, the building, the central office, and other agencies.
2. Coordinates research activities within the I & R Unit.
3. Guides the administration of experimental treatments—instructional methods, materials, media—by subexperimenters (teachers or others) to ensure continuous adherence to the specified experimental design and to a schedule for collecting information.
4. Guides the collection and, as time permits, the analysis of information collected.
5. Keeps abreast of relevant research results and methods.

For development:

1. Plans the development activities of the unit with appropriate personnel of the unit, building, central office, and other agencies.
2. Coordinates the development of a system of individually guided education within the unit, including a statement of objectives, the assessment of the capabilities of students, the instructional program, and evaluation procedures.
3. Participates directly in preparing instructional materials, diagnostic procedures, measurement instruments, etc.

Unit leaders and staff teachers have been involved in research and development since the beginnings of IGE. What is called an Instruction and Research Unit (I & R Unit) today was initially designated as a Research and Instruction (R & I) Unit. Practical research and development to improve instruction were key activities of the earliest units in elementary schools. Initially, within the school district, R & I Units were to serve as test sites for evaluating innovations prior to systemwide adoption, to carry out controlled experimentation on elements of instructional programs such as content, methods, materials and media, and to work with research groups within or outside the district. R & I Units were conceived as unique school-based research, development, and evaluation organizations. Unit leader responsibilities in those areas were correspondingly extensive. Indeed, a major part of staff development activities for unit leaders was devoted to research (Klausmeier, *et al.* 1966).

In the decade during which IGE has evolved, priorities have shifted and one rarely hears of a unit staff as heavily involved in research as was initially suggested. The true priority among unit functions is instruction, of course. This fact was recognized in 1969 when the name of the R & I Unit was changed to the present I & R Unit. Instead of research, development of instructional programs and procedures has typically been emphasized as I & R Units have attempted to carry out instructional programming for individual students according to the IGE instructional programming model and thereby improve education. What most IGE schools need is to raise questions and seek answers about the effectiveness of these developments; they must continue to carry out some research, too.

As IGE reaches a higher level of maturity in many schools, one might hope that I & R Units will find more time to carry out their research mission. A commitment to research on the part of a school staff, moreover, is an acknowledgment that education is a science as well as an art, and that scientific methods of hypothesizing, collecting data, and inferring hold much promise for the improvement of instruction. The unit leader is in a key position to determine whether or not research is valued and undertaken, and needs knowledge and techniques to carry out a leadership role in this area. Several kinds of research that have relevance for the IGE school and the unit leader's role in research are described below.

WHAT IS RESEARCH?

Research can be defined in both narrow or broad terms. In Chapter 2, research as a restricted activity designed to advance knowledge was discussed. The unit leader was portrayed as a user of research knowledge rather than as a stimulator and participant in such basic research.

Another kind of research is carried out to secure information for use in educational decision making. Research can also be defined to include applied as well as basic research activities. Whereas basic research has as its purpose the advancement of knowledge, decision-oriented or development-based research is carried out to improve practice. An outgrowth of development-based research is instructional evaluation which can be defined as "nothing more or less than good research conducted in a school setting" (Cooley 1971). The usual intent of evaluation, however, is to study a particular program or procedure, whereas several procedures, methods, or sets of materials are often studied comparatively in other kinds of decision-oriented research. These various kinds of research are perhaps understood best by the unit leader in the context of a model that explains their interrelationships in the development of IGE.

IGE: A Research-based System

The relationship between two kinds of research—basic and development-based—has been outlined in Figure 7.1. This model and the following discussion are of particular interest to unit leaders because they indicate the source of the claim that IGE is a research-based system of education. Here, basic research to generate knowledge about learning (I) on the one hand and instructional processes (II) on the other, leads directly to development of school applications. These procedures and products, in turn, are tested and refined in school settings (III), with the result that educational practice is improved.

The *Prereading Skills Program* (PRS) illustrates the flow from basic research to development and subsequent applied research (Venezky, *et al.* 1974). First, studies were carried out to determine the correlates of success in early reading. (Box II.) After a substantial amount of information was gained, instructional activities were designed to teach nonreading youngsters skills that successful readers exhibited (C Arrows). Tryouts in individual classrooms followed, and for several years the development-based research activities served to provide input to the developers as they attempted to refine the product (C Arrows). Unit leaders and teachers working with the project staff substantially affected the evolving characteristics of the program. The C sequence is fundamental to the development of high quality instructional products.

In the *Developing Mathematical Processes* (DMP) project, curriculum development followed the same paths (C sequence) but the research was more theoretical (Romberg 1974). Points of view about the sequence of concrete, pictorial, and symbolic representation of number and about the usefulness of activities and games in mathematics education were incorporated in translating a theoretical analysis of the desirable sequence of introducing mathematical concepts into a curriculum product. Some experiments comparing two approaches to teaching the same skills—for example, multiplication—were conducted prior to development to determine particular procedures that would be incorporated into the program. The product was tested in IGE and other schools over and over again to provide information both about children's learning and about the reactions of youngsters and teachers to the materials.

Other pathways also built the research base of IGE. Early studies of the multiunit organization and of teacher satisfaction sprang from organizational and sociological theory about group relations. The multiunit organization provided a setting to test these theories (D Arrow), and the largely positive findings had implications for the further development of the I & R Unit concept. The report commented particularly upon I & R Unit staff size and the tendency for grade-level divisions to surface as the

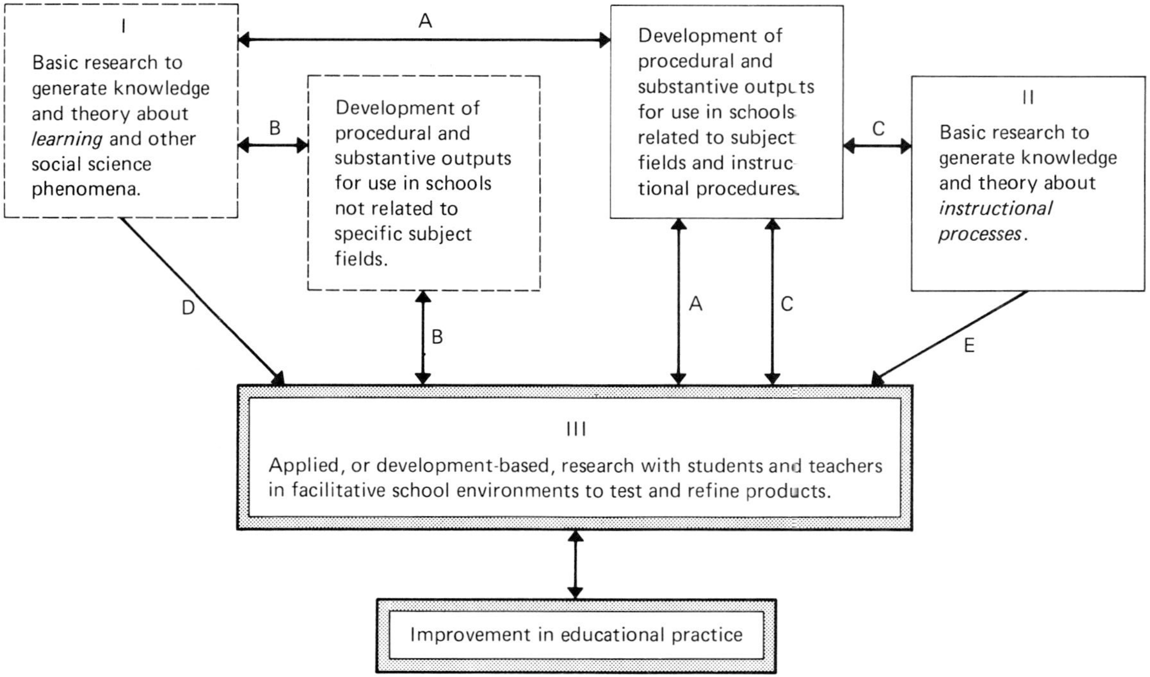

Fig. 7.1 Relationships among research and development activities. (Adapted from Klausmeier 1968, p. 2.)

unit became too large. (Pellegrin 1969). This research helped make more specific recommendations regarding unit staff size (subgroups according to former graded levels form if the teaching team gets larger than six or seven persons) and today there are only a few I & R Units with more than six or seven teachers.

The preceding illustrations show how researcher-initiated activities have changed educational practice by offering carefully designed new procedures and products. Development-based research, including evaluation, occurred prior to the dissemination of the end product. Additionally, numerous studies which were undertaken to refine test instruments, to experiment with alternative approaches, and to secure opinions of experts and practitioners attested to the care with which components of IGE were developed. It is also noteworthy that similar efforts and sophistication were used in the development of products at other Research and Development Centers and Regional Laboratories. Instructional products from such institutions, even if published commercially, generally have a research base.

SCHOOL-INITIATED RESEARCH

It would be a mistake to conclude that research and development organizations alone generate the research base for educational practice. Schools can and should have as active a part in initiating and carrying out development-based research as they have need and desire. In the multiunit organization in the IGE school, there is an explicit expectation that the I & R Unit will carry on some practical research or evaluation, even if such an activity is deferred a year or two after first year changeover until the unit operates smoothly.

The purpose of school initiated research is to improve instructional programs and practices for individual students. Successful evaluations and positive research outcomes should be reported, however, so that I & R Units in IGE schools have an opportunity to utilize effective materials and techniques developed by others. Thus, the I & R Unit may also have a dissemination role as a result of its research activity.

Three types of research activity are particularly effective in securing answers to questions about instructional strategies and programs. After developing or identifying an instructional program, I & R Units may (1) evaluate the overall outcomes of instruction; (2) study the effects of the program for various groups of students; and (3) set up an experiment contrasting at least two different treatments. Each type of research activity is discussed below, along with illustrations from the school setting.

The purpose of school-initiated research is to improve instructional programs and practices in the I & R Unit.

Evaluating the Outcomes of Instruction

It is always appropriate for the unit leader to ask whether or not the outcomes of instruction have been attained. Some specific suggestions for objective-based evaluation are given in Chapter 16. However, the unit leader should note that the question of instructional effectiveness may go beyond the *immediate* attainment of objectives. For instance, retention of reading skills over the summer by seven-year-olds using the *Wisconsin Design for Reading Skill Development* was studied. Criterion-referenced tests were given to children at the end of their second year of school and the beginning of the third year of school. As would be predicted, there was some loss of skill over the summer. Since only about 15 percent of spring mastery ratings on 13 Level B (grade one) skills changed to nonmastery in the fall, the loss was not deemed sufficient to warrant fall placement testing at a substantial cost of time and money (Rude 1973).

In evaluating the outcomes of instruction, the unit leader should not overlook noncognitive outcomes such as student attitudes and teacher judgment.

Studying Program Effectiveness for Particular Groups of Children

Teachers often question the effectiveness of instruction for particular individuals or groups of children. Systematic collection of data can provide information that will answer these questions. For example, one upper I & R Unit in an inner-city school felt very unsuccessful in its ability to involve the older boys in science. It also appeared that varied materials and activities did not meet the expectations of the teachers. Finally, a member of the unit wondered what would happen if they separated the boys from the girls and therefore had a class for boys only. With the unit leader's help they requested that a research project be carried out and data collected to answer the question. It was agreed that they would continue to plan and teach science in this grouping configuration for ten weeks. The data collected indicated that the boys' attitudes (when boys and girls were separated) toward science improved and so did their achievement; there was no change in the girls' attitudes (Center for Educational Research and Services 1968).

Experimenting with Instruction

One lower primary unit raised the question, "Is achievement of young children greater when older children tutor the younger children in a particular subject matter?" (Quilling, *et al.* 1968) In order to investigate this question, mathematics was identified as the subject matter, and the content was organized into weekly topics on the basis of an educational TV program. Ten- to twelve-year-old boys and girls were identified as potentially good tutors by their teachers and were briefed in a half-hour weekly session on the concepts presented on the TV program. One day a week each tutor played games and carried out other activities with his or her tutee. The tutees had been chosen randomly from the entire set of six- to seven-year-olds. A criterion-referenced achievement test administered near the end of the year indicated that the tutees participating in the tutoring program attained significantly more mathematical concepts than did their nonparticipating peers.

This experiment illustrates the nature of research activity as follows:

- A significant question was clearly stated.
- An experimental treatment was devised and made explicit, that is, the

weekly training sessions for tutors and weekly tutoring period occurred in addition to regularly scheduled mathematics class for all children.

- A sample of younger children was selected on a random basis to participate so that the experimental and control groups could be presumed to be equivalent in many respects as they began the treatment.
- A criterion measure related to the program content was utilized at the conclusion of the experiment to assess the effectiveness of the treatment.

To be sure, there was more information available on which to base decisions on program continuation or expansion than that provided by the one criterion-referenced measure. The estimated benefit to older children of tutoring and the logistic problems of coordinating schedules of older and younger students were among the factors that were considered, along with the positive results. Actually, further studies on benefits to tutors and effects of various tutor-tutee matching strategies were suggested by the first experiment. Some of these lines of research were subsequently pursued by research staff and a tutoring procedure was developed (Klausmeier, *et al.* 1973). This sequence illustrates an important principle of research:

Follow-through on an initial study may help refine procedures and thereby improve practice.

In a school setting, an experiment such as the one described above might lead to adoption of the procedure that was first studied. Thus, the second study is an evaluation focusing on the procedure alone, rather than an experiment comparing it with another treatment.

Some Experimental Considerations

The I & R Unit has several advantages over self-contained classrooms for experimentation. The larger number of children in the I & R Unit is, first of all, advantageous for carrying out experimentation. The possibility of flexible staffing and assignment of students to teachers is a second factor that simplifies some of the logistical problems encountered whenever careful research is undertaken. In designing experiments, the unit leader may want to take into account further considerations. For example, one procedure or program may build upon another so that the treatments are more and less intensive. In one motivation experiment, for instance, the amount of achievement was compared when (1) both teacher-child conferences were conducted and rewards were given; (2) when conferences alone were held; and (3) when no conferences were held or rewards were given (Schwenn, *et al.* 1970). The amount of time may also be varied in intensity, using as variables the amount of time spent on a procedure or the relative frequency of an activity.

A useful experimental technique for classroom research is the rotation of teachers among the treatments. If one teacher carries out one program and another teacher a second program, the results really indicate the joint effect of each program and its teachers. To be sure that programs rather than teachers are evaluated, teachers may be switched at intervals from one program to another. For instance, if there are four teachers and two programs, each teacher might teach one program for the first half of the study and the other program for the remainder. Not only does this "equalize" the effect of each teacher on each program, it also gives the teachers a chance to gain experience with the programs and make personal observations about each.

A sequence of research, development, and evaluation is especially powerful in improving instruction. Answers to initial questions may be secured in a first experiment in which a fraction of the students in the I & R Unit have a new treatment while others have no treatment. Next, the program or procedure is further developed in light of the experimental results. Subsequent implementation of the refined product with the remaining children in the unit is evaluated to ensure the continued effectiveness of instruction. In the development of a unit of instruction—creative writing, for example—the program may be presented first to a randomly selected class-sized group of students while other teachers carry out unrelated units of instruction with other children. At the end of the creative writing unit, all children might be assessed to determine whether the target unit of instruction produced differences in achievement between the participants and nonparticipants. If children had benefited from participating in the creative writing unit, then the procedure can next be refined both on the basis of the data collected and teacher comments about the particular lessons. The children in the I & R Unit who have not yet experienced the creative writing instructional program can then receive the benefit of validated and improved learning instruction. Their learning can be evaluated using scores obtained earlier as a baseline. In such a case, the development of an excellent unit of instruction is accomplished within a single semester or school year because the staff has the opportunity to test it more than once.

In order to carry out a project such as the one described above, the unit leader and staff teachers might follow the sequence of practical procedures depicted in Figure 7.2. It should be noted that an educational experiment requires adherence to carefully designed procedures. Most unit leaders will need the assistance and support of research personnel to carry out the project successfully.

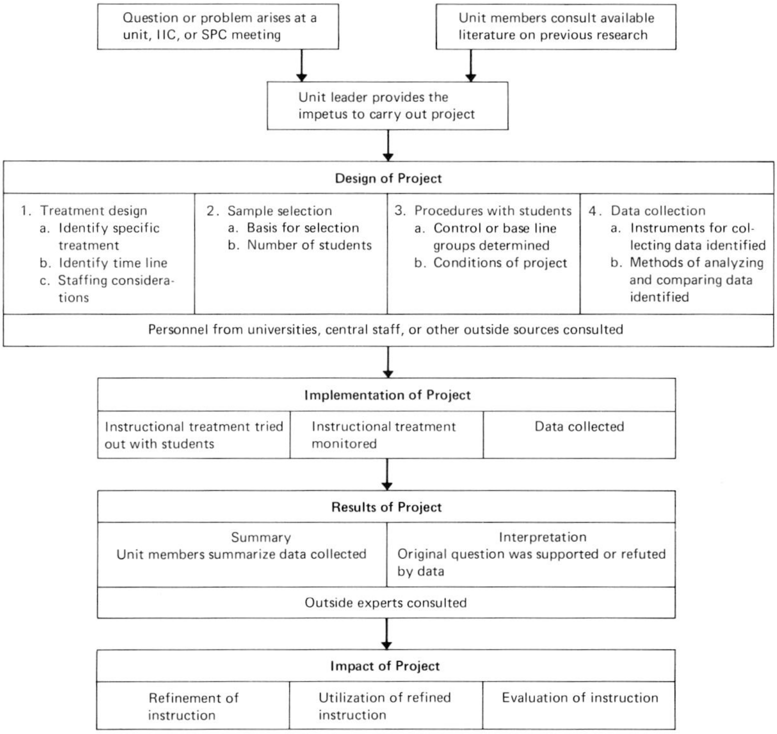

Fig. 7.2 Flowchart for I & R Unit involvement in locally initiated research.

RESEARCH ROLES FOR THE UNIT LEADER

The unit leader, although not necessarily a researcher, can be involved in research. The first requisite is that the unit leader have a positive attitude and noticeable enthusiasm toward the vital role of research in the IGE school. The unit leader must recognize that the ultimate purpose of research is to improve instruction for the children in the I & R Unit and in the school. The unit leader also has a responsibility for transmitting this attitude to the members of the unit staff.

The unit leader needs to develop a questioning attitude toward instructional and organizational practices in the I & R Unit and in the school. The unit leader and staff should ask questions of themselves and their activities such as:

- Is there another way to teach . . . ?
- Can my feelings about . . . be supported by data?
- What effect does self-selection have on the children's attitudes?

Once an idea or question is identified the next logical steps are (1) to talk it through in the unit meetings; (2) to look in educational literature for relevant information; and (3) to seek an outside consultant who is a specialist in the subject matter or in research design. Although the unit leader need not be a researcher, it is within the role expectation that he or she understand enough about research to know how to approach the question.

The unit leader role in research can be depicted four different ways: (1) interpreter of IGE as a research-based system of education; (2) leader in the application of research results; (3) leader in planning and conducting practical research; and (4) a link between the I & R Unit and researchers. Each of these roles is described below.

An Interpreter of IGE as a Research-based System of Education

IGE differs from some other educational innovations in the fact that it is research based. Teachers and others may have questions about the reasons for various practices. While there are certainly arguments to be taken on both sides of some issues, there oftentimes *are* answers to questions practitioners and parents raise about IGE. The unit leader who reviews studies about research and development in IGE will be in a good position to answer some of these questions. Also, the unit leader who has studied the earlier part of this chapter should be able to explain how research, development, and evaluation have been interlinked as the system has developed.

A Leader in the Application of Research Results

Through professional reading, participation in courses, and attendance at professional meetings, the unit leader may become acquainted with research findings and applications dealing with the curriculum, with child development, and with learning and motivation. Any professional person has some responsibility to "keep up" through planned exposure to new information, but the unit leader has a special obligation in this regard. First, his or her roles both as unit leader and as a member of the IIC presume a commitment to instructional improvement. Stimulation for such improvement can come in part from sources outside the IGE school. Second, if we accept education as, in part, a science, then rational behavior includes the use of scientific results. Finally, the values the unit leader holds for research and its applications are apparent to colleagues, and may be presumed to influence their thinking.

As the I & R Unit plans to develop instructional programs for the students of a unit, it is appropriate for the unit leader to ensure the use of well-known principles of learning and instruction. For instance, in planning a handwriting program, what is known about developmental stages of motor control, about effective procedures for motor-skill training, and about the development of habits should be applied. Research is consistent in suggesting that short, frequent practice sessions are more effective than longer, less frequent ones. The instructional program is planned with such information in hand. Unit leaders who supervise student teachers will also find that communication of such rationales assists them in their planning. For example, the principle of short practice sessions was discussed with a preservice student who wanted to tutor a child once a week for a half hour in handwriting. Actually two or three shorter sessions would be more beneficial to the child than one 30-minute session. Shorter sessions take into account that younger children have short attention spans.

As another example, consider concept formation a primary objective of the elementary school. One way to teach concepts which is highly effective is the suggestion that the child be taught what the concept is *not,* so that the child will have a properly delimited notion of the concept (Harris and Harris 1973). The death of an animal, for instance, is not extinction. In securing further information about research-based learning principles that should be applied in instructional design, unit leaders are referred to *Principles of Instructional Design* (Gagne and Briggs 1974), and to educational psychology textbooks as useful references.

What about less certain results of research than those discussed above? Critical thinking about the merits of the research and appraisal of its applicability to the given school situation are essential steps in research utilization. The critical thinking step involves asking questions of the following kinds:

- Does the person, institution, and/or publication reporting the results and making recommendations have a good professional reputation?
- Is there conflicting research evidence of alternative interpretations of the findings?
- Is the situation in which the research was conducted much like mine? Can I safely generalize the findings to my school, age level, or environment?

In answering these and other questions the unit leader may want to do further reading and to get the reactions of specialists as well as colleagues to the research itself and to its planned translation into instructional practice.

In designing or adapting a research-based procedure for the local school situation, a spirit of tentativeness is appropriate. Never does a researcher say, "I have proven that. . . ." The unit leader appropriately prefaces expectations of outcomes with words like "perhaps" and "possibly." Limited application of the results is in order, with larger scale application awaiting further trial. Evaluation of the application or experimental comparison of the procedure with alternatives are appropriate next steps. In the next section specific suggestions for school research are given.

A Leader in Planning and Conducting Practical Research

The unit leader usually needs to take initiative if research is to be conducted in the I & R Unit. Research, however, is not in itself an end, but is a means to solve some instructional problems. Therefore, the unit leader can approach a research project indirectly, linking it to some projected development or unanswered questions. Time for planning research and carrying out the experiment needs to be budgeted if the project is to be successful.

Before the experiment is begun the tasks listed earlier in the chapter should be accomplished: First, a good question needs to be formulated; second, available literature should be consulted to determine what is already known in the area; third, treatments need to be carefully designed and communicated to the staff; and fourth, experimental procedures, such as random assignment of youngsters to treatment and rotation, need to be considered. In each of these matters, the I & R Unit may either take personal responsibility for it or coordinate the activities with others. In such a matter as research, someone who has expertise in research in a school district or at a university or other research institution may be consulted. During the experiment, the treatment should be periodically reviewed by the I & R Unit staff to solve problems that may have arisen and to ensure consistency of implementation.

Other procedures include asking staff to keep records of lesson plans and logs of their reactions to various materials and events. Student opinions may also be sought periodically about particular activities and materials and at the end of the experiment about the program procedure in general. Criterion-referenced data need to be gathered as carefully as one would gather other important data. This includes selecting optimal times of the day and week for testing, scoring tests, and recording scores accurately, as well as summarizing the scores and subjective reactions. Some suggestions for these activities are given in Chapters 13 and 16 of this book.

The unit leader has a further role in making certain that the data are utilized to make curricular decisions. The teachers and others need to see that their efforts in carrying out research were worthwhile and that results of the experiment can positively affect educational practices in their own I & R Unit and school.

The unit leader's role, in short, is one of making and taking time for experimentation, of careful planning and monitoring of the research activity, and of reporting and concurrently ensuring the use of the results.

A Link between the I & R Unit and Researchers from Universities or Other Institutions

Schools and I & R Units within them are often asked to participate in studies by researchers, especially if nearby institutions have educational research programs or if school personnel are completing research degrees. Also the natural association between schools and colleges with preservice and inservice IGE programs often leads to research requests. Should the school and unit participate in such research at the possible expense of the time youngsters spend in the instructional program? Each case has to be weighed separately, but the answer can be affirmative in many cases. First, the research question may have a direct bearing upon practices in the unit, and the data collected in the course of research can be useful for both the researcher and the I & R Unit staff. Second, researchers who ask the cooperation of an I & R Unit may in turn be requested not only to explain carefully what is to be done, but to provide interpretive feedback. It is the responsibility of the unit leader to plan the data collection and follow up with the researcher so that research findings are utilized.

Because research activities are often unfamiliar to school staff, the unit leader needs to ensure explicit planning and explanation of all such activities. Careful research procedure often necessitates constraints on everyday teacher and pupil behaviors. The unit leader who seeks an understanding of the need for such constraints can help the unit staff appreciate rather than resent the research conditions. The unit leader models values regarding research activities. In contrast, if research is presented as artificial, there can be little incentive to utilize research results and the possibilities of improving instruction through research-based techniques is minimized.

What about research that seems to have no clear bearing on the school's needs? It is often difficult for the school to make a commitment to theoretical or longitudinal research. If research, however, is to shed its image of artificiality, which comes in part from data collection on unrepresentative samples in laboratory settings, there must be access to the schools. Some basic questions take priority over the applied ones in which school people are interested. Just as we have accepted a professional obligation to undertake a fair share of teacher education in many schools, so do we have an obligation to further educational science. The unit leader, who with other school district officials, critically evaluates requests for unit participation in basic research can reasonably ask the questions:

- How might this research increase our knowledge?
- What practical applications might result from this study?
- How extensive is our commitment to be?

The researcher bears the burden of presenting enough information in answer to these questions that the members of the IIC can make a decision whether or not to become involved in the study.

Research activity in IGE schools may lead to suggestions for the development of innovative instructional designs, assessment practices, content and curricular organization, materials and numerous other strategies. However, the reverse is equally true in that newly developed techniques and materials may be tested and researched before decisions regarding their effectiveness can be made and their use recommended. It would appear, too, that development-based research and development of instructional materials are also interrelated. This relationship is discussed in the final section of this chapter.

THE UNIT LEADER AND DEVELOPMENT ACTIVITIES

Research activity in IGE is not an end in itself but a means to an end—continual development and refinement of the instructional and organizational elements of education. As was indicated in Figure 7.1, development is both an outcome of involvement in research and a stimulator for subsequent research.

Unless special attention is given to the development phase of IGE, the entire system can become static. Unlike research which seeks an unknown, instructional and organizational strategies and materials are developed to accomplish certain objectives which are clearly defined. The goal of a development activity is to prepare and test new curriculum materials, instructional programs and systems, grouping arrangements, organizational plans and materials. These products are often the outcomes of knowledge gained from research involving the following areas: learning theory, motivational principles, instructional strategies, and child growth and development.

The unit leader's role in development is probably one of the most practical to be considered. The actual idea for development of materials and techniques might come from within the I & R Unit, a building, a system, or from agencies outside of the school such as were discussed earlier in this chapter. Regardless of where the development project originates, it must be conducted, often within the framework of controlled variables, in the real world of the classroom and with live and impatient children to find out if it "works." Requirements in terms of time, record-keeping devices, and evaluation techniques must be met by every teacher using the material. Information must be collected, compiled, and returned for discussion with the designer. These are the responsibilities of the unit leader. This requires the same willingness, flexibility, and cooperation as does the research component. In fact, the members of the unit staff are likely to become more deeply involved in development activity because they may be the implementors, the users, the workers in the field.

The usual sources of and reasons for development activities are needed changes in classroom conditions that will promote more effective learning for children. Materials and/or techniques are then developed in terms of objectives, expected pupil performance, necessary conditions, cost, etc. In other words, a prototype is developed and implemented in a school or number of schools for evaluation and field testing. The development phase of educational change literally depends on the cooperation of the unit staff members in any given IGE school. The need for leadership skills on the part of the unit leader is vividly apparent.

Perhaps the most useful developments are initiated by I & R Unit members. For example, many excellent instructional units are written by the unit staff. Creative activities are designed by school teachers. Organizational formats are changed and new ones tested. New procedures for home-school-community relations are evaluated. As new ideas are generated and tested in I & R Units and schools, they become steps in further development of IGE especially when they are shared and used in other I & R Units or in other schools. When feedback is given to the developers, and revisions completed if necessary, these ideas become a bank from which many other I & R Units can draw.

For example, a director of a systemwide media center desired to capitalize on the knowledge and creativity of the many IGE teachers in the system. She offered to pay for well-designed instructional units and materials and for any new ideas to improve the IGE schools in the system. Because of limited funds, she paid each contributor in services, such as laminating, duplicating, and constructing services, for which there was ordinarily a charge. An evaluation form was included in each package and each user was asked to critique the material. The unit leaders were asked to organize the work of each unit staff in this development effort.

A variety of examples of development by teachers in an I & R Unit or building is given in Chapters 11, 12, 14, and 17. Very often this development is carried out on an ongoing basis through systemwide inservice or college course work.

SUMMARY

In this chapter, several kinds of research and development activities which have relevance for instruction have been described. Development-based research, including evaluation, was identified as the kind of research most relevant to teachers. Several approaches to research were illustrated through examples of studies that have been conducted in IGE schools. Specific tasks in research techniques such as random assignment of children to a program or procedure were also described. Then, several roles for the unit leader in research were stressed. The unit leader models the value of research through emphasizing and explaining its use in solving instructional problems. The unit leader encourages the conduct of research in the I & R Unit whether the study is initiated by teachers in the school, an I & R Unit, or by personnel from universities or other institutions.

Finally, development activities, especially those initiated by the teachers in the I & R Unit, building or system were discussed.

REFERENCES

Center for Educational Research and Services, University of Toledo, 1968.

Cooley, W. W. 1971. *Methods of evaluating school innovations.* Invited address to 79th Annual Convention, Washington, D.C., Sept. 3.

Gagne, R. M., and L. J. Briggs 1974. *Principles of instructional design.* New York: Holt.

Harris, M. L., and C. W. Harris 1973. *A structure of concept attainment abilities.* Madison, Wisc.: Wisconsin Research and Development Center for Cognitive Learning.

Hilgard, E. R. 1964. A perspective on the relationship between learning theory and educational practice. In E. R. Hilgard (ed.), *Theories of learning and instruction.* Thirty-sixth Yearbook. Chicago National Society for the Study of Education.

Klausmeier, H. J., J. T. Jeter, M. R. Quilling, and D. A. Frayer 1973. *Individually guided motivation.* Madison, Wisc.: Wisconsin Research and Development Center for Cognitive Learning.

———, M. R. Quilling, J. S. Sorenson, R. S. Way, and G. R. Glasrud 1971. *Individually guided education and the multiunit elementary school: guidelines for implementation.* Madison, Wisc.: Wisconsin Research and Development Center for Cognitive Learning.

———, J. L. Wardrop, M. R. Quilling, T. A. Romberg, and R. E. Schutz 1968. *Research and development strategies in theory refinement and educational improvement.* Technical Report No. 15. Madison, Wisc.: Wisconsin Research and Development Center for Cognitive Learning.

———, W. L. Goodwin, J. Prasch, and M. R. Goodson 1966. *Project MODELS: maximizing opportunities for development and experimentation in learning in the schools.* Technical Report No. 3. Madison, Wisc.: Wisconsin Research and Development Center for Cognitive Learning.

Pellegrin, R. J., A. T. Slagle, and L. Johansen 1969. *Some organizational characteristics of multiunit schools.* Working Paper No. 22. Madison, Wisc.: Wisconsin Research and Development Center for Cognitive Learning.

Quilling, M. R., D. M. Cook, J. L. Wardrop, H. J. Klausmeier, R. Baldwin, and C. Loose 1968. *Research and development activities in R & I Units of two ele-*

mentary schools of Milwaukee, Wisconsin, 1966–1967. Technical Report No. 46. Madison, Wisc.: Wisconsin Research and Development Center for Cognitive Learning.

Romberg, T. A., and M. Montgomery 1974. *Developing mathematical processes: resource manual.* Chicago: Rand McNally.

Rude, R. T. 1973. *Sex, intelligence, and school reading curriculum as factors influencing summer retention and overall reading ability and specific reading skills of first grade subjects.* Technical Report No. 263. Madison, Wisc.: Wisconsin Research and Development Center for Cognitive Learning.

Schwenn, E. A., J. S. Sorenson, and J. L. Bavry 1970. *The effect of individual adult-child conferences on the independent reading of elementary school children.* Technical Report No. 125. Madison, Wisc.: Wisconsin Research and Development Center for Cognitive Learning.

Venezky, R. L., *et al.* 1974. *PRS (The prereading skills program): teachers' guide folder #10 history of PRS.* Chicago: Encyclopaedia Britannica Educational Corporation.

8

Improving Home-School-Community Relations

Marvin J. Fruth
B. Dean Bowles

Objectives

After reading this chapter, the reader will be able:

- To identify at least six basic principles of home-school-community relations.
- To describe the four primary interaction patterns of home-school-community relations.
- To explain the concepts of analysis, communication, involvement and resolution, and indicate the role of the unit leader in developing each.
- To describe major communications and involvement activities for the unit leader in home-school-community relations.

There are three general goals of a home-school-community relations program for an IGE school.

1. To make the IGE staff more aware of and responsive to the educational expectations and available resources of the community, parents, and students;
2. To make the community, parents, and students more aware of and responsive to the requisites of the instructional program as implemented through IGE; and
3. To identify and utilize ways and means of actively involving both staff and community in the awareness, commitment, changeover, refinement, and renewal phases of implementing IGE in the school.

To achieve these goals the staff must become more actively and effectively involved in the school community.* Moreover, ways must be found whereby the principal, unit leaders, and staff of IGE schools involve the various subpublics within the school community in both policy development and important operational decisions which will not only be generally functional for good school community relations but also contribute to effective implementation of IGE.

The unit leader plays a pivotal role in the home-school-community relations program of an IGE school. The unit leader is not only the leader of the I & R Unit, but also represents the I & R Unit on the IIC—the paramount decision-making body of the school. In both roles the unit leader interacts with school community: children, certified staff including other unit leaders, and the principal, aides, student teachers and interns, parents, and the general citizenry. Hence, if an IGE school is to have an effective home-school-community relations program, the unit leader must function effectively as a leader in the home-school-community relations effort.

This chapter delineates the home-school-community relations program for an IGE school and the role of the unit leader in a smoothly

---

* The concepts "school community" and "subpublics" are used rather synonymously throughout this chapter. Both refer to the various individual, group, or organizational interests which may be found in any school district. The terms are inclusive of both governmental and nongovernmental and formal and informal groups. The concepts are intentionally not meant to distinguish between "school people" and "nonschool people." Examples of elements of the school community or subpublics are the school board, handicapped children, athletic booster clubs, taxpayers associations, individual influentials, teachers unions, and central office. The only exception to synonymous usage comes when "school community" is employed to distinguish between the service area of a specific school and the wider school district or community.

functioning program. It parallels a similar chapter on the principal's role in improving home-school-community relations in the text on *The Principal and Individually Guided Education* (Lipham and Fruth 1976). In both chapters the major concepts are the same. In addition, as the home-school-community relations model illustrates, in some instances their roles are quite similar: the principal has primary responsibility at the school level and the unit leader at the unit level. However, the unit leader also has a role as a member of the IIC and, in this instance, shares responsibility with the principal. A major difference between these chapters is that the present chapter reflects a lesser emphasis on the political aspects.

One of the objectives of the Wisconsin Research and Development Center's research effort in home-school-community relations is to identify the specific responsibilities of principals, unit leaders, and other staff of IGE schools in bringing about an effective home-school-community relations program. That research is presently underway but has not yet been completed. Consequently, the conclusions and suggestions in the chapter reflect both the results of research to date as well as the experiences of a great number of participants in the IGE experience.

This chapter is organized into five principal sections. The first section sets forth several principles about home-school-community relations which bear on the role and function of the unit leader. The second section discusses the primary interaction patterns expected in a home-school-community relations program for an IGE school. Specific concepts and competencies for the unit leader in pursuing an effective home-school-community relations program are systematically explored in the third section. The link between home-school-community relations and the instructional program is briefly examined in section four. Finally, section five illustrates several communication and involvement aspects of the home-school-community relations program for the unit leader through the vehicle of abbreviated cases and suggested activities.

PRINCIPLES OF HOME-SCHOOL-COMMUNITY RELATIONS

First, if organizational changes associated with IGE, such as the multiunit organization, are going to be implemented, their benefits must be not only visible but also tangible to the various subpublics in the school community. This means that unit leaders, as members of the IIC, will be expected to cooperate with the principal to involve subpublics early in the implementation process and to present information clearly and in terms that the various subpublics can understand. At present, the benefits of facilitative environments, the instructional programming model, and the multiunit organization are probably neither visible nor tangible to most subpublics of the school community. Rather, subpublics want answers to such questions as: "Will my child be a better reader as a result of IGE?," "Why all this permissiveness—why don't you just tell them what to do and when to do it?" "My child is too immature to have so many teachers—won't he be frustrated?" and "Doesn't my child need a structured classroom?" Answers and outcomes should be provided in visible and tangible terms, products, and activities.

Second, unit leaders, and the I & R Unit staff teachers will have to work closely with parents. This will mean parent volunteers working in the schools, classroom observations by parents, home visits and parent participation, and involvement in making educational policies and operational decisions which affect the instructional program and school life of their children. Such participation will enhance the IGE program. Educators will have to expand the current "open-door" policy and adopt a "go-out-the-door" policy in relating to the school community.

Third, in planning instruction, unit staffs must avail themselves of the educational resources of the community. These resources should not only help children learn but also expand the knowledge of professional educators about the community. Such knowledge of the community would include, but not necessarily be restricted to, the influence of the political and social factors on the instructional program.

Fourth, principals, unit leaders, and staff should adopt and encourage a more inclusive and elastic concept of community. Educators have too long held to a "we/they" or "friends of education/foes of education" orientation. Similarly, some educators see only the subpublics "outside" the school building as the community when perhaps the most effective subpublics, the children and staff, are right in the schools. Typically the concept "community" is limited to those involved directly in education. It should include not only students and staff but also the nonparent adult and senior citizens. Unfortunately, in some districts educational affairs are considered to the exclusion of general community affairs and municipal issues.

Fifth, as a corollary to the concept of a more inclusive and elastic concept of community, the IGE staff, because of their direct influence on each student's instructional program, should be aware that the most important subpublic in any home-school-community relations program is the students. Often taken for granted, children not only are the purpose for which schools exist but also are the most consistently influential subpublic with which the school must deal. Students communicate their perceptions about school to adults, particularly parents, and therefore are the primary source of information about teachers, classes, school, and IGE. Moreover, this fact applies to the primary school child as well as to the adolescent. This observation has long-range as well as short-range home-school-community relations implications because children bring many of the perceptions

Educators will have to expand the current "open-door" policy and adopt a "go-out-the-door" policy in relating to the school community.

and experiences about school which were learned in childhood into their adult experience. In short, the premier efforts of the unit leader and staff in any home-school-community relations program should be focused on the students.

Sixth, IGE schools should avoid the general "crisis management" orientation of most home-school-community relations. All too frequently, home-school-community relations programs respond to crises and are passive and impotent rather than active and preventative. In this regard the maxim for effective, long-term home-school-community relations is simple.

A long-term, effective home-school-community relations program is built in times of peace and relative pacificity, not in times of crisis and turmoil. It is an ongoing, interactive, and meaningful relationship among home, school, and community.

Seventh, the unit leader, in order to make a significant contribution to the home-school-community relations program, should recognize that interest, participation, and stakes in the policies and practices of the public schools are no longer limited to the cadre of professional employees and a handful of involved and interested parents. Home-school-community relations require communication and involvement with many more subpublics today than they did several years ago. For a variety of reasons many subpublics which were once disorganized and mute concerning school affairs are now organized for collective action and voice their demands persistently. For example, ethnic and racial minorities, women's groups, students, organized teachers, and many other general public interest groups were not heard many years ago. Now however, the best home-school-community relations practices are required to (1) build these groups into the equation of operations; (2) adopt and adapt new and more effective means of communications; (3) seek genuine and authentic involvement of these subpublics in the alternatives impinging upon the critical decisions affecting both policy and practice; and (4) develop means to resolve actual or potential conflict among the school, home, and the newly organized and enfranchised subpublics.

Eighth, educators do not hold a monopoly on the expertise about educational philosophy and practices. The educational system and current affairs have succeeded in developing a public which, even if they do not have equivalent expertise about educational matters, know how to get it, or failing that, know the right questions to ask. In the future, educators will be dealing with better informed, more knowledgeable, and generally more sophisticated subpublics than they had to deal with in the past.

Ninth, and finally, all educators need to understand more fully the political context of an effective home-school-community relations program. The political process encompasses two principal functions:

1. The resolution of actual or potential conflict in the school community and among its various subpublics; and
2. The allocation, through both policy and practice, of scarce economic resources, the choice among differing social values, and unequal political power for various educational objectives and for the benefit of the various subpublics.

The political objective of any effective home-school-community relations program is the resolution of actual or potential conflict among the various subpublics which may be associated with policy decisions or administrative practices which determine (1) the use of available, scarce resources, (2) value choices to be made regarding the educational program, and (3) locus of power in the educational enterprise.

In this context unit leaders and other IGE school personnel should be aware that many of the concepts and practices associated with IGE are inherently political. Nongradedness, differentiated staffing, shared decision making, criterion-referenced assessment, and resource reallocation all contribute to actual or potential conflict among various subpublics within a school community. For example, in what proportion should an IGE school allocate its resources for paraprofessionals, teachers, or materials? Who is involved in shared decision making: unit teachers, paraprofessionals, and/or parents? Can the decisions of the I & R Unit stand relatively plenary or are they subject to outside vetoes? Should mainstreaming of special education children be practiced within the I & R Units? Is differentiated staffing a management or union matter? Do nongradedness and individualized instruction mean more, or less, competition, or more, or less cooperation? What values do various subpublics place on the ideas of competition and cooperation? The functions of resolving actual or potential conflict and allocating resources, choosing values, and distributing power associated with these problems, and others like them, are both crucial and political.

One may logically conclude that an effective home-school-community relations program is good, practical politics. In this context politics is not of the national, partisan variety, but of the variety which determines the kind of community in which we will live, the kind of schools we will have, and the kind of educational program our schools will conduct. Hence, all the media, all the committees, all the crisis management, all the techniques of analyzing the school community, all the modes of communication, and all the involvement activities are but means to accomplish the twin objectives of (1) resolving conflict, and (2) allocating resources, choosing values, and distributing power. The unit leader, along with the principal and other staff members, shares the responsibility for the politics involved in the implementation of IGE. If this responsibility is to be fulfilled effectively, the unit leader must, by necessity, understand the critical concepts and competencies of effective home-school-community relations: analysis, communications, involvement, and resolution.

PRIMARY INTERACTION PATTERNS IN THE HOME-SCHOOL-COMMUNITY

The Home-School-Community Relations Model for IGE Implementation which is presented in Figure 8.1 includes two major dimensions: primary interactions patterns and concepts and competencies. That portion dealing with concepts and competencies is the subject of the next section of this chapter and will be considered systematically at that point. Primary interaction patterns in the home-school-community for the IGE school are set forth here.

As may be observed in Figure 8.1, home-school-community relations are simultaneously operative at four interdependent levels. Each level represents an aspect of community and school interaction which ultimately influences the kind and quality of the instructional program in the IGE school. More specifically the primary interaction patterns are between the child and the teacher, the home and the unit leader and staff, the school community and the principal and the IIC, and the district community and the administration and Systemwide Program Committee (SPC). Although these interaction patterns are most prevalent in actual practice, there may be frequent, even persistent, home-school-community interactions across stated primary patterns.

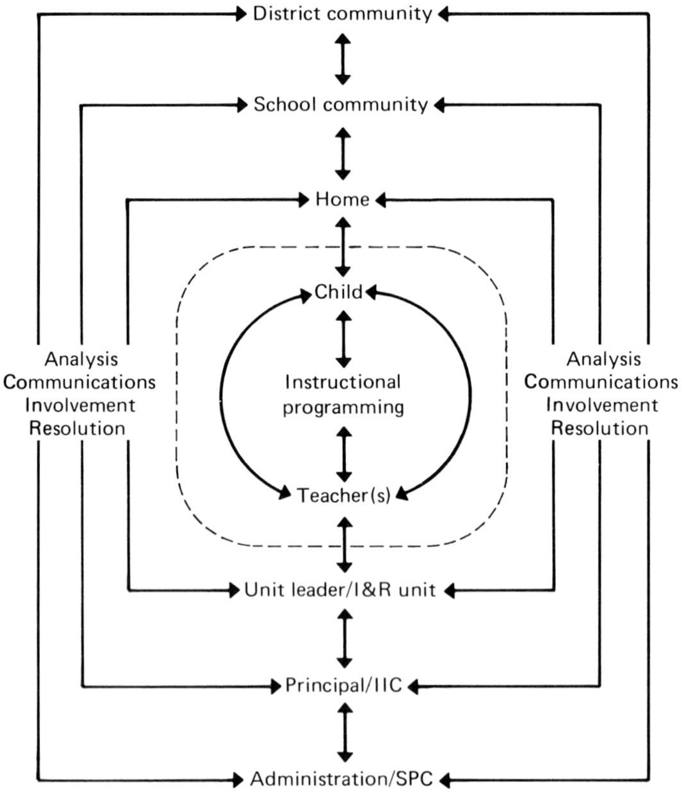

Fig. 8.1 A model for home-school-community relations.

District Community and Administration/SPC

The outer ring in Figure 8.1 represents the larger school district. In the final analysis the community controls the school through its willingness to expend power and resources on programs which mirror its values and interests. The interactions at this level are customarily between school boards, administrators, SPCs, teachers' associations, community influentials, and the like. While the district community-administration/SPC interactions are critical to the combined support of individual schools, this chapter focuses on the primary interaction patterns at the unit and school levels and on the role of the unit leader in facilitating those interactions.

School Community and Principal/IIC

A community establishes schools to meet the needs of both society and its children, and the subpublics in each attendance area have certain expectations as to how these needs are to be best met. If the values held by the community are communicated to the staff and the staff is responsive to these expectations, the community is more likely to use its power and resources to support the values represented by the instructional program. Conversely, if the staff does not satisfactorily accommodate the expectations of the community, then the community is certainly less likely to continue its full support and will either withdraw resources—witness the fate of many bond referenda—or use its power to reallocate resources and/or to replace staff with personnel who will accomplish the tasks expected in a manner acceptable to the demands of the community.

The staff expectations for the community are that they will furnish the resources and support to implement the instructional program. Although the principal, unit leaders, and staff have power in their expertise and the capability to withdraw their services if they do not receive adequate support, staff members are ultimately agents of the community and must either accommodate community demands or change them.

Open and clear channels of communication must be maintained in order to optimize the instructional program. The message for those who would like to implement instructional improvements is that the benefits and rewards of the innovation must be within the parameters of community expectations. The principal and unit leaders play crucial roles in identifying these expectations in the short run and possibly expanding them in the long run. Thus, under the guidance of the IIC, the school and its community influence each other and the cyclical process continues.

Home and Unit Leader/I & R Units

The focus here is on one specific sector of the community, namely parents, who have expectations for the school which are quite specific. Often these expectations are influenced by their own children's situation and, therefore, are less objective than those of the wider community. Parents also have a great and direct effect upon the input of each individual child into the instructional program. Because of this intense interest in both the ultimate objectives of the school or I & R Units and in the means for the achievement of the objectives, parents generally make up the most influential school-related group and may have the greatest impact on community awareness and educational policymaking within the larger community.

Because of the changing allocation of tasks and expertise within the multiunit organization, parents must be presented with a clear picture of the cognitive, affective, and psychomotor development of their children and the procedures used in promoting such development. This responsibility belongs to the unit leader and staff teachers. From the point of view of the unit, the reality of the intense family influence on children elucidates the necessity of parental inputs. The unit leader and teachers must understand the home to truly understand the child. Moreover they depend upon the home to support their instructional program for individual students.

Student and Teacher(s)

At the center of Figure 8.1, the teacher utilizes the instructional programming model to monitor the instructional program of each individual child. As the figure indicates, the child's family and community ties influence the child's attitudes, ability, and skills. Each teacher's understanding of these influences as well as an awareness of the available resources in the home and the community provide the teacher with maximum operational input, thereby increasing each child's potential for maximum operational output. This inner level of the home-school-community relations model is discussed later in this chapter.

CONCEPTS AND COMPETENCIES

There are four concepts and competencies to develop in order to establish and maintain an effective home-school-community relations program for the implementation of IGE. These are analysis, communication, involvement, and resolution. The unit leader is required to focus particularly on communication and involvement since these concepts and competencies relate to reporting pupil progress, parent conferences, utilization of parent volunteers, paraprofessionals or aides, and student teachers or interns. However, the unit leader also plays a major role as a member of the IIC in setting and interpreting school policy and practices to staff, children, and parents through honest, open, two-way communication. When actual or potential conflict threatens to come from existing or anticipated school policies or practices, the unit leader is sometimes responsible for the effective resolution of problems both small and large. Successful resolution, communication, and involvement depends largely on thorough analysis of both participants and issues. While the four concepts and competencies are frequently interdependent, each can be examined separately.

Analysis

Analysis entails three distinct functions. First, it requires that the issues and issue elements be identified. Second, it demands the identification of the participant individuals and subpublics. Third, the identified issues and issue elements must be associated with the participant individuals and subpublics in order that some plan for communication, involvement, and/or resolution of actual or potential conflict might be developed.

In relation to schoolwide policies or practices, the major responsibility for analysis lies with the principal. As a member of the IIC, the unit leader may be involved in some analysis activities. The unit leader assumes responsibility for analysis when the issues and participants involved are directly related to the I & R Unit. Therefore, it is important that the unit leader have a thorough understanding of the way analysis functions.

Issue identification. There are a number of ways in which issues can be identified. The most obvious is the customary "on-the-job sense" of the practitioner about the issues. The unit leader who knows there is "something in the wind" when some aspect of IGE is being implemented has a handle on possible issues. While this is certainly the most effortless way to know the issues, it is not always as reliable as it might appear because the unit leader can be isolated from the source of some issues for any number of reasons, such as (1) newness in the community, (2) being outside of the customary lines of communication in the community, (3) the issues are incipient and have not reached the institutional or governmental stage, (4) factionalism in the community which sometimes causes a unit leader identified with one faction to be outside the mainstream of communication about issues from another faction, and (5) the issue is only tangentially related to a particular unit. "On-the-job sense" tends to pick up only the vocal issues and people.

A second means of identifying issues is the use of a systematic survey. The utilization of this method is recommended in order to assess periodically the demise or emergence of issues in a school community. Its utility comes from its relatively objective format and from the fact that the periodical use of surveys can catch changes over time.

A third common means of identifying issues involves in-depth, open-ended interviews with persons in the school community (Lipham and Fruth 1976). The advantage of this method is that the in-depth interviews provide some flesh on the skeleton of response whereas the survey method provides a range of issues but little explanation. An in-depth interview can not only yield the issues but also suggest several courses of action for resolution of the issues and persons to involve in the course of the resolution. Moreover, the in-depth interview, when done periodically and without crisis attending it, creates little concern and is, in itself, a tremendously effective home-school-community relations technique. The text, *The Principal and Individually Guided Education* (Lipham and Fruth 1976), provides a detailed explanation of the use of interviews as an analysis activity.

A fourth means of identifying issues in a community is to employ some planned, participatory group dynamic process (Delbecq and Van de Ven 1971). Participatory techniques have the advantage not only of identifying issues but also of developing priorities among them as to their relative importance. A properly selected community group can set priorities and begin some simultaneous work toward issue resolution. This has been used successfully in IGE schools with I & R Unit, school staff, and parent groups.

Issue identification means more than the simple cataloguing of topical concerns. If the identification of issues is to be effective in a home-school-community relations program, then the issues must be analyzed into their component elements. Hence, the larger issue of, say, "discipline" in an open-concept IGE school, may have several elements. For example, some may understand the "discipline problem" to be one of "noise"; to others the problem may be one of "movement"; still to others it might be "unevenness of punishment for whites and blacks"; others might view it as the "arrangement of space"; and still others might see it as the lack of a "command presence" of the teacher(s). Yet the "discipline" problem can neither be completely understood nor adequately resolved unless and until the staff knows what individuals and groups mean by "discipline." "On-the-job sense" and surveys are less adequate than in-depth interviews and participatory techniques in isolating and analyzing such issue elements.

Identification of participant subpublics. By participant subpublics is meant both individuals and groups, whether social or organized, who are active or who one could anticipate being active on a particular issue. There are three recognized means of identifying participants in a home-school-community relations program.

The first is the "role-position" technique. Role-position is the simple process of identifying participants from their formal roles or positions in the community. For example, a participant is assumed to be one who is in a position or role to exercise influence, such as the principal, the parent-teacher organization president, the banker, board member, etc. This method both assumes and ascribes an interest and influence to the person or group in the school community. This is one approach and usually a starting point. It has flaws, however, because neither an interest in participating nor influence in controlling the resolution of an issue in a school-community necessarily follows from either formal roles or positions.

A second method in identifying participants is the reputational technique (Hunter 1953). This technique determines participant interest and influence by asking participants to interview persons who they think or know to be interested and influential in the affairs of a particular school community. The result is *always* a catalog of persons some of whom are reputed to have great influence, others little or no influence. The disadvantages are several. First, the method always supplies the names of a cadre of influentials whether such a cadre exists in reality or not. Second, the interest and influence of this cadre is perceived by the persons asked to supply the names and are perhaps not real. Finally, it is difficult to associate the named people with the issues. The chief advantage is that the reputational technique can be done quickly and easily to identify persons for in-depth interviews and initiating issue analyses.

The third technique for identifying participants is the "issue analysis" method (Dahl 1966). This technique requires that interviews be obtained with a number of persons. During the course of interviews, past issues are identified and the history or story of those issues explored. The respondent is asked to identify participants simultaneously with the discussion of the issues. Those persons identified with the issues are assumed to be those with a continued interest and influence in school-community affairs. The advantage is that those identified have been associated with the affairs of the school community. Issue analysis has some disadvantages. The issue analysis technique is neither quick nor easy. Moreover it relies heavily on history, and what may have been the case in the past may not be so today due to our highly mobile society. To its advantage there is some ease in obtaining this data, however. Respondents are less reluctant to discuss people in conjunction with past events than they are about discussing people associated with current affairs. This method also identifies persons who do not necessarily occupy formal roles or positions.

Subpublic participants and issues. The next step in school-community analysis is to associate the participants with the issues and issue elements. It is very important that this step be taken because the processes of communication, involvement, and resolution are meaningless unless this association is made. After all, communication has to be to someone about something; involvement has to include someone for some purpose, and resolution requires that actual or potential conflict be resolved between two or more participant subpublics relative to specific issues. Moreover, participants have an interest in a school community relative to specific issues and issue elements. Their interest is not abstract and disassociated from the real political questions of allocating resources, values, and power and resolving the actual or potential conflict. The association of participants with issue elements will reveal the "stakes" * which various parties have in the resolution of an issue.

Let's take just one issue and its several elements and develop a matrix which illustrates the stakes associated with the process of resolution. One IGE school was undergoing tremendous community pressure on a variety of issues. It was charged by the "Basic Education Group" that the open-concept building was creating an atmosphere of permissiveness (Issue #1). Another group in the community criticized the poor discipline in the school (Issue #2). The reading program was said to not "get at the fundamentals" (Issue #3). The individualized teaching stations were labeled as the source of discipline problems (Issue #2a). There were other charges in the general attack to return the school to more traditional ways.

In this case, the principal and two unit leaders undertook to have 30 interviews with community members. They averaged two hours each and explored the whole array of home-school-community problems, including the "IGE problems." Participants were identified by using the issue analysis technique. After the issues were identified in the interviews, interviewers pressed for the issue elements. This is what they discovered. First, permissiveness (Issue #1), it was learned, was only symbolically associated with the building design; the real culprit issue element for Issue #1 was the change to a new reporting system (it was only coincidental that the new building came when ABCs went). Relative to Issue #2, it was soon learned that it, too, was not what it seemed, but was also associated with the new parent-teacher conference which no longer included a "citizenship" grade as had the old report card. The reading program (Issue #3) was found to be, upon more in-depth issue analysis with the interview respondents, not really questioned at all. The only element at stake in this

---

* "Stakes" is the direct, immediate association of an issue element with the individual participant or group making the demand. For example, for the issue of "open space" schools, individual A may demand "strict discipline and control"; group B may seek "a return to physically structured classrooms." Simultaneously, group C may demand wider, freer utilization of the open space, and individual D may want some structured space as an alternative for some children. While the issue, broadly conceived is "open space," the issue elements or demands are linked or associated with the various participant individuals and groups. This linking or associating elements and demands with participants is the identification of "stakes." The final objective of analysis is understanding "stakes" because both communication and resolution are difficult if not impossible without this form of analysis.

instance was the anxiety expressed by parents that their children "were no longer getting a normative evaluation as they did with the old report card." The high quality of the reading program was praised, much to the surprise of the interviewers. The teaching stations and discipline issues also proved to be a report card problem. There were also other issues associated with the school program which will not be elaborated upon here.

With this information the IIC resolved the issue(s) by (1) incorporating some aspects (normative elements) of the old reporting system, (2) retaining all other aspects of the newly adopted reporting system, and (3) changing nothing else at all in the IGE program. IGE in this school is now moving ahead due to the home-school-community relations program brought about through effective techniques of analysis and resolution. By contrast, the school had lost two principals and several unit leaders had returned to staff teaching positions in the three years prior to this because of their inability to handle such "hot" issues as "permissiveness," "poor discipline," "the reading program," and "teaching stations."

Communication

Both the media (the means of communication) and the message (the substance of the communication) are vital to effective communications. The influence of home, community, and school on the student have the potential to be supportive or inhibitive of learning. In order to maximize the former and minimize the latter, it is necessary that communications be open and clear, and that the media and message be compatible. Communication has both form and direction; it can be verbal or written. In addition, communication may be the nonverbal cues which sometimes belie the unit leader's comment to a parent that "Jimmy is doing just fine." It may also take the form of the "public relations" overkill that often accompanies a hard-sell campaign for school bonds or tax increases. This section will focus on several concepts and competencies of communications which are of particular interest and importance to unit leaders as well as other staff members in an effective home-school-community relations program: one-way/two-way communications, communication style, vehicles for communication, conditions for effective communications, and quality of the message.

One-way/two-way. With regard to the element of direction in communication, it is important that a great deal of the communication be two-way (school $\leftrightarrows$ home) rather than restricted to a one-way (school $\rightarrow$ home) for several reasons (Thiemann and Bumbarger 1971). What are the advantages and disadvantages of one-way and two-way communications?

One-way communication has generally been found to be (1) faster and more orderly, (2) less accurate, (3) more enjoyable for the sender,

(4) more frustrating for the receiver, (5) placing responsibility for understanding on the listener, (6) treating all listeners as having the same physical and mental capabilities, (7) causing the communicator, who receives no feedback, to interpret this as if it were positive feedback, and (8) forcing the listener to greater concentration.

Two-way communication, on the other hand, (1) is slower, (2) is less orderly, (3) is more accurate, (4) is more enjoyable for the receiver, (5) is less enjoyable for the sender due to the realization of the sender's oversights and mistakes, (6) places responsibility on the receiver to seek clarification and on the communicator to clarify, (7) forces the communicator to pace himself or herself to the slowest listener, and (8) allows one listener to receive additional cues from the questions of other listeners.

Thus, some reasons for using one-way communication are (1) to maintain orderliness and control, (2) to communicate messages which are simple and concise, (3) to speed up the communication process, (4) to hide mistakes or to maintain ambiguity, (5) to be able to scapegoat others for the sender's mistakes and ambiguities, and (6) to divide members of a group. Some reasons for using two-way communication are (1) to increase accuracy of communication, (2) to ensure that the intentions (nuances) are understood, and (3) to increase participation and satisfaction.

Therefore, if time is limited and the message is simple, one-way communication should probably be used. However, many teachers have had the experience of sending home what they thought was a simple note, only to find several responses from the parents of their pupils indicating misunderstanding, misconception, and misinterpretation. On the other hand, if there is available time, if the message and its nuances are complex, and if there is a desire for improving satisfaction and group cohesiveness, two-way communication is absolutely essential.

Communication style. In terms of communication style, the concepts and principles discussed above are relevant here as well; however, there are some primary concerns that are particularly important to the one-to-one relationship between staff members and parents.

Communication initiated by unit leaders or staff where vocalized on a one-to-one basis or written in a message sent home, should begin on a positive or neutral note. Even if the message in some way reflects a failure of the child, positive human relations require that initial communication be positive. Likewise, communication should continue on a positive note, and contact between teacher and parent should not be limited to negative instances of the child's behavior.

Communication should be attempted in the vocabulary that the parent will understand. While educators must avoid jargon, parents also resent being "talked down to." Some ethnic minority parents avoid contact with teachers because of cross-cultural conflict, and language is an essential factor in these instances.

Vehicles for communication. The vehicles for staff-parent communication produce another area of concern. Four modes of communication are face-to-face, telephone conversation, written notes, and mass media techniques. Among the most effective means of getting a message across are face-to-face interaction and telephone conversations. However, schools, for the most part, use mass media and written messages, the least effective techniques. In choosing the most appropriate vehicle, there should be a consideration of the degree of importance of the message, the time available for communication, the complexity of the message and the specific receiver of the message. Failure to consider such variables will result in vehicles of communication that are perhaps dysfunctional to an effective home-school-community relations program.

Conditions for effective communications. Apart from the primary concerns of one-way/two-way communications, communications style, and vehicles for communication, there is another important concern for effective communication between the I & R Unit and parents, and that is the condition under which communication is conducted. Where face-to-face interaction is required, the conditions to be considered are time, location, and quality control.

For example, face-to-face communication needs to be made at the reasonable convenience of the parent, not solely as a result of the schedule of the staff member. This is not to suggest that instructional or planning time is to be taken from the unit leader, teachers, or children, but alternatives and contingencies should be available to meet parents at their convenience. Provisions may sometimes have to be made for released time, replacement, or an inservice allocation to allow time for parents and teachers to meet at their mutual convenience. The time should also be sufficient to allow analysis, communication, and resolution of the problem or to allow a communication of a mutually agreed upon plan of action for the subsequent resolution of the problems or concerns.

The location of communication activities is of prime importance. Here is a good opportunity to exercise the "go-out-the-door" policy and meet the parents on their grounds rather than simply have an "open-door" policy that all communications take place at the school. Occasionally there is a problem with parents not wanting school personnel to come to the home. In any event, a place should be set aside where parents and unit leaders can interact in an environment free of disturbances and conducive to productive conversation and effective communication.

A final consideration concerning the conditions for effective communication is whether the communication is public or private. While the communication with a parent is public in the sense of contributing to a more effective education of the student, unit leaders and teachers need to develop a sharpened sense of that which is strictly confidential (given to the staff member alone), that which is professionally sound and required for effective functioning of the unit relative to the child in question (given to the unit leader or teacher for sharing with other staff members of the unit for the benefit of the child), and that which is extraneous information or gossip. Long-term as well as communitywide communication requires the development of trust among teachers and parents as to the relative confidentiality and professional use of their shared communications. Gossip and violated trusts on the part of a staff member quickly terminate any potential for ongoing, long-term, communitywide communications on a professionally sound and candid basis. Indeed, the breakdown of trust by one staff member often infects the trust and builds suspicion for all units in dealing with all parents in the school community. In this regard there are no gimmicks and no substitutes for unit leaders and teachers who are professional, socially sensitive, intellectually honest, and mature in the conduct of both their social and professional obligations.

Quality of the message. Finally, the quality of the message, whether verbal or written, ought to reach a standard that will assure communication. Too often a note is written hastily and sent to parents with insufficient information and mistakes (technical and factual). While a conversational and somewhat extemporaneous quality ought to permeate verbal communications between unit leaders and parents, these qualities ought not to be understood as synonymous with "playing it by ear" or lack of preparation as to information base and objectives, style, and conditions. Communication ought to be factual, based on anecdotal and other records, not just opinions. Parental communications should be planned so as to avoid the problems of creating conflict on the one hand and consuming time in irrelevant conversation on the other.

In short, the I & R Unit staff ought to be more rationally conscious of the factors contributing to effective communications and plan for their effective utilization when communicating with parents and other participant subpublics in the school community.

Involvement

Although communication is a form of involvement, in the present context involvement means the active participation of various subpublics of the school community in various aspects of analysis, communications, and actual or potential conflict resolution. The outcome is expected to be an improved educational and instructional program. Involvement can be planned and relatively organized such as parent teacher organization meetings, back-to-school nights, volunteer programs, simulation activities, or structured group processes; or involvement can be unplanned and/or relatively unorganized such as in spontaneous confrontations between parent and unit leader, parent advisory meetings with parent groups in control of the agenda, unannounced visitations, brainstorming sessions, or problem-solution sessions growing out of structured group processes.

Planned, structured involvement is defined as that in which the staff member has some reasonable ability to predict the course of events and some degree of control over the agenda of issues and/or participant subpublics. An unplanned, unstructured involvement is that in which the I & R Unit staff has relatively less control over the agenda of issues and participant subpublics and certainly less power to predict the ultimate course of events. This section will discuss involvement activities which are essentially planned and structured rather than those which are relatively unplanned and unstructured.

The I & R Unit staff must necessarily reflect on the kinds of activities that will provide effective communication between the home, school, and community. Five of these activities—activities which are customarily used in IGE schools—are as follows: (1) home visits, (2) parent visits to the school, (3) parent conferences, (4) use of parent volunteers, and (5) parent representatives and participation in I & R Units and/or the IIC.

Regarding home visits, dates and times must be the option of the parent; a written message or phone call should precede each visit; the interaction should begin on a positive note; and the visitor not only must tune in on the values and expectations of the parent but also avoid overstaying the welcome. Access to the home comes from the notion that parents and educators are working in a cooperative fashion for the education of the student with the invitation to visit being initiated perhaps by the child. Frequently, members of the staff such as the nurse or social worker will have a more direct contact with the parent and the access can come through such persons.

Parent visits to the classroom are particularly productive for staff-parent interaction. Apart from the consideration of time and place discussed above, it is important that parental expectations, parental input, teachers' expectations for the role of the parent and, in general, the responsibility of the school be considered in setting up parent visits. Frequently the use of an aide in a visit with parents is an effective means of releasing anxieties and linking the common interests of staff and parent. For all parent visits, whether they be on a one-to-one basis, small group or large, some formal or informal plan for the meeting is a must. In practice, this usually is an agenda for large-group sessions, but too often the content of a one-to-one encounter is left to chance. Finally, the parent and the staff member(s) should have the benefit of a two-way reaction session at the close of the visit.

Many of the same concerns as expressed for home and school visits also pertain to parent conferences. It is important to have an agenda, mutually agreed upon objectives, and an opportunity for two-way communication. In many cases the child may be present as an active participant in the conference. In this instance, more than any other, it is important that a previous positive interaction has already taken place. In some schools more than one staff member of the unit meets, in others only the "homeroom" teacher meets. Parents may have a preference in this regard since some may be ill at ease with more than one professional staff member present. The important thing is that the staff participant has comprehensive objectives and subjective information on the individual child and knows who the child is. Nothing is more destructive to the philosophy and practice of IGE than to have a staff member say, "I don't know anything about that. It is Mrs. Smith's area." A pointed parental query might be, "Then why isn't Mrs. Smith here?" The concern that "nobody knows anything about my child" should not be validated by the conference.

Many parents and teachers are apprehensive about conferences. An analysis of the neighborhood and previous communication either in large groups or by phone or written messages will add rapport to the conference as will concerns already mentioned such as privacy, candor, and a sensible choice of time and location. These are crucial to the improvement of instructional programming and the resolution of potential conflicts between the school and the home.

A fourth activity suggested is the use of parents or other citizens as volunteers in the instructional program. The activity can be passive in terms of having volunteers merely listen to children read, or active via participation in actual instruction of students. Volunteering, as an activity for interaction, is frequently met with fear and trepidation by both volunteers and teachers. Such fear is quite likely a function of the lack of previous interaction, a fear of the unknown, and a result of being placed in a highly vulnerable environment. However, once the decision is made to recruit parents and other citizens as volunteers, there are a few considerations. First, the volunteer is participating on the school's terms and is bound by the policies, objectives, and procedures set forth by the school. Second, volunteers should not be thrown into a situation they can't handle or asked to give more time than they have. It may take special effort, perhaps a schoolwide effort, to train volunteers to go from a more passive role to a more active one. Third, the purpose of an activity is not only to involve volunteers in routine tasks but also to make the role divergent enough to maintain volunteer interest. This suggests a carefully thought out inservice program for both volunteers and I & R Unit staff.

A fifth suggestion is to enlist parent involvement in meetings and activities of the I & R Unit or IIC, as casual observers or as permanent representatives. Their inputs can be a valuable source of information relative to the student population. Obviously some considerations regarding role expectations of parent participation must be clarified—particularly as it might involve the discussion of individual students.

Most of the suggestions and concerns above relate to the refinement of the staff-parent interaction. Implicit in the suggestions is the notion that if parents and other citizens become involved, children will benefit directly. A further implication is that, as a result of productive involvement, parents of children in IGE schools, parents of children in other schools, parents of preschool and post-elementary school children, and nonparents will perceive IGE as a viable program for the education of children and support its implementation.

Resolution

The fourth concept and competency is that of resolution. The processes of analysis, communication, and involvement are employed to bring about a resolution of the actual or potential conflict in allocating resources, choosing values, and distributing power. Thus resolution is the objective of an effective home-school-community relations program. There are several modes of resolution in a home-school-community relations program, and the practitioner requires judgment in knowing when to employ one or another mode of resolution and skill in implementing this judgment. The four modes of resolution are (1) rational decision process, (2) persuasion, (3) bargaining, and (4) power play (March and Simon 1963).

Rational decision process. Rational decision process is the process most described in administration textbooks as "decision making." Rational decision processes assume that the goals which participant subpublics have at stake are the *same*. In such instances, the participants can work together for the achievement of their common objectives. This form of resolution is most amenable to the usual committees and group processes as communications and involvement mechanisms.

Persuasion. Persuasion is used when the goals which participant subpublics have at issue are *different*—but the differences are *changeable*. That is to say, the participants enter into the process of resolution with differences, but the differences are not sufficiently intense or firmly held that evidence, argumentation, and rhetoric would not suffice to change the goals of one of the participants to coincide with the objectives of the other. In this instance, the participants employ both reason and emotion to alter the stakes of the other participant. When that is accomplished, the party which changed feels comfortable and adopts as his or her own the objectives of the other participant(s).

Bargaining. Bargaining is employed when the goals which participants have at issue are both *different* and *not changeable* but *negotiable.* Bargaining assumes that there will be no persuasion of either participant to the objectives of the other participant and that the parties can negotiate in order that one participant can gain one goal and lose another, and the other participant can gain or lose, too. Hence bargaining involves a *quid pro quo* where both parties gain, and both lose, but neither is brought to adopt the objectives of the other as in the case of persuasion. By contrast with rational decision processes and persuasion, bargaining is a conflict, not a consensus, mode of resolution. The stakes tend to be greater, risks to be greater, and, because an accommodation on common objectives cannot be reached, it will always be in the interest of the participants to seek new, more advantageous *quid pro quo*s as the participants self-interest would dictate and as available power will allow.

Power play. Power play is employed when the goals which participants have at issue are not only *different* but the goals are also *not changeable* and *not negotiable.* In a case where neither persuasion nor bargaining are useful means of resolution, one participant must prevail in the goal over the other participant due solely to a power advantage. Obviously, the use of power play does not necessitate a great deal of involvement—only a raw exercise of power. Power play results in a loser and a winner and considerable residual animosity on the part of the loser toward the winner, animosity which can always come back to disrupt the tranquillity of the system.

In the implementation of IGE, it is necessary to employ several modes of resolution of home-school-community relations problems. The art rests on the ability of the school staff to properly analyze the problems, communicate, involve, and utilize the best mode for resolution—the mode which provides the optimal outcome for the instructional programming for students. The skill rests with the staff's utilization of rational decision making, persuasion, bargaining, or power play techniques as the situation may dictate.

IMPLICATIONS OF THE HOME-SCHOOL-COMMUNITY RELATIONS MODEL FOR THE IPM

The Instructional Programming Model discussed in Chapter 1 assumes an understanding of the individual child which can only be gained through a comprehensive understanding of the home and community of the student population as they affect the individual student. One cannot, for example, "state the educational objectives to be attained by the student population . . ." or "assess the level of achievement, learning style, and motivation level of each student . . ." without an understanding of the home conditions. If, for another example, from the Instructional Programming Model (IPM), the decision was reached that "the objectives were not attained," what form would the reassessment of the student's characteristics take? If the home does not support the school program or if the teacher unknowingly transgresses cultural norms, will recycling in the same cognitive, affective, or psychomotor field be effective?

Figure 8.2 presents the major concepts of the Home-School-Community Relations Model in a functional flowchart and relates them to the IPM. The top row of rectangles is merely an abbreviated version of the primary interactors specified in Figure 8.1. A major assumption underlying this flowchart is that learning results should be increased if there is agreement among the major participants within the school community on the allocation of resources, choice of values and/or distribution of power regarding educational issues. A second assumption states that in instances where differences occur, where there is an accurate analysis of what those differences are, and where there is effective communication and involvement of the major participants, then conflict over instructional programming is likely to be resolved and learning results should be improved. Another assumption is that inaccurate analysis, inaccurate communication, and/or inappropriate involvement of the major participants will have an adverse effect upon the instructional program. Students will not get the requisite home and community support and the effect upon learning will be questionable.

COMMUNICATIONS AND INVOLVEMENT ACTIVITIES FOR UNIT LEADERS

This section explores exemplary activities which are aimed at improving home-school-community relations in IGE schools. These activities are principally those associated with better communications and effective involvement and are selected as cases or activities which are suitable for use by unit leaders. Some of the activities were identified in a series of case studies on home-school-community relations conducted by the Wisconsin Research and Development Center in Madison (Miles, *et al.* 1975). Others were contributed by principals, unit leaders, and teachers in IGE schools across the nation or have been employed by the authors in their work over the years with the home-school-community relations problems

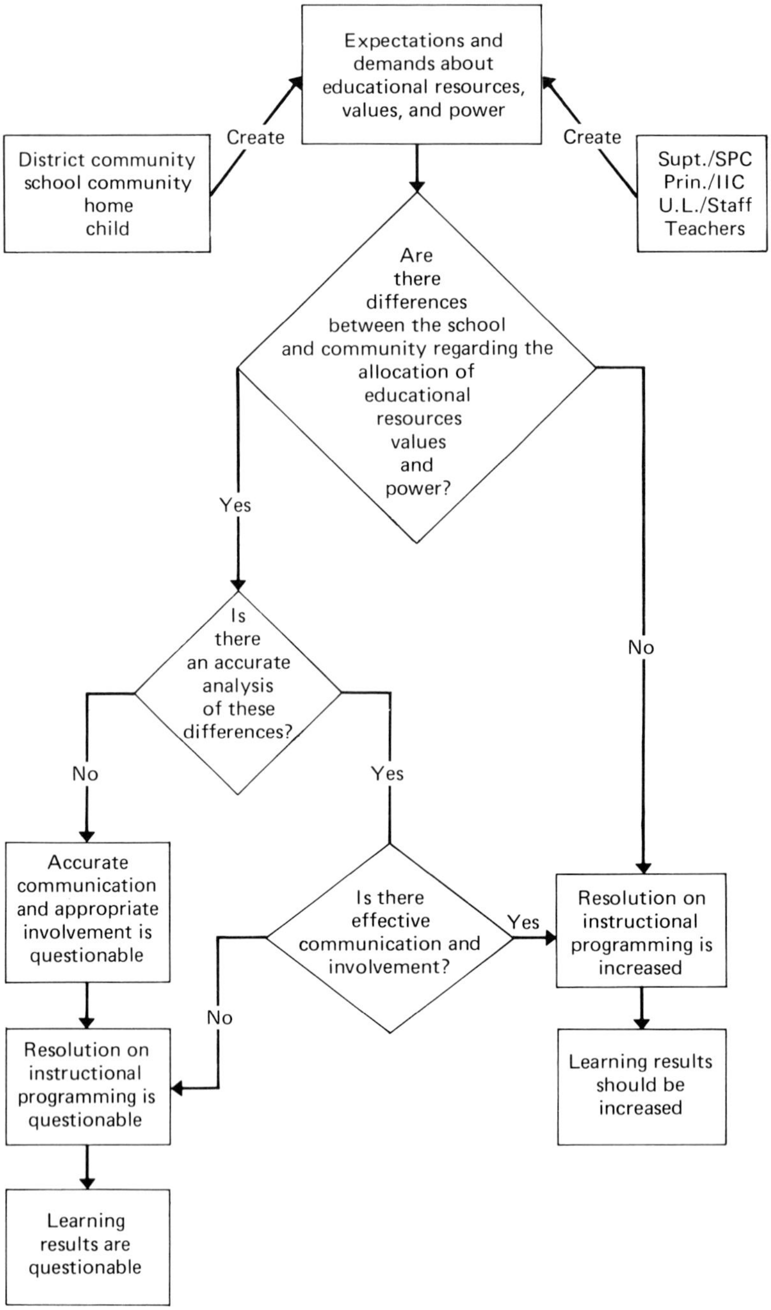

Fig. 8.2 Functional interactions between home-school-community relations and instructional programming.

of both IGE and non-IGE schools. Where an activity has been observed in an individual school, the school has been identified. This does not mean that the activity originated there, only that the authors or center staff observed it there.

Reporting Pupil Progress

Round-robin telephone calls. In addition to the periodical use of report cards and parent-teacher conferences, unit leaders in several IGE schools have assumed the responsibility of assuring telephone contact with the parents of at least two pupils each night by each unit teacher and leader between the opening of school and the first reporting period. If begun rather early in the school year, this system can ensure some contact with the parents of every child before the first customary six-week reporting period. Typically the calling is not done alphabetically but identifies pupils who have demonstrated positive behavior and performance. A teacher or unit leader just says, "I'll make the call to Julie's parents tonight; her work on the social studies project will make a good, positive entrée." Usually almost all of the pupils in an I & R Unit can be identified and associated with some positive behavior and performance and calls made that same night even if the telephone calls include nothing more than, "It certainly is a pleasure to have someone as enthusiastic as Larry in class this year." The calls average three to four minutes on the first contact, use the positive behavior and performance as an entrée, encourage parent involvement in unit activities and communication with the school, enumerate two or three instructional highlights during the first semester in which the parents might be interested, and generally keep the call on a brief, informative, two-way, positive note. This activity fullfills one of the home-school prerequisites for effective communications: make the first contact both positive and brief. The only administration required is a few minutes in a unit meeting to rehearse how the calls are to be made and what is to be said (and not said). Some encouragement is required to ensure that the calls are being timed so that they all are not made in the last week before the first reporting period. As teachers make the calls, they simply check the names off a pupil roster in the unit office, indicating the date and who made the call; during the last week and a half it is sometimes necessary to allocate the remaining 10 or 12 pupils to ensure that everyone will be contacted. There is nothing to prevent two calls to the same family, but one is the targeted objective. At least one more interim telephone contact per family is the unit objective between the sixth week report and the end of the semester and another contact during the second semester is also set as a goal. The typical telephone call format follows.

- introduction of caller
- reason that prompted the call (positive behavior or performance)
- invitation to visit class and/or unit teachers (best days and times)
- highlights of the first semester
- solicit questions and/or concerns of the parent

One final suggestion: it is sometimes wise to make the first positive contacts with the parents of children who one might anticipate to be behavioral or academic problems. This not only forces the unit staff to "discover" some positive behavior, but guarantees that the *first* contact with the family is positive. All in all, the round-robin telephone call system provides an added dimension to unit-and-home communications, reporting pupil progress, and home-school relations generally.

Parent-teacher-unit leader conferences. The use of the report card is typically coupled with the employment of a parent-teacher conference which is held in November, February, and April of each school year. The conferences follow a typical pattern in IGE schools: the total team provides input into the development of the material for the conference, and then the conference is conducted by one of the staff members. Some variations on this pattern among IGE schools and I & R Units may be of interest and value, however. Conferences have been conducted involving all members of the unit with the unit leader acting as a moderator. The pupil is sometimes included in the conferencing format; this, of course, does inhibit some communication but certainly encourages other types of communication and goes a long way to bring the child into the "mystique" of the conference.

One of the reported frustrations with multiunit schools and pupil reporting is that the teacher or unit leader reporting is not the teacher with whom the child is having difficulty academically or interpersonally or is not the person who has the information or expertise desired by the parent, often necessitating another trip for the "preliminaries." Unit leaders have overcome this in two ways in addition to the system of having the entire team involved in the conference: (1) the card or letter informing the parents of the conference requests that they indicate other teachers, the unit leader, reading specialist, etc., whom they would like to have participate in the conference. This allows for scheduling of the resource people requested and for increasing the time required for the conference depending on the numbers participating; and (2) the unit leader and staff anticipate the persons both they and the parents would like to have participate in the pupil reporting conference.

Finally, it has proven to be a good practice to allow for a "conference-in-the-home" option when scheduling pupil progress report periods. Again, the unit leader and staff could anticipate some parents having transportation problems or who might be inhibited in coming to school and, therefore, take the initiative in seeking a conference in the home. The card or letter sent home could include the conference in the home as an option to coming to school in words such as these: "While time will not permit the unit staff to meet with every family at home during the pupil progress reporting period, if you would prefer a conference in the home, please let us know, and we will contact you to establish a specific time." In Ravenswood, California, city schools, the pupil progress reporting period also serves as an excuse for a "conference in the home" at the initiative of the unit leader or teacher for the families of children who would benefit from a home visit in any event.

Introduction to IGE Concepts

Simulation activities to introduce parents to IGE concepts. One technique developed to get parents knowledgeable and actively involved in aspects of IGE is to involve them in simulation activities. These activities combine the processes of presenting information about IGE concepts with the actual participation of parents in simulation experiences. The simulations consist of a sequence of activities that provide small-group experiences for parents with concepts underlying the following IGE concepts and/or components:

- *Wisconsin Design for Reading Skill Development*
- Instructional Programming Model
- Multiunit School Organization and Operation
- *Individually Guided Motivation*
- *Developing Mathematical Processes*

The simulations are designed to provide the participant an IGE learning experience developed according to the steps of the Instructional Programming Model (IPM). Each module furnishes the participant with a sequence of activities based on the model that contribute to a knowledge of IGE concepts and an understanding of how the program can provide for the individually guided education of children. The simulation results not only in increased knowledge and understanding of IGE but (1) more effective two-way communication between parents and staff, (2) an increase in parental feedback of their values and interests in IGE implementation, and (3) an opportunity for both parents and staff to share the challenges of IGE.

Simulation modules are direct links between the general information activities of initial installation and the dynamic interaction between the parent-staff-community program of the refinement and renewal phases. Creative and well-planned use of simulation modules or other activities to involve parents and citizens can be a key not only to effective IGE installation within the school but to productivity in terms of changing negative or neutral parental attitudes toward innovation in general and IGE specifically (Moser, *et al.* 1975).

The "parent" information pamphlets. Unit leaders could identify a parent with some flair for writing and commission the translation of IGE "educationese" into "parent language." The key to this successful practice is to have pamphlets dealing with various IGE concepts and practices written by parents, for parents, and in parent language. One apparently successful use of this technique involves a parent writing a series of pamphlets dealing with the following topics:

"Many Years Ago!"
"How Come My Child Has So Many Teachers?"
"Why Do They Call Them Units?"
"Just How Do You Individualize?"
"But It's So Different!"
"Where Do I Come In?"

The format is quite simple, but effective. The pamphlets are approximately 8″ × 9″ and are folded to present a pamphlet of 4″ × 9″. The front cover has the topic title, an IGE logo, and a small title *A Parent Pamphlet—IGE*. The back cover introduces the parent, explains why the pamphlet is being written, is written in personal terms in the form of a letter, and is common to all the pamphlets. Inside is the heart and body of the message and is presented in 500 words or less (Murray undated).

Welcome-wagon committee. Another effective practice has been the formation of parent teacher organization welcome-wagon committees designed to introduce IGE concepts and practices to "new" parents in already established IGE schools. (While the practice has been noted in established IGE schools, there is nothing to prevent it from being used during the initial phases of implementation.) The welcome-wagon committees customarily take the IGE concepts and practices and translate them into parent language. The next step is to pay a home visit to those new to the school, community, or IGE and introduce "their" school to the parents (and children too). The new parents appreciate the thoughtful introduction and are made to feel welcome. Unit leaders and staff normally don't have to start at "ground zero" with the new parents during the first contacts or conferences. Finally, the Marion Emmons McKeown School in New Jersey found that the parent teacher organization and welcome-wagon committee help develop a feeling of having a greater stake in the IGE school as a result of their contributions.

Student-produced slide show. The unit leader and staff work with the students to prepare a slide-narrative show of their school, I & R Unit, and activities related to IGE concepts and practices. The key to the success of the slide show is that the content is taken from the perceptions of the children. Hence, the selected visual scenes and narrative should grow out of the experiences of the children and should not be dictated by either unit staff or parents. The Beattie Elementary School in Fort Collins, Colorado, found that the student-produced slide show can be used at parent teacher organization meetings, small group discussions, community panel presentations, and for introduction of IGE concepts and practices for visitors to the school, including parents and children who may be new to the school and/or to IGE.

Unit staff-produced videotapes. Along the line of the student-produced slide show is the development of a series of videotapes by the unit leader and staff which illustrates the various IGE concepts as practiced by that particular unit. For example, the videotapes could deal with the concept of "the I & R Unit" and then devote most of the tape to unit practices and activities. Similarly, other tapes could be devoted to the reading program or reporting pupil progress within the IGE framework. Such videotapes have been most successful when they have skillfully combined the idealized, abstract IGE concepts with current practices including both highlights and deficiencies. The videotape approach which was successfully used by Dickason Elementary School in Columbus, Wisconsin, also provides an opportunity to suggest possible changes or courses of action for future unit policies and practices—on a trial-balloon basis.

The Volunteer-aide Program

One distinction has to be made between the expectations of *parents with children in school* and others who participate in volunteer-aide programs whether paid or unpaid and whether full-time or part-time. Our research has shown that distinction to be that parents with children in school expect their job assignment and duties to place them in frequent interaction with the *teachers* of their children. Persons who did not have children in school held no such consistent and persistent expectations. Put another way, job satisfaction on the part of participant parents and overall success of the volunteer-aide program depended on parent contact with teachers far more than any other factor. As a footnote to this finding, it might also be of interest to the unit leader to know that many of those who volunteer in any of these capacities have internalized the norm that "It is the job of the teachers to teach without 'interference' from parents." The same parent volunteers viewed parent-initiated school visits and conferences as either "interference" or inadequate in frequency or quality of parent-teacher interaction. On the other hand, parent volunteer-aides have found volunter participation to be both a satisfactory and a legitimate means to the end of seeking frequent, quality interaction with the *teachers* of their children. The operational conclusion for unit leaders is simple: Parents with children in school require assignments which will afford interaction with the *teachers* of their children. The authors have attempted to bear this conclusion in mind when exploring the following cases and description of activities.

School-unit inventory of volunteer resources. Typically the inventory of potential volunteer resources is a schoolwide and parent-teacher organization function. A letter is sent home describing the nature of the volunteer program with a return card indicating how the parent could and would be willing to assist the school. Follow-up telephone calls are made by several schools to ensure and encourage a full response to the inquiry. An even more elaborate effort, and one which will attract a wide range of community resources, is to extend the invitation to *all* citizens in the community, including a systematic effort at soliciting senior citizens. IGE schools have certainly found that this course of action increases the range of experiences and resources available to them. The information is then put on key sort cards and turned over to unit staffs for their use. Teachers in Public School #27 in Paterson, New Jersey, found that unit leaders can solicit the necessary voluntary assistance ranging from well-trained persons who can and will assist with some instructional activities on a frequent basis to those who would provide one-time visits to the classroom to share their expertise or experience from an inventory list.

"Community teachers." The concept of "community teacher" has been successfully practiced in at least one school district much to the improvement of home-school-community relations and the increased effectiveness and implementation of IGE. The concept is very simple. The home-school-community is conceived of as a unitary, interactive, and cooperative entity; the school is not considered a separate entity from the community, and professional staff are considered as integral parts of the community fundamentally without the status differentials which are associated with other home-school-community relations problems. In fact, in one community, the home-school-community is officially and commonly termed a "family" by both staff, parents, and students. In this environment the parent volunteers (some paid, some not) are both customarily referred to and officially designated as "community teachers." Whatever status differential which might be associated with the words aide, volunteer, or paraprofessional is lost. The community teachers are, in fact, full participants in unit activities, meetings, and decisions. While they tend to function as traditional aides, their duties are expanded particularly in areas of (1) working with disruptive children on a one-to-one basis, (2) maintaining consistency and frequency of home-unit contacts, (3) fielding questions and working with parents on common inquiries and complaints, and (4) responsibility for recess, after-school, and weekend educational and recreational programs. The key prerequisites include, among others, (1) not being a professionally trained teacher, (2) living in the community, and (3) commitment to the goals of the educational program.

The "Community Teacher" program is especially effective in school communities where there are existing social, racial, or language barriers between the professional staff and community. The primary prerequisites for a successful "Community Teacher" program at Kavanaugh Elementary School, East Palo Alto, California, include (1) a genuine adoption of a sense of community and the abandonment of social and professional status distinctions between unit staff and community, (2) full integration of the community teacher into unit activities, (3) selection of community teachers who are indigenous to the community and who are not unique to the community by either education or training, and (4) the provision of appropriate inservice training and/or orientation to the functioning of the unit.

I & R Unit Meetings with Parents

Having I & R Unit meetings with parents has proven to be a successful home-school-community relations practice. Within the school each unit leader is given responsibility for coordinating the parent-unit meetings during the course of the school year, including the development of a set of activities for the initial meetings. The parent-unit meetings are held on different nights each month so that conflicts are minimized and all parents can attend several of the joint meetings. Typically the initial meeting in September is informational; staff and parents meet in small groups for question-and-answer sessions. The September meeting concludes by having something of an agenda established for the subsequent meeting and a tentative plan for the meetings for the remainder of the year. Each unit can function relatively independently of other units: some operate on a question-and-answer plan all year; others work with smaller groups of parents more infrequently yet more intensively. One unit in Beattie Elementary School, Fort Collins, Colorado, operated the program for the first five weeks and then began the regular conferencing; the same unit then only had three periodical meetings for the remainder of the year with the final meeting with the parents of children who would be in the unit the following year.

SUMMARY

This chapter has identified the goals of the home-school-community relations program as those which make the staff of an IGE school more aware and effective in its work with the school community, make the community more aware and effective in its work with the school, and has identified ways and means of encouraging the implementation of IGE by involving both staff and community. To this end the authors have set forth several operational assumptions about home-school-community relations, including the assumption that home-school-community relations are, in the last analysis, a political process operating within a complex social system of home, school and community, and that the objective of any home-school-community relations program is the resolution of actual or potential conflict over the allocation of scarce resources, differing values, and unequal authority and power.

The authors then set forth a two-part model of home-school-community relations: (1) Primary Interaction Patterns in the Home-School-Community, and (2) Concepts and Competencies. The former included primary interactions as those between school community and principal/IIC, home and unit leader/unit staff, and student and teacher(s); the latter included a discussion of the following concepts and competencies: analysis, communication, involvement, and resolution. The implications of the home-school-community relations model for the instructional program was explored briefly.

Finally, communications and involvement activities for I & R Units were documented including several dealing with reporting pupil progress, introducing IGE concepts, the volunteer-aide program, and joint parent-unit meetings. Of course, the latter was not exhaustive of either all desirable activities or all successful activities.

REFERENCES

Dahl, R. A. 1966. *Who governs? Democracy and power in an American city.* New Haven: Yale University Press.

Delbecq, A. L., and A. Van de Ven 1971. "A group process model for problem identification and program planning," *Journal of Applied Behavioral Science* **7:** 466–491.

Hunter, F. 1953. *Community power structure: a study of decision makers.* Chapel Hill, N.C.: University of North Carolina Press.

Lipham, J. M., and M. J. Fruth 1976. *The principal and individually guided education.* Reading, Massachusetts: Addison-Wesley.

March, J. S., and H. Simon 1963. *Organizations.* New York: Wiley.

Miles, W. R., B. D. Bowles, and M. J. Fruth 1975. *Casebook on home-school-community relations programs and activities and the implementation of IGE.* Madison, Wisc.: Wisconsin Research and Development Center for Cognitive Learning.

Moser, R. H., M. J. Fruth, and W. Klenke 1975. *Simformation: introducing parents to the Wisconsin reading design.* Madison, Wisc.: Wisconsin Research and Development Center for Cognitive Learning.

Murray, A. undated. *Parent Pamphlets: IGE.* Chelmsford, Massachusetts: Merrimack Education Center.

Thiemann, F. C., and C. S. Bumbarger 1971. One-way and two-way communication exercise book. In ERNSTSPIEL, *CASEA's task group development series,* Eugene, Ore.: University of Oregon.

9

Preparing for and Keeping Current in the Unit Leader Role

Max Poole
Juanita S. Sorenson

Objectives

After reading this chapter, the reader will be able:

- To describe the needs of the unit leader and staff teacher as they assume their new roles.
- To identify ways prospective and present unit leaders can prepare for and keep current in the role in each of the five phases of IGE implementation: (a) awareness, (b) commitment, (c) changeover, (d) refinement, and (e) renewal.
- To identify agencies that can help the unit leader in the preceding objective.
- To describe briefly the content of IGE programs at college/universities in the renewal phase of IGE.

The purpose of this chapter is to describe alternative ways in which a person can prepare for and keep current in the role of unit leader. Topics include a review of the needs of the unit leader followed by a description with illustrations of how successful unit leaders in smoothly functioning IGE schools have prepared for and kept current in the role.

NEEDS OF UNIT LEADERS

The responsibilities, opportunities, and requirements of the unit leader have been described in detail in Chapters 2 through 8. They are reviewed here briefly in the context of the topic of this chapter.

As stated earlier, the great majority of elementary teachers have not been trained for the unit leader role. Their formal college training, graduate and undergraduate, and experience through years of teaching have focused on teaching children. While the skills for teaching children remain very important, the unit leader role requires many other skills if the IGE program is to succeed and the persons who assume the role are to be happy in it.

In this changed role, the unit leader becomes a "teacher of adults" as well as of children. This skill is involved almost immediately when the unit leaders, together with the principal, take responsibility for the inservice workshop for the entire staff prior to implementing IGE. Here they teach their fellow staff members content and procedures that they themselves have learned at a workshop a few weeks or months earlier. Developing techniques, organizing a program, and evaluating their own success in teaching adults is a complete change for most teachers. Probably their greatest experience for this part of the role comes from social or professional groups in which they have held leadership positions, not from teaching.

As leader of the unit team, the unit leader needs skills to help people function together constructively and to accomplish their goals. Leadership skills are needed in the areas of both human relations and instruction. This is a position of leading peers with similar educational backgrounds and salaries. The unit leader must be prepared to face the reality of problems involved in this kind of leadership.

The unit leader as a member of an IIC becomes a decision maker and two-way communicator. Decisions are made for the entire school building as opposed to 25-30 children in a traditional classroom. Traditionally, many decisions were made by the principal or central office and were handed down. In an IGE school, the IIC and I & R Unit staffs make many decisions. These include input on the hiring of new staff members and identifying objectives for the instructional program.

The next section of this chapter will deal with helping people who have the appropriate background and desire to prepare and continue to function successfully in the role of unit leader.

WAYS TO PREPARE FOR AND KEEP CURRENT IN THE ROLE

Since the inception of IGE, the Wisconsin Research and Development Center has been involved in suggesting ways for unit leaders, staff teachers, principals, and other public school personnel to prepare for and keep up to date in their roles. For example, the state networks (Figure 1.4) and the Association for Individually Guided Education (AIGE) which were described in Chapter 1, were developed to help implement and refine IGE. The Research and Development Center implementation model includes five phases of activities (Walter, *et al.* 1975):

1. Awareness
2. Commitment
3. Changeover
4. Refinement
5. Renewal

Activities in each of these phases will be described here primarily as they relate to present and prospective unit leaders. This includes (1) primary purposes of the activities, (2) sequential time in which they occur, (3) agencies involved in carrying out the activities, (4) examples of what happens during the activities, and (5) how activities in one category relate to those in other categories.

A time line indicating suggested progression of the five phases is presented in Figure 9.1.

Awareness Phase

The purpose of this phase is to acquaint school personnel with IGE and to provide enough information to decide whether or not they want to adopt it. Awareness activities include a one-day conference and visits by teachers and other school personnel to smoothly functioning IGE schools.

The primary purpose of the awareness conference is to give district decision makers enough information to tell others about the opportunities IGE offers for children and the changes it will involve in the school and district functions. It also tells the requirements of school district commitment and opportunities for inservice education to make the changeover to IGE. It is particularly important that teachers who are leaders, and therefore prospective unit leaders, attend this conference since they form a

Phase	Months elapsed	Activities
AWARENESS	0	One-day awareness conference (central office personnel, principals, prospective unit leaders)
	1-6	Visits to IGE schools (central office personnel, principals, prospective unit leaders)
		Meetings within school district for decision makers to share IGE information (teachers, principals, unit leaders, central office personnel, Board of Education, parents, community representatives)
COMMITMENT	2-6	Decision to implement IGE (school district decision makers)
		Commitment to implement IGE (central office personnel, staffs of potential IGE schools, parents, Board of Education)
CHANGEOVER	3-12	3 to 5-day principal and unit leader workshop (PUL) (principals, prospective or designated unit leaders)
	6-18	3 to 5-day all-staff workshop (total staff of school(s) committed to IGE)
	4-20	Four half-days of buildingwide inservice (total staff of school(s) committed to IGE)
REFINEMENT	Ongoing	Institutes Conferences League support School visits Inservice programs
RENEWAL	Ongoing	Expanded network activities Continual inservice University courses Masters and Doctoral programs

Fig. 9.1 Implementation time line.

communication link between the staff teachers and the principal and central office personnel. The state education agency personnel usually take initiative for organizing this conference. A prototypic agenda for a one-day awareness conference* follows:

The objective of the one-day workshop is to develop within building administrators and central office personnel an awareness of the IGE concept. This conference should provide enough information for the participants to explain IGE to their building and district staffs.

9:30-10:15 A.M.	Greetings, history and rationale of the Research and Development Center/implementation agency effort Discussion of workshop objectives Overview of IGE. Film: *The Teacher in Individually Guided Education* Seven components of IGE
10:15-10:30	Break
10:30-11:00	The prototypic multiunit organization Systemwide Policy Committee (SPC) Instructional Improvement Committee (IIC) Instruction and Research Unit (I & R Unit)
11:00-11:30	The Instructional Programming Model (IPM) for the individual student
11:30-12:00	Instructional programs and curriculum materials compatible with the Instructional Programming Model; e.g., the *Wisconsin Design for Reading Skill Development*
12:00- 1:15 P.M.	Lunch
1:15- 2:00	An IGE Principal presents: "Through the Eyes of the Principal"
2:00- 2:45	A Unit Leader presents: "The Role of the Unit Leader—The Team Approach"
2:45- 3:00	Break
3:00- 3:30	Question-and-answer session: "Where Do We Go from Here?"

The second awareness activity is visiting smoothly functioning schools in the region and/or state or nearby states. A team, or if possible, several teams of three to five people (including prospective unit leaders, the principal, and central office personnel) should participate in the visits. Such

* Adapted from Klausmeier, Walter, and Lins 1974, p. 87.

visits can be arranged through the state coordinator or personnel from regional educational agencies.

Visits can be initiated by teachers, the principal, or central office personnel but need approval by appropriate system administrators. Visitations allow school personnel to see "IGE in action" and to enter into a two-way communication with their appropriate counterparts. Many important questions concerning the decision to adopt IGE can be answered through these visitations. Perhaps the most important value of visitations is that school personnel can see how elementary students react to the IGE program.

These visits are particularly important to prospective or designated unit leaders. Since this is a new role, most teachers have never known a unit leader and their only source of meaningful answers to questions about it is a practicing unit leader. Visits to two smoothly functioning IGE schools, at least one with characteristics similar to the home school of the visitor, are recommended for prospective unit leaders.

Staff members considering IGE should prepare for the visits by meeting together and preparing a checklist of observations to make and questions to ask. They should also read and/or view materials which present an overview of the IGE concept. These materials are available from the office of the state coordinator or regional education agency. Following the visits, the group should meet again to share their observations and other information gathered. Material from visits should be collected together and made available to all people involved in the decision of changing to IGE, particularly teachers or other staff who did not participate in the visits.

Commitment Phase

Commitment activities begin with sharing information from the awareness conference and school visits with teachers, principals, central office personnel, Board of Education members, parents and community representatives. The information could be shared through meetings such as:

1. faculty meetings for one or more buildings to inform the total staff(s).
2. a special meeting of the Board of Education and central office personnel.
3. a PTA or community meeting which includes interested parents and community representatives.

The presentations at these meetings are made by a team of people who attended the awareness conference and visited IGE schools. A film and other materials for the presentation can be borrowed from the state or regional education agency. These meetings would last about one hour with opportunity for discussion.

Following these meetings, school district decision makers must compile and weigh the information about and implications of implementing IGE. If they decide they want to implement IGE in a school or schools, they must secure the necessary commitments from the system central office staffs of potential IGE schools, teacher, parent and community groups, and the Board of Education. Once this commitment is obtained, the district normally enters into an agreement with an implementation agency (e.g., the state or regional education agency).

Prospective or designated unit leaders should attend both the awareness conference and the IGE school visitations. It is important they understand the IGE concept and the duties of the unit leader before they accept the responsibility of the role.

Awareness and commitment activities should occur 3 to 12 months before the program is implemented.

Changeover Phase

These activities include a minimum of (1) a 3- to 5-day workshop for the principal and unit leaders during the semester prior to implementation; (2) a 3- to 5-day workshop for all staff of a school building before implementation; and (3) four half-day workshops during the first year (e.g., one-half day in October, January, February, April, respectively) (Klausmeier, Walter, and Lins 1974, pp. 50-51).

Principal-unit leader workshop (PUL). This 3- to 5-day workshop is designed for principals and prospective or designated unit leaders from schools that have made the decision to implement IGE. It should occur from three to six months before actual implementation occurs. This workshop is usually conducted by state or regional education agency personnel along with persons from teacher education institutions and experienced unit leaders and principals. A prototypic agenda for a Principal/Unit Leader Workshop follows:

Prototypic Agenda for a 3- to 5-day Principals and Prospective Unit Leaders (PUL) Workshop*

Session I	Overview and workshop objectives
	Origin of IGE
	Report of IGE national implementation
	Film: *The Teacher in Individually Guided Education*
	Seven components of IGE

* Adapted from Klausmeier, Walter, and Lins 1974, p. 88.

Session II	Workshop objectives and IGE: A simulation	
	Phase 1:	Preassessment
	Phase 2:	Instructional sessions: Instructional programming in IGE Roles and responsibilities The multiunit school—its organization and operations Grouping patterns Instructional objectives Assessment in IGE Independent activity
	Phase 3:	Summary and evaluation of the day's activities
Session III	Phase 1:	Overview of Session III
	Phase 2:	Problem identification process
	Phase 3:	Instructional sessions: Use of auxiliary and special area personnel Grouping students for instruction Logistics of implementation—organization of instructional materials Logistics of implementation—curriculum, staff, and pupil scheduling Managing pupil progress—record keeping Reporting pupil progress Impact of teaming Open discussion session on topics such as: Selecting an IGE curricular area Establishment of visiting and visitation policies
	Phase 4:	Curriculum products
Sessions IV & V	Phase 1:	Overview and objectives of IIC tasks
	Phase 2:	The IIC from each school works to accomplish the following: a. a possible multiunit organizational design for their school. b. the proposed curricular area for which the Instructional Programming Model will be applied. c. identification of ways in which IGE performance objectives will be utilized in planning and evaluation d. the proposed roles and responsibilities for the various staff positions.

e. a tentative staff inservice program.
f. suggested ways of obtaining three to five hours of planning time for each unit.
g. plans for utilization of space in the building.
h. plans to obtain professional assistance on a paid basis, and/or alternative plans to obtain paraprofessional assistance if not available on a paid basis.
i. time line of first year changeover to IGE.

Session VI Workshop evaluation

The objectives of this workshop are to provide participants with instruction on IGE concepts and practices so they will be able:

1. to describe the multiunit organizational structure (MUS).
2. to identify the roles of the differentiated personnel in the IGE school.
3. to describe and explain the purpose and sequential steps of the Instructional Programming Model (IPM).
4. to develop procedures and a time line to install IGE in their building.
5. to conduct inservice programs on IGE for the entire building staff.

At this workshop, unit leaders and principals are preassessed about their knowledge of IGE. After the topics on which they need further instruction are identified, participants select the materials, grouping arrangements and procedures which are most suitable for their needs. About half of the workshop time is spent in studying basic IGE concepts.

The second half of the workshop is devoted to actual IIC meetings. This is the point at which the IIC begins planning for its changeover to IGE.

Planning must occur for curriculum, staff deployment, space and time utilization as well as for inservice programs for the entire building staff. During the workshop the IIC should strive:

- to develop two or three alternative designs for organizing all children in the school (K–6) into multiage units.
- to evaluate each design considering staff in terms of subject matter strengths, teaching style, and special talents, and also in terms of experienced teachers, first-year teachers, and aides or instructional secretaries.
- to choose the most appropriate design.
- to begin assigning staff to units.

- to arrange daily and weekly schedules to allow planning time for unit and IIC meetings during the school day.
- to evaluate present utilization of space in the building and assign space to each unit.
- to discuss ways in which IGE performance objectives will be utilized in planning and self-evaluation.
- to decide on the curriculum area(s) in which instructional programming for individual students will be developed during the first year or two.
- to write a role description for each type of differentiated staff position.
- to prepare a draft of 3- to 5-day inservice program they will conduct with the entire staff prior to implementation of IGE in the building.

All-staff workshop. After the PUL workshop, it is the responsibility of the unit leaders and principal to conduct the 3- to 5-day workshop for the staff of their building. This should take place soon after the PUL workshop and at least two months before implementation of IGE. The content for this workshop is drawn from the PUL and focuses on the basic content and procedures of IGE. Content areas include the multiunit organization, instructional programming, roles and responsibilities of the differentiated staff, grouping patterns, assessment in IGE, and instructional objectives. Procedures include use of auxiliary and special area personnel, grouping students for instruction, scheduling, organizing instructional materials into a resource file, record keeping, reporting pupil progress, and team-building skills.

The workshop program should provide time for each I & R Unit team to work together. At this time, the unit leader assumes the responsibility for guiding the I & R Unit. A prototypic agenda for an all staff workshop follows:

Prototypic Agenda for a Three- to Five-Day All-Staff Workshop

Session I	Same as Principal-Unit Leader (PUL) Workshop	
Session II	Same as PUL	
Session III	Same as PUL	
Session IV	Phase 1:	*Schoolwide meeting:* Overview of I & R Unit responsibilities Discussion of curricular area for instructional programming for individual students according to the IPM Identification of minimum schoolwide objectives for this area

	Phase 2:	*Meetings of each I & R Unit:*
		Identify instructional objectives for children in the unit in curricular area selected for instructional programming
		Inventory materials which will be available for instructional programming in selected curricular areas
		Develop resource files for some of the objectives
Session V	Phase 1:	*Schoolwide meeting:*
		Identification of space allocations for each unit
		Guidelines for assignment of students to I & R Units
	Phase 2:	*I & R Unit meetings:*
		Team-building skills
		Assessment of staff strengths
		Identify assessment instruments or activities for curricular area selected for instructional programming
	Phase 3:	*Schoolwide meetings:*
		Evaluation of workshop: "Where Do We Go from Here?"

One of the most important considerations for the unit staff at this workshop is developing instructional programming according to the model in the curriculum area selected by the IIC. For example, if reading skills have been selected, the primary I & R Unit will probably focus initially on Word Attack skills and the intermediate unit on Study skills or Comprehension skills. Several sessions of this workshop should then be devoted to helping staff members become acquainted with or to develop materials related to these areas. If the *Wisconsin Design for Reading Skill Development* (WDRSD) is used, inservice training materials are available for these workshop sessions. If the IIC has chosen a curriculum area for which adequate instructional materials but not inservice materials are available, the inservice sessions must be designed to accommodate this changeover from traditional instruction to instructional programming for IGE. Teachers must be thoroughly acquainted with materials and their planned uses before utilizing them in the instructional process.

Careful preparation should go into the inservice workshop to ensure its success. If the rest of the staff recognizes that their unit leaders and principal are well prepared for IGE and will be able to help them when problems arise, the building will be off to a good start. Unit leaders should evaluate themselves and ask others to evaluate their part in this workshop. As indicated earlier, this workshop will be the first time many unit leaders have taken the role of "teachers of adults." This is a difficult role and one for which they need to be well prepared. If possible, personnel from the local IGE league, state or regional education agency and/or teacher education institution should be involved where appropriate in this workshop.

Four half-days of buildingwide inservice. It is desirable to schedule these sessions to extend over a period of four months to a year, within the limits of the time line for changeover to IGE. These sessions should be planned by the IIC and include those areas which are of particular concern to the building staff. Topics might include the curriculum area selected for instructional programming, skills for building and functioning as a team, or development of needed instructional materials.

The IIC can request help from staff members, experienced IGE personnel, representatives of state or regional agencies and teacher educators for direction at these sessions. The quality and reception of inservice during the first year affects the attitude of the entire staff for the future. The better these sessions are, the more likely the staff will view inservice as an ongoing part of IGE.

The agencies within the state and regional networks provide a vehicle for ongoing inservice. If a school is in an area where a local league of IGE schools is established, the members of this league are its best source of help. If a school or several schools are starting IGE in an area where there is no league, they will have to get help from the regional or state agencies.

Refinement Phase

Continuing refinement of concepts and practices is required for a school to keep an IGE program alive and growing. Activities in this phase focus on substantive concerns—cognitive, affective, psychomotor—which often require learning of new skills and knowledge. Refinement programs should be planned to make it possible for every staff member in an IGE school to attend at least two activities each year. School staffs can participate in the refinement phase in a number of ways, and several of these are discussed below.

Institutes. One way is through short-term, intensive institutes that run from one to four weeks. Such an institute might be held during summer or during the school year in afterschool and/or evening sessions. The institute may be offered with or without college credit. Content of the institute focuses on problems encountered in IGE schools, and is conducted primarily for experienced IGE personnel including unit leaders, staff teachers, and principals. However, staff members of schools contemplating the change to IGE during the following year may sometimes enroll in this kind of institute.

An institute might be coordinated by personnel from a local league, a regional agency, or a teacher education institution. The staff should include a variety of personnel such as outstanding practitioners from IGE schools, state and regional IGE personnel, and teacher educators. The impetus to set up such an institute can be initiated by the school staffs or any of the agencies mentioned here.

A sample outline for a one-week advanced leadership institute for unit leaders* follows:

Prototype Agenda for Advanced Leadership Institute

Monday	9:00-10:30 A.M.	Introduction to the institute Preassessment
	10:30-12:00	The multiunit school and its organization
	1:00- 2:00 P.M.	The preparation of instructional objectives
	2:00- 5:00	IGE
Tuesday	9:00- 9:30 A.M.	Question and discussion session; designation of small groups for work in IGE by area
	9:30-12:00	IGE—small group sessions
	1:00- 4:30 P.M.	IGE—small group sessions
	4:30- 5:00	Large group feedback session
Wednesday	9:00-10:30 A.M.	Presentation of supplementary curriculum products available from the state department of education
	10:30-12:00	IGE—small group sessions
	1:00- 2:15 P.M.	Evaluation, research, and development in the multiunit school
	2:15- 4:30	IGE—small group sessions
	4:30- 5:00	Large group feedback session
Thursday	9:00-10:00 A.M.	Inservice programs for the multiunit school at the school level
	10:00-12:00	IGE—small group sessions
	1:00- 4:30 P.M.	IGE—small group sessions
	4:30- 5:00	Large group—questions and discussion of inservice programs

* Klausmeier, Walter, and Lins 1974, p. 97.

Friday	9:00-10:00 A.M.	Simulated IIC operation (conducted by staff and selected participants)
	10:00-12:00	IGE—small group sessions
	1:00- 3:00 P.M.	Discussion of postinstitute activity Postassessment Evaluation of institute (written) Critique of institute (oral)

This institute is designed to provide in-depth, concentrated instruction for experienced IGE personnel. The content of this outline could be arranged in various ways and could be given during a quarter, semester, or even a year rather than during one week if the school so desired. Institutes for principals and other IGE personnel can follow a similar format. Institutes should provide for variation in the type of schools involved in the training, and emphasize needs appropriate to the group for which they are intended. Also, allowance should be made for the amount of experience of the group as a whole. For example, if most of the group is relatively inexperienced (e.g., 1-2 years in IGE), the institute program should probably spend more time on basic information about the seven components of IGE and strategies to implement them. If the group has more than two years experience in IGE, interest may focus on implementing instructional programming in additional curricular areas, schoolwide evaluation of the IGE program, or leadership strategies.

The content of the institute outlined above focuses on problems related to the multiunit component of IGE. Other institutes might be concerned with various aspects of instructional programming for individual students, evaluation and assessment, home-school-community relations, motivation or values education, decision-making processes or areas of interest and need.

The following guidelines are suggested for planning such an institute (Klausmeier, Walter, and Lins 1974, p. 53):

1. Prepare the rationale and broad purpose for the institute.
2. Identify the target audience and specify eligibility and selection criteria.
3. Prepare a brief statement of any participant commitments prior to the institute, if there are some to be made (e.g., study to be completed, purchases to be made, or problems to be identified).
4. Formulate objectives of the institute in terms of the expected behaviors of the participants upon completing the workshop.
5. Prepare a detailed schedule of activities.
6. Inform the participants of postinstitute commitments (e.g., follow-up reports), if any, to be made.

7. Determine in advance the methods and processes to be used during the institute through consulting with participants and experienced institute leaders.
8. Identify the staff for the institute, including consultants and local personnel.
9. Prepare the assessment and evaluation instruments and procedures in advance, but be ready to improvise and revise.
10. Attend carefully to logistical concerns and housekeeping details, such as checking all spaces and equipment before their actual use, collecting monies and issuing receipts, and having supplies and materials in readiness.

Conferences. Another way to keep up to date in IGE is to attend a drive-in conference. This is one-half day or one day in length and can be sponsored by a local league, regional implementation agency, or teacher education institution. The conference offers an opportunity to combine the expertise of practitioners and others knowledgeable in IGE (e.g., state or regional facilitators, experienced practitioners, teacher educators) into one program.

Drive-in conferences might be scheduled once or twice a semester. This frequency allows input from teachers in IGE schools so that urgent topics can be included in the program. Drive-ins can vary. They might have a theme of language arts, instructional games, or social studies, with the featured speaker and smaller interaction sessions dealing with the theme. Another conference plan would have a variety of topics dealing with several cognitive, affective, and psychomotor areas. An agenda for a half-day drive-in conference focusing on the theme of language arts follows:

Fourth Semiannual Drive-in Conference Agenda
Saturday, April 3, 1976—Student Union, University of Wisconsin—Eau Claire

8:00 A.M.	Registration, coffee and conversation
9:00	Overview of conference—Davies Theater
9:15	Individualizing the Language Arts for Elementary Children Professor, University of Minnesota, School of Education
10:15	Coffeebreak—Skylite Lounge

10:30 *Concurrent Sessions*

Creative Writing for 10- to 12-year-olds
  Teacher, Mt. Washington Elementary, Eau Claire

Individualized Language Arts for 9- to 12-year-olds

11:30 *Concurrent Sessions*

The Administrator's Role in the IGE League
  Graduate Student, University of Wisconsin—Madison

Individualized Spelling
  Teacher, St. Olaf, Eau Claire

Fourth Semiannual Drive-in Conference Agenda (Cont.)

Unit Leader, Roosevelt Elementary, Eau Claire	
Incorporating Special Ed Children in the Units in the IGE School Spec. Ed. Director, Minn. Valley Coop., Waconia, Minn.	Using Children's Literature in the Language Arts Program Principal, Cherry Knoll Elementary, Traverse City, Minn.
Using Magazines in the Learning Program Teacher, Lexington Elementary, Eau Claire	Same as 10:30 session
Language Arts and the Gifted, Grades 1–6 Professor, UW-EC with student teachers	Same as 10:30 session
Small Group Work for 5- and 6-year-olds Teacher, Jim Falls Elementary, Jim Falls, Wisc.	Same as 10:30 session
Individualizing Language Arts, 11- to 14-year-olds Teacher, St. Charles Jr. High (Gr. 6–8), Chippewa Falls, Wisc.	

It should be noted, however, that two additional topics of urgent concern in regional schools were included on the agenda, even though they were not in the area of language arts. These dealt with special education and the role of the administrator in the IGE league. This conference included teachers, unit leaders, principals, and teacher educators as resource persons.

Information about these conferences is usually circulated to all elementary schools within driving distance of the conference location. Central office personnel, principals, unit leaders, and staff teachers are encouraged to attend. A small registration fee may be charged to cover the expenses of resource people. School districts will often pay this fee for personnel that attend. These conferences are often held on Saturday and thus allow any interested person to attend without involving special release time or substitute pay. This kind of conference also appeals to teachers who have an interest in individualizing instruction, but are not yet in IGE.

Other conferences that help unit leaders and teachers prepare and keep up to date in their roles are sponsored by groups of individuals who have specific or general topic conferences on IGE. Sponsors include /I/D/E/A/ of the Kettering Foundation which has worked with IGE since 1970 and other regional and state groups.

League support. One of the most available agencies to help unit leaders and teachers is the local league. While a league might sponsor implementation activities as the PUL conference just described, its greatest responsibility lies in the area of maintenance and refinement. As the number of IGE schools in a region grows, it becomes almost impossible for any one individual (be it a league facilitator or state coordinator) to provide direct assistance in the identification and solution of problems, concerns, inservice needs, development of learning programs, and community relationships. Thus, the league directs its efforts to the development of effective leadership and continuous improvement programs within its member schools.

One of the major goals of IGE is to help students become more self-directed in their learning—to help them to learn how to learn. The same could be said for the member schools of the league. The league must help each of the schools, in a sense, to learn how to learn, to acquire the skills necessary to deal effectively with their own problems and to create their own changes. This improvement process for each school is described as a systematic procedure for discussing and diagnosing its own problems, formulating solutions, taking action on recommended solutions, and then trying to obtain evidence about the effects of such action (Institute for the Development of Educational Activities 1973). The abilities of unit leaders and principals in providing leadership to help their schools carry out this process are directly related to the success of their IGE programs. This responsibility starts when the IIC is formed and continues as long as the school is conducting an IGE program. Unit leaders and staff teachers need continued help to (1) improve their existing skills and add new ones as the needs of the unit and building change, and to (2) train unit leaders and teachers who assume the roles after the initial implementation period.

Many leagues sponsor one- or two-day workshops either for unit leaders or principals or for the IICs of the building. This has been a common practice in southwest Minnesota where a series of one-day workshops have been held over the past several years. Some of the topics they have discussed include:

- leadership assessment
- improving schoolwide communication
- developing ongoing inservice programs

- building a philosophy and program goals
- techniques for identifying and solving problems
- the role of the unit leader: a perspective
- small group-sharing sessions
- opportunities in graduate education related to IGE

As suggested earlier, active leagues might also sponsor three-day or one-week institutes for unit leaders and principals. One advantage of a league sponsoring a workshop is that the greatest input into the agenda comes from the people most involved—unit leaders and principals in the area in which the workshop will be held. This ensures that the subjects of the workshop are relevant to the problems of the personnel who will attend.

School visits. Visiting schools that have successfully implemented various aspects of IGE is an effective way to help staff keep up to date and to learn more about IGE. Visitors can seek new ideas and suggestions on any areas, (e.g., team-building skills, objectives, scheduling, student goal setting in content areas, planning strategies) in which they wish to improve. Visitations also give staff members an opportunity to evaluate their own schools more objectively as they interact with the staff of the other school and see the program in operation.

Arrangements for visits can be made through the league, by a district, by central office persons or, in some cases, by staff members themselves.

Inservice programs. Systemwide, buildingwide or unit inservice sessions can be devoted to topics that help IGE staff meet an identified need in their ongoing program or to inform them of new materials, procedures, and skills that will benefit them in their program implementation. Utilization of already budgeted inservice time to improve the IGE program can take the form of a single session or the entire inservice program for a year or two depending on the need and depth of the topics identified. These sessions need to be worked out cooperatively between the staff of a building and central office personnel. In a system where there are several schools, this could be handled through the Systemwide Program Committee (SPC).

Renewal Phase

The fifth phase, renewal, is an extension of the refinement phase. It is concerned with the development of networks to support IGE schools. During the renewal phase individual schools, educational agencies, and teacher education institutions meet the following objectives: (1) to identify and resolve unanticipated problems, (2) to develop improved ways of implementing the concept of IGE, and (3) to prepare successive generations of personnel to assume roles in the various agencies (Walter, *et al.* 1975).

Fulfilling the third objective, that of the preparation of personnel for IGE roles, is mainly the responsibility of colleges and universities. This may occur at the undergraduate or graduate levels or both and involves the design and development of courses to provide an in-depth study of the IGE concept. Since this book is concerned with the unit leader role, only programs at the graduate level will be discussed. The reader is referred to Klausmeier, Walter, and Lins (1974) for a description of undergraduate programs in IGE.

University programs at the graduate level offer unit leaders and staff teachers opportunity for in-depth training in the components and processes of IGE. In addition, they can gain expertise in such related areas as learning theory, measurement and evaluation, human relations, educational administration, or specific curriculum areas as they have need and/or interest.

The following section deals with descriptions of two programs that have been in operation for five or more years. The universities that offer these programs differ in location, student characteristics, and needs. In addition, these two universities have different missions in the educational process. At both universities, unit leaders or teachers may take the IGE program as a major or emphasis, as a portion of a masters or other degree in a department such as Elementary Education or Curriculum and Instruction, or as separate courses for professional and personal advancement. It is hoped that the reader will relate to one or both of these programs in terms of preparing for and keeping current in the role.

University of Wisconsin—Eau Claire (UW—EC). This university is located in a small city (population 50,000) in northwest Wisconsin about 100 miles from the Minneapolis—St. Paul metropolitan area. Most of the area surrounding UW—EC is rural and the teachers that come for training generally teach in small school districts. The graduate program at UW—EC is limited to the masters level. Most of the graduate students in the elementary education department are practicing teachers who take one course a semester in late afternoon or evening, and courses during summer session. The total student population of UW—EC, graduate and undergraduate, is about 9500 (1974).

From the very beginning, the IGE graduate program at UW—EC has been founded on needs of unit leaders and teachers in IGE schools. The Department of Elementary Education first became involved with IGE in 1968 when the staff selected IGE as a favorable environment for the field experiences of undergraduate student teachers and interns. As a result of the department's experience with staffs in schools where these students were placed, several needs became apparent. These included training for staff of IGE schools to (1) assume the new leadership and team roles required by IGE, (2) develop curriculum materials to carry out instruction according to the IPM, (3) provide more information about the organizational-administrative component—the multiunit organization, and (4) develop expertise in implementing the IPM in new curriculum areas and in refining operations in curriculum areas where the IPM had already been implemented. Concurrent with these needs for experienced IGE personnel was the need for basic knowledge about IGE for teachers and principals who had no previous knowledge or experience with the concept.

Development of IGE graduate courses for unit leaders and staff teachers began in the spring of 1971. By the 1975-76 academic year, 12 graduate courses had been developed, approved, and taught. These courses are constantly being revised and refined. Credits earned in these courses are applicable to the Master of Science in Teaching (MST) degree.

One cluster of these courses provides an introduction to IGE and its basic concepts, development of curriculum materials to implement instructional programming, and roles and responsibilities of differentiated staff. A second cluster focuses on leadership, with one course on skills related to people and tasks, another on performance in piloting materials with children in a real classroom setting, and a third on planning inservice and other programs for IGE staffs. A third cluster includes a seminar which encompasses a variety of IGE-related topics, a course on the role of the media center in IGE, and a course in Individually Guided Motivation (IGM). While courses focus on the practical matters of IGE, they also provide the necessary background knowledge and learning theory relevant to the course content. Courses are structured sequentially and the objectives are related to Bloom's Taxonomy in the cognitive domain. A brief description of the 12 courses follows.

IGE Graduate Courses at the University of Wisconsin—Eau Claire

Introduction to IGE (ELED 401/601), 3 credits, deals with a survey of the seven components of IGE, the *Wisconsin Design* reading program, Individually Guided Motivation, and team-building skills

Individualization of Instruction (ELED 720), 3 credits, is concerned primarily with instructional programming and the preparation of teacher-made curriculum materials.

Individualizing Metric Instruction for the Elementary School (ELED 722), 1-2 credits, considers the metric system in terms of its content (1 credit) and a plan for teaching metric to elementary students (second credit).

The Media Center and Individualized Learning Programs (ELED 736), 3 credits, deals with background information about and participant creation of instructional products to be utilized in the media center.

Educational Leadership (ELED 750), 3 credits, focuses on development of effective leadership skills in terms of the objectives, people, and organizational hierarchy.

Individually Guided Motivation (IGM) (ELED 751), 3 credits, focuses on the system of IGM and its four procedures. The participant implements and evaluates one procedure with 4-6 children in a school setting.

Differential Staffing: A Support System for IGE (ELED 752), 3 credits, is concerned with roles, responsibilities, and operations of the multiunit organization and human relations techniques appropriate to the MUS hierarchy.

Program Planning in IGE (ELED 754), 3 credits, focuses on development, implementation, and evaluation of long and short range plans for inservice, instructional, motivational, or other programs.

Human Relations in the Team Environment (ELED 755), 3 credits, will enhance the student's ability to interact positively in a team setting. Experiences include examination of techniques of interdependence, simulations of group problem solving, and the diagnosis of the causes and solutions of team problems.

The Unit Leader and Individually Guided Education (ELED 756), 3 credits, is concerned with the leadership roles of the unit leader in terms of personal and instructional leadership skills, and knowledge in implementing an IGE system of instructional programming in cognitive and affective areas.

Leadership Practicum (ELED 757), 3-6 credits, provides opportunity for the student to *demonstrate* skills in terms of curriculum, developmental inservice, and/or instructional leadership in an actual school and/or system setting.

Seminar in IGE (ELED 770), 1-3 credits, deals with various aspects of a single topic or a variety of topics according to the interests and/or needs of the participants. Requirements include preparation, presentation, and evaluation of a paper on a topic selected by the participant.

In keeping with the philosophy of IGE, the courses are taught in modules with a performance-based format. This allows students to experience the process of IGE in terms of assessing and accommodating their own knowledge and experience, learning rates, and learning styles. The performance-based format also allows for accountability of both student and faculty member and lends itself to the revision of content that is so essential in a dynamic concept like IGE.

Each module deals with a specific facet of course content such as instructional programming, roles and responsibilities, multiunit organization and operations, developing a unit of instruction according to the IPM, setting general educational objectives or encouraging independent reading (IGM). Modules contain specific objectives, suggested activities to meet these objectives, and requirements for demonstrating mastery of the objectives. The complexity of a module varies with the course structure and topics. A sample module on instructional programming is shown below. This basic module is required in the introductory course (ELED 401/601) and is a prerequisite for several other courses.

Instructional Programming Module—Level 1

Objectives

The participant will be able:

1. to identify instructional programming rationale and procedures appropriate for IGE.
2. to describe the Instructional Programming Model for IGE in writing indicating the correct sequence of steps.
3. to illustrate each step of the Instructional Programming Model with examples from a content area or a program like the *Wisconsin Design for Reading Skill Development.*

Suggested Activities to Meet Objectives

1. Study handout of Instructional Programming Model (IPM) for IGE.
2. Study pp. 17-19, 25-27, and 53-65 in Klausmeier *et al.,* 1975.
3. Review filmstrip/tape on *Instructional Programming in IGE.*
4. Read reprint of article from the *Elementary School Journal* on instructional programming for the individual pupil.

Illustration of Mastery

1. Complete IGE concepts test on instructional programming with 80 percent accuracy.
2. List steps of IPM in sequence and illustrate each step with examples from any content area with 90 percent accuracy (one-page assessment).

Students may work on the modules in a variety of learning modes—independently, one-to-one with a peer or instructor, small, medium-sized, or large group—according to their preferences, background, and the characteristics of the subject matter to be learned. Students may attempt to demonstrate mastery of an area without completing the suggested learning activities if they feel they already have sufficient knowledge and experience, or they may work on the activities and attempt mastery when they feel ready.

Activities in the modules, as well as the projects, allow students to work at their own rates and give them a choice in learning style. For example, each of the suggested activities in the module on instructional programming covers essentially the same information in a different way. Methods and media utilized in suggested activities also vary between modules. For example, students participate in simulations in the "Unit Meeting" and "Home-School Communication" modules and are involved

The University of Wisconsin—Eau Claire Instructional Materials Center complements the IGE program. (Courtesy Media Development Center, UW—EC.)

in an activity with children and videotaping in the "Individually Guided Motivation" modules.

The UW—EC Instructional Materials Center complements the IGE program. It is equipped with carrels for individual viewing and listening, small-group rooms for discussion and film viewing, and has an adjoining classroom which accommodates up to 60 people for large-group sessions.

Differentiated staffing, team planning and teaching, and shared decision making are utilized by the UW—EC staff. The differentiated staff includes professors, graduate assistants, senior assistants, a secretary, work-study students, and resource persons such as experienced IGE teachers, unit leaders, principals, state and regional IGE facilitators, and personnel with special expertise from public schools, the community, and other universities. Roles of the differentiated staff can be summarized as follows:

- Professors take major responsibility for course design, direction, and conduct.
- Graduate assistants are involved in preparation of new materials, maintaining the individualized resource file, working with small instructional groups, and other related activities.
- Senior assistants, who earn credit for their work, participate in a variety of learning experiences related to orientation of teachers to materials and procedures in the university IMC, organization of individualized materials, preparation of learning modules under direction of professors, and other activities appropriate to their interests and talents.
- Work-study students (undergraduates) are involved in typing, tabulating, filing, assembling, and summarizing data and materials related to the program.
- A secretary is essential to type and format modules and other printed materials, as well as to handle regular clerical duties.
- Resource persons from the "working world of IGE" are a most important part of the staff and very popular with teachers who are graduate students; they "tell it like it is" in the school situation and add be-

A team of professors and graduate assistants provides the impetus for IGE course development and instruction.

lievability and excitement to the courses. Sessions involving resource persons are often held in the school setting.

A team of professors and graduate assistants (usually four to six persons) provides the impetus for IGE course development and instruction and handles the coordination of university staff, student personnel, and resource persons. They also maintain communication with teachers and other personnel in IGE public and parochial schools and systems. The team has regular planning meetings at least once a week and ad hoc sessions as required.

Decisions on conceptualization, development, and evaluation of courses are made by the team of professors with input from practitioners. All courses have been subjected to the regular approval procedures by the department and the university.

Besides on-campus offerings, the IGE team takes these credit courses off campus to teachers in local school districts as part of the university's outreach program.

The University of Toledo (UT). This university of 15,000 students is located on the south shore of Lake Erie. It serves the city of Toledo and the surrounding urban area. UT offers degrees in education at the baccalaureate, masters, specialist, and doctoral levels.

IGE has been one viable alternative for elementary schools in the Toledo area since 1967. While teachers have provided individualized learning experiences for pupils consistent with different learning modes and conceptual styles, the need for additional trained practitioners in the IGE concept was soon identified. This need was manifest at both the undergraduate and graduate levels of education within the college of education.

First, there was a particular need to help potential teachers in preservice teacher education programs develop the unique skills and competencies for the implementation of IGE. This need was met by the development, implementation, and the institutionalization of the Competency Based Teacher Education Program for the training of elementary school teachers. This program is based upon the completion of a set of learning modules which have a variety of specified objectives, alternative instructional strategies, specified criteria for successful performance by students, and assessment procedures (Dickson and Saxe 1974). These modules are implemented by a team of university professors who form interdisciplinary teams not unlike the differentiated staffing concept of the IGE model. Among the requirements for completion of modules is a mandatory field experience.

Second, there was a special need to provide inservice training experiences for veteran teachers in the field who wanted to expand their skills and competencies in order to better meet the challenges of providing IGE for their pupils. Some of this renewal effort could be handled by awareness conferences and inservice training workshops. It soon became apparent that teachers wanted an increased professional program of courses which could function as the focus for a graduate program leading to a masters degree program and even to an educational specialist degree for those who desired to go beyond the masters degree program. This need led to the development of a set of courses which were specifically designed to provide the training and experiences necessary to have an optimal level of application for teachers functioning in an IGE environment and to have a level of academic scholarship and excellence to satisfy the requirement of graduate courses for graduate credit at the masters degree, educational specialist degree, and even the doctoral degree at UT.

The courses developed included courses which had the primary purpose of fostering development of skills and competencies in the individualization of instruction in several subject matter curricular areas, in the administration of multiunit schools, in the guidance and counseling functions for IGE environments, in the role of the unit leader, in group processes, human relations and group dynamics, and evaluation. The specific course titles, descriptions, and quarter credit hours follow:

IGE Graduate Courses at the University of Toledo

Administration of Multiunit Schools (352:604/804), 4 credits. The course provides a general overview of all aspects and levels of the multiunit school. The systemwide program committee will be studied and particular attention will be given to the IIC and I & R Unit meetings. The personal and sociological problems associated with personnel changing from traditional to multiunit organization will be considered.

Community Analysis (352:621/821), 4 credits. School communities and their various subpublics are studied in this course. Power structures and influence patterns are considered in detail with findings applied specifically to educational operations.

The Teacher-Counselor in the Elementary School (354:502), 4 credits. A study of guidance functions and procedures as they relate to the roles of elementary school teachers and counselors. Emphasis will be placed on practical application of guidance objectives, responsibilities, and approaches in classroom settings.

The Counselor in the Multiunit School (354:604/804), 4 credits. An examination of the role and function of the counselor in the multiunit school. Particular attention will be given to the counselor working in a team setting, the development of facilitative communication skills, student assessment, practical research, and student adjustment problems related to IGE and team-based approaches.

Rationale, Planning, and Evaluation of Competency-Based Education (CBE) (336:640/840), 4 credits. The course will aid the teacher in developing skills in (1) recognizing the sociopsychological basis for CBE, (2) disciplines approach; (3) how to write and evaluate CBE curriculum in different physical and social settings; and (4) how to establish proficiency levels and evaluate students using a CBE model.

Group Processes in Education (336:539/739), 4 credits. A study of formal and informal group processes which emphasize the concepts of norms, roles, and leadership as they relate to effecting curriculum change in the schools. Particular emphasis will be placed on analyzing problems and devising strategies for change in educational settings involved in multiunit staff organization and competency based education.

The Elementary Mathematics Teacher: Mathematics Laboratory and Differentiated Staffing (312:535/735), 4 credits. The course is designed for experienced elementary teachers. The course focuses on the role and responsibilities of personnel in the elementary schools where differentiated staffing is practiced and/or where mathematics laboratories are located.

Individualizing Mathematics Instruction in the Elementary School (312:525/725), 4 credits. This course is designed for experienced elementary teachers. The course focuses on the needs of the inservice teacher. It allows for the development and involvement of materials that the teacher can use in the school math program and for the acquisition of up-to-date information on individualizing math programs.

IGE in Elementary Social Studies (312:523/723), 4 credits. An inquiry into strategies and techniques to individualize the teaching of social studies skills. New commercial learning packages as well as free and inexpensive materials will be analyzed. Emphasis will be on adapting available resources to individual learning needs. Students will participate in the design of a social studies laboratory.

Biological Science Information and Concepts for Elementary Teachers (312:531/731), 4 credits. An advanced course to enable elementary school teachers to review and update their biological science background and to prepare science based instructional activities for classroom use. Students will have the opportunity to field test materials developed and to evaluate their effectiveness.

The Unit Leader in a Multiunit School (312:630/830), 4 credits. The role of the unit leader in a multiunit elementary school is a new dimension in the teaching profession. This course is designed to aid unit leaders to (1) develop the new skills necessary in this role; (2) update skills needed for curriculum development for individualization; and (3) facilitate effective home-school communications.

Independent Study in Curriculum Development (312:599/799), 4 credits. The student will have the opportunity to develop modules of instruction to be taught and field-tested in the schools. A faculty member will direct the independent study.

Physical Science Information and Concepts for Elementary Teachers (312: 502/702), 4 credits. An advanced course to enable elementary teachers to review and update their physical science background and to prepare science-based instructional activities for classroom use. Students will have the opportunity to field-test materials developed and to evaluate their effectiveness.

Organization and Supervision of the Reading Program (312:615/815), 4 credits. The content of this course includes the study of techniques for evaluating the reading program, continual assessment and monitoring techniques, staff development, and inservice in reading practices, materials and resources.

Advanced degrees at UT are designed to meet individual student needs through interaction between the student and faculty advisor at the masters and specialists level and the student and a committee at the doctoral level. Brief summaries of the graduate program at the masters, specialist, and doctoral levels describing how a unit leader or staff teacher might prepare for the role at UT are presented below.

Masters program. This program requires a total of 48 quarter-hour credits. Requirements of the program are a 16-hour core and a 1 to 4 hour project or thesis. This allows 28 hours of choice for the student. An area of concentration is encouraged, although training for the "generalist in curriculum" may also be elected. Students may elect to take IGE courses within the 28 elective hours including courses focusing on the unit leader as well as specialized courses in content areas (e.g., IGE in math, science, language arts). They may also write a project or thesis related to IGE. In the IGE course descriptions applicable to the Masters of Education degree, presented above, courses for the degree cut across departments and divisions within the college of education in order to capitalize on the full resources of the college. A typical masters degree program would include election of up to seven of the courses.

Specialist program. This program requires a practicum of 1 to 5 credits with specific numbers of required hours. Students may elect to do their practicum in an IGE school, (e.g., study a curriculum problem in the C and I division), or in the case of educational administration or guidance and counseling departments, serve the required service hours in an IGE school.

Doctoral programs (Ph.D. or Ed.D.). This program has a minimum of 50 hours in major and 25 hours in minor areas as well as 15 credit hours for the doctoral dissertation. Traditional qualifying major and minor oral examinations, as well as a qualifying examination, are part of the total program. Here, too, the student may elect several courses related to IGE and conduct research for the dissertation on some facet of IGE.

This section has dealt with involvement of two universities in the renewal phase. Many other colleges and universities are developing IGE courses and programs. It is now possible for educators in most parts of the country to take courses related to their needs in relation to their IGE programs.

Teachers and principals who desire IGE courses which are not yet available should make their interests known to the appropriate personnel in a nearby teacher education institution. Those institutions are usually more than willing to provide courses for which there is an expressed need. Or they may be willing to offer short-term workshops and institutes in the interim while the necessary planning for new courses takes place.

The adoption of new concepts and ideas is a slow, careful process. Unit leaders, as well as staff teachers and principals, need to assume some responsibility in keeping colleges and universities aware of their needs in preparing for and keeping up to date in IGE.

SUMMARY

The purpose of this chapter was to provide present and prospective unit leaders with alternative ways to prepare for and keep current in their roles.

The five phase strategy for implementing IGE was discussed. In the first phase, awareness, local school personnel are given an overview of the seven basic IGE concepts. Phase two, commitment, requires the school district to receive commitment from all involved parties to adopt the total IGE concept. The changeover phase involves preparing the staff for the change from their past teaching practices to an IGE program. Ongoing staff development occurs during the refinement phase through inservices, institutes, and workshops. The final phase of renewal involves the colleges and universities in preparing staff personnel to fill IGE roles.

Two university curriculum programs were described in detail to help motivate the readers to understand and accept the idea of self-renewal of professional skills throughout a teaching career.

REFERENCES

Dickson, G. E., *et al.* 1973. *Partners for educational reform and renewal.* Berkeley: McCutchan.

Institute for the Development of Educational Activities 1973. *Guide to an improvement program for schools.* Dayton, Ohio.

Klausmeier, H. J., J. E. Walter, and L. J. Lins 1974. *Manual for starting and maintaining state IGE networks.* Madison, Wisc.: University of Wisconsin/Sears-Roebuck Foundation IGE Teacher Education Project.

Walter, J. E., B. T. Gardner, and H. G. MacDermot 1975. *A status report on the national implementation of IGE: 1971-1974,* Technical Report No. 345. Madison, Wisc.: Wisconsin Research and Development Center for Cognitive Learning.

SKILLS
MARINE SERVICE
PUBLIC SERVICE
HEALTH
TRANSPORTATION
BUSINESS & OFFICE
COMMUNICATIONS
CONSTRUCTION

Part III

Planning, Implementing, and Evaluating Instruction

The complex task of providing for individual differences is accomplished through developing an instructional program appropriate for each individual student. This involves consideration of objectives, student readiness, materials and media, student and teacher characteristics, evaluation procedures, and the feedback of progress to students. The guidelines for this process are provided in the Instructional Programming Model (IPM) which was presented in detail in Figure 1.3. The key points of this model along with the chapters of this part of the book that relate to each step are presented below.

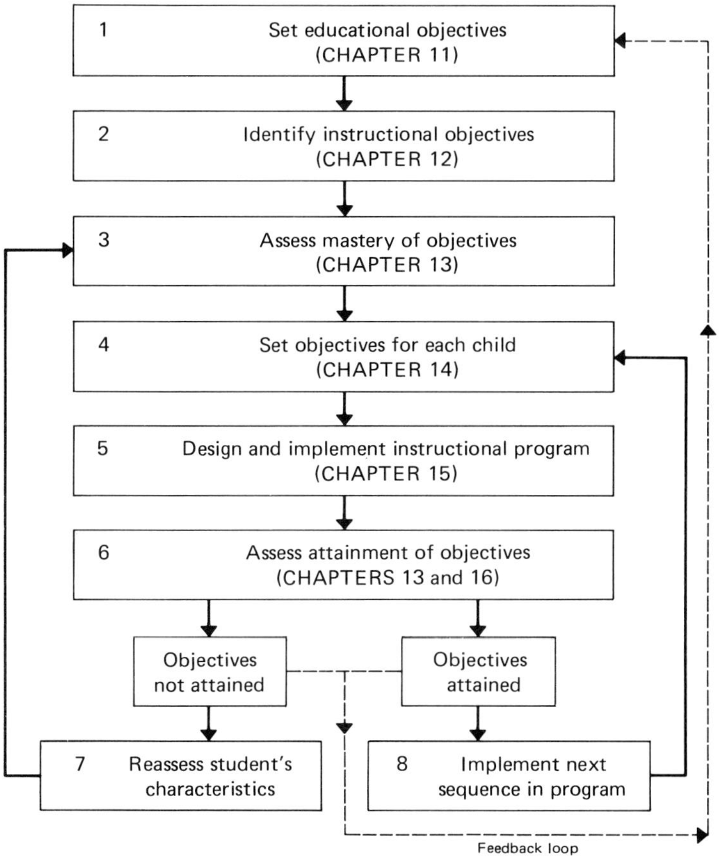

Instructional programming for the individual student is a process designed to adapt learning to three key variables: (1) what a student already knows; (2) the rate at which the student learns; and (3) the style or way in which the student goes about learning. In addition, involving the student in the instructional program increases his or her motivation to participate in the program. In the instructional process teachers need to recognize and utilize student potential in creating and contributing to their learning programs and children need to experience decision making about their own education.

The needs of each individual child can be met only by efficient coordination of:

- student characteristics and achievement in learning activities
- student relationships with staff members
- staff roles and responsibilities
- expertise and interests of unit staff members
- unit meetings with specific purposes
- general and instructional objectives
- long- and short-range planning

After an IGE instructional program has been implemented, it is necessary to evaluate it to see if the objectives of the program were met. Whether planning an instructional program for an individual student, students in the I & R Unit, or the entire building population, it should be remembered that all the personnel, materials, and facilities are there for no other reason than to meet the needs of the students.

10

Developing a Planning Strategy

Juanita S. Sorenson
Lloyd H. Joyal

Objectives

After reading this chapter, the reader will be able:

- To indicate five aspects of cooperative planning and explain how each operates in an I & R Unit.
- To describe the eight kinds of meetings in the IGE planning strategy and the purposes of each.
- To indicate the relationships between the IGE planning strategy meetings and the IPM.
- To describe the appropriate roles and responsibilities of the unit leader, staff teacher, aide, and student teacher/intern in the IGE planning process.

In an IGE school, planning for instruction is carried out by the I & R Unit staff under the direction of the unit leader. As you will recall from the diagram of the multiunit organization in Figure 1.2, the unit staff is made up of the unit leader, certified staff teachers, instructional and/or clerical aides, and student teachers and/or interns.

Planning is carried out on a cooperative basis with a team of professionals (the I & R Unit staff) rather than a single teacher making instructional and management decisions for each individual child. Team planning and subsequently team teaching "validates the best use of teacher competencies . . . because team planning and teaching make it possible for teachers to offer an educational program tailored to meet needs of the individual elementary child" (Johnson and Hunt 1968, p. 122). In the past we have asked too much of any one teacher in the self-contained classroom to be all things to all students. In addition, team planning and teaching can provide more flexible scheduling and better use of materials and equipment to meet individual student needs.

Team planning allows for the development of teaching strengths and growth not possible in the traditional self-contained classroom arrangement (Hillson and Hyman 1971, p. 123). Further, team planning assists in unifying instructional practices and programs, tends to eliminate caprices of instruction, and assures some degree of uniformity and structure for all students to accomplish certain necessary basic skills in the curriculum. Moreover, team planning leads to (1) improvement of instruction by encouraging colleague observation and self-criticism; (2) focusing teachers' attention on the need to review instructional objectives as well as reassessing teaching techniques and redeploying teaching personnel; and (3) teacher analysis and adaption of new teaching materials, groupings for instruction, and better use of space and facilities.

Team teaching is based on the premise that teachers can accomplish more when they combine their talents and work together than they can working alone (Murray and Wilhour 1971, p. 134). The key words in team teaching are "team planning." Without planning, team teaching can erode into a "teacher exchange." Cooperative planning involving the complete staff on a regularly scheduled basis is necessary for success of programs involving the concepts of nongradedness, differentiated staffing, team teaching, and programming for individual students. Success in a team approach to teaching depends *more* upon people than on other factors. Planning meetings serve as a mutual place for exchange of ideas and information among the regular members of the team and as a place for specialists, media directors, the principal, and others to have two-way communication with the team members.

Each planning meeting should have a predetermined purpose (Murray and Wilhour 1971, p. 135). Purposes might include (1) identifying

Team planning and teaching make it possible for teachers to offer an educational program tailored to meet the needs of the individual child.

children for instructional groups, (2) selecting instructional materials appropriate for certain groups of children, (3) consideration of facilities for the intended learning program, and (4) designing units of work for the children assigned to the team. Other important aspects of team planning include long- and short-range planning, designation of appropriate roles for the differentiated staff, utilization of resource personnel in the building, system or region, and development of a strong inservice program concerned with both cognitive and affective dimensions. The inservice program should be continuous and focus on the team members. It should include the principal, specialists, interns and student teachers, aides, and all other personnel who will work with the team. Cooperative team planning should include designation of inservice needs, and planning should be thorough. Inadequate planning may be a prelude to failure.

Most teams realize the need for short-range plans, but fail to see the perhaps even greater need for long-range plans (Bair and Woodward 1964, p. 84-104). Long-range plans are necessary not only for meeting goals, but also as an opportunity for team members to collect ideas and information over a longer period and thus provide a broader base from which to make decisions. They also help staff stay on course toward their objectives and thus avoid mistakes and wasted effort.

In IGE, planning occurs along a continuum with a progression of meetings designated to accomplish a number of objectives (DiPego 1970, pp. 55-62). A general set of guidelines termed the "planning system" includes four kinds of meetings:

1. *Goal-setting meeting.* This meeting is the first step in planning an instructional program, and includes:
   a. identifying the objectives (cognitive, affective, and psychomotor) of the work unit (e.g., science for 8- to 10-year-olds);
   b. selection of topic(s) within the unit (e.g., astronomy);
   c. assignment of a resource teacher to prepare the specific instructional objectives for the topics considering the strengths and/or interests of the staff; and
   d. evaluation of strengths and weaknesses of materials and procedures previously used by the staff teachers for teaching the selected topic.
2. *Design meeting.* This meeting occurs two to three weeks after the goal-setting meeting. Activities include:
   a. a presentation of the plan for the unit of work (e.g., astronomy) by the resource teacher who had accepted the assignment at the goal-setting meeting;
   b. a subsequent critique and modification of the plan for the unit of work by the team staff;
   c. assignment of teachers to teaching responsibilities related to the unit of work;
   d. preparation of a teaching schedule; and
   e. development of a plan for assessment of the unit of work.
3. *Grouping and scheduling meeting.* At this meeting students are placed in initial instructional groups based on assessment (e.g., test scores, interests, performances, work samples) and at least the first week of the unit of work is scheduled.
4. *Situational meeting.* This meeting occurs while the unit of instruction, (e.g., astronomy) is in progress and deals with any problems that have come up. In the "planning system" any meeting is situational that deals with daily operations of the unit.

Planning—especially planning by the I & R Unit staff—is at the heart of IGE success (Klausmeier, *et al.* 1971, pp. 114-116). Thus unit meetings should be regularly scheduled and incorporate the following criteria:

- Unit planning time amounts to at least *two* hours per week with one hour in a single block.
- Unit meetings are held during the regular working day.
- Unit meetings are chaired by the unit leader (or the chairpersonship is delegated in certain instances).
- Unit meetings are always attended by the unit leader, all certified unit staff teachers, and student teachers or interns assigned to the unit.
- Upon request of the unit, consultants, teachers, IMC/media director, aides, and others attend unit meetings.
- Prior to the meeting an agenda is prepared and distributed to unit staff, the principal, and others who will be involved in the meeting.
- Discussion focuses on the agenda.
- A secretary is identified and minutes of the meeting are kept.
- Minutes of the unit meetings are duplicated and distributed to all unit staff, the IIC, and others who attended the meeting.
- Unit meetings of special kinds are held as
  a. goal setting (at least once each semester)
  b. design (at least monthly)
  c. grouping and scheduling (at least once every two weeks)
  d. situational (at least once per week)
  e. evaluation of instructional units and programs and of unit operations (at least once per quarter)

For the actual planning process in a subject matter area, the following strategies are suggested to the I & R Unit staff (Klausmeier, *et al.* 1971, pp. 106-107):

1. Evaluation of past curricular procedures, materials, and assessments in the subject matter area under consideration, and adaptation of successful elements to IGE instructional programming.
2. Assignment to teachers of development responsibilities as writing objectives, developing assessment instruments, keying materials, and evaluating pupil performance.
3. Development of a plan that includes:
   a. a timetable for implementation with dates for preassessment and duration of groupings established.
   b. strategies for grouping children and assigning staff to groups.
   c. an assessment of material needs to carry out the plan.

It is important that the I & R Unit meets to develop long- and short-range plans especially before school starts in the fall. At this time the I & R Unit should focus on:

1. Long-range plans for the entire year in the design and goal-setting meetings (e.g., social studies units of work are blocked out for the entire year).
2. Short-range plans for the first 1 to 2 weeks of school are made during grouping and scheduling meetings.

It is also suggested that the unit staff meet for at least one day per semester when children are not at school to extend long-range IGE planning.

Authors cited here have discussed a variety of general strategies for team planning to prepare for team teaching. A summary of their points of view indicates a planning strategy should include:

- assessment of the expertise and/or interests of the team staff.
- designation of responsibilities for members of the differentiated staff relative to cognitive and affective aspects of the instructional program.
- identification of a long-range planning sequence or system for a semester or year particularly in curricular area(s) where team teaching will occur.
- identification of short-range planning sequence or system for development and execution of instructional units (2 to 4 weeks long).
- assignment of appropriate roles and responsibilities and assignment of duties to noncertified members of the team staff.
- utilization of a format for planning and executing the instructional process with students.
- identification of purposes for planning meetings.

CARRYING OUT COOPERATIVE PLANNING

A basic part of the IGE philosophy is that several professional teachers can make better judgments for each individual student than one professional can. This is reflected in the multiunit organization component in which three to five certified staff teachers are assigned to units or teams along with appropriate noncertified personnel as aides and perhaps student teachers or interns. This organization was discussed and presented in diagrammatic form in Figure 1.2 of this book. The unit leader takes responsibility for directing, planning, and coordinating the activities of the I & R Unit or team. Some 150 students with a three or more year age span (e.g., 5- to 7-year-olds) are assigned to the unit. The unit assumes responsibility for planning, executing, and evaluating the instructional programs for these children.

In order to teach effectively, the unit staff must carry out cooperative planning. Experience in IGE schools has indicated that planning time should be (1) designated during regular school hours, preferably when the students are not there; (2) three hours per week, in one, two, or three sessions; (3) regularly scheduled (e.g., Tuesdays and Thursdays from 3:00 to 4:30 P.M. or on Monday, Tuesday, and Thursday from 8:00 to 9:00 A.M.); (4) held at the same time for all I & R Units in a building to allow for cross unit planning when necessary and uniform scheduling throughout the building.

The planning process should be structured carefully to include: (1) efficient and effective use of expertise and interests of certified and non-certified staff; (2) designation of roles and responsibilities for all members of the unit staff; (3) identification of personnel resources in the building/system/region/state; (4) identification of long- and short-range plans in both the cognitive and affective areas; and (5) development or identification of a planning strategy in which purposes for planning meetings are designated.

Cooperative planning on a unit or team basis is new to most teachers and should be started slowly. This allows teachers to do a satisfying job and to avoid being overwhelmed by the number of variables they deal with or become so overworked they become discouraged. In planning for instructional programming for 75-150 children with a three or more year age span, a unit usually starts with one content area (e.g., reading) or some portion of a content area (e.g., Word Attack in reading). They implement instructional programming in this area for a semester or two and evaluate it continuously. When they are satisfied that instructional programming in one content area is functioning smoothly from a staff point of view and that the children are learning effectively and the general atmosphere is harmonious, they initiate plans to add another content area or portion of a content area. By moving slowly, but consistently, they can use the experience they gained in planning instructional programming in one area and apply it to the next one. Also, by having a successful experience and developing a workable schedule, the planning for the second and subsequent areas moves much more rapidly than it did for the first area.

This chapter deals with several topics that are essential to carrying out cooperative planning such as:

- determining expertise and interests of unit staff members
- utilizing the Instructional Programming Model as a base for planning instruction
- designating staff roles and responsibilities

- identifying personnel resources
- identifying long- and short-range planning objectives and sequences
- developing an IGE unit meeting planning strategy

In all cases there is an attempt to keep the content of the chapter practical and relevant to everyday experiences in the school situation.

Determining Staff Expertise and Interests

To carry out successful cooperative planning for instruction, the strengths and interests of team members must be determined. In IGE, the unit leader takes main responsibility for this. Some formal and informal sources of this information would include: (1) college preparation of staff members in terms of content minor or major; (2) leadership positions and/or participation in organizational or extracurricular activities; (3) college courses, institutes, or conferences attended by staff members during the past three years; (4) observed areas of expertise as noted by the principal, unit leader, or fellow staff teachers; and (5) expertise acquired through inservice programs.

The unit leader might accumulate this information by (1) preparing a brief questionnaire on which staff members are asked to volunteer their self-assessed areas of expertise and/or interest, (2) developing a simple needs assessment in relation to a unit of instruction coming up during the semester or year and asking teachers to assign themselves to a task, (3) asking for volunteers to take the main responsibility for preparing and assembling the outline for a unit of work, or (4) developing a brief questionnaire asking staff members to indicate what they consider the most successful units of work they have taught during the past two years. The unit leader or a staff member designated by the unit leader should summarize data from whatever method or methods used and gather it into a simple format that will be available for reference during assignment of responsibilities of staff. More detailed suggestions for these activities are given in Chapter 6.

Planning Instruction According to the IPM

In IGE, the Instructional Programming Model (IPM) provides the guidelines for planning instruction. A detailed version of this model was presented in Figure 1.3. A working version of this same model appears in Figure 10.1. In the following narrative, cooperative planning procedures and personnel are related to the IPM.

Step 1 of the model deals with planning in terms of setting general educational objectives for the students of the building. This process is primarily a function of the IIC with input from unit staff members, central

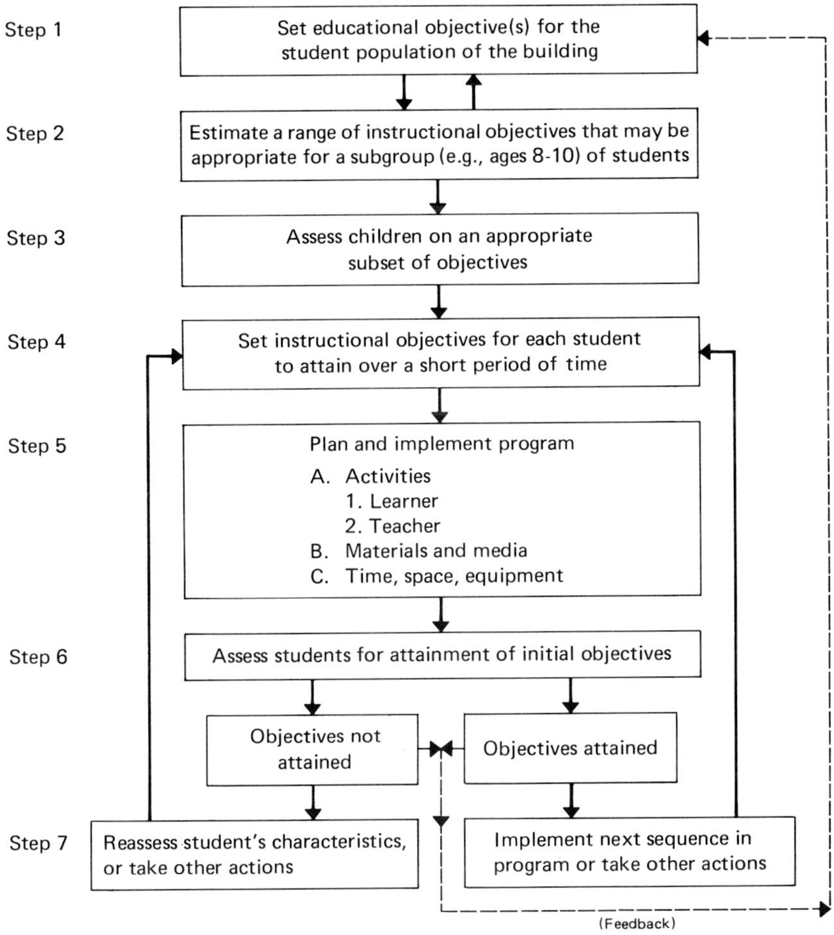

Fig. 10.1 Instructional Programming Model in IGE, simplified from Fig. 1.3.

office personnel, and others with special expertise in data interpretation and psychological services. This part of the planning strategy involves setting tentative objectives in a curriculum or other area selected for development of instructional programming during the first year of operation under the IGE plan, and systematic evaluation of these objectives after the program has been in operation for one year, with periodic review each year thereafter. Each time a new curriculum area is selected for instructional programming, the sequence is repeated.

Step 2 is concerned with planning as it relates to identification of specific instructional objectives in a curriculum area and is most effectively carried out by the unit staff members. This step involves selecting objectives for skills/concepts/processes for blocks of time, (e.g., a nine-week segment of work), in the curriculum or other area being emphasized for instructional programming. Instructional objectives may be identified initially by the entire unit staff or by one or two members of the staff after the concepts/skills/processes for the block of time, (e.g., nine-week period), have been identified and agreed upon by the entire staff. Objectives which have been selected/adapted/developed by the one or two staff members should be reviewed and agreed upon by the entire unit staff. Objectives should also be divided into reasonable units of work, (e.g., three-week periods), and sequenced appropriate to the content of the unit of work and age/grade level of the students in the unit. When Step 2 in the model has been completed, the unit staff cooperatively assumes the responsibility for planning the instructional strategies appropriate to the instructional objectives. These strategies are indicated in Steps 3, 4, 5, and 6 of the Instructional Programming Model.

Step 3 involves planning for preassessment of student performance. This may be carried out in a number of ways. For example, students may have been assessed over most of the material to be covered in a one-year period and these data may already be available to the unit staff. It is common practice to carry out assessment in this manner in skill areas like reading or mathematics. By another method, students may be assessed only over skills/processes/skills to be covered in one or two units of instruction, (e.g., three to six weeks). In all cases, it is necessary for the I & R Unit staff to agree upon assessment procedures appropriate to the type of material to be covered. Assessment plans should include consideration of general methods for assessing which include paper-and-pencil tests, performance tests as in physical education, work samples as writing a poem or story, observations, or student interest in a topic or topics. The teacher or teachers who are assuming responsibility for planning and developing a unit of instruction should recommend appropriate assessment procedures. (See Chapter 13.)

Step 4 of the model involves planning based on assessment data, teacher judgment, consideration for student learning styles, and teaching styles of staff to assign students to groups for instruction. Planning the type of grouping pattern, (e.g., small group, one-to-one, independent study, large group), or a combination of patterns appropriate to the content to be learned also needs to be carried out. (See Chapter 14.) The teacher responsible for preparing the outline for the unit of work also makes recommendations on group sizes. Grouping procedures may be carried out by the entire unit staff at a planning meeting, or one or two members of the staff may carry out the process with review and acceptance by the entire staff. A plan for monitoring students' progress should also be developed.

Step 5 involves planning for the actual instructional process. This planning includes assignment of staff, (e.g., unit leaders, staff teachers, student teachers and interns, aides and others), to groups of students along with designation of materials, equipment, space, and time. Planning for Step 5 is coordinated by the unit leader at a meeting of the entire unit staff.

Step 6 involves planning for procedures to postassess students.

Step 7 utilizes the data gathered from the postassessment to determine the next areas of instruction, appropriate actions for students who attained and who did not attain mastery, and evaluation of instructional techniques and/or materials for the total unit of instruction.

Designating Staff Roles and Responsibilities

Cooperative planning is based on the premise that the members of the unit or team will assume differentiated roles and responsibilities to bring about more effective planning and teaching. In IGE, the unit leader acts as coordinator of planning activities in terms of providing agendas for the unit meetings and chairing unit meetings. In planning for instruction, the unit leader delegates appropriate responsibilities to members of the unit staff. The unit leader is also responsible for providing an environment in which a group of professionals—the unit staff—will interact to present a variety of points of view to plan instruction for individual children and subsequently groups of children in the unit.

In the planning process, the staff teacher assumes responsibility for preparation of a tentative procedural outline for a unit of instruction in a content or other area. This outline includes (1) identification of the instructional objectives to be accomplished during the unit of instruction; (2) sources of print, audiovisual, manipulative, and creative materials in the building, system, region, state; (3) sources of personnel outside the unit staff that may be utilized from the school or general community; and (4) suggested methods of preassessment appropriate to the content to be learned.

Aides can function in planning by helping staff teachers locate sources of materials and personnel, especially in the community. Aides may also type and duplicate the outline so it may be presented to the entire unit staff for critique.

Student teachers and interns may assist staff teachers in locating material resources in the school or system IMC, in suggesting new assessment techniques appropriate to the unit of instruction being planned, and recent sources of appropriate learning materials and equipment.

While roles such as unit leader, staff teacher, aide, student teacher/intern are designated initially by title based upon previously determined education, expertise, and experiences, specific responsibilities should be assigned with additional consideration for special expertise and interests of the individuals involved, and according to the curriculum area under consideration. For example, a student teacher or aide may have considerable expertise in directing an artistic exercise in connection with a unit of instruction on westward expansion or a staff teacher may have more expertise and training in assessment techniques than the unit leader has.

Identifying Personnel Resources

Teachers are so busy doing things that they do not identify and utilize people who are excellent resources in their own schools, systems, and communities. In IGE, involvement of all appropriate personnel is recommended, with special emphasis on using resource persons who are parents and community members. Such resources might include volunteers identified from organizational lists, by word of mouth, or from leadership roles in the community.

Within a given educational system, personnel resources are available from the entire K-12 staff. However, elementary schools seldom share teachers from another elementary school, nor do elementary schools utilize secondary staff members and vice versa. Within geographic areas, many states support regional educational agencies. These agencies usually serve several counties or districts and offer special services and provide centralized resource materials, equipment, and facilities not found in the school systems in the region. At the state level, general elementary and secondary consultants, as well as persons with special expertise in curriculum areas are available at no or minimal cost upon request of the local school and/or system.

In identifying resource people, consideration should be given not only to subject matter-related activities, such as people who have traveled and can present narrative and slides on a country or countries students are studying in social studies, but also to areas like human relations, career development, motivation, and aesthetics. IGE involves all aspects of the student's life. The community is where the child lives and will eventually work. Its resources and challenges become a vital part of the curriculum in IGE.

Identifying Planning Objectives and Sequences

Effective, cooperative planning by a unit necessitates identification of both long- and short-range objectives. Both kinds of objectives must be identified and agreed upon by the unit staff members if they are to be effective in guiding the instructional program.

Long-range planning objectives are based on identification of (1) the curricular area of instructional programming to be emphasized for the current school year and following school year, (e.g., mathematics might be the area for the present year and social studies for the following year); (2) skills/concepts/processes to be covered by students in the curriculum area of emphasis for the current school year; (3) areas of general teaching practice to be emphasized for the current and subsequent school years as small group interaction and learning stations and contracts; (4) affective areas to be considered as motivational procedures, values clarification, measurement of attitudes, beliefs, values; and (5) inservice program topics and schedules to carry out long-range plans.

Short-range planning objectives include identification of (1) skills/concepts/processes to be covered by the students in the unit of instruction for curricular areas for at least one quarter of the school year, (e.g., nine weeks), at a time; (2) instructional objectives for at least one three-week block of the topics in (1) above; (3) pre- and postassessment procedures and materials for at least one three-week block; (4) learning activities and instructional materials for carrying out the objectives in at least one three-week block and (5) an evaluation plan for one teaching period (e.g., a three-week block) in advance of the period presently being taught.

A chart showing one way to designate long- and short-range planning blocks is presented in Figure 10.2. This chart has been completed for science for 9- to 12-year-olds. It should be noted that the science class meets daily for 40 minutes.

Long-range plans in Figure 10.2 are exemplified by:

1. the topic of "living things" for the year (36 weeks); and
2. a breakdown of the year into quarters (9-week blocks)
   a. plants—classification/use for Quarter 1.
   b. plants—systems/functions for Quarter 2.
   c. animals—classification/use for Quarter 3.
   d. animals—systems/functions for Quarter 4.

Short-range plans shown for Quarter 3, a nine-week period, are a further breakdown of the long-range topic of animals—classification/use. Here the nine-week block was divided into three three-week blocks and a unit of instruction designed for each block as follows:

1. (three-week unit of instruction): *Animals with backbones* (vertebrates) focusing on the five vertebrate classes:
   a. mammals
   b. birds
   c. fish
   d. amphibians
   e. reptiles
2. (three-week unit of instruciton): *Animals without backbones* (invertebrates) which centers around the five commonly known phyla.

Long-range plans

Science — Living Things — One Year of 36 Weeks											
Plants Classification/Use Qtr 1 (9 weeks)			Plants Systems/Functions Qtr. 2 (9 weeks)			Animals Classification/Use Qtr. 3 (9 weeks)			Animals Systems/Functions Qtr. 4 (9 weeks)		
Units of work			Units of work			Units of work			Units of Work		
3 wks.	3 wks.	3 wks.	3 wks.	3 wks.	3 wks.	3 wks.	3 wks.	3 wks.	3 wks.	3 wks.	3 wks.

Short-range plans

Animals: Classification/Use — Quarter 3 of 9 Weeks		
Unit of work (3 wks.)	Unit of work (3 wks.)	Unit of work (3 wks.)
Animals with backbones (vertebrates) Mammals Birds Fish Amphibians Reptiles	Animals without backbones (invertebrates) Protozoa Echinoderms Mollusca Annelida Arthropoda	How animals affect our daily lives Food chains Environment Pets/recreation Protection/research/health Destruction/disease

Fig. 10.2 Long- and short-range planning chart.

a. Protozoa (amoeba, paramecium)
b. Echinoderms (starfish, sea urchins)
c. Mollusca (clams, snails, oysters)
d. Annelida (earthworms)
e. Arthropoda (spiders, insects, crayfish)

3. (three-week unit of instruction): *How animals affect our daily lives* which focuses on the interrelationships of the child (as one representative of the mammal class) to both vertebrates and invertebrates in terms of:
   a. food chains
   b. environmental pollination, pollination of fruit blossoms by insects, plowing of the soil by earthworms, etc.
   c. pets/recreation
   d. protection/research/health
   e. destruction/disease

When a unit staff makes provision for long- and short-range planning, they avoid the too common team disease of last-minute or "panic" planning. They also establish a sound base for ongoing curriculum development, evaluation, and revision that is relevant for the students in their building and system. In addition, long- and short-range plans provide a means of relating the curriculum from one unit to another, lay the groundwork for a comprehensive view of a given curriculum area for the entire elementary program, and provide a meaningful record of what a child has been introduced to and mastered. Secondary staff can use this information to build a relevant program for the student in appropriate areas, rather than having the too frequent problem of not knowing what background a student brings along from an elementary program.

DEVELOPING A UNIT MEETING PLANNING STRATEGY

All of the activities described above in relation to cooperative planning need to be combined into a total strategy for unit planning meetings. If such a strategy is to be successful, unit meetings must have specific purposes. One strategy which lists eight types of meetings and/or unit meeting segments, the content to be taken up in these meetings, and their approximate frequency is presented in Figure 10.3. This strategy assumes an I & R Unit which holds two 90-minute meetings each week. In practice, however, meetings vary in length from one to three hours and the amount of content covered may vary accordingly. In addition, more than one type of meeting or segment may occur during a unit's scheduled meeting time, (e.g., 90 minutes). The length of the units of instruction relative to these meetings was arbitrarily set at three weeks. A discussion of what happens at each meeting and/or meeting segment, along with the suggested frequency is presented below.

Ongoing Operations Meeting

This is an eclectic type of meeting where the unit staff deals with announcements and decisions related to a wide variety of day-to-day operations of the unit, school building, and system. Daily operations include routine attendance matters, collecting monies for milk and hot lunch, bus schedules, library procedures, schedules, as well as responsibilities of special teachers, budgeting, etc. More time is devoted to routine kinds of matters early in the school year, but a few minutes, (e.g., about 10), should be allocated to ongoing operations at the beginning of most planning meetings. Ongoing operations meetings might also deal with feedback from or input to the IIC meetings, in addition to the printed IIC minutes that are circulated to all unit staff members. Since most IGE schools tend to have few complete staff faculty meetings, it is necessary to communicate infor-

Type of meeting or meeting segment	Content	Suggested frequency
Ongoing operations	Handle daily problems Carry out team communications (written/oral) from and to IIC Plan field trips Assign tasks to staff	Once each week (10–90 min)
Objectives setting	Identify/review long-range objectives Identify/review short-range objectives	Once each 9 weeks or as needed Once each 3 weeks or as needed
Designing	Present overall plan for 3 weeks: Critique, modify, approve, plan Assign teacher to special tasks Outline schedule in general	Once each 3 weeks or as needed
Assessment	Plan assessment—kind, time Plan for summary of assessment data	Once each 3 weeks or as needed depending on overall plan
Grouping	Group pupils Assign groups to teachers	Once each 3 weeks or as needed
Scheduling	Assign time, space, equipment to teachers/groups	Once each 3 weeks or as needed
Monitoring	Discuss progress of student in unit of work Discuss student accomplishments Regroup students	Once each 3 weeks or more frequently as needed
Evaluation	Evaluate postassessment data Identify alternatives for masters/nonmasters Evaluate effectiveness of total unit of work	Once each 3 weeks

Fig. 10.3 Unit meeting planning strategy outline.

mation at the unit meetings so staff members feel they are in touch with what is happening in their building and system, as well as what is happening in the unit.

As the year progresses, other activities such as plans for field trips and overall planning for the activities of the unit would be taken up at ongoing operations meetings. Problems and ideas that arise as the program progresses are also topics for these meetings. For example, a need for more effective use of the IMC or integration of the kindergarten into a primary unit might become meeting topics and be labeled Ongoing Operations—IMC or Ongoing Operations—K in the unit, respectively.

Many units, as they function over a period of time, call spur-of-the-moment meetings to meet the needs of ongoing operations in order to keep their regular unit meeting time clear for more instruction-related purposes. Such an arrangement has to be worked out by the unit staff members according to the needs of the unit and the schedules of their buildings.

Objectives-setting Meeting

This type of meeting deals with planning for and identifying both general objectives for the students in the building and specific instructional objectives relative to Steps 1 and 2 of the Instructional Programming Model, respectively. General objectives need to be identified for the students in the school building by the IIC and subsequently related to students in the unit. General objectives in curriculum areas at the building level need to be identified initially on a tentative basis during the first year of changeover to IGE. An example of a general objective in math would be: 90 percent of the students will be able to multiply using the standard algorithm through 10 times 10 by age ten, and 99 percent by age 12. During the first year after general objectives are set, they should be reviewed by the I & R Unit every nine weeks and modifications in the objectives suggested to the IIC according to progress and experience with the program. Thereafter, objectives should be evaluated and reviewed annually and modified as needed. Chapter 11 of this book deals in detail with the purposes, content, and procedures for setting and evaluating general objectives in the IGE program.

Specific instructional objectives for curricular areas should be planned for nine-week to several-year periods. Plans should include provision for students to progress appropriately within a curriculum area relative to a set of specific instructional objectives. For example, in math a set of specific instructional objectives for multiplication might be stated as: The student will be able to multiply the following with 80 percent accuracy for:

- any combination of one-digit numbers by one digit numbers using the standard algorithm.
- any combination of two-digit numbers by one-digit numbers.
- any combination of two-digit numbers by two-digit numbers.

Unit decisions on which instructional objectives should be mastered include consideration for rate of progress appropriate to the age level, verbal skills, achievement levels, and other characteristics of the students in the unit. The unit staff must also consider that some students are working at a level below the generally accepted average for commercial instructional materials and that others are working well above that level. Specific instructional objectives should be reviewed with each block of teaching or unit of work (e.g., every three weeks). Responsibility for review may be assumed by a single staff teacher with approval of the unit staff or by the entire unit staff.

Designing Meeting

Responsibility for the presentation at this meeting is usually assumed by a staff teacher who is working in his or her area of interest or expertise. This meeting deals with presentation and critique of a plan for a unit of work (e.g., three weeks). This includes listing of specific instructional objectives, identification of sources of print and audiovisual material available in the building/system/region to help staff develop a learning program in relation to the objectives, a general plan for assessment and suggested instruments appropriate to the subject matter to be learned, tentative assignment of teachers to special tasks, and tentative assignment of space, equipment, and a time line. After the plan is presented, the entire unit staff is involved in critiquing, modifying, and approving it. A designing meeting is held at least two or three weeks, and preferably four to six weeks, prior to teaching the unit of work. This interval is necessary to allow time for organization of available materials and for development and preparation of materials not readily available. If considerable teacher time is needed to prepare for the unit, unit teaching schedules need to be arranged to free one or more teachers from their teaching duties for an hour or so a day during a team teaching block to prepare the material for the next unit of instruction. As an I & R Unit staff functions together, they are able to make plans in advance more easily. Also, the second year of operation is much easier because they can revise both procedures and/or plans they used and evaluated during the first year, rather than starting from the beginning for each unit of instruction.

Assessment Meeting

The assessment meeting deals with selecting, adapting and/or developing assessment procedures and instruments to assess the content to be learned according to the specific instructional objectives identified for a curricular area selected for IGE instructional programming. In addition, a plan for scheduling assessment time and a mechanism for summarizing the assessment data so it can be used to group students should be developed. Responsibility for this meeting can best be carried out by one or two unit teachers who develop and present the plan which is then critiqued and modified by the entire unit staff. Aides and student teachers or interns as well as staff teachers should be involved in summary and preparation of the data for use in grouping students and preparing scores for record sheets, keysort cards, or computer input. When necessary, plans for interpretation of the assessment data should also be made at this meeting. Assessment meetings should be held in connection with every unit of instruction in IGE. Remember, however, that the kind of assessment used may vary widely from test scores in a skill area to student interest in social studies or performances in physical education or art.

Grouping Meeting

This meeting involves assigning individual students to groups for instruction on the basis of assessment data along with teacher judgment, information on the student's learning style, and his or her reaction to the teaching style of various unit staff members. The sizes of groups to which the students are assigned depends on the nature of the curricular matter to be learned, the age of the children, and the facilities and staffing pattern in the unit. After children are assigned to groups on the basis of the aforenamed variables, teachers are assigned to the groups for teaching. A grouping meeting is held each time a new unit of instruction is to be taught (e.g., every three weeks). The grouping process may be carried out by the unit staff the first two or three times students are grouped; thereafter, at least preliminary grouping can be done by the unit leader or a staff teacher prior to the grouping meeting to speed up the process and save time.

Scheduling Meeting

This meeting may be handled in connection with the grouping meeting or at a separate meeting, depending on time restrictions and the amount of work to be done. After the groups are formed and teachers assigned to them, time, space, equipment, and materials need to be assigned so several groups are not using the same things at the same time. Scheduling, like grouping, can be carried out by the entire unit staff or preliminary scheduling can be worked out by the unit leader or a staff teacher prior to the scheduling meeting. Then the entire unit staff can react to the plan and modify it if necessary. A scheduling meeting is held in relation to each grouping meeting, (e.g., every three weeks).

Monitoring Meeting

At this meeting, the progress of each individual student in the unit of instruction is considered. One strategy of monitoring often used is to assign about 30 students to each staff teacher in the unit. This teacher then acts as "advisor" to those 30 students (sometimes called the advisees) and is available for informal conferences. This teacher also initiates a conference for the student to review progress from time to time. The "advisor" teacher has a record of the assignments of each student to groups and receives notice periodically, (e.g., every week), when the student has attained mastery on skills or other objectives. During an ongoing unit of instruction (e.g., the second week of three weeks), the unit staff should discuss its overall impression of how students are progressing and identify students who seem to be having problems mastering the objectives. They should also identify which students need to be regrouped. Constant monitoring is necessary in an instructional program like IGE in order to find problem situations quickly and correct them before the student becomes lost or discouraged. Also, monitoring helps the staff identify students who are having trouble working in the grouping pattern or with the types of materials assigned to them. Careful monitoring of students gives them a sense of individuality and a special relationship with one adult (their advisor) even though they are a part of a group of 150. This kind of meeting or meeting segment should occur once during every unit of instruction, (e.g., once every three weeks), and at ongoing operations meetings as needed. The unit leader usually assumes responsibility for this meeting.

Evaluation Meeting

At this meeting, postassessment data is presented in summary form, and identification of alternatives for students who attained and who did not attain relative to the unit of instruction are identified. Overall effectiveness of the total unit of instruction is also discussed with appropriate rationale and suggestions for its improvement or elimination. One meeting or meeting segment dealing with evaluation occurs after every unit of instruction, (e.g., every three weeks). While the whole unit staff should be involved in the final decisions, one or two staff teachers may prepare a summary of the postassessment data and suggestions of alternatives for masters and nonmasters, and present it for reaction by the entire unit staff. This type of meeting is essential for development and improvement of an IGE program.

ILLUSTRATING THE UNIT MEETING PLANNING STRATEGY

The purpose of this section is to present a step-by-step narrative of how one I & R Unit in one school, Unit B in Willow School, carried out its planning and decision making from the onset of school in late August to the day before Thanksgiving vacation. The agendas and minutes of their unit meetings provide the vehicle for this narrative. A brief description of the staff and students at Willow School precedes the agendas and meeting minutes.

Willow School is starting its first year in the IGE program. It is one of 12 elementary schools in a midwestern city of 50,000 people. There are 625 students in Willow School and their overall achievement tends to be slightly below the national average and the next to lowest in the system.

In order to prepare for implementation of IGE in fall of this year, the principal and unit leaders from Willow attended 24 hours of intensive inservice training conducted by an IGE facilitator from the state network and experienced practitioners during the previous February and March. Then during late April and May they assumed primary responsibility for training the entire Willow staff in IGE. This training of 18 hours consisted of three 6-hour intensive training sessions. The state IGE facilitator, along with a principal and a unit leader from an IGE school in its third year of operation in a nearby city, helped the Willow principal and unit leaders conduct these sessions. Again this fall, two more sessions of six hours each were arranged by the principal and unit leaders along with a staff member from the local university. The spring inservice sessions for the Willow staff focused on the seven basic components of IGE, along with an overview of the *Wisconsin Design* and Individually Guided Motivation (IGM). The fall inservice sessions went into greater detail on the *Wisconsin Design,* with emphasis on the preparation of a resource file for Word Attack skills and on the procedures and rationale for instructional programming in IGE.

The 625 students at Willow are divided into four units of 150-160 students each. Willow has 21 regular staff teachers with areas as art, music, and physical education taught by specialists from the system. Each unit also has one aide who handles both instructional and clerical duties, and two of the units, including Unit B, have a student teacher who is assigned to the unit full-time for one semester. Unit B, the unit to be focused on in this illustration, has a unit leader, four staff teachers, one aide, one student teacher, and 150 students, ages eight to 10 (approximately third and fourth graders). Staff names and positions are:

Ms. Goldsmith — Unit Leader
Ms. Flynn — Teacher
Ms. Fords — Teacher
Mr. Frost — Teacher
Ms. Jones — Teacher
Ms. Wynn — Aide
Ms. White — Student Teacher

Last April, the principal and unit leaders, functioning as an IIC, along with input from the total staff, decided their major focus in curriculum during their first year in IGE would be reading skills. To help them become acquainted with appropriate materials for IGE instructional programming they decided to purchase materials of the *Wisconsin Design for Reading Skill Development* in the areas of Word Attack, Study skills and Comprehension.

At the August 30 meeting of the unit, they made the long-range decision to implement the Word Attack skills program during the first semester and to add Study skills and Comprehension during the second semester. They also decided that their target date to begin teaching Word Attack skills with the students would be early to mid-October.

Using these decisions and time line as a guide, the unit leader, Ms. Goldsmith, developed a tentative schedule for unit meetings for the first twelve weeks of school from September 4 to November 20. The schedule is shown in Figure 10.4. Unit B had scheduled three hours per week planning time during the school day on Tuesdays and Thursdays from 3:00 to 4:30 P.M. In setting up the tentative schedule, the unit leader, Ms. Goldsmith, utilized the IGE unit meeting planning strategy discussed earlier in this chapter and outlined in Figure 10.3. Ms. Goldsmith presented this schedule to the unit staff at the September 4 ongoing operations meeting. The agenda for this meeting had been duplicated and distributed to staff members, including the aide and student teacher, by the unit leader three days in advance of the meeting. Agenda topics included:

- general announcements for the first week of school
- long-range plans for the year
- short-range plans for the first two weeks including the meeting schedule for September 4 to November 20

The September 4 ongoing operations meeting proceeded with announcements dealing with procedures for attendance, changes in schedules for specialists, additions to the library, and other related items. Time for announcements was limited to 15 minutes. The rest of the meeting was concerned with discussion about the long- and short-range plans as outlined in the Unit B Meeting Schedule presented in Figure 10.4.

During the discussion, it was pointed out that since this was the first time the unit had attempted to arrange their instruction according to the Instructional Programming Model for IGE, the schedule was *tentative* and subject to revision as the program progressed. It was also agreed that while meetings were identified as having specific purposes, items relative to ongoing operations could be taken up at any meeting as the need arose. Ms. Goldsmith reminded the staff that in order to get off to a good start and not overload themselves, instructional programming would be limited to reading Word Attack skills for this semester. Other areas in reading and other curricular subjects would be taught according to the same plan as in previous years with one teacher assigned to about 30 children. There would be no attempt to carry out systematic grouping in other areas until a smoothly functioning method for grouping and moving children had been worked out on a unitwide basis for Word Attack skills.

It was also agreed that agendas for unit meetings would be distributed to staff 48 hours prior to any regularly scheduled unit meeting, and that the recorder's job would rotate alphabetically among the staff teachers so it would not become a burden to any one individual. The person who was secretary for the meeting would be responsible for getting the minutes to the school secretary and/or aide promptly for typing and duplicating so they could be distributed the following day to the principal, unit staff, and

September 4 to November 24

	Sun	Mon	Tue	Wed	Thu	Fri	Sat	
	2	3 Labor Day	4 Ongoing operations	5	6 Ongoing operations	7	8	
September	9	10	11 Objectives setting	12	13 Designing	14	15	
	16	17	18 Assessment (for 9 wks)	19	20 Ongoing operations (assessment)	21	22	
	23	24	25 Ongoing operations (assessment)	26	27 Ongoing operations (assessment)	28	29	
	30	1	2 Grouping	3	4 Scheduling	5	6	
	7	8	9 Ongoing operations	10	11 Monitoring	12	13	
October	14	15	16 Ongoing operations (monitoring)	17	18 Objectives setting	19	20	Block 1
	21	22	23 Designing	24	25 Grouping/ scheduling	26	27	
	28	29	30 Ongoing operations	31	1 Evaluation Block 1	2	3	
November	4	5	6 Monitoring	7	8 Objectives setting	9	10	Block 2
	11	12	13 Designing	14	15 Grouping/ scheduling	16	17	
	18	19	20 Evaluation Block 2	21	22 Thanksgiving	23	24	

Fig. 10.4 Unit B meeting schedule.

anyone else attending the unit meeting. Promptness is especially important after Tuesday meetings because the minutes from that meeting need to be available for acceptance and for reference at the Thursday meeting.

Other decisions at this meeting dealing with operating procedures for the unit included:

- information from IIC meeting minutes that was not clear to unit staff or about which the unit members had questions would be discussed at unit meetings
- items for the agenda of unit meetings would be given to the unit leader *in writing* 24 hours prior to the meeting
- unit staff members will assume responsibility for major portions of many unit meetings as the program progresses; agendas will include indications of this responsibility
- agendas will indicate names and areas of expertise of outside resource people from the system, region, state university who will be attending unit meetings
- the aide and student teacher would attend all unit meetings during the first 12 weeks of school

Planning for Unit B is indicated in the following sections of this chapter by presentation of the agendas and subsequent meeting minutes. These agendas and minutes follow the dates of the meeting schedule presented in Figure 10.4. It is hoped that the reader might join Unit B as a "silent staff member" as he or she follows their progress in beginning an IGE instructional program.

September 6—Ongoing Operations Meeting—Agenda

(Goldsmith)	1.	Announcements	10 min
(Staff)	2.	Discussion of schedule for first 12 weeks of school that was handed out at September 4 meeting	20 min
(Goldsmith)	3.	Review of *Wisconsin Design* program with emphasis on the Word Attack portion	30 min
(Goldsmith)	4.	Discussion of purposes and assignment of responsibilities to staff for three future meetings September 11: Objectives setting meeting September 13: Designing meeting September 18: Assessment meeting	30 min

September 6—Ongoing Operations Meeting—Minutes

1. Announcements by Ms. Goldsmith included:

   a. unit schedules for special teachers in physical education, art, and music for the first semester will be available tomorrow, September 7, and special teachers will start teaching at Willow during the week of September 12.
   b. notice of the first districtwide inservice meeting to be held on September 19 on the subject of preparing individualized learning stations.
   c. directions for how to handle shortages of books and materials were read and distributed.
   d. the PTA Executive Committee meeting schedule.
   e. the school nurse schedule.
   f. procedures for handling monies and reservations for milk and hot lunch.

2. Discussion continued on the purposes of unit meetings on the unit meet-schedule presented on September 4. Staff concerns centered on:
   a. how the Word Attack skills program coordinates with the present basal reading program.
   b. how the common time block (10:00-10:30 every day) for the Word Attack skills program which had been worked out the spring before would be utilized for teaching skills 90 minutes a week.
   c. utilization of the aide and student teacher in the common time Word Attack skills block, as well as their duties in the regular classroom portions of the unit program.
   d. utilization of IMC staff and materials.

3. Review of the *Wisconsin Design* program included:
   a. philosophy and use of *Wisconsin Design* and the list of 45 skills with designation of the subset most likely to be appropriate for a majority of 8- to 10-year-olds at Willow.
   b. agreement among staff that more inservice on the *Wisconsin Design* was needed. They suggested the last half hour of the unit meetings on September 20, 25, and 27 as a good time for this inservice since they would be gaining more information about the program and more questions would arise as they prepared for implementation. Also, they suggested the unit leader contact the leaders of other units at the IIC meeting to find out if they wanted more inservice on the *Design*. If they did, the inservice could be carried out on a cooperative basis.

      Mr. Frost volunteered to take responsibility for the *Design* inservice segments. They reminded him that the filmstrips/cassettes *Design in Review, Instructional Programming in IGE,* and *The Resource File* from the *Wisconsin Design* series had been reviewed and discussed previously.

4. Staff teacher responsibilities for the objectives setting, design and assessment meetings were discussed and summarized as follows:
   a. For *objectives setting meeting,* staff teacher responsibilities would include:
      (1) identifying the range of skills and objectives for the 8- to 10-year-old students in the unit.
      (2) locating skills and objectives from the *Design* in the basal reader(s) using the *Wisconsin Design* compendium when possible.
      (3) planning for unit staff to make further contributions of materials and ideas to the resource file that was started during the preschool inservice meeting.
      (4) presenting the objectives and related material along with a scheme for critiquing by unit staff members.
   b. For the *designing meeting,* staff member responsibilities would include:
      (1) designation of the number of skills to be taught in the first 3-week block.
      (2) tentative assignment of unit staff including aide and student teacher to skill groups and other duties.
      (3) presentation of rationale for initial assessment to cover the semester and/or year.
      (4) identification and location of physical space for assessment and skill teaching.
      (5) preparation of an inventory of available materials and equipment (outside of the resource file) for skills teaching.
      (6) presentation of design at September 13 meeting.
   c. For the *assessment meeting,* staff member responsibilities include:
      (1) selection of levels for initial testing of the 150 students in the unit, utilizing previous records and teacher judgment; estimates of levels are to be made in advance of the September 18 meeting.
      (2) development of schedule for administering assessment tests.
      (3) working with aide during period of September 13-19 to prepare for administration during period of September 20-26.
      (4) development of an efficient plan for correcting and summarizing test data by October 2 grouping meeting.
      (5) assuming responsibility at September 18 meeting for unit to judge the appropriateness of the suggested testing levels.
   d. Staff teacher assignments for the three meetings were worked out as follows:
      (1) Ms. Flynn, who had taken a workshop on objectives for individualized learning programs during the past year, volun-

teered to take the major responsibility for the objectives setting meeting on September 11.

(2) Ms. Fords, who had attended the one-week *Wisconsin Design* inservice program the previous spring, volunteered to handle the designing meeting on September 13.

(3) The unit staff felt the assessment meeting on September 18 and the subsequent preparation of data for the meetings of September 20, 25, and 27, and October 2 involved large amounts of work and suggested that at least two staff teachers be assigned. Ms. Jones volunteered to chair the assessment operation. They suggested Ms. Flynn, who had worked on a district evaluation project, work with her. She accepted. In the ensuing discussion, it was decided further that the student teacher, Ms. White, who had just completed a course in evaluation techniques, work with the two staff teachers.

September 11—Objectives Setting Meeting—Agenda

(Goldsmith)	1. Announcements	10 min
(Flynn)	2. Review of assessment data from basic testing programs: Gates-MacGinitie Iowa Tests of Basic Skills	20 min
(Flynn)	3. Review of *Wisconsin Design* Objectives, Levels B, C, and D	10 min
(Flynn)	4. Selecting appropriate objectives for instruction from *Wisconsin Design,* Levels B, C, and D and designation of tentative teaching procedures	50 min

September 11—Objectives Setting Meeting—Minutes

1. Announcements by Ms. Goldsmith included:
   a. a reminder to students to follow suggestions of patrol boys and girls at the crossings.
   b. the dinner for new teachers in the system will be held on September 14 at the Holiday Inn at 7:30 P.M. This does not affect Unit B personnel since no one was new this year.
   c. fall film orders are due in the principal's office by September 18.
   d. elementary teachers will meet at the Third Street School for a districtwide inservice day on Wednesday, September 19. The topic of "Developing Individualized Learning Stations" will be of particular interest to Unit B staff.
2. Ms. Flynn opened the meeting by reminding staff that prior to the selection of objectives all available information about the students in the area being considered should be reviewed. For example, in preparation

for selection of an appropriate cluster of objectives for Word Attack skills from the *Wisconsin Design,* we will want to consider test scores for children in the unit from the vocabulary sections of the Gates-MacGinitie and Iowa Test of Basic Skills, along with student progress reports and information from teachers who worked with the children during previous years.

Ms. Flynn also reminded the unit staff that the IIC had reviewed this information as a part of their selection of the *Wisconsin Design* for Willow, and as a basis for setting tentative long-range objectives for the school. Ms. Goldsmith then handed out a summary of the data from the two standardized tests for the students in Unit B. Ms. Flynn reviewed the data with the unit staff and pointed out that most of the children tended to be six months to one year below the norm for their grade level.

Mr. Flynn asked each unit member to refer to the list of *Wisconsin Design* objectives in the Teacher's Planning Guide. Since the children in Unit B ranged in age from 8 to 10 years, but tended to work below grade level, objectives at Levels B, C, and D with major emphasis on those at Levels C and D were identified as appropriate for the 150 students. Each objective at these levels was reviewed with the unit staff.

3. Ms. Flynn distributed lists on which the 150 students in Unit B had been randomly assigned to one of the five certified teachers. The 30 students assigned to each teacher would form a homeroom group. This teacher would also become an advisor for these students. This arrangement would form the basis for an advisor-advisee program which would be developed during the semester.

   Ms. Flynn pointed out that assignment of an advisor was desirable so students would have someone to talk to when necessary, and for monitoring student progress. She asked staff to review their lists and to indicate any student they felt would relate better to another teacher than to themselves. Names of six students were exchanged.

September 13—Designing Meeting—Agenda

(Goldsmith)	1. Announcements	10 min
(Fords)	2. Presentation of design for 3-week skill block (Block 1)	40 min
(Fords)	3. Critique and modification of design by unit members	20 min
(Fords)	4. Assignment of teachers to general responsibilities for Block 1	20 min

September 13—Designing Meeting—Minutes

1. Announcements by Ms. Goldsmith included:

a. the area teachers' convention is scheduled for October 11th and 12th and will be held at Central High School in Falls City. Tickets can be purchased from our building representative, Ms. Jones, for $4.00.
b. because of the convention schedule, the monitoring meeting scheduled for October 11th will be rescheduled for October 10th.
c. the first lyceum program for Willow School students will be presented on Wednesday, September 26th from 9:00 to 10:00 A.M. in the multipurpose room. The program will feature a puppet presentation.
d. numerous complaints have been received in the office about Willow School pupils cutting through private yards going to and from school, especially in the Gray Street area. Please speak to the boys and girls in your homeroom/advisee group about this.
e. any boys 9 years or older who are interested in a touch football league should meet with Mr. Valdez on Monday, September 17, immediately after school.

2. Ms. Fords, using the objectives designated at the September 11 meeting, presented suggestions for grouping students for the skills program along with several ways of teaching the content. She suggested that one of the teachers in the unit *not* be assigned to an initial teaching responsibility of a skills group. This teacher would then be available to work with pupils who move out of the assigned skill group before the conclusion of the three-week period. The teacher can supervise these students on independent work, another skill, or exploratory work in the learning center.

   Ms. Fords pointed out that this arrangement would not only provide greater flexibility in the skills program, but would provide additional planning time for one member of the unit. At the beginning of the three-week skills block, when this staff member would not have an assigned skill group, he or she could be developing plans, working on curricular materials, designing learning activities or working on other educational problems as identified by the unit. Ms. Fords suggested that this "floating" role could be rotated systematically among unit members during the year.

   "In long-range planning, for example," Ms. Fords pointed out, "the unit could identify a particular problem and ask the staff member not assigned to a skill group to gather data, list alternative solutions, locate material and so forth. Over time, the unit could get many problems solved in this manner."

   Ms. Fords also suggested that two or three unit members could work with more than one small skill group of five to six students at a time. Remaining unit members could be assigned to larger skill groups with Ms. White, the student teacher, and Ms. Wynn, the aide, assigned to assist them.

3. Three alternate plans for time scheduling of skill instruction as adapted from the Teacher's Planning Guide for the *Wisconsin Design* program were presented to the unit by Ms. Fords. After some discussion, the unit members agreed that they liked the two plans with skill instruction on alternate days. They felt that this would lend more flexibility to their entire schedule. They unanimously agreed that the time of 120 minutes per week for Word Attack skills seemed a bit long and suggested a shorter schedule.

   Ms. Fords reported that several schools with a student population similar to Willow were using the Monday, Wednesday, Friday skill group schedule, with 30-minute blocks of time each day. The unit adopted this latter plan.

4. Teachers were assigned to general responsibilities for the first three-week period as follows:

   Ms. Goldsmith: unscheduled
   Ms. Jones: two small reading skill groups
   Mr. Frost: two small reading skill groups
   Ms. Flynn: one larger reading skill group
   Ms. Fords: one larger reading skill group
   Ms. White (student teacher): assigned to work with Ms. Fords and Ms. Flynn
   Ms. Wynn (aide): assigned to work with Ms. Jones and Mr. Frost

September 18—Assessment Meeting—Agenda

(Goldsmith)	1.	Announcements	10 min
(Jones)	2.	Presentation of assessment plan and schedule with responses from staff members	30 min
(Jones, Flynn)	3.	Assignment of students and staff to testing levels	30 min
(Goldsmith)	4.	Assignment of responsibilities for grouping and scheduling meetings	20 min

September 18—Assessment Meeting—Minutes

1. Announcements by Ms. Goldsmith included:
   a. a list of new instructional materials on reading skills that had arrived in the IMC. She suggested that the aide, Ms. Wynn, key these materials, along with others available in the building, to the *Wisconsin Design* skills and add this information to the resource file.
   b. PTA meets on October 26th and she will explain the parent conference procedure for the current year.

c. advance plans should be developing for the unitwide field trip on November 27th to the nearby county museum. The trip correlates with a unit of instruction on the westward movement in social studies.

2. The assessment plan and tentative schedule, presented by Ms. Jones, indicated:
   a. testing for initial placement in the *Wisconsin Design* will involve all staff members, including the aide and student teachers.
   b. testing time would be scheduled during the reading language arts block from 10:00 to 10:30 each morning on September 20th, 21st, 24th, 25th, 26th, and 27th. Hopefully most testing would be completed by September 26th.

3. Ms. Jones reported that she, along with Ms. Flynn, Ms. White, and Ms. Wynn, had determined tentative testing levels for the students. "First, we used the standardized scores from the Gates-MacGinitie and Iowa areas of vocabulary as a guide and categorized students as 'below,' 'at,' or 'above' grade level. Then we related these scales to the *Wisconsin Design* levels and arranged the children in the unit on a chart. I have a chart for each of you with the names of the children to be tested at each level. Now, please look at the summary at the bottom of the sheet which shows the numbers of children to be tested at each level."

   Level A— 15 children
   Level B— 25 children
   Level C—100 children
   Level D— 10 children

   Ms. Flynn pointed out, "This means we'll have four test groups and will have to assign staff accordingly." Earlier, the unit had decided to assign staff so one teacher would be free to handle problems and to handle retesting of students who had been assigned at the wrong level. In order to do this, they had asked the principal, Mr. Valdez, to take a small group for testing. The principal had indicated that he would feel most comfortable with Level D material. Thus, staff assignments for testing appeared as follows:

Level B— 40 children	Mr. Frost, Ms. Fords
Level C—100 children	Ms. Jones, Chair.
	Ms. Goldsmith
	Ms. Wynn
	Ms. White
Level D— 10 children	Mr. Valdez
Roving (problems, retesting)	Ms. Flynn

After designating testing assignments, Ms. Flynn handed staff members a floor plan of the unit area, and space was assigned appropriate to the size of each test group.

Ms. Fords asked, "How do we get the right tests and what do we do with the results?" Ms. Jones replied that Ms. Wynn and the student teacher, Ms. White, had been assigned to handle correcting and punching with all staff members assisting from 3:00-4:00 P.M. each day except Friday during the testing period of September 20th, 21st, 24th, 25th, 26th, and 27th. Mr. Frost exclaimed, "This is going to be a tough schedule with teaching other subjects and all!" Ms. Goldsmith agreed and reminded the staff that this intensive testing only occurs once in an area like Word Attack and would never be this time consuming again.

4. Time was running short and Ms. Goldsmith reminded the group that responsibilities for the grouping and scheduling meetings on October 2nd and 4th, respectively, need to be designated. Mr. Frost volunteered for grouping and Ms. Flynn for scheduling.
5. The group agreed that ad hoc unit meetings should be called before school or at noon during the testing period as needed.

This series of meetings has indicated how one I & R Unit initiated instructional programming in Word Attack skills. A description of the meetings from September 20th to November 20th is presented in Appendix A.

SUMMARY

This chapter has dealt with cooperative planning in terms of (1) determining the strengths and expertise of members of the I & R Unit staff, (2) planning instruction for students in the unit according to the IPM, (3) differentiated staff roles and responsibilities, (4) identifying and using personnel resources available, (5) identifying and developing planning objectives. Then a unit meeting planning strategy which identified eight types of meetings was presented. Finally, five unit planning meetings—September 4th, 6th, 11th, 13th, and 18th—illustrated how one I & R Unit handled the problems of introducing IGE into their school, and how they planned and carried out instructional programming using the *Wisconsin Design* materials for the Word Attack skills.

Agendas and minutes for the I & R Unit meetings from September 20th to November 20th indicated in Figure 10.4 are presented in Appendix A.

REFERENCES

Bair, M., and R. G. Woodward 1964. *Team teaching in action.* Boston: Houghton Mifflin.

DiPego, G. 1970. *Individually guided education: unit operation and roles.* Dayton, Ohio: Institute for Development of Educational Activities.

Gates-MacGinitie reading tests 1965. Columbia University, New York: Teachers College Press.

Hillson, M., and R. T. Hyman (eds.), 1971. *Change and innovation in elementary and secondary organization.* (2nd ed.) New York: Holt.

Iowa test of basic skills 1964. Boston: Houghton Mifflin.

Johnson, R. H., Jr., and J. J. Hunt 1968. *Rx for team teaching.* Minneapolis: Burgess.

Klausmeier, H. J., M. R. Quilling, J. S. Sorenson, R. S. Way, and G. R. Glasrud 1971. *Individually guided education and the multiunit elementary school: guidelines for implementation.* Madison, Wisc.: Wisconsin Research and Development Center.

Murray, E. M., and J. R. Wilhour 1971. *The flexible elementary school: practical guidelines for developing a nongraded program.* West Nyack, New York: Parker.

Wisconsin design for reading skill development 1971. Madison, Wisc.: Wisconsin Research and Development Center for Cognitive Learning.

11

Setting General Objectives

Juanita S. Sorenson
Kathleen L. Nolan

Objectives

After reading this chapter, the reader will be able:

- To describe the role of general educational objectives in IGE and their relationship to specific instructional objectives.
- To identify examples of general objectives for a cognitive and an affective area.
- To indicate the sequential process by which general objectives might be identified, adapted, and evaluated for a curriculum area.
- To describe the role of the unit leader in identifying and evaluating general objectives.

General educational objectives, often called goals, have long been a part of the American educational scene. In IGE, general objectives are set for the student population of each school building. They are set by the professional staff of the building to reflect the needs and characteristics of the students. They should also be in harmony with statements of philosophy for the building and/or system.

General objectives form the structure upon which the instructional program of the school is built. It should be noted that general objectives as discussed here are different from specific instructional objectives. General objectives deal with long-term outcomes such as what is expected of the student population of the building at the end of seven years of elementary school or at intermediate steps during this period.

General objectives become criteria by which materials are selected, curriculum content is outlined, instructional objectives and procedures are developed, and assessments are prepared. All aspects of the educational program are really means to accomplish general objectives. If an educational program is to be studied systematically and intelligently, general educational objectives must be specified (Tyler 1969, p. 3).

The term curriculum as used here denotes "a group of courses and planned experiences which a student has under the guidance of the school"; further it implies "a pattern of instruction which seeks to promote learning through cooperative group activities; is concerned with development through group interaction of effective habits and skills of cooperative planning, fact-finding, and evaluation and with development of socially effective citizens; includes teacher participation with pupils in planning and executing learning activities while establishing and practicing basic principles of democratic living" (Good 1973, pp. 157-158).

Objectives are defined in a broad sense as attainable and potentially directive statements. They are signposts to recognizable and well-rounded features rather than pointers to a promised land. Objectives should be able to speak plainly for themselves (Brown 1970, p. 60).

A primary purpose of objectives is to provide a route or map for pupils to use to arrive at desired outcomes. Since objectives do specify routes and hopefully alternative routes to arrive at outcomes, they can form the basis for planning the curriculum and instructional program (Alexander, Saylor, and Williams 1971, p. 144).

General objectives for a school are statements of educational aims or outcomes that provide direction for competencies and behaviors which the professional personnel of a given school believe are necessary to attain the ultimate goals or purposes of that school. They set the stage for the identification of instructional objectives. Development of general objectives includes identification of the values of the society that supports the school. This is followed by an analysis of what is required to translate those

A primary purpose of objectives is to provide a route or map for pupils to use to arrive at desired outcomes—formal and informal.

values into increasingly more specific learnings until the teacher has a clear idea of what behavior each learner should be capable of performing. General objectives determine the general direction and quality of the more specific instructional objectives (Allen and Seitman 1971, p. 210).

The role of general educational objectives in IGE is given in Step 1 of the Instructional Programming Model: "The [general] educational objectives are to be attained by the student population of the building after a year and longer time periods in terms of level of achievement and other performance related to each curriculum area and in terms of other values and action patterns." (Klausmeier, *et al.* 1971, p. 19) An example of a general educational objective for Word Attack skills would be stated as follows: "Ninety percent of the children will attain independence in word attack by age ten; 95 percent by age eleven; and 99 percent by age twelve." The responsibility for setting general educational objectives should be assumed by the principal and unit leaders meeting as an IIC (Klausmeier, *et al.* 1971, p. 25). Input to the IIC comes from I & R Unit staff teachers and other personnel in the building and/or system.

General educational objectives in IGE are schoolwide objectives which focus the attention of the staff on priorities, including setting instructional objectives for individual children and groups of children and carrying out related instructional programming to help individual children meet those objectives. For example, if tutoring were possible in only one curriculum area, it would probably be carried out in the area in which the school staff was emphasizing instructional programming. Therefore, if a school was carrying out instructional programming in Word Attack skills in reading, tutoring would be implemented in connection with acquiring and using those skills. It is further suggested that the attainment of the objective, rather than the age or grade level of the child, will determine when Word Attack instruction in skills ceases for an individual child.

General objectives should deal with affective areas like motives, self-concept, interests, attitudes, values, and psychomotor skills such as handling of equipment, use of materials and physical coordination, as well as with cognitive areas.

SELECTING GENERAL OBJECTIVES

General educational objectives form the foundation for the IGE component of instructional programming for individual students previously discussed in Chapter 1 of this book and presented in model form in Figure 1.3. General objectives relate to students in a particular school building and are identified, adapted, and evaluated by the IIC of that building, along with other personnel from the building with special expertise. Such personnel might be the IMC director (if not an IIC member in a building), resource teachers, or a staff teacher with special expertise in the curriculum or affective area for which the objectives are being identified. System personnel should also be involved in formulating general objectives, since each building is a part of the larger system and objectives must be appropriate for the system as well as the building. Also, system personnel have special expertise and should be utilized to carry out this sometimes difficult process.

Careful planning should be carried out in connection with setting general objectives for a building. The principal, as chairperson of the IIC, should provide leadership for this process. While general objectives are identified for a group of students in a given building, it should be remembered that the work of staffs in other districts and experts in a given curriculum area can provide a good base from which adaptations can be made.

Setting general educational objectives logically appears as the first step in the model for instructional programming in Figure 1.3 and in the working version of the model in Figure 10.1. However, in practice, it is not always possible or practical to set general objectives before identifying specific instructional objectives and carrying out the other steps in instructional programming for a year or longer. Therefore, many staffs have implemented steps 2 through 7 of instructional programming (identifying specific instructional objectives, assessing pupil performance, setting objectives for individual students, implementing the instructional program, postassessing student performance, and selecting alternatives for attainers and nonattainers, respectively) in a subject area for a year or so before they set general objectives. Readers of this book are encouraged to set general objectives as soon as possible (at least within one year) after implementing instructional programming in an area, but not to delay implementing programming until general objectives are set.

General objectives are crucial in the long term evaluation of IGE. They are needed to help a staff know where their students are now, how they change over a period of several years, and how implementing of instructional programming affects student performance in a curricular or affective area. The content of this section has been divided into two areas:

1. locating sources and content of general objectives
2. identifying, adapting, and evaluating general objectives for a school building

Locating Sources and Content of General Objectives

In IGE, general objectives are identified by the IIC to meet the needs of children in a building. The IIC should consider the following points prior to identifying general objectives (Sorenson 1973, p. 4):

1. achievement scores from standardized tests in the area(s) where instructional programming is to be implemented.
2. formal and informal information about the students from cumulative and other records.
3. expectations of the parents and community.
4. chronological sequence of priorities for implementing instructional programming and/or personalizing the educational program in curriculum and/or affective areas.

    For example, in one school the IIC, with input from the staff teachers and other building/system personnel, had decided during the first two years in IGE to give priority to implementing instructional programming in reading and motivation. In reading, the skill areas of Word Attack, Study skills, and Comprehension would be implemented in that order. Motivation would focus on procedures to develop positive self-directed behaviors so the children could function more effectively in the reading skills program, as well as in the general school setting.

General objectives should be stated clearly, communicated widely, and agreed upon by the staff of the building. Five questions to help the IIC set general objectives for a school are (Institute for the Development of Educational Activities 1970, p. 70):

1. What do children need to learn today that will help them live tomorrow?
2. What skills are necessary for all children who grow up to live in America in 1985?
3. What attitudes about self, family, community, nation, and world do we want our children to possess?
4. What information is relevant today that will be relevant tomorrow?
5. What foundations do our children need—the techniques of learning and processes of thinking?

While general objectives in IGE should reflect local needs and characteristics, they should also be challenged, reviewed, and refined by those who work with them. In order to develop purposeful general educational objectives, a school system or building must have a comprehensive philosophy of education. Three obvious and relevant sources to study in deciding on a philosophy and educational objectives which relate to it are (Tyler 1969, p. 3):

1. The learners themselves. By looking at the learners, we consider education as a process of changing the behavior patterns of people and

include thinking and feeling as well as overt action. General objectives developed in this way represent the kinds of change in behavior that an educational institution seeks to bring about in its students.

2. Contemporary life outside the school. Here objectives grow out of the difficult task of accomplishing all that has been laid upon the schools with the increased body of knowledge that exists today. It also involves selecting objectives from a contemporary life that is complex and changing, and demands focusing of educational efforts on the critical aspects of this complex life.
3. Suggestions about objectives from specialists in curriculum and other areas.

General objectives can be adapted from curriculum guides and courses of study prepared by public schools, universities, state departments of education, and other educational groups. They must be related to learning experiences and serve as guidelines for future thinking. If objectives are useful, they must be stated in a manner which is meaningful to students and parents, as well as to the educators. Five principles that should be kept in mind when identifying general objectives for students are (Tyler 1969, p. 65):

1. A student must have experiences which provide the opportunity to practice the kind of behavior implied by the objective. For example, if the objective is to develop skill in problem solving, it cannot be attained unless the learning experiences in the school program give the student ample opportunity to solve problems.
2. The learning experience must be such that the student obtains satisfaction from carrying on the kind of behavior implied by the objectives. For example, in the case of learning experiences to develop skill in solving health problems, it is important that the experience not only gives the student an opportunity to solve health problems, but also poses problem solutions which are both effective and satisfying.
3. Reactions indicated in the experience should be within the range of possibility for the students involved. For example, the experiences should be appropriate to the student's present attainments, predispositions, and the like. If the learning experience involves the kind of behavior which the student is not yet able to make, then it fails in its purpose.
4. A variety of experiences can be used to attain the same educational objective.
5. A given learning experience usually brings about several outcomes. For example, while the student is solving problems about health, cer-

tain information, such as attitudes, interests, and likes or dislikes about the health field are also being acquired.

Objectives can also grow out of discussions by an elementary staff. This is illustrated in relation to an affective objective such as (Manolakes 1965, p. 34): Each child will develop an adequate concept of self which leads to considering oneself a worthy human being. This objective is based on the idea that a child learns best when relieved of great pressures to compete, and when the child feels confident of accomplishing that which is expected. This objective resulted from teacher questions similar to these:

1. "How can we expect every child to do the same assignment within the same period of time?"
2. "I wonder how many children are being asked today to do things they cannot possibly accomplish?"
3. "Is this a valid reason for calling such a child a failure?"
4. "Do our report cards help a child to develop an adequate self-concept, or do they merely reinforce the feelings of failure that some children have lived with all their lives?"
5. "Are we really being helpful when we segregate children for instruction into middle, high, and low groups for the year? I wonder how successful we are in hiding from children the fact that theirs is a slow group by calling it the Yankees?"
6. "Do all individuals have an opportunity to feel successful in what they are doing, especially in those areas that they value and that we value?"

Using the questions above as a guide, a school staff might generate the following general objectives for "improvement" for a year:

1. To reduce the competitive activities that tend to place some children in superior and some in inferior classifications.
2. To continue to seek ways to differentiate instructional activities within the classroom.
3. To reevaluate the reporting system as a professional staff.
4. To seek ways for each child to find some success in school experiences.

Identifying, Adapting, and Evaluating General Objectives

The IIC and school staff of a building should identify the general objectives for its student population in both cognitive (curriculum) and affective areas. In IGE, many staffs have identified general objectives in a cognitive area (e.g., reading, mathematics, social studies) first. This occurs because cognitive objectives are usually easier to identify and staffs have more experience and background in the cognitive areas. After they have identified objectives and have had experience with them in one subject area, they identify objectives in the affective and additional cognitive areas in successive years. Priorities in identification of objectives also depend on the needs of the students in a building or system, and on the staff and/or system expertise available at the time objectives are to be identified. For example, if the students in a school have achievement scores well above the national average in curriculum areas but have noticeable need for more positive self-directed behaviors and creativity, the staff may give priority to developing objectives in the latter affective areas.

Priorities in identification of cognitive and affective objectives should also relate to the general program objectives of the school. For example, if the staff has selected mathematics as the area in which they will first implement instructional programming, then math should be the first area for which general objectives are identified. The task of identifying objectives involves many people and is time consuming. Thus, a time line for the process should be established. For example, a school which has decided to give priority to the curriculum areas of mathematics and reading skills, and to the affective areas of motivation (goal setting), might have a time line that looks like this:

Year 1	a. mathematics	identify general and specific instructional objectives
Year 2	a. reading	identify general and specific instructional objectives in reading areas of Word Attack and Study skills
	b. goal setting	identify general and specific objectives for goal setting in mathematics skills
Year 3	a. reading	identify general and specific instructional objectives in Comprehension skills
	b. goal setting	identify general and specific objectives for goal setting in reading skills

General objectives designed for the children of a building according to their characteristics become *realistic* objectives for the children to meet. This contrasts to the traditional pattern where "average" grade level norms (local, state, national) formed the guidelines. Objectives based on these were often not relevant to any particular building since no group of children in a particular building is "average." Using "average" data (for example, the 50th percentile) in a curricular area as a basis for general objectives means the objectives are too low for some children in the buildings, and out of reach for others.

However, grade line and/or norm information is very useful as a starting point in the process of initial identification of cognitive objectives. For example, if national norms in mathematics indicate students at the 50th percentile can multiply *a given two-digit number by any two-digit number using standard algorithm* by age 12 (approximately the end of sixth grade) then a staff selecting objectives for a school building with students who consistently achieve "above average" could set tentative objectives in multiplication for its students as: By completion of elementary school (approximately age 12),

99 percent of the students will be able to multiply a given two-digit number by any two-digit number using the standard algorithm

80 percent of the students will be able to multiply a given two-digit number by any three-digit number using the standard algorithm

50 percent of the students will be able to multiply a given three-digit number by any three- or four-digit number using the standard algorithm

On the other hand, objectives in multiplication for a school whose students have consistently achieved "below average" could be set as: By completion of elementary school (approximately age 12),

90 percent of the students will be able to multiply through 10 times 10 using the standard algorithm

60 percent of the students will be able to multiply a given two-digit number by any two-digit number using the standard algorithm

40 percent of the students will be able to multiply a given two-digit number by a three-digit number using the standard algorithm

General objectives like those given above for mathematics refer to student accomplishments of skills/concepts/processes. They form the basic guidelines for unit staffs in IGE schools to select specific instructional objectives in mathematics, and serve also to direct staff input in terms of identifying media and grouping patterns and materials to help students meet the specific instructional objectives.

General objectives in skill areas like mathematics and reading are fairly easy to identify because of the generally accepted need to master these skills. In other curricular areas like science, social studies, art, and physical education, objectives may vary widely from system to system, as well as among school buildings within a system. Objectives in the affective areas are even more difficult to identify. However, affective objectives should be identified in the same manner as cognitive objectives, that is, to meet the needs of the students in each building and in relation to the priorities of the school's instructional program.

Setting general objectives, as indicated earlier, is a complex process and the staff of a school building should draw on resource personnel to help them. For example, in setting general objectives in math, special math teachers, mathematics consultants, and junior and/or senior high math teachers who are available in a system are all potential resource persons. All of these people have a strong content background in the subject matter of mathematics and can help the IIC and staff teachers to interpret statistical terminology and develop expectations in mathematics for a total elementary program. They also have information on what will be expected of students in mathematics in a particular system on leaving the elementary building. Persons from the central office staff, such as the system and/or school psychologist or others with expertise in measurement and evaluation, are helpful to elementary staffs in interpreting and summarizing data as norms, grade equivalents, percentile scores, and ability scores from standardized tests.

Central office personnel, as an elementary coordinator or supervisor if a system has one, or the superintendent or a representative in charge of instruction, should be involved in the objective-setting process. These people work in several school buildings and have valuable and practical suggestions to contribute about expected outcomes for children.

A suggested sequential procedure the IIC could use for setting and evaluating general objectives in an IGE school is presented in Figure 11.1. The narrative that follows describes each step of this procedure.

The numbers below correspond to the numbers in Figure 11.1.

1. The IIC has identified *reading* as the curricular area in which it will implement instructional programming. This decision was based on the fact that the standardized test scores of the fifth graders in the categories of vocabulary and comprehension were the lowest among the 12 buildings in the city last year.
2. The characteristics of the children could be summarized as follows:
   a. General achievement scores are slightly below the national average, but these students rank seventh among the 12 buildings in the system.
   b. Achievement scores in reading vocabulary and comprehension for fifth graders last spring were at the 30th percentile. On the same standardized test two years earlier, the fifth graders were at the 39th percentile.
   c. Information from anecdotal and cumulative records indicated that the student population is fairly mobile with 35 percent of the students being new to the district last year, while two years ago the mobility factor was about 25 percent.

d. About 10 percent of the students have been identified as having some type of emotional or mental problem.
e. About 40 percent of the students come from broken families, mostly through divorce; about 30 percent of the students are supported by government social services.
f. The student population is about 70 percent white, 25 percent black, and 5 percent Chicano.
g. About 50 percent of the fathers and mothers work at one of two local industries producing either agricultural implements or furniture with both industries employing a large number of unskilled workers.

3. To find out how other schools had handled this problem, the IIC members, along with several staff teachers, wrote to other districts and to central resource pools for individualized instruction to obtain copies of general objectives they had already set. In addition, the IMC director and the unit leader from the intermediate unit had volunteered to contact the IGE league facilitator, state network coordinator, and local university professors, and to search the local university education library for sources and examples of general objectives in reading. These efforts had resulted in only a few good examples of general objectives.
4. Resource personnel, a time line, and exemplary objectives were designated as follows:
   a. Resource persons selected to help the IIC and staff teachers select general objectives would be: (1) the system elementary coordinator; (2) a classroom teacher who recently received certification as a reading specialist; and (3) the local university IGE facilitator who has a strong background in reading and teaches reading methods. IIC members, the IMC director, and the three resource persons formed what came to be known as the Objectives Committee.
   b. The time line called for development of a tentative set of general objectives for reading Word Attack, Study skills, and Comprehension by October 15th. The Objectives Committee would meet each Thursday at 2:30 P.M. prior to this period. Individuals or small committees of two or three people would carry out specific tasks between committee meetings. It should be noted that the information referred to in steps 1, 2 and 3 was available to this committee.
   c. General objectives in reading from two schools—one in the midwest and one in the far west—along with instructional objectives in Word Attack and Comprehension from four schools were identified as guides for the committee in developing general objectives.
5. A set of tentative objectives for Word Attack was developed by the end

Suggested Sequential Procedures for Setting and Evaluating General Objectives

1. Identify the area(s) in which objectives are to be set.
2. Investigate and summarize the characteristics of the children in the building in terms of:
   a. achievement scores from standardized tests
   b. formal and informal anecdotal and other relevant records
   c. expectations of the parents and community.
3. Review objectives set by other schools.
4. Designate personnel, time lines, and examples such as:
   a. resource persons who will work with the IIC in setting the objectives
   b. a time line and meeting times for the IIC to carry out the project
   c. objectives from other schools that might be used as guidelines.
5. Develop a set of tentative objectives.
6. Have unit staffs react to the objectives (in writing).
7. Revise the initial objectives, incorporating reactions from unit staffs.
8. Duplicate and distribute the revised objectives to all personnel.
9. Evaluate the objectives periodically:
   a. at the end of the first semester for:
      1. indications of tentative revisions that seem to be needed
   b. at the end of the first year for:
      1. necessary revisions as indicated by one year's experience
      2. language changes as indicated by staff to make objectives easier to interpret
   c. at the end of each succeeding year for:
      1. needed revisions based on experience with the objectives and student gains or shifts in population.

Fig. 11.1 Suggested sequential procedures.

of the second meeting of the Objectives Committee. They appeared as follows:

> 80 percent of the children will be independent in Word Attack by age 10 (end of five years of school);
>
> 90 percent will be independent by age 11 (end of six years of school); and
>
> 99 percent by age 12 (completion of seven years of school).

At the end of the fourth meeting of the committee, a set of general objectives for Comprehension had also been devised:

60 percent of the students will achieve independence in Comprehension, e.g., be able to read daily newspaper articles not requiring a specialized vocabulary, by age 10 (end of five years of school);

60 percent will achieve independence by age 11 (end of six years of school); and

90 percent by age 12 (end of seven years of school).

6. The tentative objectives developed by the committee in Step 5 were duplicated and unit staffs were asked to react to them in writing by October 30th. Responses were to be specific and to indicate instances of agreement and disagreement with the objectives, along with appropriate reasons.

7. Objectives were revised according to the reactions from unit staffs. A summary of the reactions indicated teachers felt percentages for independence in Word Attack were a bit too high for the students. Thus, they were revised as follows:

   75 percent of the students will be independent in Word Attack by age 10 (end of five years of school) as indicated by a score of 75 percent or higher on each of the Word Attack skill tests;

   85 percent will be independent by age 11 (end of six years of school); and

   95 percent by age 12 (end of seven years of school).

   Reactions to the general objectives for Comprehension were more varied than those for Word Attack, but generally the staff felt the percentages were too high. The revised comprehension objectives appeared as follows:

   40 percent of the students will achieve independence in Comprehension, e.g., be able to read a daily newspaper, by age 10 (end of five years of school);

   50 percent will achieve independence in Comprehension by age 11 (end of six years of school); and

   85 percent will achieve independence in Comprehension by age 12 (end of seven years of school).

8. The objectives were duplicated and distributed to appropriate building and system personnel by November 15th. It was noted on all copies that these objectives were the results of a systematic process, but were subject to further revision after evaluation.

9. A plan for periodic evaluation of the objectives was set as follows:

a. At the end of the first semester, the Objectives Committee would meet and compile a list of interim reactions to the objectives. Since the program would have been in operation for only a semester, these comments would act as indicators for future evaluation and revisions.
b. In late May of this year, the Objectives Committee would meet and consider the need for revision. Unit leaders were instructed to gather data from staff teachers in a systematic manner to bring to this meeting. Data would deal with both changes in percentages as originally written and appropriateness of the language in which the objectives were stated.
c. At the end of each succeeding year, the Objectives Committee would meet in late May to consider revisions based on number of skills mastered by the students, standardized scores in the Word Attack and Comprehension areas and teacher judgment.

One of the philosophical tenets of IGE is to incorporate flexibility into the school program to meet the needs of individual children. Thus, general objectives must be set so they can be responsive to changes within a school building and/or district. This calls for ongoing evaluation of the objectives and willingness of the IIC to make appropriate revisions.

The first school in a district that sets general objectives faces a difficult task. It has no models to follow and no summarized data from curriculum areas to use as guidelines. Therefore, the IIC and staff of the building will have to initiate procedures and contacts with relevant personnel. They will also need to provide explanations to parents and community of why the objectives are being developed, how they will be used, and how they relate to the IGE program. Answers to questions like those proposed above help form a basis for the objective-setting process and its acceptance by the parents and community.

GENERAL OBJECTIVES IN PRACTICE

The last section of this chapter contains illustrations of general educational objectives that have been developed and used in the school setting. They reflect the characteristics and needs of different student populations in different types of communities.

Examples of Objectives from Four School Districts

General objectives presented here encompass both the cognitive and affective domains. They vary widely in their intent, specificity of purpose, and type of language. Background information on each district and/or school precedes its general objective statements. Since there are many

IGE schools in Wisconsin, some of which have existed since 1967, examples were drawn from that state.

Janesville, Wisconsin (Wilson School). This school has been organized and operating in the IGE mode since 1967. It has a student population of about 750 children and is located in an industrial city of 48,000. Wilson's students tend to be slightly below average in academic achievement and a large percentage of the children come from families on government social service. Wilson is organized into five I & R Units. The five unit leaders meeting with the principal as an IIC have set objectives in both cognitive and affective areas. By their sixth year of operation, the IIC had established five overarching general objectives, with subsequent learner performance objectives and multiunit management objectives. Using these as a base, each unit staff sets four or five general objectives for the year. The overarching general objectives presented below are excerpted from the Wilson School brochure (Janesville, Wisconsin):

1. The learner develops a positive self-image by having successes every day.
2. The learner becomes self-directed through self-evaluation and self-selection.
3. The learner uses accurate and reliable communication skills to structure his or her reality and maintain good human relations.
4. The learner solves problems by examining alternatives and making wise choices in relationship to self and society.
5. The learner uses interdisciplinary principles to cope with life.

IGE learner's general performance objectives are:

1. Each learner develops a positive self-image by having the following daily experiences:

   The learner's feelings are accepted.
   The learner grows at his or her own rate.
   The learner has a voice in making decisions that affect him or her.
   The learner has positive life experiences.

2. Each learner will demonstrate growth in reading commensurate with his or her apparent ability as measured by the Gates-MacGinitie tests given in the fall and spring, and the spring Metropolitan tests.

3. Each learner will demonstrate growth in mathematics commensurate with his or her apparent ability as measured by the spring Metropolitan Achievement tests, Holt Placement tests, and the Developing Mathematical Processes tests.

4. Each learner will spend time during each week in the areas of spelling and mathematics computation.

Multiunit management objectives indicate:

1. The IIC will meet weekly to develop priority guidelines and strategies to implement IGE concepts.
2. The staff will develop research products with the Wisconsin Research and Development Center in the areas of math, Prereading skills, Study skills, and Individually Guided Motivation throughout the school year.
3. Each staff member will utilize the recently established reading goals for Janesville learners.
4. Staff development will be brought about by having each staff member attend at least one small group inservice program conducted by Central Office consultants in the areas of reading, AAAS science, art, music, physical education, and learning centers during the school year.
5. The staff will bring about better home/school communication by individualizing conferences, by using parent talents in our school's programs, by contacting parents when a child has problems initially, and by having each teacher and the principal send home a minimum of five commendations during the year.

Each I & R Unit has also established priority objectives that will enhance the general objectives for the building.

Unit A—Initial Primary Level Objectives

1. Information from the Gates-MacGinitie Readiness tests given in May, prereading results of the previous year, and Ginn 360 assessment material will be used to place children in instructional reading groups early in the fall.
2. Pretest data will be utilized to establish more workable math and science groups using small groups and apparent achievement during the first month of school.
3. The unit will continue to use parents as resource people during the school year.
4. The unit will broaden the use of student models in the prereading and physical education programs during the school year.

Unit B—Lower Primary Level Objectives

1. During the year, study skills for children as outlined in the *Wisconsin Design for Reading Skill Development* will be integrated in the cur-

riculum as follows: maps, graphs, and tables into developmental math processes, social studies, and science; reference skills will be introduced by IMC directors and reinforced by teachers during the communications time block.

2. Children with deficiencies in motor skills will spend time each week receiving special help, outside of the regular physical education programs, for their individual needs.
3. Learners will spend time each week in a math and science lab on math computation and individual science exploration.
4. Students will have weekly opportunities to participate in teacher/student goal-setting conferences for improvement of prosocial behavior.

Unit C—Upper Primary Level Objectives

1. During the school year, more parental and class participation via telephone, conferences, notes, newsletters, and through parental volunteer work, will be provided.
2. Children will be able to state reasons and objectives of the lesson for any class they are in or interests they are pursuing.
3. The unit will continue doing research on the Research and Development Center's Developing Mathematical Processes program and provide more daily math computation activities.
4. The unit will do long-range planning during the school year to define learning projects and tasks for better evaluation procedures.
5. The unit will use accurate record keeping and detailed individual reading programs during the daily communications program.

Unit D—Lower Intermediate Level Objectives

1. The unit will give weekly individual opportunities to those who are interested in pursuing fine arts (music and art) in depth.
2. The unit will provide opportunities for individual work in SAPA Science by completing the priority experiments in Levels C and D during the school year.
3. The unit will work with experimental versions of Developing Mathematical Processes, levels 6 and 7, during the school year.
4. The unit will continue the Word Attack and Study skills program, and use additional materials to give them more practical application in content areas.

5. The unit will expand the child's ability to set goals by using more conferences during the school year.
6. As soon as a problem is identified, unit staff members will contact the parents so they become aware of the child's problem.

Unit E—Upper Intermediate Level Objectives

1. The learners will participate in at least five experiences with outside resource people or places during the 1972-73 school year.
2. The learners will exhibit proficiency in spelling, commensurate with their ability, as measured by the Metropolitan tests given in the spring.
3. Within one month of the opening of school, all children will be placed in science groupings according to skill needs as determined by the Study skills testing done in the spring of 1972.
4. The unit staff will develop a strategy during the first semester to incorporate the present Janesville social studies structure into a more relevant, flexible, and individualized format.
5. The unit will devise a strategy during the first month of school by which a child will be given recognition for accomplished work.

In addition, the Wilson IIC has set general objectives for teachers and parents. The objectives indicate teachers would exhibit:

1. competence at assessing individual learners.
2. acceptance and desire to work with all children.
3. job satisfaction and self-fulfillment.
4. spirit of cooperation.
5. ability to match styles of teachers and learners.

Objectives for home-school relations with parents called for:

1. participation of parents in school activities.
2. informal, open communication between school staff and parents.
3. general positive reactions in relation to students.

Appleton, Wisconsin. Appleton is a city of 58,000 located in the Fox River Valley area of Wisconsin. It is industrial and the students in its schools vary widely in academic and other characteristics. It does not have any schools that would be classified as inner city. The first Appleton schools began operating under the IGE concept in 1970. However, Appleton, as a system, has been involved in nongrading, team teaching, and differentiated staffing in some way since 1960. This long-time effort at individualization is reflected in their curriculum guides which present general objectives, specific instructional objectives, and activities at three levels: a "minimum" performance (for all children); "extensions"; and "suggested conceptual development through practical experience."

For example, under the general category of "Listening and Speaking" for children ages five to seven, the Appleton curriculum guide lists the following objectives for *listening*:

1. General objectives statement:

   Listening is the first means of communication a child uses. It becomes increasingly important as the child matures and meets more and more situations which require listening. Listening skills *must be developed.* Each pupil should be trained in the art of listening thoughtfully, critically, imaginatively, and creatively in order to be able to:

   1. choose wisely *what* to listen to.
   2. know *how* to listen effectively.
   3. *interpret* and *evaluate* what is heard.

2. General philosophical objectives topics:

   1. realization of the need for attentive listening
   2. skills in the use of listening as a tool for learning
   3. selectivity in listening habits
   4. skill in the use of listening in interpersonal relations

3. Specific instructional objectives for the topic of "Skill in the Use of Listening" as a tool for learning:

   Minimum Program for All Students

   The student will be able to:

   1. recognize complete ideas as opposed to fragments
   2. develop the ability to hear likenesses and differences in sound, rhyming words, initial consonants, medial sounds, and different endings
   3. listen to recognize different types of sentences
   4. listen to form sensory images from oral description

   Extensions

   The student will be able to:

   1. follow a speaker's sequence of ideas and organization
   2. know the values of note taking
   3. interpret idioms and unusual language
   4. perceive analogues used by the speaker

Suggested Conceptual Development through Practical Experience

The student will be able to listen:

1. to follow directions
2. to follow a sequence of ideas
3. to answer questions
4. to understand relationships
5. to understand the main points
6. for supporting details
7. to predict outcomes
8. to judge a story or report
9. to distinguish between fact and fiction

The guide also has a reminder box for the teacher, indicating that correct speaking habits and skills are an inherent part of listening, and that the listening process is important to learning in all areas of the curriculum.

Neenah, Wisconsin (Hoover School). Hoover has been an IGE school since 1970. It has a student population of about 350 and is located in a paper-producing city of 22,000. Hoover students are about average in terms of achievement scores and average in socioeconomic background factors.

Hoover has developed general objectives for students in the curriculum areas of mathematics and reading, and in the affective area of motivation, along with general objectives for the staff in the areas of communications and self-improvement. They have designated time lines in all areas except self-improvement.

The general objective for reading is: given the existing staff, supporting staff members, and the current budget, a reading curriculum will be developed which will result in 90 percent of the students enrolled in grades 1-6 at Hoover School achieving within thc range of their reading potential as indicated by the test instruments now in use. Tasks and target dates identified to meet this objective are presented below:

- September — Determine which students have achieved at less than their potential according to the standards set by the Comprehensive Test of Basic Skills (CTBS).
- October — Request that these students be tested by the reading teacher to be sure that the determinations are correct.
- October — Have the reading teacher determine the needs of the students who are not achieving at their potential.
- November — Ask the reading specialist to work with those students that can be helped by the specialist and offer prescriptions to

the teachers of students who can be helped by the classroom teacher.

- December — Meet with reading specialist to determine whether or not all requests have been carried out and to discuss further steps.
- January/February — Carry out preliminary testing to determine if progress is being made.
- January — Put into practice an additional reading class for some students in the third grade in an effort to determine if this will help prevent future reading problems.
- February to April — Carry out discussion with teachers to determine strengths and weaknesses of present program.
- May — Final testing by reading specialist.
- May — Comprehensive Test of Basic Skills testing of students.
- August — Analyze results of test to determine degree of accomplishment of objective.

The general objective for mathematics was stated similarly to the one for reading: given the existing staff, supporting staff members, and the current budget, a math curriculum will be developed which will result in 85 percent of the students enrolled in grades 2-6 at the Hoover School achieving within the range of their potential as indicated by the test instruments now in use. The tasks and target dates to meet this objective are:

- September — Analyze problems of those who have achieved at a level lower than their potential indicates they are capable of achieving.
- September — Set up committee to make recommendations for change in our curriculum.
- October — Present analysis of problems to the teachers of children involved.
- January — Committee recommendations should be ready to present to the staff.
- January to March — Discuss progress made by those not achieving to their potential.
- May — CTBS test.
- August — Determine the degree of success in achieving the stated objective.

Self-improvement objectives for teachers centered around:

- gaining a better knowledge of the SCIS science program by attending a three-week workshop on the subject.

- participating in an in-depth study of English.
- gaining a better understanding of Individually Guided Motivation (IGM) by attending a workshop or being oriented by a unit leader who has worked extensively with IGM.
- becoming a better writer of objectives and their use in implementing IGE, and measuring outcomes related to objectives by attending in-service and workshop sessions.
- becoming a better student-teacher supervisor by reading and gaining a better understanding of their role in the I & R Unit.
- becoming a better leader by thoroughly reviewing the set of tapes on leadership skills.

Outcomes for self-improvement were to be measured, insofar as possible, through discussions with the principal or fellow colleagues who would evaluate each teacher's knowledge and decisions relative to the areas selected for self-improvement.

Communication objectives for parents, teachers, pupils, and the principal will be met as follows:

- The IIC will function as the main body for communications.
- The principal will make it a point to see each teacher informally at least once a week.
- Staff meetings will be held each month during the school year.
- A weekly notice will be sent to staff to handle routine matters.
- Monthly bulletins will be sent home to parents from each unit.
- Letters will be sent to parents by each unit upon completion of a set of skills.
- An assembly will be held for the student body at least once a month.

Achievement of objectives will be measured by checking off each item on its appropriate time line on a record keeping form.

Objectives dealing with IGM, a focus of the next school year, were being introduced during the present year. Unit leaders and teachers who had worked with IGM at statewide workshops or in a graduate program had developed the program and an accompanying timetable to introduce the entire staff to the subject. A general IGM committee, plus subcommittees for each procedure, had been set up. Following introduction to IGM, plans were made to develop a time line for selection and implementation of procedures during the following year.

Introduction to IGM and its timetable appeared as follows:

- September — Initial meeting to introduce IGM topic.

- October — View and discuss film, *Guiding Children toward Self-directed Behaviors.*
- November — View and discuss film, *Guiding Children as Tutors.*
- December — Meeting of IGM committee and subcommittee chairmen.
- January — View and discuss film, *Setting Individual Goals for Learning.*
- February — View and discuss film, *Encouraging Independent Reading.*
- March to May — Discuss needs of Hoover student body in relation to the four motivation procedures viewed and discussed above, and select procedure(s) to be implemented at Hoover next year.
- June — Develop a timetable for implementation of procedure(s) selected during the next school year.

Racine, Wisconsin (*Unified School District*). This district includes 36 schools in the eastern third of Racine County which includes the city of Racine. The area is highly industrialized and is located between Milwaukee and Chicago on the western shore of Lake Michigan. The school district serves rural, urban, and suburban communities. There is a great diversity among the student populations in the schools of the district. Overall, the school population of the Unified District is approximately 80 percent white, 14 percent black, and 6 percent Mexican-American and other backgrounds. This district has been involved with IGE since 1967 when four of the first seven completely organized IGE schools were started here. Previous to this time, the Racine district had been a leader in educational innovations at both the elementary and secondary levels and had developed an outstanding inservice program for introducing and sustaining the innovations.

In 1974, the district revised its philosophy of education to include broad general objectives. Concurrently, they are revising their specific instructional objectives at three levels—for "above average," "average," and "low" achievers—to meet the diversity of students in the district. The general objectives which reflect the district's philosophy appear below (Racine County Unified School District 1973):

> Within the priorities listed above, the school district shall coordinate its resources to develop an educational program to ensure that each student will reach maximum achievement toward the following interrelated educational goals:
>
> Acquiring mastery of basic skills in the use of words and numbers.
>
> Learning how to learn and attaining a lasting positive attitude toward the learning process.

Developing an inquiring mind and proficiency in the use of basic tools of quantitative reasoning and scientific problem-solving as preparation for successful living in a world of rapid change.

Developing proficiency in the skills of communication, including ability to express oneself clearly and accurately, both in writing and speech, and the ability to listen effectively and critically.

Learning the responsibilities and rights of man as a citizen, as revealed by the study of the social sciences.

Developing an understanding of the struggle of humans toward the aesthetic as revealed by a study of the arts.

In addition, the Board recognizes that it shares, with other agencies, the responsibility to help every child develop:

The personal discipline and moral integrity that are necessary for productive and satisfying citizenship.

A positive self-image, which is a prerequisite for maximum educational, social, and vocational achievement.

An understanding of the opportunities that offer preparation for a productive life in the world of work, and enable the child to take full advantage of those opportunities.

An understanding and appreciation of persons belonging to social, cultural, and ethnic groups which differ from those of the child.

Developing to the maximum, knowledge and practice of personal and community health, safety, and physical well-being.

Creativity and satisfying self-expression in one or more fields of endeavor.

The Board recognizes that the accomplishment of these objectives demands the tailoring of the instructional program to the needs of the individual child.

The input of such individualization or personalization of instruction should result in an output best described as the complete development of inborn capacities to enable each student to contribute politically, socially, economically, and morally at optimum level in our democratic society.

SUMMARY

The purpose of this chapter was to acquaint the reader with general educational objectives, their use in IGE, and the process of setting them. The discussion included identifying sources and content of objectives, steps for adapting them to the needs of the student population of a building and evaluating them after they have been used with children.

Examples of objectives from four different school districts have been presented. These included general objectives for both students and staff. The examples of objectives were drawn from several curriculum areas and included both cognitive and affective objectives.

The next chapter will focus on instructional objectives which are derived from the general educational objectives.

REFERENCES

Alexander, W. M., J. G. Saylor, and E. L. Williams 1971. *The high school: today and tomorrow*. New York: Holt.

Allen, D. W., and E. Seifman 1971. *The teachers' handbook*. Glenview, Ill.: Scott Foresman.

Appleton, Wisconsin Schools 1970. *Guide for early childhood education*. Unpublished curriculum guide, Appleton, Wisconsin.

Brown, L. M. (ed.) 1970. *Aims of education*. New York: Teachers College Press.

Good, Carter V. 1973. *Dictionary of education*. New York: McGraw-Hill.

Hoover School, Neenah, Wisconsin 1972. *Guide to general objectives*. Unpublished objectives guide, Neenah, Wisconsin.

Institute for the Development of Educational Activities 1970. *The principal's handbook*. Dayton, Ohio: I D E A.

Klausmeier, H. J., M. R. Quilling, J. S. Sorenson, R. S. Way, and G. R. Glasrud 1971. *Individually guided education and the multiunit elementary school: guidelines for implementation*, Madison, Wisc.: Wisconsin Research and Development Center.

Manolakes, G. 1965. In R. R. Leeper (ed.), *The elementary school we need*. Washington: ASCD Commission on Elementary Curriculum.

Racine County Unified School District, No. 1, 1973. *Teacher's handbook: reporting pupil progress*. Racine, Wisc.: Racine County Division of Instructional Services.

Sorenson, J. S. 1973. *Implementing instructional programming in individualized learning programs*. Eau Claire, Wisc.: University of Wisconsin—Eau Claire.

Tyler, R. W. 1969. *Basic principles of curriculum and instruction*. Chicago: University of Chicago Press.

Wilson School, Janesville, Wisconsin 1973. *Individually guided education in a multiunit organization*. Unpublished brochure, Janesville, Wisconsin.

12

Identifying and Formulating Instructional Objectives

Juanita S. Sorenson
Lloyd H. Joyal

Objectives

After reading this chapter, the reader will be able:

- To describe at least one procedure for selecting content (skills/concepts/processes) for instructional objectives (cognitive or affective) in a curriculum area.
- To explain at least one strategy a unit staff could use in identifying instructional objectives as a base for instruction.
- To describe at least three ways in which the children of the unit could be involved in the process of identifying instructional objectives.
- To identify the role of instructional objectives in patterns of instructional programming.
- To describe the role of the unit leader in the total process of identifying and evaluating instructional objectives.

IGE is an objective-based instructional program. General educational objectives which form the overarching framework for the building program were discussed in Chapter 11. This chapter is concerned with identification and formulation of objectives directly related to instruction in a curriculum area. These objectives will be referred to as instructional objectives. Instructional objectives are noted in the second step of the Instructional Programming Model (IPM) with the statement that the I & R Unit staff will "estimate a range of objectives that may be attainable for subgroups of the student population" (Klausmeier, *et al.* 1971, p. 10). The subgroups referred to here are the children assigned to the I & R Unit and usually span three or more age levels (e.g., 5- to 7-year-olds).

DEFINITIONS AND TYPES OF INSTRUCTIONAL OBJECTIVES

Using instructional objectives as the foundation for the instructional program is common to many individualized instructional programs and has considerable basis in the literature. Instructional objectives help perform three functions (Vargas 1972, p. 3): (1) selecting appropriate learning experiences, (2) communicating to others (particularly to the student) what is expected, (3) providing both student and teacher with standards for evaluating progress.

It is important to relate instructional objectives to general objectives. General objectives are important in program planning and the general overall framework, while specific instructional objectives form the guidelines for what outcomes are to be expected from the student.

Instructional objectives should always be written at the appropriate level. Also, they should not contain more specific references to critiquing standards or evaluations than the identified goal merits. This may be stated more simply as: "Do not specify any behavioral outcome for which evaluation data will not be available or for which the data will be too suspect." (McAshan 1970, p. 4) Many critics of behavioral objectives point to the specificity of the objectives, saying that teachers are writing in too much trivia. In other words, a desk should not be measured with a micrometer when a meter stick will do.

An objective is defined as "an intent communicated by a statement describing a proposed change in a learner—a statement of what the learner is to be like when he has successfully completed a learning experience." (Mager 1962, p. 3) There are three main reasons for objectives. First, they form a framework for operations and a sound basis in educational programs for selecting appropriate materials, content, and instructional methods. Without this basis we often flounder in education. By comparison, a machinist does not select a tool without knowing what operation is to be performed, nor does a composer orchestrate a score without knowing what effects are to be achieved. A second reason relates to the degree to which the learner is able to perform in a manner described. Here objectives are useful in that they measure performance in terms of goals. And third, objectives provide the means for students to evaluate their own progress at any place along the route of instruction. This enables students to organize their efforts toward relevant activities.

The rationale for establishing instructional objectives includes the following criteria (Teacher's Handbook 1973, pp. 17-22):

1. Instructional objectives are categorized into three somewhat overlapping domains: cognitive, affective, and psychomotor.
2. Attainment of outcomes in one domain does not necessarily entail attainment of outcomes in the other domains.
3. Objectives are derived from basic concepts of the unit of instruction.
4. Instructional objectives should range from simple to complex.
5. Instructional objectives are culminated in terms of projected pupil outcomes.
6. Degree of outcome specificity will vary, depending on whether it is a minimum essential or developmental outcome.
7. Instructional objectives with specified outcomes provide a sound basis for subsequent instructional and evaluation experiences.

Most authors agree that behavioral objectives contain three minimum components. These are:

1. A description of the kind of behavior the learner is expected to perform. (Task)
2. A description of the important conditions under which the behavior will be expected to occur, that is, the context for the action. (Conditions)
3. A description of how well the learner must perform to attain this behavior. (Attainment or mastery level)

Criteria above apply primarily to behavioral objectives. However, not all instructional objectives should be behavioral. Another kind of objective is "expressive" (Eisner 1969, pp. 14-15). An expressive objective is one of intent that does not specify the behavior of the student but rather one that describes an educational encounter. Expressive objectives identify a problem or task, but they do not specify what is to be learned from the encounter. An expressive objective encourages diversity of response among students, not homogeneity as is the case with behavioral objectives. Expressive objectives help the teacher provide a situation in which meanings are more personal and students produce products, both theoretical and qualitative, that are as diverse as they are. Expressive objectives are not evaluated by applying a common standard to the products produced. Rather, evaluation is reflecting upon what was produced in order to reveal its uniqueness and significance. The result of a product in the expressive area is likely to be as much of a surprise to the maker as to the teacher. The following statements are examples of expressive objectives (Eisner 1969, p. 16):

1. to visit the zoo and discuss what was of interest there.
2. to interpret the meaning of *Paradise Lost.*
3. to develop a three-dimensional form through the use of wire and wood.

The IGE instructional program utilizes both behavioral and expressive objectives. Instructional objectives range from highly behavioral to highly expressive. Four places on the continuum are presented in the following illustration:

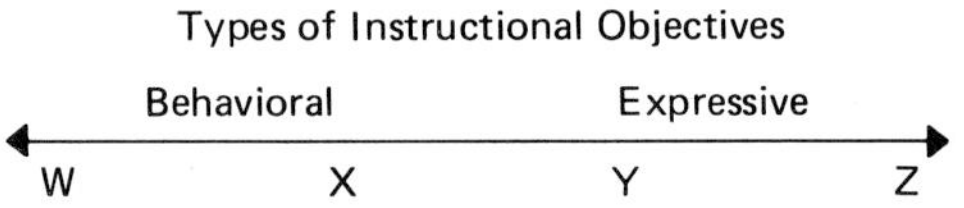

The four places along the continuum are illustrated using the topic, planets, as subject matter.

Objective W is highly behavioral:

> Given the names of the nine planets in our solar system, the student will be able to order them from closest to most distant from the sun with 80 percent accuracy.

This objective prescribes the *conditions* within which the student is to work (nine planets), the *task to be accomplished* (order from closest to most distant from sun), and the *level of attainment* (80 percent).

Objective X is somewhat less prescriptive, yet behavioral in tone:

> The student will be able to describe the proportionate distances between each of the nine planets in our solar system with 80 percent accuracy.

Here the *task* is definitely prescribed and the *level of attainment* is indicated, but the conditions under which the student carries it out are not. The student has the choice of description using words, visuals such as transparencies or slides, a model indicating the appropriate proportions, a simulation where fellow students would simulate the planets and stand at the appropriate distances from each other on the playground, or some combination of *conditions.*

An expressive objective is one of intent that does not specify the behavior of the student but rather one that describes an educational encounter.

Objective Y which is located toward the expressive side of the continuum is one of intent, yet contains some prescription of task:

> The student will describe recent findings about the possibility of life on planets other than earth.

Here the student has considerable latitude in the *conditions* selected such as a play, essay, radio broadcast, or poem, but all efforts are to be focused on the *task* of describing the possibility of life on planets other than earth.

Also, no specific attainment level is or can be indicated. Usually, "satisfactory" as agreed upon by student and instructor is used for evaluation.

Objective Z is highly expressive in nature:

The student will develop a project of his or her own design about planets.

Here, the only constraint prescribed is the word "planets" which represents the general topic of the unit of instruction. No condition, task, or attainment level is specified. The project could take any form from a scientific research project dealing with astronomical observations and data analyses to writing a play or poem. Such an objective allows for great creativity on the part of the student.

An overview of the definition, uses, and types of instructional objectives has been presented here. Suggestions for utilizing objectives as the base of the IGE instructional program are discussed in the next section of this chapter.

OBJECTIVES AS THE BASE OF THE INSTRUCTIONAL PROGRAM

Instructional objectives are identified for the children in the I & R Unit by the unit staff. Within a curriculum area, they should be in harmony with objectives selected by the other units in the building, and appropriate to the general educational objectives identified by the IIC. The selection of instructional objectives is coordinated by the unit leader at both the unit and IIC levels.

The job of identifying instructional objectives must be carried out early in the process of instructional programming for individual students. These objectives form the guidelines for everything else that is planned and implemented. They must be selected carefully, and appropriate time and personnel should be allotted to the task. In identifying instructional objectives, it should be remembered that their purpose is to facilitate instruction, not to stifle it. Objective-based programs at the elementary level have come under much criticism because they have too often required that all students proceed in a given manner through a set of objectives, just as previously all students were often required to proceed through a set of basals. In IGE, objectives are not used in this manner. Here they facilitate learning by providing a basic framework into which flexibility can be built to help individual students learn in cognitive and affective areas to function to their maximum potential in today's society. Thus, the unit leader and staff members assume great responsibility when they identify instructional objectives for the children in their unit. This section focuses on this process and presents examples under the following headings:

1. Selecting the content for instructional objectives.
2. Identifying and organizing instructional objectives.
3. Involving the students in selecting instructional objectives.
4. Instructional objectives in patterns of instructional programming.

Selecting the Content for Instructional Objectives

The content for curriculum areas must be selected before objectives can be identified. *Content can take the form of skills, concepts, or processes.* For example, traditionally the term "skills" has been used to talk about content in reading or mathematics; the term "concepts," for social studies; and the terms "concepts and processes," for science. The term "skill/concept/process" will be used here to refer to content in any curriculum area in the instructional program. Skills/concepts/processes form the skeleton outline around which an I & R Unit staff develops a unit of instruction. For example, at the beginning level of Study skills in reading, the content could be divided into the general areas and specific instructional skills (Otto and Askov 1972, pp. 142-143):

General Area	Content in the Form of a Skill
1. Location	a. locates objects in relation to self
2. Measurement	a. describes relative size b. determines relative distance
3. Beginning Work	a. follows simple directions b. remembers details c. has suitable attention and concentration span d. has beginning independent work habits
4. Basic Book Handling	a. selects, handles, refers to books

Objectives appropriate to the age/grade level of the students are developed from the content—in this case, an instructional skill. For example, content of the location skill, "locates objects in relation to self," might be stated in objective form for 5- to 6-year-olds as: "The child describes or responds to descriptions of the positions of objects in the environment in relation to self and the following terms: up-down, on, between, near (beside), behind-in front of (back-front), below-above (under-over)."

The job of selecting skills/concepts/processes is important and puts curriculum decision-making responsibility on the unit staff under the guidance of the unit leader. This is a new role for the unit leader and unit teachers. In the self-contained organizational pattern, most teachers tended to follow the sequence of the textbook for a given curriculum area, and the content of the text made up the curriculum. Here, decisions about curriculum were made by the textbook author and did not involve the teacher. However, there have always been creative and dynamic teachers who supplemented and reorganized textual material and sequence, created instructional materials, and used more than one text. They were involved in curriculum decision making.

The multiunit organizational structure in IGE facilitates decision making and makes it possible for an experienced staff to make relevant decisions for the children they know best—the children in their building. This allows the staff to fit the curriculum to the needs of the children, rather than fitting the children to a curriculum designed for some "average" group by experts who have no information about the children who will be using it. The unit staff, however, uses the materials—texts, plus all available materials that have been produced by people with expertise in an area—and adapts them to the needs of the children in their unit.

A series of steps the IIC and unit staff should consider in the selection of skills/concepts/processes in a curriculum or other area for children in a building and/or unit has been developed (Sorenson 1973, p. 4). These steps, along with a description of how the IIC and I & R Unit could carry them out, are presented below:

I. Identify general components

A. *Select the curriculum area* such as mathematics, reading, language arts, science, social studies, art, music, physical education.

B. *Identify the characteristics of the students* in the building. These include:

1. The age and/or grade levels for which instructional programming is to be implemented. Consider the content which precedes and follows the selected age/grade level so that skills/concepts/processes at the one level are not identified in isolation from those at other levels.
2. General ability (IQ) and/or achievement scores of students in selected curriculum area.
3. Information from cumulative records—formal and informal.

C. *Set general objectives for students in curriculum area.*

As a starting point, the IIC, with input from unit staffs, might consider "expected" norms of widely accepted curriculum materials for the selected grade/age level in relation to the characteristics of the students in the building. The general objectives should be set tentatively by the IIC *before* instructional programming is implemented and be evaluated *continuously after* it is in operation.

An example of a general objective in the Word Attack portion of the

Wisconsin Design for Reading Skill Development for a target population slightly below average in ability: 90 percent of the students will be independent in Word Attack by age 10, and 99 percent by age 12 (Otto and Askov 1972).

II. Identify skills/concepts/processes to be included in the selected curriculum area.

Instructional programming in IGE utilizes a criterion-referenced approach in which a child's performance is compared to a predetermined mastery level (e.g., 80 percent) or condition (e.g., satisfactory). This approach contrasts to the traditional, norm-referenced approach in which a child's performance is compared with that of other children at the same age/grade level. In using the criterion-referenced approach, common sense suggests that not all children will be able to master all the skills/concepts/processes designated for an age/grade level or levels in texts, curriculum guides, or other instructional materials. Likewise, they will *not* be able to master all the skills/concepts/processes selected by the unit staff for a year or a unit of instruction.

For example, children who learn more slowly will not be able to and should not be asked to cover the same quantity or difficulty of material that children who learn more rapidly would cover during the number of years traditionally reserved for elementary school, i.e., seven years. This means new decisions about the content need to be made by I & R Unit staff and the principal of a building, along with appropriate central office personnel and subject matter specialists.

One plan for making decisions about content in a given subject matter area is presented here. Skills/concepts/processes are classified into three levels—A, B, and C. These levels are defined as follows (Sorenson 1973):

Level A—basic, concrete skills/concepts/processes necessary for a child to function successfully in a society and/or prerequisite to learning more advanced, concrete skills/concepts/processes.

Level B—higher level, somewhat abstract skills/concepts/processes relative to a content area.

Level C—higher level, more abstract and more complex skills/concepts/processes in a content area.

Examples of mathematics skills classified into these three levels (A, B, and C) are presented below:

Level A Skills

basic addition facts
basic subtraction facts

basic multiplication facts through 6s
simple (one-step) story problems using appropriate addition, subtraction, and multiplication facts listed above
recognition of simple geometric shapes

Level B Skills

basic multiplication facts through 10s
basic division facts through one-digit divisor and two-digit dividend
more complex (two steps or more) story problems
construction of simple geometric forms

Level C Skills

exploring simple logic problems
multiplying using a variety of techniques
computing with number bases other than 10
illustrating interrelationships of geometric figures

All students would meet mastery on Level A objectives with fewer students meeting mastery on objectives in Levels B and C. Figure 12.1 presents these levels in graph form and indicates percentages of students that might meet mastery at each level.

Some commercially produced materials use a similar system of levels. For example, performance objectives for mathematics have been written at three levels (Addison-Wesley 1972, p. 2):

1. *red* objectives which represent minimal performance standards for the particular unit or chapter.
2. *yellow* objectives which are either somewhat more difficult than the red, or less essential to the students' progress at that level. Many of these objectives are well within the capabilities of average students.
3. the *green* objectives represent a maximum level of achievement of the unit or chapter.

Suggested use of these objectives indicates two alternatives for students who have mastered red objectives for a given level. They can either (1) proceed to work on the yellow objectives for that level or (2) continue on to the next chapter and again work on the red objectives.

A larger number of the skills/concepts/processes dealing with basic knowledge are normally suggested for Level A for 5- to 8-year-olds with a smaller number assigned to Levels B and C. Larger numbers would be assigned to Levels B and C for 9- to 12-year-olds.

The levels suggested here are arbitrary, and no child should be held within the limits of any level. Some children may achieve more than the

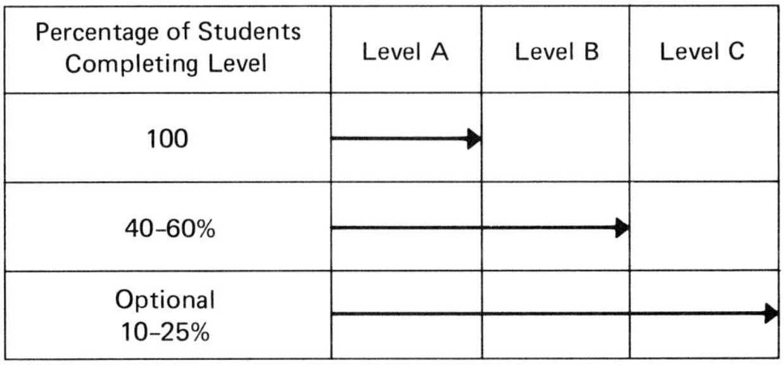

Fig. 12.1 Relationships among skill/concept/process levels and percentages of students expected to complete each level. The percentages are arbitrarily selected and would vary from building to building, depending on the characteristics of the learners.

staff selected for them initially and some will be able to achieve less. These goals should be reviewed periodically by the unit staff, e.g., every three to six weeks, and changes made as necessary.

Three steps in identifying the content for objectives are presented below:

A. *Select skills/concepts/processes.* They can be identified in a variety of ways depending on the philosophy of the school, its staff, and the system. A method commonly used by a unit staff is to start by evaluating the skills/concepts/processes currently designated for a subject matter area in the system's curriculum guide and/or texts. Those suggested in other sources as curriculum guidelines from state departments of education and national studies, and courses of study from other systems should also be reviewed. In addition, student interests in the subject matter area should be assessed in a class "brainstorming" session and/or completion of a simple survey instrument.

   During preparation of the skills/concepts/processes list, the unit staff should utilize the services of local, state, and regional resource persons with expertise in curriculum design and the subject matter area they are working in. In addition to system specialists, subject matter consultants might include junior or senior high school teachers in the selected curriculum area. These skills/concepts/processes will be the base for instructional programming, and should be classified into Levels A, B, and C.

B. *Critique skills/concepts/processes selected.* Ask "outsiders" (i.e., teachers, curriculum coordinators, subject matter specialists) not involved in the selection of the skills/concepts/processes to evaluate their relation to the general objective(s) and/or characteristics of the children in the building. This process can be accomplished by furnishing critics with a list of skills/concepts/processes, along with the general objectives for the program and student characteristics. They can critique the list independently and meet with the school staff to discuss their comments. This group should also critique the classification into levels.

C. *Finalize skills/concepts/processes list.* The unit staff should designate skills/concepts/processes to be included in the curriculum according to the outcomes of the critique process in "B" above. Resource persons should be called in to help as needed.

The selection and organization process described above is best carried out for the entire building at one time. Each I & R Unit can work on selecting skills/concepts/processes for the age range of their children. Coordination is handled by the principal and unit leaders at the IIC. If one I & R Unit initiates the process, their efforts must be coordinated with those of other units in the building to develop a meaningful program.

Skills/concepts/processes, and subsequently the objectives identified relative to them, should be grouped into meaningful content areas (Edling 1970, p. 6). This has been done in traditional teaching. Arithmetic has designated units of instruction or areas as: numeration, place value, addition, subtraction, etc. Such grouping helps in meaningful development of instructional materials and diagnosis of pupil achievement while not precluding the possibility of cutting across other areas. Further breakdown within a given area, (e.g., numeration in arithmetic) or sequencing of skills and objectives where one builds on preceding ones and acts as a prerequisite to those that follow, is also helpful.

While sequencing is necessary in some areas like arithmetic, it should not be employed unless needed. Too much sequencing can "lock" children into a program that can make grouping difficult and push an individualized program toward too much independent study. Small group interaction with fellow students and the teacher and other adults is essential to the IGE program.

Content selection has been described in considerable detail because it lies at the foundation of instructional programming for individual students in IGE. At this point, teachers have the opportunity to meet the needs of students of all abilities and develop a relevant curriculum designed specifically for their school population.

Identifying and Organizing Instructional Objectives

The I & R Unit staff will need to consider several variables in the process of identifying instructional objectives as the framework for instructional programming for students in a curriculum area. These include strategies to:

a. relate the instructional objectives to the general objective(s).

b. state the objectives so they represent the skills/concepts/processes previously identified.

c. utilize a hierarchy or schema for the objectives which is based on sound learning and psychological theory to ensure that students:
   (1) learn at a variety of levels that encompass factual information, problem solving, and creativity in the cognitive domain;
   (2) develop positive self-concepts, attitudes, values, beliefs, interests, and motivation in the affective domain; and
   (3) develop appropriate mental and motor skills in the psychomotor domain.

d. select objectives that are manageable for unit planning and appropriate to student, staff, and building capabilities.

The discussion that follows expands and illustrates each of these points.

Relate instructional objectives to general objectives. Instructional objectives must be identified so they provide appropriate experiences for the children in the unit to meet and/or move toward the general objective(s) set for the building. They should also further define the general objective(s) and be stated in a manner which enables teachers, parents, and students to understand what outcomes are expected and how they will be measured.

Relationships between general and instructional objectives for 5- to 7-year-olds, along with criteria for measurement and suggested activities, are illustrated below (adapted from the Appleton, Wisconsin, *Guide for Early Childhood Education* 1972).

General Objective: 90 percent of the children will demonstrate basic information about animals by age 7, and 99 percent by age 8.

Instructional Objectives: The child will be able to:

1. categorize animals according to their kinds (birds, mammals, reptiles, insects).
2. differentiate between wild and domesticated animals.
3. identify how animals are helpful to man such as supplying food, clothing, and protection.
4. locate animal habitats such as fields, forests, swamps, trees, parks, zoos, etc.
5. define needs of animals such as care, food, protection, hibernation, rest, exercise, migration, etc.
6. categorize the ways animals move such as hopping, running, crawling, flying.

7. discuss how animals bear their young.
8. identify relationships among animals and plants.

Mastery: Student mastery will be measured by teachers on the basis of performance and/or correctness of answers related to:

1. taking care of pets in the classroom.
2. collecting pictures of animals of the forests, fields, etc. and properly categorizing them.
3. observing life cycles of insects to become familiar with metamorphosis (complete and incomplete).
4. examining real animal homes or models of animal homes.
5. collecting animal products such as leather, fur, hair, etc.
6. using models of animals to categorize them according to wild, domestic, field, forest, swamp, etc.
7. making pictures of animals and their needs.
8. dictating stories about how animals protect themselves.
9. role playing—how animals get ready for the various seasons.

Suggested Activities:

1. Encourage children to bring pets to school.
2. Keep several animals in school and care for them properly.
3. Collect pictures of animals that live in fields, swamps, and trees, and arrange in groups.

Note that here the rather vague term "basic information" in the general objective is further defined in the statement of the instructional objectives. Also, the instructional objectives are stated to measure both knowledge in and performance of the subject matter.

State objectives in the context of skills/concepts/processes. Instructional objectives must be stated in a manner that is representative of each skill/concept/process selected. In many instances subobjectives must also be identified. For example, the Word Attack skill of consonant blends might be divided into three subobjectives as follows:

Given real or nonsense words that begin with the consonant blends *bl, cl, fl, gl, pl, sl, br, cr, dr, fr, gr, pr,* and *tr,* the child will be able to:

1. identify the two letters that stand for the initial blend in words pronounced by the teacher; and/or
2. identify words that begin with the same blend as a stimulus word pronounced by the teacher, and
3. pronounce words that begin with the blends listed above from a written list.

These objectives cover both factual knowledge and application of the skill.

The number of objectives stated for a skill/concept/process depends on the detail with which the staff has stated the skills/concepts/processes, the age/grade level for which the material is being designed, and the nature of the subject matter of concern. Usually, skills in math and reading are more precisely stated than are concepts and processes in science and social studies. Thus, the three objectives stated previously are adequate for the primary level Word Attack skill of consonant blends. A science concept, e.g., vertebrates, for upper intermediate children might be broken down into several objectives and the objectives classified into three levels as presented below.

Objectives for a Unit of Instruction on Vertebrates

Level	Instructional Objectives
	The student will be able to:
A	1. differentiate between vertebrates and invertebrates in terms of attributes and examples—concept labels (e.g., fish, lobster) and pictures.
A	2. differentiate among the five classes of vertebrates—amphibians, birds, fish, mammals, reptiles—in terms of attributes (e.g., fish have gills), examples (concept labels and pictures), definitions, and relationships.
A	3. exhibit the scientific processes of observation and classification in terms of objectives "1" and "2" above.
B	4. develop a classification system for a class or subset of a class of animals and compare it with other classification systems developed by students about the same age.
B	5. develop a game for a group of animals such as "kinds of mammals" or "kinds of birds" and try it out with students about the same age.
C	6. investigate the evolutionary development of one or more of the classes of animals and construct diagrams, a diorama, or other pictorial material to illustrate this development; also, include written material that explains the development.

C 7. rate the five classes of vertebrates from highest to lowest according to their importance to human survival in the 1970s; give reasons for your ratings.

It is suggested that all students attain mastery on Level A objectives with lesser percentages of students attaining mastery on objectives for Levels B and C. It should be recalled (Fig. 12.1) that completion of Level A objectives will be a terminal point for some children, with completion of Levels B and/or C for others, depending on their characteristics, interests, and motivation.

Utilize a hierarchy to identify and formulate objectives. In selecting objectives in all content areas and at all age/grade levels, the unit staff should rely on some hierarchy or schema. This ensures that students will have opportunities to learn more than just facts.

In the cognitive domain, a taxonomy with a hierarchy of educational objectives has been developed (Bloom 1956). This taxonomy has six levels. These levels, with a brief explanation of each, are presented below:

1. *Knowledge.* This involves the lowest level of learning, including recall and memory. Here the learner deals with recalling specifics with concrete references. It includes terminology as specific facts, dates, events, persons, places, and so on.
2. *Comprehension.* This represents the lowest level of understanding. Here the individual is able to make use of the materials or ideas without relating them to other ideas or materials.
3. *Application.* This entails the use of information in specific situations. The information may be in the form of general ideas or concepts, principles, and theories which must be remembered and applied.
4. *Analysis.* This involves taking apart the information and making new relationships. The purpose here is to clarify by discovering hidden meaning and basic structure.
5. *Synthesis.* This level involves a recombining process which permits the emergence of a new pattern or structure not previously apparent. This involves the learner reassembling the component parts to develop new or creative ideas.
6. *Evaluation.* This is the highest level of cognition. It involves making judgment on the material, information, or method for specific purposes, using a distinctive criterion as a base for decision. It relates to the problem-solving process of selecting one of the proposed alternatives over all the rest if action is to be taken.

Intellectual or cognitive learning varies from simple (knowledge level) to the complex (evaluation level) and from concrete to abstract. It should be remembered that attainment of higher cognitive levels depends on satisfactory progress at the lower levels. This relates directly to the selection of objectives and planning and implementation of individualized programs like IGE.

The affective domain deals with feelings and emotions. Common qualities in this domain are attitudes, interests, self-concepts, opinions, values, beliefs, and motives. A hierarchy of objectives which provides for a range from neutrality through mild to strong emotion has been developed (Krathwohl and Bloom 1964, p. 28). This taxonomy, like the cognitive one, ranges from simple to complex. It is best described in terms of internalization. Internalization is defined as a process beginning with an incomplete and tentative adoption of the desired emotion, with progression to a more complex adoption of feeling in the later stages of learning. The five levels of the affective taxonomy can be summarized as follows:

1. *Receiving* (attending.) Here the learner becomes aware of an idea process and is willing to listen or attend to a given communication. At this point the learner takes a passive role of receiver.
2. *Responding.* This level involves doing something with or about a phenomenon, other than just receiving it. For example, a student might display an interest in it, or may advance to voluntary response. Finally, the student may express a pleasurable feeling or satisfaction. This feeling may be expressed as the student "writes short stories for personal pleasure."
3. *Valuing.* At this level, behavior reflects a belief or attitude, and it might be said that an individual "holds the value." Here the individual makes a commitment about personal behavior. Within this level, the individual might start by holding the belief somewhat tentatively, and while proceeding through the level, the belief becomes one of conviction, at least "beyond the shadow of a doubt" or perhaps even to the point where the individual might persuade others to this way of thinking.
4. *Organization.* Here the individual has established a conscious basis for making choices and has organized his or her values into a system or a set of criteria for guiding behavior. The individual will be able to defend choices and be aware of the reason for them.
5. *Characterization.* Internalization is complete at this level. Values are integrated into some kind of internally consistent system, and the person is described as having certain controlling tendencies and a recognized philosophy of life.

Writing objectives in the affective domain is usually more difficult than writing them in the cognitive domain. This might be due to the fact that the levels of organization and characterization are not reached in any one segment of study (Krathwohl and Bloom 1964).

The third domain, the psychomotor, deals primarily with mental and motor skills. In education, these include certain instructional activities in which skills are developed. For example, motor skills are involved in playing tennis or basketball, while mental skills are used in the cognitive program for writing and talking. All of these skills require understanding and are usually accompanied with varying degrees of emotion. However, emphasis in this area must be placed on development of the skill. This psychomotor taxonomy clarifies the essentials of the process as follows (Simpson 1966):

1. *Observing.* Here the learner observes a more experienced person performing an activity. Usually this observation includes cognizance of the sequence in relationship with particular attention to the finished product.
2. *Imitating.* The learner advances to this level when he or she has begun to acquire basic rudiments of the desired behavior. The learner performs and follows directions in sequences under close supervision and is conscious of deliberate efforts to imitate the model.
3. *Practicing.* The sequence is performed repeatedly at this level. All aspects of the act are performed in sequence. Conscious effort is no longer necessary as the performance becomes more or less habitual in nature. At this level, we might say the person has acquired the skill.
4. *Adapting.* At this terminal level, the learner has perfected the skill. This process involves adapting minor details which, in turn, influence the total performance. This is the process by which a good performer becomes a better one.

Hierarchies for each of the learning domains—cognitive, affective, and psychomotor—have been summarized here. Examples of how schools utilize cognitive and affective objectives as the basis of the instructional program are presented in the last section of this chapter.

Select objectives that are manageable and appropriate. In a program like IGE, a key task is to identify and/or formulate instructional objectives specific enough to guide the staff in preparation of assessments, activities, and evaluation of pupil outcomes. Yet they should not be so specific that the continuity of the content is lost nor so numerous that they cannot be monitored by an elementary staff without a computer. The objectives must allow for flexibility, creativity, and adaptability to the capabilities and interests of the students. They must also be appropriate to the expertise of the unit staff and available materials and physical plant.

For example, if the Word Attack program in reading contains 35 objectives for primary age students, these objectives would span ages of children in two units (i.e., ages 5-10). A small number of older children —those who had not yet mastered the skills—would also work with them. Related skills should be clustered into areas to make them more manageable. An example of how a staff might provide flexibility for a wide range of student abilities for the skill "possessive forms," is presented below (Otto and Askov 1972):

Area:	Structural analysis skills
Skill:	Possessives
Objective:	The child will be able to identify the possessive forms of nouns used in context.
Assessment excerpts:	Color in the area in front of the phrase where the italicized word is a *possessive.*

1. [a] *apple* butter	2. [a] *I'll* walk
[b] *brown* shoes	[b] *teacher's* pencil
[c] *Charlie's* aunt	[c] *grass* hut

Activities:
1. Skill group instruction (5 to 10 students).
2. Worksheet on possessives.
3. Games (from a kit, or teacher- or student-made).
4. Audiotape with an accompanying worksheet emphasizing the "sounds" of commonly used possessives in the context of sentences.
5. Students develop a game or activity using possessives.

Possessives are considered an *essential skill* (Level A) that all children need to know. Possessives appear in the curriculum for all reading programs, regardless of the characteristics of the school population. Therefore, the area, skill, and even the objective may appear exactly alike for diverse groups of students. The opportunity for the unit staff to make the learning relevant to their particular group of students arises in the areas of assessments and activities. Using "possessives" as an example, a unit staff in an inner city area should examine the assessments to be sure the general language of each item is appropriate for their children. For example, the item, "Last night I viewed the planet Mars through my dad's new telescope," would not be appropriate for children whose opportunities to become familiar with a telescope are limited. Activities should be selected in a context that is familiar to the student population using them. Adaptation of objectives can occur within the activities and assessments as well as in the statement of the objectives.

In summary, skills/concepts/processes and the instructional objectives related to them may be selected from a wide variety of sources and adapted to the needs of the students in a unit and building. Objectives should be formulated by a unit staff only in cases where they are not available or cannot be adapted. Formulating objectives is a time-consuming task and objectives developed by experts are available in most areas. An I & R Unit is often "reinventing the wheel" when they write their own objectives. Their time can usually be better spent in developing activities, materials, and assessments related to the objectives. There are, however, some circumstances where objectives are not available and must be formulated. At the beginning of this chapter, the components and types of instructional objectives were stated, and several books dealing with steps in writing objectives were noted. In addition, easy-to-understand books on writing objectives are available in any college/university bookstore or library, and most school-system and public libraries.

Instructional Objectives and Patterns of Instructional Programming

Several patterns of instructional programming are utilized in IGE in order to provide for differences in individual students and differences in the nature of the subject matter taught in the elementary school. Instructional objectives, attainment levels, and sequence across units of instruction are considered in these patterns (Klausmeier, Rossmiller, and Saily, in press, Ch. 3).

Before proceeding further it is necessary to define a unit of instruction. Here a unit of instruction refers to any grouping of related instructional objectives in any curriculum area for which there is a beginning point and a terminal point. Activities in units of instruction vary. For example, activities in units of instruction in art or physical education are usually different from those in reading or in science. A unit of instruction may be as short as a week or longer than a school year. It is also assumed that there is more than one instructional objective for each unit of instruction.

There are eight possible patterns of instructional programming if two aspects for each of three variables—(1) common or variable objectives, (2) full mastery or variable criteria for attainment of objectives, and (3) invariant or variable sequence of instructional units—are considered. These patterns are:

a. Common objectives, full mastery, invariant sequence across units
b. Common objectives, full mastery, variable sequence across units

c. Common objectives, variable attainment, invariant sequence across units

d. Common objectives, variable attainment, variable sequence across units

e. Variable objectives, full mastery, invariant sequence across units

f. Variable objectives, full mastery, variable sequence across units

g. Variable objectives, variable attainment, invariant sequence across units

h. Variable objectives, variable attainment, variable sequence across units.

These patterns are presented in diagrammatic form in Figure 12.2. From the diagram, it is noted that Patterns *a* through *d* have common objectives and Patterns *e* through *h* have variable objectives.

The word *variable* as used in the patterns implies a range. In connection with objectives, for example, it implies all the possibilities ranging from most but not all the objectives being the same for a group of individuals to no objectives being the same for any two individuals. In sequence, it implies that if there are six units of instruction during a year, they may be taken in any order or that only one of the units may be taken out of sequence. Criteria for attainment may vary from a specified percentage in a skill area to "satisfactory" for a poem or project.

A brief description of how instruction may be carried out under each of the eight patterns of instructional programming follows: Examples of curriculum areas where each pattern may be used and how products developed to be compatible with IGE utilize the patterns are also discussed.

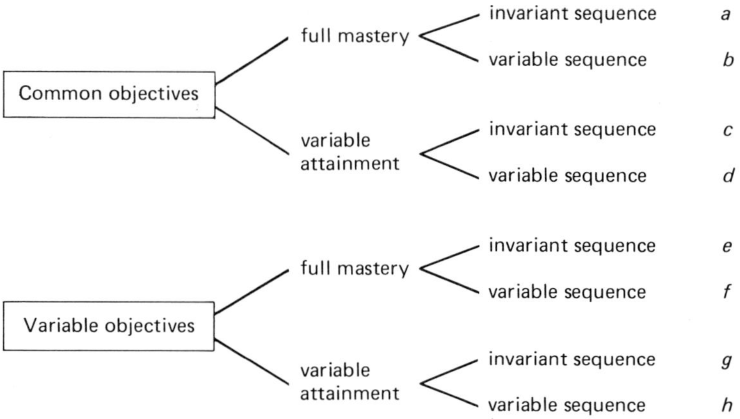

Fig. 12.2 Patterns of instructional programming.

Pattern a: common objectives, full mastery, invariant sequence across units. Here, instructional programming for the individual student is organized so that all students work on the same objectives, attain to the same criteria of mastery and proceed through the units of instruction in the same sequence. Within a unit, the objectives may or may not be sequenced invariantly. When this pattern is implemented, each student attains the objectives at his or her own rate, but not all students attain the same number of objectives during a year, or some other time interval.

Three of the six areas of the *Wisconsin Design for Reading Skill Development* (WDRSD)—Word Attack skills, Study skills and Comprehension skills—follow this pattern. The other three areas are described later under Pattern *d*.

In the WDRSD, the objectives within each area are organized according to levels, e.g., four levels—A, B, C, D—in the Word Attack area. Within each level, the objectives are not sequenced invariantly. Therefore, every student is expected to attain all the objectives within a given level to the same specified criterion of mastery before proceeding to the next successive level; but within any level, the student does not need to pursue the objectives in an invariant sequence.

Pattern b: common objectives, full mastery, variable sequence across units. Instruction may be organized so that all students pursue the same units of instruction to attain the same objectives to the same criterion of full mastery. However, mastery of one unit is not prerequisite for starting another one. Therefore a student may start any one of the several units at any point in time during a semester or year, and groups of students may be pursuing different units during any given week or month. Objectives may or may not follow an invariant sequence within each unit.

Some units of instruction in both elementary science and social studies follow this pattern. When students are grouped for instruction in this pattern, provisions are needed for early attainers and late attainers. This generally requires that several units, preferably of variable difficulty level but of about the same duration, be available simultaneously for students to pursue.

Pattern c: common objectives, variable attainment, invariant sequence across units. In this pattern, all students pursuing a particular unit attain the same objectives but not to the same criterion. The criteria of attainment are set so as to be different but appropriate for particular students; and for convenience in managing instruction or because of the hierarchical nature of the knowledge and skills, the units of instruction are sequenced invariantly during the school year. The objectives may or may not be sequenced within a particular unit. Some units of instruction in mathematics and science follow this pattern. It implies that some knowledge about a topic is essential for proceeding to the next one but the amount may vary among students.

Pattern d: common objectives, variable attainment, variable sequence across units. This is much like Pattern *c* except that the units of instruction are not undertaken in a fixed sequence. Three areas of WDRSD—Self-directed Reading skills, Interpretive Reading skills, and Creative Reading skills—conform to this pattern. *Individually Guided Motivation* (IGM) and most of the geometry topics of DMP follow this pattern. All students are to attain the same objectives as incorporated in the units of instruction; they need not attain them to the same specified level; and they need not take them in a fixed sequence.

Pattern e: variable objectives, full mastery, invariant sequence across units. Instruction may be arranged so that not all students attain the same objectives; however each objective set for any student is mastered to the same criterion. The units of instruction are undertaken in an invariant sequence.

Instrumental music may follow this pattern. Here the students who learn to perform on different instruments have different objectives. However, those learning to play the same instrument are required to attain objectives for successive units in an invariant sequence and also to reach the same level of full mastery before proceeding from one unit to another.

Pattern f: Variable objectives, full mastery, variable sequence. Instruction follows the same pattern as in Pattern *e* except that the units are not sequenced. In connection with the previous example from instrumental music, the difference according to this pattern is that the sequence by which the students attain their objectives is not fixed, or invariant.

Pattern g: Variable objectives, variable attainment, invariant sequence across units. Some units of instruction in mathematics follow this pattern. Although no particular level of attainment of objectives is required, the invariant sequence presumes that some knowledge or skill about a particular topic is needed before moving to the next topic. Therefore students who pursue the units of instruction follow an invariant sequence.

Pattern h: variable objectives, variable attainment, variable sequence across units. Topics of DMP dealing with statistics and graphing follow this pattern. The topics are not sequenced and not all students are expected to attain the same objectives. Those who do pursue the same objectives are not required to reach any particular level of mastery nor to pursue them in any special sequence.

Elective limits of instruction in all curricular areas, most outdoor education in camps and forests, and some in-school enrichment activities also follow this pattern.

Involving the Students in Selecting Instructional Objectives

The student must be involved in the process of selecting instructional objectives (Bloom, *et al.* 1971, pp. 8-9). Students must accept, and to some degree understand, the objectives if they are to self-assess the learning outcome. In the case of very young children, and older learners who have difficulty in participating in goal setting, perhaps the best that can be hoped for is that they will accept the objective. At the other extreme, there are students who must have some sense of participation in setting objectives. However, the full responsibility for setting them cannot be placed on the student, who in many cases will not be able to foresee the alternatives available and cannot fully appreciate the implications. The teacher, to an appropriate degree, is involved in the task of determining the objectives for instruction.

Objectives also influence evaluation techniques and methods for individual students and groups of students to accomplish the objectives. Objectives may be modified and adjusted to the actualities of the learning environment. Whether we like it or not, textbooks and syllabi have a strong effect on the aims of instruction. This occurs because teachers depend, in many instances, on the work of others in thinking through the content and objectives of instruction, especially in subject matter areas. Objectives are a good way for teachers to go beyond curriculum specifications to include outcomes and procedures which are in some sense an advancement over what others have been able to do (Bloom, *et al.* 1971).

In determining instructional objectives, teachers should consider two basic criteria: (1) what is possible for students and (2) what is desirable for students. Student input can be utilized here. It has been suggested that many teachers believe the decision about what is possible should be based not on the student's characteristics but on the teacher's (i.e., teaching style, ability, experience, and personality). However, the teacher should not represent the major factor in determining the objectives which are possible.

Perhaps a more difficult problem is that of determining which objectives are desirable. This involves a value problem and is partly dependent on student characteristics and their goals and aspirations. Some help in determining the appropriate range of objectives for groups of students may be found in the study of existing society as suggested in the following questions (Bloom 1956, pp. 26-28):

1. What are the activities that individuals are expected to perform?
2. What are the problems they are likely to encounter?

3. What opportunities are they likely to have for service and self-realization?

Student input in the area of objectives can also be gained by asking them what their desired outcomes are for a unit of instruction. This is particularly effective with intermediate children. For example, they might form into small groups with a chairperson and discuss what they would like to know or be able to do about oceanography or space. A compilation of ideas by the teachers could form the framework for the objectives for the unit of work. Teachers can always add objectives dealing with basic knowledge the students will need to master their desired objectives. A small group of students could react to the objectives for clarity and relevance to their needs and interests.

This section has been concerned with various facets of the process of identifying and selecting instructional objectives. The last section of the chapter provides examples of how these procedures are handled in the actual school situation.

OBJECTIVE-BASED PROGRAMS IN ACTION

Three examples of how different schools carried out the processes of using instructional objectives in three different curricular areas are presented here. These include:

1. Objectives for an elementary math program
2. How we developed our unit of instruction for map skills
3. The challenge of identifying affective objectives

Each example is written as if it is being related by the staff that carried it out.

Selecting Instructional Objectives for an Elementary Mathematics Program

Our school is in its second year of IGE operation. We spent the first year ironing out the organizational wrinkles and implementing the Word Attack section of the *Wisconsin Design for Reading Skill Development.* Our IIC agreed that during our second year we would work toward improving mathematics instruction and formulated the following general objectives.

General Educational Objectives in Mathematics for Children in the Building

Children—Ages 5–8

Addition:	By age 8 the student will be able to add a one-digit number to a three-digit number with regrouping, with 80 percent mastery.
Subtraction:	By age 8 the student will be able to subtract a one-digit number from a two-digit number without regrouping, with 80 percent mastery.

Children—Ages 8–10

Addition:	By age 10 the student will be able to do column addition with four-place or five-place addends with regrouping, with 80 percent mastery.
Subtraction:	By age 10 the student will be able to subtract a number with one or more digits from a number with three or more digits with regrouping, with 80 percent mastery.
Addition-subtraction:	By age 10 the student will be able to identify the inverse relations between addition and subtraction sentences, with 80 percent mastery.
Multiplication:	By age 10 the student will be able to multiply a number with three or more digits by multiples of 100 up to 9000, with 80 percent mastery.
Division:	By age 10 the student will be able to divide a three-digit number by a one-digit number, with remainders, with 80 percent accuracy.

Children—Ages 10–12

Addition:	By age 12 the student will be able to add rational numbers expressed in "terminating" decimal form, with 80 percent accuracy.
Subtraction:	By age 12 the student will be able to subtract rational numbers expressed in terminating decimal form, with 80 percent accuracy.
Multiplication:	By age 12 the student will be able to use sentence forms to generalize the commutative property of multiplication for rational numbers in any form, with 80 percent accuracy.
Division:	By age 12 the student will be able to divide rational numbers expressed in repeating decimal form, with 80 percent accuracy.

Our school is organized into three I & R Units: ages 5–8, 8–10, and 10–12. The units have 130, 110, and 120 children, respectively. Each unit has a staff of a unit leader, four staff teachers, one instructional aide and a one-quarter-time clerical aide. The students in our building might be considered "average" in terms of abilities.

We agreed to use the Instructional Programming Model (IPM) as a guide to organizing our efforts in mathematics. We selected mathematics objectives from *A Hierarchy of Student Behavioral Objectives K–8* (Wisconsin PACT School Mathematics Committee 1973). These objectives were developed by a team of teachers and math experts to help teachers who want to individualize instruction of elementary mathematics. The objectives are listed in a prerequisite and sequential order.

We selected the four strands dealing with addition, subtraction, multiplication, and division (strands D, E, F, and G) as our first area of focus. A sample of the grid system showing the strands and 32 of the 115 horizontal levels and code key is presented in Figure 12.3 to help you understand the organization of the objectives.

Each entry in the grid represents a specific objective in the hierarchy which is coded by a number (row) and a capital letter (column). The objectives in each column of the grid represent a prerequisite order for presenting the objectives. For example, objective 13D is a prerequisite for 16D, 16D is a prerequisite for 17D, and so on. The objectives that appear in the same row (horizontal levels) are judged to be about the same level of difficulty but are not prerequisites for one another. For example, objectives 16D and 16E can be presented at about the same time, in any order, provided all of the column prerequisites for these objectives have been met.

The 115 horizontal levels are designed to be increasingly difficult as the student moves from level 1 to 115. You will notice that there are not always objectives listed for addition (strand D) at each level. As explained in the previous paragraph, this was done to allow for the clustering of related objectives in different strands.

We also classified objectives as "Level A," "Level B," and "Level C," as presented earlier in Figure 12.1. At the early primary ages most, if not all, objectives were classified as "Level A." The "Level B" and "Level C" categories play an expanding role as the student progresses through elementary school.

A summary table listing our objectives as we classified them according to strands—addition, subtraction, multiplication, and division—and levels—A, B, and C for difficulty—are presented here. Objectives for ages 5–8 are given in Figure 12.4; for 8–10-year-olds in Figure 12.5; and for ages 10–12 in Figure 12.6. Objectives numbered 87–115 are designated for ages 13–15 and are not included.

	A	B	C	D	E	F	G	H	J	K	L	M	N	P	Q	R	S	T	V	W	X	Y	Z
1															q								
2															q								
3															q				v				
4															q								
5	a													p	q			t					
6	a													p					v				
7	a																						
8	a	b																t					
9	a	b	c						j									t					
10		b	c																				
11	a		c																				
12		b	c					h			l												
13			c	d																			
14					e																		
15			c								l												
16	a	b	c	d	e						l	m								w			
17			c	d	e			h															
18		b	c						j		l				q					w			
19			c								l				q								
20			c												q								
21			c	d					j		l												
22			c		e						l	m								w			

Fig. 12.3 Hierarchy of mathematics content objectives, K-8. (From the Wisconsin PACT School Mathematics Committee 1973.)

	A	B	C	D	E	F	G	H	J	K	L	M	N	P	Q	R	S	T	V	W	X	Y	Z
23					e						l	m											
24											l	m											
25				d								m											
26				d	e													t					
27				d														t					
28				d																			
29				d																			
30			c	d											q								
31			c	d	e										q								
32			c	d	e										q								
111																							
112																							
113																							
114																							
115																							

A sets
B counting
C numeration
D addition
E subtraction
F multiplication
G division
H fractions
J number theory and order
K integers
L writing sentences
M solving sentences
N ratios
P 3-dimensional figures
Q 2-dimensional figures
R similarity and congruence
S symmetry
T "money" and "time"
V measurement
W number line
X constructions
Y ordered pairs
Z probability and statistics

1 through 115 are horizontal "levels"
A through Z are column headings

Fig. 12.4 Mathematics content objectives for ages 5–8.

Level No.	Addition Strand D	Subtraction Strand E	Multiplication Strand F	Division Strand G
13	Identify the process of addition through experience with joining two sets of objects. (A)			
14		Identify the process of subtraction through experience with separating a subset from a set of objects. (A)		
15				
16	Recognize examples of the commutative property for addition in the set of whole numbers. (A)	Recognize that subtraction is not commutative. (A)		
17	Recognize zero as the identity element for addition in the set of whole numbers. (A)	Recognize zero's special role in subtraction. (A)		
18				
19				
20				
21	Recall the addition facts through the sum 18 (A)			

22		Recall the subtraction facts for sums through 18. (A)		
23		Subtract a one-digit number from a one-digit number. (A)		
24				
25	Use the associative property of addition in the set of whole numbers: for example, $(3 + 4) + 6 = 3 + (4 + 6)$. (B)			
26	Add a one-digit number to a two-digit number without regrouping. (A)	Subtract a one-digit number from a two-digit number without regrouping. (A)		
27	Use the vertical algorithm in the addition of three addends with one-place numerals: for example: (3, 4, + 5) (A)			
28	Add two-digit and three-digit numbers. No regrouping necessary. (A)			
29	Add a one-digit number to a two-digit number with regrouping. (A)			
30	Add a one-digit number to a three-digit number with regrouping. (A)			

A = Level A objectives
B = Level B objectives

Fig. 12.5 Mathematics content objectives for ages 8–10.

Level No.	Addition Strand D	Subtraction Strand E	Multiplication Strand F	Division Strand G
31	Add two-digit numbers with regrouping. (A)	Subtract a two-digit number from a two-digit number without regrouping. (A)		
32	Add numbers with four or more digits, without regrouping. (A)	Subtract a number with one or more digits from a number with three or more digits, without regrouping. (A)		
33	Add numbers containing three or more digits, with regrouping. (A)	Subtract a one-digit number from a two-digit number with regrouping. (A)		
34	Estimate the sum of two numbers. For example, 287 + 520 is approx. 300 + 500 or 800. (B)	Subtract a two-digit number from a two-digit number with regrouping. (A)		
35	Find solutions for sentences like: "___ + 239 = 239 + ___ and 1984 + (___ + 548) = (1984 + ___) + 548" to generalize the idea of the commutative and associative properties of addition. (B)	Subtract a number with one or more digits from a number with three or more digits, with regrouping. (A)		
36			Use the multiplication facts through the product 18. (A)	

37			Recognize the role of 1 as the identity element for multiplication in the set of whole numbers. (A)	
38				
39			Use the commutative and associative properties of multiplication in the set of whole numbers. (A)	
40		Recognize the inverse relation between addition sentences and two subtraction sentences, such as $725 + 342 = 1067$ and $1067 - 725 = 342$ and $1067 - 342 = 725$. (B)	Recognize the distributive property of multiplication over addition in the set of whole numbers; for example, $3 \times (2 + 4) = (3 \times 2) + (3 \times 4)$. (B)	
41			Recall the multiplication facts through 10×10. (A)	
42				
43				
44			Use the vertical algorithm to carry out multiplication with one factor less then 10 when regrouping may be involved. (A)	

A = Level A objectives
B = Level B objectives

Fig. 12.5 cont.

Level No.	Addition Strand D	Subtraction Strand E	Multiplication Strand F	Division Strand G
45			Multiply a one-digit number by 10, 100, 1000. (A)	Demonstrate with sets of objects the relationship between such sentences as $4 \times 7 = 28$, $28 \div 4 = 7$ and $28 \div 7 = 4$. (A)
46			Multiply a one-digit number by 10, 20, 30, . . . , 90 (A)	Recognize for each multiplication combination ($0 \times 0 = 0$ through $9 \times 9 = 81$) the corresponding division combinations, excluding division by zero. (A)
47			Multiply a two-digit number by 10, 100, 1000. (A)	Use repeated subtraction to do division computation. (A)
48			Multiply a two-digit number by a one-digit number. (A)	Recognize the special role of 1 as a divisor. (A)
49			Multiply a two-digit number by 10, 20, 30, . . . , 90. (A)	Divide a one-digit or a two-digit number by a one-digit number, with no remainders. (A)
50			Multiply a one-digit number by 100, 200, . . . , 900, 1000, . . . , 9000. (A)	Divide a three-digit number by a one-digit number, with no remainders. (A)

51			Multiply a two-digit number by 100, 200, . . . , 900, 1000, . . . , 9000. (A)	
52			Multiply a number with three or more digits by 10, 100, 1000. (A)	
53	Do column addition with several four-place or five-place addends with regrouping. (A)		Multiply a number with three or more digits by a one-digit number. (A)	
54			Multiply a number with three or more digits by 10, 20, 30, . . . , 90. (A)	Divide a three-digit number by a one-digit number, with remainders. (A)
55			Multiply a number with three or more digits by 100, 200, . . . , 900, 1000, . . . , 9000. (A)	

A = Level A objectives

Fig. 12.6 Mathematics content objectives for ages 10–12.

Level No.	Addition Strand D	Subtraction Strand E	Multiplication Strand F	Division Strand G
56			Multiply a two-digit number by a two-digit number. (A)	Divide a number with two or more digits by 10, 20, 30, . . . , 90, with or without remainders. (A)
57			Multiply a number with three or more digits by a two-digit number. (A)	Divide a number with three or more digits by 100, 200, . . . , 900, 1000, . . . , 9000, with or without remainders. (A)
58			Estimate the product of two numbers. For example, 21×88 is approximately 20×90. (B)	Estimate the quotient of two numbers. For example, $795 \div 23$ is approximately $800 \div 20$. (B)
59			Find solutions for sentences like "$723 \times \square = \triangle \times 723$," to generalize the idea of commutative property of multiplication. (B)	Divide a number with two or more digits by a two-digit number, with no remainders. (A)
60			Find solutions for sentences like "$\square \times (176 \times 19) = (\triangle \times 176) \times 19$," to generalize the associative property of multiplication. (B)	

61			Find solutions for sentences like "3 × 13 = (□ × 10) + (△ × 3) and △ × □ = (5 × 7) + (5 × 8)," to generalize the distributive property of multiplication over addition. (B)	Divide a number with two or more digits by a two-digit number, with remainders. (A)
62			Multiply a number with three or more digits by a three-digit number. (A)	Divide a number with three or more digits by a three-digit number, with or without remainders. (A)
63			Use the abbreviated form of multiplication algorithm with both factors having at least three digits. (A)	
64				
65				Use the conventional division algorithm. (A)
66				
67				
68				
69				

A = Level A objectives
B = Level B objectives

Fig. 12.6 cont.

Level No.	Addition Strand D	Subtraction Strand E	Multiplication Strand F	Division Strand G
70	Add simple rational numbers by the use of physical objects, diagrams, etc. (A)	Subtract simple rational numbers by the use of physical objects, diagrams, etc. (A)	Multiply simple rational numbers by the use of physical objects, diagrams, etc. (A)	
71				
72	Add rational numbers whose fractions have like denominators (not including conversion to mixed numerals). Examples: 2/7 + 3/7 + 3/2 + 7/2. (A)	Subtract rational numbers whose fractions have like denominators. (A)		
73	Recognize that zero is the identity element for addition in the set of positive rational numbers as well as in the set of whole numbers. (A)	Recognize that subtraction is not always possible in the set of positive rational numbers. (A)		
74	Add rational numbers whose fractions have unlike denominators. (A)		Multiply rational numbers expressed in fraction form. (A)	
75		Subtract rational numbers whose fractions have unlike denominators. (A)	Recognize that 1/1 or 1 is an identity element for multiplication of the set of rational numbers. (A)	Express the quotient of positive integers as a mixed numeral: for example, 24 ÷ 5 = 4 4/5. (B)

76				Recognize that the operation of division is the inverse of multiplication in the set of positive rational numbers. For example, the sentences "3/4 × 2/3 = 1/2," "1/2 ÷ 3/4 = 2/3," and "1/2 ÷ 2/3 = 3/4," have this relationship. (B)
77	Add rational numbers expressed in mixed numeral form. Example: 1 2/3 + 2 5/7. (A)		Multiply rational numbers expressed in mixed numeral form. (A)	Recognize the multiplicative inverse (reciprocal) for every positive rational number except zero and use it in the division of rational numbers. For example, 1/2 ÷ 3/1 = 1/2 × 4/3. (B)
78		Subtract (without regrouping) rational numbers expressed in mixed numeral form. (A)	Use the commutative and associative properties of multiplication for positive rational numbers. (B)	Divide rational numbers expressed in fractional form. (B)
79		Subtract (with regrouping) rational numbers expressed in mixed numeral form. (A)		Divide rational numbers expressed in mixed numeral form. (B)
80	Use the commutative and associative properties for addition in the set of positive rational numbers. (B)		Use the distributive property of multiplication over addition with respect to positive rational numbers. (B)	Rename a fraction as a decimal. (A)

A = Level A objectives
B = Level B objectives

Fig. 12.6 cont.

Level No.	Addition Strand D	Subtraction Strand E	Multiplication Strand F	Division Strand G
81	Use previously described sentence forms to generalize the commutative property of addition and the associate property of addition for positive rational numbers in fraction form. (C)		Use previously described sentence forms to generalize the distributive property of multiplication over addition for positive rational numbers in fractional form. (C)	
82	Add rational numbers expressed in "terminating" decimal form. (C)	Subtract rational numbers expressed in terminating decimal form. (B)		
83			Multiply rational numbers expressed in terminating decimal form. (B)	
84				Divide rational numbers expressed in terminating form. (C)
85			Use previously described sentence forms to generalize the commutative property of multiplication for rational numbers in any form. (C)	Divide rational numbers expressed in repeating decimal form. (C)

B = Level B objectives
C = Level C objectives

How We Developed Our Unit of Instruction for Map Skills*

There are 115 children, ages 6–8, in our I & R Unit. About half of them are from broken homes and nearly all of them are white. Our unit staff consists of a unit leader, three staff teachers, and an aide. We have a student teacher for a nine-week period from time to time.

Before we started work on the map skills unit of work, we looked at the student achievement scores on study skills on our standardized achievement test and, overall, found our students to be slightly below the national average. As a result of our planning meeting discussion, we made an informal survey and found that most of the children did not have a globe at home and very few had used a map of their state or an atlas. This information helped us decide that we needed to develop a "get acquainted" session for children so they could feel at ease with the basic tools—maps and globes.

We have found from experience that the most efficient way to develop a unit of instruction is to divide our labor. For example, the teacher who has special expertise or interest in the area—in this case, map skills—brings together the information and develops a draft of the specifications and teaching guidelines. Then the total unit staff critiques the draft. After revisions, the teacher who developed the unit of instruction is responsible for having the materials duplicated and to make sure materials from the IMC and other sources are available when the unit of instruction is taught. Thus, one teacher can be getting ready for one unit of instruction while someone else is working on another one. In this manner, a unit staff can prepare a large number of materials without burdening anyone.

In our school, we use Bloom's (1956) cognitive taxonomy as a guideline for developing a unit of instruction. In fact, we have designed a form used in planning. On this form, Bloom's cognitive levels are listed from simple (knowledge) to complex (evaluation) on the left side. Specifications (skills/concepts/processes), objectives and teaching guidelines (activities and materials) are printed across the top.

Our completed planning form for map skills is shown in Figure 12.7. Note the logical sequence of skills, objectives, and activities that emerges in using Bloom's taxonomy. They build from simple to complex, and also skills learned at each level are used again in the next higher level. This way, the student gets opportunities to practice newly learned skills over and over again in a variety of learning situations. By checking mastery at each level, as we do in IGE, we can be sure a child has the lower level skills before attempting a higher level. This ensures student success and usually a happy learning situation. Also, by using preassess-

---

* Adapted from a unit of instruction at Fahey Elementary School, Fond du Lac, Wisc.

Fig. 12.7 Guidelines for test specifications and teaching strategies using Bloom's cognitive levels.

Content area: Map skills   Age/Grade level Ages 6–8

Specifications			Teaching guidelines	
Cognitive level	Skill/concept/ process	Objective(s)	Activities	Materials
Knowledge	Defining	The student will be able to: 1. define the terms map, globe, map directions. 2. identify basic map colors (land, water), codes, and terms. 3. list four different kinds of maps.	1. Provide children with all types of maps and list the differences and likenesses. 2. Discuss maps and globes, and establish definitions. 3. Guide the children in finding new words that relate to maps.	World map, United States map, city map, airport map, road map, map of a room, atlases, globes
Comprehension	Identifying	4. verbally interpret what they have seen on a map and seen and/or heard about maps from a teacher, or audiovisuals.	1. Verbal interpretation and demonstration of what they read, saw, and heard on filmstrips/records.	*Learning to Use Maps and Globes,* Beginning Unit A, Produced by Classroom World Production, Inc., Green Lake, Wisc. 54941.
Application	Locating	5. illustrate map directions on paper or manually. 6. identify map symbols, oceans, continents, etc., in games, puzzles, and other materials. 7. locate places, oceans, continents, etc., on maps and globes.	1. Indicate direction in some manner from verbal instructions. 2. Work with board games, pictures, puzzles, riddles, and mazes to identify map features. 3. Locate places on maps and globes used in class activity.	*Map Fun and Activity Book* by Walter B. Gibson, Treasure Books. *The First Book of Maps and Globes* by Sam and Beryl Epstein, Franklin Watts, Inc.

Analysis	Differentiating	8. locate each state of the United States on a map. 9. relate parts to the whole.	1. Name and match a state on a puzzle part with its counterpart on a larger United States map. 2. Put puzzles of the United States together. 3. Card game on states.	Maps, transparencies and puzzles of the United States.
Synthesis	Planning	10. utilize their skills about maps and globes in a new situation.	1. Have children build their own nation on a newly found land. It is surrounded by water, has a desert area, water inlets, forest areas, mountains, lakes, rivers, and so on. Given a key for symbols, they will identify areas with the symbols, name the areas (cities, rivers, etc.), and put in industry and farm area. They will culminate all of this into one large map.	Large piece of tagboard, paints or crayons, basic outline of area to be used, construction paper.
Evaluation	Critiquing Revising	11. criticize systematically what has been developed and make suggestions for refinement.	1. The children will discuss the project in light of all learned, to see if their newly erected nation is well mapped out and the objects are located in good areas to produce easy every-day living. 2. Posttest.	Projector and handouts to facilitate the critique. Duplicated sheets with posttest questions.

ment, students who have lower level skills can move immediately to a higher level where they will be challenged. Note that our activities for the higher level skills are open-ended and allow opportunity for extensive work. They also encourage creativity.

During the map skills unit of instruction, the 115 children in our unit experience a variety of grouping patterns. These range from total unit (large group) for a film and overview to class-sized group (20–30 students), medium-sized group (11–19), small group (2–10) and independent study. These patterns are selected according to preassessed needs and interests of students and the nature of the content to be learned. For the map skills, the pretest was oral and the posttest written. Items for these tests were selected and developed by the unit staff as a part of the planning.

The Challenge of Identifying Affective Objectives

Our unit was in its third year of operation in IGE. We had, we believed, been successful in selecting objectives and carrying out the subsequent steps of instructional programming in Reading and Math skills during the first two years. We had also implemented the motivational procedure of "older students tutoring younger students" and it had been a big success. Instructional objectives for all of these programs were available from a variety of sources and our job as a group of teachers had been to select and adapt them for the 138 children in Unit Snowball (ages 5–8).

Our school is located in an urban area and students' achievement and ability, while quite varied, tends to be "average" according to national norms. Therefore, our task in selecting instructional objectives had been fairly easy. Also, the math resource teacher for our school and the junior high math teacher who lives across the street from one of the unit teachers were a great help.

This fall we decided to start setting affective objectives for our unit and we ran into some real roadblocks in getting started. We searched objectives of other schools, and telephoned resource people, principals, and unit leaders in nearby IGE schools for examples. From all of this, we gathered a few samples to use as guidelines.

One day while we were struggling with this problem, I had a long talk with our university facilitator and another professor. My question was "Why are affective objectives so hard to find? And why are the ones we do get so vague and difficult to measure?" They said that people in research also have difficulties with the affective domain. Some of the reasons they gave for the problems with affective objectives relate to the nature of affective qualities. These include:

1. the idea that affective qualities are personal in nature. This leads to answers that are "socially" acceptable, depending on the question and circumstances, rather than real or honest answers.

2. the lack of a "right" answer. For example, we have no concrete evidence to indicate a child must have a positive attitude toward math to be successful in it. Yet positive attitudes toward subject areas provide a desirable environment for teaching and learning. This contrasts with math in the cognitive domain where we generally agree that $2 + 2 = 4$.
3. Present-day statistical procedures cannot be as reliably applied to data from affective research as they can to cognitive research.
4. Affective qualities are sensitive to a person's physical surroundings as temperature, fatigue, environment, hunger and so on. So while qualities are generally stable from month to month or year to year, they may vary widely over short periods of time.
5. lack of clear-cut definition from one quality to another. For example, attitudes, values, and beliefs overlap. Interests and self-concepts may overlap all of these and motives may be influenced by any or all of the qualities mentioned.

After this brief mini-lesson about problems others have with affective qualities, I sighed and decided to share my "new" knowledge with the unit staff. Their response to my presentation was "Wow, we sure took hold of a tough one this time." But they weren't about to quit, and we went ahead with our objectives.

We decided to set priorities on the qualities we wanted to set objectives for. We decided on values and interests for this year. The objectives we developed for our 5- to 8-year-olds on values appear below.

The students will be able to:

1. identify and express their own values and order them from highest to lowest priority.
2. respect the values of others without ridicule or negative comment.
3. give reasons for their values and their order of priority.

The staff worked out a series of group exercises to help students meet these objectives. One that worked particularly well was to put cards up along the wall with three faces depicting happy 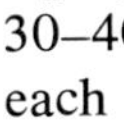, unhappy 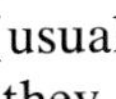, and in-between 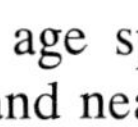. We discussed these expressions with the children to be sure that we agreed on what they meant. Then we prepared a series of statements that we read one at a time to groups of 30–40 children (usually of a two-year age span). After they listened to each statement, they were asked to stand near the face that matched their feeling about it. Some sample statements were:

Talking while someone else is talking.

Sharing my toys with others.

Playing alone.

Giving away my Snoopy toy.

Taking things that aren't mine.

Breaking something that someone else likes.

Looking at books.

After we'd completed the exercise, we discussed various aspects of each statement. The students enjoyed this and it gave all of us a chance to hear how others felt. We also had other exercises and games dealing with values. The combination of activities gave the children experiences to move toward the objectives. We'll evaluate our program and make changes as necessary.

SUMMARY

This chapter was designed to help practicing and prospective unit leaders and teachers better understand the place of instructional objectives in IGE and to more effectively carry out the process of identifying instructional objectives in their I & R Units. The ideas stressed were:

- IGE programs use a variety of types of instructional objectives
- Instructional objectives should be designated into levels so not all students are expected to master or complete all objectives
- Instructional objectives form the basis of the instructional program in terms of:
    - selecting and organizing the content for objectives
    - identifying the objectives
    - involving students in the selection process
- Instructional objectives are utilized in different ways in different curricula or other areas as:
    - the math program
    - map skills
    - affective education

Examples from the school setting were used to illustrate each idea wherever practicable.

REFERENCES

Addison-Wesley Publishing Company 1972. *Guide for individualizing elementary school mathematics.* Menlo Park, Calif.: Addison-Wesley.

Appleton, Wisconsin Schools 1970. *Guide for early childhood education.* Unpublished curriculum guide, Appleton, Wisc.

Bloom, B. S. 1956. *Taxonomy of educational objectives: the classification of educational goals, by a committee of college and university examiners.* New York: McKay.

———, J. T. Hastings, and G. A. Madaus 1971. *Handbook on formative summative evaluation of student learning.* New York: McGraw-Hill.

Edling, J. F. 1970. *Individualized instruction: a manual for administrators.* Corvallis, Ore.: Continuing Educational Publications.

Eisner, E. S. 1969. *Instructional objectives.* American Educational Research Association Monograph Series on Curriculum Evaluation. Chicago: Rand McNally.

Klausmeier, H. J., R. A. Rossmiller, and M. S. Saily (eds.) in press. *Individually guided education: concepts and principles.*

———, M. R. Quilling, J. S. Sorenson, R. S. Way, and G. R. Glasrud 1971. *Individually guided education and the multiunit elementary school: guidelines for implementation.* Madison, Wisc.: Wisconsin Research and Development Center for Cognitive Learning.

Krathwohl, D. R., and B. S. Bloom 1964. *Taxonomy of educational objectives: the classification of educational goals.* New York: McKay.

Mager, R. F. 1962. *Preparing objectives for programmed instruction.* Palo Alto, Calif.: Fearon.

McAshan, H. H. 1970. *Writing behavioral objectives: a new approach.* New York, Evanston, and London: Harper & Row.

Otto, W., and E. Askov 1972. *Wisconsin design for reading skill development: rationale and guidelines.* Minneapolis: National Computer Systems.

Simpson, E. J. 1966–67. The classification of educational objectives, psychomotor domain. *Illinois Teacher of Home Economics* **10** (Winter): 110–144.

Sorenson, J. S. 1973. *Implementing instructional programming in individualized learning programs.* Eau Claire, Wisc.: University of Wisconsin.

Teacher's handbook (Dwight Allen, ed.) 1976. Glenview, Ill.: Scott Foresman.

Vargas, J. S. 1972. *Writing worthwhile behavioral objectives.* New York: Harper & Row.

Wisconsin PACT School Mathematics Committee 1972. *Individualizing mathematical learning in the elementary school: a hierarchy of student behavioral objectives, K–8.* Madison, Wisc.: Wisconsin Department of Public Instruction.

13

Assessing Pupil Performance

William Wiersma
Stephen Jurs

Objectives

After reading this chapter, the reader will be able:

- To explain the meaning of terms used in the assessment process.
- To explain the assessment and evaluation process as it applies to Step 3 of the Instructional Programming Model for IGE.
- To identify and indicate appropriate uses of four different types of assessment instruments.
- To identify and develop techniques for organizing assessment results.
- To illustrate different interpretations of one set of assessment results.
- To explain the role and functions of the unit leader in the assessment and evaluation within the I & R Unit.

The content of this chapter is specifically directed toward the aspect of instructional programming for the individual student which is described in the third step of the Instructional Programming Model (IPM). That step is stated as (Klausmeier, *et al.* 1971, p. 19):

> Assess the level of achievement, learning style, and motivation level of each student by use of criterion-referenced tests, observation schedules, and work samples with appropriate-sized subgroups.

The activities suggested by the third step are many and varied. They include the cognitive, affective, and psychomotor assessment activities that occur in the day-to-day instruction of the I & R Unit. In order to conduct the relatively comprehensive assessment required in IGE, a variety of measurement procedures and instruments are required.

As with the entire operation of the I & R Unit, it is the unit leader's role to assume the leadership for assessment and evaluation. Although the emphasis of this chapter is on activities related to Step 3 of the Instructional Programming Model, some general background on the topic is provided early in the chapter. It is important that there be a consistency of meaning in the terminology. Also, the unit staff, especially the unit leader, should have a broad concept of assessment and evaluation in an IGE school which goes beyond that described in the third step of the Instructional Programming Model.

ASSESSMENT AND EVALUATION IN IGE

Inspection of the Instructional Programming Model indicates that instruction in IGE is clearly objective-based. It logically follows, then, that the assessment and evaluation within IGE are also based upon objectives, primarily instructional objectives which were described in Step 2 of the IPM, and discussed in Chapter 12 of this text. In order to conduct assessment and evaluation, well-prepared and realistic instructional objectives appropriate to the characteristics of the students and curriculum area under consideration are necessary. Thus, in the discussion here, we are assuming the prerequisite of such instructional objectives.

Meaning of Terms

There are a number of terms used in connection with IGE assessment and the activities involved. Those most relevant to the discussion here are test, measurement, assessment, and evaluation. Each of these is defined and examples indicated below. All are related and at times are used interchangeably in education. However, the terms are more useful if distinctions are made among them.

Test. Generally, test is considered the narrowest of the terms. It usually connotes the presentation of a defined set of questions, items, or stimuli to which individuals respond under controlled conditions. A test may be in paper-and-pencil form, oral form, or it may involve presenting a physical stimulus such as in the case of a psychomotor performance test where a child is asked to carry out a specific task. Controlled conditions might be a time limit, the requirement of responding to the test alone, or the use of special equipment. In an IGE school, tests can be prepared by the I & R Unit staff or they may be purchased from a commercial source. Tests can be described as norm-referenced or criterion-referenced.

Norm-referenced tests are used for the purpose of comparing a student's performance with the performance of other students who have taken the same test. Most teachers are acquainted with *standardized* tests which are one type of norm-referenced test. Tests are "standardized" through a procedure which includes giving the test to a large number of students and identifying norms or averages based on the obtained scores and the age/grade levels of the students. Some standardized tests, such as the Gates-MacGinitie reading tests (1965) cover only one academic area. Other standardized tests are more comprehensive and are used for testing in several curriculum areas. The Iowa Test of Basic Skills (1964) and the Stanford Achievement Test (1964, 1965) are examples of comprehensive standardized achievement tests.

Criterion-referenced tests are those which are designed to measure an individual's status with respect to some criterion (Popham 1971, p. 20). Criterion-referenced measurement provides information as to the degree of competence attained by a particular student which is independent of reference to the performance of others (Popham 1971, p. 8).

Some publishers whose instructional materials are objective-based include appropriate criterion-referenced tests for the objectives. An example of an objective and the related test from *Metric Measurement* is presented below (Imperial International Learning Corporation 1973):

Objective: Given a plane figure, all dimensions of which are less than 15 centimeters, the student measures any specified dimension to the nearest centimeter and records the answer using the unit "centimeter" or "cm."

Checkup questions: Take the blue triangle from the envelope.
20. How long is side A?
Write your answer on the answer sheet.

21. How long is side B?
Write your answer on the answer sheet.

22. How long is side C?
Write your answer on the answer sheet.

23. Start at the triangle on your answer sheet, and draw a line that is 8 cm long.

24. Is the centimeter a unit of volume, mass, or length?
Write your answer on the answer sheet.

Measurement. Measurement is a broader concept than test and generally means quantification, the assigning of numbers to performances or attributes according to certain rules. A variety of instruments and procedures can be used for measuring. These include rating scales and teacher observation, as well as tests. Measurement can be a simple or uncomplicated act such as determining the height of a student, or it can be an extensive procedure such as the administration and scoring of an entire battery of tests.

Measurement has associated with it a body of concepts and principles usually referred to as "measurement theory." These concepts relate to the meaning that can be assigned to the numbers or scores obtained when measurement takes place. This chapter contains very little reference to formal measurement theory since the emphasis is upon application. See Wiersma and Jurs (1976) for a discussion on the subject.

Assessment. Assessment is a term closely related to measurement in meaning. Assessment might be descriptively defined as the *practical application of measurement.* If reading skills were being assessed, the students might be tested using a paper-and-pencil test, asked to read orally, and required to write a report about something they had read. As actual scores are assigned to these various tasks and the resulting products, measurement takes place. Assessment usually implies performing measurement of some type.

Evaluation. The meaning of evaluation comes from the interpretation that is made of the information obtained through measurement and assessment. Is the assessed performance good or bad, above average or below average, facilitative or inhibiting of subsequent learning? The answers to these questions form the basis for instructional decisions about a student. Evaluation has been characterized as (Stufflebeam 1968, p. 6):

> . . . the provision of information through formal means, . . . to serve as rational bases for making judgments in decision situations . . . stated simply, evaluation is the science of providing information for decision-making.

This definition is quite comprehensive and is consistent with the concept of evaluation necessary for IGE. In order to have a decision situation, we must have two or more alternatives. Judgment is the assignment of values to alternatives, usually on the basis of a criterion. In order to make decisions, information must be provided through assessment. All of these characteristics are present in the implementation of the instructional programming for individual students in a school situation.

Planning for Assessment and Evaluation in the I & R Unit

Assessment and evaluation within an I & R Unit is objective-based. That is, the judgment made relates directly to whether or not the objective under consideration has been met. The process of going from the objective to the judgment can be described through a sequence of activities (Klausmeier and Goodwin 1975):

- Develop instructional objectives including the criteria of acceptable performance
- Measure performance
- Compare the measured performance to the performance indicated by the criteria
- Judge the measured performance
- Act on judgment

The sequence above supports objective-based assessment and evaluation which are inherent in the instructional programming process. Note that there must be criteria of acceptable performance or achievement. The criteria may be explicitly or implicitly contained in the objectives, or a published statement of objectives may be supplemented with stated criteria. In this regard there may be some objectives that call for precise criteria, e.g., 80 percent correct, others that call only for some progress toward mastery, and still others that merely call for some participation in certain activities, e.g., in creative activities or in interest groups.

Measurement, assessment, and evaluation in the IPM. The model on which instructional programming for individual students is based is presented on the left side of Figure 13.1. An inspection of the various steps in the model indicates numerous measurement and assessment activities either explicitly stated or implied. It should be noted that these activities are relevant to both types of decisions—those pertaining to individual students and those related to their instructional programs. These ongoing measurement, assessment, and evaluation activities are specifically indicated for each step on the right side of the figure. The culmination of instructional programming consists of a decision point with the various alternatives indicated. At each decision point, the decision alternatives that exist must be judged. The decision making which occurs in connection with the IPM (Figure 13.1) can be illustrated with content from the language

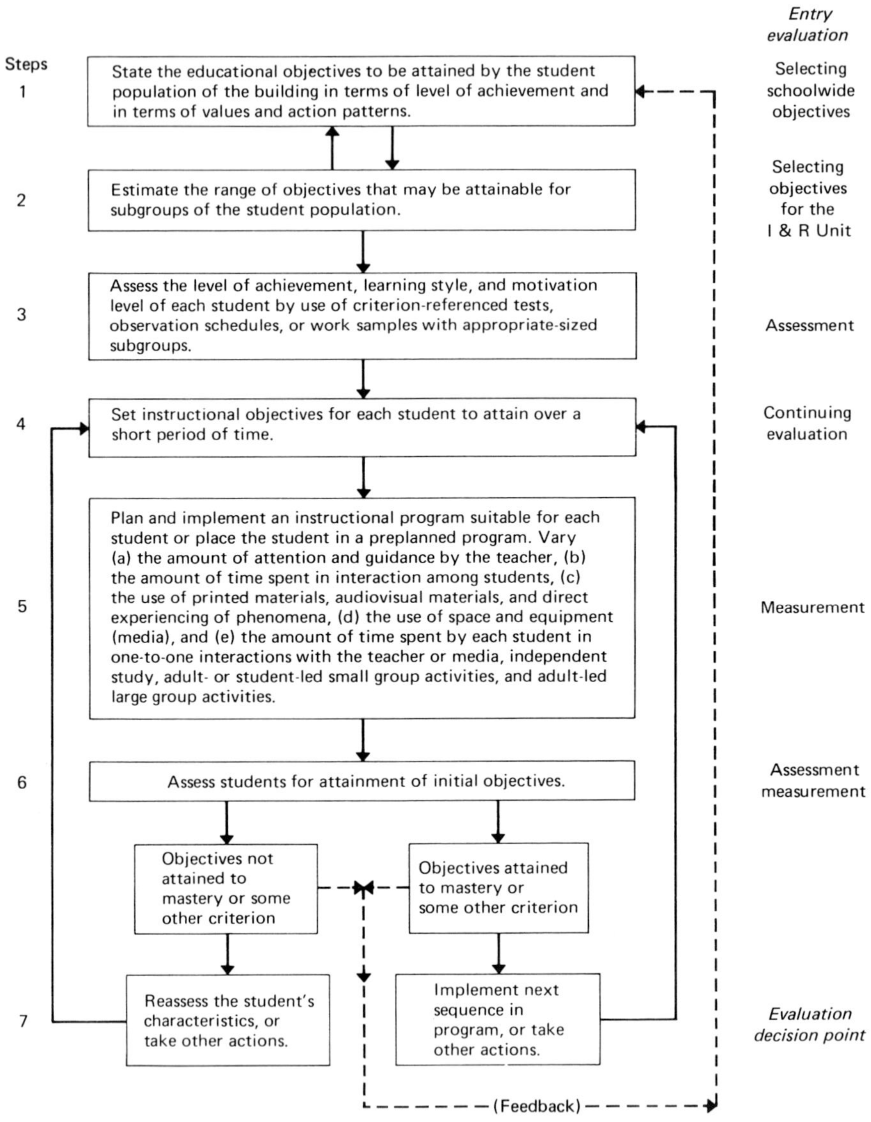

Fig. 13.1 Decision points for measurement, assessment, and evaluation in the Instructional Programming Model.

arts. In an actual school situation an I & R Unit would make many other decisions simultaneously.

The steps of the IPM are illustrated with examples as follows:

Step 1. Schoolwide objectives are set by the IIC. An example is: Ninety percent of the students will be able to use capital letters correctly in all forms of written work.

Step 2. The I & R staff working with children aged 9–11 chooses instructional objectives appropriate for their student population, such as: The student will capitalize the names of cities and states whenever they are used in written work.

Step 3. Assessment instruments are identified and students are assessed. These include:

(a) a paper-and-pencil test with the following directions: Write answers to the questions given below:

(1) Where do you live?
(2) What is the capital of our state?
(3) Where are the world headquarters of the Sears, Roebuck Co. located?

(b) assessment of learning style using an instrument such as the one presented in Figure 14.2

(c) assessment of motivational level through observation.

Step 4. Based on the results of assessment in Step 3, instructional decisions are made about each student. Those students who have not mastered this particular usage of capital letters will be put into an instructional sequence to receive appropriate instruction and practice. Students whose assessments indicate mastery of this objective will be grouped to receive instruction on other objectives which they have not yet mastered.

Step 5. At an I & R Unit planning meeting, the activities for the students working on the objective stated in Step 2 are identified. The activities might include:

(a) use of maps to locate certain cities and states
(b) practice in writing lists of cities and states
(c) practice in addressing envelopes
(d) creative writing about a hobo who went to many places in his travels

Plans are also made for assignment of personnel to instructional groups, grouping arrangements, space assignments, and possible activities for students who will not be working on the objective.

Step 6. Assessment and evaluation of the students who worked on the sample objective could include:

(a) evaluation of work samples written during the instruction
(b) a paper-and-pencil test which requires writing the names of cities and states.

Step 7. The unit staff makes decisions about each student. Those who mastered the sample objective could proceed to other objectives about capitalization *or* be assigned language arts objectives with another emphasis such as letter writing. Decisions for students who did not master the objective might lead to having the student carry out more activities related to the given objective *or* to directing the student into another set of objectives. These decisions must take into consideration the students' ability, the reasons for nonmastery, motivational level, grouping arrangement, and other related factors.

This example has illustrated the use of measurement, assessment, and evaluation in making appropriate decisions for each student.

All staff members are involved in making decisions about instruction for the children in the I & R Unit. It is the responsibility of the unit leader to ensure that all teachers are involved in planning for evaluation, including (1) means of assessment, (2) analysis of assessments data, and (3) decision making based on available information. The unit leader must provide the leadership to ensure that the assessment and evaluation sequence is implemented and carried out as planned.

Sources of information for decision making. The primary source of information in the I & R Unit is the student. From the student, information can be gathered about knowledge level, attitude, interests, learning styles, and motivation. Procedures for gathering the desired information include paper-and-pencil tests, performances, observations, and work samples. These procedures are discussed in detail later in this chapter.

Teachers outside the unit, including those who have worked directly with students in the past or in other situations, can also provide assessment information. This includes previous records from former teachers. School personnel such as the nurse, speech therapist, other specialists, and teachers of art, music, and physical education should also be called upon for their input.

The home is another valuable source of information about students. This includes information about attitudes, learning styles, interests, and motivation which often provides insights not always recognized through inschool assessment techniques.

Uses of information in decision making. Information as it has been gathered is seldom usable in its original form. It must be summarized into a workable quantity of information and presented in a usable form. The unit leader is not responsible for preparing all the reports, but must assume the responsibility for leading the unit staff in making decisions about: (1) information to be contained in the report, (2) format of the report, (3) identifying when the report will be needed, and (4) who will be responsible for completing the report. The format for the report may be as simple as a listing of performance scores for a specific student, or as complex as a proposal which indicates objectives, instructional procedures, and a plan for evaluation. The report is used when decisions are being considered at a unit meeting.

Although decisions are made by the unit staff in a unit meeting, the decision point is a point in the instructional process when a course of action is taken by a student or a group of students. For example, suppose a student is completing a unit of instruction dealing with ecology. Several instructional objectives are involved and the instruction deals with both the scientific and political aspects of ecology. The student works on the unit as appropriate for two weeks, at which time it is anticipated that the objectives have successfully been met. The specific objectives the student is attempting to attain would have been cooperatively established by a unit teacher and the student.

A decision point has been established; that is, two weeks after instruction begins, a decision will be made as to whether or not the objectives have been satisfactorily met. However, the decision does not stop there. The decision point really consists of two alternatives for the teacher: (1) the student may be moved on to another unit of instruction if objectives have been attained, or (2) the teacher makes adjustments in the student's instructional program that will enable attainment of the objectives. When the decision is to be made, the unit staff will require the necessary information.

During the course of the two weeks, the student may have worked with several of the teachers in the unit in attempting to meet the objectives of the ecology unit. Information from the different teachers would be collected and summarized. The unit leader must ensure that one teacher will assume the responsibility for this summary and that it is completed at the appropriate time. The summary can then be presented at a unit planning meeting. At this point, the unit staff will discuss the information, make a judgment as to whether or not the objectives have been met, and make a decision as to a course of action for each student.

All the decision making which takes place at the unit meetings would have little effect if the decisions were not implemented. The decision point involves implementing one of the alternatives with the student. If evaluation is adequately conducted, the information will be available when it is necessary to make decisions. If instruction has been adequately structured, decision points will exist and be identified. Without decision points, there would be no need to evaluate.

NORM-REFERENCED AND CRITERION-REFERENCED MEASUREMENT

Before we consider specific assessment activities necessary for instructional programming for the individual student, it is well to consider norm-referenced and criterion-referenced measurement and the distinctions between them. Traditionally, the majority of assessment in the elementary school has been norm-referenced. However, since IGE is an objective-based program, a student attempts to meet objectives, and performances are compared to the criteria of the objectives, not to performances of other children (criterion-referenced measurement).

Whether an item or a test is norm-referenced or criterion-referenced depends upon the interpretation. A test score is neither until an interpretation takes place. If the interpretation of an individual's performance is based on a comparison with the performance of a group of children, it is norm-referenced; if it is based on a comparison with a criterion, the interpretation is criterion-referenced.

Interpretations can be best explained with an example. Suppose a student takes a 20-item, paper-and-pencil test and correctly responds to 14 items. On the basis of 100 points the student has a score of 70. Fifty students have taken the test with a mean (average) score of 80; a score of 70 falls at about the 40th percentile of the distribution of scores. The score of 70 can be interpreted with respect to how it places in the distribution of scores. The information indicates that about 60 percent of the students scored better than the student with a score of 70. This first interpretation is norm-referenced. If grades were being distributed, the student might receive a C grade, to a large extent arbitrarily designated.

Now suppose that the 20 items are directly related to an objective that has as the criterion "the student will respond correctly to 80 percent of the items." In interpreting the score of 70 it is clear that the student has not attained the criterion. This interpretation is based on the premise that an 80 percent correct response represents minimum performance for mastery of the content reflected by the objective. The criterion of the objective, and hence the objective, has not been met. No reference is made to how other students performed on the 20 items. This second interpretation of the score is referenced to the criterion—thus, it is criterion-referenced. It should be reiterated that the assessment is norm-referenced or criterion-referenced according to the interpretation placed on the performance, *not* according to the type of items.

Before selecting or writing items for either norm-referenced or criterion-referenced tests, there are several qualities of tests such as difficulty level, discrimination power, validity and reliability which should be understood.

Difficulty level. When using criterion-referenced assessments, the method of interpreting results has direct implication for the difficulty levels of the items. In criterion-referenced assessment, the difficulty of items depends on the nature of the tasks being learned. There is no attempt to obtain a spread of scores. On the other hand, adequate norm-referenced assessment requires a spread of scores. In order to obtain the maximum spread of scores in norm-referenced assessment, it is desirable to have fifty percent, or thereabouts, of the group (on which the test is normed) respond correctly to each item. No such condition is necessary or even desirable for criterion-referenced assessment. Here the spread of scores is basically a dichotomy—those that have met the criterion and those that have not. Practically, the entire group of students measured may pass most of the items as the students approach mastery of the content. This condition is desirable if the items reflect the instructional objectives.

Discrimination power. When dealing with norm-referenced measures, it is usually desirable to have high discrimination power of the items. That is, the items should discriminate between individuals who possess what is being measured to varying degrees. In criterion-referenced measures, discrimination power is of concern only to the extent that the item discriminates between those who have attained the criterion and those who have not. As the students are achieving mastery and attaining the criterion, there would be very little variability among the scores.

Validity and reliability. Although there are several types of validity which are considered in the construction of tests, the type most relevant in the measurement of academic achievement is content validity. *Content validity* is the extent to which a test truly reflects and fully covers the objectives which it was designed to measure. Careful examination of test items in relation to the following questions can help teachers determine their content validity (Stanley and Hopkins 1972, p. 102):

- Does the test content parallel the curricular objectives in content and process?
- Are the test and curricular emphases in proper balance?
- Is the test free from prerequisites that are irrelevant or incidental to the present measurement task?

Reliability refers to the accuracy with which a test measures what it is intended to measure. A test which is reliable should yield results that are consistent and pertinent to the specific purpose the tester has in mind (Stanley and Hopkins 1972, p. 114).

Procedures for establishing reliability and validity of assessment instruments depend upon the variance in scores. Because criterion-referenced measures are designed to measure a single criterion which most students will have mastered (except when used for pretests), very little variance occurs in the scores. Therefore, criterion-referenced measures will tend to produce low reliability and validity coefficients. Users of criterion-referenced measures should be aware of this characteristic.

Criterion-referenced Assessment in IGE

Since instruction in IGE is based on instructional objectives which contain criteria for student performance, it follows that the majority of assessment in the daily operation of the I & R Unit is criterion-referenced. Information gathered from criterion-referenced tests is used as the basis for making decisions about each student in determining the next steps to be taken in each individual's instructional program.

Instructional objectives are identified by an I & R Unit team in Step 2 of the IPM. Then the team must prepare, or locate from some available source, criterion-referenced tests which will provide a measurement of each student's level of achievement for the objectives. These results are used as the basis for grouping children for instruction.

One use of criterion-referenced pretests is to identify the skills, concepts, or processes which a student needs to learn. For example, pretests are often used in reading to determine which word attack or study skills should be included in each child's instructional program; in math, pretests can be used to identify the computational skills which certain students need to learn.

A second use of criterion-referenced pretests is to determine the level of instruction needed by each student on a particular skill. For example, a student's math pretest might indicate that mastery has been attained in subtraction for most three-digit numerals, but that further instruction is needed at a level which involves regrouping when there are zeros in the minuend. A pretest in reading might show that a student succeeds in identifying unknown two-syllable words, but lacks the skills needed for attacking words of more than two syllables.

A third use of criterion-referenced tests as pretests is to determine where a student should be placed in a unit of instruction which focuses on concepts. An example of such a unit would be "The Economics of Our Community." Three levels of concept development could be identified: (1) understanding that money is used to acquire goods, (2) understanding that money is used to acquire services, (3) understanding that those who sell goods or services use the money they earn in many ways. Through pretesting, each student's level of understanding can be determined. The unit team then uses this information in placing each child in the most appropriate group for instruction.

Criterion-referenced tests are also used as posttests to determine if, and how well, each child has mastered the objective(s) of the instructional program. Posttests can be composed of the same type of questions or testing procedures as were used in the pretest. However, it is suggested that the posttest consist of different questions or items than the pretest to avoid any tendency to just "learn the answers" for the posttest.

While teachers are encouraged to utilize existing criterion-referenced tests, they may not always be available. Then teachers must develop the test. Writing criterion-referenced tests may be a new experience for many unit leaders and teachers in IGE schools. Thus it is essential that an effort be made to prepare test items which accurately reflect the criterion behavior (Popham 1971, p. 25). Unit leaders may find it necessary to provide help in the form of inservice education or resource personnel for the team to prepare criterion-referenced tests which meet their intended purposes. Further information about preparing criterion-referenced test items can be found in several of the references given at the end of this chapter.

Norm-referenced Assessment in IGE

All of the assessment relative to the curriculum areas is not necessarily criterion-referenced. Some norm-referenced measurement is useful in IGE situations. One such situation is for the general assessment of students at the beginning of a school year. For example, when standardized achievement tests are used, comparison of scores with a normative group may be helpful for developing educational objectives and for initially structuring instruction.

Some schools use norm-referenced tests (standardized achievement tests) as a basis for keeping ongoing year-by-year records of the performance of all students. These are often given late in the school year, and scores are recorded in the cumulative records. A comparison of scores for each year indicates whether or not a child is progressing at a reasonable rate in comparison with the normative group.

Many school systems continue to do standardized, systemwide achievement testing once per year. Data from these tests are used for overall evaluation. This allows for qualitative comparisons of students in a single school from year to year, or from one school or district to another and provides a kind of quality control benchmark.

Both norm-referenced and criterion-referenced assessment are found in IGE. However, in the assessment of performance using instructional objectives as a base, the majority of assessment in the daily operation of IGE schools and I & R Units is criterion-referenced.

Norm-referenced and criterion-referenced assessment have been discussed briefly. It should be recalled that a measure is norm-referenced or criterion-referenced depending on the method of interpreting the results of the assessment—by comparison to a group or to a criterion, respectively. Theoretically, any test or measure could be used in either way. Practically, the distinctions discussed above apply when the two types of assessment are used in the instructional setting.

IDENTIFYING APPROPRIATE ASSESSMENT INSTRUMENTS

The purpose for using any assessment instrument is important in identifying or developing the instrument. In instructional programming for individual students, information obtained from both pretesting and posttesting is used for structuring the students' instructional programs. As indicated earlier, pretesting is used primarily to determine the student's readiness for the instruction or to place the student at the appropriate point in the instructional sequence. The primary purpose of posttesting is to determine student progress. The information is used to make decisions about progress and also about possible adjustments in the instructional programs.

In order to accommodate great variation in both students and curricular materials, several different types of assessment instruments are utilized. Four widely used types—paper-and-pencil, performance, work samples, and observations—are discussed here. They are also presented schematically in Figure 13.2. In interpreting this figure, it should be noted that a formal testing situation is established when a student is asked to: (1) complete a paper-and-pencil assessment, or (2) perform an activity which a teacher will evaluate. Assessment can also occur informally in the normal school environment through: (1) collecting and evaluating work samples, or (2) teacher observation of student behavior.

	Written work	Overt behavior
Formal testing situation	Pencil-and-paper assessment	Performance tests
Normal school environment	Work samples	Observations

Fig. 13.2 Types of assessment instruments according to situation and behavior.

Paper-and-pencil Assessments

The purpose of this chapter is not to present a discussion of principles and procedures of construction of written tests. The topic is too extensive to be condensed into part of a chapter, and textbooks exist which very adequately cover the topic. However, some comments on objective and essay tests are in order.

Objective tests. Objective tests are those for which a single answer key can be used, so that scorers cannot disagree as to whether responses are to be scored right or wrong (Stanley and Hopkins 1972, p. 453). Those which are commonly used in elementary schools are multiple-choice, true-false, short answer, and matching.

The *multiple-choice item* consists of a statement or question, called the stem, and two or more options. The student is to select the option that correctly completes the statement or answers the question. Multiple-choice is the most popular of the objective-type items and it can be used effectively in assessing a wide variety of student outcomes.

An example of a multiple-choice item is as follows:

1. Colt is to horse as kitten is to:

   a. dog
   b. cat
   c. pony
   d. rabbit

This particular item is of the analogy type (Mehrens and Lehmann 1973).

Probably the most difficult part of constructing multiple-choice items is to develop good distractors or foils, the incorrect options of the item. Good distractors should be such that the student might select them as the result of a specific, plausible error; all distractors should be reasonable to the student. Items should be carefully reviewed by the unit staff in order to eliminate any ambiguities, grammatical inconsistencies, and poor distractors.

The *true-false item* is very straightforward and simple. The student is presented with a statement and is directed to indicate whether it is true or false. An example item is:

T F The individual credited with the invention of the phonograph was Alexander Graham Bell.

True-false items should be used sparingly because they have some definite weaknesses. They invite the use of guessing. Also, it is difficult to construct items that measure higher-level learning outcomes such as analysis and synthesis. They are best used for measuring lower-level learning outcomes, but even for that purpose would not be used extensively in IGE.

When using the *short-answer type of item* the student supplies a response rather than selecting a response from two or more given options. The item consists of a statement to be completed, or a question that can be answered. The answer is usually brief, sometimes a single word. An example of a short-answer item is:

The name of the individual credited with the invention of the phonograph was ______________________.

a.

b.

c.

d.

a. Paper-and-pencil assessments, *b.* work samples, *c.* performance tests, and *d.* observation.

Note that this item is basically the same item as the true-false item put into the short-answer format. However, in the true-false format the student could respond correctly without knowing who invented the phonograph by simply knowing that Alexander Graham Bell did not. In the short-answer item the student is required to know the inventor in order to respond correctly.

The *matching item* usually appears in a two-column format, one column called the premises and the other the responses. The student is directed to match responses to the premises by a number or letter designation. An example of a matching item which relates to elementary science instruction follows:

> What thoughts do these words bring to your mind?
>
> List A contains words that you used in the chapter.
>
> List B contains phrases that might be thoughts.
>
> Choose the phrase in List B that best matches a word or words in List A.

LIST A (premises)	*LIST B* (responses)
____1. fuel	a. fuel and oxygen giving off energy
____2. heat energy	b. light measured by needle movement
____3. radiant energy	c. energy traveling through space
____4. solar energy	d. matter for burning
____5. electrical energy	e. electricity produced from light
____6. fire	f. one kind of matter disappears in another kind
____7. chemical reaction	g. energy from the sun
____8. light meter	h. one kind of matter changes into another kind
	i. most common source of energy in homes
	j. results when radiant energy is absorbed

Matching items should be constructed using homogeneous content. We would not, for example, include political personalities and science concepts in the same item. The optimum length for matching items is from 5 to 8 premises per item, but occasionally longer items are used. Having more responses than premises avoids having the student identify a correct match through the process of elimination.

Matching items have the advantage over multiple-choice items of not requiring plausible distractors, although the response for any premise should also serve as a plausible response for the other premises. Keeping the content of the item homogeneous aids in meeting this condition.

Essay tests. There are two major characteristics that distinguish essay tests from objective tests such as those described in the preceding sections. These are (1) the length of the response, and (2) the type of anticipated response. The response to an essay item consists of up to several paragraphs of narrative produced by the student. The student is required to structure the response according to the way the question is asked.

One of the reasons for using essay tests is that essay items, properly constructed, can measure learning outcomes of objectives in the higher levels of the taxonomy of instructional objectives. Higher levels refer to analysis, synthesis, and evaluation outcomes, in contrast to the lower levels of knowledge, comprehension, and application.

Essay tests have been criticized because of some distinct disadvantages. One is scoring which tends to be unreliable and costly in scorer time. Another limitation of essay tests is that they frequently have poor content validity.

Although the limitations of essay tests are very real, there are procedures that can be used to improve the items. These procedures are directed primarily at enhancing the objectivity of scoring and improving the reliability of the test in which the items appear.

Essay items used at the elementary school level should require restricted, rather than extended, responses. As an essay item is developed, the teacher should attempt to define the students' task as much as possible and still require them to select, organize, and express the ideas. Restricting the item to some extent provides direction, but the unit staff must be careful to require the kind of student behavior that was intended.

The preparation of good essay items depends most on providing an adequate framework for the student so that the desired student behaviors are required in the response. Teachers have a tendency not to provide enough directions and structure for the response, rather than to overstructure the item. Items should be carefully checked for vague or unfamiliar wording. Definite description of what the student is expected to do should be included in the item. The text *Evaluation of instruction in individually guided education* (Wiersma and Jurs 1976) provides more detailed information on the construction and use of essay tests.

Rating scales. Paper-and-pencil instruments such as rating scales can be used to obtain information about a student's motivation, learning style, and attitude. Rating scales provide for the student the opportunity to indicate personal feelings on some continuum. The continuum is usually a scale with anywhere from three to seven positions, although sometimes the two options of "agree or disagree," and "like or dislike" are adequate. Rating scales developed by the unit staff tend to be quite short, perhaps 10 to 15 items. Let us consider some example items that might go into such a scale for elementary students.

Suppose the unit staff is interested in the learning arrangement preferences of the students. A five-point scale from like to dislike could be used. The students would be given appropriate directions and definitions regarding the points on the scale. Examples of items are as follows:

Working by yourself on arithmetic problems	Like	☐ ☐ ☐ ☐ ☐	Dislike
Working with 5–10 other students and one teacher	Like	☐ ☐ ☐ ☐ ☐	Dislike
Preparing reports with one or two other students	Like	☐ ☐ ☐ ☐ ☐	Dislike

The information provided by these example items does not order the learning arrangements or activities, but it does provide the information on likes and dislikes directly.

Performance Tests

As contrasted with paper-and-pencil tests, a performance test is one which requires motor or manual response on the examinee's part, generally involving manipulation of concrete equipment or materials (Stanley and Hopkins 1972, p. 454).

The performance of the child is interpreted as indicative of some level of achievement in areas such as concept attainment, thinking skills, and psychomotor skills. Because performance tests usually require the manipulation of materials, they may test both cognitive and psychomotor learning (Haney and Sorenson 1976).

Performance tests are quite common in some curricular areas such as physical education, music, and language usage (oral). A student knows the objective which is to be mastered. After the necessary instruction and practice, the teacher asks the student to carry out an activity which will demonstrate that the objective has been mastered. Appropriate performance tests might be to (1) catch the ball when it is thrown from three different distances, (2) play a selection on the recorder, (3) give oral directions for the path to follow from the school to the ice cream store.

In mathematics instruction, students often use concrete materials to demonstrate a concept. At an early level of instruction, an objective might be "to group (classify) objects correctly by shape." In a performance test, the student would arrange a collection of circles, squares, and triangles into correct groups. At a higher level in mathematics, a student might be asked to rearrange sets of popsicle sticks to demonstrate an understanding of the concept of place value.

Work Samples

In addition to formal testing situations, assessment can take place in the normal classroom environment. Consider the assessment of skills such as writing, drawing, or organizing a report about a science experiment. Since these types of skills can be evidenced in written products, the unit staff can collect work samples from the students. A work sample is a subset of the products resulting from a student's learning activities. It is not likely that a unit staff would assess every bit of written material for handwriting skills, but if a certain level of proficiency in handwriting is an outcome specified by one or more instructional objectives, work samples can be collected to assess this outcome.

Learning activities which result in a three-dimensional product are also assessed by an objective evaluation of the product. For example, a comprehension activity in reading may suggest that the reader make a diorama showing a certain scene in a story. Evaluation is based on the teacher's judgment as to whether or not the student succeeded in creating a diorama which conveyed the idea of the scene as it was presented in the story.

Activities such as creative writing are also assessed through an evaluation of work samples. When an evaluation is to be made, several samples collected over a period of time are available for each student. These are then used to determine the quality of the student's work as well as the student's unique style and approach to creative writing.

Work samples can be in many forms. For example, the student might produce them by creating a biological model, preparing and narrating a cassette recording, or carving an art object from soap. Whenever an instructional activity leads to the creation of a visible product, the product may be used as a sample for evaluating a child's work.

Work samples can relate to numerous outcomes. They are especially effective for the evaluation of expressive or open objectives. The evaluation of work samples should be objectively established by the unit staff on a checklist or similar device.

Observations

Student characteristics in the affective and psychomotor areas are best assessed through observations. In fact, for many outcomes, observation is the only appropriate means of assessment. Affective behavior such as cooperation, effectiveness in a team situation, and acceptance of others must be observed to be evaluated. Other affective outcomes of concern to the unit staff would include social behavior, attitudes, interests, motivations, and appreciations. Assessment of a student's use of time, persistence, and initiative is also conducted through teacher observation. Development and use of psychomotor skills can be evaluated through observation. After the teacher has recognized that a child has a particular skill, observation may be used in an effort to determine if the child is using or applying the skill appropriately. For instance, in a formal testing situation a girl may have demonstrated that she can serve a volleyball correctly; later, observations are made to evaluate whether or not this girl uses that skill in an actual volleyball game.

All of the types of outcomes above can be assessed through the use of teacher observation and be recorded on rating scales, checklists, or anecdotal records.

In using observations for these purposes, it is desirable to keep the observations as unobtrusive as possible. To assure an atmosphere of normality, children need not be informed when they are being observed for assessment of work habits, application of skills, social attitudes, and affective behavior.

Since teacher observations will to some extent be subjective, it is best to limit observation to those outcomes which cannot be assessed by other more objective means. Any observation should be directed to a limited number of outcomes to avoid confusion in interpretation. Limiting the number of students involved at any one time is also necessary. It is not reasonable to attempt observation of all students in a 150-student I & R Unit simultaneously for social skills or attitudes.

Anecdotal records. Anecdotal records can be prepared in a very informal way, but if a unit staff decides to systematically use anecdotal information in evaluation, it is best to construct a record form. Such a form need not be elaborate. An example of a simple one appears in Figure 13.3.

It is not likely that the teacher would have planned to observe John Smith at the outset of the small group science experiment. But the incident developed and it seemed worth noting. The record of the incident would have been completed when the teacher (J.M.) had an opportunity to fill in the form after the instructional session had concluded. The teacher would not have obtained a blank form and commenced recording while the incident was in progress.

An anecdotal record should be made as soon after an incident occurs as is possible. The description of the incident should be brief, but contain all the relevant information. The headings at the top of the form provide the usual factual information. The interpretation of the incident could be done by the observer, or it could be done by the unit staff at their meeting. In any event the interpretation would certainly be discussed by the unit staff.

A limitation of anecdotal records is the time required for obtaining

Student	John Smith	Unit	Intermediate
Observer	J. M.	Date	11/25/75
Group Size	Small – 9 students	Subject	Science

Description of Incident

As the science experiment got underway, John was very helpful in assembling the equipment and making necessary preparation. He seemed to know very well how to approach the experiment, and perform the necessary steps in sequence. When the group asked for explanations of various steps, John was willing to explain what he was doing and did a good job of explaining the mechanics of the experiment. When asked to read the description of the experiment from the text, John became hesitant, and read it with some difficulty. Following the reading he sat down and failed to participate in the conclusion of the experiment.

Interpretation of Incident

John tends to be mechanically oriented and likes to manipulate things with his hands. When he can manipulate things, he is "confident" in what he is doing, and confident in explaining his actions. He has difficulty reading, and becomes shy and insecure when asked to perform. He is very sensitive about his reading difficulty, to the extent that it defeated the confidence shown early in the experiment.

Fig. 13.3 Anecdotal record form.

and discussing the information. This can be counteracted somewhat by limiting the length and complexity of the record of the incident. A unit should use anecdotal records sparingly and only when appropriate.

The unit leader is responsible for directing the development of a total assessment program which includes instruments appropriate to a variety of situations. The actual logistics of information-gathering techniques would be finalized in a unit planning meeting. Based on the results of the data which are collected, the unit staff discusses the courses of action to be taken with each student. In some cases a conference between a student and teacher may be warranted. Possibly some students could benefit from a change in learning mode. All this information is used for making decisions in the evaluation process.

ORGANIZING ASSESSMENT RESULTS

Since IGE is an individualized program, assessment information (academic performance, attitudes, motivation, etc.) must be organized so the results for individual students are easily available to the I & R staff. Several ways in which IGE staffs organize data are discussed in subsequent sections.

Charts and Grids

Large wall charts are useful for keeping track of student progress on units of instruction and major objectives for all the students in a unit. These include the names of the children, usually arranged in alphabetical order, listed vertically on the side of the chart, and symbols or terms which indicate the objectives across the top. This chart would be kept on the wall near the unit planning area for easy reference when instructional decisions are being made.

An example of part of a language arts chart for a unit of children ages 8, 9, and 10 is shown in Figure 13.4. This example covers a three-year period (1974–1976). The headings at the top refer to units of instruction or major objectives in language arts skills. The topics and objectives are divided into three levels according to whether they are (1) required of all children, (2) desirable for most children, or (3) available as a choice for children who wish to pursue them. These divisions are explained in detail in Chapter 12 as Levels A, B, and C.

A review of this chart provides the following information about C.

	Required						Desirable				Choice			
	Cursive writing	Capitalization	Punctuation	Friendly letters	Creative writing workshop		Business letters	Creative dramatics	Literature unit		Oral presentations	Puppet show	Video – TV show	
Anderson, C.	5/75	4/76		10/74	10/75		12/75		10/75 Poetry				1/76	
Bolger, B.				12/75	10/75				10/75 Science			11/75		
Brown, A.	9/75	4/76		5/75				1/76	10/75 Biography		10/74			
Cantrell, M.		4/76			10/75				10/75 Animal			11/75	1/76	
Conrad, K.	5/75	1/76	4/76	10/74					10/75 Fiction		10/74			
Daiker, S.					10/75			1/76	10/75 Fiction			11/75		
Dulgarian, R.	10/74	1/76		10/74	10/75		11/74		10/75 Science		10/74			
Eshbaugh, W.	9/75	1/76		12/75	10/75			1/76	10/75 Fiction			11/75		

Fig. 13.4 Wall chart for record keeping.

Anderson. He achieved mastery in cursive writing in May, 1975, mastery in capitalization in April, 1976, and mastery in writing friendly letters in October, 1974; he completed a creative writing workshop in October, 1975; he mastered writing business letters in December, 1975, and participated in the poetry section of the literature unit in October, 1975; he completed a video TV show in January, 1976. He has not achieved mastery in punctuation nor participated in creative dramatics or puppet shows and has not completed an oral presentation. The chart indicates that B. Bolger has achieved mastery in writing friendly letters and in the creative writing workshop; completed the science section of the literature unit; and participated in a puppet show. He has not achieved mastery in cursive writing, capitalization, punctuation, and writing business letters; he has not participated in creative dramatics, oral presentations, or puppet shows.

The unit team may refer to this chart to see what should be included in the instructional programs for certain individuals. Or the team may review the areas of instruction to help decide which area should be included in their planning in the near future. Such information is also helpful if the team chooses to repeat the unit of instruction and wishes to encourage students to explore a different area. A wall chart such as this one serves a general purpose as a guide in planning. It does not provide specific information about mastery of instructional objectives.

A grid such as the one shown in Figure 13.5 would be used for keeping records of individual mastery of instructional objectives. It uses the same format as the wall chart, but is prepared on standard-size paper suitable for filing. Listed across the top are math skills or concepts that refer to instructional objectives. The grid has spaces to record scores on pre- and posttests for many math skills. The percentage score for the first pretest is recorded under column 1 if mastery is not achieved; if mastery is achieved, the percentage score is recorded in the column labeled M. Column 2 is provided for recording of the posttest if mastery is not achieved on a second trial. If mastery is achieved, the posttest score is recorded under M.

From the data provided in such a detailed grid, the unit team can make instructional decisions for each child. For example, the grid indicates D. Aaron has attained mastery in three skills and has not reached mastery in two others—subtracting three-, four-, and five-digit numbers and adding and subtracting numbers through ten thousands.

The unit staff may choose to look at specific skills and group the children who need instruction in that skill. A quick glance at the grid suggests that L. Abdol, S. Abel, A. Abrahamson, and others need instruction in adding three-, four-, and five-digit numbers. The pretest scores also help the team anticipate how much instruction each child needs in a specific skill. For example, students with scores of 50–70 percent, using 80 per-

Math skills/concepts

Data Grid / Student names/ Numbers		Add three-, four-, and five-digit numbers			Subtract three-, four-, and five-digit numbers			Use addition and subtraction to solve word problems			Add and subtract numbers through ten thousands			Add with three and four addends											
		1	2	M	1	2	M	1	2	M	1	2	M	1	2	M	1	2	M	1	2	M	1	2	M
Aaron, Dennis	1			80	60					90	70					100									
Abdol, Linda	2	70			70			60					80	50											
Abel, Sam	3	60					80			80	50			60											
Abrahamson, Ann	4	50					100			80			90	50											
Acker, John	5	40			70					90	50			60											
Adams, John	6	60			40			60			70					80									
Adams, Sue	7			90	30					80			90			80									
Adler, Kay	8			100	50					100	70			60											
Ash, Don	9	60			40			60			70			60											
Baxter, Jim	10	50					80			80			80			80									
Beebe, Tom	11	40					90			80	70			50											
Bingham, Mary	12	30					80			80	60					90									
Bloom, Ed	13	70			70					80			80			90									
Brant, Ed	14			90			80	70					90			80									
Cameron, Jim	15	70			60			70					90	60											
Carlson, John	16	60					80	50					80			90									

Fig. 13.5 Data grid for recording mastery of instructional objectives.

cent as mastery, would need only a short period of instruction compared to those who scored between 0 and 49 percent.

Checklists

Checklists are one of the most useful instruments for recording student performance information. The checklist shown in Figure 13.6 is used to record an individual's performance in handling the two-pan balance scale in science activities. The unit team must first decide what is to be considered as good, fair, or poor performance. A team member then observes the child at work with the two-pan balance scale. The checklist may be dated, and checkmarks placed in the appropriate column for each behavior. Or, the same sheet can be used for periodic evaluations by noting the date of the observation in the column indicating the child's performance. (Haney and Sorenson 1976)

Information about learning styles can also be recorded on a checklist. An instrument for such observations is shown in Figure 14.2. If time allows, measures can be taken independently by unit staff members and shared at a unit staff meeting. This provides a check on the consistency of the teachers' perceptions.

	Rating scale		
Item	Good—3	Fair—2	Poor—1
1. Removal of scale from storage area			
2. Placement of scale on table/counter			
3. Placement of object to be weighed on scale pan			
4. Placement of counterweights on scale pan			
5. Adjustment of "fine" weight on scale			
6. Adding or taking away counterweights to balance weight of object			
7. Removal of metal object from scale			
8. Removal of counterweights on scale			
9. Return of counterweights to proper box			
10. Replacement of scale to storage area			

Fig. 13.6 Performance checklist for handling two-pan balance scale.

Checklists are also useful for recording affective behavior. The unit team should first decide what behaviors are to be evaluated. These might include items such as "works well with classmates"; "completes activities in a reasonable amount of time"; "uses time well when choosing own activities"; "displays acceptable behavior in situations outside the unit area." The team must then decide on an observation schedule, including answers to the following questions: Who should be observed? Who will do the observing and recording? When will children be observed? What are the standards expected for the chosen ratings?

Keysort Cards

An efficient way of keeping records of individual achievements of objectives is through the use of keysort cards. Some commercial materials, such as the *Wisconsin Design for Reading Skill Development* (1971), provide cards which are keyed to the objectives of the program. If a unit team prefers to use their own list of instructional objectives, they may purchase *blank* keysort cards such as the one shown in Figure 13.7. In addition to keeping records of objectives which have or have not been achieved, this particular card provides space for recording evaluative comments about a child's academic development.

The major advantage of using keysort cards is that they provide an easy means of identifying groups of children who need instruction in a given skill. As children achieve mastery in a skill, the card is punched out at the edge beside the area and number of the skill. For grouping, the cards are placed in a stack and a skewer is run through the hole beside a given objective. Those cards which are punched out will drop off; those which are not remain on the skewer. The cards on the skewer show immediately which children need instruction in a particular skill. In a short time, the unit team can identify those children who will compose the different instructional groups for work on certain skills.

Computers

In an effort to make large amounts of information available in a more efficient, manageable form, many schools are turning to the use of computers. There are five functions of a computer system which are of benefit to school record keeping: input, storage, control, arithmetic, and output (Klausmeier and Ripple 1971, p. 176).

The Mounds View Public Schools in St. Paul, Minnesota have established a record-keeping and monitoring system through the use of a centrally located district computer (Gunderman 1973, p. 4). Their system is designed so that the computer can handle the following tasks: (1) score and record all pre- and posttests in the skills area; (2) reproduce desired skill groupings; (3) produce concise and explicit status reports for in-

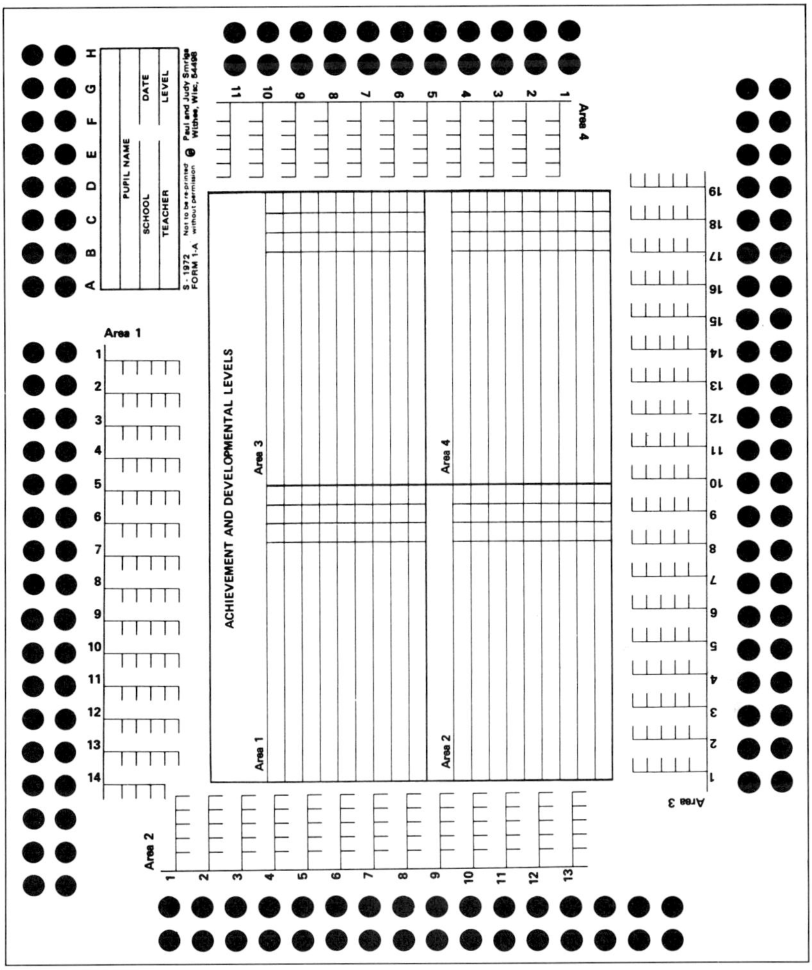

Fig. 13.7 Keysort card for an individual student. (Courtesy of P. and J. Smriga.)

dividual students; (4) provide scope and sequence of skills yet to be achieved; and (5) provide a research base for studying the overall program.

In addition to skills information about individual children, the computer can also store information such as curriculum profile, pupil profile of demographic data, materials file, teacher style, and staff development program.

Organizing assessment results is an important task when implementing IGE. It is essential that a unit team have sufficient information with which to make instructional decisions. This information is useful only if it is accessible to the team in a manageable form and at the time it is needed.

The unit team, including the unit leader, staff teachers and aides, is responsible for assembling the necessary information. The exact format for the information must be developed cooperatively in unit planning meetings. It is the unit leader's responsibility to prevent the procedures from breaking down. If information is incomplete, student records are omitted, or information is late, it is the unit leader's responsibility to locate the difficulty and make appropriate corrections. In preparing the agenda for a unit planning meeting, the unit leader should check on the assessment information required and make certain that it will be available.

INTERPRETATION AND UTILIZATION OF ASSESSMENT RESULTS

The procedures of interpreting and utilizing assessment results are combined because the interpretation of results is directed to the instruction which, of course, involves the utilization of results. There is little point in interpreting results if no use is going to be made of the interpretation. Interpretation of results is part of the assessment and evaluation process in the I & R Unit. Not only is meaning assigned to the results but value is also placed on the various courses of action that might be followed. For example, if the results indicate performance at criterion level, we interpret the results as indicating mastery of skills or content. The most "valuable" course of action for the student is then to proceed to the next objectives in the instructional sequence. Suppose a student has not performed up to the level of the criteria. The results are interpreted to indicate that mastery has not been attained and that a defined recycling is the appropriate activity.

Interpreting a Variety of Information

Suppose that a unit staff has the following information about the performance and characteristics of a student. The information has been obtained through the use of a variety of assessment instruments: diagnostic tests, pretests, posttests, observation schedules, anecdotal records, and a brief attitudes indicator. Performance in mathematics is under consideration, specifically the attainment of ten instructional objectives, which represent a unit of instruction. The facts are these:

1. The results of the diagnostic test indicated that the student was prepared to begin working on the attainment of the ten mathematics objectives.
2. The pretest performance indicated no attainment of any of the criteria of the ten objectives.
3. The posttest performance indicated the attainment of the criteria for five of the ten objectives.
4. Two anecdotal records were consistent in indicating that the student had been very reluctant to participate in small group activities when receiving mathematics instruction.
5. An observation schedule showed that the student was rather withdrawn when large group instruction in mathematics was being conducted. Subsequently, the student was less than enthusiastic about learning activities such as problem solving in mathematics.
6. The attitude indicator showed that though the student was not hostile toward participating in the mathematics instruction, the student preferred to read and work in language arts activities.
7. The anecdotal records gave no indication that the student was being rejected by the group. Popularity with peers was satisfactory.

It should be noted that the seven points above are facts. They have not been interpreted and they really have no meaning until they are interpreted. The unit staff, under the leadership of the unit leader must interpret and utilize the information. (In a real situation there might be more facts, and the information would be available in detail since the summary forms and some of the assessment instruments would exist and be in the possession of the unit staff.)

What can be made of these facts? Since the criteria of the objectives have not been met, will the unit staff simply repeat instruction in an attempts to have the student attain the objectives? Hardly. More perceptive interpretation of the facts can be made. But it is important that the unit staff have an opportunity to discuss this student's performance. Not only will all unit staff members aid in interpretation but they may also have relevant input which was not contained in the assessment results.

The interpretation of the pretest performance (Fact 2) was that the student did not possess the skills or knowledge to omit any of the ten objectives. However, the diagnostic test results (Fact 1) did show that the student was ready to begin work on the objectives. Therefore, the course of action was that the student worked on all ten objectives. The results of the posttest (Fact 3) are interpreted to mean that the student has not adequately mastered the skills and knowledge required. Clearly, some type of additional instruction is necessary, but it is not necessarily true that simply repeating instruction in an attempt to meet the five unattained objectives is the most appropriate course of action. Other assessment information is available.

The anecdotal records (Fact 4) consistently indicated that the student did not participate well in the small group learning mode for the mathematics instruction. Therefore, it does not seem advisable to persist with this mode. It would be a good idea to have a student-teacher conference, not only to obtain additional information about the student's motivation in mathematics but also to discuss some of the student's own perceptions about why the objectives were not met. It may be that some one-to-one instruction is the best course of action, or possibly independent study could make up part of the instruction. Information from Facts 5, 6, and 7 along with information already used, is helpful in developing the instructional activities.

There is no indication that this student's difficulty in mathematics is caused by a reading deficiency. However, this possibility could and should be checked. The teacher who is most familiar with the student's reading performance could comment on whether there has been any difficulty in comprehension. There would likely be reading test scores available which could also be checked.

If the mathematics exercises used were, for the most part, drill exercises, it would be wise to switch to mathematics problems in verbal or story form. These would perhaps be more appealing to the student, especially since the student shows a preference for reading activities. It may be possible to incorporate mathematics problems into the student's reading materials.

If the outcomes of the five instructional objectives that were not met are not prerequisite for the next mathematics objectives in the instructional sequence, the student could be given some alternative mathematics objectives. This tends to keep motivation higher and keep the student from becoming discouraged. The student-teacher conference would provide information as to the desirable course of action.

There are any number of combinations of evaluation results and student characteristics that can arise. Evaluation results come from numerous sources, certainly not limited to those of pretesting and posttesting. The important thing is that information is acquired, interpreted, and used in decision making. There is always a risk that results may be misinterpreted and that the course of action decided upon may not produce the desired results. Learning modes may have to be changed to include other types of activities. It could be that a student's motivation is so low that persisting with unattained objectives is futile. Judgments and decisions need to be made, and they must be made with adequate information by a knowledgeable unit staff.

SUMMARY

This chapter has discussed the ideas and procedures of assessment, primarily as they apply to the third step of the Instructional Programming Model. Assessment in IGE is both criterion-referenced and norm-referenced although the majority is criterion-referenced. Assessment is objective-based; the criteria of the instructional objectives provide the base from which assessment and evaluation proceed.

The evaluation process within a unit begins with the identification of a decision point and continues through the process of information acquisition, interpretation, and utilization back to the decision point. This process involves the entire I & R Unit staff and it is a continuous process. At any time, the evaluation with respect to several decision points is simultaneously in progress. Data for evaluation is obtained through paper-and-pencil tests, performance tests, work samples, and observations. Charts, grids, checklists, keysort cards, and computers are used to record evaluation data and to make them readily available for use by the I & R Unit team.

The unit leader's participation in the assessment and evaluation within the unit is very much like that of any staff teacher. The added responsibility of the unit leader is that of providing leadership by ensuring that the process does not break down. Assessment is a broad and ongoing activity, but it is made up of specifics. Specific students must be tested with specific tests. Specific teachers must collect specific work samples, and so it goes. Results must be summarized and interpreted. From the interpretations, decisions must be made. The unit leader is not only a participant in the assessment activity and evaluation process but the overseer as well.

REFERENCES

Gates-MacGinitie reading tests 1965. Columbia University, New York: Teachers College Press.

Gunderman, A. 1973. Reeder school makes the computer work for individuality. *Minnesota Elementary School Principal* **15,** (3):4-6.

Haney, R., and J. Sorenson 1976. *Individually guided science.* Reading, Mass.: Addison-Wesley.

Iowa test of basic skills 1964. Boston: Houghton Mifflin.

Klausmeier, H. J., and W. Goodwin 1975. *Learning and human abilities.* (4th ed.) New York: Harper & Row.

———, M. R. Quilling, J. S. Sorenson, R. S. Way, and G. R. Glasrud 1971. *Individually guided education and the multiunit elementary school: guidelines for implementation.* Madison, Wisc.: Wisconsin Research and Development Center for Cognitive Learning.

———, and R. E. Ripple 1971. *Learning and human abilities.* (3rd ed.) New York: Harper & Row.

Mehrens, W. A., and I. J. Lehmann 1973. *Measurement and evaluation in education and psychology.* New York: Holt.

Metric measurement. University of Pittsburgh, Pa.: Imperial International Learning Corp., 1973.

Popham, W. J. 1971. *Criterion-referenced measurement: an introduction.* Englewood Cliffs, N.J.: Educational Technology Publications.

Stanford achievement tests 1964–65. New York: Harcourt.

Stanley, J. C., and K. D. Hopkins 1972. *Educational and psychological measurement and evaluation.* (5th ed.) Englewood Cliffs, N.J.: Prentice-Hall.

Stufflebeam, D. L. 1968. Toward a science of educational evaluation, *Educational Technology* **8,** (14):5-12.

Wiersma, W., and S. Jurs 1976. *Evaluation of instruction in individually guided education.* Reading, Mass.: Addison-Wesley.

Wisconsin design for reading skill development 1971. Madison, Wisc.: Wisconsin Research and Development Center for Cognitive Learning.

14

Providing for Needs of Individual Students

Lloyd H. Joyal
Juanita S. Sorenson

Objectives

After reading this chapter, the reader will be able:

- To describe grouping techniques, patterns, and criteria appropriate to IGE.
- To recognize elements of learning style relevant to elementary students and describe how they can be assessed.
- To identify media appropriate to the grouping process.
- To describe how the objectives above can be utilized in an IGE program.
- To apply, in a simulated group situation, grouping techniques, criteria, learning style, and media appropriate to a selected age/grade level and curriculum area.

This chapter deals with providing for the needs of individual students as indicated in Step 4 of the instructional programming model (Klausmeier, *et al.* 1971, p. 19). In IGE, these needs are met by utilizing assessment data, cognitive and affective, along with teacher judgment, to identify objectives and the appropriate learning environment for each student. Students with common needs are grouped together for instruction in groups of various sizes according to their characteristics and the content to be learned.

The practice of grouping is not new in American education. A review of grouping practices used since colonial times shows that most educational groups were formed on the basis of economic or geographic needs, rather than strictly educational demands (Ragan and Shepherd 1971, pp. 9-42). In colonial times, grouping was largely done on an individual basis because of the scattered population. Small schools served a mixed population of students, and children usually recited their lessons individually to the teacher. As the country grew in population, people moved to cities. By the early 1800s, additional ways of handling the numbers of children were needed. The monitorial system developed in England seemed to provide a cheap and quick solution to the problem of educating these increasing numbers of students. This system was basically a one-room school, but because of the large numbers of pupils, monitors or additional teachers were made available to help with the instruction. After 1830, pupils were gradually sorted into grades and classes according to reading ability.

The movement for graded schools as they exist today received strong support from Horace Mann in the 1840s. The first graded school was organized in Boston. Its organization for instruction was a single teacher per grade or per class. By 1860, most towns or cities of any size had their own system of schools organized on a graded basis. With the advent of the graded school and prescribed courses of study, the textbook, usually chosen by the state or the city, became the primary source of instruction.

Following the Civil War, drastic social, political, and economic changes posed many new problems for American education. Among these were the expanding school population and a shift from rural to urban living. There was also a continued influx of immigrants from Europe. Child labor laws and compulsory school attendance legislation were enacted. Educators began to recognize the individual differences of children and their varied abilities to learn the subjects in the prescribed curriculum.

The method of instruction in graded schools did not differ greatly from that established in the earlier monitorial system. In graded classes, it became easier to establish grade curriculum primarily on graded textbooks. Children had prescribed lessons to learn. Many of these lessons were geared to the bright children. As a result, by the end of the 1800s, a serious problem had developed in that many children in our schools were failing. This caused a number of educators to take a look at other ways of grouping students. Some of the earliest grouping plans were those developed by William T. Harris in St. Louis in 1869. In his plan, promotion was established on a quarterly basis so that the child could move through the curriculum in a continually readjustable process.

Several other pioneering efforts followed Harris's plans (Morganstern 1966, p. 8). One was the Elizabeth plan developed in 1866 in Elizabeth, New Jersey. Its essential feature was the division of each grade into three or four sections. A child could be moved from one section to another, or to the next grade at the completion of the grade requirements. Other plans like the Cambridge plan, Double Tillidge plan, and the Batavia plan had one feature in common. They recognized that children learned at different rates, and pupils were given the opportunity to work in prescribed courses as fast as possible. Those who finished first were sent ahead. Instruction in all curriculum areas was given to the whole class or to a large group. In 1888, in Pueblo, Colorado, Preston W. Search set up a loud voice to protest whole-class, lockstep methods of teaching, and he urged complete individual progress for each pupil.

By 1919, two new plans were introduced. They were the Dalton and Winnetka plans under which children mastered their assignments as fast as they could, regardless of the grade limits. The Dalton plan, providing for individual instruction, was introduced in the public school system in Dalton, Massachusetts. The Winnetka plan, initiated by Superintendent Carleton Washburn at Winnetka, Illinois, provided for a curriculum which was divided into two main parts. One part consisted of the common essentials, the other of group activities and self-expression subjects. Like the Dalton plan, work was on an individual basis in the essentials, reading, writing, and arithmetic. But in other activities, there were no definite goals. The common feature of these two plans was an emphasis on individual instruction. Perhaps the most serious flaw in these laboratory plans was that they attempted to provide for different rates of progress in the academic areas, but did not pay attention to the personal, social, and emotional needs of the pupils.

The appearance of easily administered measures of intelligence and achievement during World War I made it possible for schools to measure children in terms of their ability to master prescribed subject matter. The rapid development of such testing instruments after World War I resulted in wide and somewhat indiscriminate administration of intelligence tests. They were often used as a basis for grouping of students, and helped promote the practice of ability grouping in the public schools in the 1920s. During the 1920s and 1930s many questions and doubts as to the advantages and disadvantages of the grouping were raised as the result of experience and of research studies. Reports of the conclusions of these studies were not in general agreement (Morganstern 1966, p. 11). Of 33 studies, there were 13 which had or approached significance favoring homogeneous groupings, 15 which found no differences in homogeneous or heterogeneous groups or which found homogeneous grouping detrimental, and five studies which gave mixed results, partially favorable and partially unfavorable to homogeneous grouping.

The need for grouping can be summarized as follows (Harris and Bessart 1969, p. 95): "It is not only necessary for practical purposes but desirable for educational reasons that pupils be grouped for instruction for a significant portion of their time in school." Further, grouping can be flexible or inflexible and range from tutorial arrangements to large group instruction. The question of grouping is not one of desirability, but one of determining what system of assigning pupils and teachers to instructional spaces will best facilitate the accomplishment of schoolwide goals and instructional objectives for learners. There is little evidence to support the contention that better teaching or more learning occurs when homogeneous groups are formed so this should not be given undue attention when determining group structure.

It should be recalled that the role of assessment in grouping is very important. It is essential that unit leaders and staff teachers be aware of assessment techniques and utilize available data when considering grouping procedures and learning style. Chapter 13 of this book deals with assessment, both norm-referenced and criterion-referenced, and its use in Individually Guided Education programs, and you are referred to it for an in-depth discussion.

As indicated above, educators have long attempted to use grouping as a means to improve instruction. Grouping is explored in this chapter in term of: (1) techniques; (2) criteria; (3) learning style; (4) media to facilitate grouping practices and learning styles; and (5) application of grouping practices in the I & R Units.

GROUPING TECHNIQUES

Interest in grouping procedures showed a marked increase during the 1950s and 1960s. Dawson (1961, p. 146) issued the following statement:

> In the school of the future, with the kinds of flexibility we have been talking about, school organization may be a term used mainly in discussing the history of education from 1800 to 2000. The emphasis will not be upon organizational structure geared to a specific number of children and teachers, a particular kind of school plant, and a relatively static curriculum. The emphasis will be on the coordination of vast educational resources into programs geared to the individual needs of a child and the common needs of children.

Typical Techniques

Homogeneous grouping and other methods of grouping in accordance with ability tend to be organized within a year group, and the resultant classes therefore consist of a narrowly prescribed age range. It is pointed out that one of the major criticisms leveled against a system of one-year grading is its lack of flexibility (Yates 1966, pp. 26–28). Brighter children who are promoted solely on the basis of ability are often confronted with problems of adjustment; other students who are older but slower in ability may become poorly motivated and sometimes rebellious. Yates suggests that more satisfactory groupings can be achieved if other characteristics are also taken into account. These include mental age or maturity, social and emotional development, or a child's aptitude or readiness for a specific educational activity. Grouping by chronological age has been used for a long time, probably because it is administratively simple and has been accepted by parents and by the pupils themselves.

Grouping has been typically classified into seven forms (Yates 1966, p. 54):

1. *Grading.* This form is based on the pupil's levels of attainment and rates of progress. It is commonly used and usually involves children of a given age placed together in a particular grade.

2. *Special classes.* These could be formed in schools based on the particular needs of a group of children such as the physically handicapped, the emotionally or socially maladjusted, or those whose assessed intelligence is below what is considered the minimal level for educability in an ordinary class.

3. *Tracking within the school.* Tracking is the allocation of pupils to different classes or courses within a school. This might take place at the very beginning of the school year, or perhaps after the students have pursued a common course for a time. This practice is particularly common in secondary schools, with courses labeled "college preparatory," "vocational," or "engineering."

4. *Streaming and setting.* These are devices for securing relatively homogeneous groups for instructional purposes. Streaming is the practice of teaching children of different levels of ability separately, for all or most of the subjects of the curriculum. Setting applies to a few key subjects (e.g., a child may be assigned to one particular group for reading, another in mathematics, and so on) and does not necessarily last for the duration of the course.

5. *Clubs or free activity groups.* These would be informal groups designed to serve a variety of purposes—intellectual, social, cultural, recreational—and are usually directed by teachers or by the pupils them-

selves. They could be set up for a specific age group, or for pupils of all ages. These are usually interest groups, and are not compulsory.

6. *Planned heterogeneous groups.* Pupils are often grouped heterogeneously as a matter of deliberate policy. In the United States this form of grouping owes much to Dewey's influence. Planned heterogeneous groupings can be achieved in a number of ways. One way is to have parallel classes. Within each age group, children may be divided into classes so that each contains pupils from all levels of ability. A second way is to have an ungraded school in which children are permitted to progress as rapidly as their abilities permit. Here grade levels are abandoned, and within each class subgroups are formed to allow for a variety of academic standards. This is sometimes termed a continuous progress plan. A third way is multiple or multi-grade grouping. This procedure involves a grouping of students from two or more standard grade levels. Multi-grade grouping has been defined as that "type of elementary school class in which the pupils are not identified by any standard level and which includes more than one grade usually provided for in the standard system." A fourth way is inter-age or multi-age grouping. Here there is a deliberate attempt to group pupils of different ages for instructional purposes. The spread is over several years and is greater than would normally be found in a graded classroom. Classes of this kind have been introduced in a number of English primary schools.
7. *Teachability grouping.* This term is applied to a plan for grouping not on the basis of objectively defined types of students, but rather on the conditions required for effective teaching and learning. The plan suggests that effective grouping should make use of three principles; compatibility, homogeneity, and complementation. The major variables that should be considered in teachability grouping are:
    1. the student's value attitude system
    2. the student's sophistication and maturity
    3. the sort of teacher with whom the student can identify
    4. the student's susceptibility to threat from other students
    5. the student's generalized tendencies to deal with stress
    6. the student's goal in the special sense of the kind of experience he or she seeks

Considerations to Improve Grouping

The most important curricular function of grouping is "to place a child in the human environment in which he can learn best and learn most" (Manning 1971, p. 134). There are a number of practices which need consideration to improve the grouping process (Manning 1971, pp. 140-144).

The first of these is a flexible admissions policy to allow maturity to be a factor in admission in addition to chronological age. A second way is planned diversity. This can be accomplished by deliberately building certain kinds of differences into the composition of each class or unit of students. The third process is a humanistic factor in grouping procedures. Such a procedure would "balance" the groups so that each child could be a leader or could excel in some group. Team learning, the fourth suggested practice, consists of combining pupils into small groups of two or three for mutual assistance in learning. Research results suggest that team learning groups do achieve more, and the quality of learning is enhanced. Fifth, students benefit from cross-age relationships where older peers or adults provide models for pupils to follow. Sixth, personal needs can form the basis of grouping. This is a concept which recognizes psychological as well as academic needs of children and tries to respond to these needs. Finally, flexible regrouping, a concept necessary in order to keep pace with the changing abilities and growth rate of the pupils is suggested. These previously mentioned grouping adjustments provide no unusual problems in a multiage, nongraded school. The total concept of flexible grouping requires the crossing of grade lines if the ultimate in improved learning opportunities for children is to be accomplished.

During the 1966-1967 academic year, the University Elementary School, University of California at Los Angeles, conducted a case study with a team of three teachers working with 75 pupils from 9 through 12 years of age (Fischer and Fischer 1969, pp. 298-303). In this study, concepts of nongrading or continuous progress, as well as team teaching principles, were utilized. This study was based on the assumption that individualization of instruction requires careful placement of pupils into instruction groups, and careful consideration of what goes on in such groups. Records and observations made during the first few weeks of school showed a great change in the children's learning style, interests, autonomy in learning, achievement, attitudes, and skills.

The results of the study would indicate that it is important that the learning environment includes:

1. small group learning opportunities
2. teachers with varied teaching styles
3. tapping of the child's immediate interest whenever possible
4. short-term goals with highly predictable success
5. immediate feedback whenever possible; frequent self-evaluation and conferences with the teacher
6. a variety of activities within a period, utilizing varied learning materials

In a project to reorganize the Franklin Elementary School in Lexington, Massachusetts, a team organization was selected because it was felt that this would "permit more flexible and appropriate grouping arrangements to meet individual interests" (Anderson, Hagstrom, and Robinson 1960, pp. 71-72). At the conclusion of the first year of operation it was reported that more flexible and appropriate grouping arrangements had been utilized. There was also more discussion regarding criteria for grouping and evaluating students, as well as ways in which the curriculum could be improved to present better learning opportunities for students.

Seven "Guidelines for Action" for grouping are suggested below (Westby-Gibson 1966, pp. 12-20):

1. Educators must design grouping practices that encourage pupils to see themselves as learners. Grouping procedures must foster feelings of self-worth, acceptance, and achievement.
2. Grouping practices must be planned to avoid accentuating racial and social biases. Wherever possible, grouping procedures should facilitate the interaction of children from different social backgrounds.
3. Grouping practices must take into account the variety of learning styles. Grouping procedures must make possible curriculum development embodying the use of teaching strategies which adapt content, methods, and media to the requirements of individual pupils.
4. Grouping practices must provide special opportunities for disadvantaged children and youth. The specific needs children bring to the school should dictate the specific programs.
5. Grouping practices must take into account the nature of the groups they make possible. Grouping procedures should provide opportunities to work together for children who can contribute to one another's learning.
6. Grouping practices should make available teachers of both sexes and of differing personalities to increase the possibilities of placing each child with some teachers especially supportive of him or her.
7. Grouping practices must promote a variety of excellences. They must help students to realize not only the kinds of potential that are demonstrated by mental ability or achievement tests, but also the kinds that are demonstrated in many other ways.

Techniques used for grouping students vary widely, but there appears to be general agreement among authors that grouping for instruction is most effective in a nongraded or continuous progress situation. The next section deals with criteria for forming groups.

CRITERIA FOR GROUPING

Teachers, especially at the elementary level, have grouped children for a long time for special purposes. They have seen grouping as a way to:

1. diagnose and evaluate individually what children learn and how they learn it.
2. teach children, placing particular emphasis on their individual abilities, achievement, and interests.
3. give individual children particular attention and recognition designed to help them see themselves as learners.
4. help children learn effective group participation.
5. enable a small group to explore in depth some aspect of a problem on which a larger group or the entire class is at work.

According to their purposes, teachers may choose to group children by a number of different criteria: abilities, achievement, interest, sociometric choice, and the task at hand.

Abilities

Abilities in the sense of special aptitudes are frequently criteria for grouping. Students with comparable aptitudes for music, for example, may be placed in the same vocal or instrumental group. Students with comparable physical abilities may similarly be grouped into teams for sports activities.

The most commonly used criterion involving ability, however, is probably that of mental ability. Mental ability as measured by scores on standardized tests is rarely used as a sole criterion for grouping. In most classes where teachers consider mental ability test scores as a basis for grouping, achievement scores are also taken into account. Social studies groups, for instance, may be based on mental ability as well as past achievement in social studies.

Ability and achievement test scores in recent years have frequently been the basis for differentiating the academically talented or gifted. Much of what has been done in the name of the talented, however, has been an attempt to identify them so that they could be given more of the existing curriculum. As has been the case with pupils of other levels of ability and achievement, relatively little has been done to create learning situations which would take into account their individual differences.

Achievement

Reading achievement data has been most frequently used as the basis for classroom grouping. It has been used not only to determine reading groups but also for groups in social studies and other subjects. The greatest shortcoming in such grouping is the danger that, given a group relatively homogeneous in reading achievement, teachers will expect the group to be relatively homogeneous in other ways. They may, for instance, expect all of the children with the same reading achievement to be interested in reading the same books. The fact is, of course, that children similar in reading achievement still have a wide range of other differences. Thus, achievement data from the curriculum area in which the groups are to be formed must be utilized, and in IGE a further breakdown within the curriculum area according to the instructional objectives is necessary. For example, a student might have high achievement scores in mathematics in sets and geometry, but medium to low scores in computational areas.

Interest

As a criterion for grouping, interest takes into account an important dimension of learning that grouping by ability and achievement may neglect —namely, motivation. If a child is to be motivated to use his or her ability, he or she must be interested in the task at hand. Many teachers, understanding the role that motivation plays in learning, group for interest. Children interested in learning about Germany, for example, will be more likely to work effectively if grouped together than if forced to choose some other country in which they have little interest.

Sociometric Choice

This is another basis for grouping. Most teachers have learned methods of diagnosing the sociometric structure of their classes. By informal means and by using sociograms or sociographs, they are able to analyze the patterns of social interaction in their classes. They can identify the students who are at the center of clique groups, the students who make mutual choices, and those who are isolated. They are aware of the roles different children play in different classroom groups.

Teachers can use their sociometric knowledge to help place apparently isolated and rejected children in group situations where they are most likely to interact effectively with others. They can assign such children to work and play groups that include at least one or two of the children they would choose and, if possible, one who would choose them.

Task at Hand

This often affords teachers the opportunity to bring together children of varied backgrounds to work together on a common project. Work groups invite a diversity of abilities, achievements, and interests. Children studying Mexico, for example, may be variously skilled in reading, map work, arithmetic, art, and music. The children can pool all these skills to communicate with each other and share with the larger class their findings about Mexican people and their culture. For example, a sixth grade work group was studying the economic flow of goods between Mexico and the United States, using a handbook on Latin America as their source. One academically talented child compiled a variety of figures presented in the handbook and reduced them to comparable bases. Two boys who could not read well enough to analyze the figures were able to assist in making a chart to present them.

In grouping for instruction in IGE, a variety of criteria—including achievement scores, interests, sociometric choice, and the task at hand, along with teacher judgment—are used to help form groups. The process of gathering data as a basis for these criteria was discussed in Chapter 13.

Learning style also presents criteria for grouping, but because of its importance and complexity, it is discussed in a separate section of this chapter which follows. Media appropriate to grouping and learning styles is also discussed in a separate section.

LEARNING STYLE IN GROUPING

As an I & R Unit staff becomes experienced in developing instructional programs for individual students, data from learning style can be added to the other criteria for grouping. This section will deal with definition of learning style, facets of learning style, and instruments of observing and reporting learning style.

What is learning style? It has been defined in individualized instructional programs as "those factors that ease and facilitate learning for an individual student in a given situation" (Bechtol 1973, p. 46). An individualized program recognizes that each student is an individual who learns in a unique way and at a particular pace. Educators who are concerned with learning styles are asking new questions such as, "Which students learned with the new treatment?" "Which students learned with the old treatment?" "Which students are placed in programs where the treatment is not effective?" (Bechtol 1973, p. 47)

Learning style is also defined "as personal ways in which the learner processes information in the course of learning new concepts" (DeCecco 1968, p. 75).

A number of variations in learning styles which unit staffs may wish to consider in describing the ways children show diversity in their handling of learning tasks in the classroom include (Shumsky and Shumsky 1968, pp. 162-168):

1. tempo in learning
2. independence in work
3. attentiveness
4. reactions to new situations

Twelve elements of learning style should be considered (Dunn and Dunn 1972, pp. 29-30). These are presented in summary form in Figure 14.1. Teachers already have much existing information or could easily gather it about individual students and organize it in a useful way.

Learning style diagnosis	*Questions to consider*
1. Time	When is the student most alert? In the early morning, at lunchtime, in the afternoon, in the evening, at night?
2. Schedule	What is the student's attention span? Continuous, irregular, short bursts, concentrated effort, forgetting periods, etc.?
3. Amount of sound	What level of noise can the student tolerate? Absolute quiet, a murmur, distant sound, high levels of conversation?
4. Type of sound	What type of sound produces a positive reaction? Music, conversation, laughter, working groups?
5. Type of work group	How does the student work best? Alone, with one person, with a small task group, in a large team, a combination?
6. Amount of pressure	What kind of pressure (if any) does the student need? Relaxed, slight, moderate, extreme?
7. Type of pressure and motivation	What helps to motivate this student? Self, teacher expectation, deadlines, rewards, recognition of achievement, internalized interest, etc.?
8. Place	Where does the student work best? Home, school, learning centers, library, media corner?
9. Physical environment and conditions	Floor, carpet, reclining, sitting, desk, temperature, table lighting, type of clothing, food?
10. Type of assignments	On which type of assignments does the student thrive? Contracts, totally self-directed projects, teacher-selected tasks, etc.?
11. Perceptual strengths and styles	How does the student learn most easily? Visual materials, sound recording, printed media, tactile experiences, kinesthetic activities, multimedia packages, combinations of these?
12. Type of structure and evaluation	What type of structure suits this student most of the time? Strict, flexible, self-determined, jointly arranged, periodic, self-starting, continuous, occasional, time-line expectations, terminal assessment, etc.?

Fig. 14.1 Elements of learning style. (From R. Dunn and K. Dunn 1972, *Practical approaches to individualizing instruction, contracts, and other learning strategies,* Englewood Cliffs, N.J.: Prentice-Hall.)

The teachers, aides, or student teachers can help analyze and determine each youngster's learning style. Unit staff will need to plan to reassess periodically to confirm the original analysis and to make adjustments for changes in mental growth, attitudes, or interests. In addition, students should be encouraged to analyze their own learning styles. One way to do this is through interviews with the student, followed by analysis by unit members.

Student Preferences in Learning Style

An instrument utilizing information from Figure 14.1 and teacher suggestions is presented in Figure 14.2. Here an older elementary student (i.e., ages 10 or above), or an adult interviewing younger students, is asked to react to the elements of learning style (presented on the left side of the instrument) on a five-point continuum between a bipolar word pair. For example, the respondent is asked to respond to the item of "alertness" in terms of five spaces between morning and afternoon. Thus, if a student is most alert in early to midmorning, spaces 1 or 2, respectively, would be checked; if greatest alertness is at midday, space 3; early afternoon, space 4; and late afternoon, space 5. The respondent (or observer) should react to each item in a similar manner.

Directions: Check the box between the two words or phrases that best describes your reaction to the item on the left.

		1	2	3	4	5	
1. Alertness	morning						afternoon
2. Attention span	continuous						short bursts
3. Noise tolerance							
a) amount	absolute quiet						high level conversations
b) type	random (foreground)						organized (background)
4. Grouping pattern							
a) alone	like						dislike
b) one-to-one (adult)	like						dislike
c) one-to-one (peer)	like						dislike
d) small group	like						dislike
e) medium-sized group	like						dislike
f) large group	like						dislike
5. Learning environment							
a) location							
1. learning center (IMC)	like						dislike
2. instructional area	like						dislike
3. isolated study area	like						dislike
b) structure	low						high
6. Self-directedness (task completion)	low						high

Fig. 14.2 Learning style checklist. Continued next page.

		1	2	3	4	5	
7. Media							
a) print	like						dislike
b) visual	like						dislike
c) audio	like						dislike
d) manipulative	like						dislike
e) kinesthetic involvement	like						dislike
8. Self-evaluation	well developed						undeveloped
9. Mode of operation	inductive (parts to whole)						deductive (whole to parts)

The I & R Unit staff may want to assess the learning style for all students for general information or they may decide to assess and evaluate in depth 10-20 percent of the students who are having the greatest learning problems. Noncertified personnel can gather and then summarize the data for a group of students on an unused copy of the instrument. However, decisions for groups and individuals should be made by certified personnel. This could be handled by one teacher who is not assigned to a skill or instructional group as illustrated in Chapter 10.

Adult Observation of Student Learning Style

Another instrument, Observation of Student's Learning Style (OSLS), presented in Figure 14.3, was used and refined in a study (Joyal 1973). OSLS is designed to be used to observe three students at any given time and should be used by an adult. A total of 45 minutes is necessary for each classroom observation, with 15 minutes being devoted to each student (A, B, and C) on an alternate minute basis. The first minute is spent recording the observation about student A regarding (1) his/her activity, (2) number of students in the room, (3) number of students in A's group, (4) what adult is interacting with A, (5) the materials being used, (6) number of students using the same material, and (7) whether the activity noted is teacher or student directed. A new entry is made for student A each time there is a change of activity or materials during that minute. Minute 2 is recorded on a new form while observing student B; minute 3, student C; and minute 4 is again devoted to student A.

In order to facilitate observation notes, categories of activities and materials are noted at the bottom of OSLS. Numbers 1a through 1h refer to various listening and speaking activities; numbers 2a through 2h refer to reading and writing activities; and numbers 3a through 3f refer to miscellaneous categories such as learning games, nonacademic behavior, and art-related activities. Each of the three general categories allows for

	1	2	3	4	5	6	7	8
Minute number	Activity	Number of students in room	Number of students in same activity	Interaction with Adult—specify which adult	Materials being used	Number of students using same material	Check if activity is assigned by teacher	Comments

1. Listening and speaking activities
   a. Listens to teacher speak
   b. Listens to teacher give directions
   c. Listens to teacher read
   d. Listens to student speak
   e. Listens to student read
   f. Asks question
   g. Answers question or contributes point to discussion
   h. Makes a report
   i. Other—specify

2. Reading and writing activities
   a. Reads silently in textbook
   b. Reads other material silently—specify
   c. Follows oral reading in book
   d. Reads orally
   e. Works in workbook
   f. Works on worksheet
   g. Works with programmed materials
   h. Answers questions based on assignment
   i. Other—specify

3. Miscellaneous
   a. Uses an educational game or kit
   b. Works in another subject—specify
   c. Nonacademic behavior (talking to neighbor, doing nothing, etc.)
   d. Using AV material
   e. Waiting for materials
   f. Drawing or painting
   g. Other—specify

Name ______________________________ School ______________

Date ____________ Teacher ____________________

Fig. 14.3 Observation of student's learning style.

"other" activities with a column provided for comments on the nature of the activity.

The major categories specified on OSLS are listening and speaking activities and reading and writing activities. It was felt that regardless of subject matter involvement of the students being observed, most of the learning skills would fall into one of these categories. Any exceptions to this were noted under the "miscellaneous" section and were explained in the "comments" column. The personal data noted on each observation form was for identification purposes.

This instrument, OSLS, could be used by practicing IGE schools as an evaluation device for their ongoing instructional program. If the present school goals, in terms of instructional strategies, are known, OSLS could help a staff determine current practices in their school. Careful evaluation could tell them if their goals are being met, and subsequent uses of OSLS could present a profile of ongoing trends for continuous program evaluation.

Schools using OSLS should consider including at least 20 percent of their students in the observation schedule and should use the instrument at least once each quarter. It would also be well to consider stratifying the observation schedule to include observations of specific subject matter activities and specific learning modes (e.g., large group, small group, and independent study group). This could provide a profile of what is occurring across specific subject areas and learning modes.

It should be noted that OSLS is intended to be a survey-type instrument only. It can provide elementary staffs with a broad-spectrum look at some of the learning style patterns of elementary students. It could identify broad areas that may need further attention.

MEDIA TO FACILITATE GROUPING PRACTICES AND LEARNING STYLES

A number of instructional media are available to accommodate different grouping practices and learning styles. These media can give new dimensions to programs for individual study, small-group activities, or large-group presentations. Those considered here are (1) projected materials, (2) audio equipment, (3) educational kits, (4) programmed instruction, (5) television and videotape, and (6) instructional games. In the last part of this section, the integration of these media will be discussed.

Projected Materials

A great variety of projected material now exists and can be used for many instructional purposes. These materials include 16mm films (in both reel and cartridge form), 8mm film loops, filmstrips, slides, and transparencies.

Films are an appropriate means of instruction for large groups because the quality of the picture is not lost when it is projected on a large screen. However, their use for small group or individual work should not be overlooked. Children who need further information on a topic or project should be encouraged to use films from the school system film collection, the public library, or other local sources such as universities or commercial sources. Children can be taught proper ways to handle the necessary equipment and can then work individually or in small groups to view films, seeking answers to their questions.

Most schools have at least a small collection of filmstrips which can also be used by students. Slides are available from many community resources as well as through the school and public library collections. Whenever additional information is needed by students, these sources should be considered. Equipment is available which is extremely simple to operate so that students can work without adult supervision. It is usually possible to find a nook or cranny where a sheet of paper can be taped to a wall to serve as a screen, and a small group can project slides or filmstrips without disturbing others who are working nearby.

Not only do projected materials provide needed information for many situations; they also provide an excellent means for students to share their own ideas. Making overhead transparencies requires no technical expertise. Many students find transparencies an effective means to illustrate presentations for reporting to the class, teach younger children, or plan as a small group. Kits are available for making slides and filmstrips; cameras are a common possession and can be used to carry out learning activities. Making a film is an exciting way to culminate a unit of instruction. Such an activity could provide a complete review of what had been learned as the students summarize the unit and decide on important aspects to be filmed. It would also provide opportunities for growth in working together toward a common goal, reaching group decisions, serving as a leader, cooperating as a follower, planning ahead, coordinating activities, and reaching a desired goal.

Either as receivers of information or as producers of materials, children are generally enthusiastic about the possibilities available through projected materials. These media are extremely adaptable to different grouping arrangements as well as to individual differences in learning abilities.

Audio Equipment

One of the most accessible forms of audio equipment today is the cassette tape recorder because it is comparatively inexpensive and easy to use. A listening area can be set up where small groups can work on activities which require listening or recording. Children who prefer listening, rather than reading, as a means of acquiring information, can listen to tapes on the topics being studied. Beginning readers can get extra practice by reading along in books as they listen to recorded stories. Commercially recorded cassettes are available from most publishers of educational materials. Teachers may prefer to tape their own material using older students, parents, and aides as sources of help for recording.

Cassette recorders are also excellent tools for students to use for projects and creative activities. Every area of study lends itself to use of cassette recorders. For instance, in social studies children might record a simulation of a meeting of people they are studying. In science, a student could tape the directions for the use of certain equipment or materials for use by other students. Children who are shy about speaking in front of a group can often express themselves more openly on tape.

Cassette recorders can be useful tools for individuals, paired learners, and small groups. Given an opportunity, students will very often find that the use of a cassette makes learning experiences more meaningful.

There are also times when a large group would be involved in a listening activity. A unit of instruction might begin with all children listening to a taped narration which accompanies a filmstrip. The large group might meet together to listen to music, hear a recorded debate, or listen to a recording of a speaker. For use with large groups, phonographs or reel-to-reel tape recorders should be used because the fidelity of the sound can be maintained when high volume is required.

Educational Kits

Kits come in many shapes, sizes, and arrangements, and are a very effective means of organizing a variety of media on a particular topic or subject. A kit might contain printed matter, films or filmstrips, cassettes, and materials needed for exploration of a topic. Some social studies kits about a specific country contain artifacts such as clothing, tools for eating, and writing materials, as well as printed or recorded information. A mathematics measuring kit might contain tapes, rulers, weights, volume containers, and scales in addition to suggestions for activities.

Many kits are available commercially and can be useful tools for learning. They should be chosen with care to ensure that the materials are appropriate for the purpose they are to serve. If the necessary time and talent are available within the school staff or community, excellent kits can be put together to meet specific needs of a school.

An important feature of kits is that they are designed to serve individual needs of students. They can be used by individuals or by groups; they can be used as a whole, or parts can be used separately as needed; they can be used by teachers in instructional situations or by students who are pursuing self-selected objectives.

Kits came into being to meet a variety of needs and to provide varied ways of learning. They can be adapted to any number of uses as teachers and students choose what is most important for their purposes.

Programmed Instruction

Programmed instruction offers highly individualized instruction which requires a minimum of supervision by teachers. It is, therefore, especially suited to individual study. Programs, whether presented in a programmed book or a teaching machine, present information to students and control their reactions in a predetermined way. The student participates actively in the teaching-learning process by responding to frequent questions. He or she, in turn, receives immediate feedback as to the correctness of responses. The student can move at any pace through the programmed materials.

Some students can probably profit greatly from the use of programmed instruction. But it has been pointed out that a word of caution is in order (Cronbach 1970). Programs may or may not be the most effective and efficient means of providing particular students with instruction. Students, for example, must be motivated to use programs, but well-motivated students may profit more from reading than from responding to a programmed text. Similarly, although programmed instruction may be especially suitable for certain kinds of highly structured material, few programs are appropriate for less structured content.

It is important that educators choose such materials with care to ensure that programs they acquire are appropriate to their goals and to the needs of the students who will use them.

Television and Videotape

Television provides another medium with special potential for effective use in a variety of grouping situations. Programs for educational purposes can be found on commercial television as well as on channels devoted to educational purposes. Closed-circuit broadcasting is available in most school systems and offers materials which are closely related to the school curriculum. Teachers who use these programs are encouraged to become well acquainted with the program descriptions which are available from the broadcasting service. It is then possible to determine what programs are relevant for specific learning situations. Small groups of children may be asked to watch certain programs to learn or to review skills. Other programs may have special interest for large groups. With some care in planning and in the placement of the television set, it is possible to use this medium for groups of any size.

Because television is also a medium for home use, it becomes especially important for teachers to help students learn how to use television with discrimination. The challenge to teachers is to help students become critical, effective users of this mass medium which promises to play a continuing role in education both at home and in school.

Learning experiences of a somewhat different nature are made possible through the use of videotape equipment. Television programs can be recorded to be used at a more appropriate time or to be used in a situation where repeated viewing is needed to achieve an objective. Videotape also allows for creative involvement by students. With a minimum of encouragement, they will become totally engrossed in preparing "television shows," newscasts, learning materials, and drama for taping. Any of these activities can be vehicles for improving skills and attitudes such as preplanning, working cooperatively, and sharing creative ideas.

Instructional Games

Most children enjoy instructional games or activities. Walk into a classroom where games are available to children and the atmosphere is alive. In such a classroom pupils show great interest and curiosity in what is happening in school.

The beneficial qualities of games are well-known. A reasonable amount of research from 1967-71 produced findings supporting the worth of games as a teaching technique (Cratty 1971). Many of the techniques employed with games do not need research data to indicate that they transfer to classroom operations, as they are classroom operations conducted in a different form.

Games are intrinsically motivating because their form is characterized by the dramatic (Gordon 1970). The object of the game may be to win, but the student is usually motivated to further study of the topic.

Games and activities are adaptable to a wide range of subjects and mental abilities. They have been found to be challenging to the bright student and effective in teaching the slow learner. Games can be played alone, with another person, in small groups, in structured and unstructured classroom situations, and under supervision or without supervision.

Games encourage experimentation and nurture an intellectual approach that can be applied to other problems (Gordon 1970). Practicing analytical skills in games should cultivate the habit of analysis in other situations.

Teachers are becoming more and more adept at creating games which serve specific instructional purposes and are competitive with commercial materials in quality and appeal. Students can also develop games appropriate for review, extended practice, or introduction of concepts or skills. Substituting games for other less appealing materials can lead to improved student attitudes and motivation, as well as to increased learning.

Integration of Media

As teachers become more involved in planning instructional programs to meet the needs of their students, they are creating more ways in which to present exactly the right combination of materials in the most desirable ways to achieve specific goals. Many teachers do this through learning stations. Each station has a specified purpose and is set up to include information for the student, necessary materials, and step-by-step directions to guide the learner through the activity and the practice needed to achieve the goal. Another technique for guiding students through learning activities is the learning activity packet. In this situation, a printed packet contains directions for activities as well as information about the topic. In following the directions, a student might view a film, make a tape recording, play instructional games, and develop a learning kit.

Learning stations and packets provide excellent opportunities for encouraging student choice of media. For instance, a learning station might include books, a sound filmstrip, and a game, all of which provide the basic factual information. In working toward the objective, each student could select the media which best suits his or her learning style.

These suggested learning activities may be prepared for students to use singly or in small groups. Or, arrangements can be made that large numbers of students will use them, but at different times. Preparing a number of learning stations or packets, then having students rotate in using them, has been found to be an effective way to have large numbers of children work toward the same objective. At the same time, this procedure provides for differences such as rate of learning, depth of understanding, friendship preferences, and choice of media.

Students can also be involved in integrating media to achieve their own goals as well as to provide learning materials for others. For example, while studying about the environment, students might make slides, build models, prepare overhead transparencies, and tape information or an explanation on a cassette. This collection could be put into the Media Center for use by students and teachers in other units.

Educational media offer a wealth of possibilities for interesting learning experiences which are suitable for any grouping arrangement. Flexibility in grouping can be enhanced through the wise use of media which are selected or prepared to meet the instructional needs of the students.

APPLICATION OF GROUPING PRACTICES IN THE I & R UNITS

This section deals with the application of grouping practices using achievement and learning style data along with teacher judgment as the main criteria. Examples are given for students at the primary level in language arts and at the intermediate level in science.

Creative Writing—Paired Learning for 5- to 7-Year-Olds*

Unit A (children ages 5-7) used an interesting technique to improve the student's ability to (1) tell a story in sequence, (2) write a story using good sentence structure, and (3) improve creative writing skills. The unit leader reported that the members of this unit were concerned with improving the writing skills of primary students, and also wanted to find better ways of involving the younger students with the older students in the unit.

After some discussion, the unit staff members hit on an idea to involve children ages 5–7 in creative writing/paired learning, and to help the students reach some of the instructional objectives of the primary language arts program.

The objectives that unit members identified for each student are as follows:

1. The student will be able to tell a short story to another student or to a group of students keeping the events in proper sequence.
2. The student will be able to write a short story dictated by another student and will be able to use good sentence structure and spelling in writing the story.
3. The social atmosphere/peer relationships between the 5- to 7-year-olds will improve as a result of an opportunity for one-to-one relationships as evidenced by friendlier attitudes toward one another in the school and playground environments.

In carrying out these objectives, the unit leader reports that unit members helped the 5-year-olds decide on a story to tell. This story could be based on a feeling, or something they had made, an experience they have had—in short, just about any idea that would encourage 5-year-olds to express themselves.

Unit staff members would then help the 5-year-olds select and dictate a story to an older primary student. This technique helps the 5-year-olds learn to share their thoughts with others. It also provides the older primary child an opportunity to practice language skills in a meaningful way.

As this program has continued, unit members have observed the increasing language skills of the children ages 5-7. Their written stories are shared with other children in the unit. And an increasing vocabulary development has been noted as well as the improved peer relationships.

The unit leader reports a high pupil interest in this project and her unit

---

* McKinley Elementary School, Appleton, Wisconsin.

The social atmosphere/peer relationships will improve as a result of an opportunity for one-to-one relationships.

is now using this paired learning technique on a weekly basis. There is a decreasing need for teacher direction as children learn to identify their story idea, select their own peer "helper," and proceed to dictate the story with very little teacher direction.

Learning about Vertebrates for Children 9 to 12 Years Old

This illustration groups children for instruction utilizing data from three basic areas:

1. cognitive data from tests, observations, performances, work samples;
2. personal data on learning styles, and
3. affective data such as interests, attitudes, and motivational level. A diagram of this grouping procedure would look like this:

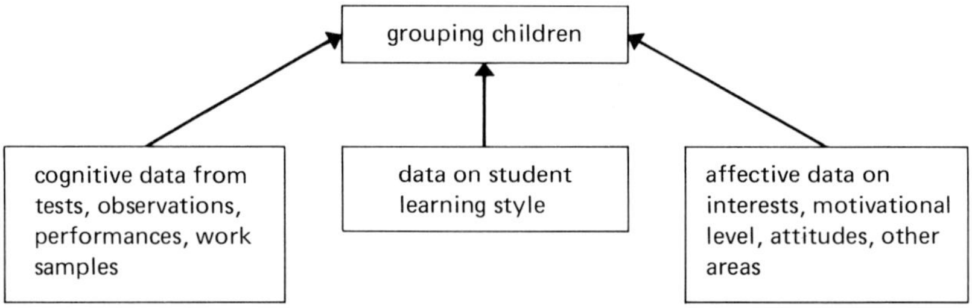

When the unit leader and the unit staff sit down to group children for instruction, where do they start this complex process? In IGE, this process starts with the objectives and follows through to monitoring and evaluating of student progress. For example, if a unit staff is going to group children ages 9 to 12 for a unit of work on vertebrates in science, they might proceed as follows:

1. identify the instructional objectives.
2. gather the cognitive, personal, and affective data on the students and organize it into a usable form.
3. assign students to groups, and groups to physical space.
4. assign unit staff to groups.
5. monitor/evaluate student progress.

The remainder of this section will discuss these five points for the unit of instruction on vertebrates outlined above. The format of the discussion will be told from the viewpoint of a unit leader.

Before we talk about grouping students for instruction in science, I'd like to tell you something about our school, Greenwood. It is located in an outer city area in Connecticut, but it would not be considered suburban. All the schools in our city are integrated and Greenwood has a student population which is 30 percent black, 10 percent Oriental, and 60 percent white. The achievement scores of the students are about at the national average. The parents of the children hold a variety of jobs from unskilled labor to highly professional. Greenwood is one of 30 schools in the district.

We're in our second year in the IGE program. We started the instructional programming process in reading skills, and are presently working on instructional programming in math. We are also starting to develop units of instruction according to the IPM in science. We want to individualize instruction through instructional programming in all areas, but do not want to move faster than we can handle the programs successfully. Our unit has four teachers including myself, one aide, one student teacher, and 120 students ages 9–12. Vertebrates will be the third unit of instruction in science that we have planned and will be taught on a team basis.

Identifying instructional objectives. Our first step was to identify instructional objectives for each individual student. The objectives were selected from a pool of objectives which had been previously identified for the vertebrates unit of instruction at the objective setting meeting. The instructional objectives for all students for vertebrates are presented below.

The student will be able to:

1. differentiate between vertebrates and invertebrates in terms of examples—concept labels (e.g., fish, lobster) and pictures.
2. differentiate among the five classes of vertebrates—amphibians, birds, fish, mammals, reptiles—in terms of attributes (e.g., fish are gill-breathing throughout life and have fins), examples (concept labels and pictures) and definitions.
3. utilize the scientific processes of observation and classification in terms of objectives "1" and "2" above.
4. develop a classification system for a subset of living things—plants or animals—different from that developed by scientists. Try it out with other students about the same age.
5. develop a game for a group of animals such as "kinds of mammals or birds" and try it out.

Since students had had some prior work on vertebrates, and some children tend to do a lot of reading, museum visiting, hobby work, and television viewing on their own, the unit staff decided to pretest the students on a multiple choice test. The pretest had equal numbers of items on each of the five classes of vertebrates, so it was easy to identify strong or weak areas the students might have within objective "2." Thus, objective "2" became the first objective on which students were grouped. Their mastery of objectives "1" and "3" was interrelated to objective "2" and objectives "4" and "5" were available for children who wanted to do creative work, and for those who might have mastered the basic subject matter on vertebrates on the pretest.

We find working with objectives in science quite different from working with math or reading skills. In the latter areas, each skill is easily related to a single objective. In science, objectives tend to become interrelated and we found we had to make a decision to start grouping on one or two clear-cut objectives and then work the other objectives into whatever group we were teaching. As explained earlier, our decision for vertebrates then was to group on objective "2":

> The student will be able to differentiate among the five classes of vertebrates—amphibians, birds, fish, mammals, reptiles—in terms of attributes, examples, and definitions.

Since there are five classes of vertebrates, this objective can really be broken into five subobjectives and one or more of these subobjectives would be identified for each student.

Gathering data. The second step we took was to gather and organize our data. We've found that grouping goes smoothly if we have prepared the data in usable form *before* the grouping meeting. Another tip for efficient grouping is to have various teachers in the unit "specialize" in an area such as cognitive data, learning style data, affective data, and so on. This way, one person can keep records on students up to date and we can keep ongoing, as well as unit-of-instruction, data available for the use of our unit staff. We handled it like this: One teacher was assigned to organize the data from the vertebrates pretest so it would be easy for the unit staff to use at the grouping and scheduling meeting. Another teacher who had a strong interest and background in learning style summarized learning style data which had been gathered at the beginning of the year.

Data on student interests, motivational level, and general attitudes had been discussed at previous meetings. At this point, the staff had agreed on general motivational level of students, but had not pinpointed it to specific content areas. To make the motivational information more relevant to science, the staff had decided to survey the science motivational level of each of the students by the consensus method. One teacher who was the "specialist" on affective data for the unit, in this case yours truly, would read the student's name aloud. The other teachers would rate each student on a three-point scale: three points for high motivation level; two for medium, and one for low. To do this very rapidly, they would hold up the number of fingers to indicate their best judgment of the student's level according to the three-point scale. Usually the teachers were in agreement about the student's level and I could jot down a numeral "1," "2," or "3" next to the student's name. In cases of disagreement, we stopped and gave reasons for our judgments. It took about 30 minutes to rate the student's motivational level toward science, but it was worth it since the data would be available for future as well as present use.

Our staff felt that data on interests were valuable, and administered a science interest inventory. Two of the older students were able to tally these data and one of the teachers summarized them so we could use them for grouping.

Also, we had done very little work on collecting attitudinal data. The only way we had involved attitudes in grouping to this point was via teacher judgment. Since I was our "specialist" in affective matters, I developed the following instrument on attitudes toward curriculum areas:

Attitude Inventory Card

Directions: Put a "1" in front of the subject you like best; a "2" in front of the subject you like next best, and so on until you have a number in front of each subject.

SUBJECTS

____ art
____ language arts
____ mathematics
____ music
____ physical education
____ reading
____ science
____ social studies

Circle one word: Boy Girl

(Leave blank): ____ ____

I presented it to the staff and then gathered data from the children in the unit. You'll note that it is a rank-order instrument and is designed to provide data about how children feel about various content areas. Students in our unit ranked science next to the lowest. While this instrument gave us general data, it did not allow for the student to express a positive or a very negative attitude toward all subject areas, nor did it allow for individual attitudes. At our unit meeting, we decided we would like to have this information to do more effective grouping and will work on it in the future. Meanwhile, the low rating of science by the students has motivated us to try to improve our science units of instruction and the vertebrates unit is one effort to do this. We carried out grouping in the following steps for the vertebrates unit of instruction.

Assigning students to groups. I had scheduled a 90-minute planning meeting for grouping and scheduling the students for vertebrates. At the designing meeting earlier, the unit staff had decided vertebrates would be blocked into a three-week period and that all teachers, the aide, and the student teacher would be involved in teaching. One teacher had selected the objectives, references, and activities for all of us. Also, I had asked the teachers who were "specialists" in their areas to provide summaries of test data, learning style data, and affective data.

With the responsibility for preparation of summary data delegated among three teachers, the unit staff tackled the grouping problem in three successive stages:

1. Form groups according to assessment data.
2. Reconsider groups formed in "1" and/or form subgroups from groups formed in "1" on the basis of learning style.
3. Reconsider groups and/or subgroups from "2" above on the basis of interests, attitudes, and motivational level.

This sounds rather complicated, so let's look at how we did it.

The teacher who had assumed the responsibility for summarizing the assessment data had already placed the 120 children in the unit into four groups and had duplicated the names of the students. These appeared as follows:

(40 students) 1. students who did *not* meet the mastery level (90 percent) for any of the five classes of vertebrates and needed work on all of the material.

(30 students) 2. students who needed work on three of four classes: mammals, fish, amphibians, and reptiles.

(40 students) 3. students who needed work on two of three classes: mammals, amphibians, and reptiles.

(10 students) 4. students who met the mastery level on all five classes and did not need basic work on vertebrates.

This completed the initial grouping step and took only five minutes of meeting time.

The second step in grouping was to reconsider the initial groups formed on the basis of assessment scores. Reconsideration is based upon learning style. A quick glance at Group 1 (40 students) suggests they might start out together in a seminar situation with one teacher, and then be broken down into smaller groups for learning activities. The teacher "specialist" on learning style and media preference had worked with the teacher "specialist" who had formed the groups from assessment data. She had added in data on learning style which included (1) attention span—continuous, irregular, short bursts; (2) sound tolerance—low, medium, high; (3) group size—alone, one-to-one, small, other; (4) assignment type—teacher or student-selected; (5) perceptual strengths and styles (preferred media). As the teacher who was our specialist in affective data, I suggested we look at the needs of these 40 students who did not meet the mastery level for any of the five classes of vertebrates and place them in subgroups.

Group 1. Forty students needing instruction in all five processes.

(10 students) Subgroup A.

learning style	continuous attention span low tolerance for noise small group (3–13 students) self-selected assignments a combination of printed and audiovisual materials
affective	medium interest medium motivation low to medium attitude toward science

(17 students) Subgroup B.

learning style	short bursts of concentrated effort tolerated distant noise well small group teacher-selected tasks mainly audiovisual and activity-oriented materials
affective	low interest low motivation medium to low attitude toward science

(13 students) Subgroup C.

learning style	irregular attention span high level of activity/noise one-to-one and small group teacher-selected tasks high interest, audiovisual materials and activities

affective	low interest low motivation low attitude toward science

The three remaining initial groups formed on the basis of assessment were reconsidered in the same manner as the first one: Reconsidered groupings appeared as follows:

Group 2. Thirty students needing instruction in three of four classes: mammals, fish, amphibians, reptiles.

(10 students) Subgroup D.

learning style	irregular attention low noise tolerance small group teacher-selected tasks audiovisual materials/activities
affective	low to medium interest low to medium motivational level medium attitude

(20 students) Subgroup E.

learning style	short bursts of concentration tolerates medium noise level small to medium-sized group teacher-selected tasks audiovisual material/activities
affective	medium interest medium motivation medium attitude

Group 3. Forty students who need work on two of three classes: mammals, amphibians, reptiles.

(25 students) Subgroup F.

learning style	continuous to irregular attention span medium to high noise tolerance one-to-one to small group teacher-selected tasks audiovisual materials/activities
affective	low to medium interest low to medium motivation medium attitude

(15 students) Subgroup G.

learning style	continuous attention medium to high noise tolerance alone to small group student-selected tasks printed and audiovisual materials
affective	medium interest medium motivation medium to high attitude

Group 4. Ten students who had mastered all basic work in vertebrates.

(10 students) Subgroup H.

learning style	continuous attention varied noise tolerance alone to small group student-selected tasks printed, audiovisual combination
affective	high interest medium to high motivation medium to high attitude

I drew a schematic of the groups as they now existed on the chalkboard and it looked like this:

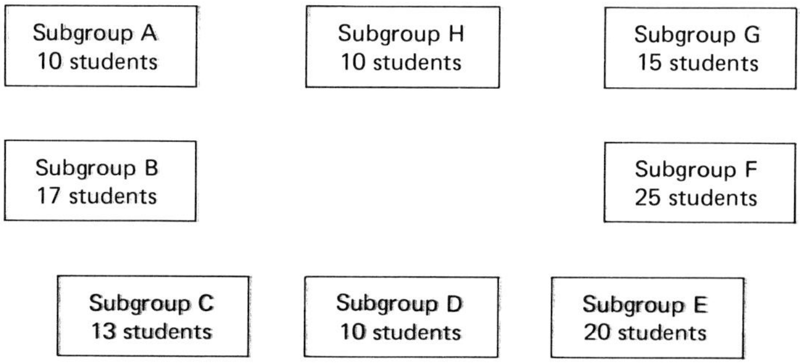

Then I projected a transparency of the unit's space diagram on the screen next to the schematic on the chalkboard so space for the groups could be assigned easily and quickly. Space was assigned primarily on the basis of students' needs relative to (1) noise level, (2) heavy use of audiovisual equipment, and (3) facilities for one-to-one and independent study work.

The assignment of students to groups and groups to space had taken about 35 minutes. Only one more task remained for this unit meeting—to assign teachers to student groups.

Assigning staff to student groups. Eight instructional subgroups had been designated. These had to be staffed by four teachers, one aide, and one student teacher. At this point, I opened up the discussion for comments. "Where do we start, staff?"

One teacher pointed out that the ten students in Subgroup H had mastered the basic content of the unit and would be working on self-selected tasks like developing games or new classification systems. They would need a minimum of teacher instruction beyond the large group seminar, and could be assigned to the aide for supervision with periodic meetings with a teacher. We suggested they hold their periodic meetings with the teacher who had designed the science unit and was our science "expert."

Then someone suggested one teacher could handle both Subgroups F and G, since they had so many similar needs. Perhaps the two groups could have formal work together, with Subgroup F doing additional independent work.

This left Subgroups A, B, C, D, and E to be assigned. I volunteered to work with Subgroups A, B, and C who had similar needs and to take the large group seminars at the beginning for the entire group. Another teacher agreed to help me. The aide would also work with us some of the time.

This left one teacher and the student teacher to handle Subgroups D and E who had similar needs. They agreed.

This completed our assignments and we all felt good about what we'd done. In grouping, some compromises have to be made as we simply don't have enough staff positions to do as much small group work as we'd like to. Compromises we made in our unit of instruction on vertebrates include:

1. assigning more than one group to a teacher.
2. putting students with slight variations in affective levels (e.g., medium and high interests, motivational level, attitude) into the same group.
3. assigning teaching duties to all teachers in the unit. When we teach skills in reading and math we have one teacher "floating" to pick up unforeseen problems and develop materials we need in our work. We simply couldn't arrange it this time, but two teachers will be "free" to work on materials the first two days when we conduct the large group seminars.
4. limiting the amount of one-to-one instruction. However, we plan to use the ten students who have mastered the content in a tutoring situation for three or four days. Most of these ten students are 12 years old and most of the students who need one-to-one help are 9 or 10 years old, so this should work out.

Monitoring and evaluating student progress. We refer to monitoring as the last step in grouping. We've developed a science card that is our adaptation of a keysort card. We have these printed in large quantities and then write in the objectives we expect the students to master. We feel we have to do it this way, because we're still putting our science material together and can't afford to print every time we individualize a new unit of work. A copy of our card was presented earlier in Figure 13.7. We got this card from a unit leader in a nearby town. She and her husband had developed it. With these cards, initial groups based on assessment can be formed in a few minutes and the aide can type out the names for each group so they are ready for use at the meetings. We also want the students to get involved in record keeping, so we have them keep track of their own progress on a sheet which is a Xeroxed copy of the card. They color in the circles (which we punch out on the card) as they meet an objective. They do this in math and reading, too.

In addition, each certified teacher is "advisor" to about 30 students and each also has a Xeroxed copy of the card that the aide updates periodically. The advisor system allows us to check on students every two or three weeks and to pick up problems like students who don't work well alone or are not progressing, or are progressing more rapidly than we expected. We also use these cards for the learning style and affective data.

You may think we're "card happy," but we find grouping with cards so much faster and easier than a chart that we use them for everything. We also like the idea of a Xeroxed sheet for the student and the "advisor" teacher. Students need to be involved in monitoring their own progress, and teachers need to have a practical way to monitor progress. Not everything can be done as a team and this way the "advisor" teacher can check on student progress on her own at her convenience.

You might ask, "Is all this effort worth it?" and "How can you live with all these compromises?" We sometimes talk about this and we feel that grouping students gives them a much better education, and they enjoy learning a lot more. We have data from our standardized tests to indicate this is true in reading, and we hope we will have similar data in math, science, and other areas after we've worked in the program for two or more years.

SUMMARY

This chapter has been concerned with setting objectives for individual students and grouping students with common needs or interests together for instruction.

The historical development and research behind many grouping techniques were reviewed along with considerations for improving grouping techniques.

The criteria for grouping which are most relevant to implementing the instructional programming model are student abilities, achievement interests, sociometric choices, and tasks at hand.

Techniques for identifying useful information about student learning styles were presented, along with two instruments for recording learning style data. These included student preferences in learning style and adult observation of student learning style.

Media to facilitate grouping practices and learning styles were discussed with particular emphasis on their appropriateness for use in different grouping patterns. The media categories presented were projected materials, audio equipment, educational kits, programmed instruction, television and videotape, and instructional games.

The application of grouping practices in two I & R Units were given as examples of grouping procedures used in two different school settings.

Many of the ideas presented in this chapter will reappear in the next chapter which deals with the dynamic process of implementing the instructional program.

REFERENCES

Anderson, R., E. A. Hagstrom, and W. M. Robinson 1960. Team teaching in an elementary school. *School Review* **68** (1): 71–84.

Bechtol, W. M. 1973. *Individualizing instruction and keeping your sanity.* Chicago: Follett.

Cratty, B. J. 1971. *Active learning: games to enhance academic abilities.* Englewood Cliffs, N.J.: Prentice-Hall.

Cronbach, L. J. 1970. *Essentials of psychological testing.* (3rd ed.) New York: Harper & Row.

Dawson, M. (ed.) 1961. *Elementary school organization.* National Elementary Principal Yearbook, Washington, D.C.: National Education Association.

DeCecco, J. 1968. *The psychology of learning and instruction: educational psychology.* Englewood Cliffs, N.J.: Prentice-Hall.

Dunn, R., and K. Dunn 1972. *Practical approaches to individualizing instruction: contracts and other effective teaching strategies.* West Nyack, New York: Parker.

Ekstrom, R. B. 1959. *Experimental studies of homogeneous grouping.* (Office of Naval Research Contract No.–2214(00) Project Designation, N. R., 151–74). Princeton: *Educational Testing Service* **3.**

Fischer, B. B., and L. Fischer 1969. Toward individualized learning. *Elementary School Journal* **69,** (3):298–303.

Gordon, A. K. 1970. *Games for growth.* Chicago: Science Research Associates.

Harris, B. M., and W. Bessent 1969. *Inservice education.* Englewood Cliffs, N.J.: Prentice-Hall.

Joyal, L. 1973. Curriculum and instruction in elementary school mathematics education. Unpublished curriculum guide. University of Wisconsin–Eau Claire.

Klausmeier, H. J., M. R. Quilling, J. S. Sorenson, R. S. Way, and G. R. Glasrud 1971. *Individually guided education and the multiunit elementary school: guidelines for implementation.* Madison, Wisc.: Wisconsin Research and Development Center for Cognitive Learning.

Manning, D. 1971. *Toward a humanistic curriculum.* New York: Harper & Row.

Morganstern, A. 1966. *Grouping in the elementary school.* New York: Pitman.

Ragan, W. B., and G. D. Shepherd 1971. *Modern elementary curriculum.* New York: Holt, Rinehart and Winston.

Shumsky, A. 1968. *In search of teaching style.* New York: Appleton-Century-Crofts.

Westby-Gibson, D. 1966. *Grouping students for improved instruction.* Englewood Cliffs, N.J.: Prentice-Hall.

Yates, A. 1966. *Grouping in education: a report sponsored by the UNESCO Institute for Education, Hamburg.* New York: Wiley.

15

Implementing the Instructional Program

Lloyd H. Joyal
Mary P. Melvin

Objectives

After reading this chapter, the reader will be able:

- To identify appropriate uses for the four basic grouping patterns.
- To explain ways to keep materials accessible and usable for students and staff.
- To describe different ways space can be used in implementing instructional programs.
- To identify a variety of time schedules which enhance flexibility in implementing instructional programs according to the needs and characteristics of individual students.

The fifth step of the Instructional Programming Model (IPM) involves the implementation of the instructional program. This occurs after general and instructional objectives have been identified, students have been assessed, and short term instructional objectives for individual students have been determined.

In Step 5 of the IPM all of the previous planning comes together and focuses on the needs of the learner. The implementation of the instructional program involves (1) attention and guidance from the teacher; (2) time spent in interaction among students; (3) the use of printed materials, audiovisual materials, and direct experience; (4) the use of space and equipment; and (5) time spent by each student in one-to-one interactions with the teacher or media, independent study, small group activities, and large group activities (Klausmeier, *et al.* 1971, p. 19).

Creating an instructional program in which all these variables function simultaneously and smoothly is a complex task. In this chapter, special emphasis is given to instructional groups, instructional materials, physical facilities, and use of time. It has been necessary to separate these topics for purposes of discussion. However, the reader must keep in mind that all of these facets of the instructional program occur simultaneously in any actual school situation.

INSTRUCTIONAL GROUPS

The previous chapter focused on ways to determine the most appropriate grouping patterns for individual children. Once these decisions have been made, the unit team decides how each group will function, based on the information about students and on the strengths of the I & R Unit staff. In this section, we will look at four basic grouping patterns and ways to match teaching styles with them.

Basic Grouping Patterns

The four basic grouping patterns—independent study, one-to-one, small group and large group—need to be considered by staff teachers as they plan instructional activities for students. Consideration of students' learning styles, needs, and interests demands that each of these groups be available at some time for all students. Each of these grouping patterns is discussed below in relation to implementing the IGE instructional program.

Independent study. Independent study assumes that the student will accept increasing responsibility for directing his or her own learning. It assumes, too, that staff teachers are committed to a new role—that of assisting and guiding the students in learning how to work well independently and how to make sound learning decisions by themselves.

Being able to make decisions for oneself is one of the important goals for a happy life, but it is a skill often lacking in many adults. Experience has shown that when independent, rather than dependent, student behavior is encouraged, more comprehensive use is made of learning materials (Glasser 1971, p. 80). This is certainly understandable, for when students assume the responsibility for seeking answers to questions, they often will explore many sources and will not limit the search to those materials "assigned" by the teacher.

Experience with numerous undergraduate and graduate students would support the earlier statement that many adults do not possess the skills necessary for self-directed study simply because no one has asked them to assume such a responsibility earlier. Thus, it is important to provide elementary children and adults with ongoing experiences in making decisions regarding their learning programs.

One of the most important factors in self-directed learning is motivation. Students are more motivated to learn when they are allowed to make some of the decisions about what they will study and how they will proceed. Provision can be made to let children study topics of their own choice or to choose from options identified by the I & R Unit staff. Opportunities for self-selection should start early and, as children mature, an increasing amount of time should be provided for them to select their own activities. Opportunities for self-evaluation should also be provided to help children set goals and develop criteria for independent learning.

In providing opportunities for independent study, teachers must be prepared to help the student locate and interpret sources of information. In one elementary class, the students were planning to spend a month pursuing a science topic of their interest. These 11- and 12-year-olds had been exposed to a variety of topics and materials during the year and were allowed to select a topic that was of interest to them. One girl was convinced of the superior intelligence of the horse over the dog and wanted to prove it to her friends. She selected the topic, "The Comparative Rank of Animal Intelligence." She had a need for references that she could understand and interpret to the class. It took much guidance on the part of the teacher to help this student locate sources through library research, interviewing members of the psychology department on a university campus, and using the personal libraries of these professors.

A boy in the same class was fascinated by the prospect of space travel and the effect of Einstein's theory of relativity regarding traveling faster than the speed of light and simultaneously aging more slowly than in earth time. He went through a similar process of locating information that he and the teacher could both understand and interpret.

These kinds of individual projects require the cooperation of the I & R Unit staff, the media center director, and others to assist students in locat-

a.

b.

a. Independent study, *b.* one-to-one, *c.* small group, and *d.* large group.

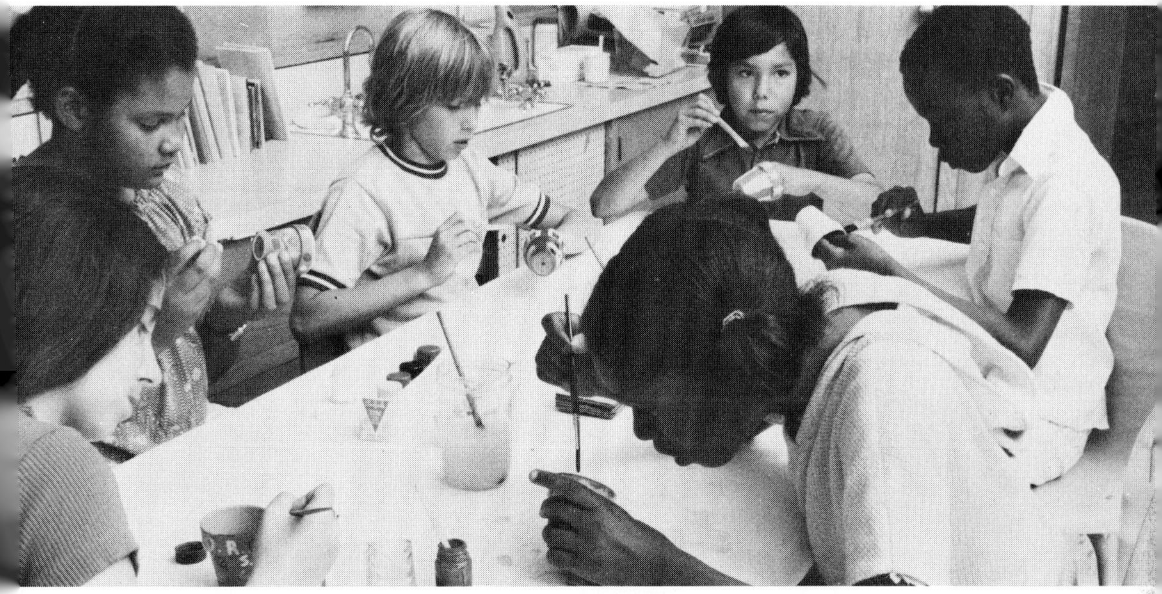

c.

d.

ing answers to questions of interest to them. The process is highly worthwhile and highly motivating to many students and will help them to assume increasing responsibility for their own learning.

Students who enjoy and can benefit from independent learning activities can be identified by teacher observation or by using a learning style assessment instrument such as the one which was described in Figure 14.2. Once a child is involved in independent study, progress needs to be monitored. A simple checklist that can be used to monitor student progress in independent study is given in Figure 15.1.

Students, too, should assume responsibility for assessing their progress toward self-direction. They can get perceptions of their progress at the conclusion of a unit of instruction by summarizing and discussing the strengths and weaknesses indicated on a form like the one presented in Figure 15.2.

Independent Study Skills	Always	Sometimes	Never
1. Completes a teacher-assigned project			
2. Completes a self-assigned project			
3. Shows motivation while working alone			
4. Explores a variety of learning sources			
5. Can functionally use:			
(a) card catalog			
(b) AV equipment			
(c) reference material (dictionary, encyclopedia)			
(d) other print material (books)			
(e) periodicals			
6. Pupil can work ____ hours per week independently.			

____
Student Name

____
Date

Fig. 15.1 Checklist for monitoring independent study.

1. I set learning objectives best when I ____________

____

____

2. When I work in the IMC, my favorite sources of information are ____________________________

____

____

3. I can work best alone when I ____________________

____

____

4. I would like to know more about ________________

____

____

5. The thing I like best about working independently is ____

____

6. An interesting fact or idea I discovered recently is ____

____

7. In order to improve my skills in working independently, I have found that I need to ______

____

____

____
Student's name

____
Date

Fig. 15.2 Pupil-teacher assessment for independent study.

This discussion between student and teacher might be five to ten minutes in length and could be held while the teacher is supervising several children working independently or as part of a scheduled student-advisor conference.

One-to-one. These groups may be composed of one teacher working with one child, a student tutor helping a child, or two children working together on the same activity. Teachers work individually with children to provide help on unique problems, to assist students in the course of independent study, and to work on goal-setting activities. Student tutors, often older children, can assist children by providing information on special topics, guiding a series of learning or practice activities, or helping to carry out projects. Peers often choose to work together not only to enjoy the social interaction but also to benefit from each other's strengths. Children who enjoy this way of learning may choose to be together for reading, quiet activities such as working on math problems, and doing creative writing. Project work, research, and creative drama are other areas where a child may enjoy and benefit from working with a peer.

One-to-one, like independent study, places much responsibility for learning with the student. In both areas the role of the teacher in relation to these learning groups, might be generally described as a "director of learning activities" (Glasser 1971, p. 152). The student must make decisions in relation to use of time, speed or pace of progress, and the area or space in which it is to be done. In these patterns teachers can encourage students to explore learning materials with which they are not presently familiar. For example, a student who normally uses print material might be encouraged to utilize appropriate cassette tapes, filmstrips, records, or other available media.

Small group. The small group is one of the most versatile, usable forms of grouping students for instruction. Small groups (1) can be formed on the basis of need or interest, (2) can effectively utilize all forms of media, and (3) can utilize small spaces wherever they are available.

Small groups are the most common arrangement for teacher-directed learning activities in IGE. Common objectives can be identified and a teacher can prepare lessons to meet them. In a small group setting, it is possible for all the children to be actively involved in learning activities because each child can be close to the teacher, hear what others are saying, and see the materials which are being used.

Many basic skills are most effectively taught in small groups. A detailed description of planning small groups for Word Attack skills was presented in Chapter 10. An example of forming small groups for science instruction was given in Chapter 14. These grouping arrangements were formed on the basis of cognitive data, learning styles, and affective data.

Small groups can utilize spaces wherever they are available.

Small groups are also a means of helping children learn effective group participation. Shy children can be given the support they need to feel secure in speaking to a group. Overly assertive children can be given help and experience in expressing themselves in ways which are acceptable to others. Strengths and talents which might go unnoticed in a large group can be identified and developed within a small group.

Working with a program like IGE that stresses instructional programming for individual students does not mean that instruction is carried out only through independent, one-to-one, or small groups. Larger instructional groups are also important vehicles for instruction.

Large group. Although many, perhaps most, of the daily teaching and learning activities occur in the smaller sized groups, there are times when groups of 25 or more children are appropriate. Large groups can be used for general presentations of information, for guest speakers whose time is limited, or for films which are of general interest. Culminating activities resulting from a unit of instruction may be shared with the total I & R Unit student population.

The large group can also be used creatively. One team of five teachers selected the large group mode as a motivating activity for an entire unit of 120 primary children. Near the end of the school year, the unit members determined that there would be at least one month in which no specific content or specific objectives needed to be taught as an essential part of the science program. In order to provide some options in terms of content for students, four of the teachers agreed to provide four content options. The fifth team member agreed to provide motivation for these content areas by presenting a brief overview of each option to the entire student population of the unit. The students would then elect their choices on the basis of this presentation.

In this case, the unit was able to keep one member free from direct teaching responsibilities to be available to assist in the preparation and presentation of other teaching materials and to handle the unexpected situations which always occur. The unit staff planned and carried out this program combining student interests with the interests and strengths of each unit teacher.

Discussion of matters affecting all the students in a unit can also be effectively handled in a large group situation. Acceptable conduct in the school building or a review of ways to care for school materials are examples of topics that would be appropriate for large group presentations.

Matching Teaching Styles and Grouping Patterns

Different kinds of teaching styles were discussed in Chapter 4. Techniques for identifying the strengths of each unit member were presented in Chapter 6. This information should be put to use at the time instructional groups are formed. When assigning unit members to groups, consideration should be given to each teacher's preference regarding group size and teaching atmosphere, as well as to individual talents and expertise.

Preferred group size. Some teachers enjoy directing activities which are appropriate for large groups. A member of the unit staff who can keep the attention of large groups of children and, at the same time, create an effective learning situation should be encouraged to assume the responsibility for large group instruction. Another staff member may enjoy working with a large number of children but not in direct instructional situations. That person could be responsible for overseeing the independent learning activities of many children.

Teachers who are especially good at organizing and preparing materials to meet a specific instructional goal might be encouraged to use these materials with small groups. Those teachers who have difficulty maintaining control of 30 or more children could contribute more to team effectiveness by working with smaller groups.

It may not always be feasible for each teacher to work with exactly the group size which each prefers. However, preferences should be considered whenever groupings are made or changed so that the strengths of each person are used as often as possible.

Preferred teaching atmosphere. Some teachers like a very quiet learning atmosphere; others enjoy a noisy buzz. Some prefer that children sit still; others encourage the children to move around. Many teachers prefer an area that has a feeling of privacy; others like to be in areas which are exposed to the movement and activities of other groups. All these preferences can be recognized in implementing the instructional program. The purpose of each group will, to some extent, dictate the atmosphere in which it could function best. The unit team can decide together what will happen in each of the I & R Units and can assign teachers to locations where they can work most successfully.

Talents and expertise. Expertise in subject matter and talents in certain kinds of activities are strengths which should be considered to make the instructional program as effective as possible. In IGE, each teacher is involved in all curriculum areas. However, there are occasions when it is desirable for a person with an excellent background in one subject to assume responsibility for certain lessons. At the upper elementary level, someone with a strong background in mathematics may be needed to clarify difficult concepts for students. In social studies, a teacher who had traveled widely might be expected to do a social studies presentation on holiday customs in other lands.

Meeting the needs of each individual student requires a large variety of learning activities. Different approaches would be needed for activities such as (1) helping children locate resources in the Media Center, (2) directing a values clarification activity, (3) guiding the construction of a complicated art project, or (4) explaining a mathematics concept to students who have difficulty understanding the number system. No one person can be an expert in conducting all these activities. Therefore, it is to the advantage of the students and the staff that all team members be allowed to utilize their talents. By sharing their talents, teachers are not only giving students the best instruction for the activity but they are also teaching each other how to handle similar situations that may arise in the future.

It will seldom, if ever, be possible to give equal consideration to all the qualities that make up each teacher's teaching style. However, the unit leader should be alert to the strengths and weaknesses which exist and should help the team consider these qualities when making grouping decisions.

The purpose of grouping is to provide for the needs of each student. Instructional groups may vary from only one student to a large number of students, depending on the purpose to be achieved. Flexibility in grouping patterns is necessary when the instructional program is designed to provide the best learning situation for each student.

Within any I & R Unit, there are teachers who have different strengths and preferences. These should be utilized as much as possible when delegating the responsibilities for the variety of groups and activities in each unit.

INSTRUCTIONAL MATERIALS

Materials and media which are appropriate for different grouping practices and learning styles were presented in Chapter 14. Successful implementation of the instructional program will be greatly affected by the way these materials are arranged and cared for. Suggestions for managing materials to keep them accessible, in usable condition, and available in sufficient quantities are presented below.

Accessibility

During the planning of all instructional activities, the unit leader must be certain that the materials which will be needed are identified and plans made to acquire materials which are not available in the building.

Regardless of the physical arrangement of an I & R Unit learning area, one section should be designated as a place for materials. A management system should be devised so that each team member knows where and how materials are stored. Equipment such as projectors and tape recorders can be stored on shelves. Other shelves can hold textbooks and paperbacks which are kept in the unit area. A filing cabinet or cardboard boxes can hold printed matter such as worksheets and learning packets. Books and other printed matter should be grouped by curriculum area.

A special place should be designated for materials in current use. This makes it possible for each teacher to retrieve the necessary materials at the time they are needed for a lesson. The unit leader should help all unit members develop a habit of returning materials to their places when not in use so they will be there when someone else needs them.

Children should also know the basic arrangement of materials so they can locate those which are needed for independent learning activities. The possibilities of borrowing materials from sources outside the school such as the public library, district Media Center, and community resource people should also be made known.

Condition and Quantity

It is important that the unit leader help the staff and students develop practices for keeping materials and equipment in usable condition. Procedures should be developed so that each person knows what to do when a projector light burns out, when the last printed activity sheet is used up, and when the cassette recorder doesn't work properly. Lack of concern about such matters causes unnecessary problems in carrying out learning activities.

In the course of some units of instruction, different teachers or students may need to use the same materials (e.g., textbooks, transparencies, projectors). The management system should include a way to plan ahead so that different groups aren't planning to use the same materials simultaneously.

The management of materials is one of the more mechanical necessities of an IGE program. However, a good system for handling materials is important to keep instructional programs alive and moving.

PHYSICAL FACILITIES

The physical structure of a school does not in any way inhibit the implementation of IGE. Some very successful IGE programs exist in buildings constructed before 1900; others are in "egg-crate" buildings which are made up entirely of halls and classrooms; and many are occurring in buildings which have been planned to provide the variety of spaces and settings which are desirable for an IGE school.

Regardless of the style of the building, arrangements should be made to use all the available space in the most effective way. One area should be designated for a Media Center, as this is essential for full implementation of instructional programming for individual students. Each I & R Unit should have an identifiable area of the building. This area might be four classrooms and the area hall space. It might be three old classrooms, a wide hall, an old coat closet, and a former storage area. Or it might be a pod in an open-design building. In addition to the Media Center and unit areas, space should be available for art, music, and physical education classes. In this section we will examine how space can be used for unit areas and for the Media Center.

Utilizing Space Assigned to the I & R Unit

There are many ways to utilize space in an IGE program. One way to decide how to use the available space is to list the purposes for which space is needed. Then the unit team should study the available space and designate certain areas to be used for each purpose. Most areas will have to be used for more than one kind of activity. An area should be arranged to accommodate its primary purpose, yet be flexible enough to be rearranged easily for other purposes. Usefulness of all areas is increased when children are not assigned to specific desks, but are free to move to areas designated for particular purposes.

In a *traditional building,* the team may decide to designate each room for a specific function. One way of arranging four rooms according to function is shown in Figure 15.3.

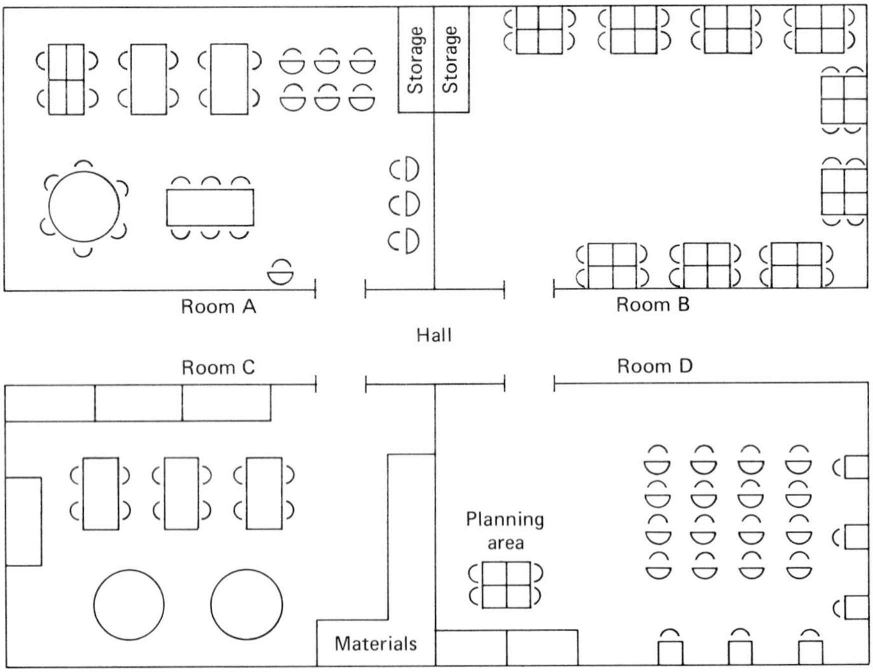

Fig. 15.3 Room arrangements according to function.

The small group and individual desk arrangement in Room A would be appropriate for independent study, one-to-one, or small group activities. In Room B the desks (or tables) are arranged in clusters around the perimeter of the room, leaving a large open area in the center. The room could be used for independent, one-to-one, or small group activities, but is also designed to accommodate large groups. A large group could sit on the floor in the open space, or chairs could be taken from the desks around the room and from other rooms to provide sufficient seating space.

Room C could be designated as an activities room. The noisier, more active educational activities could be conducted here. A space is included for storage of materials to be used during these activities. Most learning games would be kept here. Room D could be designated as the "quiet" room. Class-size, small group, or individual assessment could be held here. Students who felt they were ready for assessment or teachers who wanted to assess a group could utilize this room. When not being used for assessment activities, Room D could be used by individual students who need or desire a quiet work area.

It should be emphasized that the arrangement described above provides for a maximum amount of flexibility. Each room has a purpose, but can be adjusted to meet other needs as they arise.

Depending on local regulations, it may also be possible to use part of the hall area for instructional space. Learning stations can be attached to hall bulletin boards with occasional desks placed nearby so children can complete the station activities there. Narrow bookcases can be set against the wall to hold educational kits, books, or concrete materials. When children are working in different rooms, but using materials from the same sources, the hall is often the most central area for placing materials for easy accessibility.

Similar space utilization techniques can be employed in an *open-space building* such as the one presented in Figure 15.4. The open-space arrangement here includes the area for independent, one-to-one, and small group activities (Area A), space for large groups (Area B), the activity area (Area C), and the quiet work area (Area D). In this setting, the space available for the unit has increased as the hall space from the traditional building has been included in the unit area.

It is important that space be available for different grouping arrangements and for different kinds of activities. There should be space for teaching small groups, for independent work (e.g., learning stations, carrels, listening center, quiet reading area) and for large group meetings. Space arrangements should also be based on consideration of noise level and type of activity. Learning situations are most effective when children—and teachers—aren't unnecessarily distracted by nearby activities.

Regardless of the type of building, one small area should be desig-

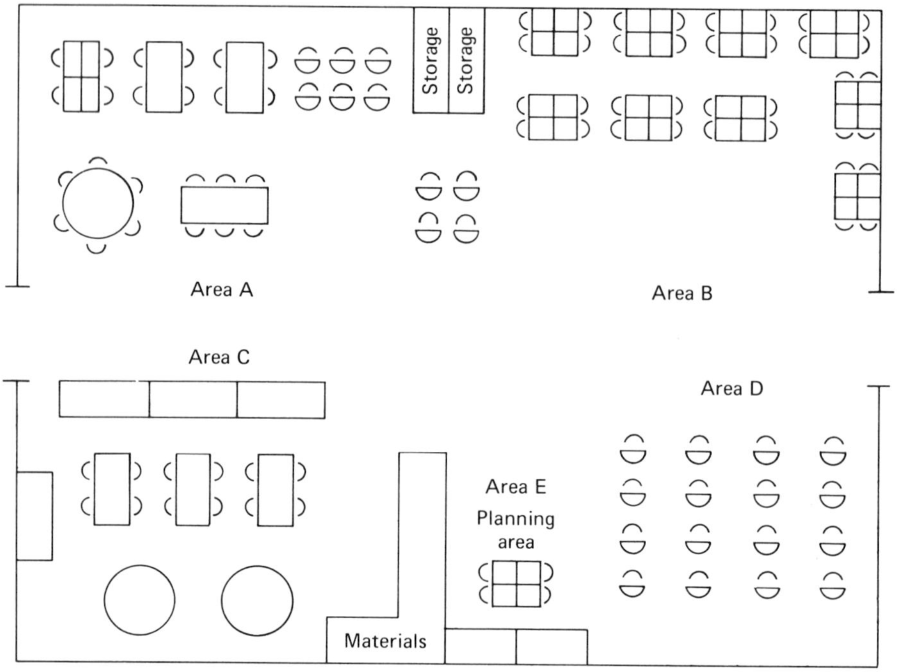

Fig. 15.4 Arrangement of I & R Unit areas in an open-space building.

nated as the I & R Unit planning area (Area E in Figure 15.4). The teachers' desks can be arranged in a cluster in the area where teaching materials are stored. Having a planning area can increase interaction among the team members as well as provide a central location for the materials which they all use.

The Media Center

It is crucial in a program like IGE to have an area of the school designated as a Media Center, Instructional Materials Center (IMC), Learning Center, or some other title. This refers to space designated to house a variety of materials and to encourage exploration of learning opportunities. The Media Center is the hub of any IGE program, and certainly a key factor in independent and one-to-one study.

In developing the Media Center, as in any other part of the IGE program, there must be a willingness on the part of all staff involved—Media Center director, unit members, principal—to find an increasing variety of ways to accommodate children's interests in learning. Commitment of the staff, a plan for developing the Media Center in accordance with the objectives of the school, workable space in the school, and a flexible schedule are necessary for the successful operation of a Media Center (Glogau, *et al.* 1972).

Planning for a Media Center. As a member of the IIC, the unit leader will have some responsibility either for creating a Media Center or for evaluating and improving an existing one.

In the planning stages, consideration must be given to: (1) selection, acquisition, and organization of a materials collection; (2) processing of materials; (3) accessibility of materials; (4) staff; (5) materials to be included in the collection; (6) AV equipment; (7) professional collection; and (8) expenditures (Wisconsin Department of Public Instruction 1972). Minimum guidelines for establishing a Media Center can be found in *Media Programs: District and School* published jointly by the National Education Association and the American Library Association (1974).

To provide for the variety of learning experiences which are part of an IGE program, a Media Center should have: (1) listening area; (2) viewing area; (3) story and quiet area; (4) reference and study area; (5) discussion area; (6) display area; (7) circulation area; and (8) enough equipment and materials to serve the school and its program (Glogau, *et al.* 1972).

Most schools have some form of library or Media Center already in existence. The task of the IIC, in cooperation with the media specialist, will be to analyze what is already available, determine what should make up the Media Center which is desired for their IGE program, and set priorities for reaching the goal. The document, *Planning Instruments for School Library/Media Programs* (Liesener 1974), provides guidelines for planning and setting priorities. An outline of factors to consider, with suggestions for setting priorities, is reproduced from this document in Appendix B.

The decision about size of the media budget will be made by each school, depending upon their educational objectives. Many IGE schools have found that they need to budget more of their money to purchase materials for the Media Center. When materials and equipment are located in a centralized area, they can receive the widest possible use by all students and staff. As the IGE program expands, there is less need for having identical books in the hands of each student, and more use is found for a variety of instructional materials.

Effective use of the Media Center. In order for the Media Center to be an effective part of the IGE program and provide the maximum amount of service to the staff and students, an *open schedule* should be established. The Media Center should be available to any student or group of students at any time of the day, rather than on a scheduled weekly basis. Having the Media Center specialists' time as well as staff and student time operating on a flexible basis will do a great deal to implement the instructional programs.

When *developing instructional programs,* it is important to inform the Media Center personnel of the goals and objectives so that materials to support these goals can be located or developed. A variety of media to support individual and small group studies should be available to students who are pursuing various interests (see Chapter 14). Nothing will dismay eager students more than having their curiosity aroused and then having no means to satisfy it.

As mentioned earlier, one of the goals of IGE is to help students become more self-directed. Learning to use the Media Center is an important step toward this goal. *Location skills* are necessary tools for wise use of the Media Center. These skills may be taught as a unit of instruction or through a series of activities which students carry out independently. The media specialist and the I & R Unit staff should work cooperatively to plan the activities and prepare the materials for this purpose.

It is important to provide opportunities to strengthen listening, viewing, and reading skills for use in the Media Center. As individuals and groups of students work in the Media Center, they will be able to develop and use these skills as needs or interests arise. Much of the necessary skill instruction can be an integral part of the Media Center program, and should be carried out in close cooperation with the staff members in each I & R Unit.

Instructional techniques such as student contracts, "unipacs," and learning stations can be encouraged and supported through an active, adequate Media Center program. Students who are using such activities should be encouraged to work in the Media Center where the necessary resources are readily available.

Research experiences are an important part of any program to stimulate intellectual curiosity. Research skills, from the simple skill of finding a picture in the vertical file to the difficult job of coordinating notes from many sources for a written report, can be sequenced and the Media Center director can help elementary students master these skills when appropriate. Many techniques and activities designed to help children learn to locate and use media material can be found in Chapters 5 and 6 of *Developing a Successful Elementary School Media Center* (Glogau, *et al.* 1972) and in *The Elementary School Library in Action* (Palovic and Goodman 1968).

All curriculum areas contain possibilities for research activities. An example would be a unit of instruction on environmental education. Research activities could be used to interest students in environmental concerns as well as to provide some guidance for exploratory activities. An example of a concept with suggested activities based on research is given in Figure 15.5.

Exploratory activities can be encouraged in other areas. In mathematics, there are many topics related to basic skills that can be explored by students. These include probability, the historical development of numbers, and use of logic and reasoning.

Research Activity on Environment

Concept: Energy is supplied to an ecosystem by the activities of green plants.

Instructional Objective:
The learner will be able to interpret a labeled drawing of the relationship between plants and the ecosystem.

1. *Activities:*
   a. Listen to the *Environmental Reader* tape, Chapter 3. Complete the activity sheet to check your learning.
   b. Research, read, and write a report on the relationship and interaction of plants, animals, and decomposers, such as fungi, bacteria, and mushrooms.
   c. In the classroom, view a film or filmstrip on photosynthesis. Tell another pupil the process. Make an illustrated chart to help explain this process.
   d. Each pupil will write a pupil definition of the words listed:
      (1) community (5) direct consumers
      (2) ecology (6) decomposers
      (3) dominant (7) food chain
      (4) producers (8) food web
   e. In a small group, prepare a bulletin board illustrating an ecosystem of specific plants, animals, and decomposers. Write questions pertaining to the ideas and attach in an envelope for others to answer.
   f. In a small group, set up a terrarium or aquarium that displays a sample ecosystem. Include cards of explanation of the relationship of plants and animals.
   g. With a pupil-selected commercially prepared overhead transparency or a set of selected transparencies, prepare an oral explanation to present to a small group.

Fig. 15.5 Example of a research activity on environment. (From J. S. Sorenson 1973, *Implementing instructional programming in individualized learning programs,* Instructional Paper No. 3, Department of Elementary Education, University of Wisconsin—Eau Claire.)

Some students may apply what they have learned to constructing instructional games to assist other students. One intermediate group boy had completed the necessary mathematics skills and had several days of "unscheduled" time. He enjoyed mathematics and could work alone with little direction. One of the unit teachers asked him if he would like to develop a game or activity which would help other students improve computational skills. The boy accepted the challenge and came up with a game he called "Football Math." His board was modeled after a playing field. There were sets of cards under the headings of "kickoff," addition, subtraction, multiplication, division, fractions, and "bonus."

A "kickoff" card was drawn to determine where the football was to be placed. The other stacks contained problems and the number of yards gained or lost, depending on whether or not the correct answer was provided. Four tries or "downs" were given each turn to make the necessary ten yards in order to continue playing. A "touchdown," of course, was the goal.

This game proved so popular that the student constructed a simpler version for use by younger students. The materials and equipment used in producing this game came from the Media Center. The completed games were filed in the Media Center to be available to anyone who wished to use them.

In language arts, most elementary children can be stimulated through activities dealing with interpretive skills, examining the plot of the story, or creating their own short stories. These could be small group activities with five or six students in each group. The Media Center provides an excellent environment in which to work.

In order to excite children about reading books they might not otherwise look at, one teacher used the technique of reading from the "Book of the Week." Children enjoy being read to, even at 12 years of age, and the teacher would spend about ten minutes each day reading from the selected book. It was so planned that by Friday a crucial or interesting point would be reached in the book. The teacher would then return the book to the Media Center and stand back! Invariably, many children would try to secure the book to complete the story. Often, this technique would ensure the book's circulation for several months.

The important point to remember is that once the teacher arouses the interest or curiosity of students, an attempt must be made to provide methods and materials necessary for the interest to grow.

Interests can also be encouraged by providing opportunities for children to demonstrate or illustrate an idea to be shared with their peers. Children are natural "sharers" and can be easily motivated to produce something to share with others.

Small groups of children can collaborate on setting up a "book corner" in the Media Center. This corner could contain books selected by these children according to interest or centering around a theme. Tape recorders could be used to present recorded book talks. A simple camera could be used to make slides or pictures to accompany the tapes.

Children enjoy writing dialogue and individuals or small groups could produce a short play from a book using very simple props. These demonstrations could be given in the Media Center. Similar techniques can be used for a "You Were There" production from some historical book.

For those who like to draw, "book illustrations" or a poster can be made that will help "sell" the book to other students. The possibilities are endless. Accomplishment of many of these tasks is very satisfying to children and will help make learning activities an exciting experience.

The Media Center should be one of the busiest places in an IGE school. Children can carry out many learning activities such as those described in this section. They should also have time available in the Media Center to explore, to find, to touch, to look, to listen, to sense, to reject. At these times, the Media Center personnel and unit teachers should remain in the background and be available only when requested. By providing flexible scheduling and subtle adult guidance, and by making a variety of materials readily available, the child's natural curiosity can be encouraged. This is an essential step toward the goal of developing self-directed, independent learners.

Much of each child's school day will be spent in the unit learning area and the Media Center. The unit leader must be involved in making deci-

The Media Center should be one of the busiest places in an IGE school.

sions about where these areas will be located. After the areas are identified, the unit leader's responsibility is to provide the necessary leadership for effective use of the facilities of each area.

USE OF TIME

The use of time is one of the most important factors in creating and implementing instructional programs for all students. One of the responsibilities of the unit leader in the I & R Unit is providing leadership for making decisions regarding the use of time. The unit leader must help the team look at time, not just as a six- or seven-hour school day, but more importantly as a daily investment of six or seven hours of each child's educational experience.

Basic Considerations for Scheduling

It is not possible in the context of this book to prescribe "the best schedule possible," but some examples will be presented. Many factors influence decisions about the use of time in each I & R Unit situation. Scheduling decisions will be affected by local characteristics such as (1) the length of the school day; (2) state and local guidelines; (3) availability of teachers for music, art, and physical education; and (4) the characteristics of the student population. However, there are some basic ideas about the use of time which can serve as guidelines in scheduling instructional time.

Time can be utilized most flexibly by considering the total amount of time available each day. How much instructional time is available for each student? How can we best utilize this time to the advantage of each individual student?

One important fact should be kept in mind: It is easier to keep a schedule flexible if *large blocks* of time are set up rather than using smaller segments where frequent changes are scheduled. When larger blocks of instructional time are planned, the unit team has more alternatives for providing instructional flexibility. These include:

1. Allowing students with long attention spans to work without interruption for a large block of time and, at the same time, permitting students whose attention spans are shorter to move through several different activities.
2. Freeing several teachers to work on plans while one or two members of the team accept responsibility for all the students in the unit for a block of time.
3. Having one teacher supervise a large group of children working on independent studies while each of the other staff members conducts directed learning activities with smaller groups.

The unit team will have to work cooperatively to arrange a schedule which will provide these large time blocks. An example of such a schedule is given in Figure 15.6.

	Mon.	Tue.	Wed.	Thu.	Fri.
7:45	Unit planning	Individual planning	Unit planning	Unit or individual planning	Individual planning
8:45	Student interaction — discussion — plans for the day				
9:00	Communications block — includes reading, writing, spelling, speaking, and listening skills			*	
11:00	Mathematics				
12:00	Lunch	Lunch	Lunch	Lunch	Lunch
12:45	Special subjects — art, music, physical education				
1:45	Science and social studies — alternating units of instruction in each area				
3:00	Student interaction — discussion — evaluation				

Fig. 15.6 Weekly schedule for Unit B.* A detailed schedule for the use of this time block is presented in Fig. 15.7.

Once the basic schedule has been outlined, the unit leader guides the team in planning the use of time within each block. Consideration is given to all the information which has been gathered during planning sessions such as (1) what instructional objectives are being emphasized, (2) what characteristics of each student are relevant to his or her schedule, (3) what is the nature of the grouping arrangements for the different curriculum areas.

Student Schedules within a Large Time Block

Within a given time block, different students will be guided to use their time in different ways. The Thursday communications block which is shaded in Figure 15.6 is expanded and shown in greater detail in Figure 15.7. Three options (A, B, and C) for the use of this communications block are presented and discussed below.

Some students work quite well with a minimum of teacher guidance. They may be given directions about a number of objectives which could, or should, be accomplished over a period of time, then be allowed to de-

	Option A	Option B	Option C
9:00	Independent reading activities	Study skills	Word Attack skills
9:15			Listening
9:30		Written work	Drawing
9:45	Reading books	Reading books	Handwriting
10:00	Learning station	Creative dramatics	Spelling game
10:15			Directed reading
10:30	Puppet show	Group reading conferences	
10:45			Creative dramatics

Fig. 15.7 Flexible scheduling within a two-hour communications block. This figure shows a detailed schedule of the shaded area in Fig. 15.6.

termine their own schedules to achieve them. One of these students might follow Option A of the schedule in this way:

1. 45 minutes—work on a given reading task (e.g., reading from a set of individualized reading materials and completing the follow-up written work)

2. 20 minutes—read self-selected books
3. 25 minutes—work at a learning station for practice in writing business letters
4. 30 minutes—plan and/or practice a puppet show

Other students who have similar learning styles could proceed in the same manner to achieve their objectives. Their time might be used to practice handwriting, work on grammar lessons, write creative stories, read assignments from basal readers, or complete other activities which are part of their instructional programs and which are readily available in the form of study guides, learning stations, ongoing activities, activity packets or other means. During the week, some time will be scheduled for these students to meet with a teacher to discuss their progress, solve any problems, evaluate work completed, and plan for new activities. The unit team can plan to have one teacher available for a half hour at a specified time every two or three days to provide this help.

Every unit will probably have some students who can achieve their objectives through much independent work, but most children in a unit will need to spend more time in teacher- or student-directed activities. In the communications block, these students might work on study skills as a group and complete other activities using a schedule similar to Option B:

1. 30 minutes—use dictionary
2. 20 minutes—complete written work about the dictionary
3. 20 minutes—read for pleasure
4. 30 minutes—participate in creative dramatics
5. 20 minutes—meet with a teacher for a group reading conference

At the same time, other students could be meeting in instructional groups which were planned to meet objectives in such areas as reading vocabulary, syllabication, cursive writing, or English usage.

A few children will need more teacher-directed activities, and some will need to work in shorter time segments. Their needs might be met with a schedule such as Option C:

1. 20 minutes—directed lesson in word attack skills
2. 10 minutes—use of headphones to read along with a taped story
3. 20 minutes—making drawings to accompany the taped story
4. 15 minutes—directed handwriting activity
5. 20 minutes—spelling learning game
6. 20 minutes—directed reading lesson
7. 15 minutes—creative drama activity

The schedules above are certainly not exhaustive of the possibilities for using large blocks of time. However, they do show that the varying needs of children can be met through flexible scheduling. The example described above is just one way of using large time blocks to make it possible to schedule time to meet different needs of individual children in one unit.

Teacher Schedules within a Large Time Block

In the examples above, sample student schedules for the communications block were given. To help put these schedules into better perspective in terms of all the members of an I & R Unit, an outline of what each adult team member might be doing during this same time block is presented here.

For this example, we will use the same I & R Unit which was described in Chapter 10. You will recall that this is a unit of 150 students, ages 8 to 10, with a unit leader, four staff teachers, one aide, and a student teacher. The following example can be assumed to have taken place at least a year after the experiences described in Chapter 10. To provide a more comprehensive picture of how this time block is used by the entire unit, the teachers' schedules include a greater range of activities and groups than were presented in the sample student schedules. The teachers' schedules are as follows:

Ms. Flynn, Teacher
50 minutes—conducting reading conferences
15 minutes—teaching small group handwriting lesson
25 minutes—teaching a reading group
30 minutes—supervising a large group activity (e.g., viewing a film, working on creative writing, listening to a story)

Ms. Fords, Teacher
20 minutes—teaching Word Attack skills (small group)
40 minutes—conducting reading conferences
35 minutes—teaching a spelling lesson (small group)
25 minutes—supervising student-directed small groups

Mr. Frost, Teacher
30 minutes—teaching study skills
20 minutes—teaching a reading group
40 minutes—directing students in goal-setting activities
30 minutes—directing preparations for a puppet show

Ms. Jones, Teacher
45 minutes—supervising student-directed reading activities
20 minutes—teaching a reading group

25 minutes—supervising learning stations
30 minutes—conducting reading conferences

Ms. Wynn, Aide
20 minutes—organizing materials
10 minutes—supervising reading/listening activity
20 minutes—supervising completion of written work and drawing assignments
20 minutes—supervising independent reading of self-selected books
50 minutes—supervising as needed (e.g., learning stations, student-directed small groups)

Ms. White, Student Teacher
65 minutes—supervising students working on reading assignments
20 minutes—supervising learning games
20 minutes—teaching a directed reading lesson
15 minutes—conducting reading conferences

Ms. Goldsmith, Unit Leader
30 minutes—teaching a small group language lesson
40 minutes—conducting reading conferences
50 minutes—directing creative dramatics (2 different groups)

It is apparent that the teachers as well as the students do not use the entire time block for a single activity. Having the large block of time makes it possible to allocate an appropriate amount of time for each activity and lesson.

A Student's Daily Schedule

Up to this point, we have focused only on the time used for the communication arts. The same basic assumptions apply in scheduling during the rest of the day. To show how this would work, a possible schedule for one child on a particular day is presented.

Sarah Green is a 9-year-old in Unit B. Her favorite areas of study are science and mathematics. She acquires new mathematics concepts readily and has no difficulty applying them in problem-solving situations. Sarah has a more neutral attitude toward reading and hasn't yet acquired sufficient skills to read independently in materials which are considered to be fourth grade level. Sarah has an indifferent attitude toward social studies—some lessons are interesting but, for the most part, she could ignore this area of study.

Sarah uses her time most effectively when she is working on mathematics or when she can be involved in making something. It is difficult for her to use print materials for learning if she is expected to work alone.

Using the schedule presented in Figure 15.6, a school day for Sarah might look like this:

	8:35	Arrive at school
	8:45	Meet in class size group to discuss plans for the day
Communications	9:00	Work on Word Attack skills in a teacher-directed group
	9:20	Use a phonics learning game
	9:45	Meet in a small group for reading practice
	10:05	Take a break (drink, toilet, etc.)
	10:10	Work on a spelling lesson in a teacher-directed small group
	10:25	Read a science book with a friend
	10:45	Illustrate a poster for "Be Kind to Animals Week"
Mathematics	11:00	Work on introductory concepts for long division in a teacher-directed group
	11:20	Practice using long division
	11:40	Help three children who are working on beginning geometry
	12:00	Take a break for lunch and playtime
Special subjects	12:45	Participate in art class
	1:15	Participate in physical education class
Science/ Social Studies	1:45	Work on a science project—diorama of animals in the meadow
	2:10	Tape a narration to explain a series of dioramas
	2:30	Meet in a teacher-directed social studies group for a film and discussion about Canada
	3:00	Meet in a small group to discuss and evaluate the day
	3:15	Depart for home

Sarah's schedule provides the time she needs to carry out the activities which are appropriate for her. Other students in the unit would have the same large time block schedule but the time allocation within each block would differ according to individual needs. Students who like to concentrate for long periods of time, those who work slowly, and those who want to be able to complete time-consuming activities need schedules which allow for these learning styles. At the same time, schedules should be arranged to accommodate students who have short attention spans and those who prefer to change activities often and work for short periods of time on each one. Planning the basic daily schedule in large time blocks makes it possible to meet the needs of all these students in a way which is not possible with strict scheduling in short time segments.

In this section we have described ways to achieve flexible scheduling which are responsive to student learning styles and instructional needs as well as to teacher strengths and styles. Schedules will vary from school to school, depending on factors unique to each situation. It is the responsibility of the unit leader, in cooperation with the I & R Unit team, to plan schedules which are sufficiently flexible to permit implementation of instructional programming for each student.

SUMMARY

This chapter has focused on the implementation of a suitable instructional program for each student as described in Step 5 of the Instructional Programming Model. It deals specifically with instructional groups, materials, physical facilities, and the use of time as they relate to specific teaching strategies.

The section on grouping provides examples of the ways in which the four basic grouping patterns are used for different purposes. A short section on materials gives ideas to help keep materials readily available to staff and students. The discussion of physical facilities encourages an open, creative look at the instructional space available to each I & R Unit to encourage the most flexible use of space whether in a traditional or open-space building. The use of large time blocks, utilized in various ways to achieve maximum flexibility, was illustrated.

This chapter also deals with the importance of the Media Center in IGE schools. It shows how a well-organized, smoothly functioning Media Center can actively support the components of instructional groups, materials, space, and time. A Media Center Planning document is presented in Appendix B.

Implementation of the instructional program is the most complex step of the IPM. It involves the integration and orchestration of all the efforts of the previous steps into a unified whole—a great variety of activities occurring simultaneously. Careful planning and effective leadership by the unit leader are of paramount importance in implementing the instructional program.

REFERENCES

Association for Educational Communications and Technology and the American Association of School Librarians 1974. *Media programs: district and school.* Chicago: American Library Association.

Division for Library Services 1972. *Standards for school library/media programs: 1972-75.* Madison, Wisc.: Wisconsin Department of Public Instruction.

Glasser, J. F. 1971. *Learning centers for independent study.* West Nyack, N.Y.: Parker.

Glogau, L., E. Krause and M. Wexler 1972. *Developing a successful elementary school media center.* West Nyack, New York: Parker.

Klausmeier, H. J., M. R. Quilling, J. S. Sorenson, R. S. Way, and G. R. Glasrud 1971. *Individually guided education and the multiunit elementary school: guidelines for implementation.* Madison, Wisc.: Wisconsin Research and Development Center for Cognitive Learning.

Liesener, James W. 1974. *Planning instruments for school library/media programs.* College Park: University of Maryland.

Palovic, L., and E. B. Goodman 1974. *The elementary school library in action.* West Nyack, New York: Parker.

Sorenson, J. S. 1973. *Implementing instructional programming in individualized learning programs.* Instructional Paper No. 3. Eau Claire, Wisc.: Department of Elementary Education, University of Wisconsin—Eau Claire.

16

Evaluating the Instructional Program

Stephen Jurs
William Wiersma

Objectives

After reading this chapter, the reader will be able:

- To indicate the ways in which evaluation of the instructional program differs from evaluation of a student.
- To specify criteria which can be used for evaluation of an instructional program.
- To explain ways in which program evaluation aids the staff in making instructional decisions.
- To be aware of the structure needed for establishing ongoing evaluation of the instructional program.

Instruction based on objectives with corresponding criterion-referenced assessment does not ensure an effective program. Careful and systematic evaluation is necessary to assess how well the program is operating and to suggest what modifications, if any, need to be made. It is the intent of this chapter to provide information that will help the staffs of I & R Units and the IIC of a building evaluate the IGE program that has been implemented in their building. Special attention will be given to the role of the unit leader in these activities. Such evaluation may also be carried out as a part of a district evaluation if there is more than one IGE school in the district.

THE PURPOSE OF PROGRAM EVALUATION IN IGE

It is one thing to evaluate individual students as they are progressing through the program but quite another to evaluate the instructional program itself. In the context of program evaluation, the term "evaluation" has a connotation that tends to make teachers reluctant to become involved in it. The unit leader and staff teachers may perceive evaluation of the instructional program as much more of a direct reflection on them than on the individual students. It is quite natural to defend an instructional program which is the product of many hours of hard work. If evaluation is seen as a threat to program development efforts, it will surely be feared, mistrusted, and avoided. However, when properly considered, program evaluation can be helpful. Evaluation of the instructional program can give the unit leader and staff the appropriate feedback about the consequences of their efforts so that accomplishments can be analyzed and used for program revision and improvement. It is important that the unit leader transmit this proper concept of program evaluation to the I & R Unit staff.

The purpose of program evaluation in IGE is to ensure that decisions about program efficiency, program effectiveness, and program modification are based on the best data possible. This means that all relevant data must be provided for each decision and that these data must be accurate and up to date. A useful definition of evaluation in this context is, "Evaluation is the process of delineating, obtaining, and providing useful information for judging decision alternatives" (Stufflebeam 1971, p. xiv). The discussion that follows is concerned with aspects of evaluation that are specific to IGE as well as those that are absolute and relative to any educational program.

Aspects of Evaluating the IGE Program

An important point to remember in evaluating the IGE program is that in most instances the evaluator is also the decision maker. That means that most of the decisions about program revision are made by the unit staff under the direction of the unit leader. The unit staff also has the responsibility of gathering and interpreting data in the evaluation. Such a dual role should do a great deal to ensure a commitment to the use of the results of the evaluation. It also provides the unit staff an understanding of the evaluation process so that evaluation activities will not be perceived as a threat. The unit staff is concerned with evaluation as it promotes changes in the instructional program. Such "formative" evaluation is the responsibility of the program implementers, the unit staff, because they are the closest to the program. They know the students, the materials, and the teaching techniques. The evaluation merely ensures that decisions about the program are based on all the relevant information and that this information is collected and reported in a systematic manner.

Another kind of program evaluation, "summative" evaluation, deals with an overall appraisal of the worth of the program. Essentially this kind of evaluation reaches a conclusion about whether the program is good or bad. However, data from a summative evaluation are *not* intended to be used for modifying instructional procedures. Such data would be used for selecting the most appropriate curriculum for a school, for example. It is also the case that a summative evaluation should *not* be conducted by persons directly involved in the instructional program. Since the unit leader is closely involved in the instruction, conducting summative evaluation is not an appropriate unit leader function. This does not mean that summative evaluation would never occur in IGE, though. Central staff of the school system might at times find it appropriate. However, because summative evaluation is not the responsibility of the unit leader and I & R staff, it will not be developed in this chapter. Rather, the emphasis is on formative evaluation focused on the instructional program decisions that face the I & R Unit staff.

Perhaps the clearest way to show the kind of evaluation of the instructional program the unit staff is involved with is to look at the information presented in Figure 16.1. Here, the shaded area in the figure represents the type of evaluation which is the concern of the I & R Unit staff. First, it is *formative* and it is designed to find the deficiencies and successes in developing an instructional program so that orderly revision can take place. Second, it is an *internal* evaluation conducted in-house by the persons responsible for implementing the program. And third, the evaluation is *based on the explicit objectives* of the program. That is, the learning program is judged relative to whether the stated objectives are achieved in the most efficient and effective way. Readers are referred to the suggested references at the end of this chapter.

Absolute and Relative Aspects of Evaluation

The evaluation of the instructional program would have two components —absolute and relative. The goal of both of these components would be to

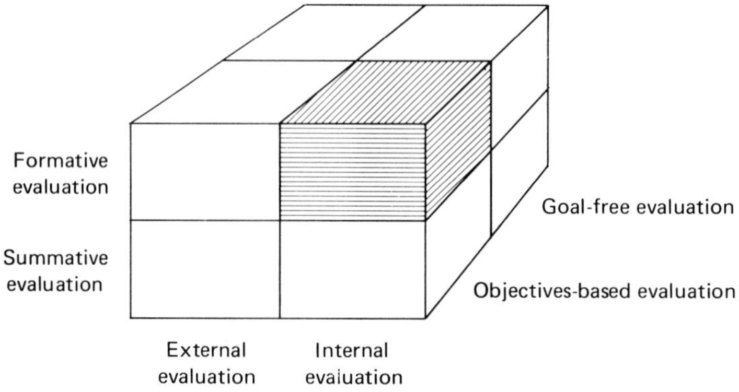

Fig. 16.1 Formative internal evaluation of program objectives.

provide the appropriate information to the unit staff to facilitate decisions among alternatives for program revision. In the absolute approach, the I & R Unit staff would set objectives for themselves in the same way in which they write objectives for students. In this way the instructional program would be evaluated according to how well the program objectives have been met. This approach is similar to the one in which the objectives of the principal, unit staff, and others are described in terms of the steps suggested for implementing an IGE program (Klausmeier, *et al.* 1971). These teacher objectives would be in the form of standards of student performance. For example, an objective might be that 80 percent of the students in the I & R Unit correctly master a particular instructional objective or set of objectives. Then the evaluation of the instructional program would be based on how well these unit objectives were met. Such information would help the unit staff identify where program revisions are needed.

In the relative approach to evaluation, which is really complementary to the first approach, one makes judgments relative to the performance of others. Comparisons can be made with other units, other schools, or previous classes. The goal statements of the I & R Unit in this context would be similar to "more of the students this year will master a particular objective(s) than mastered the same objective(s) last year." Again this kind of evaluative data would indicate where program revision should take place.

COLLECTING AND REPORTING DATA FOR PROGRAM EVALUATION

Regardless of whether either or both of the approaches described in the previous section are used, it is necessary for the unit staff to keep accurate records of student performance on the instructional objectives. For reasons discussed in Chapter 13, such records are essential for assessing pupil performance. Much of the data that can be used for evaluative decisions about the instructional program are the same data that were used in making programmatic decisions about individual students. However, the emphasis in program evaluation would be on the results of groups of students with an eye toward deciding what aspects of the instructional program seem to be successful and what aspects need additional attention.

Much of the data that can be used for evaluative decisions about the instructional program are the same data that were used in making programmatic decisions about individual students.

Collecting and Recording Data from Student Performances on Objectives

The initial format for collecting these data should be quite comprehensive although the data will probably later be summarized and reduced. The evaluation of the instructional program must consider the interaction of the students, the objectives, and the instructional strategies used to achieve these objectives. An example of the kind of reporting format that might be used for this purpose appears in Figure 16.2. In this record the progress of each student is recorded so that the unit staff can see which objectives required a great deal of recycling and which teaching strategies worked with different kinds of students. In Figure 16.2 the symbols M and X are used to indicate mastery and nonmastery, respectively. Some unit staff might choose to provide columns for additional recycles or for some descriptors of the students. However, the goal of such a recording format is to present a large amount of information as succinctly as possible so the record does not become too unwieldy.

Objective: Given a root word, the student is able to add or select affixes to make the context of the given sentence correct.

Student	Materials/strategy	Evaluation	Recycle strategy	Recycle Evaluation
Adams	Workbook/indep. study	X	Workbook/small group	M
Brown	Workbook/small group	M		
Cole	Workbook/small group	M		
Davis	Exercises/large group	M		
Early	Exercises/large group	X	Workbook/indep. study	M
.	.	.	.	.
.	.	.	.	.
.	.	.	.	.
.	.	.	.	.
.	.	.	.	.
.	.	.	.	.
.	.	.	.	.

Fig. 16.2 Record of a group of students on one objective.

In Chapter 13, suggestions were provided for summarizing the performance of individual students. At this point the emphasis is shifting from individual results to results of groups. Figure 16.3 deals with performance on a single objective, summarized over a group of students.

Objective	Students succeeding on first attempt	Students requiring 1 recycle	Students requiring 2 recycles	Students requiring more than 2 recycles
1	80	42	8	0
2	76	27	16	11
3	111	19	0	0
4	64	51	10	5
5	83	43	3	1
6	66	40	18	6
7	53	42	25	10
8	82	16	15	17
9	42	57	18	13
10	51	37	35	7

Fig. 16.3 Summarized performance data for 130 students.

Recording information in this way allows efficient comparisons across objectives as well as within objectives. A tabulation of student performance could be easily gathered from the reports of the separate objectives. For example, Figure 16.3 illustrates a chart of student performance for a unit of 130 students across a set of ten objectives. These data were gathered from ten charts like the one in Figure 16.2. Data reduction is critical because the record of each student's performance on every objective is too detailed for most decisions on the program level. Some form of reporting should be used to summarize these large amounts of data. In the following section several methods are presented as illustrative suggestions.

The unit leader is not responsible for collecting and summarizing all the data; that is the responsibility of the I & R Unit staff. However, the unit leader is responsible for organizing the evaluation within the unit and ensuring that the various tasks get done. The evaluation of the instructional program cuts across the several units in a school. This type of evaluation should be planned by the IIC. The unit leader as a member of the IIC is expected to participate in the planning and assist in the evaluation tasks.

Summarizing and Reporting Data from Student Performances on Objectives

There are several useful ways to report the performance of groups of students on the objectives in a reduced, synthesized form. One technique is to report at intervals along the sequence of objectives. Since IGE has in its instructional program an explicit statement of a continuum of objectives, reports of student performance could be reduced by reporting only for important objectives along the continuum. If objectives were judged to be equally important, then it might be reasonable to report what proportion of the students had mastered, say, every tenth objective. If some objectives are judged to be more important (weighted more heavily) to parents or more essential to later objectives, then these should be the objectives which are reported. In any event, such a reduction of data should facilitate decisions about whether the instructional program is as successful as is expected.

Another method is to report from clusters of homogeneous objectives. Here, the performance of each student in the unit on each objective would be synthesized by clustering objectives and reporting for clusters. For example, the report might indicate that 85 percent of the students in the unit have mastered all of the objectives which deal with the concept of "telling time." The problem with this approach is that it could be used effectively only when the students have all had the opportunity to attempt all the objectives in a given cluster.

The suggestions above deal only with a reduced description of student performance. No judgments have been made about the meaning of the reduced description. The evaluation of the instructional program suggests that judgment will be made about the worth of the program. Such judgments can be improved by explicitly stating the criteria to be used in the judgment. The following suggestions incorporate such criteria into the reporting of student performance data.

For example, the unit staff could decide to report along an expected time line for objectives. They could then establish a minimally acceptable schedule for the expected mastery of objectives, in much the same way that criteria levels are specified in instructional objectives for students. The synthesized reports of student data could be written to coincide with that schedule. It may be necessary to create two or three schedules for different student types, for example, rapid, average, or slow learners. It would also be wise to include only a few of the more important objectives on this time line of anticipated student performances. A more complete listing would lead to the curriculum rigidity that IGE was developed to overcome.

Finally, it might be decided that the unit staff would report for a weighted combination of objectives. The most concise reduction of student performance data could be done by assigning weights to each of the instructional objectives. Objectives would be assigned points according to their importance. Then the proportions of students who were successful on each objective and the weights (points) for those objectives would be combined to provide a single number which indicates program performance. Although the latter technique is potentially the most useful, it is probably the least used. Establishing weights can be a very complicated procedure but it does cause the unit staff to evaluate the objectives that they teach. This in itself is useful.

LINKS BETWEEN INTENTIONS AND ACTIVITIES

The description of student performance on the instructional objectives may be the most important data used in the evaluation of the instructional program, but it is not the only data to be considered. It is helpful to determine whether student achievement is congruent with the expectations of the I & R Unit staff. It is also very important to determine whether the instruction has actually taken place in a manner consistent with the intentions of the unit staff. For example, if the method of reporting combinations of weighted objectives were used, a unit staff would be required to establish the single numbers (representing the combinations of weights) that indicate minimal expectations. Then the actual weighted combination could be compared with the minimal expectation.

The evaluation of the consistency between the actual and intended instructional procedures would be quite subjective. It would, to a large extent, be based on the perceptions of the individual teachers of the unit. However, it would be relatively easy to identify gross departures from the intended procedures. These points would be discussed in the I & R Unit planning meetings and plans made to determine and correct the problem.

For example, suppose that upper intermediate students are working on objectives which deal with computing volumes of geometric solids. The unit staff has decided to supplement the textual material with a film which develops volume from animated cross sections of figures. Finally, a set of five plastic geometric solids is to be given to each student to manipulate to reinforce the points which were made in the text and in the film. Then for some reason, the film is not available. In such an instance, the evaluation of the effectiveness of the instructional program would have to take into consideration the possible effects of not following the intended plan. Since the plastic figures were designed to supplement the film, their effectiveness can only be partly assessed. The unit staff will not know how these materials would have worked in combination with the film.

Another example of a lack of correspondence between intended and actual classroom activities would be when an inquiry or discovery lesson evolves into a lecture dominated by the teachers or by a single student. The teachers monitoring such a group might not even be aware of the transition, but observers or tapes of the class would immediately make the problem known. Additional comments are made about this type of evaluation in the following section. It is the unit leader's responsibility to make certain that the unit staff evaluates agreement between intended and actual activities, and attempts to keep lack of agreement to a minimum.

Comparing What Was Planned with What Happened in the Instructional Program

It is difficult to make decisions about the instructional program without an accurate description of what actually goes on in the classroom. Successes and failures as indicated solely by student achievement data are insufficient clues about which techniques worked and which techniques failed. Before a technique can be judged successful or not, it must be shown that the technique was implemented in a manner which agrees with its design.

Suppose, for example, that a science unit of instruction on eclipses is taught for one week. After that time, it is reported that none of the students mastered all of the objectives for that unit. If taken at face value, it might suggest that the unit was poorly designed or, at least, that instruction was somehow inadequate. Such may be the case, but without additional information, that conclusion is not warranted. It may be that the objectives were not appropriate. It might also be that the unit was not taught in the manner in which it was expected to be taught.

If such is the case, a comparison would be made between the intended classroom activities, as specified in lesson plans, manuals, and curriculum guides and the actual classroom activities that took place. A record of the time spent in discussion of activities, in reading about eclipses, and with other materials would provide much of the descripticn of the classroom events. Students could indicate the availability of supplementary resources and any difficulty they had with the readings or other materials. Additional information could be taken from videotapes, interaction analyses, or other relevant data that might be available. When it is clear that the unit on eclipses was taught the way it was intended, then it has been given a fair chance to work and can be evaluated accordingly. Too frequently units, or whole curricular approaches, are rejected when they have not been tried out in the way they were designed to operate.

Comparing Student Progress under a Variety of Conditions

The purpose of an evaluation of the instructional program is primarily to suggest what program revisions might be desirable to improve student performance on the instructional objectives. This evaluation should provide data which allow the unit staff to determine whether decisions which have been made about students have resulted in satisfactory levels of student achievement.

Making decisions about student progress in the sequence of objectives was discussed in Chapter 13. Decisions about advancement, total recycling, or partial recycling are based on a wide range of data from a variety of sources. Although the decisions are the most reasonable judgments at the time, the evaluation of the instructional program provides a careful look at the consequences of those decisions.

For example, if for a particular set of instructional objectives there were a lot of recycled students, it would be wise to compare those students who were partially recycled to those students who were totally recycled. If those who were completely recycled did much better later on related objectives than did those who were partially recycled, it would suggest that the decision rule for partial recycling might not be adequate.

In the same manner, decisions to skip objectives or to change the sequence of objectives for particular students can be investigated. If these decisions result in no achievement losses, then they might suggest building additional options into the program.

The evaluation of the instructional program allows other kinds of interesting comparisons. It would probably be worth comparing the progress of students who worked on the same objective with different materials or modes of instruction. Another interesting comparison would be between those students who spent different amounts of time on a particular objective. All of these ministudies relate directly to the evaluation of the instructional program. Perhaps some combinations of time and materials are particularly ineffective with some kinds of students. If these comparisons are included as part of the evaluation, improvements and adjustments in the program may result. The whole matter of learning style which was discussed in Chapter 14 is relevant to this point, but since it is tangential to the focus of this chapter, it will not be pursued here.

Another critical comparison that should be made in any evaluation of the instructional program would be a comparison among success levels for objectives which require a great deal of recycling before most students complete the objective. This indicates possible points for a more intensive follow-up designed to isolate the reasons for so much recycling. It could be that some objectives have been left out of the sequence or that the criterion level is unrealistic or a host of other possibilities. However, these possibilities will not be investigated unless the unit staff takes a step back and looks at the program from a different perspective than just teachers immersed in the daily tasks of instruction. An evaluation of the instructional program will permit this desired perspective.

A related comparison that needs to be made is the objective-to-objective interface in the sequence of objectives. For example, there are many objectives which are considered to be essential prerequisites to more complex learning. Such an objective is called an enabling objective for subsequent objectives involving the more complex learning. The value of these enabling objectives can be somewhat established by determining how well students master the more complex behavior. Failure on the more complex task might suggest that the criterion level was set too low on the enabling objective. Success on the more complex task with minimal performance on the enabling objective might cause the unit staff to question how essential the enabling objective really is.

Comparing Short- and Long-Term Retention

A final suggested evaluation activity would be to include a delayed posttest of some of the objectives. Some students might perform above criterion on a posttest immediately following a unit of instruction but not be able to meet that same criterion a month later. If an objective dealt with a skill that was a component of a subsequent topic, it is likely that mastery would be retained because of its continued use. This would not be the case of other objectives. If a delayed posttest indicated that the level of mastery was not maintained over time, the unit staff would have to decide whether the effort spent teaching for that objective was wasted or if the efficiency that would be gained in remastering the objective is worth it.

For a specific example, think of a social studies unit on American Indians. An objective might be to match 20 Indian nations with their geographic locations. On a delayed posttest given two months after completion of the unit on American Indians, only half of the students can reach the criterion of 18 correct matches out of 20, although 90 percent of the students mastered it when the unit was taught. The I & R Unit staff would then have to decide among several alternatives. One choice might be that factual nature of the objective would suggest that such forgetting would naturally occur and should be of no concern. Another choice might be that perhaps the objective was a poor one in the first place and should be discarded. A third explanation might be that the objective was worthwhile because such exposure is desirable and perhaps some future anthropologist was given inspiration in that unit of instruction. Clearly these example explanations are hypothetical and perhaps contradictory, but the point to be made is that an evaluation of the instructional program needs to consider the long-term retention of mastery levels of student performance.

The purpose of the kinds of critical comparisons which are suggested here is to get unit leaders and unit staff thinking about the kinds of data that might be collected which would provide a base for decisions about program improvement. A checklist to help teachers in this process is presented on pages 497-499. When evaluation of the instructional program is ongoing, the interpretation of this kind of information provides ensurance that program revision will be based upon the most accurate and relevant data available. It is important that the evaluation of the instructional program helps the unit staff make decisions about the program while not imposing a time or resource burden. To do so efficiently, some structure needs to be maintained.

Checklist for evaluating a unit of instruction

Explanation:

1. Under each section space has been provided for any additional questions to be added by the unit staff.
2. A check in box "1" indicates a definite "yes" answer for an item; a check in box "5" indicates a definite "no" response; boxes 2, 3, and 4 are for varying degrees of attainment between yes and no.

I. Did the students:

A. Objectives	1	2	3	4	5	
1. help state the objectives?						1.
2. understand the objectives?						2.
3. accept the objectives as reasonable?						3.
B. Tasks						
1. help select activities to meet the objectives?						1.
2. understand the directions?						2.
3. use their time effectively?						3.
4. work on learning activities until they were completed?						4.
5. enjoy their activities?						5.
C. Performance						
1. meet objectives at the predetermined level?						1.
2. gain satisfaction from their achievements?						2.
3. work cooperatively with others in group situations?						3.
D. Other						
____________________						
____________________						
____________________						

II. Did the teachers:

A. Objectives						
1. correlate the instructional objectives with the general schoolwide objectives?						1.
2. clearly formulate the objectives in preplanning?						2.
3. state the objectives so that parents and students had a clear understanding of each objective?						3.
B. Activities						
1. identify activities for students appropriate to each objective?						1.
2. provide sufficient activities for attaining each objective?						2.

	1	2	3	4	5	
3. provide a variety of activities appropriate for different learning styles?						3.
4. maximize performance by using the talents and expertise of each team member?						4.
5. provide supplementary explanations and/or activities for the students who encountered difficulties?						5.

C. Performance

	1	2	3	4	5	
1. perform their duties as planned?						1.
2. work cooperatively with other team members?						2.
3. adjust their program to meet unanticipated needs or situations?						3.
4. enjoy teaching the unit of instruction?						4.

D. Assessments

	1	2	3	4	5	
1. provide paper-and-pencil assignments?						1.
2. use work samples for assessment?						2.
3. assess student performances?						3.
4. observe student behavior for assessment purposes?						4.

E. Other

	1	2	3	4	5
______________________					
______________________					
______________________					

III. Were the instructional materials and media:

A. Objectives

	1	2	3	4	5	
1. identified during planning?						1.
2. sufficient in number and variety to enable students to meet the objectives?						2.

B. Usefulness

	1	2	3	4	5	
1. readily available to meet student needs?						1.
2. accessible to unit staff members?						2.
3. properly scheduled to meet unit needs?						3.
4. coordinated with group size?						4.
5. in workable order?						5.
6. returned to their proper location after use?						6.

C. Other

	1	2	3	4	5
______________________					
______________________					
______________________					

	1	2	3	4	5	
IV. Did the facilities have:						
A. Space						
1. sufficient space available to meet all the planned activities?						1.
2. enough room to accommodate each group size?						2.
B. Quality of learning area						
1. appropriate furnishings (e.g., sink, rugs, tables, etc.)?						1.
2. an adequate acoustical atmosphere?						2.
3. freedom from distractions?						3.
4. a room atmosphere consistent with that of the activities and teaching style of the team member?						4.
5. a comfortable room temperature?						5.
C. Other						
______________________						
______________________						
______________________						

A STRUCTURE FOR EVALUATING THE INSTRUCTIONAL PROGRAM IN THE I & R UNIT

The same structure might not fit all units in IGE schools but some components are common to all of them. These components are presented in Figure 16.4 and each one is discussed below.

Identify Decision Points

For the evaluation to serve the decision makers, it is necessary that decision points must be identified well in advance. This allows enough time so that all necessary information and discussion can be brought to bear upon the decision. For example, if the decision is whether to revise the instructional program to improve the teaching of a particular objective, the lead time might be quite great if that objective was not to be taught again until the following year. However, for the purpose of efficiency it might be wise to restrict decisions about revision to two or three weeks after the completion of instruction for that objective. This ensures that experiences and data will be fresh in the minds of the unit staff. Such a time restriction would limit the kinds of data that could be gathered and synthesized before any decision was made.

Another example of the kinds of decisions that need to be identified well in advance would be with respect to deadlines that principals have for ordering materials and equipment. The selection of such materials is

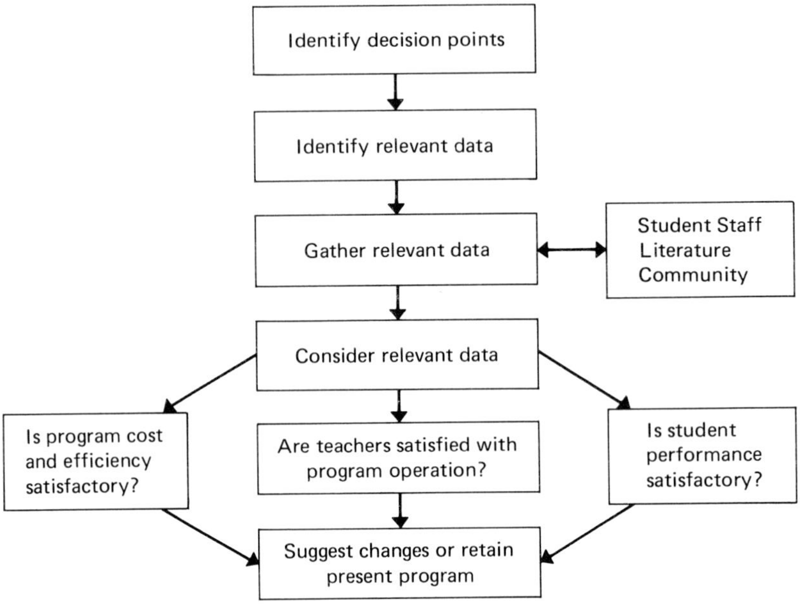

Fig. 16.4 Components of I & R Unit program evaluation.

frequently quite separated in time from the teaching of the corresponding units. These decision points are relatively inflexible and the evaluation of the instructional program must be timed so that adequate evaluative data can be presented to facilitate these decisions.

Identify Data Relevant to the Decision Points

Once the decision points are determined, the second step would be to identify the data which are relevant to those decisions. These data will be as varied as the decision requires. Certainly for most considerations, student and teacher opinion about previous attempts at solutions to similar problems and the record of student performance relative to the decision will need to be looked at. It is usually worthwhile to include input from as many sources as possible—students, teachers, administrators, and parents. In addition, the professional literature is helpful to the staff in making most of these decisions.

Gather Relevant Data

Once the pertinent data for the decisions are identified, it is necessary to provide for the collection and synthesis of the data. It would probably be the responsibility of the unit leader to make certain that these tasks get done. Different tasks would be assigned to different people in the team, but one person in the team would probably be assigned the responsibility of all the data collection. Surely, though, the task of synthesizing the various kinds of data would be a responsibility of all of the unit staff. Such a synthesis would likely require extensive discussion of the relative importance of the various kinds of information relevant to a decision. For example, in the decision on how to teach for a particular objective the next time around, it is likely that the cost of the present techniques in terms of personnel and materials would be compared to the cost of alternative techniques. Also the performance of students would be compared to the expected performance levels that the unit staff thought was reasonable. These considerations would be most fully developed at a unit meeting where all could provide input. Clearly the final decision would probably emerge from such a session where alternatives are weighed and consensus is reached. The decision must be a decision of the unit staff as a whole if it is to be functional. In IGE, the multiunit organization and the IPM provide for this kind of deliberation and implementation. In summary, when a decision point is identified, all relevant data need to be available.

Consider Relevant Data

Relevant data would be defined as all information which bears on the effectiveness and efficiency of the instructional program with regard to the decision in question. Effectiveness would surely be determined by the student performance on the objectives. The important consideration would be whether student performance was in agreement with the expectations of the teachers, the parents, and society. To make such judgments, an assessment must be made of these criteria as well as the student performance data.

Information on the efficiency of the instructional program would include costs in terms of money and time. Student time as well as unit staff time would have to be recorded to see whether particular strategies require more resources than expected. Time spent in planning and time spent in instruction should be analyzed separately so that specific corrective decisions could be made as necessary. The comparative resource needs of different instructional activities would provide part of the rationale of program change.

Check Teacher and Student Satisfaction

Points of satisfaction with the present instructional program should be obtained from teachers and students so that corrective measures can be taken when appropriate. Satisfaction ratings could be obtained from a sample instrument on which teachers and students were asked to rate a number of relevant items on a five-point scale. The scale could range from very satisfied through fairly satisfied, no special feeling, somewhat dissatisfied, and very dissatisfied. Also it should be determined whether what is being taught and the methods for teaching it are consistent with the best thinking in the discipline. For example, a unit of instruction on black scientists should be able to stand on its own merits if reviewed by historians.

Both of the points discussed above could be carried out by subcommittees within the I & R Unit or the IIC. Teachers with special expertise or interest in the topic could act on the appropriate committee. This is more efficient than the entire unit or IIC staff attempting to work on all problems.

Decide to Change or Retain the Present Instructional Program

When all of the data from the components discussed previously are considered, the I & R Unit staff, coordinated by the unit leader, has to make the decision about whether to make minor or major changes or to retain the present instructional program. Most instructional programs undergo minor changes as the result of an evaluation. This is the way in which programs are kept vital and up to date. If major changes are to be made in a program, it means a lot of work for the unit staff. Such a decision should be based on sound data from the evaluation. If the decision points have been selected carefully and relevant data identified and gathered accurately along with careful evaluation of satisfaction, the unit staff should have little difficulty choosing among the alternatives. A lack of consensus in making decisions about the instructional program might suggest that some additional data are needed. Or it may suggest that the consequences of any compromise decision should be carefully monitored to provide a better basis for similar or related decision points in the future.

COORDINATING EVALUATION ACROSS UNITS

Many of the decisions served by the evaluation within a given I & R Unit require relevant information from other units. In other instances, the data gathering and recording can be done consistently in several units. This minimizes inefficiency and misinterpretation when the several units share the data. A systemwide evaluation structure ensures that these issues are considered. Input into such a systemwide evaluation should clearly be one function of the IIC. Responsibility for the systemwide evaluation should rest with the SPC.

Although the unit staffs have autonomy in their evaluation activities within the unit, the IIC members have a unique opportunity, and in fact a responsibility, to share both their evaluation activities and the results of the evaluations of their separate units. Such sharing may help some units avoid problems encountered by others. This sharing also shows what relevant information used by one group may have not been used by others. Ideas, suggestions, and pooled results obtained at an IIC meeting would surely improve the evaluation activities within the units.

Another function that the IIC could provide is that of selecting evaluation instruments for the units. If an attitude questionnaire is to be given to the students of two or more units, the IIC members could select or develop the appropriate instrument and provide guidelines for its administration. When the same scale is given under consistent conditions, the data may be meaningfully combined and comparisons can be made between different groups of students.

The IIC would also have the responsibility for selecting standardized norm-referenced achievement tests so that student performance can be interpreted relative to a wider base than just the students within that particular geographic location. Such norm-referenced tests can be useful when the items of the test are representative of the objectives of the IGE program. Any mismatch would unfairly penalize the IGE program because student knowledge in some areas would be unmeasured and some of the test items would be over topics that were not taught among the IGE objectives. If the IIC can select an appropriate achievement test which closely matches the objectives of their program, then comparison can be made between the achievement of the students in the units and the students in the norm group.

The coordination of evaluation across the units will probably not take up a great deal of the time of the IIC. It will, though, provide a communication link and a consistency of methods that will help unite the units in a total effort to improve the instructional program.

EXTERNAL EVALUATION OF THE INSTRUCTIONAL PROGRAM

The evaluation of the instructional program discussed thus far has dealt with the decisions that the unit leader and unit staff must make to facilitate its ongoing improvement. These decisions are primarily concerned with the instruction in a specific I & R Unit for a specific group of students relative to the criteria levels established in the unit's objectives.

A broader kind of evaluation of the instructional program might also be considered. The components of this type of evaluation would include comparison with other IGE and traditional schools. Much of this evaluation could be done with norm-referenced tests. It is also conceivable that some of this evaluation might be done by an outside evaluator, not a part of the unit staff. Such evaluators would present an objective perspective because they would have no vested interest in the development of the learning program to that point. In either case, whether the external evaluation is from norm-referenced tests or from an outside evaluator the purpose is to provide a kind of comparative quality assessment.

For example, a school which is just beginning to implement the IGE model might be interested in using an external evaluator for two reasons. First, this evaluator might monitor the implementation to confirm whether the development is consistent with IGE philosophy. Rates of change, faculty and student attitudes would provide most of the relevant data. A second reason for using an external evaluator would be for comparative quality control reasons. The focus of this investigation would be to assure parents and school boards that the transition to IGE has not been accompanied by a lowering of performance during the changeover. The external evaluator would be more credible than in-house staff who are promoting the curricular change.

It must be understood that the goals for these internal and external evaluations are quite different. The internal evaluation is done by the unit staff so that day-to-day program operation can be improved. The external evaluation is done to judge whether the program is working as well as alternative or similar instructional programs.

It is unlikely that an external evaluation would provide the detailed information needed by the unit staff for effective decision making about the instructional program. The usefulness of an external evaluation is acknowledged but not elaborated on in this chapter because it is not an immediate or major concern of the unit leader.

SUMMARY

This chapter has been concerned with the process of evaluating the instructional program with emphasis on the role the unit leader and members of the I & R Unit staff plays in it. The discussion has considered the purpose of program evaluation in IGE, procedures for collecting and reporting data, the links or comparisons between the intentions of the unit staff and what actually occurred during the implementation, along with a structure or model for the unit staff to use in evaluating their program. It also included information on how coordination across units could make the evaluation more effective and efficient, and the place of external evaluation in program evaluation.

The chapter emphasizes that improvement of the instructional program is dependent upon a careful and systematic evaluation of the strengths and weaknesses of the present program. Only then will revision decisions be based on all the pertinent data instead of on the whims and hunches of teachers and administrators. The evaluative process within the unit should be systematic, comprehensive, and open. In that way, evaluation will improve the instructional program. When the unit leader and unit staff understand and participate in the evaluation, then the evaluation is not feared, but rather it is welcomed.

REFERENCES

Klausmeier, H. J., M. R. Quilling, J. S. Sorenson, R. S. Way and G. R. Glasrud 1971. *Individually guided education and the multiunit elementary school; guidelines for implementation.* Madison, Wisc.: Wisconsin Research and Development Center for Cognitive Learning.

Scriven, M. 1972. Pros and cons about goal-free evaluation. *Evaluation Comment* **3:** 1-4.

——— 1967. The methodology of evaluation, in *Perspective of curriculum evaluation.* AERA monograph, No. 1. Chicago: Rand McNally.

Stake, R. E. 1967. The countenance of educational evaluation. *Teachers College Record* **68:** 523-540.

Stufflebeam, D. L. (ed.) 1971. *Educational evaluation and decision making.* Itasca: Peacock.

Worthen, B. R. and J. R. Sanders 1973. *Educational evaluation: theory and practice.* Worthington, Ohio: Jones.

17

Two Years of IGE in Our School: A Case Study

Barbara B. Berry
Juanita S. Sorenson

Objectives

After reading this chapter, the reader will be able:

- To indicate the strategy used by one I & R Unit staff to carry out instructional programming for individual students in mathematics, ages 8-10, over a two-year period.
- To adapt the strategy used by one I & R Unit to plan and implement instructional programming in mathematics or some other content area for the particular students in their I & R Unit and building.

In this chapter, a unit leader shares her experiences of how her I & R Unit staff implemented instructional programming in mathematics and two procedures in Individually Guided Motivation (IGM) in her school. This case study covers a two-year period and is told informally by the unit leader. The reader is asked to note how content and procedures described in the preceding chapters of this book are used in a practical school setting.

OVERVIEW AND DESCRIPTION OF THE SCHOOL

Our school is completing its third year of operation as an IGE school. As with many schools, we implemented the Word Attack area of the *Wisconsin Design for Reading Skill Development* (WDRSD) first, and then added Study skills and Comprehension. After the first year of using the WDRSD, we wanted to implement instructional programming in another content area, and our IIC decided on mathematics. We felt the organization and management techniques of the WDRSD could be applied to mathematics. The organization of the WDRSD was systematic, yet it allowed the teachers to teach the skill in their own style and for the benefit of the students. We felt we were truly meeting all children's reading needs because we were able to determine each student's specific needs and then group together those who needed to learn a particular skill. The WDRSD program seemed very workable for the teacher who still taught a group, but with each child learning a needed skill. Many skills could be taught, but one teacher wasn't responsible for all of them at one time.

During the two years of implementing instructional programming in Word Attack skills (WDRSD), we had used a "modern math" program based on a textbook from a well-known publisher. We grouped the students by age/grade level and then by achievement. Each group was taught page by page with little regard for the student's knowledge of the material or rate and style of learning. But before we talk about how we developed our mathematics program, let's look at the characteristics of our school and its students.

Our school is located in a white, middle-class neighborhood in an industrial city of about 20,000. Economic background of the families is about 10 percent supported by government social service and 10 percent in the upper middle-class. The remaining families would be classified in the low-middle and middle-income group. About 50 percent of the mothers work outside the home.

The students generally score "average" to "above average" in achievement on national standardized tests. Each grade level seems to have two or three students who are much lower than average.

The school is organized into three I & R Units: Unit A, ages 5-8; Unit B, 8-10; and Unit C, 10-12. Each unit has about 120 students and four teachers. One teacher is the unit leader. We have volunteer parents and a Neighborhood Youth Corps girl that do clerical work. Parents also work with some students on a one-to-one basis in the reading program and help staff the library. Special teachers that are part of the staff include a librarian who is in the building a day and a half each week, gym teachers who have each class twice a week, and a music and an art teacher who come once a week. We have a full-time principal who is very much in favor of teaching to the child's individual needs and who gets involved with our instructional program.

Development and Implementation of the Mathematics Program—The First Year

After our IIC decided that our school would develop a mathematics program using the WDRSD format as a model, we had to decide what kind of program to have. Would it be continuous progress? Would it be for all students? These and similar questions were discussed by teachers and unit leaders and their ideas summarized for presentation to the IIC.

Background on the Mathematics Program

Prior to the IIC's decision, there had been much criticism of the existing mathematics program. Many teachers felt that the better students were not being challenged enough, and that some of the poorer students were frustrated because they were being pushed along whether they really learned the concepts or not. A few teachers had experimented on their own with some type of individualized mathematics. For example, one teacher let the able students work at their own rates and tested them every 5 to 10 days. These students made excellent progress—some finishing all the work for their grade level and part of the next grade's work. They did well on the tests for the units of instruction and generally developed good study habits.

At one IIC meeting when we talked about developing instructional programming for individual students in mathematics, we found that many teachers had similar ideas. Most of the teachers of slower students felt they were pushing them along without mastering very much. This lack of accomplishment dampened these students' interest or motivation for mathematics.

Setting Schoolwide Objectives in the IIC

It was a consensus of the I & R Unit staffs that instructional programming for individual students in mathematics should be the emphasis the following year. The IIC then appointed a committee of teachers interested in mathematics to write the schoolwide, general objectives. The principal, one teacher from each unit, and a unit leader (the writer of this chapter) were on this committee. The committee agreed to use the Instructional Programming Model (IPM) as a guide to organizing their efforts. Instead of "reinventing the wheel," they adopted the general objectives listed in the *Guidelines to Mathematics* (Wisconsin Department of Public Instruction, 1972). These formed the schoolwide, general objectives as stated in Step 1 of the IPM. Excerpts from these objectives are presented in Figure 17.1. Members of the committee then took the general objectives for the age level students in their I & R Units back to the unit meeting and discussed them with the unit teachers.

Addition:
70 percent of the students will be able to add rational numbers expressed in "terminating" decimal form by age 12;
90 percent by age 13, and
99 percent by age 14.

Subtraction:
65 percent of the students will be able to subtract rational numbers expressed in "terminating" decimal form by age 12;
80 percent by age 13, and
99 percent by age 14.

Multiplication:
60 percent of the students will be able to use sentence forms to generalize the commutative property of multiplication for rational numbers in any form by age 12;
75 percent by age 14, and
99 percent by age 16.

Division:
50 percent of the students will be able to divide rational numbers expressed in repeating form by age 12;
70 percent by age 14, and
99 percent by age 16.

Fig. 17.1 Excerpts from Hoover School's general objectives in math. Hoover Elementary School, Neenah, Wisconsin.

Setting Instructional Objectives in the I & R Units

Once the general objectives were agreed upon, each I & R Unit identified the instructional objectives for their age/grade level of children. The remainder of this narrative will focus on the 120 children, ages 8-10, in my unit, Unit B, and the teachers and aide who worked with them.

For specific instructional objectives, one resource was *A Hierarchy of Student Behavioral Objectives K-8* (Wisconsin PACT School Mathematics Committee, 1973). These objectives had been developed by a team of teachers and mathematics experts to help teachers individualize their instruction of elementary mathematics. The objectives are listed in a prerequisite and sequential order. (These objectives were presented for 5- to 12-year-olds in Chapter 12 of this book).

Another source of specific objectives was the textbook used throughout the school system. It listed an objective for each lesson. This organization was a great help in fitting an already developed textbook program into an individualized program with its own objectives.

Coordinating and Developing Materials

Once the specific instructional objectives were selected by our I & R Unit for the 8- to 10-year-olds, the actual organization of the program could begin. We had already gotten rid of the complaints of the "old" program, so now we were ready to begin planning for the new program. From our experience with the WDRSD, we knew that once we had the objectives, we needed to identify pretests, posttests, and instructional materials.

Over the previous summer, the unit leader had written the contracts for the addition and subtraction parts of the grade 4 book to correlate with the objectives and the materials available in the school. This was done as the project part of a university graduate course in individualizing instruction. In this course, the unit leader also learned a great deal about IGE instructional programming for the individual student and test construction.

The format of these contracts provided a base for development of the program. Each unit of instruction for addition, subtraction, multiplication, division, geometry, and fractions was subdivided into several parts. Then, a contract was developed for each part. Each contract contained one to four related objectives, blanks for pretest and posttest scores, assignments, and activities. Contracts were designed for use by the child, teacher, and parent. The child would use the contract to find out what was to be learned to keep track of assignments, and as a source of games and activities that were available for learning the material. The teacher would use the contract as a teaching guide, an instrument to monitor the child's progress, a record of information, and as a report to the parents. Parents would use it to find out what and how their child was learning. An example of a contract on addition and subtraction facts is given in Figure 17.2.

For several reasons the contracts were written to be short enough to fit on one page. First, the child should be able to complete the contract in a few days to three weeks, thus experiencing a feeling of success. The second reason was management. The contracts were stapled to the outside of a folder kept by the student. It would be cumbersome to manage a contract more than one page long. The third reason was testing. When the contracts were kept short with only a few objectives, the tests could be thorough, but take only a few minutes to administer.

Devising Assessment Instruments

At least five pre- and postassessment items were developed for each objective. Preassessments were designed to be used as diagnostic tests at the beginning of each part of a unit of instruction. The postassessments were

Name ________________
Date begun ________________

Minimum

Objectives: (Note: All the objectives will have an accuracy level of 80 percent unless otherwise indicated.)

You will be able to:

1. write addition and subtraction facts through the sums of 18.
2. use the associative property of addition in the set of whole numbers.

Pretest score: If your score is higher than 80 percent, take Pretest B. If your score is lower than 80 percent, do the assignments.

Score .... ________

Assignments: Write your score for the page or pages after you correct your work. Unless another book is given, the work is from the Houghton-Mifflin book.

Date	*What and how much to do*	*Score*
________	28/1-7; 29/1-4, 9-17	/ 20
________	30/1-47	/ 47
________	34/1-9, 15-20; 35/odd	/ 33
________	37/1-16	/ 16
________	Workbook page 10/1-13	/ 13
________	Program practice, 13/1-10	/ 10

Activities: Dealer Up, Partners, Lonesome George, Ferris Wheel, Lost in the Woods, Concentration, Flash Card Race, Find the 10s

Posttest A: Take this test when you have done the assignments and have corrected any mistakes.

Score .... ________
Signed ________________
Date completed ________________

Fig. 17.2 Contract for addition and subtraction 4, Part A.

to be used after a student completed the activities for each part of a unit of instruction. Assessments usually covered from one to three objectives, depending on their difficulty. An assessment was divided into sections which corresponded to particular objectives. To aid the teachers, the assignment pages covered by the sections were included on the test. An example of a posttest is presented in Figure 17.3.

A vital part of any instructional programming for individual students is the immediate correction of tests and feedback to the student. If correcting is cumbersome, it slows down the process and weakens the feedback. To alleviate this problem, our tests were organized in a vertical format, and a simple correction card like the one in Figure 17.4 was developed. This card was used to score a two-page test with 14 items on one page (see lefthand column of answers) and six items (see righthand column answers) on the other. At a glance, the teacher or aide could correct the test.

Name ______________________

Score ______________________

Addition and Subtraction 4
Posttest A (Minimum)
Use after Program practice, p. 13

I. Write the sums or missing addends.

1. 3 + 6 = ________
2. 2 + 4 = ________
3. 10 − 4 = ________
4. 4 + 9 = ________
5. 5 + 6 = ________
6. 11 − 2 = ________
7. 6 + 7 = ________
8. 7 − 4 = ________
9. 4 + 7 = ________
10. 14 − 8 = ________
11. 2 + 9 = ________
12. 16 − 8 = ________
13. 5 + 7 = ________
14. 18 − 9 = ________

II. Rewrite the equations, grouping the way the mark ( ) tells you.

15. 8 + (3 + 6) = ________
16. (3 + 4) + 9 = ________
17. 4 + (2 + 5) = ________
18. (2 + 5) + 6 = ________
19. 3 + (6 + 2) = ________
20. 5 + (4 + 3) = ________

Fig. 17.3 Example of a posttest for addition and subtraction 4, Part A.

The middle columns are a score table. To make storing and organizing the cards easier for a given unit of instruction, all cards were made the same color and size. Note that the answer card in Figure 17.4 is for the posttest in Figure 17.3.

Implementing the Program

To begin a unit of instruction, a student took the pretest for Part A. Anyone who scored at least 80 percent, our mastery level, on the test was not required to do the assignment for Part A. On the student's contract would be recorded the pretest score, teacher's signature, and date of pretest to be taken home as a progress report. The student then began the pretest for Part B, and so forth.

If a student did not master a pretest, the teacher determined what assignments in that part should be done. Missing all the objectives required doing all the assignments. However, if the student missed questions on one objective only, the teacher decided if it was appropriate for the student to work on that objective only.

When a student began work on a part of a unit of instruction, the contract was stapled to the outside of a folder. The contract was dated as to when it was begun and completed. The student recorded progress on the sheet and kept the work inside the folder. Upon completion of the assignments, the folder was reviewed by the teacher for accuracy in the

Answer card

Addition and Subtraction 4 Posttest A (Minimum)			
Answer	Number wrong	Percent score	Answer
I.			
9			8 + 9
6			7 + 9
6			4 + 7
13	−1	95	7 + 6
11	−2	90	3 + 8
	−3	85	
9	−4	80	5 + 7
13	−5	75	
	−6	70	
3	−7	65	
11	−8	60	
	−9	55	
6	−10	50	
11	−11	45	
	−12	40	
8	−13	35	
12	−14	30	
	−15	25	
9	−16	20	

Fig. 17.4 Posttest answer card.

work, and the student took the appropriate posttest. The teacher signed, dated, and wrote the posttest score on the contract, which was then taken home as a student progress report.

The objectives were included on the contract and written in simple language that both 8- to 10-year-olds and parents could understand. The total number of problems covered in one assignment was given on the sheet so students could record their results and the teacher could quickly check their progress.

Grouping the students. Students were grouped for instruction according to the skills they had not mastered on the pretest. Teachers were assigned to student groups based on their strengths, interests, and different teaching styles. One teacher had students who needed addition work, another multiplication work, and so on. With attainment of mastery of objectives on all the contracts in that particular area, the student was transferred to another group which was working with contracts which contained objectives the student had not mastered. This became quite a logistics problem. Sometimes one room would be overflowing with students while another had only a few students. Each week at the unit meeting we discussed the numbers problems and reassigned students to make the groups more equal in size.

Developing a resource file. After seeing the benefits of a well-supplied teacher's resource file (in the WDRSD program) the I & R Unit staff decided we should make one for mathematics. We used some unit planning time to scour catalogs and ordered second, third, and fourth grade math workbooks from many companies. During the inservice day we pulled them apart and arranged them as a resource file. Now, if teachers need more resources to teach a particular objective they can go to the file and pull out what is needed.

It took time to build up a supply of materials that could be used in a program. At spring budgeting time during the first year in the mathematics program, the unit staff decided it needed still more material to use as reinforcement or supplement. We ordered tapes and kits and games, and branched away from all written material. With the new materials, the program was even stronger. An aide or volunteer now can monitor the students using the tapes. The tapes can be used either for remedial work or for introduction to a new skill. As with any program, as time goes by refinements and additions will be made.

Evaluating and Improving the Program

We constantly evaluate the programs we use in our I & R Unit. However, the major evaluation comes at the end of each year of the program—usually in April. First, we brainstorm to get a list of all the problems we've had, or areas that need improvement. In April of the first year of the mathematics program, we agreed to make the following changes:

1. put more emphasis on basic mathematics facts
2. differentiate objectives and assignments according to the achievement of the students
3. develop more games and activities as learning materials
4. gear activities to different learning styles of students

Making these improvements became our goals for the next school year. Some teachers started on these during the summer and made games to accompany the contracts. The games were designed to fit into a manila envelope for easy filing and storing. Each envelope was labeled with the name of the activity. When the set of games is complete there will be at least one game or activity for each objective. The students may use the games as an instructional tool, as a review, or, depending on the group they are in, as a reward for finishing their work before the end of the day.

All during the first year, it had bothered us that lower achieving math students were being required to meet the same objectives as the others but at a different rate. Many of them became frustrated and discouraged with so many different ways of doing problems in "new math." We decided that the unit leader should discuss this problem with the IIC for their opinions. We wanted to develop a minimum program for low achieving students. This would affect how much they would be exposed to when they got into the upper I & R Unit.

The problem was brought up at the next IIC meeting. The IIC discussed it and the other unit leaders then discussed it with their staff teachers. We found that our unit was not alone in this opinion. The IIC decided, after considerable discussion, that a three-level mathematics program would be appropriate to meet the needs of all individual students. The A level would contain mathematics objectives to be mastered by all students and would include the computational skills of addition, subtraction, multiplication, and division. The B level would contain objectives to be learned by students who completed A level. We estimated that 40-60 percent of our students would complete B level objectives. The C level objectives would be for the students who completed B level and would generally be the higher achieving students. (The rationale for leveling objectives and examples of levels of objectives in math are discussed in Chapter 12 of this book.)

The IIC asked each I & R Unit to classify the objectives in the program according to these levels. The mathematics committee then made slight revisions so that the total skill would be learned sequentially within a level.

Besides differentiating objectives according to children's achievement, our unit staff felt skill groups should be geared to different styles of learning. We had some students who learned best in an independent atmosphere. These students could follow written directions well and would ask questions of a teacher when they did not understand something.

We also had some students who had not achieved at grade level on standardized tests in mathematics. Most of them also learned best in a structured learning situation where a lesson is presented by the teacher, worked on by the students, and corrected when finished. These were the ones who had not been successful in math and found it confusing and frustrating. And, of course, there were the students who were a combination of the extremes. There were also students who learned best from manipulative materials and games. These considerations fit well with the designation of objectives at three levels (see Figure 12.1).

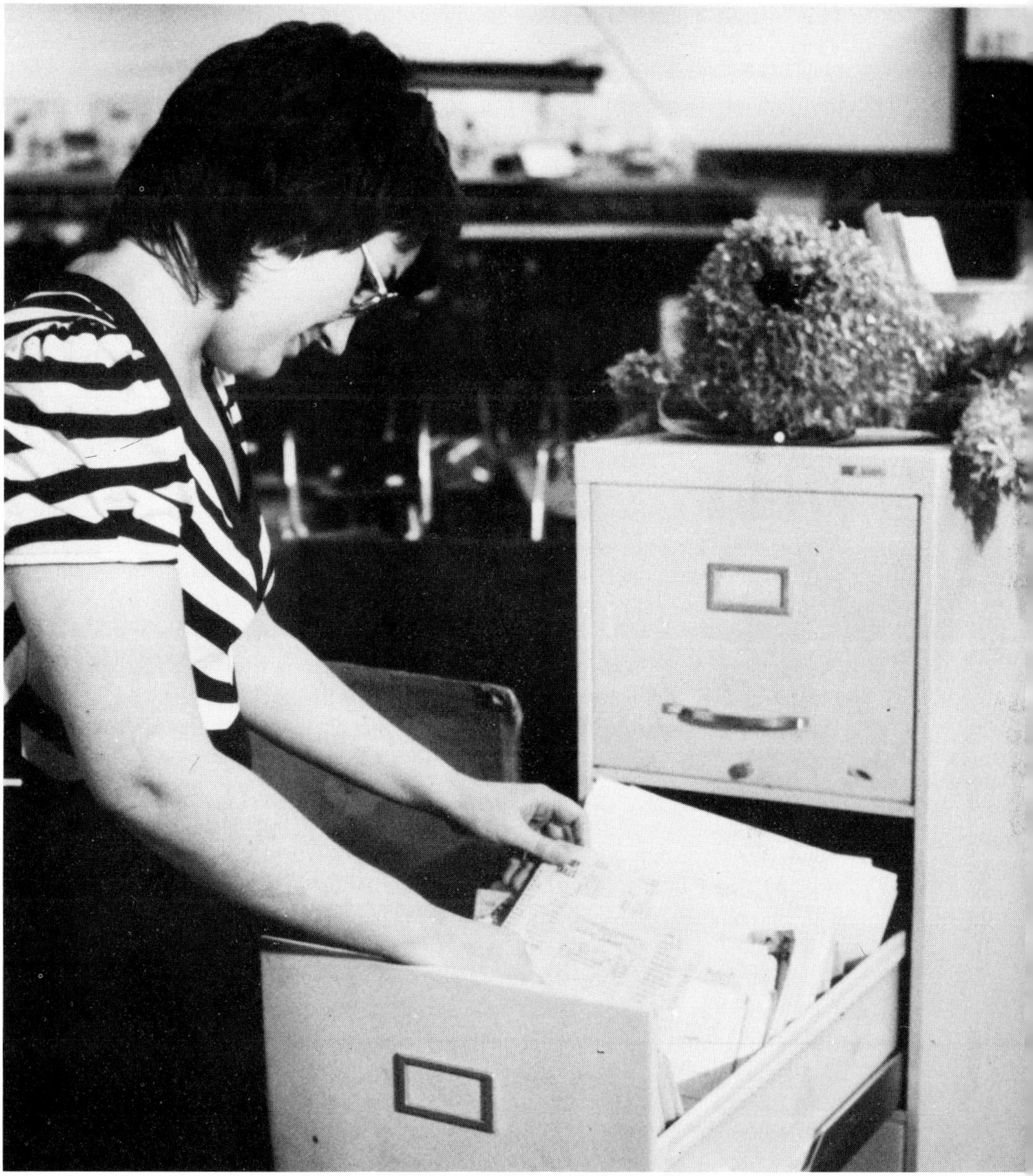

After seeing the benefits of a well-supplied teacher's resource file, the I & R Unit staff decided to make one for mathematics.

The Second Year: Continuing Mathematics and Adding IGM

During the second year of the mathematics program, the unit staff decided to form eight groups. Each teacher had two groups. Two teachers had very structured groups working on the A level objectives and an independent group working on all three levels of objectives. A third teacher taught the younger children on B and C level objectives and the fourth taught older children who were working on B and C level objectives. The two teachers with structured groups each began with one group of 25-30 children, but soon divided them into two or three smaller groups. These students had a specified amount of time in which to complete the work.

The contracts were revised so that the objectives, assignments, and tests were on the three levels. Objectives for computational skills of addition, subtraction, multiplication, and division were at Level A. Fractions were added to Level B, and plane and solid geometry, bases other than 10, and exponents were part of the Level C program.

Children progressed through the program basically the same regardless of the type of learning situation they were in. First, the independent group functioned as it had the previous year. These students used all three levels of objectives. The students using the Level A objectives in a structured class were given a pretest at the beginning of a part of the unit of instruction. Very seldom did any students pass a pretest. If they passed, they could work on the next contract or with the activities for the test they passed. Students who did not pass the pretest worked on assignments each day with the teacher presenting the lesson. The group worked on problems together, and then completed the assignment. The teacher deviated from the assignments whenever the students needed more reinforcement. When assignments were completed, students took the posttest. Those that passed it worked with the activities or could have "vacation" (working on something they brought to class). Those students that didn't pass worked on more assignments with the teacher or with another student.

Students in a semistructured situation were allowed to work at their own rate, but teachers found that some of them didn't get much done and others were not passing the posttests consistently. They decided to divide the group into four subgroups. Each subgroup took a pretest, and those who passed could take the next test and were allowed to work completely on their own. Those that did not pass the pretest, which was often most of them, began the contract together. The teacher explained a new procedure about every two days. After most of the students had completed half of the contract, a testing date was set. Students who finished their contracts before the testing date could use the games and activities for that contract as enrichment or work on more advanced objectives that were appropriate to independent study. Other students were expected to be finished by the testing date. After the test, a few days were allowed for those who did not pass the test to do additional work.

ASSIGNING AND REASSIGNING STUDENTS TO GROUPS

About this time, you might be wondering, "How are the students assigned to the groups?" In the first year, students had been assigned to groups during the first three or four weeks of the school year. During this time, all students in the unit were taught the same material on sets and numeration. At the end of the unit of instruction, the teachers decided where the children would be placed. Students definitely would be changed later as the need arose. To determine students for each group, the unit teachers used the following criteria:

1. mathematics achievement on a standardized test
2. progress in the program during the first three to four weeks
3. student's best style of learning
4. teacher judgment of maturity and needs

The criteria cannot be followed in any set order, but we tried to fit the child's need to the kind of learning situation first. We felt that children must first be in an environment or situation where they can perform best. Then we considered the achievement level or how much is expected of the child.

The students in the structured classes were at least one year below "grade level" according to achievement scores. They also were the ones who made slow progress while working on sets and numbers. Some of these students originally were in the less structured class, but were not able to complete their work and had trouble following directions.

The students in the independent group generally were above average in ability and achieved at least one year above "grade level." They also finished their work quickly and correctly at the beginning of the year. They followed written directions and worked well by themselves.

Not all of the students in the middle group were able to do well in an independent situation. Some started in the independent group but did not make very good progress. They were transferred into the more structured situations. These students had average ability and achievement, with some exceptions. A few students who had lower ability were placed in the independent group and functioned well there. This gave them a chance to practice more independent work habits.

Whenever a child didn't seem to be making appropriate progress in the learning situation, the teacher discussed it informally with the unit leader. The teacher and unit leader usually had some ideas that were tried. If no change occurred, the entire unit staff discussed the situation. Sometimes it was a personality clash or something else the child's mathematics teacher was not aware of. Unit teachers were able to help find the problem by observing the teacher's group and talking to the student. Other teachers sometimes had other information that helped to explain the student's poor progress. This discussion and search for solutions took cooperation and professionalism on the part of the unit members. If it was not there, the unit leader had to bring the teachers to that point by example and guidance.

When we placed students into groups according to their needs and learning styles, we had to remember to remain flexible. Even though we used many criteria to group students, sometimes they just didn't function effectively in the group they were placed in. We always allowed room for regrouping individual students to suit their particular needs.

Monitoring Student Progress

In instructional programming for individual students, there has to be accurate monitoring of what the child learns. In a self-contained classroom the teacher does not have to be concerned about another teacher understanding her or his grading system. However, in an IGE program all teachers in the I & R Unit will need to be able to interpret every other teacher's record keeping.

Our teachers decided at the beginning of the second year to keep student's tests in separate files. They would be available at conferences and to analyze for remedial work. This worked well except that tests often piled up before they got filed. It was also hard to compare the child's progress with that of other group members quickly. Two teachers tried recording test results in a record book, and another teacher enlarged upon the idea. The idea was to record the scores on a chart like the one in Figure 17.5. This chart was stapled to the outside of a file folder. When a child completed a test and it was corrected, the teacher recorded the test score and slipped the test into the folder. Periodically, our Neighborhood Youth Corps person would file these tests in the child's individual folder and record the scores on a form like Figure 17.6. This seemed an answer to our problems. We all adopted the method. This also allowed one teacher to monitor and act as advisor for a group of 25-30 children.

Reporting to Parents

One important aspect of record keeping is reporting it to the parents. Our I & R Unit was worried about this at first. How much should we tell parents? How often? What are they interested in? Last year our school

Student's name	Addition and subtraction									Multiplication and division													
	A	A		B	B		C	C		A	A		B	B		C	C		D	D		E	E
Scott A.	80			40	80		28	93		65	90												
Eric E.	40	85		0	90		21	80		0	60												
Robert H.	85			75	100		79	100		45	95												
Mike K.	95			15	85			93		55	95												
Tammy L.	95			80	100		57	93		45	90												
Lori L.	95			60	95		43	93		85													
Lori M.	85			20	95		79	64 / 86		30	95												
Todd M.	75	85		50	95		50	57 / 80		20	90												
David O.	80			55	95		57	50 / 93		45	95												
Jon S.	85			55	100		71	93		20	95												
Elaine S.	95			70	95		79	100		60	100												
Linda S.	95			55	80		71	100		25	100												

Fig. 17.5 Homebase advisor chart.

Name ______________________ CTBS Score __________ __________

Addition and subtraction	Pre	Post	*Fractions*	Pre	Post
Part A	______	______	Part A	______	______
Part B	______	______	Part B	______	______
Part C	______	______	Part C	______	______
			Part D	______	______
Multiplication and division			*Geometry*		
Part A	______	______	Part A	______	______
Part B	______	______	Part B	______	______
Part C	______	______	Part C	______	______
Part D	______	______	Part D	______	______
Part E	______	______			

Fig. 17.6 Individual student record form.

system revised its reporting system. The committee that carried out the revision was made up of parents, administrators, and teachers from throughout the system. The committee felt that parents' first concern was how their children were working, second whether they were making satisfactory progress, and third, how they were getting along with other students. Our mathematics program fit well into the reporting system the committee developed. It was mainly a report on the child's progress according to what he or she should be able to accomplish. To supplement this quarterly report we decided to send the contracts home. This would give those parents who were interested a chance to see their child's work, test scores, and objectives covered. At the first parent-teacher conference in the fall, we described the program to the parents, told them where their child was and why. We showed them the child's standardized test score in math, and also where their child ranked in relationship to the other students in the same age/grade group in the school, system, and nation.

These parent conferences were held with the child's teacher-advisor and homeroom teacher. This teacher had each child's test folder and a short written report about the child's work habits and progress.

Using the IGM Goal-setting Procedure

Several of the teachers in our I & R Unit used the goal-setting procedures as described in the Individually Guided Motivation (IGM) materials along with the mathematics program. One teacher identified six children in her math groups who seemed to need motivation to get their work done each day and to do it well. A particular day was set aside for a conference with those students. The teacher arranged to have a volunteer or aide in during that time. The teacher presented the lesson to the groups. Then the volunteer or aide corrected tests or answered student questions while the teacher conducted goal-setting conferences with each of the six students.

During the first conference they discussed their own goals and compared them with how athletes set goals and work to achieve them. Using a contract, the student then set a goal on what he or she would be able to do in one week. Sometimes the child set the goal of being able to master an objective or two or set goals by assignments. Then the student set how many pages or problems to do in a day or week. If the goal was set on a daily basis, the completed work was shown to the teacher each day for reinforcement.

Each week the teacher held these conferences with students until they developed self-motivation. Rewards were used with some students. For example, if the student wrote the goal on the inside cover of the math folder, it was always there as a reminder. When the child reached the goal for the day or week, he or she received a star or seal to put on the folder. This conference procedure seemed to work well.

Pairing Students (Tutoring)

Besides the conferences, another IGM procedure of older students tutoring younger students was quite successful. Pairing students was not new—most teachers had used the method at one time or another. There were some students who seemed to have questions constantly because they were unsure of themselves. Each of these was paired with a student who had already mastered the objective(s). If a teacher couldn't help at the time the unsure student had a question, the partner could help. The partner, at times, checked the first few problems done by the unsure student to give immediate feedback and to make sure he/she was off to a good start. The partner was chosen for good work habits to act as a model for the other student.

Review of the Second Year and Looking Ahead

In April when we reviewed the second year of the program we felt it had been quite successful. Our main goal in mathematics for next year was to enlarge the activity file and to add more manipulative materials to our resource file. We also were happy with the relative ease with which the two IGM procedures of goal setting and tutoring had been utilized to motivate students working in the mathematics program.

Now that the WDRSD and the mathematics programs are running smoothly, our IIC is discussing which area to implement instructional programming in next. This decision, like the one for mathematics, will be made cooperatively by the IIC and the unit staffs.

RESPONSES TO THE CASE STUDY

The reactions of two teachers to the preceding narrative are presented here. These teachers are familiar with the IGE concept and have taught in two different types of communities. They tell the background about their schools and indicate which procedures they would adopt and which ones they would change if they were to successfully implement the mathematics and motivation programs in their schools.

An Inner-city Unit Leader's Point of View

Our school is located in an urban area with a population of 250,000 in a northeastern state. The school system comprises 35 elementary schools, two middle schools, three high schools, numerous preschools and four alternative learning centers. The majority of the parents are employed in the insurance business, federal positions, and industrial jobs. The city's school population is distributed in the following manner: black, 55 percent; Spanish surnamed, 25 percent; white and other ethnic groups, 10 percent each.

Our school building is about five years old, and located in an inner-city setting in the community that it serves. It has an open-space architectural design. The student population of 900 is 90 percent black and 10 percent Spanish surnamed. The students and adults are organized into 10 I & R Units as follows:

4 I & R Units of 5- to 7-year-olds	3 teachers, 80-90 children and 2 paraprofessionals per unit
3 I & R Units of 8- to 10-year-olds	4 teachers, 100-120 children and 2 paraprofessionals per unit
3 I & R Units of 10- to 12-year-olds	4 teachers, 100-120 children and 2 paraprofessionals per unit

Nearly 80 percent of the students' mothers work and 75 percent of the families are supported by government social service. Inner-city schools are fortunate to have supplemental funding from the federal government because of the makeup of the student population. In our school, this funding is used for instructional materials, staff, hardware, software, and media.

There are many full- and part-time resource people in the building who are available to students throughout the school day when the need arises. In addition to teachers, administrators, and aides, full-time personnel include an IMC director, a communications-media teacher, a teacher of educable mentally retarded, a learning disabilities teacher, a reading consultant, an English-as-a-second-language teacher, nurse, guidance counselor, social worker, secretaries, and custodians. Part-time staff includes a psychologist, psychological examiner, dental hygienist, speech therapist, doctor, behavior modification specialist, and personnel to help the gifted student.

If we were to implement instructional programming for individual students in mathematics in our school, we would use the systemwide objectives for mathematics that were developed by our Board of Education. Even though the system's population is diverse, these objectives can be implemented at any of the schools with appropriate modification by the IIC and teachers in each building. Also, because of this diversity, there are no systemwide textbooks for mathematics or any other subject. The staff of each building chooses the textbooks for their students. Also, in some buildings, a variety of texts and other materials are selected instead of a set textbook.

Another difference is that we would set up our mathematics program so that there is an integration of subject matter. For example, fractions would be taught with addition, and the basis for multiplication would be introduced in first year mathematics. We don't like to isolate the facts of mathematics when we teach them as was done in the program described in the preceding narrative.

In the area of communication, we generate a feeling of openness in our instructional areas. Students are encouraged to talk over their problems with any one of the teachers, and we do not assign a teacher-advisor or homeroom teacher. They talk about whatever is on their minds and this helps us discover what might be hindering a student's progress. Student-teacher conferences are scheduled as they are needed. Whenever a problem arises, a child will meet several times a week with a teacher. Then as progress is made, the number of conferences decreases. We have found that one conference a week as mentioned in the preceding narrative was just not enough to help us get at the student's problem.

In reporting to parents, we have found that we are most successful if we go out into the community and meet with the parents in their homes. This helps break down the barriers that are sometimes created between the home and the school. It also leads to a friendly atmosphere between the school staff and the parents. When conferences are held at the school, they usually include the student, along with the parent and the teacher. This procedure fosters the idea of three groups—the home, school, and the child—working together for common goals.

A Rural-urban Teacher's Point of View

Our school district is semirural, semiurban, and is often called a "bedroom community." It is located near a large industrial city in the midwest. The city provides most of the employment for the people in the school district. Recreation facilities are located at the more than 15 lakes within our district. Children are bused in from six neighboring communities. Most of the school population and teaching staff are white. The population is transient since families are constantly moving out to our rural area from the large city nearby, and the school population is steadily growing. There are three elementary schools, one middle school, and one senior high school in the district.

In more than half of the families, both parents work. About 60 percent of the families are blue-collar workers, 20 percent are professionals or semiprofessionals and 20 percent are in the lower economic bracket or on government social service.

Our school building has 18 self-contained classrooms and one special education room. Four of the classrooms have moveable walls to provide large group spaces. We have 530 students. We are not yet an IGE school, but have been team teaching in kindergarten and grades 1-5 in reading and math for several years. This experience would make the change to I & R Units easier. We have 19 teachers, two playground aides that also supervise the lunchroom, and one paraprofessional who works in the Media Center. Parents work as volunteer aides in the classroom. They help children with one-to-one activities and the teachers with clerical duties. Special teachers include a music teacher and a gym teacher who meets once a week with each class, and two band directors who work with students ages 10-12. We also have a speech therapist, a remedial reading teacher, a reading consultant, and a learning disabilities consultant.

Leveling of instructional objectives. Many ideas in the preceding narrative of implementing instructional programming for individual students in mathematics could be applied in our school. The idea of three levels of objectives for students is especially relevant. It would help us meet the state-assigned minimum mathematics objectives while simultaneously meeting the needs of students who can work more rapidly. In our state, accountability has been a very important topic in public education. In order to measure accountability to some degree, the state has issued minimum objectives to be met by all students in grades four and seven. We would use the state minimum objectives as a starting point for our math program. They would probably be comparable to Level A objectives. We would then add Level B and C objectives to provide a well-rounded program for our diverse student population. (See Fig. 12.1).

Home-school-community relations. The unit staff in the preceding case study felt a need for motivation of individual students. In our district, the problem is more than motivating the student. It also includes educating the parents. Many parents felt left out when "modern math" was brought into our district a decade ago. The influence on the attitudes of their children could be seen in the classroom. If we are going to make another change in the mathematics program, parental understanding of what we were attempting to do would be an initial concern.

In order to allay the parental "fears" of another new program and to help parents communicate with their children in the area of mathematics, we would want to explain the program to them in full detail. Unit meetings with parents would be an effective home-school-community practice for this purpose. The unit leader along with unit teachers could brainstorm ideas on how to present the new program to the parents during the parent unit meeting. Since about 100 parents would attend we could hold a large group meeting first to give them an outline of the general objectives of the program. Then we could break the group into smaller groups ranging from 20–30 parents and have a 20-minute student simulation in which they would review learning stations, contracts, and learning pacs under the direction of a unit teacher. After the parent involvement activities, a 20-minute question-and-answer session could be held by each unit teacher. We believe this kind of involvement would give the parents an understanding of the program and motivate them to help the students have a more positive attitude toward mathematics. Also we would hope it would eliminate the negative idea that "my father says the old way is best."

Student goal setting. The ideas in the preceding description about individual student motivation were encouraging. In our system we have used a tutor-tutee program between twelve- and seven-year-olds that has been successful in improving student motivation in the area of reading. It has also enhanced student relationships between different age groups. It seems highly possible that it could be extended to the mathematics areas.

The idea of goal setting is a new one to our system and has some unique characteristics. It should definitely be an area that we would implement into our mathematics program. The intriguing aspect of goal setting is getting the student involved in deciding the amount of work he or she wishes to accomplish and giving the student the responsibility to see that the work is completed. This seems to be an ideal approach to student self-direction and motivation.

SUMMARY

This chapter has related the experiences of one I & R Unit with four teachers, an aide and 120 children, ages 8-10, over a two-year period. During this time they implemented instructional programming in mathematics and integrated two IGM procedures—goal setting and tutoring—into the mathematics program. The narrative, as told by the leader of this unit, dealt with the implementation process in a sequential and practical manner.

It has also presented reactions to the narrative by two teachers who teach in different types of schools in different areas of the country.

REFERENCES

Wisconsin Department of Public Instruction 1972. *Guidelines to mathematics, K-6*. Madison, Wisc.

Wisconsin PACT School Mathematics Committee (K. Zahn, Chairman) c. 1973. *Individualizing mathematical learning in the elementary school: a hierarchy of student behavioral objectives, K-8*. Wisconsin Department of Public Instruction, Madison, Wisc.

Appendix A

Unit B Planning Meetings: September 20 to November 20

The unit planning meetings' agendas, and minutes presented here are a continuation of those for Unit B at Willow School that were described in Chapter 10.

Five meetings—September 20, 25, and 30 and October 2 and 4—deal with problems that occurred during *Wisconsin Design* testing, along with grouping and scheduling students and staff for skill instruction during Block 1. Special features to note include (1) how Unit B is developing an inservice plan to meet ongoing needs; (2) the advantages of having one teacher (in this case, Ms. Flynn) unassigned so she can handle problems as they arise and help out where needed; (3) the roles of the aide and student teacher who attended all of these meetings because they were involved in the business being conducted; and (4) the delegation of responsibility among all members of the I & R Unit staff.

Successive meetings—from October 9 to November 20—are a record of how the staff functioned more smoothly as they worked together, and how they accomplished more during their planning meeting time including combining meeting segments like grouping and scheduling into one planning meeting. The two-way communication between the I & R Unit and the IIC should also be noted.

September 20—Ongoing Operations Meeting: Assessment—Agenda

(Goldsmith)	1. Announcements	10 min
(Jones)	2. Review and evaluation of first day of testing with feedback from staff of necessary changes	30 min
(Flynn)	3. Reminder of testing schedules for September 21, 24, and 25	20 min
(Frost)	4. *Wisconsin Design* Inservice	30 min

September 20—Ongoing Operations Meeting: Assessment—Minutes

1. Ms. Goldsmith called the meeting to order and made two or three brief announcements. She could tell the group was anxious to talk about the events of the first day of testing on the *Wisconsin Design.*

Before Ms. Goldsmith could ask how everything went, a student knocked on the door and presented a note from Mr. Valdez. Ms. Goldsmith read the note aloud: "Congratulations to all of you on the smooth manner in which the first day of testing was handled. I noticed the children were receiving the appropriate materials and were working very attentively on the tests. The group of ten students I had all appeared to be able to handle Level D tests without noticeable difficulty. I enjoyed helping with the testing and look forward to future sessions." They gave a unanimous sigh of relief.

2. Ms. Jones asked staff from each testing level to indicate the names of students who appeared to be placed at too low or too high a testing level. Mr. Frost, who was handling Level B testing, said he had two students who were having minor difficulties. He suggested, however, that they be retained in Level B for another day of testing before they were moved. He also had three students who were completing the tests very quickly with more than 80 percent accuracy and who should be moved to Level C. Names of students were given to Ms. Flynn who was roving and would handle re-testing.

Ms. Goldsmith, who was supervising Level C testing, had checked with the other testers and reported that 14 students should be retested at Level B and nine at Level D. These names were also given to Ms. Flynn.

Ms. Flynn had devised a plan for retesting which she asked the unit to react to. "Since I can't retest at all levels during the testing time, and since these skills are not generally sequential, I suggest the students start testing tomorrow with the groups at their newly assigned levels. Then, I'll pick them up one by one or in clusters for the tests they missed today." She would attempt to retest students during free reading time starting to-morrow, and would have the 27th open to complete retesting. The unit agreed that this was a practical approach, and Ms. Jones volunteered to help Ms. Flynn by testing the Level C students on the 27th if needed. The unit asked Ms. Flynn to monitor the students carefully tomorrow so that any students who were having problems but were not noticed today could be found before they got too far into the testing. Also, teachers were to report any further problems to Ms. Flynn by 1:00 P.M. tomorrow.

3. Ms. Flynn reviewed the testing schedule for the four levels for the 21st. Ms. Wynn and Ms. White indicated tests were ready for tomorrow's testing, including extra copies to accommodate changes in levels.

4. Mr. Frost went ahead with the *Wisconsin Design* inservice program which included the showing of the filmstrip on grouping called *Focusing Instruction*. After the filmstrip, he led a discussion on how the principles in the filmstrip would apply to the situation in Unit B.

September 25—Ongoing Operations Meeting: Assessment—Agenda

(Goldsmith)	1. Announcements	10 min
(Flynn)	2. Report on testing and retesting schedule to date	20 min
(Goldsmith/ Wynn)	3. Report on correcting and punching of test data	20 min
(Frost)	4. *Wisconsin Design* Inservice	40 min

September 25—Ongoing Operations Meeting: Assessment—Minutes

1. Ms. Goldsmith spent about five minutes on announcements, including the problem of a shortage of Level D tests that was solved when the school secretary ran off extra copies at the last minute. She also asked Ms. Wynn to check again on numbers of tests so this wouldn't happen at other levels in the future.

2. Ms. Flynn reported that testing was proceeding well and that only two more children were recommended for retesting from Level C to Level D. She reported further that retesting for missed tests at Level C and D would occur at 10:30 A.M. on the 27th, as both teachers handling Levels C and D indicated they would have completed their group testing by then. Ms. Flynn said, "I will be able to complete retesting students in Level B on the 24th and 26th."

3. Ms. Goldsmith asked Ms. Wynn, "How is correcting coming?" Holding her right hand up in a pencil-grasp position, Ms. Wynn replied that they were on schedule and staff might not be needed for correcting on Monday, October 1st if things continued smoothly. She indicated that Ms. White had asked two friends of hers who were studying elementary education at the university to help correct tests and together they had contributed ten hours. This had freed Ms. Wynn to begin punching the record cards. Ms. Flynn had also been able to work on card punching several hours during testing time.

4. Mr. Frost started the *Wisconsin Design* inservice meeting by noting that the content of this inservice meeting was directly related to the grouping and scheduling meetings on October 2nd and 4th, respectively. He reviewed the key points of the filmstrip on grouping they had viewed on the 20th, and then started the simulation on grouping.

The grouping simulation contained a module with objectives, a handout indicating grouping procedures for unsequenced and sequenced skills, and a card deck with punched data for 80 students in five skills.

Mr. Frost acted as chairperson for the group while they proceeded through the suggested activities to learn the grouping procedure and card sort technique with the data deck. While 40 minutes had been scheduled for this segment, they were just getting into it at the end of the hour. Since it was now after five, they decided to continue on Thursday.

September 27—Ongoing Operations Meeting: Assessment—Agenda

(Goldsmith)	1. Announcements	10 min
(Flynn)	2. Report on testing and recording data	15 min
(Flynn)	3. Plans for grouping and scheduling meetings	15 min
(Frost)	4. *Wisconsin Design* Inservice	50 min

September 27—Ongoing Operations Meeting: Assessment—Minutes

1. Ms. Goldsmith made two brief announcements:
   a. children riding bicycles must park them in the racks provided at the north and south doors and not lean them against the gym windows.
   b. the aide from Unit C who was in charge of playground duty reported rubber playground balls were being used in the vicinity of the swings. She asked teachers to please discuss the dangers of this practice with their homeroom/advisor groups and ask them to use the balls only on the surfaced areas adjacent to the west side of the building.

2. Ms. Flynn reported testing and retesting were completed at 2:00 P.M. today. "I'm glad we finished. I've about had it in one stretch!" was the exclamation by Ms. Jones. All members agreed, but were satisfied that it had run smoothly. Ms. Goldsmith said, "Thanks to the cooperative effort of all unit staff members, we made it with our sanity. Are there any last minute problems you want to mention?" No problems were mentioned except the uncertain feeling about the grouping process.

3. Ms. Flynn, Ms. Wynn, and Ms. White reported that correcting was nearly complete and that punching was coming along well and should be completed by Monday noon, on October 1st. This would make punched cards available for the unit grouping meeting on Tuesday, October 2nd.

4. The staff was anxious to get back to the grouping simulation they started on Tuesday. They had an hour of meeting time left and agreed to extend the meeting an additional 20 minutes or so in order to get more experience in the grouping process.

October 2—Grouping Meeting—Agenda

(Goldsmith)	1. Announcements	10 min
(Jones)	2. Presentation of assessment data on punched cards	15 min
(Frost, Wynn)	3. Tentative designation of skill groups based on assessment scores	15 min
(Frost)	4. Discussion of appropriateness of assignments with changes as needed and finalizing assignment of staff and students to skill groups	50 min

October 2—Grouping Meeting—Minutes

1. Ms. Goldsmith announced:
   a. next week's unit meetings will be on October 9th and 10th rather

than 9th and 11th because of the area teachers' convention on the 11th.

b. the first PTA meeting has been scheduled for Tuesday, October 30th at 7:30 P.M. A panel including Dr. Thoreson, Supt. of Schools, Mr. Valdez, Principal of Willow School, and Ms. Goldsmith will discuss "The Implications of an IGE Program on Learning Opportunities for Children."

c. the ditto-paper order expected October 1st will not arrive in our building until at least October 10th. We have enough reserve supplies for normal use, but please use discretion.

2. Ms. Jones presented a resume of assessment data from the punched cards. Ms. Wynn, the aide, had assisted in punching the cards and recording data. Ms. Jones stated, "I first glanced at the punched cards to make a decision of where the largest groups of children might fall. We then started with these larger groups and checked their student makeup against other possible groups in order to avoid overlapping or omitting any student."

Examples and charts were presented by Ms. Jones showing how data had been recorded. Ms. Wynn, the aide, then assisted Ms. Jones in a demonstration in the use of sorting keysort cards to determine mastery and nonmastery of skills.

3. Mr. Frost and Ms. Wynn used the assessment scores on the cards to make preliminary suggestions regarding the makeup of skill groups. Their summary indicated most of the children tested at Level B had not mastered consonant digraphs, contractions, and plurals; at Level C many students had not mastered diphthongs, long and short *oo, r*-controlled vowels, base words with prefixes and suffixes, plural forms, and homonyms, synonyms, and antonyms; at Level D nonmastery occurred in three-letter consonant blends, syllabication, accents, and possessive forms.

Mr. Frost noted that the following skill groups were needed for ten or more students. (Some students needed more than one skill group.)

Level	*Skill*	*Pupils in Group*
B	Consonant digraphs	18
B	Contractions	18
B	Plurals	22
C	Diphthongs	27
C	Long and short *oo*	19
C	*r*-controlled vowels	26
C	Base words with prefixes and suffixes	26
C	Homonyms, synonyms, and antonyms	32

C	Plural forms	28
D	Three-letter consonant blends	19
D	Syllabication	10
D	Accent	10
D	Possessive forms	10

Since there are only five staff teachers, one student teacher, and one aide, and since it had been agreed previously to let one staff member "float" to pick up students who complete mastery of skills before the three-week skill block is complete, Mr. Frost suggested the following skill groups be set up for the first time block:

Level	*Skill*	*Pupils in Group*
B	Consonant digraphs	18
B	Plurals	22
C	Diphthongs	27
C	Base words—prefixes and suffixes	26
C	Plural forms	28
D	Three-letter consonant blends	19
D	Syllabication	10
	Total	150

The unit referred to the minutes of the September 13th meeting and assigned staff as follows:

Staff Member	*Skill Assignment*	*Pupils in Group*
Ms. Goldsmith	"floating"	—
Ms. Jones	Level C—Diphthongs	27
	Level D—Syllabication	10
Mr. Frost	Level B—Consonant digraphs	18
	Level D—Three-letter consonant blends	19
Ms. Flynn	Level C—Base words—prefixes and suffixes	26
Ms. Fords and	Level B—Plurals	22
Ms. White	Level C—Plural forms	28
Ms. Wynn	Assist Fords and White	

4. The discussion of the appropriateness of staff assignments centered around the consensus of the unit staff in meeting the needs of the pupils in the unit. Mr. Frost said, "The suggested grouping schedule appears to meet the needs of the largest number of students during this first skill group period. We have many needs in terms of smaller groups, too, but feel that for the first time we should perhaps limit the number of group offerings and the number of preparations for any one unit member. We also want to put every student in a group rather than in independent study for the first block."

Further discussion brought out the fact that while Ms. Fords' and Ms. White's groups are fairly large, the two skills are quite related and some overlap could result. In addition, Ms. Wynn would be available to assist them. Ms. Jones and Mr. Frost also have large groups to start with, but since many students in these groups had scores close to mastery (50 to 70 percent) they would become smaller after the first week.

October 4—Scheduling Meeting—Agenda

(Goldsmith)	1. Announcements	10 min
(Flynn)	2. Presentation of time schedule	10 min
(Flynn)	3. Assignment of space	20 min
(Goldsmith)	4. *Preparation for Instruction. Design* filmstrip/ tape "G"	50 min

October 4—Scheduling Meeting—Minutes

1. Announcements by Ms. Goldsmith included:
   a. The PTA unit mothers have been selected. You may call on them to help with the Halloween party and other activities. A list of mothers and their phone numbers was given to each unit member.
   b. There will be a Halloween parade again this year. It will be held from 12:45-1:15 P.M. on October 31st on the school playground.
   c. Mr. Larry Habermeyer, Unit Leader from Lincoln School in nearby Marshalltown, will meet with us on October 16th to discuss supplementary materials and activities developed by their staff for the *Wisconsin Design.*

2. Ms. Flynn reviewed the unit discussion of September 13th in which the unit staff suggested a Monday, Wednesday, Friday time schedule of 30 minutes each day for skills teaching. After a brief discussion, unit members agreed to accept the plan to use 10:00-10:30 A.M. of the reading/ language arts time Monday, Wednesday, and Friday as the reading skill time.

3. Ms. Flynn presented a building plan for Willow to each unit member and pointed out the space currently assigned to Unit B. "In addition," she reported, "Ms. Kato, the IMC director, agreed that one or two smaller skill groups could meet in the back pod of the IMC if necessary."

Since Ms. Fords and Ms. White had been assigned larger skill groups, the large open area was assigned to them. Mr. Frost and Ms. Jones were assigned to the smaller spaces in an isolated corner of the area since they indicated that they planned to have much interaction with their groups and it could get fairly noisy. The remaining space was assigned to Ms. Flynn. Ms. Goldsmith would work in the east side of the IMC.

4. The filmstrip/tape *Preparation for Instruction* from the *Wisconsin Design* set "G" was shown to the unit by Ms. Goldsmith. Brief discussion followed, and unit members made note of suggestions made in the filmstrip with plans to try out these ideas during the instructional sequence.

October 9—Ongoing Operations Meeting—Agenda

(Goldsmith)	1. Announcements	10 min
(Staff)	2. Review of first day (October 8) of *Wisconsin Design* skill group teaching; modifications needed for the second day	30 min
(Goldsmith)	3. Develop a plan to identify and posttest children who appear to have mastered the skill before the end of the three-week period	30 min
(Staff)	4. Staff input for inservice on *Wisconsin Design* for October 10	20 min

October 9—Ongoing Operations Meeting—Minutes

1. Ms. Goldsmith made the following announcements:
   a. the time for the schoolwide Halloween party has been set for 2:00 P.M. on October 31st.
   b. all Halloween decorations must be fireproof and nonedible.
   c. the IIC is formulating a plan for complete revamping of the IMC to better facilitate the IGE program. Each unit has been asked to submit suggestions in writing. Each unit member was asked to jot down his or her own ideas for discussion at the October 30 Ongoing Operations unit meeting.

2. Ms. Fords was the first to give her impression of the first day of skill group teaching. "I was really surprised how all of the students arrived in the right location at 10:30, and, on being questioned, knew the name of the skill they would be working on. The kids seemed to take to this group-

ing idea with little adjustment." Ms. Jones remarked, "Handling my two groups on *diphthongs* and *syllabication* went really smoothly. I did it in the same way I used to handle more than one reading group in a classroom situation by giving one group (syllabication—Level D) an instructional tape with an accompanying worksheet, while I introduced the skill (diphthongs—Level C) to the other group in person. Then I went through the key points of syllabication in person and gave the diphthongs group a gamelike worksheet." Ms. Fords mentioned that several children in her skill groups (plurals—Level B and plural forms—Level C) appeared to have a good grasp of the skill and would probably test out of the group by Monday (October 16th) of the following week. Generally, the first day had gone smoothly with only one or two children not finding their skill groups. This problem was corrected promptly by Ms. Goldsmith who was "floating" since she was not assigned to a skill group.

3. The remark by Ms. Fords about some children already having a grasp of the skill and testing out of the group prompted two questions:

   a. How should those who test out be handled?

   b. Should students have been subclustered (e.g., those with scores of 50-79 percent in one group and those with 00-49 percent in another) in the initial grouping process?

The first question was most urgent, and Ms. Goldsmith, who was not assigned to a skill group, had already been thinking about a plan. She asked the unit staff to react to it: "I suggest that children who test out of a skill group be assigned to another skill group or to independent study to work on another skill they have not mastered. For example, children who have mastered Level B plurals could be moved to Level C plurals easily since both levels are being handled by the same personnel—Ms. Fords and Ms. White. Students who test out of Level C plurals and other skill groups could be assigned to work on skills independently in the IMC." She noted skills for which materials are presently available for independent study, as follows:

Level B—Contractions

Level C—Homonyms, synonyms, antonyms

Level D—Possessives

Inspection and sorting of the punched cards indicated a large number of students needed work in these three skills. Mr. Frost reflected, "I didn't know we had materials for independent study for any skills." Ms. Goldsmith replied, "We didn't, but I developed these materials for independent study last week, and Ms. Wynn is typing them onto dittoes at the present time. If you have students who test out of your skill groups who don't need any of these skills, give their names to me and I'll arrange enrichment or self-selected reading for them. Let's hope this latter number isn't greater than eight or ten students."

4. Staff input for the *Wisconsin Design* inservice focused on the need for more diversity of activities and depth in the resource file for a given skill. Several teachers said they had items in their closets and at home that they needed to update and add to the file. Unanimously, the staff decided to spend the 60-minute inservice session tomorrow on organizing materials for the file. Then Ms. Wynn could file the materials early next week.

October 10—Monitoring Meeting—Agenda

(Goldsmith)	1. Announcements	5 min
(Goldsmith)	2. Problems encountered during second day of skill teaching	5 min
(Fords, Flynn)	3. Presentation of monitoring plan	10 min
(Goldsmith)	4. Designation of staff for the upcoming meetings: October 18—Objectives Setting October 23—Designing October 25—Grouping/Scheduling	10 min
(Staff)	5. Inservice on *Wisconsin Design*—Resource File	60 min

October 10—Monitoring Meeting—Minutes

1. Ms. Goldsmith announced the following:
   a. a suggestion that staff members circulate to as many sessions as possible at the systemwide inservice meeting tomorrow, especially to those sessions dealing with individualized reading. In order to do this, the staff decided to go over the agenda and selected sessions to meet their needs. They decided to share any new ideas and/or materials they gathered with the unit at the October 18 meeting.
   b. a reminder to prepare questions on *Wisconsin Design* implementation for Larry Habermeyer who will be a guest practitioner at the October 16th unit meeting.
   c. at the IIC meeting, Mr. Valdez announced that a new supply of ditto paper had arrived. He pleaded for efficient use of paper so we will still have some left in spring.

2. Ms. Goldsmith systematically asked each staff member the following questions about the skill groups they were teaching:
   a. Do you feel the children in your group are functioning smoothly?
   b. Are the children in your group able to handle the materials they're working with?
   c. Do you plan to posttest before the end of the three-week block? If so, then let me know your schedule. Please try to cluster students into small groups for posttesting, if possible.

Responses to the first question indicated that all staff, including the aide and student teacher, felt the program was working well for all but three or four of the 150 children in the unit. Ms. Goldsmith suggested she meet with the three or four children and talk to them to try to find out what was bothering them and to help them.

On the second question, teachers agreed that within a skill group children with scores close to mastery (50-79 percent) and those with low scores (00-49 percent) did not function well in a single group and should be divided into subgroups in the future. Ms. Goldsmith suggested that each teacher be responsible for subgrouping within his or her skill group. Ms. Flynn pointed out that the higher group (50-79 percent) would generally test out before the end of the block and designation of these numbers and the skill they would be completing would be helpful in advance planning for the block.

3. Ms. Fords and Ms. Flynn presented the monitoring plan they had devised and asked for unit reaction to it. Basically, it consisted of each certified teacher monitoring the 30 students assigned to them as homeroom and advisee groups. For Word Attack skills, they could use a printed duplicate of the Word Attack Profile Card like the one presented in Figure A.1. Each teacher would receive one form for each student. Skills mastered would be marked off by the aide, teacher, or others by superimposing the punched profile card over the printed form and coloring in the punched area. Ms. Fords also suggested that the level at which the student was presently working be circled on the form.

Ms. Flynn, who had appeared to be doodling while Ms. Fords was talking, then said, "If I had a student who had been tested initially at Level C and had mastered skills 1, 3, 4, 6, 8, 9, 10, 12, 14, 15, and 16, his record form would appear like this. (See Figure A.2.) Level C would be circled and the "punch areas" in front of these skills would be punched, along with the "punch areas" for all skills in Levels A and B for which mastery is assumed." The unit members looked at the card and agreed.

Mr. Frost suggested, "This whole plan is a great idea. We certainly

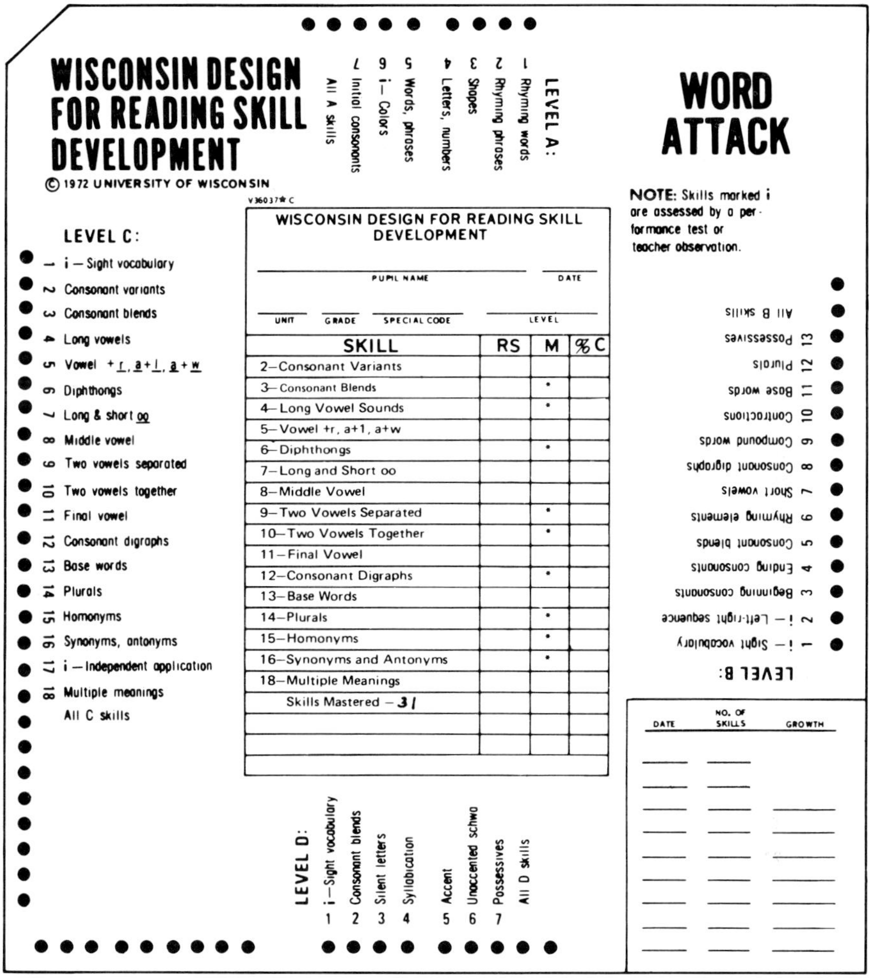

Fig. A.1 Blank Word Attack profile card.

need something to keep track of the kids and the kids need to know there is someone they can come to, to see how they're doing, and to talk to about problems or exciting ideas concerning reading." Ms. Goldsmith noted that with this plan an individual student could look at his or her own record and set goals for skills he or she hoped to master.

4. Time was running short and Ms. Goldsmith asked for volunteers to assume responsibility for upcoming meetings listed on the agenda.

Ms. Flynn volunteered for the October 18 Objectives Setting Meeting.

Mr. Frost for the October 23 Designing Meeting and
Ms. Fords for the October 25 Grouping/Scheduling Meeting.

5. Fifty minutes of the meeting time had already been used, but the staff agreed to work for an hour on the resource file according to the suggestion of Ms. Jones who exclaimed, "We might as well work later tonight since we won't be here tomorrow and Friday because of the area inservice meetings."

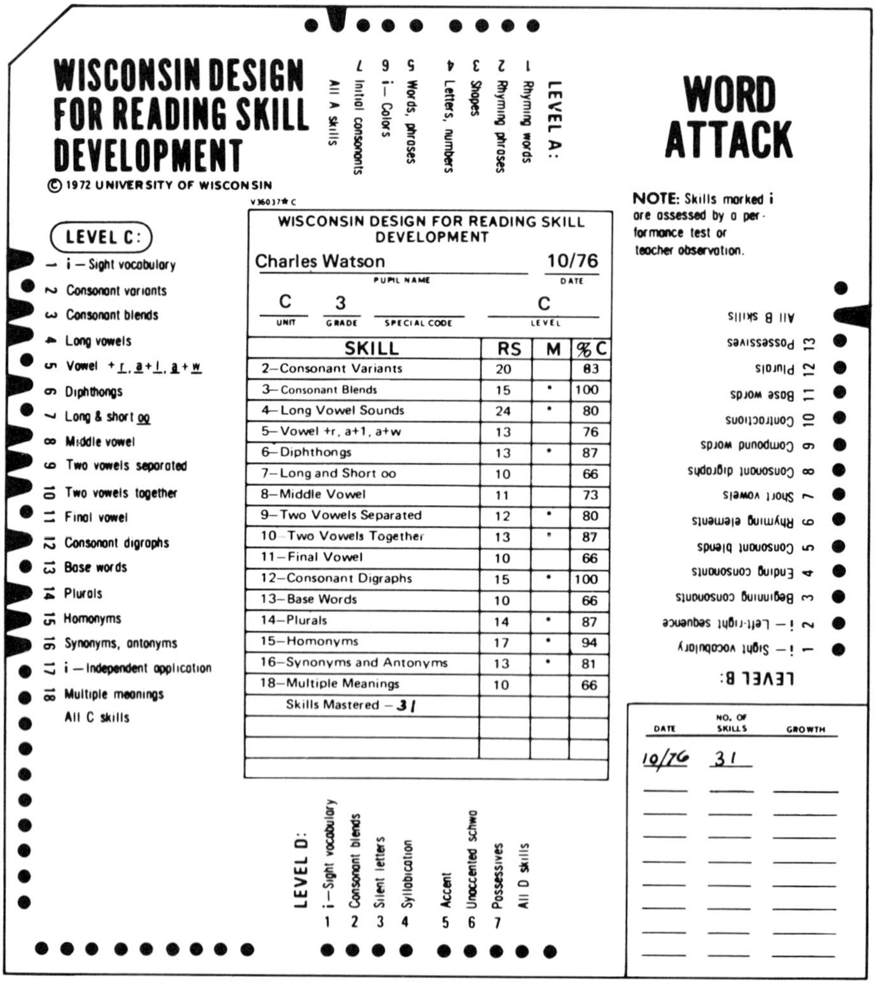

WISCONSIN DESIGN FOR READING SKILL DEVELOPMENT

© 1972 UNIVERSITY OF WISCONSIN

WORD ATTACK

LEVEL A:
1 Rhyming words
2 Rhyming phrases
3 Shapes
4 Letters, numbers
5 Words, phrases
6 i — Colors
7 i — Initial consonants
All A skills

NOTE: Skills marked i are assessed by a performance test or teacher observation.

LEVEL B:
1 i — Sight vocabulary
2 i — Left-right sequence
3 Beginning consonants
4 Ending consonants
5 Consonant blends
6 Rhyming elements
7 Short vowels
8 Consonant digraphs
9 Compound words
10 Contractions
11 Base words
12 Plurals
13 Possessives
All B skills

LEVEL C:
1 i — Sight vocabulary
2 Consonant variants
3 Consonant blends
4 Long vowels
5 Vowel +r, a+l, a+w
6 Diphthongs
7 Long & short oo
8 Middle vowel
9 Two vowels separated
10 Two vowels together
11 Final vowel
12 Consonant digraphs
13 Base words
14 Plurals
15 Homonyms
16 Synonyms, antonyms
17 i — Independent application
18 Multiple meanings
All C skills

LEVEL D:
1 i — Sight vocabulary
2 Consonant blends
3 Silent letters
4 Syllabication
5 Accent
6 Unaccented schwa
7 Possessives
All D skills

V36037★C

WISCONSIN DESIGN FOR READING SKILL DEVELOPMENT

Charles Watson (PUPIL NAME) 10/76 (DATE)

UNIT: C GRADE: 3 SPECIAL CODE: LEVEL: C

SKILL	RS	M	%C
2—Consonant Variants	20		83
3—Consonant Blends	15	•	100
4—Long Vowel Sounds	24	•	80
5—Vowel +r, a+1, a+w	13		76
6—Diphthongs	13	•	87
7—Long and Short oo	10		66
8—Middle Vowel	11		73
9—Two Vowels Separated	12	•	80
10—Two Vowels Together	13	•	87
11—Final Vowel	10		66
12—Consonant Digraphs	15	•	100
13—Base Words	10		66
14—Plurals	14	•	87
15—Homonyms	17	•	94
16—Synonyms and Antonyms	13	•	81
18—Multiple Meanings	10		66
Skills Mastered — 31			

DATE	NO. OF SKILLS	GROWTH
10/76	31	

Fig. A.2 Marked Word Attack profile card completed.

October 16—Ongoing Operations: Monitoring Meeting—Agenda

(Goldsmith)	1. Announcements	10 min
(Goldsmith)	2. Review of monitoring procedures to date, with suggestions for immediate changes if necessary.	20 min
(Habermeyer)	3. Inservice meeting on *Wisconsin Design* implementation by Mr. Larry Habermeyer, Unit Leader from Lincoln School in nearby Marshalltown. (Remember staff, bring along your nitty-gritty questions to ask Mr. Habermeyer. Here's your chance to get advice from a teacher with two years of experience with the *Design.*)	60 min

October 16—Ongoing Operations: Monitoring Meeting—Minutes

1. a. Ms. Goldsmith announced that plans for the schoolwide Halloween party seemed to be going well according to reports at the IIC.
   b. She also suggested that the IIC would be working on several buildingwide problems this year. The first one which she had told the unit about earlier would deal with a complete revamping of Willow's IMC, and the one projected after that was a set of social studies concepts/processes/skills for a better integrated program.
   c. She indicated other announcements could wait as she wanted the staff to spend as much time with Mr. Habermeyer as possible.

2. Ms. Goldsmith checked on student progress with each teacher, and responses indicated that most students had been progressing well. At the end of the first week of skill teaching, nearly 20 percent of the students had been posttested with most of them attaining mastery. Ms. Flynn said she had not expected so many to finish so soon, but that Ms. Goldsmith had been able to put most of them into independent or small group work on additional skills, and two had been assigned enrichment activities. Mr. Frost replied, "I'm glad we let one teacher 'float' during the skill block. What would we have done with all those kids if no one had been able to work with them?" Ms. Goldsmith agreed and said this would become even more crucial by the end of this week when approximately 10 percent more—or a total of 45 children—would have completed the skill assigned initially for Block 1. "Wow!" was Ms. Jones's reply. At this point Ms. Goldsmith could see that the interest of the day was talking with Mr. Habermeyer and asking him questions.

3. Ms. Goldsmith introduced Mr. Habermeyer and asked him to present a few reflections on his two years of experience with the *Design*. "We're

now starting our third year with the *Wisconsin Design* and are working in Word Attack, Study skills and Comprehension. We started with Word Attack the first year, then added Study skills the first semester of the second year, and Comprehension during the second semester of the second year. Since you're just starting, you probably feel this would be overwhelming. However, as you get accustomed to the procedures—objectives setting, designing, grouping, scheduling, monitoring, and evaluation—they take about one-third of the time you're putting on them now. Also, Study skills and Comprehension can be worked into language arts, social studies, math, and science instead of being handled as separate skills sessions. The important thing here is pre- and posttesting and monitoring. I really like the idea you're using at Willow for monitoring. When we first started two years ago, the entire unit staff tried to monitor all 135 children. After struggling with this, we found it cumbersome and inefficient. You've started off right, and I know you'll like your system."

Ms. Fords asked, "After two years of work in the *Design,* does your staff think the outcomes are worth the effort, and what evidence are you seeing in your school from the *Design?* Also, do you think the *Design* is too structured, leaving no imagination to the children?" Mr. Habermeyer replied that their school had set up an evaluation program and found that children working under the *Design* checkoff system had performed significantly better on standardized tests in areas related to Word Attack than had similar students at Lincoln in previous years. He said Study skills and Comprehension were presently being evaluated. His reply to the second question on structure was that children can gain mastery in many ways, and the checkoff of skills mastered is the only mandatory part of the *Design.* Other questions centered around preparation of materials for skills teaching, more effective use of the resource file, the arrangement of Lincoln's IMC, and the role of the IMC director in relation to the units and IIC as well as general teacher attitudes toward IGE after two years in the program.

Some 30 minutes after the end of scheduled planning time, the group broke up. Mr. Frost said, "This has been the best kind of inservice we could have. We really needed to talk to someone who has 'been through it' to help us keep our eyes on the goals we've set and to give us some ideas of where we might do better." All agreed and thanked Mr. Habermeyer. They also made tentative plans for exchange of teacher-made materials on *Wisconsin Design* skills between the two schools.

October 18—Objectives Setting Meeting—Agenda

(Goldsmith)	1. Announcements	10 min
(Staff)	2. Report back on systemwide inservice meetings	25 min

(Flynn)	3. Designate objectives for skill Block 2 (October 29 to November 16)	50 min
(Goldsmith)	4. Discussion on assignment of responsibilities for objectives setting, designing and grouping/scheduling for Block 3	5 min

October 18—Objectives Setting Meeting—Minutes

1. Announcements by Ms. Goldsmith included:
   a. a special concert for elementary students will be held on Friday, October 26th, in the University Arena at 2:00 P.M. Tickets, $.50 each, should be purchased by Wednesday, October 24th.
   b. new fall library books are now processed and ready for checkout in the IMC. Special arrangements can be made with Ms. Kato to have children preview the new selections. Mr. Frost will coordinate our units' requests.
   c. systemwide parent conference days for the first quarter have been scheduled for November 5th, 7th, and 11th from 1:00-4:30 P.M. each day. Ms. Goldsmith, assisted by Ms. Wynn and Ms. White, will set up a tentative conference schedule and report to the unit on October 23rd.

2. Ms. Goldsmith chaired a general discussion regarding the area Teachers' Convention on October 11th and 12th. The group agreed on the following points:
   a. The large general sessions were interesting, but not of specific help with classroom problems. They suggested having fewer large sessions and more small-group interaction sessions, especially sessions dealing with the problems of developing individualized programs.
   b. Most of the small-group sessions were excellent, especially those involving practicing staff members and opportunities for interaction (questions).

3. "In designating objectives for the second skill block," Ms. Flynn reported, "I feel that there were three major problems to consider:
   a. What skills from Block 1, if any, do we want to reteach?
   b. What skills do we want to suggest for independent study?
   c. What other skill groups do we want to schedule for this block?"

   The following plans were recommended:

   a. "Level B plurals and Level C plural forms need to be retaught. Since it appears that there may be only eight to ten children who need continual help and five or six more who will be starting the skill, perhaps we should form one skill group combining Levels B and C."

b. "I've tried to select objectives for one skill from each level to use as independent study skill groups. They are:

   Level B—Compound words

   Level C—Base words with prefixes and suffixes

   Level D—Accents"

   "You will note," Ms. Flynn continued, "that the Level C skill is one to be retaught. It appears that this group will be small and they should be able to handle some independent work.

   "Level D accents is also a small group, and if we made use of the tapes in the IMC so the boys and girls could hear the accents, they could also work with little direction."

c. Ms. Flynn reminded the unit that Block 1 reading skill groups were formed from those skills that showed the greatest need in terms of numbers of students. Block 2 should contain some larger groups, but the unit needs to consider working with many smaller skill groups too. "It becomes more difficult to coordinate," Ms. Flynn said, "each time you sort through the card deck and eliminate some of the more commonly needed skills."

   Ms. Flynn recommended that objectives for the following skills be included in the second block in addition to the three listed above for independent study:

   Level B—Possessive forms

   Level B/C—Plurals (repeat)

   Level C—*a* plus *w*

   Level C—*r*-controlled vowels

   Level C—Homonyms, synonyms, antonyms

   Level C—Short vowel

   Level C—Silent *e*

   Level C—Two vowels together

   Level D—Possessive forms

   Level D—Silent letter principles

After a brief discussion, the recommended objectives were accepted for Block 2 (October 29th–November 16th).

4. Ms. Goldsmith chaired the discussion regarding the assignment of responsibilities. Since the time was running late, unit members agreed that Ms. Goldsmith should assign responsibilities for objectives setting, designing, and grouping/scheduling meetings for Block 3 and announce the selections at the October 23 meeting.

October 23—Designing Meeting—Agenda

(Goldsmith)	1. Announcements	10 min
(Goldsmith)	2. Review of number of students ready for posttesting	20 min
(Frost)	3. Presentation of plans for Block 2 of *Wisconsin Design* including assignment of teachers to skills	50 min
(Goldsmith, White, Wynn)	4. Tentative Parent Conference Schedule (November 5 and 7)	10 min

October 23—Designing Meeting—Minutes

1. Announcements by Ms. Goldsmith included:
   a. The Willow Education Association meeting will be held on October 24th at 4:30 P.M. in the Junior High School cafeteria.
   b. Boys' intramurals will *not* meet on October 24th after school.
   c. An SPC meeting will be held November 29th at 2:30 P.M. in the Superintendent's Conference Room. A progress report on Willow's IGE program will be presented by Ms. Goldsmith.
   d. As requested in Item 4 of the October 18th minutes, assignments for Block 3 were made as follows:

      Objectives Setting—November 8—Ms. Goldsmith
      Designing Meeting—November 13—Ms. Fords
      Grouping/Scheduling—November 15—Mr. Frost

2. Ms. Goldsmith stated, "Several of you have indicated that you have students ready for posttesting and could move on to enrichment for the last two days of Block 1. Would each of you please report your suggestions to the unit now? Let's begin with Ms. Jones." The five teachers reported 30 more students had completed the skill assigned. This brought the total to 75 students who would not be in a skill group on October 24 and 26 during skill time. Because of the large number and because Mr. Frost and Ms. Flynn's groups had completed their skills, it was decided to have a

large group enrichment program dealing with student brainstorming techniques. Enrichment was selected because only two days of the block remained and this was too short a time to start independent study. Also, some students who had been working on independent study had completed their assignments and would also join the enrichment group. Three teachers—Goldsmith, Flynn, and Frost—would handle enrichment activities.

3. From experience in working in Block 1 and from comments from other unit members during unit meetings, Mr. Frost asked the unit to consider three points for incorporation into the teaching design plans for Block 2. These were:

   a. Teachers seemed to be able to handle two skill groups at the same time without problems;
   b. Some skill groups would not need three formal meetings each week;
   c. There is need to make better use of the facilities, materials, and equipment in the IMC.

   In the discussion that followed, unit members agreed with the points Mr. Frost had made, but suggested that the combined size of two skill groups to be taught by one teacher not exceed a normal class-size group of 30 students. Mr. Frost also suggested that the names of students who are ready for posttesting should be given to the "floating" teacher the day before the students are ready to take the test. This would give Ms. Wynn time to have the tests ready. He also suggested that the unit consider having the "floating" teacher and/or Ms. Wynn administer the posttests during Block 2 in an area (e.g., the alcove where the tests are stored) and call it the "assessment corner." This would allow the other teachers to remain full-time with the skill groups. During Block 1 it seemed like the posttesting broke the continuity of the teaching in many instances.

   The unit liked Mr. Frost's ideas and suggested he work with Ms. Fords to be sure the ideas were incorporated into the Grouping/Scheduling meeting on October 25.

4. Ms. Goldsmith distributed copies of the building master plan which had been developed by the IIC for parent conferences. "You'll note," she said, "that for those parents who have several children in our building, we tried to schedule the conferences on the same day so that they would not have to make several trips to school."

Ms. Goldsmith suggested that Ms. White look over the schedule and sit in on at least eight conferences with several staff members. Ms. White was asked to work out her schedule and check with the individual staff members involved.

October 25—Grouping/Scheduling Meeting—Agenda

(Goldsmith)	1. Announcements	10 min
(Fords)	2. Presentation of groups and schedules for Block 2, along with assignment of students to teachers with adjustments as decided by the entire staff.	50 min

October 25—Grouping/Scheduling Meeting—Minutes

1. Announcements by Ms. Goldsmith included:
   a. Suggestions are needed for equipment/materials for the IMC. There are limited funds available for purchase for second semester. Give suggestions to Mr. Valdez by November 2nd.
   b. Ms. Fords has been appointed as a representative on the system in-service committee to plan next year's programs. Please forward any suggestions or ideas to her as soon as possible. The first planning meeting for this committee is November 7th.

2. Ms. Fords, working from the objectives agreed on at the October 18th meeting and incorporating the suggestons of Mr. Frost at the October 23rd meeting, made the following assignments of teachers and students to skills:

Teacher	Skill	Number of students
Jones	"floating"	18 (independent study)
Goldsmith	Possessive forms, Level B	22
with Wynn	Possessive forms, Level D	10
Frost	*a* plus *w*, Level C	10
	r-controlled, Level C	9
	Homonyms, synonyms, antonyms Level C	11
Flynn	Short vowels, Level C	19
	Two vowels together, Level C	12
Fords	Silent *e*, Level C	13
	Silent letter principles, Level D	13
White	Plurals, Level B	8
	Plural forms, Level C	5

Ms. Flynn was concerned that Mr. Frost had assigned three groups to himself. She questioned whether this might be too difficult an assignment. Mr. Frost replied, "All of the groups are relatively small, and students in two of the groups had scores between 50 and 79 percent on the tests which means they will be ready for posttesting fairly soon. This will cut down on the numbers."

Ms. Goldsmith said, "I will not need the aide, Ms. Wynn, during every skill period. Let's plan for at least one skill period each week where Ms. Wynn will be free to work with other groups."

After a brief discussion the recommendations for grouping were accepted. The unit meeting adjourned at 4:00 P.M. This was the first time in many weeks that they had finished early.

October 30—Ongoing Operations Meeting—Agenda

(Goldsmith)	1. Announcements	10 min
(Goldsmith)	2. Review of the first day (October 29) of Block 2 skill teaching	10 min
(Staff)	3. General plans of staff for materials to be developed for more effective skill teaching	30 min
(Goldsmith)	4. Formulation of unit statement on revamping of IMC	40 min

October 30—Ongoing Operations Meeting—Minutes

1. Ms. Goldsmith announced:
   a. plans have been finalized for the Halloween party and safety precautions were to be remembered.
   b. the evaluation meeting for Block 1 will take place on Thursday, November 1st. Teachers were asked to be ready to indicate alternatives for masters and particularly for nonmasters.
   c. Ms. Wynn reported that all test data from Block 1 would be punched on cards and recorded on monitoring forms by 3:30 P.M. today.

2. Ms. Goldsmith asked how things went on Monday with the new skill groups. "It's a lot easier this time" was the response from Ms. Jones who was the "floating" teacher for Block 2. "The children seem to know exactly what to do and were anxious to get started. In fact, everything was going so smoothly that I believe I can just go ahead and develop materials for the resource file on Wednesday and Friday of this week." Ms. Jones said the ideas for compound words (Level B), base words (Level C), and accents (Level D) skills that the staff had considered appropriate for independent work at the October 18th meeting seemed to be well accepted by the students.

Ms. Fords indicated that she also felt things were going more smoothly this time and that she was more relaxed and at home with the procedures now. Ms. Flynn said, "I'd had 'my' 25 or 30 children every year for ten years. I found the idea of having different groups every three weeks frightening at first, but I think I'll like it."

3. The discussion on plans for developing more effective materials for skills learning was a lively one. In fact, everyone wanted to get ideas out at once. So Ms. Goldsmith said, "Let's have a five-minute brainstorming session." They did and generated some 25 ideas which could be summarized as follows:

a. Get kids involved with the skill by using *active* activities and not just passive ones like completing a worksheet.

b. Include a *variety* of ways to learn the same thing to accommodate the learning style of the student (e.g., tapes, writing, transparencies, games, tutors).

c. Develop independent study and small group, student-led activities for appropriate skills in Levels B, C, and D with a greater number of these in Levels C and D.

Staff members, including the student teacher, Ms. White, took assignments to develop creative ideas for particular skills. Ms. Jones who was "floating" during this block took the assignment of designating skills appropriate for independent work for all levels. The skills she selected would be brought back to the unit for their input on November 6.

Ms. Fords remarked, "This idea of designating skills for independent study is great. I feel we must start making long-range plans. So far they've been almost all short range." Ms. Goldsmith agreed and said meetings of November 1st, 6th, and 8th, as well as the meetings between Thanksgiving and Christmas, would deal with ideas for and writing of long-range plans.

4. Item 3 on materials had taken more time than Ms. Goldsmith had planned, so they proceeded directly into what Unit B would like to see in the IMC. She asked, "Let's write down ideas we would like the IIC to consider in revamping the IMC, and then select the five we give highest priority." Some 15 ideas came quickly and the five given priority were:

a. The IMC should be a work area, not a library where kids are afraid to go and someone constantly says "sh-h-h" the way it is now.

b. AV and printed materials other than texts should be catalogued, stored, and checked out by students at the IMC.

c. Teachers should be able to send students to the IMC with a clearly stated task(s) in writing without accompanying them.

d. IMC use should be coordinated by the IIC so not all units are planning extensive use of the area at the same time.

e. The IMC director should be involved in teaching on occasion, attend IIC and unit meetings on request, and work with the units in selecting and purchasing materials according to their needs.

November 1—Evaluation Meeting—Agenda

(Goldsmith)	1. Announcements	10 min
(Goldsmith and Staff)	2. Evaluation of all aspects of Block 1, including the handling of unit planning meetings in relation to the actual teaching situation.	80 min

November 1—Evaluation Meeting—Minutes

1. Ms. Goldsmith announced:

   a. The unit's ideas on the IMC reorganization were given to the IIC and would be used along with those from other units to formulate the building plan.

   b. We started talking about formulating long-range plans for our unit at the last meeting (October 30th). I, as unit leader, need to know the areas which you believe have priority for long-range planning. Will you be thinking about this and be ready to consider it on November 6th?

   c. The PTA is planning a benefit party on November 20th. Proceeds will go for AV materials and equipment for the IMC. Please have the children in your room take the notices home.

   d. The cook has been having problems with hot lunch count. Please ask the children in your homeroom to check in when they do not plan to eat hot lunch.

2. Ms. Goldsmith took major responsibility for the first evaluation meeting. She reiterated its purposes as follows:

   a. to determine the number of masters and nonmasters from each skill group in the Block 1, along with appropriate alternatives for both groups.

   b. to determine how many children were ready for the posttest prior to the last day of the skill teaching.

   c. to evaluate the overall effectiveness of the way Block 1 had been handled.

   Ms. Goldsmith called on each teacher to give the number of masters and nonmasters from their monitor group. Overall, 82 percent

(123 students) of the students had mastered the skill assigned to them during the three-week block. This left 18 percent (27 students) not mastering it.

Fifty percent, or 75 of the 150 students, had passed the posttest prior to the end of the three-week period and had been placed into independent study or enrichment. The independent study group presented a special problem since they were now part way through the work for this skill on October 29 when they were assigned to a new skill group (teacher-led) for Block 2. The unit staff struggled with this problem which involved 27 children and posed the following alternatives:

(1) The students could leave the skill they were working with and go to the new skill group; then they could return to the independent skill the next time they completed a skill ahead of the three-week schedule.

(2) Students who were completing skills early could be identified and assigned to groups where they would work on two skills instead of one in a three-week time block.

(3) All students could be enriched when they finished early, instead of working on more skills.

The unit staff felt (2) was the best alternative and planned to implement it during Block 3. During Block 2, students would proceed as suggested in (1) since they had already started with the new skill groups.

For students who did *not* master the skill, the unit suggested alternative teaching methods and a further evaluation of the students' learning styles and general problems. The staff also decided that students repeat the nonmastered skill once. If they still failed to master it, their problems should be considered by the entire unit staff at an evaluation meeting. Ten of the 27 students were already repeating Plurals—Level B and Plural Forms—Level C as these were the only skills being retaught in Block 2. Ms. Flynn volunteered to review the situation for nonmasters from skill groups for the rest of this semester, and try to work out viable solutions for the unit. Ms. White would work with her and monitor these students carefully during Blocks 2 and 3 to gain more information about their problems.

Generally, the staff felt Block 1 had gone well. Some things they would like to think about for Blocks 2 and 3 and successive blocks were:

a. identification and preparation of more materials with action and a variety of media.

b. using tutors from the nearby high school to work with small groups of students.

c. carrying out more advance planning for skill groups and assignment of teachers to groups.

Ms. Goldsmith asked Ms. Jones to take responsibility for the evaluation meeting for Block 2 on November 20.

November 6—Monitoring Meeting—Agenda

(Goldsmith)	1. Announcements	10 min
(Staff)	2. Feedback from parent-teacher conferences	10 min
(Jones)	3. Ms. Jones will present list of skills appropriate for independent study and staff will react.	20 min
(Goldsmith)	4. Setting priority areas for long-range plans	20 min
(Staff)	5. Check on student progress to date in Block 2	30 min

November 6—Monitoring Meeting—Minutes

1. Ms. Goldsmith said there were no announcements.

2. Feedback from parent-teacher conferences indicated parents had great interest in the IGE reading skills program. All except two parents interviewed on Monday (November 5th) indicated the children liked the idea of having more than one teacher, and the parents were most positive toward the idea of each child moving at his or her own rate.

Mr. Frost said, "This conference idea is great, but takes a lot of time." Ms. Fords replied, "I get to know the parents and subsequently the child a lot better with a conference than just sending out a report card."

3. Ms. Jones presented the list of skills she considered appropriate for independent study at Levels B, C, and D. The staff reviewed each skill and, after revisions, the list appeared as follows:

Level B	*Level C*	*Level D*
contractions	homonyms, synonyms, antonyms	possessives
rhyming elements		accents
	short vowel generalization	
simple consonant digraphs	silent "*e*"	three-letter consonant blends
compound words	two vowels together	syllabication
	final vowel	
	multiple meanings of words	

Materials had already been designed by "floating" teachers for several of these skills. The group decided that the format should be standardized to include *objectives, suggested activities to meet objectives,* and *illustration of mastery*. A sample is presented in Figure A.3. The group liked this idea and agreed to use the format—for independent study materials.

Objectives:

The student will be able to identify nouns and pronouns, in context, that denote ownership. For example, indicate which underlined word is a possessive:

The boys went to the show with their mother.
Answers:
boys is a plural form
their is a possessive

Suggested Activities:

1. Listen to the sound-tape and complete the accompanying worksheet, "Possessives and You," in the IMC file.
2. Complete practice sheet 3 on possessives (from the resource file), correct it yourself, and seek help from a unit teacher for any you have wrong.
3. Work the exercise on possessives in the resource book, "Possessives Can Be Fun," on p. 94.
4. Complete possessive sequence on cards 20 and 21 in EEC kit.
5. Read the section and complete exercises on possessives in Ginn Reading 360 book.

Illustration of Mastery

Complete *Wisconsin Design* posttest on possessives (Level D) with 80 percent accuracy.

Fig. A.3 Student independent study form for possessives (Level D).

4. After considerable discussion, the unit identified the following priority areas for long-range plans:

a. selection and development of materials for teaching Word Attack skills.

b. investigation of Study skills and Comprehension areas of the *Wisconsin Design* for next year.

c. identification of inservice needs for the second semester of this year.

d. development of a new student progress reporting form in cooperation with the IIC.

5. Ms. Goldsmith checked with each teacher, and students appeared to be progressing well in the second skill block. In fact, Ms. Flynn suggested, "The students are learning the skills faster this block than they did in the first one. Maybe we should assign two skills to a block instead of one." "That's OK for some kids," replied Mr. Frost, "but some are having a lot of trouble and need more individual help "

These latter comments pointed to the problems that arise when children are encouraged to work at their own rate, and the need for alternative strategies on the part of the unit to meet them. Ms. Goldsmith indicated she would attempt to accommodate these problems in her plan for the designing meeting on November 13th.

November 8—Objective Setting Meeting—Agenda

(Goldsmith)	1. Announcements	10 min
(White, Jones)	2. Setting objectives for Block 3 (November 26-December 14)	40 min
(Goldsmith)	3. Reaction of unit to IIC plan for revamping the IMC.	40 min

November 8—Objective Setting Meeting—Minutes

1. Announcements by Ms. Goldsmith included:
   a. Teachers were asked to schedule any make-up parent conferences prior to November 16th, if at all possible.
   b. A film on *Winter Safety* will be shown to all students in the unit on November 14th at 9:00 A.M. in the gym. A local traffic safety officer will present the film and answer questions.
   c. The IIC agreed that Thanksgiving parties for all units would be held from 2:00 to 3:30 P.M. on November 21st. Each unit is to arrange their own party. A fee of 10 cents per child may be drawn from the school PTA funds for party treats.

2. Ms. White presented a list of suggested objectives for Block 3 (November 26th-December 14th). Since it was not possible to put all children needing a skill in a group at the same time, Ms. White suggested that during Block 3 the unit first look at skills taught in Blocks 1 and 2 to see if some pupils still needed those skills. She reported the following results:

Block 1 Skills Needed:

Level B—Consonant digraphs

Level B—Plurals

Level C—Plural forms

Level C—Diphthongs

Level D—Three-letter consonant blends

Level D—Syllabication

Block 2 Skills Needed:

Level B—Possessive Forms

Level C—*a* plus *w*

Level C—Short Vowel

Level C—Silent *e*

Level C—Two vowels together

Level D—Possessive forms

"In addition," Ms. White reported, "there are two large groups of students who needed skills not previously taught: independent varied Word Attack skills, Level C, 33 students; and Base Words and Endings, Level B, 20 students." Ms. White thanked Ms. Jones for helping her select the objectives.

3. The IIC plan for revamping the IMC was presented by Ms. Goldsmith. "We worked hard on this at the IIC and now want your honest reaction to it. Here's the general plan:

   a. The IMC will become a work area for students. We will ask the units to pool all AV equipment for the building in the IMC. Also, teachers will be asked to place all instructional kits in the IMC area. Students will check all materials in and out at the IMC. Ms. Kato, our IMC director, will make an inventory of all materials and equipment and will work with the IIC to design a plan for moving counters and other equipment during Christmas vacation."

   b. Four areas will be designated in the IMC. One of these will be for quiet reading only, while others will be for noisy activities.

   c. A full-time aide will be assigned to the IMC to work with Ms. Kato. This will give ample help to check materials in and out, and free Ms. Kato to work with children and to locate and develop materials for the units.

   d. Teachers may send students to the IMC, but the student tasks must be clearly outlined *in writing* and the teacher must be sure the materials are available for the students to work with."

After Ms. Goldsmith had detailed the plan, she asked for questions. Ms. Fords asked, "How do I get AV equipment to use for learning stations in my room if it's all down at the IMC?" Ms. Goldsmith replied that equipment could be checked out by staff for such purposes. Other questions centered around the responsibilities of the teachers, aides, IMC director, and clerks in the IMC area. Ms. Goldsmith indicated a progress report on the IMC would take place at future meetings.

November 13—Designing Meeting—Agenda

(Goldsmith)	1. Announcements	10 min
(Goldsmith)	2. Designing plans for Block 3	70 min

November 13—Designing Meeting—Minutes

1. Ms. Goldsmith announced:
   a. This year the local Optimists Club is sponsoring a contest for Thanksgiving art by children ages 8-10. There will be three prizes of books foı the best drawings. Entry forms and contest regulations are available now in the principal's office for those who are interested.
   b. A note from the custodian has asked teachers to remind children to keep rubbers and overshoes *inside* lockers. Last Thursday when it was raining, the crew mopped the floor after lunch and picked up 20 pairs of rubbers. Children will have to go to the custodian and identify theirs to get them back.

2. Ms. Goldsmith presented her design according to the skills and objectives set at the November 8th meeting. She said, "I felt I needed to know how many students needed each skill before I could assign teachers. I contacted Ms. Flynn who had taken main responsibility for grouping and scheduling for Block 3. We worked together and arrived at the assignment of teachers and students to skills. I had a copy of this duplicated for each of you. Here it is."

Plurals	(Level B)— 8 students—Ms. Goldsmith
Plural forms	(Level C)—13 students—Ms. Goldsmith
Diphthongs	(Level C)—16 students—Ms. Jones
Short vowels	(Level C)— 7 students—Ms. Jones
Possessive forms	(Level B)—16 students—Ms. Fords
Independent and varied Word Attack skills	(Level C)—33 students—Ms. Flynn Ms. Wynn
Base words and endings	(Level B)—20 students—Ms. White
Independent Work	(Supervised by Mr. Frost as "floating" teacher)
Consonant digraphs	(Level B)— 9 students
Silent *e*	(Level C)— 6 students
Two vowels together	(Level C)— 5 students
Syllabication	(Level D)— 9 students
Possessive forms	(Level D)— 8 students

The staff felt the plan was workable. Then Ms. Flynn passed out the names of the students for each skill group. Mr. Frost remarked, "I think that Jonathan Smith and Tim Roosevelt might have problems working independently on consonant digraphs (Level B). Do they need another skill that is being taught by a teacher?" Ms. Flynn asked the teachers who were monitoring Jonathan and Tim's progress and found they both needed plural forms. Ms. White asked. "Ms. Flynn, why didn't you get this information by running a skewer through the Level B skills being taught?" Ms. Flynn replied, "The cards in the deck cannot be kept in alphabetical order when they're used for grouping. This is one reason we have the monitoring forms so we can look at individual needs. The card deck really gives us information about the common needs of children in the group, while the monitoring sheets give us information about each individual child. Since clusters of 30 children were given to teachers and alphabetized, it is easy to find an individual's record." The schedule of spaces for skill groups as presented by Ms. Flynn was also approved.

Ms. Fords remarked, "This meeting really went well, and we completed grouping and scheduling as well as designing in one 80-minute meeting. Our real need now is more materials. Since we don't need the meeting on November 15th for grouping and scheduling, let's work on materials for the resource file and independent study skills. Have your ideas and materials prepared before the meeting." The group agreed and the meeting was adjourned.

November 15—Grouping and Scheduling—Agenda

The entire meeting will be devoted to development of materials for skills.

November 15—Grouping/Scheduling Meeting—Minutes

The staff developed five modules for skills for independent study and four audiotapes with accompanying worksheets during the 90-minute period.

Ms. Jones remarked, "Let's do this again. It's the greatest way to get materials developed I've seen. You can get someone to react and critique the rough draft and then you can prepare the material to use with children immediately."

Ms. Goldsmith congratulated the group on their fine work and indicated, "I believe we got so much done because all of you were prepared to go to work at the beginning of the meeting. You selected independent study skills two weeks ago, you collected ideas and materials, then today you put the pieces together. Planning is perhaps the most important thing we do in IGE."

November 20—Evaluation Meeting—Agenda

(Goldsmith)	1. Announcements	10 min
(Jones)	2. Evaluation of Block 2	30 min
	3. Evaluation of *Wisconsin Design* program to date	40 min
	4. Plans for Block teaching after Thanksgiving	10 min

November 20—Evaluation Meeting—Minutes

1. Announcements by Ms. Goldsmith centered around IIC activities as follows:

   a. Schoolwide plans to develop a new system for reporting to parents that would better reflect the IGE philosophy are being formulated.

   b. A summary of parent-teacher conferences indicated they were well received.

   c. A schedule for staff teachers to attend IIC meetings on a rotating basis, so that every teacher would attend at least once during the school year, is being developed and will go into effect after Thanksgiving vacation.

   d. The relationship of central office consultants to the IIC and unit is being discussed.

2. Ms. Jones presented the data from Block 2 of the *Wisconsin Design*.

   a. 80 percent of the students mastered the assigned skills.

   b. About 25 percent of the students took and mastered the posttest prior to the last week of the block.

   c. All students who completed the skill prior to the last week of the skill block were assigned a skill to be studied independently, and most of them completed it. Students finishing during the last week were assigned to enrichment activities.

The staff responded enthusiastically to the presentation, but Ms. Fords said, "I still am worried about the nonmasters. Why do we still have children not learning?" Ms. Goldsmith replied, "The IGE system is good, but it does not solve all problems. We need more experience in diagnosing learning problems."

Ms. Flynn recalled that she and Ms. White had been monitoring the nonmasters and, in reviewing Ms. Jones' data on nonmasters, found that of the 30 nonmasters from Block 2, 20 of them were also nonmasters in Block 1. "This repetition indicates," suggested Ms. Flynn, "that we need to have a long look at the problem of these 20 children and perhaps put them into a tutoring program after careful diagnosis of their needs."

The unit staff agreed and the second meeting after Thanksgiving (November 29) vacation was reserved for diagnosis of problems and solutions for these children. Ms. Jones said, "I think being able to make decisions like this about kids is what teaching is all about, and I'm glad we are part of IGE." "I agree," said Ms. Flynn, "but there were times during the first weeks that I wasn't sure we'd make it to Thanksgiving."

But made it we had, and with a sense of accomplishment for the past and promise for the future. The staff parted wishing each other "Happy Thanksgiving."

Appendix B

Form for Determining Preferences for School Library/Media Center Services

James W. Liesener

College of Library and Information Services
University of Maryland
College Park, Maryland 20742

This instrument is designed to help you decide which media center services are most important. You are going to assign points according to your idea of the importance of these services. There may be some services which are of no value to you. These services should receive a "0" score.

Follow these steps in assigning points:

Step 1

You are being asked to participate in establishing service priorities for the media center. Allocate 1000 points among the broad categories (I-V) of service in such a way as to reflect your own opinion on the relative importance or value of these service categories.

Enter the number of points you assign to each of the Roman numeraled sections in the blank at the beginning of each section. The five numbers should total to 1000. Please use a pencil so that you can revise the numbers if you change your mind.

Step 2

Divide the number you have given to each Roman numeral section among the capital letter subsections. Enter the number for each subsection on the line preceding the capital letter. If a subsection is not worth any points, enter a "0."

Step 3

Follow the same procedure in breaking down the points allocated to the Arabic numeral and small letter subsections. Be careful that the points assigned to each subsection add up to the points assigned to the points allocated to the whole section.

Step 4

As you go through the steps above, feel free to change your mind about the assignment of numbers. As you work with the more specific services, you may decide that a certain section needs more points and you will need to subtract points from another section in order to accomplish this change.

Note: If you are not clear regarding what a specific service means, see the same section in the *Inventory of School Library/Media Center Services.*

_____ I. Access to materials, equipment, space

_____A. Provision of materials

_____1. Books

_____2. Periodicals, newspapers, pamphlet materials

_____3. Sound media (e.g. recordings, tapes)

_____4. Visual media (e.g. films, filmstrips, slides, maps, art)

_____5. Others (e.g. kits, games, models, puzzles, globes)

_____B. Provision of AV equipment

_____1. Equipment for sound media (e.g. tape recorders and players, radios)

_____2. Equipment for visual media (e.g. projectors, cameras, screens, readers)

_____3. Television (e.g. receivers, monitors, cameras)

_____4. Equipment for automated learning and information retrieval systems

_____C. Provision of space in media center

_____1. Space to work (individually and in groups)

_____2. Space to use audiovisual and electronic equipment (individually and in groups)

_____3. Space for special collections (reserve or class projects)

_____D. Use of materials, equipment, space

_____1. Use of media center (media center available for use)

_____a. Available for use during school hours for individual and groups

_____b. Available for use evenings and weekends

_____c. Available for use during vacations and summers

_____d. Available to parents and nonschool persons

_____2. Circulation services for materials and equipment

_____a. Provision for use of materials and equipment in media center and school (including use of *materials* outside the school)

_____b. Provision for use of *equipment* outside the school

_____c. Provision of additional circulation services such as borrowing limitations, renewals, recalls, and reservations

____E. Provision of materials not in media center collection

____1. Provision of materials from other sources outside the school (e.g. interlibrary loans)

____2. Purchasing materials for the media center requested by users for specialized needs

____3. Sale of materials

____F. Provision of special collections

____1. Provision of materials on special subject on request

____2. Provision of professional library for teachers

____G. Provision of copying services for users

____ II. Reference services

____A. Provision of collection of reference materials for self-help

____B. Assistance in identification and location of materials in media center

____C. Assistance in identification and location of materials outside the media center collection (e.g. information about other collections and referral to other sources)

____D. Alerting the user and current awareness services

____1. Notifying the users of new materials, equipment and services on a regular basis

____2. Providing programs and presentations which publicize special events, materials, services, etc.

____3. Systematically gathering information about user interests and needs, and routing relevant information and materials regarding those in terests and needs:

____a. For teachers

____b. For students

____E. Assistance in compiling bibliographies

____1. Assistance in preparing lists of references on a given subject

____2. Provision of lists of references on a given subject *for* users on request

____3. Provision of evaluative information in addition to references

_____4. Provision of access to and assistance in using computer searching services

_____F. Answer services

_____1. Provision of answers to simple questions for users on request

_____2. Provision of answers to complex questions on request, including the use of subject matter specialists (e.g. biology teacher) when necessary

_____III. Production services

_____A. Provision of materials, equipment, and facilities for users to produce instructional materials (including graphics, photography, and reprography)

_____B. Provision of technical assistance in producing instructional materials

_____C. Production of materials by media center staff for users on request (includes production of instructional television programs)

_____IV. Instruction

_____A. Directional services

_____B. Provision of formal instruction and orientation programs

_____C. Provision of inservice training programs

_____D. Provision of informal instruction on request

_____E. Provision of guidance in reading, viewing, and listening

_____ V. Consulting services

_____A. Provision of consultation to individual teachers regarding selection and use of instructional and professional materials and equipment and the design of instructional strategies and content

_____B. Provision of consultation to teaching teams and department or grade level groups

_____C. Contributing to overall curriculum planning in the school or system through participation on curriculum planning committees

_____D. The media center serves as a clearinghouse for instructional media

Glossary

Accountability a dimension of group focus that refers to the degree to which persons are held responsible for their task performance.

Accountability, educational the idea that teachers and school systems may be held responsible for actual improvement in student achievement and that such improvement is measurable.

Affective domain the area of learning or instruction pertaining to the feelings and emotions.

Affective outcomes of education results which involve feelings more than understandings. Likes and dislikes, satisfactions and discontents, and ideals and values are some of the affective outcomes that education may develop in the individual.

Age norm the average score on an aptitude or achievement test for students of a specific age group. Age norms are usually reported in tables showing the average scores of students in a series of different age groups.

Aide, clerical a paraprofessional whose duties are mainly secretarial.

Aide, instructional a paraprofessional member of the I&R Unit who, working under the direct supervision of the teachers, performs various routine duties. These duties, which depend on the experiences and skills of the aide, may include working with children in a one-to-one or small group situation, administering and scoring tests, helping students in the media center or on the playground.

Anecdotal method a technique by means of which behavior and responses are recorded as they occur.

Aptitude the capacity to learn; e.g., typing aptitude prior to practice on a typewriter. Aptitude tests are designed to predict the outcome of training; hence to predict future ability on the basis of present ability.

Assessment application of a measurement procedure; obtaining data through measurement; does not include a judgment and therefore is nonevaluative measurement; assessment is also used by some writers as a synonym for either evaluation or measurement.

Assessment, instrument a measurement tool, such as a test.

Assessment, pre- the process of gathering various kinds of information to understand the individual prior to the start of an instructional sequence; some of the information is used to evaluate the student's readiness for attaining particular instructional objectives.

Assessment, post- the process of gathering various kinds of data to understand the individual after a sequence of instruction. Some of the information is used to evaluate the students' attainment of particular instructional objectives.

Attitude an orientation toward or away from some object, concept, or situation; a readiness to respond in a predetermined manner to the object, concept, or situation.

Average a number, not always an actual score, which represents the most typical, or representative value in a group of scores. "Average" is a generic term designating any measure of a central tendency, such as the mean, median, or mode. In ordinary speech, the term "average" often means the same thing as the term "arithmetic mean."

Basic skills skills such as those involved in reading, language, and arithmetic. Their development is regarded as essential to the further study of content subjects, and they tend to be emphasized during the elementary school years.

Behavior 1. the action or activities of an individual; that is, anything that an individual does, including overt, physical action, internal physiological and emotional processes, and implicit mental activity; 2. those activities of an organism that can be observed by another organism or by an experimenter's instruments. Included within behavior are verbal reports made about subjective, conscious experiences.

Brainstorming a popular nontechnical term for certain techniques for the stimulation of creative thinking in the development of new ideas; consists of individual or, more generally, small-group activity in which a deliberate attempt is made to think uncritically but creatively about all possible approaches and solutions to a given problem, the group participating in spontaneous and unrestrained discussion which usually involves evaluative feedback.

Center, Instructional Materials (IMC) 1. an area set up by a school system consisting of at least a library and an audiovisual center which contain a variety of instructional material and equipment (*syn.* educational materials center; multimedia center; learning resource center, media center); 2. an area set aside within a single school in which the multimedia approach is utilized for individual and group teaching-learning activities.

Center, learning an area in the classroom or some designated area in the school where there is a wide assortment of resources for learning.

Cognitive domain the area of learning or instruction pertaining to attaining and using knowledge.

Cognitive outcomes of education results from education in the intellectual domain including factual knowledge, comprehension, and various intellectual skills; not to be confused with an *objective* of education, which is a desired result of education.

Competency, functional ability to apply to practical situations the essential principles and techniques of a particular subject matter field.

Comprehension the process of acquiring or developing the meaning of various types of material, including words, sentences, paragraphs, and longer material.

Concepts abstractions based on the properties or relationships common to a class of objects or ideas. Concepts may be of concrete things; e.g., the term "poodle dog" referring to a given variety of dog, or of abstractions; e.g., equality, justice, number, implying relationships common to many different kinds of objects or ideas.

Content validity that quality of an educational achievement test which is determined by the extent to which the items in the test adequately sample the areas of subject matter and the abilities that a course of instruction has aimed to teach.

Criterion a standard or norm established as a basis for making a qualitative or quantitative comparison.

Criterion, mastery a standard that explicitly indicates full or complete attainment of an objective or objectives, usually in the cognitive or psychomotor domain; e.g., 90 percent correct on a 30-item test that measures attainment of three objectives in science; walking a mile in 15 minutes without stopping to rest; or running. Mastery criteria are usually set when it is known or presumed that one objective, or set of objectives, must be attained fully before the next one can be undertaken successfully.

Criterion-referenced test *See* **Test, criterion.**

Criterion, variable a standard that implies that either (a) not all students must attain the same level of knowledge, skill, or affective outcome, or (b) that a particular lesson or unit contains several objectives, not all of which are to be attained to the same specified level. Variable criteria are generally set in connection with expressive objectives, objectives in the affective domain, and objectives in the psychomotor domain. In general, only a limited number of objectives in the skill subjects are to be attained to mastery by all students at one time during their elementary school years, and even here exceptions are made for exceptional students; e.g., the blind, deaf, emotionally disturbed, or mentally retarded.

Decision making the act of making a choice among defined alternatives concerning a defined issue or problem.

Decision making, involvement in the extent to which one engages in defining a problem, suggesting alternatives, making decisions, and evaluating decision outcomes.

Decision making, student involvement in the amount and kind of student participation in classroom interaction.

Developing Mathematical Processes (DMP) a comprehensive instructional and management program in elementary mathematics that integrates arithmetic, geometry, and probability and statistics.

Differentiated staffing dividing the roles of school personnel into different professional and paraprofessional subroles according to specific functions and duties to be performed in the school and according to particular talents and strengths evident within the human resources of any given school community.

Distribution, normal the standard symmetrical bell-shaped distribution.

Distribution of scores a tabulation or enumeration of the frequency of occurrence in each score in a given set of scores. A distribution of scores may be indicated graphically by a frequency polygon or by a histogram.

Evaluation the science of providing information for decision making; the process of delineating, obtaining, and providing useful information for judging decision alternatives.

Evaluation criteria the standards against which a person, a group, a procedure, or an instrument may be checked.

Evaluation cycle the cycle which begins with an initial determination of educational objectives for a particular course or program and ends with a final evaluation of its effectiveness.

Evaluation, formative evaluation of a student's learning during an instructional sequence, evaluation of an instructional product—textbook, film—while it is being developed; evaluation of a process while it is being carried out.

Evaluation, informal appraisal of an individual's status or growth by means other than standardized instruments.

Evaluation, initial evaluation of a student's characteristics and level of achievement before determining appropriate instructional objectives for the student; evaluation of an instructional product; e.g., a textbook, a film, before using it; evaluation of a process; e.g., planning an instructional program for a student, planning for the use of materials by the IIC, before beginning the actual process.

Evaluation instrument any of the means for obtaining information on the progress of a learner and the effectiveness of instruction. Quantitative and qualitative data, object measures, subjective impressions, tests, observations, anecdotal records, case studies, and sociometric methods may all serve as instruments for deciding whether instructional objectives have been obtained.

Evaluation of a curriculum the assessment of learning activities within a specific instructional area for the purpose of determining the validity of objectives, relevancy and sequence of content, and achievement of specified goals; leads to decisions associated with planning, programming, implementing, and recycling program activities.

Evaluation, of an instructional program of a student an estimate of the quality of the instructional program arranged for a particular student that uses as the criterion the student's attainment of the stated objective(s) of that program.

Evaluation, of staff an estimate of the quality of a person's performance based on one or more criteria such as achievement, adjustment, behavior, and the judgment of school officials, parents, students, and the role incumbent.

Evaluation, of a student a process in which information derived from many sources is used to arrive at a value judgment; includes not only identifying the degree to which a student possesses a trait or to which the student's behavior has been modified but also evaluating the desirability and adequacy of these findings.

Evaluation, summative evaluation of a student's learning at the end of an instructional sequence (this would also be considered part of the formative evaluation of an instructional program comprised of more than one sequence); evaluation of an instructional product—textbook, film, total instructional program of a student—after it is completed or finished; evaluation of a completed process.

Facilitative environments the intra- and extraorganizational agencies, groups, and individuals who contribute to installation, refinement, and renewal of innovative educational programs.

Goal an end state or condition toward which the motivated behavior sequence is directed and by which the sequence is completed.

Grade equivalent the mean or median achievement of pupils in a given school grade on a given standardized test. Grade norm tables usually present these mean scores for several adjacent grades.

Group, instructional a social system exhibiting the general characteristics of groups with the particular quality of the group being shaped by the fact that it is essentially a formal work group functioning within the institutional setting of the school.

Group problem solving collective action involving students and staff to discover or to achieve an answer or a solution to a problem or set of problems.

Heterogeneity a term which when applied to the individuals in a group or the items in a test, refers to the degree to which they are different or unlike.

Homogeneity a term which when applied to the individual in a group or the items in a test, refers to the degree to which they are alike or not different.

Individualization *See* **Instruction, individualized.**

Individually Guided Education (IGE) a comprehensive form of schooling that is an alternative to the age-graded, self-contained form of schooling. It is designed to produce higher education achievements and to attain other educational objectives through providing well for differences among students in rate of learning, learning style, and other characteristics.

Individually Guided Motivation (IGM) a program for focusing a school's efforts on motivation in accordance with instructional programming for the individual student. Four motivational-instructional procedures are designed to increase children's interest in learning related to any curricular area and also to promote their self-direction.

Inservice teacher education a school, system, or area teacher training plan that may include such activities as workshops and seminars for individuals who are already teaching. It is designed to increase staff competency or to inform them of recent developments.

Instruction, individualized as commonly used, any type of teaching-learning situation in which consideration is given to planning and arranging instruction for the individual student; more strictly, the kind of teaching-learning situations in which each student receives instruction of a different kind or at a different rate from other students; for example, in guided independent study and in proceeding through a sequence of instruction at the individual's own rate. This is in contrast to instructional programming for the individual student in which children who have similar needs and readiness to attain the same objectives are grouped for instruction.

Instructional Improvement Committee (IIC) the organizational element of the multiunit school organization structure at the school level. It is composed of the principal, the unit leaders, and a parent representative. The IIC carries out many planning and evaluating functions regarding instruction previously performed by the principal or teachers independently.

Instructional program 1. a statement or description of instructional activities over a given period of time designed to enable the students to attain specified instructional objectives; 2. That which is being taught or has been taught by the school or teacher in question and the manner of instruction.

Instructional program for the individual student 1. the teaching-learning activities by which the student attains one or more instructional objectives over a short period of time (students with the same needs and readiness may have the same instructional program in a given curriculum area); 2. the combination of all the student's teaching-learning activities in the various curriculum areas for any given period of time.

Instructional Programming Model (IPM) a seven-step model for planning, carrying out, and evaluating instructional programs for the individual students of a school building (*see* **Instructional program for the individual student).** The model takes into account these conditions: that some but not all instructional objectives should be attained by all students during elementary school; that some but not all objectives should be attained by students to a criterion of mastery, and that some, but not most, objectives are attained in a fixed and invariant sequence.

Instructional and Research (I & R) Unit an element of the multiunit school organization typically consisting of a unit leader, three to five staff teachers, an instructional secretary, a teacher aide, and 100-150 students. The I & R Unit replaces the age-graded self-contained classroom organization for instruction. The staff of the unit is a hierarchically organized team with clearly defined job descriptions.

Intelligence 1. that which a properly standardized intelligence test measures; 2. according to Binet, the characteristics of thought processes that enable persons to take and maintain a direction without becoming distracted, to adapt means to ends, and to criticize their own attempts at problem solution.

Internal consistency an attribute a test possesses if it is composed of items that all measure much the same thing and that are therefore highly intercorrelated. A measure of internal consistency provides one measure of test reliability.

Intern teacher a teacher whose teacher assignment and preservice professional growth plan conform to an internship plan of a college or of the local school system or of both. Such plans usually provide for a major portion of the day, usually for a full school year, with supervision by the college or university personnel as well as by local supervisors, and occasionally with additional provision for parallel course work and college credit. Intern teachers are usually paid by the school districts though on a lower basis than regular teachers.

Inventory a number of questions, tasks, or other stimuli, designed more to provide a comprehensive description of some aspect of an individual's characteristics than to provide a quantitative measurement of one of those aspects. Inventories are commonly used in the description of interests, attitudes, or personality traits than in the measurement of intellectual achievements.

Item analysis a study to determine the difficulty and discriminating power of a test item. The difficulty of an item is usually expressed as the percent of the group of examinees who failed to answer the item correctly. Its discriminating power may be expressed as a difference between the proportions of good and poor students who answered the item correctly. Applied to multiple-choice items, the counting of responses from students of high and low overall achievements reveals the effectiveness of each distractor.

Learning a relatively permanent change in behavior that occurs as the result of practice. Behavior changes due to maturation or temporary conditions of the organism (e.g., fatigue, the influence of drugs, adaptation) are not included.

Learning, independent learning that occurs by an individual without assistance from another person.

Maturation growth processes in the individual that result in orderly changes in behavior, whose timing and patterning are relatively independent of exercise or experience though they may require a normal environment.

Mean a measure of the central tendency or of the average numerical value of a set of scores. It is calculated by adding all of the scores and dividing the sum by the number of scores.

Measurement a process of assigning numbers to an object or the members of a set.

Measurement, educational 1. a term indicating the testing, scaling, and appraisal of aspects of the educational process for which measures are available and of the individuals undergoing the educational process; 2. the end product obtained through applying a measure to any aspect of the educational process or the individuals undergoing it.

Median the point in a score distribution that divides it into two parts containing equal numbers of scores. If the number of scores in the distribution is odd, the median is the middle score. If the number is even, the median is a point midway between the two scores nearest the middle. The median is identical with the fifth decile or the fiftieth percentile.

Motivation a general term used to indicate the activation and direction of effort, usually towards a goal.

Motive any condition of the organism that affects its readiness to start upon or continue in a sequence of behavior.

Multiunit school organization a three-level instructional organizational pattern consisting of the I & R Unit; an Instructional Improvement Committee within the building; and a Systemwide Program Committee within the school district.

Norm, test the average or typical score or other measure for members of a specific group. Norms are often presented in tables giving the typical score values for a series of different homogeneous groups, such as students in a given grade or students of a given age.

Norms the behavioral values shared by members of a group; beliefs about what the members or others ought to do under given circumstances.

Objective (*n*) aim, end in view, or purpose of a course of action or a belief; that which is anticipated as desirable in the early phases of an activity and serves to select, regulate, and direct later aspects of the act so that the total process is designed and integrated.

Objective-based instruction a system of instruction in which instructional activities and evaluation procedures are based on clearly stated objectives.

Objective, behavioral an instructional objective that includes a description of observable or measurable behavior. The behavior may be measurable, not necessarily only overt behavior that is directly observable.

Objective, educational or general an aim stated for education in general, for a school division, or for a subject in general.

Objective, expressive an instructional objective stated in terms of the kind and/or number of activities to be engaged in.

Objective, instructional a statement describing the desired results that may be expected from the particular unit or sequence of instruction.

Paraprofessional any person who works within an I & R Unit who is not being employed as a certificated teacher and is not an intern or student teacher; *also see* **Aide, clerical** and **Aide, instructional.**

Performance overt or readily measured behavior, as distinguished from knowledge or information not translated into action.

Prereading Skills Program (PSR) a program that includes materials and procedures for developing children's visual and auditory skills. It is designed to prevent reading failures by identifying and overcoming deficits in prereading skills at the preschool and kindergarten levels.

Preservice teacher education the program planned and implemented by an institution of higher education which terminates in a degree and teacher certification.

Program, education, of a building a short statement of the terminal objectives that all students are to attain at a specific point in time, e.g., after seven years of schooling, after one year of schooling, and the related learning experiences by which the various objectives are to be attained. Common objectives which are to be attained by all students and other objectives to be attained by some but not all students should be indicated.

Program planning a process by which the nature and sequence of future educational programs are determined.

Program, reading a planned instructional program in reading as contrasted with incidental teaching of reading or with unskilled and unplanned reading instruction.

Psychomotor domain the area of learning or instruction pertaining to muscular activity that follows directly from a mental process.

Questionnaire a list of planned written questions relating to a particular topic, usually intended to gather descriptive information from a number of selected respondents. An important difference between a questionnaire and a test is that in a questionnaire the responses are ordinarily summarized question by question, whereas in a test they are summarized respondent by respondent.

Random sample a sample selected in such a way as to guarantee equal probability of selection to all possible samples of this size that could be formed from the members of the universe involved.

Rating scale a device by which a rater can record his or her judgment of another person (or of himself or herself) on the traits defined by the scale.

Raw score the number first obtained in scoring the test, before any transformation to a standard score or other derived score. For objectively scorable tests, the raw score usually consists of the number of right answers, the number right minus some fraction of the number wrong, the time required for performance, the number of errors, or some other directly defined measure. On an essay test the raw score is often the scorer's estimate of the quality of the response, relative to some quantitative standard of perfection.

Regional IGE Coordinating Council (RICC) the intermediate group in a three-level organizational arrangement; the group is composed of representatives of the Systemwide Program Committees of the school districts of the region, a representative of the intermediate agency of the region, a representative of at least one teacher education institution of the region, and a representative of the state education agency.

Reinforcement 1. in classical conditioning the experimental procedure of following the conditioned stimulus by the unconditioned stimulus; 2. in operant conditioning the analogous procedure of following the occurrence of the operant response by the reinforcing stimulus; 3. the process which increases the strength of conditioning as a result of these arrangements.

Reliability the self-consistency of a test as a measuring instrument. Reliability is measured by a coefficient of correlation between scores on two halves of a test, alternate forms of the test, or retests with the same test; a high correlation signifying high consistency of scores for the population tested.

Role the dynamic aspect of a status or position which is defined by the expectations held for one's behavior.

Role playing a method for teaching principles affecting interpersonal relations by having the subject assume a part in a spontaneous play, whether in psychotherapy or in leadership training.

Sample a selection of scores from a total set of scores known as the "population." If selection is random, an unbiased sample results; if selection is nonrandom, the sample is biased and unrepresentative.

Staff development continuous improvement of teacher knowledge, skills and attitudes as planned for and with the I & R Unit, the school, and the school district.

State IGE Coordinating Council (SICC) the state group in a three-level organizational arrangement; it is chaired by the chief state school officer or designee, and composed of at least one state IGE coordinator, other key personnel of the state agency, and representatives of each RICC including a teacher educator, a representative of an intermediate agency, and a representative of a Systemwide Program Committee.

Subpublic a group holding similar positions, membership, and value orientations.

Systemwide Program Committee (SPC) the element of the multiunit school organization at the school district level. It is chaired by the superintendent of schools or designee and consists of representative central office consultants, principals, unit leaders, teachers, and community representatives.

Teacher flexibility a dimension of teacher behavior that deals with the way the teacher handles two or more issues at the same time.

Team teaching a type of instructional organization involving teaching personnel and the students assigned to them in which two or more teachers are given joint responsibility for all or a significant part of the instruction of the same group of students. The team may include paraprofessionals and student teachers; the I & R Unit is a hierarchical team with clearly defined roles for all members, and it has functions in addition to instruction.

Test a collection of items (questions, tasks, etc.) so arranged that replies or performances can be scored and interpreted.

Test, achievement an instrument designed to measure a student's accomplishment or proficiency related to some body of knowledge or skill; often used to measure achievement in arithmetic, chemistry, English, typing, and other subjects of study; most tests made by teachers for classroom use are achievement tests.

Test, aptitude an instrument given to determine the potential of an individual for development along a special line or the extent to which he or she is likely to profit from instruction along that line. Tests of academic aptitude, scientific aptitude, music aptitude, clerical aptitude, and other special aptitudes are available.

Test battery a collection of tests whose composite scores are used to appraise individual differences.

Test, criterion the instrument used to measure the end result of an instructional sequence or an experimental treatment.

Test, diagnostic an instrument designed to reveal specific weaknesses or failures to learn in some subject of study such as reading or arithmetic. In a diagnostic test the main interest is in scores on individual items or on small groups of highly similar items.

Test, group a test administered to several people at once by a single tester. A college examination is usually a group test.

Test, individual a test designed to be administered to one person at a time. Binet intelligence tests are individual tests.

Test, mastery an instrument not intended to indicate how much a student has achieved relative to other students, but only whether or not the student has achieved enough to satisfy the minimum requirements of the teacher or the examining agency.

Test, nonverbal usually an intelligence test, a test which aims to minimize the importance of language skills as a factor determining the test score. In the purest form of nonverbal test there is no use of words, written or spoken, either by the examiner giving the test or by the subjects responding to it. More commonly, a nonverbal test is one in which no written directions are employed and to which the subject responds without using language. Such tests are commonly used in testing small children, illiterates, and others with language deficiencies.

Test, objective a test that can be provided with a simple predetermined list of correct answers, so that subjective opinion or judgment in the scoring procedure is eliminated. The scoring of true-false, multiple-choice, or matching exercises is completely objective. The scoring of short-answer or completion items is partly objective.

Test standardization the establishment of norms for interpreting scores by giving a test to a representative population and by making appropriate studies of its reliability and validity.

Test, work-sample a performance test which provides a controlled tryout of the examinee's behavior under conditions as similar as possible to those to be encountered in a work situation.

Theory a set of assumptions (axioms) advanced to explain existing data and predict new events; usually applicable to a wide array of phenomena and experimental situations.

Thinking behavior carried on in terms of ideas (representational or symbolic processes); ideational problem solving as distinguished from solution through overt manipulation.

Underachievement the term used to describe the educational situation of a pupil whose aptitude test scores are substantially higher than the pupil's achievement test scores. Often such apparent discrepancies are due to a difference between the kind of achievement the aptitude test measures, and the kind that the achievement test measures (for both measure learned achievements). Sometimes the discrepancies are due to different bases used in norming the aptitude and achievement tests. Sometimes they are simply due to errors of measurement. Any marked discrepancy between the scores a student makes on different tests ought to be investigated and, if possible, explained. But teachers should guard against overly simple explanations. It is usually true that the underachieving student could do better "if the student would only try," but so also could all of the "normally achieving" or "over-achieving" classmates. Aptitude test scores may not provide valid indications of how good a pupil's achievement ought to be.

Understanding the process of acquiring or developing the meaning of various types of material.

Unit leader a certificated teacher who, in addition to teaching children from 50 to 80 percent of the time, is responsible for serving as the instructional leader of an I & R Unit, chairing meetings of the unit, and serving on the IIC of the school building; a main instructional responsibility is to lead the unit staff in planning, carrying out, and evaluating instructional programs for individual students.

***Wisconsin Design for Reading Skill Development* (WDRSD)** a reading program which describes six areas of reading skills and related behavioral and expressive objectives. It provides machine-scorable, criterion-referenced tests for assessing student attainment of behavioral and expressive objectives; it also provides the means for managing objective-based instruction in reading.

Author Index

Subject Index